Prosocial Development

Prosocial Development

A MULTIDIMENSIONAL APPROACH

Edited by Laura M. Padilla-Walker

and

Gustavo Carlo

OXFORD
UNIVERSITY PRESS

OXFORD
UNIVERSITY PRESS

Oxford University Press is a department of the University of Oxford.
It furthers the University's objective of excellence in research, scholarship,
and education by publishing worldwide.

Oxford   New York
Auckland   Cape Town   Dar es Salaam   Hong Kong   Karachi
Kuala Lumpur   Madrid   Melbourne   Mexico City   Nairobi
New Delhi   Shanghai   Taipei   Toronto

With offices in
Argentina   Austria   Brazil   Chile   Czech Republic   France   Greece
Guatemala   Hungary   Italy   Japan   Poland   Portugal   Singapore
South Korea   Switzerland   Thailand   Turkey   Ukraine   Vietnam

Oxford is a registered trademark of Oxford University Press
in the UK and certain other countries.

Published in the United States of America by
Oxford University Press
198 Madison Avenue, New York, NY 10016

Library of Congress Cataloging-in-Publication Data
Prosocial development : a multidimensional approach / edited by
Laura M. Padilla-Walker and Gustavo Carlo.
pages cm
Includes index.
ISBN 978-0-19-996477-2 (hardcover); 978-0-19-049906-8 (paperback)
1. Altruism.   2. Moral development.   3. Socialization.   4. Social interaction.
I. Padilla-Walker, Laura M.   II. Carlo, Gustavo.
HM1146.P76 2014
302—dc23
2013033916

{ CONTENTS }

SECTION 4 Cultural and Contextual Perspectives

SECTION 5 Specific Targets and Types of Prosocial Behavior

{ ABOUT THE EDITORS }

Laura M. Padilla-Walker is an associate professor in the School of Family Life at Brigham Young University. Her research focuses on how parents and other socialization agents (e.g., media, siblings) help to foster prosocial and moral development during adolescence and emerging adulthood. Dr. Padilla-Walker has published over 50 peer-reviewed articles and book chapters.

Gustavo Carlo is the Millsap Professor of Diversity and Multicultural Studies in the Department of Human Development and Family Studies at the University of Missouri. His primary interest is in prosocial and moral development, particularly on the parenting, personality, and sociocultural correlates of prosocial behaviors. Dr. Carlo has published well over 100 peer-reviewed articles and book chapters, and has coedited several volumes (*Handbook of U.S. Latino Psychology; Health Disparities in Youth and Families: Research and Applications; Moral Motivation Through the Life Span*). The National Science Foundation and National Institutes of Health have primarily funded Dr. Carlo's research.

{ CONTRIBUTORS }

Camille D. Basilio
Doctoral Candidate
Department of Psychology
Arizona State University

Christi Bergin, Ph.D.
Associate Research Professor
Network for Educator
    Effectiveness
Assessment Resource Center
University of Missouri

Gustavo Carlo, Ph.D.
Millsap Professor of Diversity and
    Multicultural Studies
Department of Human Development
    and Family Studies
University of Missouri

Alek Chakroff
Doctoral Candidate
Department of Psychology
Harvard University

Sarah M. Coyne, Ph.D.
Associate Professor
School of Family Life
Brigham Young University

Alexandra N. Davis
Doctoral Candidate
Department of Human Development
    and Family Studies
University of Missouri

Kieu Anh Do
Doctoral Candidate
Department of Child, Youth and
    Family Studies
University of Nebraska-Lincoln

Nancy Eisenberg, Ph.D.
Regents' Professor
Department of Psychology
Arizona State University

Keren Fortuna, Ph.D.
Lecturer
Department of Psychology
The Hebrew University of Jerusalem

Kathryn B. Gustafson, M.S.
School of Family Life
Brigham Young University

Maria Rosario T. de Guzman, Ph.D.
Associate Professor and Extension
    Specialist
Department of Child, Youth and
    Family Studies
University of Nebraska-Lincoln

Daniel Hart, Ph.D.
Professor
Department of Psychology
Rutgers University

Paul D. Hastings, Ph.D.
Professor
Department of Psychology
University of California, Davis

Patricia H. Hawley, Ph.D.
Professor
Department of Educational
    Psychology & Leadership
Texas Tech University

Erin Karahuta
Doctoral Candidate
Department of Psychology
Lehigh University

Ariel Knafo, Ph.D.
Associate Professor
Department of Psychology
The Hebrew University of Jerusalem,
   Israel

George P. Knight, Ph.D.
Professor
Department of Psychology
Arizona State University

Car Mun Kok
Doctoral Candidate
Department of Child, Youth and
   Family Studies
University of Nebraska-Lincoln

Asiye Kumru, Ph.D.
Associate Professor
Department of Psychology
Özyeğin University

Deborah Laible, Ph.D.
Associate Professor
Department of Psychology
Lehigh University

Heather L. Lawford, Ph.D.
Assistant Professor
Department of Psychology
Bishop's University

Mary B. Eberly Lewis, Ph.D.
Associate Professor
Department of Psychology
Oakland University

Meredith McGinley, Ph.D.
Affiliate Faculty
The Chicago School of Professional
   Psychology

Belén Mesurado, Ph.D.
Assistant Researcher
Interdisciplinary Center for Research
   in Mathematical and Experimental
   Psychology (CIIPME), CONICET
Buenos Aires, Argentina

Jonas G. Miller
Doctoral Candidate
Department of Psychology
University of California, Davis

Deanna Opal
Doctoral Candidate
Department of Psychology
University of Nebraska, Lincoln

Laura M. Padilla-Walker, Ph.D.
Associate Professor
School of Family Life
Brigham Young University

Michael W. Pratt, Ed.D.
Professor
Department of Psychology
Wilfrid Laurier University

Brandy A. Randall, Ph.D.
Associate Professor
Human Development and Family
   Science
North Dakota State University

María Cristina Richaud, Ph.D.
Director
Interdisciplinary Center for Research
   in Mathematical and Experimental
   Psychology (CIIPME), CONICET
Buenos Aires, Argentina

Nathan J. Smith
Doctoral Candidate
School of Family Life
Brigham Young University

Tracy L. Spinrad, Ph.D.
Associate Professor
T. Denny Sanford School of Social and
   Family Dynamics
Arizona State University

Michael J. Sulik
Doctoral Candidate
Department of Psychology
Arizona State University

Lawrence J. Walker, Ph.D.
Professor
Department of Psychology
University of British Columbia

Jennifer R. Wenner
Doctoral Candidate
Human Development and Family
    Science
North Dakota State University

Kathryn R. Wentzel, Ph.D.
Professor
Human Development
University of Maryland, College Park

Bilge Yağmurlu, Ph.D.
Associate Professor
Department of Psychology
Koç University

Jeremy B. Yorgason, Ph.D.
Associate Professor
School of Family Life
Brigham Young University

Liane Young, Ph.D.
Assistant Professor
Department of Psychology
Boston College

Overview of Prosocial Behavior

The Study of Prosocial Behavior

PAST, PRESENT, AND FUTURE

Laura M. Padilla-Walker and Gustavo Carlo

A baby who softly touches the hand of another crying baby, a toddler who comforts his sibling after a painful fall, a child who shares her crayons with a playmate in the hopes the act will be reciprocated; a teenager who helps his mother take out the garbage; a young adult who rushes into a burning building to save an unknown family; a woman who is kind to a man at work because she wants him to like her; a grandfather who passes out flowers in front of a grocery store; an elderly widow who has given countless hours throughout her life in community service and volunteering at local charities. All of these are examples of prosocial behavior (i.e., actions intended to benefit others) representing a wide variety of different actions at each stage of development. These behaviors also represent a set of actions crucial to human flourishing and survival.

All human societies value prosocial actions, and the expression of prosocial behavior is an integral aspect of all social animals. Such behaviors are essential to developing and maintaining harmonious relationships—from the gentle, sometimes subtle, forms that soothe and comfort others and lead to the development of caregiver-child attachment to the more sophisticated, purposeful forms committed for great social causes. The present volume is dedicated to surveying our understanding of how these behaviors originate, develop, and vary across individuals and groups. Our approach is predicated on the assumption that each form of prosocial action is unique and must be understood as such.

The notion that different forms of prosocial behavior have uniquely associated antecedents and correlates is not novel. Indeed, in one of the earliest and largest systematic studies of prosocial (and moral) behaviors, Hartshorne, May, and Shuttleworth (1930) found that morality indices are often weakly interrelated and concluded that the search for a global moral construct is futile. These scholars proposed that the field would benefit if researchers considered behavior-specific models of morality. However, most researchers since then followed the path of conceptualizing prosocial behavior as a global construct. Perhaps the pull of global, relatively simplistic models of prosocial behavior was too alluring. On the other hand, it is possible that because the predominant theories of social and developmental psychology (e.g., cognitive development, social learning) advocated universal mechanisms, this posed challenges and complexities in conceptualizing unique forms of prosocial behavior. No matter the reason, most research on prosocial behavior has conceptualized the construct as singular and unidimensional, implying that all prosocial behaviors are equal.

During the late 1960s and early 1970s, in particular, there was a surge of interest in research on prosocial behavior (Batson, 1998). The increased activity in this area began in part as a result of bystander intervention studies (e.g., Latane & Darley, 1970) and personality psychology (e.g., Staub, 1979), but spilled into social developmental psychology with the advent of cognitive developmental (e.g., Kohlberg, 1969) and moral socialization theories (e.g., Eisenberg-Berg, 1979; Hoffman, 1970; Radke-Yarrow, Zahn-Waxler, & Chapman, 1983). In most of this work, prosocial behavior was conceptualized as a relatively global construct such that common antecedents and correlates were identified and studied.

Despite the global conception of prosocial behavior, the research has resulted (and continues to result) in many advances in our understanding of these behaviors. Indeed, global conceptions of prosocial behavior have advanced the notion that there are some common mechanisms underlying the expression of such actions. For example, there is ample evidence on the biological (e.g., genetics, neurotransmitters) and environmental (e.g., parental, peer, and media influences) basis of individual differences in prosocial behavior that appear early in life and remain relatively stable across the life span (see Carlo, 2014; Eisenberg, Spinrad, & Fabes, 2006). We have also learned much regarding sociocognitive (e.g., perspective taking, moral reasoning) and socioemotive (e.g., empathy, sympathy, guilt) traits associated with such behaviors. Finally, recent research has begun to more clearly examine the central role of prosocial behavior within the broader areas of morality (including moral identity), antisocial behaviors, and physical and psychological health. No doubt, there is utility in a global conception of prosocial behavior, and such research will continue to uncover new findings.

The question then remains—What is to be gained by conceptualizing and researching prosocial behavior as a multidimensional construct? First, a more nuanced conception of prosocial behavior fits better with the body of evidence to date. Thus far, much of the contemporary research confirms the early (Hartshorne et al., 1930) and later (see Carlo, 2014) findings such that there are generally weak or nonsignificant relations among various forms of prosocial behavior. Such findings demonstrate that not all prosocial behaviors are equal and that there are unique correlates of such behaviors. Second, researching specific forms of prosocial behavior opens avenues of developing richer, more nuanced models of these actions. For example, these more nuanced models may help to account for the differences between forms of prosocial behavior that are more centrally related to morality and those that may be more centrally linked to social conventions or even personal prudence. Furthermore, individual and group (including cross-cultural groups, gender, age) differences in prosocial behavior can be more easily accommodated in this more sophisticated approach. And third, a more prosocial behavior-specific approach has important real-world implications for intervention development and policymaking. For example, the behavior-specific approach implies the need to target specific forms of prosocial behavior in developing prosocial behavior intervention programs. Developers of such programs would need to carefully consider the specific forms desired and construct programs with these actions in mind. Thus, programs to increase cooperative behaviors might differ from those designed to foster empathic-based behaviors; or those designed to foster prosocial behavior toward kin or in-group members might differ from those designed to foster such behaviors toward nonkin or out-group members. Taken together, there is a clear need for the field to build on the existing foundation of understanding that has been amassed with the study of global prosocial behavior and move toward a more nuanced and multidimensional understanding of prosocial development.

The Current Volume

Thus, the current volume includes chapters by leading scholars from diverse disciplines in an attempt to capture the highly multidimensional nature of prosocial development and to encourage continued research that takes these complexities into account and meaningfully moves the field forward. Section 1 of the volume provides an overview of the field and highlights particular areas wherein our knowledge of prosocial development is lacking and could be strengthened by further research. Specifically, in chapter 2 Eisenberg and Spinrad summarize the current state of the field and raise a number of issues that will inform the future of the field. This chapter pays particular attention to the need to consider different definitions of prosocial behavior, especially as they relate to the motivation behind the behavior. Eisenberg and Spinrad also discuss the importance of in-group–out-group distinctions and the need to more carefully consider developmental age when studying prosocial behavior, particularly during infancy and adolescence. Taken together, this section of the volume provides an overview of the field and focuses on ways to rethink how we currently conceptualize prosocial development.

In the remainder of the volume, we have sought to capture multidimensionality in a number of ways, highlighting biological perspectives in Section 2, socialization perspectives in Section 3, and cultural and contextual perspectives in Section 4. The final section (Section 5) then focuses on different targets and types of prosocial behavior. These sections represent a variety of topical areas that are often studied in isolation, which has created a somewhat inconsistent and disconnected

picture of prosocial development over time. One purpose of this volume is to con-
nect these sometimes disparate literatures in an attempt to present a clearer picture
of the current state of the field and the complexity of factors that come into play
when studying prosocial development. All chapters include meaningful directions
for future research that will help to keep the field moving in a positive direction
and will provide momentum for both basic and applied research in this area.

The Multidimensionality of Prosocial Behavior

While prosocial behavior has been defined as voluntary behavior meant to benefit
another, this definition captures a wide variety of motivations and behaviors that
are not explicitly included in the definition. Indeed, when comparing the field of
prosocial behavior to our sister field of aggressive behavior, it is clear that the idea
of multidimensionality has been well developed in the latter field. For instance, if
one were to ask the definition of aggressive behavior, a specific response would
likely require clarification regarding both the form and function of the aggressive
behavior in question (Coyne, Nelson, & Underwood, 2010). Indeed, the function
or motivation for aggressive behavior can be either reactive or proactive, both
of which have different correlates and are approached from a different direction
in regard to intervention. Similarly, aggressive behavior comes in many forms,
including physical, verbal, and relational, just to name a few, each of which also
has somewhat unique correlates.

Similarly, prosocial behavior is not a unidimensional construct, but consists
of a wide variety of behaviors and includes complexities and nuances that may be
meaningful to parents and educators who seek to promote prosocial behavior in
children. While many of these nuances have been acknowledged in the field at one
time or another, they are generally not overtly agreed on by researchers and tend
to be scattered across individual studies, making it difficult to formulate a cohesive understanding of prosocial development. Indeed, as previously mentioned,
the most common approaches to studies of prosocial development continue to use
global measures of prosocial behavior with unidentified targets, although there
are an increasing number of exceptions to this pattern. Further, a relatively large
body of research has examined prosocial behavior during childhood, but prosocial behavior during adolescence and later years is relatively less well understood,
and there are few studies that examine longitudinal change in prosocial behavior
across the teen years. There is also little consistency in the manner in which prosocial behavior is measured and studies suggest quite a bit of variability in findings
as a function of methodology and measurement (Eisenberg et al., 2006), which is
particularly problematic when examining prosocial behavior over time. Indeed,
research on prosocial behavior during childhood relies more on observation,
while research during adolescence relies more on self-reports, making comparisons across studies difficult. However, even in the case of self-reported prosocial

behavior, a wide variety of instruments are currently used, with little specificity in terms of different types or targets of behavior. While no one study can cover all the nuances of prosocial development, it is our hope that this volume will be an impetus to move the field in a direction that will increase specificity so that conclusions can be more easily made across age groups and different empirical studies.

Thus, the current volume attempts to capture the multidimensionality of prosocial development in a number of different ways, including the examination of a variety of predictors of prosocial behavior, and with careful attention to different types and targets of prosocial behavior. In addition, the current volume takes a developmental approach to prosocial behavior and examines prosocial behavior during childhood, adolescence, and young adulthood in hopes of encouraging research that will carefully consider the development of prosocial behavior over time and how the form and function of these behaviors may change as children age.

BIOLOGICAL PERSPECTIVES

There is a well-developed literature on the role of biological factors in the development of aggression and antisocial behavior, but this area is relatively less developed in the area of prosocial development (Eisenberg, Fabes, & Miller, 1990). However, there are strong theoretical approaches suggesting evolutionary, genetic, and neurophysiological determinants of prosocial behavior, and a growing body of empirical research has found support for these approaches. Thus, an important contribution of the current volume is the inclusion of a section on the biological underpinnings of prosocial behavior, as this is an area that will continue to inform the field regarding essential contributions to prosocial development. This section begins with a look at what evolutionary theory can add to our understanding of prosocial behavior (Hawley, chapter 3), raising issues regarding the confusion that can occur when trying to integrate concepts from the fields of developmental and evolutionary psychology. Hawley examines the voluntary nature of behavior and the intentions and motivations behind prosocial behavior to argue that psychological and evolutionary perspectives make different assumptions about what constitutes altruistic behavior and that clarification and accuracy are necessary and important. Sometimes confusion, mixed findings, and inconsistencies exist merely as a result of the conflation of terms and concepts that are not equivalent, and the opening chapter of this section clearly and convincingly encourages greater precision in how we define prosocial terms as we move forward in an exploration of multidimensionality, especially across disciplines. This section also considers how genetic and environmental influences vary as a function of the type and target of prosocial behavior (Fortuna & Knafo, chapter 4) and suggests that different types of prosocial emotions and responses are differentially heritable. This chapter emphasizes multidimensionality by arguing that genetic effects vary as a function of study methodology, age of the child, and target of prosocial behavior. Fortuna and Knafo highlight the relative infancy of this body of research as it relates to prosocial behavior and suggest the need for continued longitudinal studies that are genetically sensitive and that consider gene-environment correlations and interactions as they relate to various types and targets of prosocial behavior. Neural mechanisms that underlie prosocial behavior are also reviewed in this section (Chakroff & Young, chapter 5), suggesting that different areas of the brain are differentially associated with varying motivations for prosocial behavior. Chakroff and Young focus specifically on the psychological processes that underlie prosocial behavior and the neural mechanisms that are associated with these processes. More specifically, they discuss the neural mechanisms behind the perception of others, the tendency to make distinctions between entities with the mental capacity to make moral decisions, the ability to determine the mental states (e.g., emotions, desires, beliefs) of others, and the anticipation of reward for prosocial behavior. This chapter stresses the need for future research to carefully consider the prosocial brain and how both psychological and neurological characteristics are involved in multiple motivations for prosocial behavior. Finally, increased attention is being paid to the physiologic underpinnings of behavior, but as of yet has focused primarily on externalizing and internalizing behavior (El-Sheikh & Erath, 2011; Hastings et al., 2011), with relatively less focus on prosocial behavior. Thus, Hastings and Miller (chapter 6) argue that prosocial behavior is best understood when examining the interplay of physiological functioning and the more commonly studied areas of emotion, cognition, and behavior. They rely on polyvagal theory to explain complicated findings that have been made in regard to evolutionary, neurological, and psychophysiological contributions to prosocial behavior. Although this is a relatively new area of study, findings presented in this chapter suggest links between parasympathetic regulation and prosocial emotions and behaviors and highlight exciting ideas for future research. Taken together, this section offers an overview of some of the diverse ways in which biology is associated with prosocial behavior and encourages future research in an area that is replete with cutting-edge research questions that will make an important contribution to the strong theoretical support that has long existed for the role of biology in diverse aspects of prosocial development.

SOCIALIZATION PERSPECTIVES

The socialization of prosocial behavior has enjoyed a relatively long history of study in comparison with other perspectives in the current volume, with both cross-sectional and longitudinal studies supporting the import of a variety of socialization influences on children and adolescents' prosocial behavior (Grusec, 2006; Hastings, Utendale, & Sullivan, 2007). Thus, in this section we attempt to capture some of the most important socialization sources, as well as some that are relatively understudied and in need of future research. Two of the most well-established sources of socialization are parents and peers, but the current chapters on these topics take a more multidimensional approach than is typically taken. More specifically, Padilla-Walker (chapter 7) looks at a variety of different aspects of parenting and how they influence different types and targets of prosocial behavior, including parental warmth, as well as various aspects of both reactive (e.g., discipline, praise) and proactive (e.g., emotion socialization, teaching) parenting. This chapter calls for additional studies with clear theoretical frameworks that will help to clarify the often disparate findings regarding parenting and prosocial behavior and suggests that looking at both parenting and prosocial behavior from a multidimensional perspective raises a number of fruitful avenues for future research that would build on a rich body of existing literature. Peers are also commonly highlighted as an important socialization source for prosocial behavior, but in chapter 9 Wentzel examines a diversity of aspects of peer relations as they promote prosocial development. More specifically, this chapter reviews different types of peer relationships and different theoretical perspectives and suggests a conceptual framework that organizes research on motivation, peer relationships, and prosocial goal pursuit as means of fostering prosocial behavior. Although the study of both parenting and peer influences on prosocial behavior is well established, these two chapters clarify the need for continued research that will expand our understanding of the socialization process by taking a more nuanced and multidimensional approach.

In addition to these two commonly studied sources of socialization, this section also highlights two relatively new areas of study with a great deal of promise as they relate to the socialization of prosocial behavior. First, although there is a large body of research on the role of media on children's aggressive behavior (Coyne et al., 2010), there is relatively less research examining how media might socialize prosocial behavior. Thus, Coyne and Smith (chapter 8) focus on different contexts, targets, and motivations for prosocial behavior and how these might be depicted in media for children and adolescents. This chapter also examines different forms of media and how they might be associated with prosocial development at different ages and provides numerous directions for future research, especially in regard to how new media (e.g., cell phones, social networking) might impact prosocial behavior. Finally, while parents (Grusec, 2006) and siblings (Dunn, 2007; Padilla-Walker, Harper, & Jensen, 2010) have both been examined as having important influences on prosocial behavior, Yorgason and Gustafson (chapter 10) highlight the unique role that grandparents play in prosocial development and the many dimensions of grandparent-grandchild relationships that are differentially associated with prosocial behavior. This chapter presents new longitudinal research suggesting that multiple aspects of grandparent involvement are associated with both initial levels and change in prosocial development over time and highlights how these patterns vary as a function of the target of prosocial behavior (e.g., friends, family, strangers). Taken together, this section combines well-established areas of socialization with relatively understudied areas and suggests utility in considering a variety of socialization sources as a means of better understanding the development of different types of prosocial behavior.

The early studies on emergency bystander situations (Latane & Darley, 1970) aptly demonstrated the importance of contextual influences on prosocial behavior. In those studies, researchers manipulated immediate, situational characteristics and showed how such manipulations could influence helping rates. However, there was less interest in individual differences in prosocial responding in those studies. Furthermore, more distal contextual influences such as sociocultural characteristics were less explored. This section of the volume examines research that focuses on culture group and classroom cultural influences on prosocial behavior. Early research on prosocial behavior among cultural groups tended to identify and emphasize comparisons across such groups. Those studies laid the foundation for understanding the generalizability of existing models of prosocial behavior across societies. This research also demonstrated commonalities and differences between culture groups, which led to investigations designed to understand the reasons for such patterns of findings. Although such studies continue to date and provide basic information regarding prosocial behavior in nonstudied societies, more recent research has tended to focus on developing models for specific culture groups, or models that account for culture group differences in prosocial behavior.

In the current volume, de Guzman, Do, and Kok (chapter 11) provide a thorough review of culturally grounded theories and research on prosocial behavior and advocate the need for more within-culture studies using mixed methodologies (i.e., quantitative and qualitative approaches). Given the relative lack of understanding of different culture groups and the vulnerability of cultural biases in conducting research across cultures, de Guzman and her colleagues propose the adoption of anthropological methods to address these concerns and highlight the importance of interdisciplinary research in conducting cultural studies on prosocial behavior. In chapter 12, Carlo, Knight, Basilio, and Davis provide a rare example of within-culture research on prosocial behavior in an ethnic minority group by summarizing decades of studies focusing on Mexican American populations. In the most recent series of studies, their research suggests the relevance of cultural values, cultural identity, and culture-specific parenting practices for predicting different forms of prosocial behavior in Mexican American early adolescents. Moreover, in contrast to most prior research in specific culture groups, this chapter provides examples of studies designed to establish adequate evidence of measurement properties of prosocial tendencies.

McGinley, Opal, Richaud, and Mesurado (chapter 13) tackle the topics of both culture and measurement in their chapter by conducting a brief but thorough review and critique of measures of prosocial behavior, with particular emphasis

on the Prosocial Tendencies Measure (PTM). These scholars summarize the existing evidence on the reliability and validity of the measure across different cultural
groups and provide new evidence on the psychometric properties of the PTM with
a sample from Argentina. This chapter reminds us of the key issue of measurement and provides important recommendations for future research across cultures. Finally, Bergin (chapter 14) considers a different cultural milieu—that of the
school classroom. Bergin thoroughly describes the forms of prosocial behavior
often exhibited in school classrooms, age trends in such behaviors in those contexts, and the various influences of those behaviors. She cogently argues for the
importance of studying prosocial behaviors in these contexts as distinct from other
social contexts (e.g., neighborhoods, home) and outlines suggestions and recommendations for promoting prosocial behavior in schools and school classrooms.
In sum, this section tackles the essential issue of context as it relates to different
types of prosocial behavior, with particular emphasis on the cultural context, and
highlights the continued need to consider a variety of contextual variables in order
to more clearly understand the multidimensional nature of prosocial behavior.

TARGETS OF PROSOCIAL BEHAVIOR

Recent research has begun to explore different targets of prosocial behavior in
an attempt to determine if there are different predictors and outcomes associated
with prosocial behavior toward one target versus another. While several chapters
in previously mentioned sections have considered targets, this section includes
two chapters that look specifically at different family members as targets of prosocial behavior. Certainly broad social psychological approaches to in-group and
out-group helping suggest that individuals approach prosocial behavior differently
when the target is part of their in-group as opposed to their out-group (e.g., Batson,
Chang, Orr, & Rowland, 2002; Stürmer & Snyder, 2010); but a more developmental approach considering the targets of prosocial behavior is warranted. Indeed,
much of the research on prosocial behavior to date looks at helping behavior
toward strangers, or even more frequently does not distinguish between strangers, peers, and friends. A relational approach to prosocial development suggests
importance in the examination of prosocial behavior toward those with whom
one has a relationship (e.g., friends, parents, siblings, grandparents) and highlights
different aspects of these relationships as the most important predictors of prosocial behavior within that relationship (Amato, 1990; Eberly & Montemayor, 1998,
1999; Padilla-Walker & Christensen, 2011). Indeed, this type of relational prosocial
behavior appears to be far more prevalent than prosocial behavior toward strangers, because children and adolescents spend the majority of their time among family and friends rather than strangers and report more frequent prosocial behavior
toward friends and family than toward strangers (Padilla-Walker & Christensen,
2011). In addition, relational prosocial behavior is differentially motivated; with

socialization, relationship quality, and relationship roles playing a more significant role in helping behavior toward friends and family than toward strangers.

To highlight this point within the parent-child relationship, Lewis (chapter 15) provides a careful analysis of myriad aspects of the parent-child relationship that promote different types of prosocial behavior toward parents and how these resulting prosocial behaviors continue to shape the parent-child relationship. Within the focus on parents as a target of prosocial behavior, this chapter also highlights different forms that prosocial behavior might take within the parent-child relationship and how these forms might differentially impact relationship quality. Relatedly, Kumru and Yağmurlu (chapter 16) focus on a variety of prosocial behaviors directed toward both siblings and grandparents and how the complex dynamics of the relationship context, as well as culture, influence the frequency and type of prosocial behavior toward those with whom children are in a relationship. This chapter also examines the complicated role of the parent-child relationship as a moderator of prosocial behavior toward other family members and emphasizes both evolutionary and relational explanations for these processes. Taken together, these chapters argue that prosocial behavior toward family members is unique from prosocial behavior toward other targets and that future research is warranted on the role of children's and adolescents' prosocial behavior not only toward parents but also toward other immediate (i.e., siblings) and extended (i.e., aunts, uncles, grandparents) family members. This is a relatively understudied area with numerous fruitful avenues for continued research.

TYPES OF PROSOCIAL BEHAVIOR

This volume repeatedly highlights the complexity of different types of prosocial behavior and the need to more carefully define and delineate between types of prosocial behavior as the field moves forward. Broadly, both low- and high-cost prosocial behaviors are often combined within single measures but have different predictors and outcomes as well as different meanings and motivations (Eisenberg & Spinrad, chapter 2). As another example of the importance of considering the type of prosocial behavior, Eisenberg and Spinrad highlight recent research on the construct of pathological prosocial behavior, which is behavior that is intended for good but which actually harms either the recipient or the initiator of the behavior (Oakley, Knafo, & McGrath, 2012) and likely has quite different correlates than does extended volunteering or prosocial behavior toward a close friend.

Developmental age is another factor that influences the type of prosocial behavior that is prevalent. Indeed, even very young children display a variety of different prosocial behaviors that are motivated and socialized by different factors (Laible & Karahuta, chapter 17), and that may be associated with the development of different prosocial behaviors over time. This chapter focuses on three specific types of prosocial behavior that emerge within the first three years of life, namely, responsiveness, helping, and ability to work with others. Laible and Karahuta also highlight differences in the development of these behaviors as a function of target and suggest fruitful avenues for future research focusing on the ontogeny of pro-social behavior. At the other end of the developmental spectrum covered in this volume, chapter 18 (Randall & Wenner) focuses specifically on prosocial behavior among college students and highlights the different types of prosocial behavior assessed using the Prosocial Tendencies Measure (PTM; see Carlo, 2014). The PTM is a relatively recent attempt to specifically examine different types of pro-social behavior and assesses six different motivations for, or contexts of, prosocial behavior: namely public, anonymous, dire, emotional, compliant, and altruistic. While some helping behavior may be elicited by an emotionally evocative situ-ation, other helping may be extrinsically reinforced through a reward. To date, research using the PTM has resulted in a flurry of studies that demonstrate unique correlates of each type of prosocial behavior (in this volume see chapters 12, 13, and 18, in particular). Randall and Wenner suggest that although college students are often perceived as being self-centered and involved primarily in risk behaviors, they are also capable of (and engage in) a wide variety of prosocial behaviors. This chapter also presents new analyses examining correlates and gender differences in prosocial tendencies during the college years.

While the majority of prosocial behavior covered in these chapters exist in some variety of dyadic interaction, other types of prosocial behavior are much more broad and are more often directed toward strangers and groups of individuals or prosocial causes, such as in the case of volunteerism (Hart & Sulik, chapter 19) and civic engagement (Pratt & Lawford, chapter 20). Hart and Sulik briefly discuss different types of volunteering, explore cross-national and cross-cultural differ-ences in rates of volunteering, and present a compelling argument regarding the social construction of volunteering. Presenting new analyses using historical data, this chapter suggests that how different cultures and cohorts socially construct volunteering is likely associated with rates and correlates of volunteering behavior over time and across cultures. Relatedly, Pratt and Lawford (chapter 20) examine generativity, or one's focus on the needs of the next generation, as a predictor of a variety of different types of prosocial behavior, including civic engagement, envi-ronmental awareness, vocational involvement, and political activism. This chapter highlights multidimensionality in terms of differences in longitudinal relations as a function of the type of prosocial outcome as well as the type of measurement (questionnaire versus narrative).

It should also be noted that the final three chapters in this section of the volume focus on relatively high-cost types of prosocial behavior as opposed to prosocial behavior that might be considered lower cost. As previously mentioned, although research does not always make this distinction, it is clear that there are different predictors and possibly outcomes as a function of the cost of the behavior, and sig-nificant attention has been paid to those who engage in high-cost prosocial behav-ior in exemplary or supererogatory ways (Hart & Fegley, 1995; Walker & Hennig,

2004). In an attempt to explore this literature with an eye to multidimensionality, Walker (chapter 21) highlights that there are several types of exemplary prosocial behavior, or ways in which one can be a prosocial exemplar. Walker addresses the issue of motivation that is raised throughout the volume by arguing that motivation for prosocial behavior can be self-regarding (as opposed to solely self-denying) if prosocial behavior is an integral part of one's personality and moral identity. Further, he suggests that those who engage in prosocially exemplary behavior are often able to integrate agentic and communal motivations so that prosocial behavior becomes part of an individual's self-definition and therefore advances one's own interests as well as the interests of others. Taken together, this section highlights a number of different targets and types of prosocial behavior, representing diverse theoretical approaches and differing correlates and outcomes as a function of the multidimensionality of prosocial behavior. This section also covers a variety of ages, from infancy to adulthood, and suggests the need to consider these different targets and types of behavior from a developmental framework.

Conclusion

We had a simple purpose in publishing this volume—to spur much more research on prosocial behavior. Although there have been many significant advances since the early studies of Hartshorne and his colleagues, the remaining gaps in our understanding of prosocial behavior and its correlates are many. The volume does not do justice to the completeness of research on prosocial behavior, as such an endeavor would require several volumes reflecting the various disciplinary approaches. The chapter authors were challenged to summarize and critique advances within their own areas of expertise but, more importantly, to provide recommendations and directions for future research. The major common theme throughout the volume is the multidimensionality of prosocial behavior. Therefore, each chapter concludes with homage to this concept within the context of the topic of the chapter. We believe this is one, though clearly not the only, important conceptual idea that can move scholarly work in the area of prosocial behavior substantially forward. However, beyond the concept of multidimensionality, the chapters speak for themselves on the richness of ideas, models, theories, measures, and empirical evidence in the field of prosocial behavior. The resulting cornucopia provides direction for exciting new avenues of future research in the area of prosocial behavior and development.

References

Amato, P. (1990). Personality and social network involvement as predictors of helping behavior in everyday life. *Social Psychology Quarterly, 53*, 31–43.

Batson, C. D. (1998). Altruism and prosocial behavior. In D. T. Gilbert, S. T. Fiske, & G. Lindzey (Eds.), *The handbook of social psychology* (4th ed., Vol. 2, pp. 282–316). Boston: McGraw-Hill.

Batson, C. D., Chang, J., Orr, R., & Rowland, J. (2002). Empathy, attitudes and action: Can feeling for a member of a stigmatized group motivate one to help the group? *Personality and Social Psychology Bulletin, 28*(12), 1656–1666.

Carlo, G. (2014). The development and correlates of prosocial moral behaviors. In M. Killen & J. G. Smetana (Eds.), *Handbook of moral development* (2nd ed., pp. 208–234). New York: Psychology Press.

Coyne, S. M., Nelson, D. A., & Underwood, M. (2010). Aggression in children. In P. K. Smith & C. H. Hart (Eds.), *The Wiley-Blackwell handbook of childhood social development* (2nd ed., pp. 491–509). Oxford, UK: Wiley-Blackwell.

Dunn, J. (2007). Siblings and socialization. In J. E. Grusec & P. D. Hastings (Eds.), *Handbook of socialization* (pp. 309–327). New York: Guilford Press.

Eberly, M. B., & Montemayor, R. (1998). Doing good deeds: An examination of adolescent prosocial behavior in the context of parent/adolescent relationships. *Journal of Early Adolescence, 13*, 403–432.

Eberly, M. B., & Montemayor, R. (1999). Adolescent affection and helpfulness toward parents: A 2-year follow-up. *The Journal of Early Adolescence, 19*, 226–248.

Eisenberg, N., Fabes, R. A., & Miller, P. A. (1990). The evolutionary and neurological roots of prosocial behavior. In L. Ellis & H. Hoffman (Eds.), *Crime in biological, social, and moral contexts* (pp. 247–260). New York: Praeger.

Eisenberg, N., Fabes, R., & Spinrad, T. L. (2006). Prosocial development. In N. Eisenberg, W. Damon, & R. M. Lerner (Eds.), *Handbook of child psychology: Vol. 3. Social, emotional, and personality development* (6th ed., pp. 646–718). Hoboken, NJ: Wiley & Sons.

Eisenberg-Berg, N. (1979). Development of children's prosocial moral judgment. *Developmental Psychology, 15*, 128–137.

El-Sheikh, M., & Erath, S. A. (2011). Family conflict, autonomic nervous system functioning, and child adaptation: State of the science and future directions. *Development and Psychopathology, 23*, 703–721.

Grusec, J. E. (2006). The development of moral behavior and conscience from a socialization perspective. In M. Killen & J. Smetana (Eds.), *Handbook of moral development* (pp. 243–266). Mahwah, NJ: Erlbaum.

Hart, D., & Fegley, S. (1995). Prosocial behavior and caring in adolescence: Relations to self-understanding and social judgment. *Child Development, 66*(5), 1346–1359.

Hartshorne, H., May, M. A., & Shuttleworth, F. K. (1930). *Studies in the nature of character.* New York: MacMillan.

Hastings, P. D., Shirtcliff, E. A., Klimes-Dougan, B., Allison, A. L., Derose, L., Kendziora, K. T…Zahn-Waxler, C. (2011). Allostasis and the development of internalizing and externalizing problems: Changing relations with physiological systems across adolescence. *Development and Psychopathology, 23*, 1149–1165.

Hastings, P. D., Utendale, W. T., & Sullivan, C. (2007). The socialization of prosocial development. In J. E. Grusec & P. D. Hastings (Eds.), *Handbook of socialization* (pp. 638–664). New York: Guilford Press.

Hoffman, M. L. (1970). Moral development. In P. Mussen (Ed.), *Handbook of Child Psychology* (pp. 261–361). New York: John Wiley.

Kohlberg, L. (1969). Stage and sequence: The cognitive-developmental approach to socialization. In D. Goslin (Ed.), *Handbook of socialization theory and research*. Stokie,
IL: Rand McNally.

Latane, B., & Darley, J. M. (1970). *The unresponsive bystander: Why doesn't he help?*
New York: Appleton-Crofts.

Oakley B., Knafo, A., & McGrath, M. (2012). Pathological altruism: An introduction. In
B. Oakley, A. Knafo, G. Madhavan, & D. S. Wilson (Eds.). *Pathological altruism* (pp. 3–9).
Oxford, UK: Oxford University Press.

Padilla-Walker, L. M., & Christensen, K. J. (2011). Empathy and self-regulation as mediators
between parenting and adolescents' prosocial behaviors toward strangers, friends, and
family. *Journal of Research on Adolescence, 21*, 545–551.

Padilla-Walker, L. M., Harper, J. M., & Jensen, A. C. (2010). Self-regulation as a mediator
between sibling relationship quality and early adolescents' positive and negative outcomes. *Journal of Family Psychology, 24*, 419–428.

Radke-Yarrow, M., Zahn-Waxler, C., & Chapman, M. (1983). Children's prosocial dispositions and behaviors. In P. H. Mussen (Ed.), *Carmichael's manual of child psychology*
(Vol. 4, pp. 469–546). New York: Wiley.

Staub, E. (1979). *Positive social behavior and morality: Socialization and development* (Vol. 2).
New York: Academic.

Stürmer, S., & Snyder, M. (2010). Helping "us" versus "them": Towards a group-level theory
of helping and altruism within and across group boundaries. In S. Stürmer & M. Snyder
(Eds.), *The psychology of prosocial behavior: Group processes, intergroup relations, and
helping* (pp. 33–58). Oxford, UK: Wiley-Blackwell.

Walker, L. J., & Hennig, K. H. (2004). Differing conceptions of moral exemplarity: Just,
brave and caring. *Journal of Personality and Social Psychology, 86*, 629–647.

Multidimensionality of Prosocial Behavior

RETHINKING THE CONCEPTUALIZATION AND DEVELOPMENT OF PROSOCIAL BEHAVIOR

Nancy Eisenberg and Tracy L. Spinrad

After a dramatic increase in research on prosocial responding from the late 1970s to approximately the early 1990s, there was an observable decline in research on the topic for more than a decade. However, there appears to be renewed interest in prosocial behavior and emotions in recent years. The newest generation of research is stronger in some respects than the last (e.g., in terms of the use of sophisticated statistical methods and longitudinal designs, as well as clever experiments with infants); however, many conceptual issues have not been adequately discussed or resolved, and many questions remain unanswered. In this chapter, we discuss a range of issues relevant to the current and next generation of work, including definitional issues, nuances to be considered in conceptualizing prosocial behavior, and how recent empirical work requires an updating of Hoffman's theory on early empathy-related responding and of conclusions regarding the normative development of prosocial responding in childhood and adolescence. Central to all of the aforementioned issues—to varying degrees—is consideration of the multidimensionality of prosocial behavior and the importance of acknowledging the diversity of prosocial responses when discussing the development, origins, and consequences of prosocial behavior.

Definitional and Conceptual Issues

Prosocial behavior often has been defined as voluntary behavior intended to benefit another (Eisenberg, Fabes, & Spinrad, 2006). Note that this definition does not limit the range of motivations that might underlie a prosocial behavior, including motives as diverse as ingratiation, the desire to incur a debt, the desire to improve another's welfare, or acting in accordance with internalized moral values. Thus, there are many types of prosocial behavior and not all of them are motivated by positive or moral concerns. Indeed, researchers studying prosocial moral judgment have demonstrated that children and adolescents express a range of reasons for acting prosocially, including hedonistic reasons, social and normative reasons, other-oriented reasons, and internalized moral values (see Eisenberg, 1986).

Altruism is one subtype of prosocial behavior that is important to differentiate from other types of prosocial behavior. Generally it is defined as prosocial behavior motivated by concern for another and, for some theorists, by internalized moral values rather than concrete or social rewards (Batson, 1991; Eisenberg et al., 2006). A number of other, sometimes related dimensions for categorizing prosocial behaviors have been explicitly or implicitly suggested in research, including the distinction between spontaneously emitted versus compliant (i.e., requested) prosocial behavior (Eisenberg, Cameron, Tryon, & Dodez, 1981), between public and private prosocial behaviors (e.g., Carlo & Randall, 2002), between costly and less costly prosocial behaviors (e.g., Eisenberg et al., 1999, Eisenberg & Shell, 1986), and between spontaneous prosocial behaviors elicited by strong environmental cues (e.g., emergencies) and planned prosocial behaviors that tend to occur over time (Amato, 1985).

Although the motivation for performing prosocial actions is critical (Padilla-Walker & Carlo, chapter 1, this volume), it is often unknown. Researchers using experimental paradigms have often partially dealt with this problem by constructing situations in which enacted prosocial behavior is unlikely to be motivated by pleasing others (e.g., by making the helping situation appear to be anonymous) or self-gain, but often motives for prosocial behaviors in a given context can be diverse. Even more problematic are trait measures of prosocial behavior that usually elicit ratings of prosocial behavior without reference to motivation, although some investigators have developed questionnaire measures to assess different types of prosocial behaviors (e.g., anonymous, public, altruistic, compliant, or in dire or emotional contexts; Carlo & Randall, 2002). Of course, these different types of prosocial behaviors are not mutually exclusive; for example, a person can enact public prosocial behaviors in emotionally evocative circumstances. However, multiple motives for prosocial behaviors are rarely considered.

The nature of prosocial responding is relevant when studying the predictors, correlates, or potential sequelae of prosocial behavior. Although most of the aforementioned variations in prosocial behavior do not map one-to-one onto specific motives, they would be expected to relate, and sometimes have done so, to different constellations of traits, behaviors, and values. For example, spontaneously emitted prosocial behaviors that are somewhat costly (e.g., sharing an object), in comparison to prosocial behaviors that are emitted in response to a verbal or nonverbal request and/or are of low cost (e.g., passing art materials), tend to be more consistently associated with children's and adolescents' other-oriented prosocial moral reasoning, sympathy (feelings of concern or sorrow for another), and subsequent prosocial behavior, concurrently and often across time (Eisenberg et al.,

2002; Eisenberg et al., 1999; Eisenberg, McCreath, & Ahn, 1988; Eisenberg-Berg & Hand, 1979). This relation is likely because young children's (and perhaps older persons') spontaneously emitted, costly prosocial behaviors often seem to be motivated by sympathy (Eisenberg et al., 1988; Eisenberg & Fabes, 1990; Eisenberg-Berg & Hand, 1979), whereas young children who consistently comply with peers' requests for objects tend to be nonassertive (Eisenberg et al., 1981). By adolescence or adulthood, however, compliant prosocial behaviors, perhaps especially costly ones, tend to relate positively with sympathy, perspective taking, social responsibility, and ascription of responsibility to the self (Carlo, Hausmann, Christiansen, & Randall, 2003; Carlo, Knight, McGinley, & Hayes, 2011; Eisenberg et al., 2002), perhaps because, with age, compliant prosocial behaviors are increasingly motivated by internalized values or a prosocial self-image rather than nonassertiveness (Eisenberg, Hofer, Sulik, & Liew, in press).

Eisenberg (1986) argued that prosocial moral reasoning reflects motivations for prosocial behaviors and, more specifically, that the motivations reflect the hierarchy of goals, needs, and values in any particular helping situation. For example, if a child has a strong need to garner adult approval, that motive will be relevant in contexts in which an adult is likely to know he/she has helped another (e.g., a public context). If the same child assists in an anonymous context, some other need, value, or goal is likely to explain this behavior. If people tend to be motivated by sympathy, hold other-oriented values, and, as a consequence, have the goal of improving the emotional and physical state of others, one might expect them to be relatively likely to assist in contexts involving a distressed or needy other and in a context in which their behavior is likely to make a difference in the other's situation; they also should be relatively likely to assist when their prosocial behavior is anonymous and they cannot expect concrete or social rewards. In contrast, they might be less likely to help when the other person does not have a discernible need and when helping reflects normative expectations of "good behavior."

If moral reasoning reflects individuals' motives, needs, and goals, we would expect it to relate in somewhat different ways to various types of prosocial behavior. Consistent with Eisenberg's (1986) arguments, Carlo et al. (2003) found that approval-oriented prosocial moral reasoning was positively related to public prosocial behavior for both early and middle adolescents and negatively related to altruism (for both age groups) and dire prosocial behavior (for middle adolescents). Hedonistic moral reasoning was negatively related to compliant, anonymous, dire, emotional, and altruistic prosocial behavior for at least one of the age groups but was unrelated to public prosocial behavior. Internalized moral reasoning (references in internalized norms, moral emotion, or values) related to all types of prosocial behavior for one (compliant, anonymous, dire, altruistic prosocial behavior) or both (emotional prosocial behavior) age groups but was unrelated to public prosocial behavior. In a sample of college students, hedonistic and approval-oriented moral reasoning were positively related to public prosocial behavior and negatively related to altruistic prosocial behavior; internalized reasoning was negatively related to public prosocial behavior and positively related to emotional, compliant, and altruistic prosocial behavior (Carlo & Randall, 2002). Thus, even when using trait (global questionnaire) measures of various types of prosocial behavior, most of the relations between moral reasoning and prosocial behavior appeared to reflect the motivational basis of the prosocial behavior.

One would reasonably expect temperament/personality or other child characteristics to be differentially related to various modes of prosocial behavior. Carlo et al. (2011) found that sympathy was especially strongly positively related to youths' emotional prosocial behavior and prosocial behavior in dire circumstances (although, surprisingly, it was negatively related to altruism, perhaps because such behavior was more often motivated by values). Carlo et al. (2003) also reported positive relations between sympathy and both dire and emotional prosocial behavior (as well as compliant behavior); public and anonymous prosocial behaviors were unrelated to sympathy, whereas altruism was positive related to sympathy for early (and not middle) adolescents. Similarly, in a study with Mexican American college students, self-reported sympathy/perspective taking was positively related to most types of prosocial behaviors (i.e., altruism, emotionality, dire, anonymous, compliant), but not those performed that were selected to be performed in public (Carlo, McGinley, Hayes, Batenhorst, & Wilkinson, 2012). College students' sympathy was negatively related to public prosocial behavior and positively related to all other types (Carlo & Randall, 2002). Thus, although findings of relations between sympathy and altruistic prosocial behavior are not very consistent, sympathy tends to be associated with dire and emotional prosocial behavior (and often compliant behavior) and not public prosocial behavior.

The importance of context in combination with personal characteristics (and the needs and goals associated with them) when predicting prosocial behavior is illustrated in studies of young children who view adults acting as if they are hurt or sad. Whether toddlers assist or not and how they assist seems to be partly due to who needs help (e.g., someone well known or a stranger) and the child's personality (e.g., assertiveness, shyness). Shy children tend to be hesitant to approach a stranger and/or exhibit low empathy (Liew et al., 2011; Young, Fox, & Zahn-Waxler, 1999), but shyness does not appear to be a factor if the adult in the situation is a parent (Young et al., 1999). Moreover, shy children tend to go to their parent when they view a hurt stranger; they may do so to help indirectly (tell their mother so she might assist) as well as to calm themselves (Liew et al., 2011). In addition, it may be highly assertive young children—those who are also likely to be aggressive—are most likely to show concern and to attend to the other in a helping context involving contact with a relative stranger (Gill & Calkins, 2003). In preschool and beyond, children who are more sociable and more likely to approach novel people and things are more likely to help others (e.g., Stanhope, Bell, & Parker-Cohen, 1987; see Eisenberg & Fabes, 1998; Eisenberg et al., 2006), although introverts tend to help in ways that do not involve approaching another person (Suda & Fouts, 1980). Without considering the context as well as children's characteristics, motives, and goals, it is difficult to make sense of how young children behave in specific helping contexts.

The socialization antecedents of various types of prosocial behaviors would also be expected to differ (see Bergin, chapter 14, this volume; Padilla-Walker, chapter 7, this volume; Yorgason & Gustafson, chapter 10, this volume). In a study of adolescents, Carlo et al. (2011) elicited adolescents' reports of parental use of inductions (reasoning, explanations) for discipline which, according to the sample items, emphasized approval from family members or that the adolescent should feel good when he/she does things the mother likes. Inductions of this sort were positively related to most types of adolescent-reported prosocial behavior (e.g., emotional, direct, compliant, public), but less so with anonymous prosocial behaviors (significant in zero-order correlations but not in a model), and were negatively related to altruism in some analyses (but unrelated in zero-order correlations). This pattern makes sense if the inductions are viewed as discipline that highlighted the effects of the youths' behaviors for the parents and other family members but not necessarily for others outside the family. Moreover, Carlo et al. (2012) found that college students' close, positive relationship with their closest parent was positively correlated with altruism but not other types of prosocial behaviors. In a study of adolescent-reported parenting practices (Carlo et al., 2007), public prosocial behavior was associated with parental use of social and material rewards for prosocial behavior; the opposite pattern was true for altruism. Parental attempts to get their children involved in activities that provide experimental learning (e.g., volunteering) were positively associated with anonymous, compliant, and dire prosocial behavior. Parental conversations with youths about others' needs and moral themes were positively related to all types of prosocial behavior except they were negatively related to altruism, perhaps because there was little need to talk to altruistic youths about these issues. Reported parental responsiveness and demandingness were infrequently related to prosocial behavior. Although the relevant findings are not entirely as one might predict (e.g., Barry, Padilla-Walker, Madsen, & Nelson, 2008), the existing work suggests that the socialization of other-oriented prosocial behavior differs considerably from the socialization of selfishly motivated prosocial behavior or prosocial behavior motivated by the desire for approval, although research using measures other than youths' reports is very limited.

In summary, various prosocial behaviors differ in their motivation and, hence in their social and psychological significance. Thus, it is not surprising that different prosocial behaviors appear to be associated with different temperamental/personality dispositions and socialization experiences. Moreover, various sorts of prosocial behaviors would be expected to be associated with different outcomes, at least some of the time and in some contexts, sometimes due in part to differences in underlying motivation. We now turn to an example of how prosocial behaviors can vary in their outcomes for the self and others.

OUTCOME AS A DIFFERENTIATING FACTOR IN
PROSOCIAL BEHAVIOR

Prosocial behavior as defined involves the intention to help. But the intention to help and the reality in regard to the actual helpfulness of a prosocial behavior can be two different things. An important dimension of prosocial behavior is the outcome of the behavior for the other person, as well as for the self. The issue of outcome comes to the fore when considering pathological altruism.

Oakley, Knafo, and McGrath (2012, p. 4) defined a pathological altruist as "A person who *sincerely* engages in what he or she intends to be altruistic acts, but who harms the very person or group he or she is trying to help, often in unanticipated fashion; or harms others; or irrationally becomes a victim of his or her own altruistic actions." Other authors do not assume that pathological altruism necessarily involves a sincere intent to help others; for example, Turvey (2012) includes in the category of pathological altruists those who get pleasure or satisfaction from controlling or punishing others with self-sacrificing acts, including any resultant displays of suffering (e.g., a controlling parent who is generous to a child but uses sacrifice and martyrdom to get compliance with his/her wishes). Other examples of pathological altruism discussed by Turvey are masochistic altruism: "a maladaptive need to suffer or be the victim, compensating for profound envy, jealousy, anger, aggression, and/or low self-esteem and thoughts of inadequacy…a coping mechanism for masking inner negativity and conflict" (p. 179), as well as compulsive care taking of others.

O'Connor, Berry, Lewis, and Stiver (2012) discussed a type of pathological altruism when people witness someone in distress and develop pathogenic guilt: that is, they falsely believe they have caused another's distress and/or that they can relieve it. As a consequence, they may self-denigrate and inhibit their own normal behavior in an effort to avoid feeling better off than the distressed person or they may take impulsive or unwise actions they falsely believe will end the person's distress. Thus, they often perform actions that help no one or may harm others.

Maladaptive prosocial behavior in children seldom has been studied. However, there is little doubt that such behavior exists. For example, Zahn-Waxler (see Zahn-Waxler & Van Hulle, 2012) has studied children of depressed parents whose empathy can lead to pathogenic guilt, anxiety, and a sense of personal failure. Zahn-Waxler argues that genetic and environmental (e.g., familial) factors jointly cause some children, especially girls, to experience empathy-based guilt, which in turn contributes to costly prosocial behavior (e.g., toward a depressed parent) as well as depression.

Another possible example of problematic prosocial behavior in children is when they help excessively to deal with their own inadequacies. There is, for example, evidence that children who are anxious, inhibited, and emotionally unstable tend to be high in prosocial behavior performed in the presence of, or promised to, peers (O'Connor, Dollinger, Kennedy, & Pelletier-Smetko, 1979; see Eisenberg et al., 2006). Eisenberg (Eisenberg et al., 1981; Eisenberg et al., 1988) found that preschoolers high in observed compliant prosocial behavior were relatively non-assertive, prone to personal distress (a self-focused, aversive reaction to another's emotion or situation) rather than sympathy, and did not elicit positive reactions from peers when they engaged in prosocial behaviors; these children seemed to become targets for peers' requests. They also did not appear to help or share for other-oriented reasons (Eisenberg-Berg & Hand, 1979). Although their actions may have benefited their peers in small ways, being so compliant seemed to have disproportional negative consequences for the self in the peer context.

Consideration of varieties of pathological altruism (perhaps more aptly labeled pathological prosocial behavior) highlights dimensions of prosocial behavior that generally have been ignored such as the degree of negative outcomes for others, irrational costs to the self, and unhealthy motivating emotions and cognitions. In future work, it would be useful to consider motives that have seldom been examined such as pathogenic guilt and the desire to control others.

A focus on pathological altruism also highlights the need to consider cultural factors when thinking about types of prosocial behavior and their diverse motivations. Consider the extreme case of a suicide bomber who kills innocent strangers to further the cause of his/her people. In some groups such behavior is viewed as heroism, whereas in others it is viewed as pathological at best. Even when considering less extreme actions, what is considered pathological or a deviation from the norm and what is altruistic varies across cultures (Traphagan, 2012; see Eisenberg et al., 2006). Thus, there is a need to attend to the meaning of prosocial behaviors in various cultures (see Carlo, Knight, Basilio, & Davis, chapter 12, this volume; de Guzman, Do, & Kok, chapter 11, this volume).

WHAT ARE THE BOUNDARIES IN TERMS OF RECIPIENTS OF PROSOCIAL BEHAVIOR?

An underexamined issue when considering distinctions among various aspects of prosocial responding is the boundary conditions for the enactment of prosocial behavior or the experience of prosocial emotion. Consider the research of Oliner and Oliner (1988) on rescuers and nonrescuers of Jews in Nazi Europe. Rescuers and nonrescuers were similar in their endorsement of social conventional values such as the fulfillment of prescribed social roles and norms. The critical distinction was the range of persons whom they considered to be appropriate and worthy recipients of moral consideration and prosocial behavior. The rescuers reported learning from socializers that moral concerns such as justice and caring were applicable to others beyond the in-group—to the broader category of humanity—whereas such thoughts and sentiments were less common in nonrescuers.

The Oliners' findings are consistent with research showing that adults' reports of concern with and the desire to help humanity more generally were associated with concern for global human rights and humanitarian needs, low ethnocentrism, willingness to contribute to international humanitarian relief, being a member of a major international human rights or charity group, equal valuing of the lives of in-group and out-group members, and knowledge of global humanitarian concerns (McFarland, Webb, & Brown, 2012). In addition, adults for whom moral identity was very important reported more favorable attitudes toward relief efforts directed at out-group members, greater willingness to provide financial assistance to out-group members, less willingness to harm innocent out-group members not involved in a conflict, and more forgiveness of out-group members who transgressed against the in-group (Reed & Aquino, 2003).

Thus, prosocial behaviors can be partially categorized in terms of whether they are extended to people one knows and cares about, people one does not like, strangers, people in one's social in-group (i.e., groups someone belongs to), and/or people not in the in-group. Such distinctions are relevant to motivations for performing prosocial actions; for example, prosocial behaviors directed to members of an out-group or disliked others might be more likely to be motivated by internalized moral values (although they could also be motivated by self-protective and other reasons) than prosocial behaviors directed at family members and friends. Eisenberg (1983) found that elementary children and adolescents who verbalized higher level prosocial moral judgment were less likely to differentiate among potential recipients of aid in regard to whom they thought should be helped when in need.

The issue of in-group–out-group distinctions has received considerable attention in social psychological work and some attention in research on adults' empathy/sympathy (see Eisenberg, Eggum, & Di Giunta, 2010, for a review). In the social psychological work, there is evidence that people tend to see similarities between themselves and other in-group members and see out-group members as dissimilar from themselves (see Stürmer & Snyder, 2010); in general, this tendency is believed to increase perspective taking and sympathy with in-group members. Indeed, Batson and his colleagues (Batson, Chang, Orr, & Rowland, 2002; Batson et al., 1997) obtained evidence consistent with the argument that inducing empathy (defined as sympathy or empathic concern for another) through perspective taking can increase adult empathizers' valuing of the stigmatized person's welfare and can even generalize to the larger group to which the stigmatized person belongs (e.g., produces more positive attitudes toward stigmatized groups and more helping). However, some recent research on neurological responding to the emotions of in-group and out-group members suggests that adults do not easily empathize with people they do not like (Gutsell & Inzlicht, 2012). Moreover, there is evidence that adults who are induced to take the perspective of an out-group (or stigmatized) person in a context in which they may feel vulnerable (e.g., empathizing with an out-group member who contracted AIDS from unprotected sex) may want to distance themselves, and might feel negative toward, the out-group member (Batson et al., 1997).

There is very limited work on in-group–out-group considerations and children's prosocial behavior or empathy-related responding. Initial work indicates that the in-group bias in regard to prosocial behavior increases from age 3 to 8 (Fehr, Bernhard, & Rockenbach, 2008). Moreover, elementary and high school children are more likely to believe that people should help family and friends more than others, especially disliked others and stigmatized people (e.g., criminals; Eisenberg, 1983), and 5- to 13-year olds believe that other children feel more positive about, and more obligation to help, in-group members (Weller & Lagattuta, 2013).

De Guzman et al. (2008) found that children in the Philippines tended to exhibit more prosocial behavior toward relatives than nonrelatives, whereas children in the United States exhibited more prosocial behavior toward nonrelatives, often peers (the authors did not compare across groups). This is consistent with Eisenberg and Fabes's suggestion (1998) that children in traditional cultures help people they have a connection with more than children in Western, industrialized cultures, but may be less likely to assist people who are not in their in-group.

There is some evidence of relations between children's empathy-related responding and their prosocial responding toward out-group members. School children's dispositional empathy has been positively related to acceptance of individual differences (Bryant, 1982), liking of members of out-groups (Nesdale, Griffith, Durkin, & Maass, 2005), and lower aggression toward out-group members (Nesdale, Milliner, Duffy, & Griffiths, 2009). Adolescents' sympathy has been related to helping friends and strangers, but not family members (which was related only to supportive mothering; Padilla-Walker & Christensen, 2011; see Stürmer, Snyder, & Omoto, 2005, for similar findings with adults).

In a study of Colored minority-status adolescents in South Africa, youths' contact with white South Africans (friendships) was found to predict empathy, which increased positive attitudes toward whites and increased perceived variability among white people (Swart, Hewstone, Christ, & Voci, 2011). However, Nesdale and Lawson (2011) found that group norms affected the association between empathy and liking for out-group members of a different ethnicity. When children were induced to believe their group had a norm of inclusion (e.g., liking or wanting to work with members of the other team), higher empathy was positively associated with higher liking. However, when induced to believe that their group has a norm of exclusion (e.g., disliking or avoiding members of the other team who were from another ethnic group), liking of the out-group member did not differ between children low and high in empathy.

The socialization of prosocial behavior directed toward in-group members and other people may differ. Grusec, Goodnow, and Cohen (1996) found that routine (but not requested) participation in household chores was related to 9- and 14-year-olds' prosocial behavior in the family, although primarily for older youths and girls, but was not related to helping strangers. Hardy, Bhattacharjee, Reed, and Aquino (2010) reported that dimensions of adolescent-reported authoritative parenting (responsiveness, autonomy-granting, and demandingness) were related to a strongly moral identity, which in turn was positively related to the tendency to report having a moral or ethical obligation to show concern for the welfare/ interests of out-group members (e.g., those from another country, ethnicity, or religion or strangers). It is not clear whether the positive parenting reported by the more inclusive group also was coupled with parenting values and behaviors that communicated or taught children to have a broader conception of one's in-group.

In summary, an important distinction among prosocial behaviors is whether they are directed toward in-group or liked individuals versus out-group or disliked individuals. Moreover, empathy-related responding seems to play an important role in social cognitions and in the quality of behavior directed toward out-group members. Because of the huge practical implications of this distinction for harmony among people, it is important that greater attention be paid to the recipient of prosocial behavior and variables that foster prosocial behavior directed toward out-group members.

DEVELOPMENTAL CHANGE IN PROSOCIAL BEHAVIOR
IN INFANCY AND TODDLERHOOD

In understanding the development of prosocial behavior in young children, researchers have nearly exclusively relied on Hoffman's developmental theory (Hoffman, 2000). Hoffman proposed a series of phases delineating the development of empathy and prosocial behavior. Specifically, he argued that rudimentary forms of empathy are evident in newborns. This phase, known as *global empathic distress*, is observed in newborns' reactive or contagious cries. These reactions are viewed as simple precursors to empathy. Hoffman further argued that beginning around the end of the first year of life, infants exhibit *egocentric empathic distress*. In this period, infants make efforts to reduce their own distress when exposed to others' distress. Personal distress responses are likely during this phase because infants have not yet developed the ability to differentiate their own distress from that of another.

Early in the second year of life, Hoffman suggested that toddlers can show *quasi-egocentric empathic distress*. During this phase, toddlers may experience concern for others; however, because toddlers lack cognitive and perspective-taking skills, they may not provide accurate or effective helping behaviors. That is, toddlers may pat, touch, hug or give assistance to victims of distress, but they are likely to give the distressed person what they themselves find comforting. Hoffman argued that *veridical empathy*, beginning around the end of the second year of life or later, was more indicative of real empathy once toddlers have developed self-other differentiation. Thus, he argued that empathy does not develop until later into the second year of life and improves substantially with age and changes in cognitive functioning. By 9 to 10 years of age, Hoffman argued that children begin to experience empathy for those beyond the immediate situation (such as distress for another's plight or for groups/classes of people).

There has been some support for the notion that self-other differentiation is associated with toddlers' prosocial behavior and empathy-related responding. In a number of studies, researchers have shown that toddlers who demonstrate self-recognition tend to be relatively empathic and prosocial (Bischof-Köhler, 2012; Johnson, 1982; Zahn-Waxler, Radke-Yarrow, Wagner, & Chapman, 1992; Zahn-Waxler, Schiro, Robinson, Emde, & Schmitz, 2001). In each of these studies, researchers have relied on the classic "rouge on the nose" test to assess toddlers' mirror self-recognition. Lewis and Ramsay (2004) argued that with maturation, starting around 15 months of age, infants develop a mental state of "self." Thus, there is a relatively advanced level of cognitive maturation that is required before mirror self-recognition is achieved (Butterworth, 1992; Davidov, Zahn-Waxler, Roth-Hanania & Knafo, 2013).

However, recent work provides evidence that infants may develop self-other differentiation skills (or precursors to such skills) much earlier than the second year of life. For example, children begin to demonstrate an understanding of others' intentions, goals, and desires between 9 and 12 months (Woodward, 1999, 2003). Even earlier, 3- to 9-month-old infants distinguish between the experience of self-created movement versus movement produced by someone else, indicating a rudimentary conceptualization of self (Rochat & Striano, 2002).

Moreover, infants have the ability to make judgments about others' moral character early in development—an ability that suggests relative sophistication in understanding others' mental states. In recent work, researchers have shown that young infants reason about others' prosocial and antisocial goals (Kuhlmeier, Wynn & Bloom, 2003; Premack & Premack, 1997). In a series of studies, Hamlin and colleagues showed that infants as young as 3 months of age preferred a "good" puppet (one that helps a protagonist achieve a goal) versus a "bad" puppet (Hamlin & Wynn, 2011; Hamlin, Wynn & Bloom, 2007, 2010; Hamlin, Wynn, Bloom, & Mahajan, 2011). Similarly, 6-month-old infants discriminate geometrical shapes that are helping versus hindering others (Hamlin et al., 2007). In addition, toddlers have been shown to evaluate the source of information when making choices. Among a sample of 16-month olds, toddlers were likely to choose a food that a prosocial puppet expressed liking over disliking, but they ignored such information from an antisocial puppet (Hamlin & Wynn, 2012).

Thus, the development of empathy may begin well before Hoffman argued (see Laible & Karahuta, chapter 17, this volume). Of course, one issue with this claim is that few researchers have attempted to study empathy and prosocial behavior in infants and very young toddlers. As an exception, Roth-Hanania, Davidov and Zahn-Waxler (2011) studied this possibility and found that 8- and 10-month-olds occasionally showed affective and cognitive concern for others and these behaviors increased across the second year of life. These findings suggest that empathy and sympathy may be experienced earlier in development than proposed by Hoffman.

The ability to behave prosocially in the early years clearly depends on the type of prosocial behavior. Certain tasks, such as instrumental helping tasks (i.e., picking up a dropped clothespin that the experimenter is reaching for), are much easier to accomplish than are those that require higher levels of emotion understanding or self-sacrifice. Warneken and Tomasello (2007) showed that toddlers as young as 14 to 18 months behave prosocially in straightforward instrumental tasks (i.e., assisting someone in reaching their goals, such as picking up a dropped object) and that chimpanzees are also capable of this type of prosocial behavior (Warneken & Tomasello, 2006). Moreover, researchers have demonstrated that instrumental helping is relatively frequent among toddlers (Svetlova, Nicols, & Brownell, 2010) and does not require encouragement or external motivation (Warneken & Tomasello, in press; also see Warneken & Tomasello, 2008).

In contrast to instrumental helping tasks, prosocial behavior in response to others' emotions appears to emerge later in development. Svetlova et al. (2010) found that prosocial responses to adults' emotions (i.e., "I'm sad", "I'm cold") were unlikely among 18-month-olds without extensive prompts. Prosocial behaviors to these emotional tasks were more frequent and required less communication by 30 months of age. Thus, researchers are confident that instrumental helping tasks are simpler than empathic helping tasks, particularly for those tasks that require some self-sacrifice (i.e., giving something of their own to the adult).

There is less consensus regarding the development of sharing behavior, which may not require as much emotion understanding and perspective taking as cooperative tasks. Hay and Rheingold (1983) described sharing as showing objects as well as giving objects and noted its emergence around 9 to 10 months of age (with sharing being quite frequent in the second year of life), whereas others report that sharing food with an unfamiliar adult at no personal cost appears to be evident by 25 months of age but not by 18 months (Brownell, Svetlova, & Nichols, 2009).

Although the majority of work pertaining to the early development of prosocial behavior has focused on those behaviors directed toward adults, the development of prosocial behavior toward peers also is of interest. Young toddlers evidence very little understanding of peers' emotions/affective messages (Nichols, Svetlova, & Brownell, 2010), which may account for toddlers' infrequent prosocial behavior toward peers in natural settings (Caplan & Hay, 1989; Lamb & Zakhireh, 1997; Demetriou & Hay, 2004). Indeed, children do not appear to reliably cooperate with each other until 24 to 30 months of age (Brownell & Carriger, 1990; Brownell, Ramani, & Zerwas, 2006).

It is clear that young children consider aspects of the empathy-inducing context when responding to others' emotions. For example, toddlers are more likely to respond with prosocial behavior or empathy if they are not personally responsible for the others' distress (Zahn-Waxler, Radke-Yarrow, & King, 1979; Zahn-Waxler et al., 1992), although Demetrio and Hay (2004) found the opposite pattern when studying children's responses to peers' distress. Toddlers' consideration of context is also evident in that toddlers are more likely to help and show concern for their mothers over strangers (Kiang, Moreno, & Robinson, 2004; Knafo, Zahn-Waxler, Van Hulle, Robinson, & Rhee, 2008; Spinrad & Stifter, 2006; van der Mark, van IJzendoorn, & Bakermans-Kranenburg, 2002). In a recent study, Hepach, Vaish, and Tomasello (2012) showed that 3-year-old children tended to sympathize with a person whose distress was justified (e.g., a lid closes on the experimenter's fingers) but not when the distress was unjustified (e.g., a lid closes on the experimenter's sleeve). Similarly, young children show more concern and prosocial behavior toward a victim who was harmed (i.e., their picture was destroyed) than an unharmed victim, even when the victim did not express negative emotion (Vaish, Carpenter, & Tomasello, 2009). Thus, older toddlers and preschool-age children evaluate the context and cause of another's distress.

Questions still remain regarding whether Hoffman's developmental theory should be revised to acknowledge infants' earlier cognitive capabilities and the ontogeny of empathy and prosocial behavior. The evidence is consistent, however, that empathy and prosocial behaviors increase as children mature, at least in the early years, whereas toddlers' self-distress reactions tend to decrease with age (Liew et al., 2011; van der Mark et al., 2002; Zahn-Waxler et al., 2001). In their meta-analysis, Eisenberg and Fabes (1998) showed increases in prosocial behavior within the preschool period (3 to 6 years), and school-age children were higher on prosocial behavior than were preschoolers, albeit the findings varied somewhat based on study characteristics.

Despite general increases in prosocial behavior and empathy with age, Hay and colleagues have argued that prosocial behaviors become more selective during the preschool years, governed by display rules, gender roles and norms, and friendships (Hay & Cook, 2007). These changes are thought to accompany changes in other skills such as emotion understanding, gender identity, and language abilities. Hay, Castle, Davies, Demetriou, and Stimson (1999) found that sharing behaviors with peers declined somewhat as children grew older, this decline was most clear for boys, but not girls. Moreover, boys showed reciprocity in their levels of sharing, whereas girls did not. Further, children responded favorably to peers' interest in items when the peers were same-sex, but not other-sex. Thus, sharing seems to be linked with gender and perhaps to a preference for one's own sex. Moreover, consistent with Hay and Cook's argument, children have been found to show more prosocial behavior toward friends versus nonfriends (Costin & Jones, 1992; Howes & Farver, 1987; Moore, 2009), those who reciprocate (Fujisawa, Kutsukake, & Hasegawa, 2008; Hay et al., 1999; Olson & Spelke, 2008), those who were previously willing to provide a toy over one who did not (Dunfield & Kuhlmeier, 2010), and, as previously noted, those in the in-group versus those in the out-group (Fehr et al., 2008; Weller & Lagattuta, 2013). Thus, it is clear that in some circumstances, children become more discriminating about whom to help with age.

DEVELOPMENT OF PROSOCIAL BEHAVIOR IN
CHILDHOOD AND ADOLESCENCE

Recent research suggests that the issue of developmental change in children's prosocial responding after the early years also merits more attention. Researchers have discussed numerous reasons why prosocial behaviors might be expected to increase in frequency in childhood and adolescence, including growth in sociocognitive functioning (e.g., moral reasoning, perspective taking, social problem-solving) and physical changes, including strength, that allow for a wider variety of prosocial actions (e.g., Fabes, Carlo, Kupanoff, & Laible, 1999; Eisenberg & Fabes, 1998). In a meta-analysis, children's prosocial behavior was found to increase, in general, from the early years into the elementary school years (Eisenberg & Fabes, 1998). Fabes et al. (1999), in a meta-analysis using the same data as Eisenberg and Fabes (1998), found evidence of more prosocial behavior in early adolescence (13–15 years of age) than in childhood (7–12 years). Older adolescents (age 16–18) had somewhat more prosocial behavior than did younger adolescents, but this difference was not significant. The studies included in this meta-analysis were relatively few and were mostly cross-sectional.

However, there appears to be some deviation in this normative pattern of change, especially as children move into adolescence, at least for some measures of prosocial behavior. Researchers have identified multiple trajectories of prosocial behaviors across childhood, and this work suggests that some types of prosocial behaviors may not increase in childhood and may even decline in frequency. For example, Côté, Tremblay, Nagin, Zoccolillo, and Vitaro (2002) examined trajectories of French-speaking, Canadian children's teacher-rated prosocial behavior across 6 to 12 years of age. For boys and girls separately, three trajectories were found: low starting and stable (43.8% of boys and 15.2% of girls), moderate starting and increasing from 6 to 9 years then decreasing from 9 to 12 years (54.4% of boys and 58.2% of girls), and high starting and stable (1.8% of boys and 26.7% of girls). In contrast, using boys from a lower socioeconomic (compared to Côté et al.) Canadian French-speaking sample and the same measure of prosocial behavior, Kokko, Tremblay, Lacourse, Nagin, and Vitaro (2006) reported two trajectories from age 6 to 12: low starting and declining (57.6%) and moderate starting and declining (42.4%). Thus, especially for Canadian boys of lower socioeconomic status, teachers' perceptions of prosocial behavior became somewhat more negative from age 6 to 12.

Using data from late childhood to midadolescence, Nantel-Vivier et al. (2009) examined prosocial development in two samples, one with Canadian boys (across 10 to 15 years of age; the same sample as Kokko et al., 2006) and one with Italian boys and girls (10 to 14 years of age). For the Canadian boys, similar to in Kokko et al. (2006), the trajectories indicated considerable stability in mean level differences in groups of boys but a general decline in teacher-reported prosocial behavior with age. Mothers were slightly more likely to report stability than decline in their sons' prosocial behavior. In the Italian sample, self-rating as well as teachers' ratings were obtained. Self-ratings tended to be stable over time for the three trajectory groups identified (low/stable 9%, moderate/stable 50%, high/stable 42%), whereas teachers' ratings indicated a decline for the majority of the children (low/stable 8%, moderate/declining 48%, high/declining 37%, increasing 7%). Thus, the findings indicate that teacher-rated prosocial behavior declines from midchildhood into early or midadolescence, especially for boys; it is not clear whether other measures of prosocial behavior show a similar decline (recall that self-ratings did not and mothers reported more stability than decline).

Recent evidence also suggests that change with age in self-reported prosocial behavior varies with the recipient of prosocial behavior. Reports of prosocial behavior toward family members generally were relatively stable from age 11 to 14, with 25% high and increasing and 21% initially declining and then increasing slightly. In contrast, self-reported prosocial behavior directed at friends generally increased with age, although the increasing slope leveled off for about 55% of the sample (Padilla-Walker, Dyer, Yorgason, Fraser, & Coyne, in press).

A few researchers have examined change solely within adolescence or from adolescence into early adulthood using longitudinal data. Jacobs, Vernon, and Eccles (2004) found a significant increase in self-reported engagement in helping/volunteering and prosocial behaviors more generally using assessments at 7th, 8th, and 10th grades, although the increase was mostly between 7th and 8th grade. Using growth curve modeling, Carlo, Crockett, Randall, and Roesch (2007) reported that self-reported prosocial behavior of adolescents of low socioeconomic status in a rural area significantly declined on average starting in 7th grade, although there was a small increase in 12th grade (one too small to result in a quadratic trend) and significant variability in adolescents' trajectories. Eisenberg, Cumberland, Guthrie, Murphy, and Shepard (2005) found that self-reported helping increased from 15–16 to 17–18, decreased from 17–18 to 21–22, exhibited stability from 21–22 to 23–24, and increased from 23–24 to 25–26 years. Finally, Kanacri, Pastorelli, Eisenberg, Zuffianò, and Caprara (2012) obtained a quadratic growth curve for Italian adolescents' self-reported prosocial responding, with a decline from age 13 to approximately age 17 and a subsequent slight rebound until age 21. However, when they analyzed for different trajectories, they found that 18% of the sample increased in prosocial behavior from a fairly low level initially to nearly as high as the highest group at age 21 (Kanacri et al., 2013).

Thus, the longitudinal findings are not consistent regarding age-related changes in adolescents' prosocial responding. However, taken together, it appears that prosocial behavior, with the exception of volunteering, community service, and other helping activities (e.g., helping a friend with homework), declines in adolescence but tend to rebound somewhat in late adolescence or early adulthood. In the future, there is a need to identify the reasons for this decline and if it occurs only in certain settings (e.g., school) and for certain kinds of prosocial behavior.

Conclusions and Future Directions

In this chapter, we have argued for the diversity of types of prosocial behavior and the need to consider this diversity when conceptualizing, operationalizing, and studying the correlates, origins, and outcomes of prosocial responding (also see Fortuna & Knafo, chapter 4, this volume). Without consideration of this diversity, it will be impossible to obtain a coherent pattern of findings regarding differences among various types of prosocial behavior; the psychological, social, and moral significance of these differences; the origins of these differences; and their differential relations to developmental outcomes such as maladjustment, the quality of social relationships, and the development of caring, moral dispositions. Such knowledge would be helpful in understanding ways to foster other-oriented prosocial behavior. We believe a particular need is research on the development of in-group–out-group distinctions in children's sympathy and prosocial behavior and of factors related to extensivity in caring and the application of moral values.

Another understudied issue is the relation of personality to various types of prosocial behaviors and to a caring disposition. For example, one factor of personality, agreeableness, has been associated with higher levels of sympathy and responsivity to others, potentially because both agreeableness and prosocial motivation involve a high level of social responsiveness (Graziano & Eisenberg, 1997; Graziano, Habashi, Sheese, & Tobin, 2007). The personality dimension of conscientiousness also is likely to be linked to prosocial behavior. For instance, Ferguson (2004) found that conscientiousness was related to frequency of blood donation, rate, and years of donation, particularly for men. More work focusing on the associations between personality and empathy or prosocial behavior in children or adolescence is needed, and researchers might also focus on the processes underlying these relations (i.e., regulatory skills may partly mediate the relations).

Acknowledgment

Work on this chapter was supported by a grant from NICHD to Carlos Valiente and Nancy Eisenberg, PIs.

References

Amato, P. R. (1985). An investigation of planned helping behavior. *Journal of Research in Personality, 19*(2), 232–252. doi: 10.1016/0092-6566(85)90031-5

Barry, C. M., Padilla-Walker, L. M., Madsen, S. D., & Nelson, L. J. (2008). The impact of maternal relationship quality on emerging adults' prosocial tendencies: Indirect effects via regulation of prosocial values. *Journal of Youth and Adolescence, 37*, 581–591. doi: 10.1007/s10964-007-9238-7

Batson, C. D. (1991). *The altruism question: Toward a social-psychological answer.* Hillsdale, NJ: Erlbaum.

Batson, C. D., Chang, J., Orr, R., & Rowland, J. (2002). Empathy, attitudes and action: Can feeling for a member of a stigmatized group motivate one to help the group? *Personality and Social Psychology Bulletin, 28*(12), 1656–1666. doi: 10.1177/014616702237647

Batson, C. D., Polycarpou, M. P., Harmon-Jones, E., Imhoff, H. J., Mitchener, E. C., Bednar, L. L., … Highberger, L. (1997). Empathy and attitudes: Can feeling for a member of a stigmatized group improve feelings toward the group? *Journal of Personality and Social Psychology, 72*(1), 105–118. doi: 10.1037/0022-3514.72.1.105

Bischof-Köhler, D. (2012). Empathy and self-recognition in phylogenetic and ontogenetic perspective. *Emotion Review, 4*(1), 40–48. doi: 10.1177/1754073911421377

Brownell, C. A., & Carriger, M. S. (1990). Changes in cooperation and self-other differentiation during the second year. *Child Development, 61*(4), 1164–1174. doi: 10.2307/1130884

Brownell, C. A., Ramani, G. B., & Zerwas, S. (2006). Becoming a social partner with peers: Cooperation and social understanding in one- and two-year-olds. *Child Development, 77*(4), 803–821. doi: 10.1111/j.1467-8624.2006.00904.x

Brownell, C. A., Svetlova, M., & Nichols, S. (2009). To share or not to share: When do toddlers respond to another's needs? *Infancy, 14*(1), 117–130. doi: 10.1080/15250000802569868

Bryant, B. K. (1982). An index of empathy for children and adolescents. *Child Development, 53*(2), 413–425. doi: 10.2307/1128984

Butterworth, G. (1992). Origins of self-perception in infancy. *Psychological Inquiry, 3*(2), 103–111. doi: 10.1207/s15327965pli0302_1

Caplan, M. Z., & Hay, D. F. (1989). Preschoolers' responses to peers' distress and beliefs about bystander intervention. *Journal of Child Psychology and Psychiatry, 30*(2), 231–242. doi: 10.1111/j.1469-7610.1989.tb00237.x

Carlo, G., Crockett, L. J., Randall, B. A., & Roesch, S. C. (2007). A latent growth curve analysis of prosocial behavior among rural adolescents. *Journal of Research on Adolescence, 17,* 301–324. doi:10.1111/j.1532-7795.2007.00524.x

Carlo, G., Hausmann, A., Christiansen, S., & Randall, B. A. (2003). Sociocognitive and behavioral correlates of a measure of prosocial tendencies for adolescents. *Journal of Early Adolescence, 23,* 107–134. doi:10.1177/0272431602239132

Carlo, G., Knight, G. P., McGinley, M., & Hayes, R. (2011). The roles of parental inductions, moral emotions, and moral cognitions in prosocial tendencies among Mexican American and European American early adolescents. *Journal of Early Adolescence, 31*(6), 757–781. doi: 10.1177/0272431610373100

Carlo, G., McGinley, M., Hayes, R., Batenhorst, C., & Wilkinson, J. (2007). Parenting styles or practices? Parenting, sympathy, and prosocial behaviors among adolescents. *Journal of Genetic Psychology, 168*(2), 147–176. doi: 10.3200/GNTP.168.2.147-176

Carlo, G., McGinley, M., Hayes, R. C., & Martinez, M. M. (2012). Empathy as a mediator of the relations between parent and peer attachment and prosocial and physically aggressive behaviors in Mexican American college students. *Journal of Social and Personal Relationships, 29*(3), 337–357. doi: 10.1177/0265407511431181

Carlo, G., & Randall, B. A. (2002). The development of a measure of prosocial behaviors for late adolescents. *Journal of Youth and Adolescence, 31*(1), 31–44.

Costin, S. E., & Jones, D. C. (1992). Friendship as a facilitator of emotional responsiveness and prosocial interventions among young children. *Developmental Psychology, 28*(5), 941–947. doi: 10.1037/0012-1649.28.5.941

Côté, S., Tremblay, R. E., Nagin, D., Zoccolillo, M., and Vitaro, F. (2002). The development of impulsivity, fearfulness, and helpfulness during childhood: Patterns of consistency and change in the trajectories of boys and girls. *Journal of Child Psychology and Psychiatry, 43,* 609–618. doi: 10.1111/1469-7610.00050

Davidov, M., Zahn-Waxler, C., Roth-Hanania, R., & Knafo, A. (2013). Concern for others in the first year of life: Theory, evidence, and avenues for research. *Child Developmental Perspectives, 7*(2), 126–131. doi: 10.1111/cdep.12028

de Guzman, M., Rosario T., Carlo, G., & Edwards, C. P. (2008). Prosocial behaviors in context: Examining the role of children's social companions. *International Journal of Behavioral Development, 32*(6), 522–530. doi: 10.1177/0165025408095557

Demetriou, H., & Hay, D. F. (2004). Toddlers' reactions to the distress of familiar peers: The importance of context. *Infancy, 6*(2), 299–318. doi: 10.1207/s15327078in0602_9

Dunfield, K. A., & Kuhlmeier, V. A. (2010). Intention-mediated selective helping in infancy. *Psychological Science, 21*(4), 523–527. doi: 10.1177/0956797610364119

Eisenberg, N. (1983). Children's differentiations among potential recipients of aid. *Child Development, 54*(3), 594–602. doi: 10.2307/1130046

Eisenberg, N. (1986). *Altruistic emotion, cognition, and behavior.* Hillsdale, N.J: Erlbaum.

Eisenberg, N., Cameron, E., Tryon, K., & Dodez, R. (1981). Socialization of prosocial behavior in the preschool classroom. *Developmental Psychology, 17,* 773–782. doi:10.1037/0012-1649.17.6.773

Eisenberg, N., Cumberland, A., Guthrie, I. K., Murphy, B. C., & Shepard, S. A. (2005). Age changes in prosocial responding and moral reasoning in adolescence and early adulthood. *Journal of Research on Adolescence, 15,* 235–260. doi:10.1111/j.1532-7795.2005.00095.x

Eisenberg, N., Eggum, N. D., & Di Giunta, L. (2010). Empathy-related responding: Associations with prosocial behavior, aggression, and intergroup relations. *Social Issues and Policy Review, 4,* 143–180. doi: 10.1111/j.1751-2409.2010.01020.x

Eisenberg, N., & Fabes, R. A. (1990). Empathy: Conceptualization, assessment, and relation to prosocial behavior. *Motivation and Emotion, 14,* 131–149. Accessed from PsycInfo.

Eisenberg, N., & Fabes, R. A. (1998). Prosocial development. In W. Damon (Series Ed.), & N. Eisenberg (Volume Ed.), *Handbook of child psychology: Vol. 3. Social, emotional, and personality development* (5th ed., pp. 701–778). New York: Wiley.

Eisenberg, N., Fabes, R. A., & Spinrad, T. L. (2006). Prosocial behavior. In N. Eisenberg (Vol. Ed) and W. Damon & R. M. Lerner (Series Eds.), *Handbook of child psychology: Vol. 3. Social, emotional, and personality development* (6th ed.; pp. 646–718). New York: Wiley.

Eisenberg, N., Guthrie, I. K., Cumberland, A., Murphy, B. C., Shepard, S. A., Zhou, Q., & Carlo, G. (2002). Prosocial development in early adulthood: A longitudinal study. *Journal of Personality and Social Psychology, 82,* 993–1066. doi:10.1037//0022-3514.82.6.993

Eisenberg, N., Guthrie, I. K., Murphy, B. C., Shepard, S. A., Cumberland, A., & Carlo, G. (1999). Consistency and development of prosocial dispositions: A longitudinal study. *Child Development, 70,* 1360–1372. doi:10.1111/1467-8624.00100

Eisenberg, N., Hofer, C., Sulik, M. J., & Liew, J. (in press). The development of prosocial moral reasoning and a prosocial orientation in young adulthood: Concurrent and longitudinal correlates. *Developmental Psychology.* doi: 10.1037/a0032990

Eisenberg, N., McCreath, H., & Ahn, R. (1988). Vicarious emotional responsiveness and prosocial behavior: Their interrelations in young children. *Personality and Social Psychology Bulletin, 14*, 298–311. doi:10.1177/0146167288142008

Eisenberg, N., & Shell, R. (1986). The relation of prosocial moral judgment and behavior in children: The mediating role of cost. *Personality and Social Psychology Bulletin, 12*, 426–433. doi:10.1177/0146167286124005

Eisenberg-Berg, N., & Hand, M. (1979). The relationship of preschoolers' reasoning about prosocial moral conflicts to prosocial behavior. *Child Development, 50*(2), 356–363.

Fabes, R. A., Carlo, G., Kupanoff, K., & Laible, D. (1999). Early adolescence and prosocial/moral behavior: I. The role of individual processes. *Journal of Early Adolescence, 19*, 5–16. doi:10.1177/0272431699019001001

Fehr, E., Bernhard, H., & Rockenbach, B. (2008). Egalitarianism in young children. *Nature, 454*(7208), 1079–1083. doi: 10.1038/nature07155

Ferguson, E. (2004). Conscientiousness, emotional stability, perceived control and the frequency, recency, rate and years of blood donor behaviour. *British Journal of Health Psychology, 9*(3), 293–314. doi: 10.1348/1359107041557011

Fujisawa, K. K., Kutsukake, N., & Hasegawa, T. (2008). Reciprocity of prosocial behavior in Japanese preschool children. *International Journal of Behavioral Development, 32*(2), 89–97. doi: 10.1177/0165025407084055

Gill, K. L., & Calkins, S. D. (2003). Do aggressive/destructive toddlers lack concern for others? behavioral and physiological indicators of empathic responding in 2-year-old children. *Development and Psychopathology, 15*, 55–71. doi:10.1017/S095457940300004x

Graziano, W. G., & Eisenberg, N. H. (1997). Agreeableness: A dimension of personality. In R. Hogan, J. Johnson, & S. Briggs (Eds.), *Handbook of personality psychology* (pp. 795–824). San Diego: Academic Press. doi: 10.1016/B978-012134645-4/50031-7

Graziano, W. G., Habashi, M. M., Sheese, B. E., & Tobin, R. M. (2007). Agreeableness, empathy, and helping: A person × situation perspective. *Journal of Personality and Social Psychology, 93*(4), 583–599. doi: 10.1037/0022-3514.93.4.583

Grusec, J. E., Goodnow, J. J., & Cohen, L. (1996). Household work and the development of concern for others. *Developmental Psychology, 32*, 999–1007. doi: 10.1037/0012-1649.32.6.999

Gutsell, J. N., & Inzlicht, M. (2012). Intergroup differences in the sharing of emotive states: Neural evidence of an empathy gap. *Social Cognitive and Affective Neuroscience, 7*, 596–603. doi:10.1093/scan/nsr035

Hamlin, J. K., & Wynn, K. (2011). Young infants prefer prosocial to antisocial others. *Cognitive Development, 26*(1), 30–39. doi: 10.1016/j.cogdev.2010.09.001

Hamlin, J. K., & Wynn, K. (2012). Who knows what's good to eat? Infants fail to match the food preferences of antisocial others. *Cognitive Development, 27*(3), 227–239. doi: 10.1016/j.cogdev.2012.05.005

Hamlin, J. K., Wynn, K., & Bloom, P. (2007). Social evaluation in preverbal infants. *Nature, 450*(7169), 557–559. doi: 10.1038/nature06288

Hamlin, J. K., Wynn, K., & Bloom, P. (2010). Three-month-olds show a negativity bias in their social evaluations. *Developmental Science, 13*(6), 923–929. doi: 10.1111/j.1467-7687.2010.00951.x

Hamlin, J. K., Wynn, K., Bloom, P., & Mahajan, N. (2011). How infants and toddlers react to antisocial others. *PNAS Proceedings of the National Academy of Sciences of the United States of America, 108*(50), 19931–19936. doi: 10.1073/pnas.1110306108

Hardy, S. A., Bhattacharjee, A., Reed, A., & Aquino, K. (2010). Moral identity and psychological distance: The case of adolescent parental socialization. *Journal of Adolescence*, *33*(1), 111–123. doi: 10.1016/j.adolescence.2009.04.008

Hay, D. F., Castle, J., Davies, L., Demetriou, H., & Stimson, C. A. (1999). Prosocial action in very early childhood. *Journal of Child Psychology and Psychiatry*, *40*(6), 905–916. doi: 10.1111/1469-7610.00508

Hay, D. F., & Cook, K. V. (2007). The transformation of prosocial behavior from infancy to childhood. In C. E. Brownell, & C. B. Kopp (Eds.), *Socioemotional development in the toddler years: Transitions and transformations* (pp. 100–131). New York: Guilford Press.

Hay, D. F., & Rheingold, H. L. (1983). The early appearance of some valued social behaviors. In D. L. Bridgeman (Ed.). *The nature of prosocial development: Interdisciplinary theories and strategies* (pp. 73–94). New York: Academic Press.

Hepach, R., Vaish, A., & Tomasello, M. (2012). Young children sympathize less in response to unjustified emotional distress. *Developmental Psychology*, doi: 10.1037/a0029501

Hoffman, M. L. (2000). *Empathy and moral development: Implications for caring and justice.* New York: Cambridge University Press.

Howes, C., & Farver, J. (1987). Toddlers' responses to the distress of their peers. *Journal of Applied Developmental Psychology*, *8*(4), 441–452. doi: 10.1016/0193-3973(87)90032-3

Jacobs, J. E., Vernon, M. K., & Eccles, J. S. (2004). Relations between social self-perceptions, time use, and prosocial or problem behaviors during adolescence. *Journal of Adolescent Research*, *19*, 45–62. doi:10.1177/0743558403258225

Johnson, D. B. (1982). Altruistic behavior and the development of the self in infants. *Merrill-Palmer Quarterly*, *28*(3), 379–388.

Kanacri, B. P. L., Pastorelli, C., Eisenberg, N., Zuffianò, A., & Caprara, G. V. (2013). The development of prosociality from adolescence to early adulthood: The role of effortful control. *Journal of Personality*, *81*(3), 302–312. doi: 10.1111/jopy.12001

Kanacri, B. P. L., Pastorelli, C., Eisenberg, N., Zuffianò, A., Castellani, V., & Caprara, G. V. (2013). *Trajectories of prosocial behaviors from adolescence to early adulthood: Associations with personality change.* Manuscript submitted for editorial review.

Kiang, L., Moreno, A. J., & Robinson, J. L. (2004). Maternal preconceptions about parenting predict child temperament, maternal sensitivity, and children's empathy. *Developmental Psychology*, *40*(6), 1081–1092. doi: 10.1037/0012-1649.40.6.1081

Knafo, A., Zahn-Waxler, C., Van Hulle, C., Robinson, J. L., & Rhee, S. H. (2008). The developmental origins of a disposition toward empathy: Genetic and environmental contributions. *Emotion*, *8*(6), 737–752. doi: 10.1037/a0014179

Kokko, K., Tremblay, R. E., Lacourse, E., Nagin, D. S., & Vitaro, F. (2006). Trajectories of prosocial behavior and physical aggression in middle childhood: Links to adolescent school dropout and physical violence. *Journal of Research on Adolescence*, *16*, 403–428. doi:10.1111/j.1532-7795.2006.00500.x

Kuhlmeier, V., Wynn, K., & Bloom, P. (2003). Attribution of dispositional states by 12-month-olds. *Psychological Science*, *14*(5), 402–408. doi: 10.1111/1467-9280.01454

Lamb, S., & Zakhireh, B. (1997). Toddlers' attention to the distress of peers in a day care setting. *Early Education and Development*, *8*(2), 105–118. doi: 10.1207/s15566935eed0802_1

Lewis, M., & Ramsay, D. (2004). Development of self-recognition, personal pronoun use, and pretend play during the 2nd year. *Child Development*, *75*(6), 1821–1831. doi: 10.1111/j .1467-8624.2004.00819.x

Liew, J., Eisenberg, N., Spinrad, T. L., Eggum, N. D., Haugen, R. G., Kupfer, A., … Baham, M. E. (2011). Physiological regulation and fearfulness as predictors of young children's empathy-related reactions. *Social Development, 20,* 111–134. doi:10.1111/j.1467-9507.2010.00575.x

McFarland, S., Webb, M., & Brown, D. (2012). All humanity is my ingroup: A measure and studies of identification with all humanity. *Journal of Personality and Social Psychology, 103*(5), 830–853. doi: 10.1037/a0028724

Moore, C. (2009). Fairness in children's resource allocation depends on the recipient. *Psychological Science, 20*(8), 944–948. doi: 10.1111/j.1467-9280.2009.02378.x

Nantel-Vivier, A., Kokko, K., Caprara, G. V., Pastorelli, C., Gerbino, M. G., Paciello, M., … Tremblay, R. E. (2009). Prosocial development from childhood to adolescence: A multi-informant perspective with Canadian and Italian longitudinal studies. *Journal of Child Psychology and Psychiatry, 50,* 590–598. doi:10.1111/j.1469-7610.2008.02039.x

Nesdale, D., Griffith, J., Durkin, K., & Maass, A. (2005). Empathy, group norms and children's ethnic attitudes. *Applied Developmental Psychology, 26,* 623–637. doi:10.1016/j.appdev.2005.08.003

Nesdale, D., & Lawson, M. J. (2011). Social groups and children's intergroup attitudes: Can school norms moderate the effects of social group norms? *Child Development, 82*(5), 1594–1606. doi: 10.1111/j.1467-8624.2011.01637.x

Nesdale, D., Milliner, E., Duffy, A., & Griffiths, J. A. (2009). Group membership, group norms, empathy, and young children's intentions to aggress. *Aggressive Behavior, 35,* 244–258. doi: 10.1003/ab.20303

Nichols, S. R., Svetlova, M., & Brownell, C. A. (2010). Toddlers' understanding of peers' emotions. *Journal of Genetic Psychology: Research and Theory on Human Development, 171*(1), 35–53. doi: 10.1080/00221320903300346

Oakley B., Knafo, A., & McGrath, M. (2012). Pathological altruism: An introduction. In B. Oakley, A. Knafo, G. Madhavan, & D. S. Wilson (Eds.), *Pathological altruism* (pp. 3–9). Oxford: Oxford University Press.

O'Connor, L. E., Berry, J. W., Lewis, T. B., & Stiver, D. J. (2012). Empathy-based pathogenic guilt, pathological altruism, and psychopathology. In B. Oakley, A. Knafo, G. Madhavan, & D. S. Wilson (Eds.), *Pathological altruism* (pp. 10–30). Oxford: Oxford University Press.

O'Connor, M. M., Dollinger, S. S., Kennedy, S. S., & Pelletier-Smetko, P. (1979). Prosocial behavior and psychopathology in emotionally disturbed boys. *American Journal of Orthopsychiatry, 49,* 301–310.

Oliner, S. P., & Oliner, P. M. (1988). *The altruistic personality: Rescuers of Jews in Nazi Europe.* New York: Free Press.

Olson, K. R., & Spelke, E. S. (2008). Foundations of cooperation in young children. *Cognition, 108*(1), 222–231. doi: 10.1016/j.cognition.2007.12.003

Padilla-Walker, L. M., & Christensen, K. J. (2011). Empathy and self-regulation as mediators between parenting and adolescents' prosocial behavior toward strangers, friends, and family. *Journal of Research on Adolescence, 21*(3), 545–551. doi: 10.1111/j.1532-7795.2010.00695.x

Padilla-Walker, L. M., Dyer, W. J., Yorgason, J. B., Fraser, A. M., & Coyne, S. M. (in press). Adolescents' prosocial behaviors toward family, friends, and strangers: A person-centered approach. *Journal of Research on Adolescence.*

Premack, D., & Premack, A. J. (1997). Infants attribute value± to the goal-directed actions of self-propelled objects. *Journal of Cognitive Neuroscience, 9*(6), 848–856. doi: 10.1162/jocn.1997.9.6.848

Reed, A., & Aquino, K. F. (2003). Moral identity and the expanding circle of moral regard toward out-groups. *Journal of Personality and Social Psychology, 84*(6), 1270–1286. doi: 10.1037/0022-3514.84.6.1270

Rochat, P., & Striano, T. (2002). Who's in the mirror? self-other discrimination in specular images by four- and nine-month-old infants. *Child Development, 73*(1), 35–46. doi: 10.1111/1467-8624.00390

Roth-Hanania, R., Davidov, M., & Zahn-Waxler, C. (2011). Empathy development from 8 to 16 months: Early signs of concern for others. *Infant Behavior and Development, 34*(3), 447–458. doi: 10.1016/j.infbeh.2011.04.007

Spinrad, T. L., & Stifter, C. A. (2006). Toddlers' empathy-related responding to distress: Predictions from negative emotionality and maternal behavior in infancy. *Infancy, 10*(2), 97–121. doi: 10.1207/s15327078in1002_1

Stanhope, L., Bell, R. Q., & Parker-Cohen, N. (1987). Temperament and helping behavior in preschool children. *Developmental Psychology, 23*(3), 347–353. doi: 10.1037/0012-1649.23.3.347

Stürmer, S., & Snyder, M. (2010). Helping "us" versus "them": Towards a group-level theory of helping and altruism within and across group boundaries. In S. Stürmer & M. Snyder (Eds.), *The psychology of prosocial behavior: Group processes, intergroup relations, and helping* (pp. 33–58). Oxford, UK: Wiley-Blackwell.

Stürmer, S., Snyder, M., & Omoto, A. M. (2005). Prosocial emotions and helping: The moderating role of group membership. *Journal of Personality and Social Psychology, 88,* 532–546. doi: 10.1037/0022-3514.88.3.532

Suda, W., & Fouts, G. (1980). Effects of peer presence on helping in introverted and extroverted children. *Child Development, 51*(4), 1272–1275. doi: 10.2307/1129571

Svetlova, M., Nichols, S. R., & Brownell, C. A. (2010). Toddlers' prosocial behavior: From instrumental to empathic to altruistic helping. *Child Development, 81*(6), 1814–1827. doi: 10.1111/j.1467-8624.2010.01512.x

Swart, H., Hewstone, M., Christ, O., & Voci, A. (2011, July 4). Affective mediators of intergroup contact: A three-wave longitudinal study in South Africa. *Journal of Personality and Social Psychology.* Advance online publication. doi: 10.1037/a0024450

Traphagan, J. W. (2012). Altruism, pathology, and culture. In B. Oakley, A. Knafo, G. Madhavan, & D. S. Wilson (Eds.), *Pathological altruism* (pp. 272–287). Oxford: Oxford University Press.

Turvey, B. E. (2012). Pathological altruism: Victims and motivational types. In B. Oakley, A. Knafo, G. Madhavan, & D. S. Wilson (Eds.), *Pathological altruism* (pp. 177–192). Oxford: Oxford University Press.

Vaish, A., Carpenter, M., & Tomasello, M. (2009). Sympathy through affective perspective taking and its relation to prosocial behavior in toddlers. *Developmental Psychology, 45*(2), 534–543. doi: 10.1037/a0014322

van der Mark., I. L., van IJzendoorn, M. H., & Bakermans-Kranenburg, M. J. (2002). Development of empathy in girls during the second year of life: Associations with parenting, attachment, and temperament. *Social Development, 11*(4), 451–468. doi: 10.1111/1467-9507.00210

Warneken, F., & Tomasello, M. (2006). Altruistic helping in human infants and young chimpanzees. *Science, 311*(5765), 1301–1303. doi: 10.1126/science.1121448

Warneken, F., & Tomasello, M. (2007). Helping and cooperation at 14 months of age. *Infancy, 11*(3), 271–294. doi: 10.1111/j.1532-7078.2007.tb00227.x

Warneken, F., & Tomasello, M. (2008). Extrinsic rewards undermine altruistic tendencies in 20-month-olds. *Developmental Psychology, 44*(6), 1785–1788. doi: 10.1037/a0013860

Warneken, F., & Tomasello, M. (2013). Parental presence and encouragement do not influence helping in young children. *Infancy, 18*(3), 345–368. Retrieved from http://search.proquest.com/docview/1437971262?accountid=4485

Weller, D., & Lagattuta, K. H. (2013). Helping the ingroup feels better: Children's judgments and emotion attributions in response to prosocial dilemmas. *Child Development., 84*(1), 253–268. doi: 10.1111/j.1467-8624.2012.01837.x

Woodward, A. L. (1999). Infants' ability to distinguish between purposeful and non-purposeful behaviors. *Infant Behavior and Development, 22*(2), 145–160. doi: 10.1016/S0163-6383(99)00007-7

Woodward, A. L. (2003). Infants' developing understanding of the link between looker and object. *Developmental Science, 6*(3), 297–311. doi: 10.1111/1467-7687.00286

Young, S. K., Fox, N. A., & Zahn-Waxler, C. (1999). The relations between temperament and empathy in 2-year-olds. *Developmental Psychology, 35*(5), 1189–1197. doi: 10.1037/0012-1649.35.5.1189

Zahn-Waxler, C., Radke-Yarrow, M., & King, R. A. (1979). Child rearing and children's prosocial initiations toward victims of distress. *Child Development, 50*(2), 319–330. doi: 10.2307/1129406

Zahn-Waxler, C., Radke-Yarrow, M., Wagner, E., & Chapman, M. (1992). Development of concern for others. *Developmental Psychology, 28*(1), 126–136. doi: 10.1037/0012-1649.28.1.126

Zahn-Waxler, C., Schiro, K., Robinson, J. L., Emde, R. N., & Schmitz, S. (2001). Empathy and prosocial patterns in young MZ and DZ twins: Development and genetic and environmental influences. In R. N. Emde & J. K. Hewitt (Ed.), *Infancy to early childhood: Genetic and environmental influences on developmental change* (pp. 141–162). New York: Oxford University Press.

Zahn-Waxler, C., & Van Hulle, C. (2012). The development and underlying brain processes of pathological altruism. In B. Oakley, A. Knafo, G. Madhavan, & D. S. Wilson (Eds.), *Pathological altruism* (pp. 321–344). Oxford: Oxford University Press.

Biological Perspectives

3

Evolution, Prosocial Behavior, and Altruism

A ROADMAP FOR UNDERSTANDING WHERE
THE PROXIMATE MEETS THE ULTIMATE

Patricia H. Hawley

Non nobis solum nati sumus (Not for ourselves alone are we born).
—MARCUS TULLIUS CICERO *(STONE, 2005, P. 186)*

Nature does nothing in vain.
—ARISTOTLE *(LENNOX, 2001, P. 206)*

Philosophers in ancient Greece and Rome were well aware that human nature is in part consequent to our predilection to live in social groups wherein our fates are interwoven. Aristotle, in addition to observing the gregariousness of man, noted that "nature" is neither purposeless nor superfluous. These two quotes point to two fundamental truths: Humans are "naturally" social, and "nature" does not tend to construct cost-bearing qualities without balancing them with benefit. Unknown to our ancient intellectual forefathers, however, is that "nature" is largely constructed by natural selection.

The casual reader, however, is not to be blamed for assuming that evolutionists are split on whether we are *really* nice to each other or not. As I hope to show in this chapter, there is widespread agreement that we are well tuned in to others' needs and desires and have a penchant for treating others with care and concern. Disagreement arises not on questions of "whether," but rather on questions about "how?" (does other-concern develop out of a cultural veneer that breaks us of our "true natures"?) and "why?" (from what evolutionary mechanism does this other-concern come about?).

This chapter attempts to deconstruct several predominant theoretical positions on prosocial behavior and altruism in fields of interest to developmental psychologists. I will clarify the definitional landscape from developmental and evolutionary perspectives by first introducing a class of fallacy that many contemporary authors fall victim to and second proposing several tools to help organize our thinking to avoid this fallacy ourselves and identify it in others. Following this, I will explain the key differences between proximate and ultimate levels of causation and describe how serious conflation of these levels is still occurring among evolutionists and nonevolutionists alike. This continued confusion is significant because it (1) influences conclusions drawn from developmental studies, (2) impacts arguments about levels of selection (i.e., mechanisms of natural selection), and (3) has serious implications for philosophies of "good" and "evil." In the end, I hope to convince the reader that the roots of psychological altruism need not be in evolutionary altruism, even if altruistic motivation is not predominantly born of culture. I will close with a defense of prosocial strategies of resource control characteristic of resource control theory and demonstrate how they are in fact a winning strategy for humanity.

The Definitional Landscape

> Psychologists have tended to be sloppy with words. We need to become
> more intimate with their meanings, denotatively and connotatively,
> because summary labels…quickly will control—often in unrecognized
> ways—the way we think. (Block, 1995, p. 211)

> The difference between the *almost right* word and the *right* word is really
> a large matter—'tis the difference between the lightning-bug and the
> lightning. (Twain, 1888/1890, p. 87)

THE JINGLE FALLACY

The common use of language is markedly imprecise. Despite researchers' and science writers' attention to detail, imprecise language can impede effective communication, cloud a domain, or perturb paths of connection between disciplines and lines of inquiry. Moreover, as expressed by Block in the epigraph to this section, the use of language influences and constrains the way we think. We implicitly recognize this fact when we invoke a metaphor to convey a complex process; we aim to make it easier to understand by tagging it to something familiar. However, doing so can lead to fallacious applications. Indeed, the "jingle fallacy" refers to the common error of labeling different psychological, behavioral, or theoretical constructs identically. Scientists and others then use the terms interchangeably and erroneously (Thorndike, 1904). This imprecision is an issue that has historically dogged early lexical approaches to personality (e.g., Allport & Odbert, 1936). The jingle fallacy bedevils the modern bullying literature as well (where the terms "bullying" and "aggression" are used interchangeably, though they are not interchangeable concepts; Hawley, Stump, & Ratliff, 2010). For the purposes of this chapter, the scientific landscape is further muddled when historically distinct fields (e.g., developmental psychology and evolutionary biology) attempt to integrate using shared terms as points of contact, though these terms refer to unshared constructs. This confusion has infiltrated interdisciplinary attempts to understand prosocial behavior and altruism. The problems have included (1) using interchangeably the terms "altruistic" and "prosocial," (2) conflating "intention" and "motivation," and (3) referring to very different constructs by the same name (i.e., "altruism"). Each "jingle" will be discussed in turn.

Definitions of Prosocial and Altruistic Behavior in Developmental Psychology

Many developmental psychologists, especially perhaps those whose work is represented in the present volume, define prosocial behavior as "voluntary behavior intended to benefit another" (Eisenberg, Fabes, & Spinrad, 2006, p. 646), including helping, sharing, and cooperating. Important to note is that such behavior "may be performed for a host of reasons including egoistic, other-oriented, or practical concerns" (Eisenberg et al., 2006, p. 646). That is, prosocial behavior may be enacted in response to several underlying motivations. This definition has been enormously useful in defining a domain space and giving rise to a broad and deep literature that addresses motives that are purely altruistic (e.g., out of sympathetic or empathic concern for others: Eisenberg & Fabes, 1998; increasing another's welfare without the goal of increasing one's own: Batson, 1998) and, to a lesser degree, those that are more self-serving (e.g., implicit or explicit expectation of social or material reward; Carlo, McGinley, Davis, & Streit, in press; Carlo & Randall, 2002; Hawley, 1999, 2003). Because these motivations operate in the psychological domain (as do hormones, learned responses, neurological mechanisms), they are referred to as *proximate levels of causation*, especially in evolutionary circles (Tinbergen, 1963). This latter point becomes central to the thesis of this chapter.

My read on this literature suggests three key facets to the proximate level (i.e., psychological) definitions of prosocial behavior and altruistically motivated behavior. I have illustrated these facets in flowchart format in Figure 3.1 in order to clearly distinguish the levels of definitional attainment and to make clear the use of terminology. In other words, Figure 3.1 intends to address the first jingle of the jingle fallacy: The interchangeable use of the terms "prosocial" and "altruistic" one encounters often in the literature.

VOLUNTARINESS

First, to count as either prosocial behavior or altruism,[1] the behavior must be *voluntary*. Has the actor, according to his/her own will, enacted the behavior to

---

[1] The Oxford English Dictionary (2013) defines "altruism" as, "Disinterested or selfless concern for the well-being of others, esp. as a principle of action" and "altruistic" as "Of, relating to, or characterized by altruism; selfless." For the purpose of the present chapter when speaking of the psychological (vs. evolutionary) uses of the term, "altruism" will be used to refer to behavior that is altruistically motivated. Said behavior will also be referred to as "altruistic behavior" and "altruistically motivated behavior" because they are functionally equal.

benefit another? A donation to a foundation that immunizes children against fatal diseases tends to be willingly and voluntarily chosen among a host of alternate responses. Thus, we tend to consider such donations voluntary. Coerced or obligate behaviors do not pass this first level and therefore in the end are not typically considered prosocial and certainly not altruistic. Paying taxes is a case in point, as one may not opt out without committing a crime. Taxes, so goes the maxim, are as obligatory as death.

INTENTION

Second, as implied by the definition, if the behavior is voluntary, then it must pass the test of issuing forth an *intentional benefit*. If the benefit gained by a recipient was intended by the actor, then the behavior meets the conditions for prosocial behavior; namely, it is in the end "voluntary behavior intended to benefit another" (see Figure 3.1). According to the *Oxford English Dictionary* (OED, 2013), "intent" requires purposeful, conscious attention. One's donation to the children's

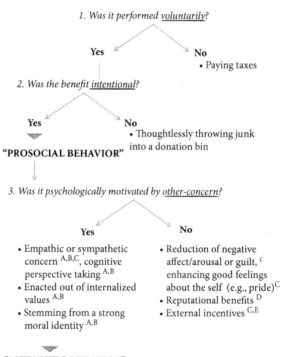

BEHAVIOR THAT BENEFITS ANOTHER PROXIMATE LEVEL

1. Was it performed voluntarily?

Yes   **No**
• Paying taxes

2. Was the benefit intentional?

Yes   **No**
• Thoughtlessly throwing junk
"PROSOCIAL BEHAVIOR" into a donation bin

3. Was it psychologically motivated by other-concern?

Yes   **No**
• Empathic or sympathetic concern [A,B,C], cognitive perspective taking [A,B]
• Enacted out of internalized values [A,B]
• Stemming from a strong moral identity [A,B]

• Reduction of negative affect/arousal or guilt, [c] enhancing good feelings about the self (e.g., pride)[C]
• Reputational benefits [D]
• External incentives [C,E]

"ALTRUISTIC BEHAVIOR"

Note: A = Eisenberg (1991); B = Eisenberg, Shea, et al., 1991; C = Batson & Shaw (1991); D = Carlo & Randall (2002); E = Hawley (2003)

FIGURE 3.1 *Prosocial and altruistic behavior at the psychological (proximate) level.*

fund intends to aid the recipient children. Behaviors that may benefit the recipient unintentionally do not meet the criteria for prosocial behavior. If one expedites housecleaning by taking old junk thoughtlessly to a donation bin, then the behavior, it could be argued, issued benefits (albeit small) that were unintentional. Thus, emptying one's closet thoughtlessly does not meet the definitional criteria of prosocial behavior.[2]

MOTIVATION

Once a behavior has been established to be prosocial, motivations must be considered to establish whether a behavior is altruistic (see Figure 3.1). Motivations "give purpose or direction to human or animal behavior" (OED, 2013) and have been accordingly defined as "goal-directed psychological force within an organism" (Batson & Shaw, 1991, p. 108). Batson and Eisenberg have most clearly articulated what these altruistic motivations include. For example, other-concerning motives comprise empathic or sympathetic concern (Eisenberg, 1991; Eisenberg, Shea, Carlo, & Knight, 1991), or the cognitive taking of another's perspective (Eisenberg, 1991). Furthermore, Eisenberg and colleagues have also argued that acting out of one's internalized value system or a strong personal moral identity also constitute an altruistic orientation (Eisenberg, 1991; Eisenberg et al., 1991).

On the other hand, altruistically motivated behavior may *not* be performed with the primary goal to reduce unpleasant emotional arousal (e.g., Eisenberg et al., 1991) or to reduce guilt for having not performed the behavior (e.g., Batson, 2011). These consequents are self-gains (i.e., "egoistic"; Batson, 2011; Batson & Shaw, 1991), as are positive feelings such as pride or righteousness (Batson & Shaw, 1991; Eisenberg, 1986). Similarly, egoistic motives include the anticipation of reputational benefits, or, the anticipation that others will issue approval for the behavior's performance (Carlo & Randall, 2002; Carlo et al., in press) or that there is an anticipation of social and/or material gains to be had for behaving prosocially (Hawley, 2003).

PROSOCIAL BEHAVIOR IS NOT THE SAME AS ALTRUISTIC BEHAVIOR

As can be seen in Figure 3.1, in deconstructing the predominant definitions of prosocial behavior and altruistic motivation, prosocial and altruistic behavior are not one and the same, and thus the terms are not interchangeable. Note that the issue of intention (question 2, Figure 3.1) does not speak directly to motivation; behaviors that intend to benefit the recipient may or may not be motivated by other-concern. Thus, motivations per se are not under consideration to establish

---

[2] I am not claiming that all donations follow this course.

the larger domain of "prosocial behavior." For prosocial behavior to be considered altruistic from this proximate view, motives must be established. Namely, for prosocial behavior to "count" as altruism, the behavior must be *primarily* motivated by other-concern (but see Batson, Duncan, Ackerman, Buckley, & Birch, 1981). It follows then that all altruistic behaviors by this definition are prosocial behaviors (see Figure 3.1), but not all prosocial behaviors are deemed altruistic. Assuming they are interchangeable is like erroneously equating cats and animals just because all cats are animals. Clearly, not all animals are cats. This point is important as it directly leads us to the first jingle of the jingle fallacy (as mentioned above): The terms "prosocial behavior" and "altruistic behavior" are all too often used interchangeably, and they should not be.

INTENTIONS ARE NOT THE SAME AS MOTIVATIONS

In many treatments of prosocial and altruistic behavior, intentions are conflated with motivations. This point leads us to the second jingle of the fallacy; the equating of intentions and motivations.

As mentioned, one's intentions require purposeful, conscious attention (but see Bargh & Barndollar, 1996). Motivations do not. That is, these goal-directed, internal psychological forces may be conscious or unconscious (Bargh & Morsella, 2008; Batson & Shaw, 1991), and as such, assessing them takes great care and ingenuity (as even Freud made plain; see also Batson et al., 1981). In principle, because intentions are consciously attended to, they can be self-reported (but as such, they are vulnerable to falsification for impression management purposes). Conscious goals and intentions interact in complex ways with unconscious processes. This issue deserves entire bodies of psychological and philosophical literature unto itself and accordingly lies well beyond the scope of the present chapter. For the present purposes, however, the presumed distinction between intentions and motivations must be highlighted because, first, it is central to the definitions of both prosocial and altruistic behavior and, second, it is unexplored and unarticulated in the developmental literature.

This lack of articulation may underlie some of the more intractable issues in the field that center on disentangling "why" someone did what they did. For example, individuals who host cocktail parties rise in rank over time because of the social connections forged. Why did they throw the party? A self-reported answer might include, "we like to entertain" or "we enjoy meeting new people." Without considering more deeply the distinction between intention and motivation, we may unquestioningly accept their response as their motivation based on its face value. However, bearing in mind that intentions do not equal motivations (and that intentions are often falsified), we should realize that motives may or may not be accessible to respondents and moreover are at best loosely related to behavior (Webb & Sheeran, 2006). This latter point is especially relevant in evolutionary approaches to behavior.

Evolutionary Definitions of Prosocial and Altruistic Behavior

Evolutionists are deeply concerned with "behavior that benefits another," such as helping, sharing, and cooperating. Indeed, such behavior has posed some of the greatest theoretical and philosophical puzzles in evolutionary circles for over a century. Definitions of such behavior, however, differ fundamentally from psychological definitions, as is illustrated in Figure 3.2.

VOLUNTARINESS

For the sake of clarity, Figure 3.2 follows the same logic as Figure 3.1 so that the disciplines can easily be compared. Question 1: *Was the behavior performed voluntarily?* Most adopting an evolutionary stance do not dwell on whether a behavior was "voluntary" or not because (1) this issue has no particular relevance for evolutionary definitions of altruism and (2) most species under study do not execute "free will" in the sense that we do. Choices are made between alternatives to be sure, and these choices constitute tests of evolutionary theoretical models. At the same time, however, very little ink is spent pondering the voluntariness in the choices of, for example, fish or honeybees. Indeed, some of the most remarkable

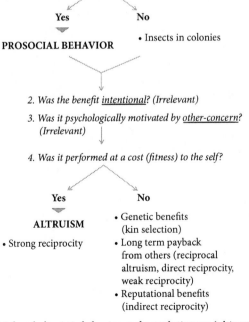

FIGURE 3.2 *Prosocial and altruistic behavior at the evolutionary (ultimate) level.*

"cooperative" behavior occurs in the eusocial insects (e.g., ants, bees, termites; Wilson, 1971). The roles of individuals in the colony, however, are determined by specialized morphology. Accordingly, their behavior is not seen as "voluntary" per se, and thus such cooperative brood care is not typically referred to as "prosocial" (but rather, "eusocial"). More cognitively advanced species such as chimpanzees, however, do appear to engage in voluntary behavior that benefits others. Work in this domain is especially compelling when the voluntary nature of the behavior is experimentally demonstrated (e.g., Horner, Carter, Suchak, & de Waal, 2011). Thus, it is not unusual to see the term "prosocial behavior" (Figure 3.2) applied to chimpanzees and other primates (Lakshminarayanan, & Santos, 2008).

Thus, unlike the psychological definitions (Figure 3.1), voluntariness does not bear on the issue of whether or not the behavior is altruistic from evolutionary perspectives. Moreover, and of critical importance, altruistic behavior in evolutionary circles need not first meet the criteria of prosocial behavior as is required in the proximate definition.

INTENTION

Similar to issues of free will, issues concerning "intention" do not bear on evolutionary definitions of altruism as they do on psychological definitions (though intentions are certainly an interesting domain of study: e.g., de Waal, 1992). First, as mentioned above, evolutionary scholars do not restrict their study to humans, but also include models derived from wildly varied species such as paper wasps (e.g., Nonacs & Reeve, 1995) and naked mole rats (e.g., Lacey & Sherman, 1997) where the concept of "intention" has little value. Relatedly, placing central importance on characteristics that might single out privileged species (e.g., having conscious intentions that presumably can be assessed) obstructs the uncovering of general biological laws (e.g., kin selection).

Finally, because intentions are presumably under conscious control, they are prone to misrepresentation by the actor. Indeed, there are sizable incentives for falsifying one's intentions. Good reputations often rely on being altruistic, or, alternatively, *appearing* to be altruistic (e.g., moral hypocrisy; Batson, Thompson, Seuferling, Whitney, & Strongman, 1999). Consequent reputational information spreads throughout the social group bringing benefits to the actor, often in reproductive success terms (Nowak & Sigmund, 2005). At some level we implicitly or explicitly recognize this connection; the probability of engaging in altruism increases when actors perceive they are being observed by others (Bateson, Nettle, & Roberts, 2006; Soetevent, 2005). Additionally, visible (and not invisible) altruism enhances status and, therefore, mating opportunities (Hardy & van Vugt, 2006). In social psychological circles, it has long been known that humans deliberately attempt to influence the perceptions of others to boost group members' evaluations of us (e.g., Leary & Kowalski, 1990). Even very young children engage in deception for impression management reasons (Polak & Harris, 1999).

Our perceptions of others' intentions (and their perceptions of ours) are a very important aspect of the social ecology; we make important social judgments and enact contingent strategies based on these evaluations (e.g., mind reading; Barrett, Cosmides, & Tooby, 2010; Byrne & Whiten, 1988; Humphrey, 1976). Yet, how many people would admit that they support a certain cause (visibly) because doing so bolsters their reputation in the community and wins them status benefits? Managing one's reputation is a matter of social learning over time. I will make a brief comment about this in the context of prosocial strategies of resource control in a later section.

Although children's daily deceptions may not be of central importance in developmental circles (but see Sodian, Taylor, Harris, & Perner, 1991), deception is fundamental in biology. Many species' key behavioral or morphological traits are designed to mislead conspecifics or predators (e.g., crypsis, brood parasitism, mimicry; Maynard-Smith & Harper, 2003). There is a very strong selection pressure for being "dishonest."

MOTIVATION

Like intentions, psychological motivations are irrelevant to evolutionary assessments of altruism. This is not to say that motivational assessment is unimportant in animal behavior circles and those entrenched deeply in evolutionary theory (e.g., de Waal & Suchak, 2010; Warneken & Tomasello, 2006); this work, however, is exploring proximate motivational mechanisms and, as such, it fits beautifully on Figure 3.1. In general, however, establishing the psychological motivation underlying a behavior is not a requirement for deeming behavior as altruistic from an evolutionary perspective.

A FOCUS ON FITNESS COST

The fourth question illustrated in Figure 3.2 (but not found in Figure 3.1) is unique to evolutionary circles: *Was the behavior performed at a fitness cost to the self?* This question illustrates the fact that evolutionary approaches focus on *effects* of *behavior* (motoric, cognitive, emotional), especially in currencies related to reproductive success (e.g., somatic development, material and social resource acquisition, hierarchy ascension, mating, offspring rearing). That is, while altruism from a psychologist's view is directed behavior that benefits another and is motivated by true other-oriented concern (and as such is considered psychologically unselfish), biologists define altruism in terms of lifetime fitness effects: A behavior is altruistic insofar as it confers a fitness benefit to a recipient at a fitness cost to the actor. Nothing at this level is stated in terms of intention or motivation, and rather than residing at the proximal level of analyses, Figure 3.2 addresses the *ultimate* or evolutionary level of analysis, which addresses how the behavior came about over multiple generations.

The most hotly debated classes of behavior in evolutionary circles are ones that involve "other-concern." The heat centers not on whether we have other-concern, or whether other-concern is "natural" to us; rather, the question is, where on Figure 3.2 does other-concern belong?

HAS A FITNESS COST BEEN INCURRED? NO

Kin Selection

Most biologists agree that so-called kin selection, the benefits of which are mea-sured by "inclusive fitness" (shared genetic material with descendent and nonde-scendent kin), is not cost-inducing in the evolutionary sense of the term. Hamilton's seminal work addressing the puzzle of cooperation (Hamilton, 1964) focused on the genetic benefit associated with aiding kin. "If a sister is concerned for the wel-fare of her brother, the sister's self-interest can be thought of as including...this concern for the welfare of her brother" (Axelrod & Hamilton, 1981, p. 7). This per-spective holds kin selection to be anything but altruistic in the evolutionary/ulti-mate sense of the term.

Reciprocal Altruism and Direct Reciprocity

Trivers's groundbreaking work on reciprocal altruism (Trivers, 1971) sought to solve the puzzle of cooperation among *unrelated* individuals and as such is the pre-dominant theoretical framework addressing the evolution of reciprocal exchange; that is, the mechanism for the evolution of cooperation would lie in the expecta-tion that the favor would be returned such that benefits would be bestowed on the actor. Such exchanges, Trivers argued, are not only present in humans, but similar patterns are evident in animals (e.g., the cleaning symbiosis of fish, warning calls in birds). Thus, in the end, Trivers's theory also claims that such exchanges are not truly fitness cost-inducing in the long term and therefore not truly altruistic (see Figure 3.2).

Regrettably, referring to the phenomenon as "reciprocal altruism" has caused no end in confusion because in the evolutionary sense of the term it isn't actually altruistic. Rather, it is driven by genetic self-interest. Presumably, it is for this rea-son that "reciprocal altruism" has come to be known as "direct reciprocity" to con-note a more or less even exchange between partners over time. Because the actors are focused on future gains, it has also been referred to as "weak reciprocity" (e.g., Guala, 2012) to contrast it with "strong reciprocity," which will be described below.

Indirect Reciprocity

As an extension of Trivers's theory on reciprocal altruism, indirect reciprocity, in contrast to direct reciprocity, operates on the currency of reputation within com-munities of potential exchange partners (Alexander, 1987; Nowak & Sigmund, 2005; see impression management and intention falsification, discussed ear-lier): people who have been helpful to others are more likely to receive help from others (Nowak & Sigmund, 2005). That is, an additional mechanism for the evolution of cooperation (at least in humans) is reputation based, with good reputations leading to long-term material rewards. Therein lays its selective mechanism. Variants that fail to cultivate goodwill and good standing are at a reproductive disadvantage to those that do.

HAS A FITNESS COST BEEN INCURRED? YES

Strong Reciprocity

The hunt for "true" altruism in evolutionary circles has led us to strong reciprocity. Behavioral economists have observed that people *are* nice to each other and, rather than being limited to "self-regarding preferences" (e.g., psychological selfishness), people also possess "other-regarding preferences" (i.e., desiring payoff for others as well as the self). These preferences appear to be associated with the tendency to punish those who "free ride" (i.e., cheat) in experimental economic games (chimpanzees demonstrate these preferences as well; Brosnan & de Waal, 2003) and led these authors to observe, "humans are born with a moral sense" (Gintis, 2012). Humans, it is argued in this literature, are strong reciprocators: We reciprocate not out of self-interest (as with weak reciprocity), but because we feel it is right to do so. Punishing others for defecting also feels right, even if we do not gain from it. Experimental games are effective tools for exploring the conditions under which people either cooperate or defect (e.g., free ride) under conditions characterized by a conflict of self- and other-interest. In so doing, these experiments assess reputedly motivations of the players. Ordinarily, players in such games realize that they can selfishly maintain their own personal stash while drawing on the group's collective goods (hence, public goods games) to which all constituents are urged to contribute. Namely, after repeated rounds, individual contributions typically fall precipitously (depending on the set parameters) as players evoke rational self-serving strategies. However, additional variants of games have shown that when allowed to punish said free riders (by imposing fines on the defector, for example), cooperation is maintained at high levels because some players punish defectors (Fehr & Fischbacher, 2004; Fehr & Gaechter, 2002).

These findings have stimulated lively debate with the "not altruism" camp. One can reason, for example, that an "altruist" punishes a free-rider, bears no real cost, *and* benefits from the defector resuming his/her contribution. This scenario would be akin to calling out a colleague for shirking on advising duties; the defecting faculty member is exploiting the goodwill of the cooperative department by bearing little cost in the advising task yet enjoying the benefit nonetheless (e.g., a good departmental reputation with administration). From the framework of a rational self-interest model, the individual who has punished this free rider enjoys (1) an enhanced reputation in the department, (2) material benefits in terms recuperated time, and (3) a lower probability of future defection by others. This is easily handled by well-accepted "nonaltruistic" models. Benefits outweigh the costs, and, moreover, the whole department benefits from the punisher's efforts.

In carefully controlled laboratory experiments, however, conditions can be set that (1) maintain players' anonymity such that no reputational enhancement can occur, (2) disallow material rewards for issuing punishment, and (3) prevent future benefits for the punisher. Will people still punish defectors so that *others* (and not themselves) will benefit? Do we still have a preference for equity and fairness? Apparently, many do. The fact that some people routinely punish under these controlled conditions seems to demonstrate "other-regarding preferences"; people will bear costs so that nonrelated others can benefit. For this reason, this phenomenon is referred to as "altruistic punishment" (also, "costly punishment," "moralistic punishment"). The emotional response (or motivational state) precipitating the punishing act has been referred to as "punitive sentiment" (Price, Cosmides, & Tooby, 2002). Importantly, groups with altruistic punishers perform better at attaining benefits than groups without, and here is the proposed mechanism for the evolution of such traits.

Critique of Strong Reciprocity

Though it is clear that under some (experimental) conditions some individuals will behave "morally" even if it bears a cost, not everyone is in agreement with the "therefore humans are inherently moral/egalitarian" rhetoric (or even with the interpretation of the games). Steven Pinker has been an outspoken critic by pointing out that the carefully controlled conditions created by the experimenters are unlikely to occur in nature and therefore lack external validity. Indeed, Pinker has called these authors "Darwinian leftists" and former "Marxists," clearly implying that their work is inextricably linked with their political ideology. Guala (2012) has additionally allowed that although the "narrow interpretation" of altruistic punishment experiments are entirely justified (i.e., the paradigm has demonstrated the conditions under which socially attractive human preferences and attitudes are elicited in some people), the "wide interpretation" of the program is nothing more than speculation; we have no evidence that costly punishment maintains cooperation either in the real world now or in the past (cf. Boehm, 1999).[3] Others argue that the motivations isolated by the strong reciprocity proponents

---

[3] Pro-altruism writers tend to heavily cite Christopher Boehm, who has claimed repeatedly that Pleistocene hunter and gatherers were "egalitarian" in that they punished dominating bullies to maintain equity in their groups. Many citing this work interpret it liberally, taking it to mean that humans are "naturally egalitarian." However, Boehm draws his conclusions from a small, select group of modern day hunter-gatherers and that this "egalitarian sentiment" explicitly does not apply to women or children. Moreover, Boehm concedes that humans are naturally wired to ascend at others' expenses thus making his hierarchy "leveling mechanisms" (punishment) necessary in the first place. Finally, Boehm opens his book observing that his findings and theory well match his democratic political ideology ("To one who is living one's life as a democrat, egalitarianism is a topic that affects not only the head, but the heart. My heart was in this book" [Boehm, 1999, p. vii]). This is all to say that the casual reader should be cautious in uncritically adopting this wide interpretation, however appealing it is.

are not psychologically altruistic at all. For example, one study demonstrated that punishment is not born out of moral punitive sentiments, but rather of the more self-serving envy (Pedersen, Kurzban, & McCullough, 2013). Moreover, punishers may not be the aggrieved "cooperators" in the group, but rather those who choose to cheat the cooperative system themselves (Eldakar, Farrell, & Wilson, 2007).

The number of studies rolling out from both sides of the debate is overwhelming at present. At the 2013 Human Behavior and Evolution Society Meeting there were no fewer than eight symposia on cooperation alone. Suffice it to say at this point, as scholars we ought to be very cautious in invoking this work uncritically because we risk appearing ideologically seduced.

Proximate and Ultimate Levels of Causation Deconstructed

Figures 3.1 and 3.2 essentially distinguish proximate from ultimate levels of thinking regarding interorganism cooperative behavior. This distinction between proximate and ultimate levels of causation lies among the four distinct foci outlined by Tinbergen as the field was emerging (Tinbergen, 1963); namely, evolutionists tend to address the adaptive *function* of behavior (the role it plays in reproductive success) and/or its evolutionary history or phylogeny. These two are ultimate levels of analysis. In contrast, psychologists tend to favor proximal causation for study (e.g., sensory, neural, hormonal, motivational underpinnings, and environmental releasers) and/or the behavior's development within the individual (i.e., its ontogeny). Tinbergen urged fellow researchers to focus rigorously on the integration of the four categories of question (de Waal's work with primates is a textbook example of this integration) and warned us urgently not to conflate them.

Yet, conflate them we do. And this conflation leads us to our third "jingle" of the fallacy; the interchangeable use of the proximate and ultimate levels' employment of the same term, "altruism."

CONFLATING PSYCHOLOGICAL AND EVOLUTIONARY ALTRUISM AND SELFISHNESS

Be warned that if you wish, as I do, to build a society in which individuals cooperate generously and unselfishly towards a common good, you can expect little help from biological nature. Let us try to teach generosity and altruism, because we are born selfish. (Dawkins, 1976/1989, p. 3)

A good deal of the ongoing confusion, acrimony, and thus lack of complete and successful interdisciplinary integration stems from the tendency to conflate psychological and evolutionary altruism on the one hand and psychological and evolutionary egoism and selfishness on the other. Biologists have long used the terms "altruism" and "egoism" (or "selfishness") metaphorically, most famously by

Richard Dawkins (1976/1989). As discussed previously, altruism in biology refers to a behavior or morphological characteristic that gives fitness advantages to others at a cost to one's own fitness. Because the terms are borrowed from a domain used to describe motivations and intentions, it is all too easy to say the organism is behaving altruistically or selfishly, as Dawkins has done in the quote cited earlier. His utterance seems to imply that selfish behavior at the ultimate level entails selfish behavior at the proximate level. This characterization is blatantly incorrect: The psychological and evolutionary dimensions are independent (see Figure 3.3).

A "selfish gene," in Dawkins' sense, is propelling its owner to behave in ways that will replicate said genetic material. "Altruistic" genetic material by definition is burdened by large hurdles to replication. The "selfishness" of the gene says nothing about whether the behavior of the organism will be self- or other-oriented, or self- or other-motivated. Evolutionarily speaking, genes that impel us to bring many, surviving children into the world are the most directly selfish; they are being carried along by our offspring into the future and presumably urging these offspring to do the same. The genes are successfully replicating themselves. This process is similar whether one is a human or an orb weaving spider. At the same time, human parenting is psychologically altruistic; a good proportion of human parents put their children's well-being well above their own and willingly endure many sacrifices on their behalf. Here, evolutionary selfishness goes hand in hand with psychological altruism. This example, like most if not all kin selection, falls in cell B of Figure 3.3. Notice here, however, that genetic "selfishness" can apply to virtually every living creature or cell. Psychological altruism does not. What does psychological altruism mean to a spider or slime mold?

Casual criticism of evolutionary psychology often portrays the field in ways that make it appear that it is focused only on cell A, where evolutionary selfishness and psychological selfishness go hand in hand. These critics suggest the field claims that in reality, we are all *really* selfish, inside and out (also implied by Dawkins's quote, cited earlier). In fact, only a portion of evolutionary work resides here, and which work would be a matter of some debate. Some might assign the more unsavory aspects of human mating to this quadrant (e.g., males intentionally focused on young, nubile females as receptacles for their offspring, or sexual coercion).

			Proximate psychological motivations, social preferences	
			Selfish	Altruistic
Ultimate evolutionary function, fitness costs and benefits	Selfish		A	B
	Altruistic		C	D

FIGURE 3.3 *Proximate and ultimate dimensions are independent.*

Some might be inclined to put reciprocity in cell A (Trivers, 1971) *if* they are think-ing in an Adam Smith sort of way (you sell your bread not out of kindness, but for money in return; direct reciprocity) but *not if* one is thinking in terms of indirect reciprocity, where one's psychological selflessness pays genetically (cell B).

Most evolutionists would agree, however, that cells C and D invoke the most debate and resist reliable and consistent exemplars. Can replicators even in prin-ciple be altruistic? If they were, would they not be culled out of the pool promptly? The biologically minded, for example, might place Mother Teresa in cell D, for her bearing a large fitness cost (evolutionary altruism) to intentionally aid others for moral reasons (psychological altruism). Mother Teresa was a singular individual to be sure, and that is precisely the point: Could a population of genetic altruists evolve? Because they forego reproduction, biologists say no.

Under what conditions would one show psychological selfishness but evolu-tionary altruism (cell C)? Perhaps we are seeing a wave of this in modern, industri-alized culture. Over the last decades there has been a shift from early reproduction to later reproduction (and fewer children) out of shifting preferences for advanced education, personal growth experiences, and accumulation of material wealth. This cultural shift stands to have evolutionary consequences (which are yet unknown) in part because large numbers of people are willingly reducing the representation of their alleles in the human gene pool.

In which cell does strong reciprocity belong? This is actually a very complicated question. So far, I have represented it on Figure 3.2 as if measuring the behav-ior occurs at the ultimate level. In fact, "altruistic punishment" addresses human psychology and motivation. As such, it belongs on Figure 3.1. What remains yet unclear, however, is whether this work is most appropriately placed in cells B or D in Figure 3.3. To clarify this muzzy landscape, a bit more must be said about natu-ral selection and discussions about the level at which selection is operating, which I will turn to in the following section.

Figure 3.3 is not intended to be a definitive categorization system, nor one that will win unanimous agreement. It is simply meant to highlight the dangers of metaphor and imprecise language and the consequences of conflating levels of analysis. In the quote above, it appears that Dawkins does not have a preference for psychological altruism. This preference, however, does not logically arise from his theory of evolutionary selfishness. In my view, he has conflated evolutionary and psychological altruism, and he has probably done multiple fields a disservice for doing so.

Similarly, de Waal himself also attempted to disentangle levels of analysis (de Waal, 2008) to clarify the definitional landscape. In my view, however, he fell short of this goal and inadvertently caused further confusion. For example, "intentionally altruistic altruism" (behavior performed truly for another's ben-efit) is distinguished from "intentionally selfish altruism" (the actor explicitly expects reciprocity for self-benefit), but it is not noted whether the "altruism" is at the ultimate or proximate level. Thus, it seems he has either created a tangle of evolutionary and psychological constructs or an oxymoron,[4] neither of which is helpful.

The Battle Between Good and Evil: Individual Versus Group Selection

An unavoidable and perpetual war exists between honor, virtue, and duty, the products of group selection, on one side, and selfishness, cowardice, and hypocrisy, the products of individual selection, on the other side.
(E. O. Wilson, 2012, p. 56)

Strong reciprocity and its accompanying empirical support have been enormously useful for those wishing to show that "humans are naturally good" or "humans have a natural moral preference." At the same time, however, whether humans are capable of altruistic motivation has really not been in debate. Where this work claims contribution over and above other proximate level work (done, for example, by authors in the present volume) is that it strives to insinuate evolutionary *underpinnings of the altruistic variety* (see Figure 3.2). The mechanism of preference for this cadre of economic researchers is group selection.

In brief, group selection refers to a mechanism of evolution that confers benefit to an individual (or an individual's genes) indirectly *through the advancement of the group.* One may engage in a behavior that is individually disadvantageous (e.g., costly punishment), but the cost is mitigated by the benefit enjoyed by the group, which includes oneself and presumably one's genetic relatives. (In contemporary circles, most now refer to such processes as "multilevel selection" because of the individual level selection effects also inherent to such models.) D. S. Wilson (2003) has proposed that such mechanisms can be fruitfully invoked to account for the adaptive value of formalized religions, within which one is part of a moral community; groups that adopted religious values, most of which include some version of the golden rule (which specifically attempts to minimize within-group competition), historically did better in terms of resource acquisition and reproduction than other aggregates. As part of the community, though one is asked (via explicitly stated prosocial norms, or implicitly through cultural values) to adopt an other-oriented posture (prosociality, cooperation, sharing) and to engage in behavior that is individually disadvantageous, one does well in the end because one is part of a flourishing social group. The group, under some conditions, can be the unit of selection. Thus, biology can inform the development of human cultural institutions (D. S. Wilson, 2003). Indeed, E. O. Wilson has recently reversed his

---

[4] Psychologists refer to "intentionally altruistic altruism" simply as "altruistic behavior" (see Figure 3.1). "Intentionally selfish altruism" makes no sense whatsoever. If it is selfish, it is not altruistic from either evolutionary or psychological perspectives.

previous take on insect eusociality to plump for group-level selective mechanisms in the venerated journal *Nature* (Nowak, Tarnita, & Wilson, 2010). Despite the commercial success of Darwin's Cathedral and E. O. Wilson's professional cachet, biologists by and large are unconvinced. Indeed, Nowak et al. (2010) were greeted by a 140-author intellectual pummeling a year later (Abbot et al., 2011). The discussions centered on the level of evolutionary mechanisms can be quite acrimonious, the low point in my view being when one author hinted that another author might be less than sane (Coyne, 2011).[5] It really is no less than a battle over the nature of human nature. However, the cautious reader should be aware that this is not a 50–50 debate in the field, but rather proponents of individual-level selection (who are also most often opponents—sometimes very hostile—of group selection) far outnumber proponents of multilevel selection (who tend *not* to be opponents of individual level mechanisms, by definition).

Arguments for or against these mechanisms lie largely in the mathematical domain and are outside the scope of the present work. Conceptually speaking in simple terms, however, cooperative groups are susceptible to infiltrators with genetic configurations that propel their owners to enjoy the benefits of group membership while at the same time *imposing costs on the other group members* by failing to contribute in kind. Here, another metaphor has been used: cheating. A pool of altruists is vulnerable to an influx of individuals who will exploit them. Instead, individual level selection mechanisms (e.g., inclusive fitness)—genes propelling the individuals to survive and reproduce—have enjoyed decades of support (i.e., kin selection, direct reciprocity, and indirect reciprocity).

Reciprocal altruism successfully addressed cooperation among unrelated individuals, like you and your neighbor. Cultivating friendly relationships among members of one's own local community pays (i.e., weak reciprocity) when it comes to emergency aid (survival), meeting opposite sex peers (mating), or aiding in child care (reproduction). Forging long-term friendly alliances assures us that we have someone to call when we need something. A recluse cannot rely on others and accordingly bears a steep cost. The degree to which one is approachable and a reliable reciprocator predicts the degree to which one is sought out as a candidate in the reciprocity pool (Frank, 1988). There are long-term benefits to being nice, and cultivating a positive reputation (Nowak, 2006) with other group members plays a critical role in gleaning benefits. Indeed, that rates of strong reciprocity increase when players believe they might be observed suggests an egoistic component (Kurzban, DeScioli, & O'Brien, 2007). Group selection mechanisms need not be invoked.

If group selection mechanisms are not at play (because they do not exist), then what is the evolutionary status of strong reciprocity?[6]

---

[5] "David Sloan Wilson is convinced that organizing Binghamton's citizens into amiably competing groups can turn it into the proverbial City on a Hill. His passion sometimes verges on obsession, as if (to paraphrase the Blues Brothers) he's on a mission from Darwin" (Coyne, 2011, p. 24).

[6] See also Guala (2012) and Henrich and Chudek (2012).

PROSOCIALITY IS EVOLUTIONARILY INSTRUMENTAL

Regardless of which mechanism one applies, note that all have in common the fact that prosociality is ultimately instrumental (e.g., evolutionarily selfish; cells A and B of Figure 3.3): I am cooperative, my group thrives, that is a win for me and my genes (multilevel selection). I am cooperative with my extended family, my family thrives, that is a win for me and my genes (kin selection). I reciprocate with my neighbor in a give and take fashion, that is a win for me and my genes (direct reciprocity). I am visibly cooperative in my community, I win social approval and accordingly am sought out as an ally, that is a win for me and my genes (indirect reciprocity). Selection at the level of the group *sounds* more virtuous to some ears. In the quote cited earlier, E. O. Wilson takes the issue mistakenly to the extreme by implying that group selection alone gives rise to virtue and individual level selection gives rise to sin. Alas, among other problems with his new conversion, he has conflated evolutionary and psychological altruism and egoism. But he has now employed a powerful rhetorical trick; if you do not want humans to be inherently evil, you had better root for group selection. This stance is simply not defensible.

Psychological Altruism Need Not Be Born of Evolutionary Altruism, Even if Psychological Altruism Emerges Early

As developmental scholars, we are invested in the proximate process of ontogeny. That is, we are still interested to know, are we born psychologically selfish (cells A or C) or psychologically altruistic (B or D)? The answer cannot be logically deduced from Figures 3.1 or 3.2. So-called veneer theories, such as that which seems to be espoused by Dawkins (we are born psychologically selfish and "broken down" by culture to be altruistic) suggest that we are born in cell A, but socialization moves us to cell B (and if therefore if you remain in cell A, socialization has failed).

Frans de Waal's work is instructive here. He has argued that "empathy evolved in animals as the main proximate mechanism for directed altruism and that it causes altruism to be dispensed in accordance with predictions from kin selection and reciprocal altruism theory" (de Waal, 2008; p. 282). Here, de Waal defines directed altruism as "helping or comforting behavior directed at an individual in need, pain, or distress" (de Waal, 2008, p. 281).[7] As a primatologist, he argues that empathy—an emotional prerequisite for coordinated action—has primacy over cognitions that serve similar roles. Accordingly, he explores the boundaries of empathy and coordinated functioning in organisms (here, species) not typically granted the social cognitive skill of adult humans.

---

[7] Note here that he indicates he is not studying altruism in the evolutionary sense, but rather the psychological sense. Thus, he places his work in cell B of Figure 3.3.

Indeed the roots of empathy likely emerged well before humans did, in species that exhibit coordinated parental care characterized by the feeding, cleaning, protecting, and warming of offspring (i.e., directed altruism). These roots of empathy would have spread and flourished by way of kin selection; those individuals who did not care for their young left fewer descendants. In turn, empathic and agreeable orientations would smooth and facilitate friendly coordinated action within one's group whether one was related to group members or not, in much the same way you enjoy a reciprocal, lifelong, mutually beneficial bond with your family dog, which, by the way, has similar empathic powers (Buttelmann & Tomasello, 2013).

The pet example is far from facetious. Several mammalian species, according to de Waal, will respond to distress of another with comforting attempts, however rudimentary (that dogs do this very well helps explain why we welcome them into our homes). De Waal has shown that bystanding chimpanzees—without the benefit of organized culture and explicit prosocial norms like humans—will contact victims of aggression more often than the perpetrators, especially when the aggression was severe (de Waal & Aureli, 1996). Monkeys, too, have other-regarding preferences (Burkart, Fehr, Efferson, & van Schaik, 2007), apparently choosing to reward both the self and a partner when given the option (the degree to which being associated with degree of relatedness and social closeness; de Waal, Leimgruber, & Greenberg, 2008). Additionally, nonhuman primates, like humans, experience a degree of inequity aversion (though it tends to be self-serving; de Waal & Suchak, 2010; Horner, Carter, Suchak, & de Waal, 2011). They even engage in directed helping (targeted helping, or aid administered in response to another's specific needs). Apes (including chimpanzees and orangutans) have been documented, for example, to aid their infants to cross from tree to tree. Distinguishing self from other may be an important precursor (de Waal, 2008); it perhaps is no coincidence that apes can pass the mirror recognition task of Gallup (1982) while monkeys as a rule cannot.

Indeed, several outstanding researchers are exploring such cognitive abilities related to perspective taking, coordinated action, and empathic responding. Most notably bridging primatology and developmental psychology is the work of Michael Tomasello and his students (e.g., Warneken & Tomasello, 2006, 2009) who are showing that even very young infants respond to needs expressed by others and will even willingly bear costs to help them (Warneken, 2013; see also Hamlin, Wynn, & Bloom, 2007). It appears that altruistic motivation is not merely a matter of cultural entrainment, but there appear to be inherent biological bases for these predispositions (the nature of which remain to be fully elucidated). Thus, the "psychological roots to cooperate" are present from very early on and residing in Cell B or D of Figure 3.3 comes rather naturally to us (presumably under normal conditions of socialization).

Domestic dogs are worth mentioning again because they appear to represent a case of convergent evolution rather than evolution via common ancestry; that is, they share some sophisticated sociocognitive characteristics with humans—unshared with our nearest ape relatives—that suggest that these skills arose independently through the same evolutionary mechanisms and processes (Miklósi, 2007). Domestic dogs descend from wolves who engage in a high degree of social coordination and cooperative breeding. Unlike wolves (and chimps), however, domesticated dogs—by definition—have evolved at the side of humans in what has presumably been a long-term mutually beneficial relationship. Accordingly, wolves and dogs have different sociocognitive skill sets, with those skills associated with the formation and maintenance of long-term reciprocal bonds (e.g., following the gaze and point of a human to a food source on first trial, reading emotions on human faces) being favored in domestic dogs (Hare, Brown, Williamson, & Tomasello, 2002; Nagasawa, Murai, Mogi, & Kikusui, 2011).

Integrating Proximate and Ultimate via Resource Control Theory

As I hope to have made clear thus far, there is quite a bit of needless acrimony in the field in large part due to the iatrogenic effects of metaphor and term conflations that bedevil the evolutionary and psychological views of altruism. As a developmentalist speaking from an evolutionary background, I see this hostility in the anonymous reviews of my work. What touches a nerve? Prosocial strategies of resource control.

RESOURCE CONTROL THEORY

Resource control theory (RCT; Hawley, 1999) is the theoretical framework within which I work. Its ancestral lineage is a mix of ethology, developmental psychology, and life history theory (Hawley, 1999, 2011). It has a foundational evolutionary premise that is rather uncontroversial in the abstract: Humans enact behavioral strategies that have evolved to compete for limited resources within the social group. Some of those strategies, like instrumental aggression ("coercive strategies" in RCT parlance), risk disrupting social bonds. There is a good deal of consensus about the function of coercion and aggression from various fields including evolutionary psychology, developmental psychology, and ethology. Aggression is in arguably an effective means to win resources when one pits oneself against others in the group. They are psychologically and evolutionarily selfish and, as such, belong in cell A of Figure 3.3. They require no controversial evolutionary mechanism to account for them. Proximate and ultimate levels are on the same page.

Prosocial Strategies

The other of these strategies, however, stands to strengthen social bonds while at the same time win resources for the actor as well as the actor's social partners. Prosocial strategies of resource control are voluntary behaviors intended to benefit others *while winning benefits for the self.*

Our self-report measures suggest that psychological/motivational altruism is not operating (see Figure 3.1). We ask participants whether they forge friendships, reciprocate, behave nicely to others, and cooperate, *for goal attainment*. The "strategy" lies in the "goal attainment" aspect of the item, and thus participants are self-reporting on their self-oriented motivation. (We additionally assess prosociality by asking about helping, sharing, and caring without reference to motivation such as goal attainment). Our work, like everyone's, is vulnerable to the vagaries of self-report; namely, we naively assume that people know why they do what they do. Better measures in my view involve behavioral observation (e.g., Hawley, 2002; Hawley & Little, 1999), even though they too are fraught with ambiguities. For example, "helping" another child in a cooperative game is positively associated with resource use because the helping child successfully commandeers the play material. What is the underlying psychological motivation? What was the intention? *Does it matter?* Is it enough to show positive behaviors are associated with resource use? To pinpoint motivation, experimentation would be required: Can a condition be devised such that "helping" yields no benefits or incurs cost to the actor? Would rates of helping decrease? (See Batson et al., 1981, for examples with adults.)

It would be interesting and perhaps very difficult to isolate a pure human motivation that is uncontaminated by other motivations. Even Mother Teresa was presumably motivated to some degree by Salvation (for a more nuanced view, see Walker, chapter 21, this volume; Batson et al., 1981). Overall, after a decade of work, my view is that prosocial strategies are not predominantly psychologically altruistic. On the whole, these behaviors win social and material rewards and many (if not most) participants explicitly recognize this. Yet, at the same time, these strategies are not without an empathic component; they reflect internalized values and are consistent with moral norms (see Figure 3.1) when enacted by most children and adults. Like most human behavior, prosocial strategies of resource control probably have multiple motives underlying them, none of which need be salient to the actor.

Prosocial strategies certainly achieve the definition of prosocial behavior as illustrated on Figure 3.1. They are voluntary, and benefits to social partners are intentional (though these benefits need not be divided equally). As far as natural selection is concerned, I favor direct and indirect reciprocity, though I don't find group level proposals particularly aversive. After all, all of these views agree that *prosociality is instrumental*. In summary, prosocial strategies reside in cell A (psychologically selfish motives), with perhaps a bit of spillover from cell B (psychologically altruistic motivation).

OBJECTIONS TO PROSOCIAL STRATEGIES

Where do the objections to prosocial strategies come from? Largely out of suspicion about whether "prosocial strategies" are really "prosocial." To some, these strategies appear to be tainted with sociopathic manipulation. Admittedly, very young children lack social grace when they enact such strategies (e.g., "If you let

me have some of your ice cream, I'll be your best friend") because they cannot well bury their "true intentions and motives" for reasons of reputational enhancement. Yet we teach our children these strategies anyway as the socially acceptable way to induce people to share their things with us. By adulthood, most of us have honed our impression management skills such that we perform these behaviors unconsciously, subtly, and seamlessly in our daily social exchange processes. Thus, prosocial strategies that emerge early in ontogeny may appear in some children as barefaced manipulation, in others as social competence. In any case, the ways these objections are framed reflect our first jingle, conflating prosocial behavior with psychological altruism.

Additionally, this disapproving interpretation of prosocial strategies probably comes most easily when considering the profiles of adolescent and adult "bistrategic controllers" (those who use prosocial and coercive strategies to a high degree) that I have described elsewhere at length, presumably because they appear to be (and indeed self-report to be) truly calculating. But their calculating natures lie not in the character of prosocial strategies per se, but rather in bistrategics' selective engagement of prosocial strategies balanced with aggression. In stark contrast, individuals who favor prosocial strategies (e.g., "prosocial controllers") show a profile across multiple studies suggesting that they are shining examples of human social competence and citizenship. If prosocial strategies were in actuality unsavory, then it would follow that prosocial controllers are psychopaths because they are best at cloaking their iniquity. In the end, this logic fails. Prosocial strategies are ultimately instrumental and their power lies in their proximate ability to strengthen—not weaken—social bonds (Hawley, 1999). Thus in the end, I see prosocial strategies as a winning strategy for humanity.

Conclusions

> Of course, a theory that predicted that everyone always sacrificed
> themselves for another's good would be as preposterous as a theory that
> predicted that no one ever did. (Pinker, 2008)

Human behavior is complex, and prosocial behavior has many motivations underlying it (Figure 3.1). Yet none of these motivations speak to whether—at the evolutionary level—humans are altruistic or not (Figure 3.2). Moreover, tenable models of human nature are much more complex than "we are inherently moral" or "we are inherently selfish." The truth lies in the middle ground.

"HUMAN NATURE" DEPENDS ON CONTEXT

Entirely missing from the discussion thus far is the role of context. The more meaningful and interesting question is not whether humans exhibit self-regarding preferences or other-regarding preferences but rather under what natural conditions do humans express self- versus other-regarding preferences, or, better still, when do they uphold prosocial norms while simultaneously serving the self in the long term? Here is where developmental perspectives stand to weigh in on the debate in important ways: We *understand context.* Indeed, in the present volume alone are several contributions outlining how early developmental contexts facilitate or hinder prosocial functioning. Cultural norms serve as contextual variables that impact our behavior; church groups are more prosocial than prisons. They have very different socially derived norms regarding what it takes to succeed. Human nature varies by the ecology, and to think otherwise doesn't make much sense.

THE MULTIDIMENSIONALITY OF HUMAN BEHAVIOR

Human nature varies by context, and thus, not surprisingly, there are many types of "prosocial behavior" that serve a myriad of important functions in the social group, all of which probably boost social cohesion. Rather than serving as a catalog for the multidimensionality of prosocial behavior, the present chapter attempted to address three major underlying issues regarding evolutionary synthesis: First, we need to be more consistent and clearer about our classification system and its descriptors. I hope Figures 3.1 through 3.3 are useful tools for guiding us in the right direction. Second, it is very difficult to draw conclusions about evolutionary processes by studying psychological phenomena, and conversely, evolutionary mechanisms ("why") say very little about psychological manifestation ("whether") and development ("how"). Future work linking proximate and ultimate should attempt to identify ideologically driven speculations in order to minimize their effect, especially those related to allusions about good and evil. Third, while the merit of interdisciplinary pursuit is inestimable, its value is enhanced when we are crystal clear about our respective languages. This last point leads back to the first. In the end, linking psychological treatments of prosociality and altruism with evolutionary models will illuminate where human instrumentality and sociality collide.

Acknowledgments

I thank Jamie Fuller and Nate Baker from the University of Kansas for background research on, and stimulating discussions about, the ideas contained within.

References

Abbot, P., Abe, J., Alcock, J., Alizon, S., Alpedrinha, J. A., Andersson, M.,...Gardner, A. (2011). Inclusive fitness theory and eusociality. *Nature, 471,* E1–E4.

Alexander, R. D. (1987). The biology of moral systems. Hawthorne, NY: Aldine de Gruyter

Allport, G. W., & Odbert, H. S. (1936). Trait names: A psycho-lexical study. *Psychological Monographs, 47*(1).

Axelrod, R., & Hamilton, W. D. (1981). The evolution of cooperation. *Science, 211,* 1390–1396.

Bargh, J. A., & Barndollar, K. (1996). Automaticity in action: The unconscious as repository of chronic goals and motives. In P. M. Gollwitzer & J. A. Bargh (Eds.), *The psychology of action: Linking cognition and motivation to behavior* (pp. 457–481). New York: Guilford Press.

Bargh, J. A., & Morsella, E. (2008). The unconscious mind. *Perspectives on Psychological Science, 3,* 73–79.

Barrett, H. C., Cosmides, L., & Tooby, J. (2010). Coevolution of cooperation, causal cognition and mindreading. *Communicative and Integrative Biology, 3,* 522–524.

Bateson, M., Nettle, D., & Roberts, G. (2006). Cues of being watched enhance cooperation in a real world setting. *Biology Letters, 2,* 412–414.

Batson, C. D. (1998). Altruism and prosocial behavior. In D. T. Gilbert, S. T. Fiske, & G. Lindzey (Eds.), *The handbook of social psychology* (4th ed., pp. 282–316). New York: McGraw-Hill.

Batson, C. D. (2011). *Altruism in humans.* New York: Oxford University Press.

Batson, C. D., Duncan, B. D., Ackerman, P., Buckley, T., & Birch, K. (1981). Is empathic emotion a source of altruistic motivation?. *Journal of Personality and Social Psychology, 40,* 290.

Batson, C. D., & Shaw, L. L. (1991). Evidence for altruism: Toward a pluralism of prosocial motives. *Psychological Inquiry, 2,* 107–122.

Batson, C. D., Thompson, E. R., Seuferling, G., Whitney, H., & Strongman, J. A. (1999). Moral hypocrisy: Appearing moral to oneself without being so. *Journal of Personality and Social Psychology, 77,* 525–537.

Block, J. (1995). A contrarian view of the five-factor approach to personality description. *Psychological Bulletin, 117,* 187–215.

Boehm, C. H. (1999). *Hierarchy in the forest: The evolution of egalitarian behavior.* Cambridge, MA: Harvard University Press.

Brosnan, S. F., & De Waal, F. B. (2003). Monkeys reject unequal pay. *Nature, 425,* 297–299.

Burkart, J. M., Fehr, E., Efferson, C., & van Schaik, C. P. (2007). Other-regarding preferences in a non-human primate: Common marmosets provision food altruistically. *Proceedings of the National Academy of Sciences, 104,* 19762–19766.

Buttelmann, D., & Tomasello, M. (2013). Can domestic dogs (*Canis familiaris*) use referential emotional expressions to locate hidden food? *Animal Cognition, 16,* 137–145.

Byrne, R. W., & Whiten, A. (1988). *Machiavellian intelligence: Social expertise and the evolution of intellect in monkeys, apes and humans.* New York: Oxford University Press.

Carlo, G., & Randall, B. A. (2002). The development of a measure of prosocial behaviors for late adolescents. *Journal of Youth and Adolescence, 31,* 31–44.

Coyne, J. A. (2011, September 11). Mr. Darwin's neighborhood. *New York Times Sunday Book Review.* Retrieved from http://www.nytimes.com/2011/09/11/books/review/the-neighborhood-project-by-david-sloan-wilson-book-review.html?pagewanted=all&_r=0

Dawkins, R. (1976/1989). *The selfish gene.* New York: Oxford University Press.

de Waal, F. B. M. (1992). Intentional deception in primates. *Evolutionary Anthropology: Issues, News, and Reviews, 1,* 86–92.

de Waal, F. B. M. (2008). Putting the altruism back into altruism: The evolution of empathy. *Annual Review of Psychology, 59,* 279–300.

de Waal, F. B. M., & Aureli, F. (1996). Consolation, reconciliation, and a possible cognitive difference between macaques and chimpanzees. In A. E. Russon, K. A. Bard, & S. T. Parker (Eds.), *Reaching into thought: The minds of the great apes* (pp. 80–110). New York: Cambridge University Press.

de Waal, F. B. M., Leimgruber, K., & Greenberg, A. R. (2008). Giving is self-rewarding for monkeys. *Proceedings of the National Academy of Sciences, 105,* 13685–13689.

de Waal, F. B. M., & Suchak, M. (2010). Prosocial primates: Selfish and unselfish motivations. *Philosophical Transactions of the Royal Society B: Biological Sciences, 365,* 2711–2722.

Eisenberg, N. (1986). *Altruistic emotion, cognition, and behavior.* Hillsdale, NJ: Erlbaum.

Eisenberg, N. (1991). Values, sympathy, and individual differences: Toward a pluralism of factors influencing altruism and empathy. *Psychological Inquiry, 2,* 128–131.

Eisenberg, N., & Fabes, R. (1998). Prosocial development. In W. Damon & N. Eisenberg (Eds.), *Handbook of child psychology: Vol. 3. Social, emotional, and personality development* (pp. 701–778). New York: Wiley.

Eisenberg, N., Fabes, R. A., & Spinrad, T. (2006). Prosocial development. In N. Eisenberg (Ed.), *Handbook of child psychology: Social, emotional, and personality development* (pp. 646–718). Hoboken, NJ: Wiley.

Eisenberg, N., Shea, C. L., Carlo, G., & Knight, G. P. (1991). Empathy related responding and cognition: A "chicken and the egg" dilemma. In W. Kurtines & J. Gewirtz (Eds.), *Handbook of moral behavior and development: Vol. 2. Research* (pp. 63–88). Hillsdale, NJ: Erlbaum.

Eldakar, O. T., Farrell, D. L., & Wilson, D. S. (2007). Selfish punishment: Altruism can be maintained by competition among cheaters. *Journal of Theoretical Biology, 249,* 198–205.

Fehr, E., & Fischbacher, U. (2004). Third-party punishment and social norms. *Evolution and Human Behavior, 25,* 63–87.

Fehr, E., & Gächter, S. (2002). Altruistic punishment in humans. *Nature, 415,* 137–140.

Frank, R. H. (1988). *Passions within reason: The strategic role of the emotions.* New York: Norton.

Gallup, G. G. (1982). Self-awareness and the emergence of mind in primates. *American Journal of Primatology 2,* 237–248.

Guala, F. (2012). Reciprocity: Weak or strong? What punishment experiments do (and do not) demonstrate. *Behavioral and Brain Sciences, 35,* 1–15.

Hamilton, W. D. (1964). The genetical evolution of social behaviour: II. *Journal of Theoretical Biology, 7,* 17–52.

Hamlin, J. K., Wynn, K., & Bloom, P. (2007). Social evaluation by preverbal infants. *Nature, 450*(7169), 557–559.

Hardy, C. L., & Van Vugt, M. (2006). Nice guys finish first: The competitive altruism hypothesis. *Personality and Social Psychology Bulletin, 32,* 1402–1413.

Hare, B., Brown, M., Williamson, C., & Tomasello, M. (2002). The domestication of social cognition in dogs. *Science, 298,* 1634–1636.

Hawley, P. H. (1999). The ontogenesis of social dominance: A strategy-based evolutionary perspective. *Developmental Review, 19,* 97–132.

Hawley, P. H. (2002). Social dominance and prosocial and coercive strategies of resource control in preschoolers. *International Journal of Behavioral Development, 26,* 167–176.

Hawley, P. H. (2003). Prosocial and coercive configurations of resource control in early adolescence: A case for the well-adapted Machiavellian. *Merrill-Palmer Quarterly, 49,* 279–309.

Hawley, P. H., & Little, T.D. (1999). On winning some and losing some: A social relations approach to social dominance in toddlers. *Merrill-Palmer Quarterly, 43,* 185–214.

Hawley, P. H., Stump, K. N., & Ratliff, J. M. (2010). Sidestepping the jingle fallacy: Bullying, aggression, and the importance of knowing the difference. In D. Espelage & S. Swearer (Eds.), *Bullying in North American schools* (2nd ed., pp. 101–115). London: Routledge.

Henrich, J., & Chudek, M. (2012). Reciprocity: Weak or strong? What punishment experiments do (and do not) demonstrate. *Behavioral and Brain Sciences, 35,* 29–30.

Horner, V., Carter, J. D., Suchak, M., & de Waal, F. B. (2011). Spontaneous prosocial choice by chimpanzees. *Proceedings of the National Academy of Sciences, 108,* 13847–13851.

Humphrey N. (1976). The social function of intellect. In P. P. G. Bateson & R. A. Hinde (Eds.), *Growing points in ethology* (pp. 303–32). Cambridge, UK: Cambridge University Press.

Kurzban, R., DeScioli, P., & O'Brien, E. (2007). Audience effects on moralistic punishment. *Evolution and Human Behavior, 28,* 75–84.

Lacey, E. A., & Sherman, P. W. (1997). Cooperative breeding in naked mole-rats: Implications for vertebrate and invertebrate sociality. In N. G. Solomon, & J. A. French (Eds.), *Cooperative breeding in mammals* (pp. 267–301). Cambridge, UK: Cambridge University Press.

Lakshminarayanan, V. R., & Santos, L. R. (2008). Capuchin monkeys are sensitive to others' welfare. *Current Biology, 18,* R999–R1000.

Leary, M. R., & Kowalski, R. M. (1990). Impression management: A literature review and two-component model. *Psychological Bulletin, 107,* 34–47.

Lennox, J. G. (2001). *Aristotle's philosophy of biology: Studies in the origins of life science.* New York: Cambridge University Press.

Maynard-Smith, J., & Harper, D. (2003). *Animal signals.* New York: Oxford University Press.

Miklósi, A. (2007). *Dog behaviour, evolution, and cognition.* New York: Oxford University Press.

Nagasawa, M., Murai, K., Mogi, K., & Kikusui, T. (2011). Dogs can discriminate human smiling faces from blank expressions. *Animal Cognition, 14,* 525–533.

Nonacs, P., & Reeve, H. K. (1995). The ecology of cooperation in wasps: Causes and consequences of alternative reproductive decisions. *Ecology, 76,* 953–967.

Nowak, M. A., & Sigmund, K. (2005). Evolution of indirect reciprocity. *Nature, 437,* 1291–1298.

Nowak, M. A., Tarnita, C. E., & Wilson, E. O. (2010). The evolution of eusociality. *Nature, 466,* 1057–1062.

Nowak, M. A. (2006). Five rules for the evolution of cooperation. *Science, 314,* 1560–1563.

Oxford English Dictionary Online. (June 2013). Oxford University Press. July 31, 2013. http://www.oed.com.www2.lib.ku.edu:2048/view/Entry/5859.

Pedersen, E. J., Kurzban, R., & McCullough, M. E. (2013). Do humans really punish altruistically? A closer look. *Proceedings of the Royal Society B: Biological Sciences, 280,* 1–8.

Pinker, S. (2013, January 18). The moral instinct. *New York Times.* Retrieved from http://www.nytimes.com/2008/01/13/magazine/13Psychology-t.html?pagewanted=all&_r=0

Polak, A., & Harris, P. L. (1999). Deception by young children following noncompliance. *Developmental Psychology, 35,* 561–568.

Price, M. E., Cosmides, L., & Tooby, J. (2002). Punitive sentiment as an anti-free rider psychological device. *Evolution and Human Behavior*, 23, 203–231.

Sodian, B., Taylor, C., Harris, P. L., & Perner, J. (1991). Early deception and the child's theory of mind: False trails and genuine markers. *Child Development*, 62, 468–483.

Soetevent, A. R. (2005). Anonymity in giving in a natural context: A field experiment in 30 churches. *Journal of Public Economics*, 89, 2301–2323.

Stone, J. R. (2005). *The Routledge dictionary of Latin quotations*. New York: Routledge.

Thorndike, E. L. (1904). *An introduction to the theory of mental and social measurements*. New York: Teachers College, Columbia University.

Tinbergen, N. (1963). On aims and methods of ethology. *Zeitschrift fuer Tierpsychologie*, 20, 410–433.

Trivers, R. L. (1971). The evolution of reciprocal altruism. *Quarterly Review of Biology*, 46, 35–57.

Twain, M. (1888/1890). Letter to George Bainton, October 15, 1888, solicited for and printed in G. Bainton (Ed.), *The art of authorship: Literary reminiscences, methods of work, and advice to young beginners, personally contributed by leading authors of the day* (pp. 87–88). London: J. Clarke.

Warneken, F. (2013). The Development of Altruistic behavior: helping in children and chimpanzees. *Social Research: An International Quarterly*, 80(2), 431–442.

Warneken, F., & Tomasello, M. (2006). Altruistic helping in human infants and young chimpanzees. *Science*, 311, 1301–1303.

Warneken, F., & Tomasello, M. (2009). Varieties of altruism in children and chimpanzees. *Trends in Cognitive Sciences*, 13, 397–402.

Webb, T. L., & Sheeran, P. (2006). Does changing behavioral intentions engender behavior change? A meta-analysis of the experimental evidence. *Psychological Bulletin*, 132, 249–268.

Wilson, D. S. (2003). Darwin's cathedral: Evolution, religion, and the nature of society. Chicago, IL: University of Chicago Press.

Wilson, E. O. (1971). *The insect societies*. Cambridge, MA: Belknap Press.

Wilson, E. O. (2012). *The social conquest of earth*. New York: Norton.

4

Parental and Genetic Contributions to Prosocial Behavior During Childhood

Keren Fortuna and Ariel Knafo

Most parents want to raise kind, caring, and helpful children. Yet we wonder regarding the extent to which we can influence our children's development of such valued skills versus the extent to which they are inherently disposed. Research over the last few decades has shown that (a)stable individual differences in prosocial behavior exist from the earliest years and (b)early environment (e.g., parents) plays a major role in the likelihood of children to act prosocially toward others in need. In addition, recent research points to a significant contribution of genetics. This chapter summarizes findings regarding environmental (e.g., parental) and genetic influences on early development of prosocial behavior. Although these are distinctive sources of influence, it is often difficult to empirically separate them and thereby differentiate their unique contributions. Genetically informed research designs are used to disentangle genetic and environmental effects. We first briefly present findings related to parenting and children's prosocial behavior, then discuss the role of genetics, and lastly introduce research that examines the interplay between genes and the parental environment in the development of prosocial behavior during childhood.

Prosocial behavior is broadly defined as voluntary behavior intended to benefit others (Eisenberg, Fabes, & Spinrad, 2006). Importantly, prosocial behavior is a complex, multidimensional construct (Padilla-Walker & Carlo, chapter 1, this volume). For example, a prosocial act may be self-initiated (i.e., spontaneous, performed without an explicit request) or performed in response to an explicit request (compliant). Likewise, prosocial behavior consists of a range of behaviors such as helping, providing comfort, and sharing. Different prosocial acts are assumingly initiated by different motivations (Eisenberg & Spinrad, chapter 2, this volume) and occasionally do not cluster together (e.g., Bryant & Crockenberg, 1980). Several related constructs such as empathy, sympathy, and altruism have been employed to describe similar (yet distinct) behaviors. *Empathy*, a vicarious response to others' affective states, positively relates to prosocial behavior (Eisenberg & Miller, 1987; Knafo, Zahn-Waxler, Van Hulle, Robinson, & Rhee, 2008), possibly being the underlying mechanism behind many cases of prosocial behavior. In this chapter we include studies related to the origins of these related constructs.

Keeping in mind the multidimensionality of prosocial behavior, in this chapter we explore whether genetic influences vary as a function of the type of prosocial behavior assessed (e.g., compliant vs. self-initiated prosocial behavior), the methodological approach being employed (e.g., questionnaires vs. observations), the developmental period (i.e., age) of participants, and the target of the prosocial act (e.g., mother, examiner).

Parental Contributions to Prosocial Behavior

Many theories of personality development emphasize parents' role in children's social and emotional development. Accordingly, much of the search for factors shaping children's prosocial development has focused on parental socialization, such as parenting quality, attitudes, and disciplinary style (e.g., Grusec, 1991; Grusec, Davidov, & Lundell, 2002; Hastings, Utendale, & Sullivan, 2007; Staub, 1992; Trommsdorff, 1991). According to Hoffman's (1975) theoretical account, three main interrelated parental attributes help foster the development of altruism (defined here as intrinsically motivated prosocial behavior) in children: providing a model of altruistic behavior, using discipline that is victim-centered (i.e., directing child's attention to another's distress, suggesting acts of reparation), and frequent provision of affection.

There is an abundance of empirical evidence for the association between parenting and children's prosocial behavior (reviewed in Padilla-Walker, chapter 7, this volume). Children are more likely to develop a tendency toward prosocial behavior when parents are authoritative (Hastings, Zahn-Waxler, Robinson, Usher, & Bridges, 2000), provide discipline based on reasoning (e.g., Krevans & Gibbs, 1996), and balance this with warmth and positivity (e.g., Denham & Grout, 1992; Padilla-Walker & Christensen, 2011; Robinson, Zahn-Waxler, & Emde, 1994). In contrast, parental negative affect and harsh, coercive discipline relate negatively to children's prosocial behavior (e.g., Eisenberg, Liew, & Pidada, 2001; Hastings et al., 2007; Koenig, Cicchetti, & Rogosch, 2004; Zahn-Waxler, Radke-Yarrow, & King, 1979). It is important to note that most of the research to date has focused on mothers, and therefore not much is known about the effects of fathers' socialization practices (but see Dekovic & Janssens, 1992; Roberts, 1999). A few studies suggest that mothers contribute more strongly than fathers to children's prosocial development (Barnett, King, Howard, & Dino, 1980; Bernadett-Shapiro, Ehrensaft, & Shapiro, 1996). In any case, the significance of parenting and the parent-child relationship to children's prosocial development is marked. That said, there are several limitations to research focusing solely on parenting and prosocial behavior (see Eisenberg et al., 2006).

First, most studies of parenting have used correlational, single-time assessments, making it difficult to infer causation. Longitudinal studies of parenting and prosocial outcomes are needed to shed light on this issue. For example, Knafo and Plomin's (2006b) longitudinal analysis demonstrated that parental feelings and discipline significantly (though weakly) predicted children's later parent-reported prosocial behavior, above and beyond prosocial behavior at earlier time points. Similarly, Hastings et al. (2000) found that authoritative mothers had children who showed more concern for others 2 years later, and Zhou et al. (2002) reported cross-time associations with maternal positive expressivity. Such findings do support the contribution of parenting (although see Carlo, Mestre, Samper, Tur, & Armenta [2011] for a study showing that early prosocial behaviors predicted later parenting).

Second, despite extensive research, the mechanisms involved in the transmission from parenting to children's prosocial behavior are not fully understood. Several researchers have suggested the development of empathy as a mediator linking parental discipline and positivity to child prosocial behavior (Krevans & Gibbs, 1996). For example, Padilla-Walker and Christensen (2011) found that mother-reported empathy mediated the relation between positive parenting and prosocial behavior toward strangers and friends. Child perceptions of the parent and acceptance of parental messages (Grusec, & Goodnow, 1994; Padilla-Walker, 2007), child emotion understanding (Ensor, Spencer, & Hughes, 2011), perspective taking, moral and prosocial moral reasoning, and self-regulation are additional potential mediators. During adolescence, personal prosocial values have been found to mediate the relations between parenting and adolescents' tendencies to engage in prosocial behaviors (Hardy, Carlo, & Roesch, 2010; Padilla-Walker, & Carlo, 2007).

Third, some null findings of associations between parenting and prosocial behavior suggest the presence of moderating factors. Some potential moderators are children's sex, age, temperament, and cultural differences (e.g., Eisenberg et al., 2001). It is well established that children's characteristics interact with parenting, such that the effects of parental behaviors on their children's development depend on the child (e.g., Rubin, Burgess, & Hastings, 2002). For example, authoritative mothering was found to predict more prosocial responding toward a researcher for less inhibited girls; for more inhibited girls *authoritarian* mothering predicted prosocial behavior (Hastings, Rubin, & DeRose, 2005). Additional parenting × temperament interactions have been documented in relation to prosocial behavior (e.g., Carlo, Roesch, & Melby, 1998; Padilla-Walker & Nelson, 2010).

Lastly, but central to the theme of this chapter, *heredity* may (partially) account for the observed associations between parenting and children's prosocial behavior. Parenting and child behavior may correlate simply because parents and their (biological) children are genetically related, and so each parent provides the child not only parenting but also half of his or her genes. This is known as a *passive gene-environment correlation* (passive rGE), since there is a correlation between the genotype children inherit and the parenting they receive (rGE is indicated when environmental exposure is associated with a genetic influence; Scarr & McCartney, 1983). Such passive rGEs are especially likely when the child's trait and the parent's behavior may have overlapping psychological and biological underpinnings, which is likely to be the case for children's empathy/prosocial behavior on the one hand and parents' warmth and acceptance on the other (Knafo & Jaffee, 2013).

Evocative rGE is a process by which children's genetically influenced dispositions (e.g., temperament) modulate parents' behavior toward them. For example, parents may respond negatively (e.g., using harsh discipline) to children who are less empathic by nature. Genetically informed studies, such as twin and adoption studies (to be further described), indicate substantial heritability of putative environmental measures including parental warmth and discipline (e.g., Plomin & Bergeman, 1991; Plomin, Reiss, Hetherington, & Howe, 1994), thus supporting the notion that children's genetic predispositions influence parenting (e.g., McGuire, 2003). Overall, studies suggest that rGEs are mediated by heritable personality and behavioral characteristics (Jaffee & Price, 2007). It is therefore imperative to employ designs that disentangle genetic and environmental effects on prosocial behavior.

Genetic Contributions to Prosocial Behavior

Empirical work on the genetic and biological sources of prosocial behavior (in humans) has emerged relatively recently, showing that genetics play a major role in prosocial development (Hastings, Zahn-Waxler, & McShane, 2005; Knafo & Israel, 2009). The most common genetically informed design to study the contribution of genes (and environment) to individual differences is the twin design, which relies on the genetic relatedness between pairs of twins (i.e., children of the same age growing up in the same family), by comparing the phenotypic (i.e., observed) similarity of monozygotic (MZ) twin pairs with the similarity between dizygotic (DZ) pairs. MZ twins carry a virtually identical genetic sequence, whereas DZ twins
• have on average only half of the genetic variance in common (like all full biological siblings). Assuming that MZ and DZ twins growing up in their biological families are equal in terms of how similar their environments are, then greater MZ twin concordance indicates a genetic basis for the measured phenotype. The proportion of individual differences that is explained by genetic variability (as applicable within a certain context, population, and age) is called *heritability*. Similarity beyond this genetic effect is attributed to environmental influences making siblings similar (*shared environment effect*), and any differences between the twins that are not due to genetic differences are ascribed to *nonshared environmental*

effects and measurement error (Plomin, DeFries, McClearn, & McGuffin, 2001). Model-fitting analyses are performed to yield estimates of these three factors, expressed in terms of proportion of the variance (Plomin et al., 2001).

Several twin studies have examined the relative genetic and environmental contributions to prosocial behavior. As will be reviewed, estimates of genetic effects are significant for the most part but differ across as well as within studies. These findings may suggest inconsistency in the literature regarding the role of genes in prosocial development. However, bearing in mind the multidimensionality of this construct, it becomes clearer that genetic and environmental influences vary in accordance to the aspects delineated at the beginning of this chapter; the type of prosocial behavior assessed, the methodology used, the age studied, and the recipient of prosocial responding. We therefore review the findings accordingly.

TYPE OF PROSOCIAL BEHAVIOR/EMPATHY

As discussed, there are various ways of expressing prosocial behavior, such that different studies tap different forms of prosocial behavior and empathy. Zahn-Waxler, Robinson, and Emde (1992) devised an observational measure to assess children's empathy toward mothers and an unknown experimenter from their reaction to simulated distress. For example, the experimenter expressed pain after pretending to close her finger in a suitcase, and mothers pretended to hurt their knee. The coding of child behavior differentiated between affective and cognitive empathy. The cognitive component was measured by children's attempts to comprehend the person's distress and was thus referred to as *hypothesis testing* or *inquisitiveness*. The affective component, indicated by expressions of apparent concern toward the victim, is referred to as *empathic concern*. At the age of 14 months, genetic effects accounted for 27% of the individual differences in hypothesis testing and 23% of the variance in empathic concern. Building on this work with an extended sample, Knafo, Zahn-Waxler, et al. (2008) reported that heritability estimates for empathic concern toward the examiner reached 18% at most between 14 and 36 months, whereas genetic effects for hypothesis testing reached 37%.

Using a similar procedure among 12- and 25-month-old twins, Volbrecht, Lemery-Chalfant, Aksan, Zahn-Waxler, and Goldsmith (2007) found heritability estimates of 30% for empathic concern toward the mother (due to a different modeling approach it did not reach significance, but intratwin correlations were similar to Zahn-Waxler et al., 1992) and 40% for hypothesis testing. Knafo et al. (2009) found higher heritability estimates for 3.5-year-old's hypothesis testing toward an examiner (44%) as compared with empathic concern (19%; although they demonstrated that the genetic effects on the two aspects of empathy overlap). A meta-analysis of twin studies at different ages (Knafo & Uzefovsky, 2012) concluded that genetics accounted for 30% of the variance in affective empathy (with no shared environment effect) and estimated genetic effect for cognitive empathy at 26%, with significant shared environment estimates (17%). Thus it appears that genetic contribution for cognitive and affective empathy is comparable, yet shared environment plays a bigger role in cognitive empathy, at least as observed in children.

Another important distinction is between self-initiated and compliant prosocial behaviors, which correlate only weakly (Eisenberg, Cameron, & Tryon, 1984; Knafo, Israel, & Ebstein, 2011) and likely convey very different underlying motivations (e.g., caring for the well-being of others vs. avoiding punishment). Knafo et al. (2011) observed both types of prosocial behavior in 3.5-year-old twins. Self-initiated prosocial behaviors included helping the experimenter pick up pencils which she "accidentally" dropped, providing emotional support when she hurt her knee, and sharing a treat. Compliant prosocial behavior consisted of looking for the experimenter's doll when asked for help finding it, providing emotional support to the doll following an explicit request, and sharing stickers with a hypothetical child when given an option to do so. Heritability estimates were modest (34%) for compliant prosocial behavior and stronger for self-initiated behavior (43%). For both, nonshared environment (and error) accounted for the rest of the variance. Van IJzendoorn, Bakermans-Kranenburg, Pannebakker, and Out (2010) also experimentally observed compliant prosocial behavior. Seven-year-old twins (N = 91 pairs) were shown a videotaped call for donation to charity (UNICEF) and were then further probed by an experimenter asking whether the child would like to donate money. Most children donated some money after being probed, yet observed individual differences were only explained by environmental influence. Conclusions from both studies suggest that compliant prosocial behavior may be less genetically based and indeed more situation-specific.

ASSESSMENT METHOD OF PROSOCIAL BEHAVIOR

Genetic studies that directly observe prosocial behavior and empathic responding are the exception rather than the rule. In order to reach greater numbers of participants to enhance confidence in the findings and provide more statistical power to detect small effects, researchers usually employ questionnaire-based assessments. This is also a way to gain knowledge from informants (usually parents) who know the child well and see him or her across time and situations. Most genetic studies assessing children's prosocial behavior with questionnaires use the prosocial scale of the Strengths and Difficulties Questionnaire (SDQ; Goodman, 1997), which comprises five items asking about child's level of consideration of others' feelings, sharing, being helpful, being kind to others, and volunteering to help. Among South Korean children, aged 2–9 years, mother-reports on the SDQ showed genetic effects accounting for 55% of the variance and no shared environmental effects (Hur & Rushton, 2007). Similar results were found for 3.5-year-old Israeli twins (Knafo et al., 2011). In a large British study of 2- to 7-year-old twins, results indicated significant genetic effects (average estimates of 32% to 61%, varying according to age), and teacher-reports at age 7 revealed high heritability estimates as well (51%–72%; Knafo & Plomin, 2006a). Strong genetic effects were replicated in adolescence (14–19), with the best-fitting model for parental reports on the SDQ estimating 61% heritability (Gregory, Light-Hausermann, Rijsdijk, & Eley, 2009).

In comparison, genetic effects on observational measures appear to be lower. Volbrecht et al. (2007) reported nonsignificant heritability estimates of 22% for observed prosocial helping among 1- to 2-year-olds toward mothers in response to simulated distress, while shared environmental effects accounted for 43% of the variance. Knafo, Zahn-Waxler, et al. (2008) found modest heritability for observed prosocial acts (9% to 24%) among 14- to 36-month-olds, with most of the variance attributed to nonshared environment.

Thus, questionnaire measures of prosocial behavior tend to yield higher heritability estimates than when children's behavior is rated by observers (discussed in Deater-Deckard, 2000). This is derived from parents making a bigger distinction between DZ twins while perceiving MZ twins as more alike relative to outside observers, possibly due to better familiarity with the individual twins' behaviors (which may also result in higher reliability for good questionnaires as compared to single-time behavioral observations). In contrast, independent observers who separately rate each of the twins unaware of their zygosity, have no preconception on how similar they are expected to be. Another possibility is that age is confounded with method, since observational measures tend to be used with younger children. However, these findings also appear within studies (e.g., Knafo et al., 2011) that have used both observational and questionnaire measures concurrently within the same sample.

AGE/DEVELOPMENT

Research typically shows a decrease in shared environment influence along with an increase in genetic influence throughout the years (e.g., general intelligence; Plomin et al., 2001), which is also evident regarding prosocial behavior. Knafo, Zahn-Waxler, et al. (2008) found small genetic effects on a common empathy factor at 14 and 20 months, yet at 24 and 36 months genetics accounted for 34% and 47% of the variance, respectively. In a longitudinal study of parent-rated prosocial behavior (Knafo & Plomin, 2006a) heritability increased from 26%–37% at age 2 to 60%–62% at age 7. Moving beyond early childhood, Scourfield, John, Martin, and McGuffin (2004) reported that genetic influences were significantly larger among older adolescents (ages 11–16; 87%) as compared with a younger group (under 11; 46%), based on teacher reports. Similar, though nonsignificant, differences were found using parent reports (47% vs. 27%). A study of adolescents' self-reported prosocial behavior at 13–17 and 14–19 years did not replicate these findings (possibly due to sample size; Gregory et al., 2009).

Increasing genetic effects during early childhood parallel cognitive and language development and growing sophistication in understanding social situations. This increase with age may also reflect stronger active and evocative rGEs over time, as children have more opportunities to actively select environments that match their genetic predispositions, and children's (partially heritable) early behavior evoke reactions from the environment, which feeds back to the child further reinforcing the initial tendency (Knafo & Jaffee, 2013). This feedback loop, mediated by environmental reaction, should increase the relative contribution of genetics. A recent simulation study shows that genetic differences between twins, reflected in their behavior and in the response of the environment to them, can eventually lead to an increase in heritability estimates with age (Beam & Turkheimer, 2013). By design, twin analyses typically include these effects under the heritability estimate even though they also reflect environmental effects.

The increase in heritability over time may be the result of the same genetic effects having stronger influence as children grow up or of new effects emerging in later ages. Although the genetic composition of individuals is, of course, fixed, some genetic influences may be relevant at early ages and new genetic influences may emerge as children mature (via genetic influences on cognitive abilities, for example; Knafo & Plomin, 2006a). To address this question, several longitudinal genetically informed studies have further looked into genetic contribution to *development* in prosocial behavior over time. Such studies report that genetics accounts for both change and continuity in prosocial behavior, with new genetic effects emerging at different ages (Gregory et al., 2009; Knafo & Plomin, 2006a; Knafo, Zahn-Waxler, et al. 2008). For example, Knafo and Plomin (2006a) found that a substantial part of the genetic effect on mother-reported prosocial behavior at age 7 was due to new influences that were not present at age 4.

TARGET OF PROSOCIAL BEHAVIOR

Only a handful of studies specify the target of prosocial behavior or include observations of multiple targets. This is important as demonstrated in Knafo, Zahn-Waxler, et al. (2008); more children performed prosocial acts toward their mother than the examiner at all ages examined. Further, hypothesis testing was more pronounced toward mothers at most ages, whereas empathic concern was overall slightly higher toward the examiner. Genetic influences on the affective and cognitive components of empathy were found mainly in the context of children's responses toward the examiner and not the mother (beyond those accounted for by a common empathy factor; Knafo, Zahn-Waxler, et al. 2008). As the authors suggested, these findings may indicate that children's natural inclination toward high or low empathy tend to be more apparent with strangers for which no relationship-specific rules have been established with time, demonstrating the importance of context.

In conclusion, twin studies teach us that generally, genetic variation is associated with variation in prosocial behavior, that genetic effects often increase with age, and that genes account for both stability and change in prosocial behavior.

Notably, we see that different types of prosocial behavior, and prosocial acts/empathy directed at different targets, are differentially heritable. In addition, questionnaire measures of prosocial behavior tend to yield higher heritability estimates than those observed. Taken together, the findings speak to the complexity of prosocial behavior and, therefore, to the importance of including multimethod designs, specifying which aspect of what is broadly called prosocial behavior is being assessed and the need to consider specific contexts when speaking of genetic and environmental contributions to prosocial behavior.

Behavioral genetic studies are important in pointing out the relative contributions of genes and environment and so begin to unfold the complexity of prosocial development. Significant heritability points out the need for further genetic research, taking the next step of identifying specific genetic markers of individual differences in prosocial behavior.

MOLECULAR-GENETIC STUDIES OF PROSOCIAL BEHAVIOR

Molecular-genetic research consists of measuring both phenotypic variation and specific genetic polymorphisms in search for links between the two. A number of genes have been highlighted in relation to prosocial/altruistic behavior in humans. One is the dopamine receptor gene and in particular a functional polymorphism on the dopamine receptor D4 gene, a variable number tandem repeat (2, 4, and 7 being the most common repeats) on the third exon (DRD4-III). Bachner-Melman, Gritsenko, Nemanov, Zohar, and Ebstein (2005) found variation in the DRD4-III gene to be related to young adults' self-reported altruism. DiLalla, Elam, and Smolen (2009) found DRD4-III to relate to preschool-age twins' sharing with each other (but not with unfamiliar peers). Knafo et al. (2011) did not find a direct association of prosocial behavior with the DRD4-7 repeat (DRD4-7R) polymorphism, but rather an interaction with parenting (see next section). Another dopaminergic polymorphism, the COMT Val158Met single nucleotide polymorphism (SNP), was found to relate to the amount of money adults donated in the lab (Reuter, Frenzel, Walter, Markett, & Montag, 2010). The dopaminergic system is associated with reward processes, and one possibility is that "We 'feel good' and are rewarded by a dopamine pulse when doing good deeds" (Bachner-Melman et al., 2005). Nevertheless, the precise processes through which the dopaminergic system affects prosocial behavior are yet to be unraveled.

Another candidate gene is the gene encoding the oxytocin receptor (OXTR; MacDonald, & MacDonald, 2010). Oxytocin is an important social hormone, facilitating social cognition, communication, and affiliative behaviors. SNPs for the OXTR gene were shown to relate to donation in the dictator game, a laboratory procedure in which participants decide regarding the split of a fixed amount of money between oneself and a stranger (Israel et al., 2009). Although effects were found in two separate Israeli samples, a Swedish study did not replicate the findings (Apicella et al., 2010). Kogan et al. (2011) used thin-slicing methodology to show that individuals who were homozygous for the G allele of the rs53576 SNP of the OXTR gene were judged to be more prosocial than carriers of the A allele. Similar results were found with regard to behavioral and dispositional empathy (Rodrigues, Saslow, Garcia, John, & Keltner, 2009).

The closely related arginine vasopressin 1A receptor gene (AVPR1A) has been associated with both human altruism and autism—two extremes of the social dimension (For a detailed review see Israel et al., 2008). Knafo, Israel, et al. (2008) found that length of the promoter region of the gene coding for AVPR1A relates to donations in the dictator game and self-reported altruism among university students. Shorter repeats of the RS3 promoter-region were associated with lower altruism. While most studies of this kind use adult samples, Avinun et al. (2011) showed a link between the AVPR1A RS3 and a lower proclivity toward altruistic behavior among preschoolers using a modified dictator game (donating stickers). A recent study (Poulin, Holman, & Buffone, 2012) found OXTR rs53576 and AVPR1a polymorphisms RS1 and RS3 interacted with perceived threat to predict engagement in volunteer work or charitable activities and commitment to civic duty.

Lastly, the serotonergic system, known for its role in various affective processes and disorders, is also relevant. Genes regulating the function of the neurotransmitter serotonin (5-HT) have been linked to aggression on the one hand (when function is low or impaired) and to cooperative, prosocial behavior on the other (high or enhanced 5-HT function). Crockett (2009) showed that lowering 5-HT relates to prosocial decision-making in the context of an economic game (increased rejection of unfair offers) and suggest that it affects prosocial responding via modulating brain region involved in responding to unfair treatment.

To conclude from existing molecular-genetic research, there is evidence that human altruistic behavior is affected by processes involving the dopamine, oxytocin, and vasopressin receptor genes, and the serotonin neurotransmitter. Additional polymorphisms may be important as well. As is the case with most psychological traits, genetic influence is not based on a single gene exerting strong influence but rather on additive and interactive effects between many genes (Plomin et al, 2001). Additional molecular-genetic studies, specifically focusing on children, will help clarify the roots for genetic effects.

HOW SHOULD EVIDENCE FOR HERITABILITY AND GENE-PROSOCIAL ASSOCIATIONS BE INTERPRETED?

As Zahn-Waxler et al. (1992) explained, "We would not assert that genes code for social emotional behaviors directly. Rather, genes code for enzymes that, in the context of the environment, influence patterns of brain chemistry and neurohormonal systems of individuals. These, in turn, affect how people act, think, and feel when exposed to distress in others." Further research is needed in order to describe the underlying temperamental basis of the heritability of prosocial behavior. For instance, Knafo, Zahn-Waxler, et al. (2008) suggest that the effects of genetics may be mediated by overall capacity to experience and regulate emotions, as well as other temperamental constellations that relate to prosocial behavior and empathy (e.g., sociability). It is also important to further explore the processes through which genetic variation affects brain functioning associated with high versus low prosocial behavior and empathy (Chakroff & Young, chapter 5, this volume; Hein & Singer, 2010).

WHAT DO GENETICALLY INFORMED STUDIES TELL US ABOUT ENVIRONMENTAL INFLUENCES?

Although we have thus far focused on genetic effects, all behavioral genetic studies conducted with children find significant effects for the environment in explaining individual differences in prosocial behavior. Simply the fact that MZ twins do not correlate perfectly points to the influence of the environment on their individual development (Deater-Deckard et al., 2001). More specifically, Volbrecht et al. (2007) report that shared environment accounted for a large portion of the variance at 19 to 25 months in empathic concern and prosocial helping directed toward the primary caregiver. Strong shared environmental influences were observed on empathy at 14 (69%) and 20 months, accounting for most of the variance (Knafo, Zahn-Waxler, et al., 2008). Importantly, some components of prosocial behavior and empathy appear to be more responsive to socialization efforts than others (Zahn-Waxler et al., 1992). For example, it may be easier to "teach" cognitive aspects of empathy as compared to concern and sympathy.

Since the estimates of the three variance components—heritability, shared environment, and nonshared environment—are expressed as proportions of total phenotypic variance, they are interdependent. Therefore, the increase in genetic effects with age entails a decline in shared or nonshared environment or both. The literature suggests that shared environmental effects are significant during early childhood and decrease with age (Gregory et al., 2009; Knafo & Plomin, 2006a; Knafo et al., 2009; Knafo, Zahn-Waxler, et al., 2008; Scourfield et al., 2004). By adolescence it appears that the shared environment does not play a role in shaping individual differences in prosocial behavior. As children get older, they become gradually more exposed to influences out of the home (e.g., school, peer relationships), such that a growing proportion of environmental influences are not shared with family members.

WHAT DO FINDINGS TELL US, IN PARTICULAR, ABOUT PARENTAL INFLUENCES ON PROSOCIAL BEHAVIOR?

The findings pointing to shared environmental effects at younger ages do confirm a role for early socialization in the development of prosocial behavior (Hastings et al., 2007). It is also possible to measure not only the phenotype of interest—prosocial behavior, but also the hypothesized environmental predictor, such as parenting, and conduct a multivariate twin modeling analysis. In this analysis, cross-twin cross-trait associations (i.e., the correlations between the parenting of one twin and the co-twin's behavioral outcome) are computed to estimate the extent to which the phenotypic relationship is mediated by genetic effects, shared and non-shared environmental effects. In such an analysis, Knafo and Plomin (2006b) found that although bivariate heritability accounted for most of the correlation between maternal negativity (negative feelings toward the child and punitive discipline) and mother-reported prosocial behavior (average of 63%; indicating rGE processes), bivariate shared environment had substantial contributions to concurrent and longitudinal associations between maternal positivity (positive feelings and discipline) and prosocial behavior (average of 51%), especially among younger children. Similarly, Deater-Deckard, Dunn, O'Connor, Davies, and Golding (2001), in a study of full-siblings and half-siblings in step-families found that the link between maternal negative feelings and mother-reported prosocial behavior was mediated primarily by environmental effects. This suggests that parental affection and discipline, shared by siblings to some extent, makes them similar in prosocial behavior, providing evidence for parental influences that are independent of children's genetics.

It is tempting to consider parenting to be shared-environment (experienced similarly by siblings). Coupled with the vast evidence reviewed for the role of parenting in children's empathy and prosocial behavior, this assumption is at odds with the findings of decreasing or nonsignificant shared environment effects (e.g., Knafo, Zahn-Waxler, et al., 2008). How can these apparently contradictory findings be settled? First, it is important to note that in the twin design, shared environmental effects represent the joint contribution of a wide range of variables that are shared by siblings growing up together (e.g., neighborhood, socioeconomic status) and not only that of parenting. Second, parental behaviors may be experienced (objectively and subjectively) quite differently by siblings and are, to an extent, of the nonshared kind. The literature on parental differential treatment (PDT) provides ample support for the notion that parenting is also a differentiating factor, exerting longitudinal effects on children over and above their own behavioral differences (e.g., Caspi et al., 2004).

The importance of environmental effects unique to each child in a family is nicely exemplified using the MZ twin-difference design. In a study by Deater-Deckard, Pike, et al. (2001), mothers were observed to treat their 3.5-year-old same-sex MZ twins differently. Furthermore, the twin who received less maternal harsh discipline, less negativity, and more positivity was also more prosocial as compared with the identical co-twin (based on mother-reported SDQ). Another study using a large sample of 4-year-old MZ twins (Asbury, Dunn, Pike, & Plomin, 2003) reported similar findings. These effects cannot be attributed to rGE, because parents are not responding to genetic differences between their children in this case.

Gene-Environment Interactions

Clearly, genetic and environmental pressures do not work independently and should not be viewed as opposite explanations for development. Biological and contextual factors are in a continuous, dynamic interplay over time (Ellis & Boyce, 2008). Thus, child development cannot simply be explained by either parenting or genes, since parental influences depend on children's genotype (e.g., Caspi et al., 2002). *Gene by environment interaction* (GXE) is the process through which an outcome is affected by a nonadditive joint effect of environmental and genetic influences. Some individuals may be more genetically sensitive than others to certain environments. Importantly, there are within-family differences in susceptibility to parenting (as may be indicated by the identified contribution of the nonshared environment during childhood; Ellis, Boyce, Belsky, Bakermans-Kranenburg, & van IJzendoorn, 2011)

An exciting body of research refers to *differential susceptibility*, the idea that some children are more susceptible than others to the influence of their rearing environment (e.g., the parenting they received) as a function of genetic, behavioral, and physiological variation. This is a type of parenting × child interaction but extending the classic "diathesis-stress" model by advocating that not only are those more susceptible vulnerable to negative parenting but also *benefit* more strongly from positive parental influences (Belsky, Bakermans-Kranenburg, & van IJzendoorn, 2007; Belsky & Pluess, 2009; Ellis et al., 2011).

Several polymorphisms involved in the serotonergic and dopaminergic systems have been shown to underlie differential genetic susceptibility to parental influence (Belsky et al., 2007) and the DRD4-III 7R allele in particular (Bakermans-Kranenburg & van IJzendoorn, 2006; van IJzendoorn & Bakermans-Kranenburg, 2006). Thus, genetic variability in dopaminergic genes appears to serve as a modulatory mechanism for limiting or enhancing the sensitivity to parental influences on developmental outcome. This is particularly relevant for the development of social behavior (Knafo et al., 2011). In one of the few GXE studies conducted concerning parenting and prosocial behavior, Knafo et al. (2011; method described in detail earlier in this chapter) provide support for differential genetic susceptibility to parenting. Whereas parenting did not directly relate to mother-rated SDQ prosocial behavior for the sample as a whole or among the children who do not carry the DRD4-7R allele, meaningful associations were found among those who do; the 7-present children receiving the lowest maternal positivity were described as the least prosocial, whereas those with the most positive mothers were the most prosocial. In addition, 7-present children whose mothers were low in unexplained punishment were the least likely to initiate prosocial behaviors toward the experimenter (helping, providing emotional support, and sharing a treat), whereas children whose mothers were high in unexplained punishment were the most likely to initiate prosocial behaviors. (This less intuitive association is discussed by Knafo et al., 2011. Also see Morris, Marshall, and Miller,

1973, for experimental findings regarding an association between unexplained [vicarious] punishment and helping behavior). DiLalla et al. (2009) did not find evidence for GXE between DRD4 and parental sensitivity on sharing behaviors during family (parent-twins) interactions. Knafo and Uzefovsky (2012) identified an interaction involving DRD4, maternal negativity, and observed empathy toward the examiner, such that a negative relationship was found between maternal negativity and child empathic concern only among 7-present children. Additional studies point to stronger environmental effects on prosociality among DRD4-7R carriers (Bakermans-Kranenburg & van IJzendoorn, 2011, for attachment security; Sasaki et al., 2011, for religion priming).

Discussion and Future Directions

This chapter emphasizes the important contributions that genetic factors, in addition to parents and other environmental contributions, make toward children's development of empathic understanding of family, friends, and strangers, and acting in ways that benefit others. These relative contributions vary in meaningful ways. Notably, children's biological factors and parental influences are in a continuous interplay in shaping their behavior toward others in need.

Further research involving longitudinal, genetically sensitive, parenting-sensitive designs are called for to identify and interpret gene-environment correlations and interactions. Large sample sizes are needed to detect effects, and growing use of molecular-genetic studies by psychologists is beneficial (Jaffee & Price, 2007). To better understand the role of rGEs in prosocial behavior further questions that should be asked are: Are the rGEs identified between parenting and a child's genes due to prosocial behavior itself or is it just one behavior in a set of child behaviors shaping parenting? Which types of rGEs are at work? For example, adoption studies can be helpful in distinguishing between parenting behaviors that are influenced by passive versus active or evocative rGE, as correlations between adoptive parents' parenting and children's genetics cannot be passive correlations. It is important to appreciate that parenting also likely mediates genetic predispositions and child behavior. Caregiving of children serves in part a regulatory function, helping regulate genetic tendencies and temperamentally based physiological processes.

The finding that the role of parenting depends on children's genotype tells us not only about parents' limits of influence but also about children's increasingly appreciated role in family processes (Knafo & Israel, 2009). As increasingly more evidence accumulates for such bidirectional parent-child processes, we come to see children as active agents in their development, shaping their environment— influencing the parenting that they receive—rather than being passive recipients of top-down parenting (e.g., Grusec & Goodnow, 1994).

We also call for future study of the processes underlying the identified genetic influences on developmental stability and change (Knafo & Plomin, 2006a) and of the epigenetic processes by which environmental processes interact with the way genes are expressed through development (McGowan et al., 2009). This type of research would move toward a fuller understanding of gene-environment processes promoting prosocial behavior.

Importantly, all of the above research avenues should take into account the multidimensionality of prosocial behavior. In this chapter we have reviewed findings pointing to differences in genetic and environmental effects depending on the type of prosocial behavior and the assessment method, the target, and age of the child at the time of assessment. An additional moderator to keep in mind when relying on questionnaire data is the informant reporting on prosocial behavior. For example, parents (in comparison with teachers, perhaps) may have biases when describing their own children's prosocial tendencies (usually valued by parents) which may result in inflation of ratings as well as greater twin similarities (e.g., Scourfield et al., 2004). In one study using both parent-reports as well as self-reports of adolescent twins' prosocial behavior (Gregory et al., 2009), there were only weak associations between reporters, with parents describing their twins' behavior as more similar than did the twins themselves.

The literature reviewed in this chapter shows that many studies are confounded by type of prosocial behavior. For example, questionnaires like the SDQ, while very useful for an overall estimation of prosocial behavior, mesh together different operationalizations of prosocial behavior (e.g., being considerate of others' feelings, being kind, sharing, and helping). Measures that better distinguish between the various forms of prosocial behavior toward others are likely to tell a more complete story regarding the origins specific to each of these behaviors. Such an approach will further promote the understanding of the development of these wonderfully complex set of behaviors performed by humans.

References

Apicella, C. L., Cesarini, D., Johannesson, M., Dawes, C.T., Lichtenstein, P., Wallace, B., et al. (2010). No association between oxytocin receptor (OXTR) gene polymorphisms and experimentally elicited social preferences. *PLoS ONE, 5*(6), e11153.

Asbury, K., Dunn, J. F., Pike, A., & Plomin, R. (2003). Nonshared environmental influences on individual differences in early behavioral development: A monozygotic twin differences study. *Child Development, 74*, 933–943.

Avinun, R., Israel, S., Shalev, I., Gritsenko, I., Bornstein, G., Ebstein, R. P, & Knafo, A. (2011). AVPR1A variant associated with preschoolers' lower altruistic behavior. *PLoS ONE, 6*(9), e25274

Bachner-Melman, R., Gritsenko, I., Nemanov, L., Zohar, A. H., & Ebstein, R. P. (2005). Dopaminergic polymorphisms associated with self-report measures of human altruism: A fresh phenotype for the dopamine D4 receptor. *Molecular Psychiatry, 10*, 333–335.

Bakermans-Kranenburg, M. J., & van IJzendoorn, M. H. (2006). Gene-environment interaction of the dopamine D4 receptor and observed maternal insensitivity predicting externalizing behavior in preschoolers. *Developmental Psychobiology, 48,* 406–409.

Bakermans-Kranenburg, M. J., & van IJzendoorn, M. H. (2011). Differential susceptibility to rearing environment depending on dopamine-related genes: New evidence and a meta-analysis. *Development and Psychopathology, 23,* 39–52.

Barnett, M. A., King, L. M. Howard, J. A., & Dino, G. A. (1980). Empathy in young children: Relation to parents' empathy, affection, and emphasis on the feelings of others. *Developmental Psychology, 16,* 243–244.

Beam, C. R., & Turkheimer, E. (2013). Phenotype-environment correlations in longitudinal twin models. *Development and Psychopathology, 25,* 7–16.

Belsky, J., & Pluess, M. (2009). The nature (and nurture?) of plasticity in early human development. *Perspectives on Psychological Science, 4,* 345–351.

Belsky, J., Bakermans-Kranenburg, M. J., & van IJzendoorn, M. H. (2007). For better and for worse: Differential susceptibility to environmental influences. *Current Directions in Psychological Science, 16,* 300–304.

Bernadett-Shapiro, S., Ehrensaft, D., & Shapiro, J. L. (1996). Father participation in childcare and the development of empathy in sons: An empirical study. *Family Therapy, 23,* 77–93.

Bryant, B. K., & Crockenberg, S. B. (1980). Correlates and dimensions of prosocial behavior: A study of female siblings with their mothers. *Child Development, 51,* 529–544.

Carlo, G., Mestre, M. V., Samper, P., Tur, A., & Armenta, B. E. (2011). The longitudinal relations among dimensions of parenting styles, sympathy, prosocial moral reasoning, and prosocial behaviors. *International Journal of Behavioral Development, 35,* 116–124.

Carlo, G., Roesch, S. C., & Melby, J. (1998). The multiplicative relations of parenting and temperament to prosocial and antisocial behaviors in adolescence. *Journal of Early Adolescence, 18,* 266–290.

Caspi, A., McClay, J., Moffitt, T. E., Mill, J., Martin, J., Craig, W. I., et al. (2002). Role of genotype in the cycle of violence in maltreated children. *Science, 297,* 851–854.

Caspi, A., Moffitt, T. E., Morgan, J., Rutter, M., Taylor, A., Arseneault, L., et al. (2004). Maternal expressed emotion predicts children's antisocial behavior problems: Using monozygotic-twin differences to identify environmental effects on behavioral development. *Developmental Psychology, 40,* 149–161.

Crockett, M. J. (2009). The neurochemistry of fairness. *Annals of the New York Academy of Sciences, 1167,* 76–86.

Deater-Deckard, K. (2000). Parenting and child behavioral adjustment in early childhood: A quantitative genetic approach to studying family processes and child development. *Child Development, 71,* 468–484.

Deater-Deckard, K., Dunn, J., O'Connor, T. G., Davies, L., & Golding, J. (2001). Using the stepfamily genetic design to examine gene-environmental processes in child and family functioning. *Marriage and Family Review, 33,* 131–156.

Deater-Deckard, K., Pike, A., Petrill, S. A., Cutting, A. L., Hughes, C., & O'Connor, T. G. (2001). Nonshared environmental processes in social-emotional development: An observational study of identical twin differences in the preschool period. *Developmental Science, 4,* F1–F6.

Dekovic, M., & Janssens, J. M. A. M. (1992). Parents' child-rearing style and children's sociometric status. *Developmental Psychology, 28,* 925–932.

Denham, S. A., & Grout, L. (1992). Mothers' emotional expressiveness and coping: Relations with preschoolers' social-emotional competence. *Genetic, Social, and General Psychology Monographs, 118*, 75–101.

DiLalla, L. F., Elam, K. K., & Smolen, A. (2009). Genetic and gene–environment interaction effects on preschoolers' social behaviors. *Developmental Psychobiology, 51*, 451–464.

Eisenberg, N., Cameron, E., & Tryon, F. (1984). Prosocial behavior in the preschool years: Methodological and conceptual issues. In E. Staub, D. Bar-Tal, J. Karylowski, & J. Reykowski (Eds.), *The development and maintenance of prosocial behavior: International perspectives on positive development* (pp. 101–115). New York: Plenum Press.

Eisenberg, N., Fabes, R. A., & Spinrad, T. (2006). Prosocial development. In N. Eisenberg (Vol. Ed.) & W. Damon & R. M. Lerner (Series Eds.), *Handbook of child psychology: Vol. 3. Social, emotional, and personality development* (6th ed., pp. 646–718). Hoboken, NJ: Wiley.

Eisenberg, N., Liew, J., & Pidada, S. (2001). The relations of parental emotional expressivity with the quality of Indonesian children's social functioning. *Emotion, 1*, 107–115.

Eisenberg, N., & Miller, P. A. (1987). The relation of empathy to prosocial and related behaviors. *Psychological Bulletin, 101*, 91–119.

Ellis, J., & Boyce, T. (2008). Biological sensitivity to context. *Current Directions in Psychological Science, 17*, 183–187.

Ellis, B. J., Boyce, W. T., Belsky, J., Bakermans-Kranenburg, M. J., & van IJzendoorn, M. H. (2011). Differential susceptibility to the environment: An evolutionary-neurodevelopmental theory. *Development and Psychopathology, 23*, 7–28.

Ensor, R., Spencer, D., & Hughes, C. (2011). "You feel sad?" Emotion understanding mediates effects of verbal ability and mother–child mutuality on prosocial behaviors: Findings from 2 years to 4 years. *Social Development, 20*, 93–110.

Goodman, R. (1997). The strengths and difficulties questionnaire: A research note. *Journal of Child Psychology and Psychiatry, 38*, 581–586.

Gregory, A. M., Light-Hausermann, J. H., Rijsdijk, F., & Eley, T. C. (2009). Behavioral genetic analyses of prosocial behavior in adolescents. *Developmental Science, 12*, 165–174.

Grusec, J. E. (1991). Socializing concern for others in home. *Developmental Psychology, 27*, 338–342.

Grusec, J. E., Davidov, M., & Lundell, L. (2002). Prosocial and helping behavior. In C. H. Hart & P. K. Smith (Eds.), *Blackwell handbook of childhood social development* (pp. 457–474). Malden, MA: Blackwell.

Grusec, J. E., & Goodnow, J. J. (1994). Impact of parental discipline methods on the child's internalization of values: A reconceptualization of current points of view. *Developmental Psychology, 30*, 4–19.

Hardy, S. A., Carlo, G., & Roesch, S. C. (2010). Links between adolescents' expected parental reactions and prosocial behavioral tendencies: The mediating role of prosocial values. *Journal of Youth and Adolescence, 39*, 84–95.

Hastings, P. D., Rubin, K. H., & DeRose, L. (2005). Links among gender, inhibition, and parental socialization in the development of prosocial behavior. *Merrill-Palmer Quarterly, 51*, 501–527.

Hastings, P. D., Utendale, W. T., & Sullivan, C. (2007). The socialization of prosocial development. In J. E. Grusec & P. D. Hastings (Eds.), *Handbook of socialization* (pp. 638–664). New York: Guilford Press.

Hastings, P. D., Zahn-Waxler, C., & McShane, K. (2005). We are, by nature, moral creatures: Biological bases of concern for others. In M. Killen & J. Smetana (Eds.), *Handbook of moral development* (pp. 483–516). Hillsdale, NJ: Erlbaum.

Hastings, P. D., Zahn-Waxler, C., Robinson, J., Usher, B., & Bridges, D. (2000). The development of concern for others in children with behavior problems. *Developmental Psychology, 36,* 531–546.

Hein, G., & Singer, T. (2010). Neuroscience meets social psychology: An integrative approach to human empathy and prosocial behavior. In M. Mikulincer & P. R. Shaver (Eds.), *Prosocial motives, emotions, and behavior: The better angels of our nature,* (pp. 109–125). Washington, DC: American Psychological Association.

Hoffman, M. L. (1975). Altruistic behavior and the parent-child relationship. *Journal of Personality and Social Psychology, 31,* 937–943.

Hur, Y. M., & Rushton, J. P. (2007). Genetic and environmental contributions to prosocial behaviour in 2- to 9-year-old South Korean twins. *Biology Letters, 3,* 664–666.

Israel, S., Lerer, E., Shalev, I., Uzefovsky, F., Reibold, M., Bachner-Melman, R., et al. (2008). Molecular genetic studies of the arginine vasopressin 1a receptor (AVPR1a) and the oxytocin receptor (OXTR) in human behavior: From autism to altruism with some notes in between. *Progress in Brain Research, 170,* 435–449.

Israel, S., Lerer, E., Shalev, I., Uzefovsky, F., Reibold, M., Laiba, E., et al. (2009). The oxytocin receptor (OXTR) contributes to prosocial fund allocations in the dictator game and the social value orientations task. *PLoS ONE, 4,* e5535.

Jaffee, S. R., & Price, T. S. (2007). Gene–environment correlations: A review of the evidence and implications for prevention of mental illness. *Molecular Psychiatry, 12,* 432–442.

Knafo, A., & Israel, S. (2009). Genetic and environmental influences on prosocial behavior. In M. Mikulincer & P. R. Shaver (Eds.), *Prosocial motives, emotions, and behavior: The better angels of our nature* (pp. 149–167). Washington, DC: APA.

Knafo, A., Israel, S., Darvasi, A., Bachner-Melman, R., Uzefovsky, F., Cohen, L., et al. (2008). Individual differences in allocation of funds in the Dictator Game and postmortem hippocampal mRNA levels are correlated with length of the arginine vasopressin 1a receptor (AVPR1a) RS3 promoter-region repeat. *Genes, Brain and Behavior, 7,* 266–275.

Knafo, A., Israel, S., & Ebstein, R. P. (2011). Heritability of children's prosocial behavior and differential susceptibility to parenting by variation in the dopamine receptor D4 gene. *Development and Psychopathology, 23,* 53–67.

Knafo, A., & Jaffee, S. R. (2013). Gene-environment correlations in developmental psychopathology. *Development and Psychopathology, 25,* 1–6.

Knafo, A., & Plomin, R. (2006a). Prosocial behavior from early to middle childhood: Genetic and environmental influences on stability and change. *Developmental Psychology, 42,* 771–786.

Knafo, A., & Plomin, R. (2006b). Parental discipline and affection, and children's prosocial behavior: Genetic and environmental links. *Journal of Personality and Social Psychology, 90,* 147–164.

Knafo, A., & Uzefovsky, F. (2012). Variation in empathy: The interplay of genetic and environmental factors. In M. Legerstee, D. W. Haley, & M. H. Bornstein (Eds.), *The developing infant mind: Integrating biology and experience* (pp. 97–121). New York: Guilford Press.

Knafo, A., Zahn-Waxler, C., Davidov, M., Van Hulle, C., Robinson, J., & Rhee, S. H. (2009). Empathy in early childhood: Genetic, environmental and affective contributions. *Annals of the New York Academy of Sciences, 1167*, 103–114.

Knafo, A., Zahn-Waxler, C., Van Hulle, C., Robinson, J. L., Rhee, S. H. (2008). The developmental origins of a disposition toward empathy: Genetic and environmental contributions. *Emotion, 8*, 737–752.

Koenig, A. L., Cicchetti, D., & Rogosch, F. A. (2004). Moral development: The association between maltreatment and young children's prosocial behaviors and moral transgressions. *Social Development, 13*, 87–106.

Kogan, A., Saslow, L. R., Impetta, E. A., Oveisc, C., Keltner, D., Saturn, S. R. (2011). Thin-slicing study of the oxytocin receptor (OXTR) gene and the evaluation and expression of the prosocial disposition. *PNAS Proceedings of the National Academy of Sciences of the United States of America, 108*, 19189–19192.

Krevans, J., & Gibbs, J. C. (1996). Parents' use of inductive discipline: Relations to children's empathy and prosocial behavior. *Child Development, 67*, 3263–3277.

MacDonald, K., & MacDonald, T. M. (2010). The peptide that binds: A systematic review of oxytocin and its prosocial effects in humans. *Harvard Review of Psychiatry, 18*, 1–21.

McGowan, P. O., Sasaki, A., D'Alessio, A. C., Dymov, S., Labonté, B., Szyf, M., et al. (2009). Epigenetic regulation of the glucocorticoid receptor in human brain associates with childhood abuse. *Nature Neuroscience, 12*, 342–348.

McGuire, S. (2003). The heritability of parenting. *Parenting: Science and Practice, 3*, 73–94.

Morris, W. N., Marshall, H. M., & Miller, R. S. (1973). The effect of vicarious punishment on prosocial behavior in children. *Journal of Experimental Child Psychology, 15*, 222–236.

Padilla-Walker, L. M. (2007). Characteristics of mother-child interactions related to adolescents' positive values and behaviors. *Journal of Marriage and Family, 69*, 675–686.

Padilla-Walker, L. M., & Carlo, G. (2007). Personal values as a mediator between parent and peer expectations and adolescent behaviors. *Journal of Family Psychology, 21*, 538–541.

Padilla-Walker, L. M., & Christensen, K. J. (2011). Empathy and self-regulation as mediators between parenting and adolescents' prosocial behavior toward strangers, friends, and family. *Journal of Research on Adolescence, 21*, 545–551.

Padilla-Walker, L. M., & Nelson, L. J. (2010). Parenting and adolescents' values and behaviour: The moderating role of temperament. *Journal of Moral Education, 39*, 491–509.

Plomin R., & Bergeman C. S. (1991). The nature of nurture: genetic influence on 'environmental' measures. *Behavioral and Brain Sciences, 14*, 373–427.

Plomin, R., DeFries, J. C., McClearn, G. E., & McGuffin, P. (2001). *Behavioral genetics* (4th ed.). New York: Worth.

Plomin, R., Reiss, D., Hetherington, E. M., & Howe, G.W. (1994). Nature and nurture: Genetic contributions to measures of the family environment. *Developmental Psychology, 30*, 32–43.

Poulin, M. J., Holman, E. A., & Buffone, A. (2012). The neurogenetics of nice: Receptor genes for oxytocin and vasopressin interact with threat to predict prosocial behavior. *Psychological Science, 23*, 446–452.

Reuter, M., Frenzel, C., Walter, N. T., Markett, S., & Montag, C. (2010). Investigating the genetic basis of altruism: The role of the COMT Val158Met polymorphism. *Social Cognitive and Affective Neuroscience, 6*, 662–668.

Roberts, W. L. (1999). The socialization of emotional expression: Relations with prosocial behaviour and competence in five samples. *Canadian Journal of Behavioural Science*, *31*, 72–85.

Robinson, J. L., Zahn-Waxler, C., & Emde, R. N. (1994). Patterns of development in early empathic behavior: Environmental and child constitutional influences. *Social Development*, *3*, 125–145.

Rodrigues, S. M., Saslow, L. R., Garcia, N., John, O. P., & Keltner, D. (2009). Oxytocin receptor genetic variation relates to empathy and stress reactivity in humans. *PNAS Proceedings of the National Academy of Sciences of the United States of America*, *106*, 21437–21441.

Rubin, K. H., Burgess, K. B., & Hastings, P. D. (2002). Stability and social-behavioral consequences of toddlers' inhibited temperament and parenting behaviors. *Child Development*, *73*, 483–495.

Sasaki, J. Y., Kim, H. S., Mojaverian, T., Kelley L. D. S., Park, I. Y., & Janusonis, S. (2011). Religion priming differentially increases prosocial behavior among variants of the dopamine D4 receptor (DRD4) gene. *Social Cognitive and Affective Neuroscience*. Advance access. doi:10.1093/scan/nsr089.

Scarr, S., & McCartney, K. (1983). How people make their own environments: A theory of genotype greater than environment effects. *Child Development*, *54*, 424–435.

Scourfield, J., John, B., Martin, N., & McGuffin, P. (2004). The development of prosocial behaviour in children and adolescents: A twin study. *Journal of Child Psychology and Psychiatry*, *45*, 927–935.

Staub, E. (1992). The origins of caring, helping, and nonaggression: Parental socialization, the family system, schools, and cultural influence. In P. M. Oliner, L. Baron, L. A. Blum, D. L. Krebs, & M. Z. Smolenska (Eds.), *Embracing the other: Philosophical, psychological, and historical perspectives on altruism* (pp. 390–412). New York: New York University Press.

Trommsdorff, G. (1991). Child-rearing and children's empathy. *Perceptual Motor Skills*, *72*, 387–390.

Van IJzendoorn, M. H., & Bakermans-Kranenburg, M. J. (2006). DRD47-repeat polymorphism moderates the association between maternal unresolved loss or trauma and infant disorganization. *Attachment and Human Development*, *8*, 291–307.

Van IJzendoorn, M. H., Bakermans-Kranenburg, M. J., Pannebakker, F., & Out, D. (2010). In defence of situational morality: Genetic, dispositional and situational determinants of children's donating to charity. *Journal of Moral Education*, *39*, 1–20.

Volbrecht, M. M., Lemery-Chalfant, K., Aksan, N., Zahn-Waxler, C., & Goldsmith, H. H. (2007). Examining the familial link between positive affect and empathy development in the second year. *Journal of Genetic Psychology*, *168*, 105–129.

Zahn-Waxler, C., Radke-Yarrow, M., & King, R. A. (1979). Child rearing and children's prosocial initiations toward victims of distress. *Child Development*, *50*, 319–330.

Zahn-Waxler, C., Robinson, J., & Emde, R. N. (1992). The development of empathy in twins. *Developmental Psychology*, *28*, 1038–1047.

Zhou, Q., Eisenberg, N., Losoya, S. H., Fabes, R. A., Reiser, M., Guthrie, I. K., et al. (2002). The relations of parental warmth and positive expressiveness to children's empathy-related responding and social functioning: A longitudinal study. *Child Development*, *73*, 893–915.

5

The Prosocial Brain

PERCEIVING OTHERS IN NEED AND ACTING ON IT

Alek Chakroff and Liane Young

In early 2011, a 9.03 magnitude earthquake struck east of Tōhoku, Japan, creating a tsunami that caused widespread destruction and the deaths of over 15,000 people. Like many tragedies, this one elicited an outpouring of aid from people around the world. American citizens alone donated over $650 million to the relief effort (Japan Center for International Exchange, 2012). Locally, hundreds of elderly Japanese citizens volunteered to clean up the Fukushima Daiichi nuclear power plant, arguing that they were less susceptible to radiation poisoning than younger volunteers and in any case had fewer remaining years for radiation effects to emerge (Lah, 2011). Why did American citizens offer aid to people who would likely never return the favor or even meet their benefactors? Why did elderly Japanese citizens form what was known as the "suicide corps," cleaning up toxic waste at their own ultimate personal risk?

Prosocial behavior, or behavior carried out with the intention to help others (Eisenberg, Fabes, & Spinrad, 2006), may be rooted in different reasons, some more noble than others. We may help others anticipating direct or indirect reciprocal benefits or, more generally, social credit; we may help others to avoid negative social consequences; we may help others for purely instrumental reasons (e.g., tax write-offs); and we may help others out of an altruistic motivation, a selfless desire to increase their well-being, without anticipated selfish benefit (Batson et al., 1989).

Debate rages about how a noncolonial social species could have evolved altruistic tendencies such that individuals incur costs to benefit others. Fitness comparisons at the level of individuals—the individual altruist and the individual miser—reveal the miser as the clear winner. Yet, groups of altruists are thought to outperform groups of misers (Boyd & Richerson, 2002; Sober & Wilson, 1998), though altruism may also emerge particularly robustly in groups that share genetic variance (West, Mouden, & Gardner, 2011). Altruism could therefore be selected for at the cultural and genetic level. Regardless of the evolutionary origins of altruistic behavior, the present review concerns the psychologically proximate motivations for prosocial behavior. Indeed, ultimate "ends" will not necessarily correspond with proximate "means" (Mayr, 1993; Von Hippel & Trivers, 2011). Thus, even in the absence of true biological altruism, we need not predict that individuals never act out of "genuine" altruistic motivations.

What psychological capacities does an individual need in order to engage in prosocial behavior as defined above (Eisenberg et al., 2006)? Acting to intentionally benefit others first requires that one perceive others—other living beings with needs and desires—in other words, acting to benefit others requires social cognition. We offer aid to living creatures, not rocks; friends, not foes; family more than strangers. However, perceiving a need in others does not always lead to sufficient motivation to help. Millions around the world are starving to death, and members of developed countries have the power to save lives by donating some or most of their income to charitable organizations (Singer, 1997). Why do they not donate more? It may be difficult to empathize with the plight of unseen others across the globe—we simply do not feel bad enough. Alternatively, we may be less likely to help those who have no power to return the favor. Prosocial behavior requires not only the perception of an opportunity to help, but the motivation to act. This motivation may be rooted in empathetic processes through feeling the pain of another and desiring to reduce the pain. The motivation to help others may also require the ability to anticipate some future reward, whether that reward is anticipated reciprocity (e.g., you scratch my back) or the "warm glow" of being a good person.

This review is organized around the distinct psychological processes underlying prosocial behavior. First, we outline the processes that are likely required for prosocial action to occur: perception of life, minds, and negative mental states in others as well as anticipation of positive outcomes. We discuss the neural mechanisms underlying each of these psychological processes and use this discussion as a lens through which to interpret research directly relating prosocial behavior to the brain. Finally, we discuss ambiguities in the interpretation of the current research and suggest future directions.

Psychological Underpinnings of Prosocial Behavior

Would you be more likely to intervene to stop a child from pulling wings off a fly, or to stop a child from pulling leaves off a fallen tree branch? To make this distinction, one must distinguish animate from inanimate forms. What if the child were trying to pull the wings off a bird? We distinguish between different kinds of minds, and some may be perceived as more capable of experiencing pain. We care about the needs of others and about our relative influence on their affective state. We are adept at distinguishing between kinds of life forms, kinds of minds, and kinds of mental states—and we adjust our prosocial behavior accordingly. In the following sections, we provide an overview of the neural processes underlying the perception of animate objects, minds, mental states, and reward anticipation and we discuss the contribution of these processes to prosocial behavior.

PERCEIVING LIFE

Humans evolved in a harsh environment, in which the ability to distinguish living from nonliving enabled people to find food and to avoid becoming food. Animacy perception is automatic. For a demonstration, watch a low-budget cartoon where a small triangle shakes and quickly moves away from a larger triangle, which then proceeds in the same direction, in what appears, unmistakably, to be a hostile pursuit (Heider & Simmel, 1944). Although the shapes bear little surface resemblance to animate agents (e.g., no eyes, no limbs), we infer agency and experience from motion that is contingent (e.g., reactive to others) or self-generated (Gelman & Gottfried, 1996; Luo & Baillargeon, 2005, Scholl & Tremoulet, 2000). We also process surface cues to animacy, such as faces, automatically (Bentin, Allison, Puce, Perez, & McCarthy, 1996; Hadjikhani, Kveraga, Naik, & Ahlfors, 2009) and from infancy on (Johnson, Dziurawiec, Ellis, & Morton, 1991). In fact, we detect agents even where they are not technically present—when we see faces in the clouds or the Virgin Mary in our toast (i.e., pareidolia).

The neural underpinnings of animacy perception have been assessed using techniques such as electroencephalography (EEG) and functional magnetic resonance imaging (fMRI), aimed at measuring, primarily, the speed and spatial location of neural processing, respectively. Research using EEG has shown that faces can be neurally distinguished from nonfaces approximately 170 milliseconds after presentation (Bentin et al., 1996), even when the "face" is a sparse schematic of three dots arranged like eyes and a mouth (Hadjikhani et al., 2009). However, more subtle cues to animacy (e.g., used to distinguish the face of a live human being from the face on a mannequin) are integrated later, around 400 milliseconds after presentation (Wheatley, Weinberg, Looser, Moran, & Hajcak, 2011).

Meanwhile, fMRI research has shown that face processing takes place near the posterior fusiform gyrus (FG; Kanwisher, McDermott, & Chun, 1997), while biological motion is processed in the posterior superior temporal sulcus (pSTS; Grossman et al., 2000; Wheatley, Milleville, & Martin, 2007). Both the FG and the pSTS are sensitive to subtle cues to animacy. For example, Looser, Guntupalli, and Wheatley (2012) presented participants with pictures of humans and dogs, both animate and inanimate (e.g., realistic dolls), and found that the FG and pSTS exhibit similar responses to animate humans and dogs, but dissimilar responses to animate versus inanimate targets, suggesting that animacy is a primary driver of these regions, regardless of form (e.g., doglike versus humanlike). By contrast, regions in the inferior and lateral occipital cortex were more sensitive to the overall form of objects (including animate entities) and responded similarly to targets with a similar form, such as an animate human and an inanimate doll (Looser et al., 2012). These occipital responses can also be used to distinguish different biological kinds (e.g., birds versus bugs; Connolly et al., 2012). Together, these results reveal complementary roles for these regions: The FG and pSTS distinguish animate agents from inanimate objects, whereas the inferior and lateral occipital cortex distinguish among kinds of animate and inanimate entities.

PERCEIVING MINDS

Bugs and birds alike are living entities, but birds may seem to possess greater mental capacity. We judge some creatures to be more capable of conscious experience (e.g., pain and suffering) than others and some creatures to be more capable of action or agency than others (Gray, Gray, & Wegner, 2007). These judgments carry consequences for empathy and moral cognition. Entities seen as highly capable of experience are more readily recognized as victims. It is worse to harm a bird than a bug. Entities seen as highly capable of agency are also deemed more morally responsible for their behavior. Theft is worse if carried out by an adult man versus a small child. Some evidence suggests that these dimensions may be inversely related; entities high in agency are also low in experience, and vice versa. In an unnerving demonstration of this trade-off, participants were more willing to inflict pain on Mother Teresa, relative to a neutral target, presumably because "super agents" are not easily seen as "patients," capable of experiencing pain (Gray & Wegner, 2009).

When judging others, we assess not only their capacity for agency and experience but also their specific intent to help or hinder us (warmth) and their ability to carry out those intentions (competence; S. T. Fiske, Cuddy, & Glick, 2007). We spontaneously sort people along the dimensions of warmth and competence: friends versus foes, strong versus weak. Compare your feelings toward the homeless (low warmth, low competence), the elderly (high warmth, low competence), businessmen (low warmth, high competence), and middle-class Americans (high warmth, high competence). Research indicates that the elderly and the middle class are perceived as similarly friendly (warmth) but different in their capacity to act on generally good intentions (competence). By contrast, neither the businessmen nor the homeless are perceived as particularly well intentioned but, because of perceived differences in competence, are regarded with envy and disgust, respectively.

Dimensions of warmth and competence roughly correspond with those of trustworthiness and dominance, as assessed through trait inferences of human faces (Todorov, Said, Engell, & Oosterhof, 2008). People judge warmth and competence based on people's facial expressions and configurations (Todorov, Gobbini, Evans, & Haxby, 2007; Todorov et al., 2008), semantic stereotypical knowledge of the person (Contreras, Banaji, & Mitchell, 2012; Mitchell, Ames, Jenkins, & Banaji, 2009), and assessments of similarity to oneself (Mitchell, Macrae, & Banaji, 2006). We judge those who are happy, similar to us, and/

or part of our group to be highest in warmth and trustworthiness. Inferring social traits (and social cognition more generally) consistently recruits the medial prefrontal cortex (mPFC; Amodio & Frith, 2006; Contreras et al., 2012; Mitchell et al., 2009; Mitchell et al., 2006). For example, similar or in-group others are more likely to elicit activation in the ventral mPFC (Krienen, Tu, & Buckner, 2010; Mitchell et al., 2006), a region also implicated in self-referential processing (Jenkins & Mitchell, 2011; Kelley et al., 2002; Morrison, Decety, & Molenberghs, 2012). Perceiving close others also increases activity in "reward areas" such as the ventral striatum (VS; Cloutier, Heatherton, Whalen, & Kelley, 2008; Mende-Siedlecki, Said, & Todorov, 2012), which are often activated when a participant receives or anticipates some kind of reward, such as money, food, or social contact (Fehr & Camerer, 2007; Knutson & Cooper, 2005). Meanwhile, dissimilar or out-group others are likely to elicit activation in dorsal mPFC (Mitchell et al., 2006), as well as regions associated with negative affect, such as the amygdala and anterior insula (Harris & Fiske, 2006; Lieberman, Hariri, Jarcho, Eisenberger, & Brookheimer, 2005; Mende-Siedlecki, Said, & Todorov, 2012). Other work suggests that individuals judged to be both cold and incompetent elicit less activation in the mPFC in general, indicating a potential neural signature of dehumanization (Harris & Fiske, 2006).

PERCEIVING MENTAL STATES

We perceive not only different kinds of minds and stable mental dispositions, but also transient mental states. We make inferences about people's feelings, desires, beliefs, and intentions (Amodio & Frith, 2006; Saxe & Powell, 2006). Mental state inferences rely on a network of brain regions including the mPFC, precuneus (PC), and bilateral temporoparietal junction (TPJ), though these regions are theorized to support distinct functions. For example, while the mPFC supports the processing of dispositional traits and preferences (Contreras et al., 2012; Mitchell et al., 2009), the right TPJ supports the inference of transient beliefs and intentions (Saxe & Powell, 2006; Young & Saxe, 2009).

Of particular interest here is perception of unpleasant mental states in others (e.g., pain or suffering), an ability required for emotional perspective taking (e.g., Batson et al., 1989). Suppose you watch a video of someone being beaten with a hammer. Even with full knowledge that the video is staged, your heart rate will increase, your palms will sweat, and you may grimace or even recoil at the sight (Cushman, Gray, Gaffey, & Mendes, 2012; see also Rozin, Millman, & Nemeroff, 1986). Emotional perspective taking may result in: (1) empathy, where one feels the same emotion as another, (2) sympathy, where one feels concern *for* another, or (3) personal distress, a self-focused response where one feels negatively because of another (Batson, 2009; Decety & Lamm, 2009; Eisenberg & Eggum, 2009). Perceiving others in pain often activates the same brain regions involved in the personal experience of pain, including the anterior insula (AI) and anterior cingulate cortex (ACC; De Vignemont & Singer, 2006; Jackson, Meltzoff, & Decety, 2005). As automatic as pain processing is, it may also be modulated by contextual knowledge. For example, as discussed previously, we are more sensitive to the pain of moral patients or victims, versus moral agents or perpetrators (Gray & Wegner, 2009). This differential sensitivity is reflected in increased activity in AI and ACC when perceiving pain in victims versus perpetrators (Decety, Echols, & Correll, 2010). Empathic reactions are also modulated by group membership (i.e., reduced activity in AI and ACC in response to the painful experiences of out-group members; Xu, Zuo, Wang, & Han, 2009). These effects may be particularly strong in the context of intergroup conflict or competition, resulting even in the recruitment of reward regions in response to the physical or emotional suffering of out-group members (Cikara, Botvinick, & Fiske, 2011; Cikara, Bruneau, & Saxe, 2011; Singer et al., 2006).

ANTICIPATING REWARD

Prosocial behavior requires the perception of another being who could bene-fit from one's own behavior. However, as we have seen, simply identifying an opportunity for prosociality is no guarantee that one will act on it. We may be more motivated to behave prosocially when the cost of such behavior is low and the anticipated benefits are high. These benefits may come in the form of reciprocation or public credit, or as a private positive feeling (i.e., "warm glow"). The reward system can be roughly divided into two processes: the anticipation of reward and the processing of a rewarding outcome. These two processes, pre-diction and the processing of prediction error, are associated with activity in distinct brain regions (Knutson & Cooper, 2005). The anticipation of reward is associated with activity in the VS and the nucleus accumbens, a subregion of the VS; the processing of a rewarding outcome is associated with activity in the ven-tral mPFC. Both regions seem to be involved in the processing of reward across multiple domains, for example, reflecting the rewarding aspects of food, money, or social contact (Fehr & Camerer, 2007; Knutson & Cooper, 2005). While this generality hints that prosocial behavior may indeed be associated with activity in reward brain regions, it also increases the difficulty of making strong infer-ences about the *kind* of reward that is anticipated by the prosocial individual. For example, one person may help another because he anticipates reputational benefits; another may do so because he finds prosocial behavior intrinsically rewarding, that is, it feels good to "do what's right." Both of these expected out-comes are rewarding in a sense and may be associated with activity in brain regions such as the VS and ventral mPFC. Notably, this ambiguity in the inter-pretation of brain data applies not only to the reward system, but also to regions involved in social cognition and the perception of negative mental states. We revisit this discussion after reviewing research directly associating brain activity and prosocial behavior.

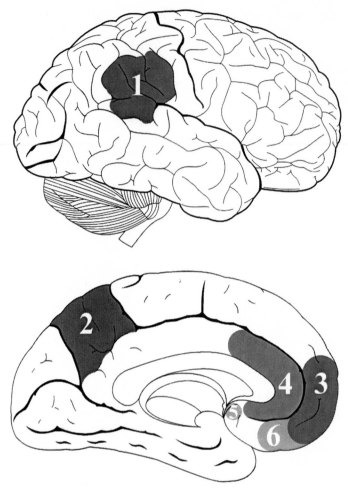

FIGURE 5.1 **The Prosocial Brain** *Prosocial behavior is associated with processing in brain regions implicated in social cognition, such as the bilateral temporoparietal junction (TPJ, 1), precune us (PC, 2) and medial prefrontal cortex (mPFC, 3); brain regions involved in processing conflict and discomfort, such as the anterior cingulate (ACC, 4) and anterior insula (AI, not pictured); and brain regions involved in reward processing, such as the ventral striatum (VS, 5) and ventral mPFC (6).*

Modified from Gray (1918, Figures 727 and 728) by Oona Räisänen.

The Prosocial Brain

Earlier, we provided a brief review of the psychological and neural processes that enable people to perceive life, minds, and mental states in others. Here we discuss research revealing a link between social cognition and prosocial behavior and in particular evidence showing that greater involvement of regions for mind perception (e.g., mPFC, TPJ), the perception of unpleasant states in others (e.g., AI and

ACC), and the anticipation of reward (VS) is associated with prosocial sentiments and behavior (see Figure 5.1). Notably, there has been little neuroscientific research associating the perception of life or animacy and prosocial behavior. This may be because, on the face of it, people are clearly motivated to aid living creatures rather than inanimate objects such as rocks. Although people sometimes admit to "animistic" tendencies, judging inanimate objects to have animate traits (e.g., my printer hates me), these judgments often go beyond mere animacy attribution, leading, ultimately, to inferences about the presence of minds as well (see Waytz, Gray, Epley, & Wegner, 2010).

Notably, the anticipated role of mentalizing and reward brain networks in prosocial behavior dovetails with work linking prosociality to neurochemicals such as oxytocin and dopamine. Oxytocin interacts with social cognitive brain regions such as the mPFC and reward regions such as the VS (Bethlehem, Honk, Auyeung, & Baron-Cohen, 2013) and plays a critical role in modulating social behavior. Polymorphisms on the oxytocin receptor (OXTR) gene are associated with individual differences in prosocial behavior (Israel et al., 2009), and oxytocin administration increases trust and generosity (De Dreu et al., 2010; Israel, Weisel, Ebstein, & Bornstein, 2012; Zak, Stanton, Ahmadi, 2007). Genetic variance in the receptors of dopamine, a neurotransmitter implicated in reward processing, is also associated with prosocial tendencies (Knafo, Israel, & Ebstein, 2011).

Brain regions involved in perception of other minds and unpleasant mental states are consistently predictive of both empathic responses and prosocial behavior. Rameson, Morelli, and Lieberman (2012) assessed prosocial tendencies by instructing participants to complete a diary over two weeks, documenting their own helpful behavior (e.g., holding a door open, lending money) directed toward friends and strangers. Participants later judged the negativity of sad images while undergoing fMRI. Correlations revealed that both empathy and self-reported helping behavior were associated with greater activity in the mPFC and ACC. Reported helping of *friends* was associated with activity in a much more robust network, including the mPFC, the ACC, and the PC, whereas reported helping of *strangers* was associated with only a relatively small section of the mPFC.

Other research directly targets the relationship between prosocial behavior and brain activity in examining participants' actual prosocial behavior toward a victim based on participants' neural response to that victim's plight. Masten, Morelli, and Eisenberger (2011) scanned participants while they viewed a game where three players pass a virtual "ball" back and forth. Partway into the game, players 1 and 2 began passing only to each other, effectively excluding player 3. Participants later sent e-mails to all players, and participants' e-mails to the excluded player were rated for prosocial (e.g., consoling) content. Viewing socially salient exclusion interactions versus inclusion interactions resulted in greater activity in the mPFC. Activity in the dorsal mPFC, along with the right AI (associated with negative affect), predicted the prosocial content of e-mails. This research presents a novel perspective by (1) measuring actual prosocial behavior, rather than self-reported tendencies and (2) predicting prosocial behavior directed toward a victim based on an empathic response to that same victim's plight. Yet, this research is limited in its focus on relatively low-cost prosocial behavior (e.g., sending an e-mail).

Waytz, Zaki, and Mitchell (2012) scanned participants while they made judgments about other individuals (e.g., "Does this person like to gossip?") and later completed a monetary distribution task that allowed participants to pay a monetary cost to benefit those individuals while also maximizing utility (e.g., you receive $1 or they receive $1.50). Following their scan session, participants were given an opportunity to spend time helping others complete a tedious quiz. Both kinds of costly prosocial behavior were predicted by activity in the dorsal mPFC.

Prosocial behavior is associated not only with functional differences (i.e., in brain activity) but also with structural differences in brain architecture. Using a monetary allocation task, Morishima, Schunk, Bruhin, Ruff, and Fehr (2012) related prosocial behavior to cortical gray matter volume using voxel-based morphometry (VBM) analysis. The task design allowed for distinct kinds of prosocial behavior to be examined. Gray matter volume in the right TPJ (involved in social cognition, as discussed earlier) was predictive of prosocial behavior across participants, but only when participants were in an advantageous position (e.g., giving to others if they are poorer but not wealthier than oneself). Interestingly, this region was insensitive to prosocial behavior that could be modeled by reciprocity (e.g., tit-for-tat strategy).

Neuropsychiatric studies of lesion patients have consistently implicated the mPFC in the regulation of social behavior. Most famously, Phineas Gage became antisocial and belligerent following an injury that disrupted function of mPFC and surrounding regions. Recent research on patients with ventral mPFC damage shows increased impulsivity and reduced sensitivity to social norms, suggesting a link between ventral mPFC lesions and "acquired psychopathy" (Bechara, Tranel, Damasio, & Damasio, 1996; Damasio, Tranel, & Damasio, 1991; Krajbich, Adolphs, Tranel, Denburg, & Camerer, 2009). Krajbich et al. (2009) found lower rates of generosity among six patients with varying degrees of ventral mPFC damage, relative to patients with damage to other regions. Ventral mPFC patients also behaved in ways suggesting that they were less trusting of others and felt less guilt after behaving selfishly. Thus, compromised ventral mPFC function may lead to deficits in prosocial behavior.

Finally, neuroscientific evidence suggests that engaging in prosocial behavior is rewarding (Harbaugh, Mayr, & Burghart, 2007; Moll et al., 2006; Rilling et al., 2002; Rilling, Sanfey, Aronson, Nystrom, & Cohen, 2004; Tabibnia, Satpute, & Lieberman, 2008; see Lee, 2008, for review). Moll et al. (2006) found similar patterns of activity in the VS (a "reward" area) both when participants received money and when participants donated money toward a charity. Moreover, activity in this region predicted the frequency (and consequent amount) of donations made by participants. Harbaugh et al. (2007) found VS activity when participants made costly donations toward a charity, even when those donations were mandatory.

Activity in this reward region was also greater for voluntary versus mandatory donations and, reflecting Moll et al. (2006), the amount of activity in VS scaled up with the magnitude of donation. These results are consistent with behavioral work documenting a positive relationship between spending money on others and happiness—a relationship that was particularly strong when the recipients of one's spending were one's family or close friends (Aknin, Sandstrom, Dunn, & Norton, 2011). However, as stated previously, donation-dependent reward activity may reflect either anticipated social benefits or the intrinsic value of prosocial behavior.

Multiple Prosocial Motivations

In the neuroscientific research reviewed earlier, prosocial behavior was associated with activity in brain regions involved in social cognition, perception of mental states in others, and anticipation of reward. However, this work alone cannot distinguish between different kinds of proximal motivations for prosocial behavior. For example, increased activity in social cognitive brain regions such as the mPFC could reflect either an empathetic focus on a victim or a kind of strategizing whereby one assesses the social benefits attainable by helping the victim. The finding that the mPFC activates more robustly for close versus distant others (Mitchell et al., 2006; Krienen et al., 2010; Rameson et al., 2012) is consistent with both accounts: close others may elicit more empathy from us, and close others are also more likely to reciprocate prosocial behavior. To inform the discussion of possible motivations of prosocial behavior, we look beyond the neuroscientific literature and highlight relevant behavioral work. We first review research that supports a strategic account of prosocial behavior and then we turn to research supporting an altruistic account.

QUID PRO QUO

It pays to be nice. Being on the receiving end of a prosocial act is rewarding (Rilling et al., 2002; Rilling et al., 2004; Tabibnia et al., 2008) and may make the recipient want to return the favor (Axelrod & Hamilton, 1981; Cialdini, 2006). More indirect benefits may come in the form of reputational credit or prestige, making conspicuous prosociality an adaptive social strategy (Barclay & Willer, 2007; Hardy & Vugt, 2006). Accordingly, people are sensitive to the reputational effects of prosocial behavior. They are more likely to donate to strangers face-to-face than to unseen strangers (Bohnet & Frey, 1999; Rege & Telle, 2004) and to named than unnamed strangers (Charness & Gneezy, 2008). People are also more likely to behave well when their actions are known to an identified third party (Andreoni & Petrie, 2004; Franzen & Pointer, 2012; Piazza & Bering, 2008; Satow, 1975). People are even sensitive to the mere idea of accountability, acting more prosocially in the presence of a picture of watchful eyes (Bateson, Nettle, & Roberts, 2006; Ernest-Jones,

Nettle, & Bateson, 2011; Haley & Fessler, 2005) and when primed with the concept of God or a watchful spirit (Gervais & Norenzayan, 2012; Mazar, Amir, & Ariely, 2008; Piazza, Bering, & Ingram, 2011; Shariff & Norenzayan, 2007). Conversely, people may withhold help or act selfishly when their identity is obscured by darkness (Hirsh, Galinsky, & Zhong, 2011; Zhong, Bohns, & Gino, 2010) or when they are unidentified in a group (Darley & Latane, 1968; Postmes & Spears, 1998; J. E. Singer, Brush, & Lublin, 1965).

This sensitivity emerges early in development. Children age six and under are more willing to share toys with a friend than a stranger (Knight & Chao, 1991; Moore, 2009). Leimgruber, Shaw, Santos, and Olson (2012) gave 5-year-olds a choice between receiving a toy on the one hand and receiving a toy and also allowing a peer to receive a toy on the other. The children were more willing to "give" the toy to the peer (at no direct cost to themselves) when the generous behavior was visible to the recipient, but not otherwise. As with adults, prosocial behavior directed at children results in positive outcomes or social benefits. Children are sensitive to others' previous actions, preferring to play with helpful versus unhelpful others (Hamlin & Wynn, 2011) and helping a former collaborator more than a known noncollaborative peer (Hamann, Warnecken, & Tomasello, 2012).

The reputational credit bestowed on a prosocial agent scales up with the costliness of their behavior (Barclay & Willer, 2007; Hardy & Vugt, 2006). The two most admired people of the 20th century, Mother Teresa and Martin Luther King Jr., are known for their selfless commitment to prosocial causes (Gallup, 1999). We revere those who sacrifice the most for others, and we may in turn be motivated to engage in costly acts in pursuit of admiration. But can this help explain why anyone would ever sacrifice his or her life to benefit others? The soldier who jumps on a grenade is not likely thinking about cashing in on the social credit his act will earn him. Reputation may help explain how altruistic motives could have developed in the first place (Nowak & Sigmund, 2005; Panchanathan & Boyd, 2004). However the question remains—what was going through the minds of these extreme altruists?

GOOD FOR GOODNESS' SAKE

Prosocial behavior may be proximally motivated through a need to maintain a positive moral identity or self-concept (Aquino & Reed, 2002; Gino, Schweitzer, Mead, & Ariely, 2011; Mazar et al., 2008; Monin & Miller, 2001; Sachdeva, Iliev, & Medin, 2009; Young, Chakroff, & Tom, 2012). Most people want to see themselves as moral individuals and may try to act in accordance with this ideal self-concept. Deviations from this ideal may create an unpleasant state of dissonance, which can serve as a proximate motivator to act morally (Stone & Cooper, 2001). We may behave unethically (or withhold prosocial behavior) only to the extent that we can still justify our moral identities to ourselves (Mazar et al., 2008). Thus, people may behave unethically when they can do so indirectly. For example, people are more likely to cheat to earn tokens worth cash, rather than cash itself (Mazar et al.,

2008); some will steal soda rather than money, which could be used to buy soda (Ariely, 2008). If one expresses egalitarian sentiments (e.g., hiring a person of a minority group), one may be less likely to express similar egalitarian sentiments in a secondary task, presumably because one has already "proven" one's prosocial sentiments (Monin & Miller, 2001; Sachdeva et al., 2009). This kind of moral "licensing" seems to depend on the perception of moral behavior as a "credit," rather than an expression of one's moral nature. Other research highlights people's need to feel consistent with their own moral self-concepts. Young at al. (2012) demonstrate that people are more willing to donate to charity after they have recounted instances of their own prosocial behavior, relative to people who recalled instances of their own past antisocial behavior.

Providing monetary incentives for prosocial behavior often backfires, resulting in less prosociality overall, despite what seems to be a better incentive structure. For example, Gneezy and Rustichini (2000a) found that providing monetary incentives for students collecting money for charity actually decreased performance. In another domain, incentivizing parents to be on time to pick their children up from school (by fining late parents in this case) resulted in more late parents (Gneezy & Rustichini, 2000b). Taking the perspective of the prosocial agents, however, renders these results less surprising. Following an example from A. P. Fiske and Tetlock (1997), how would you feel if, after preparing and serving a feast for friends and family, a guest offered to show his appreciation by writing you a check? How motivated would you be to cook for him in the future? Presumably, the original motivation for the feast was a desire to please others or, more generally, to do good—in other words the feast was not a service for a fee but an expression of love or good will. Monetary compensation for good deeds reframes moral or social events as business transactions and may therefore undermine intrinsic motivations to do good. This reframing may affect not only one's motivation to cook in the future but also others' perceptions of the act ("he did it for the money"). Thus, any social benefits of the prosocial behavior, such as reputational credit, may be undermined by secondary incentives. In an economist's terms, the intrinsic incentives (e.g., morality) were crowded out by the extrinsic ones (e.g., money; Frey & Jergen, 2001). The consequences of this effect extend far beyond daycare and dinner. Researchers provided monetary incentives to facilitate conflict resolution among Israeli and Palestinian participants. As above, the incentives backfired, resulting in emotional outrage and support of violent opposition to the resolution (Ginges, Atran, Medin, & Shikaki, 2007).

In sum, people may try to behave in accordance with their own moral self-concept (Stone & Cooper, 2001; Young et al., 2012). Discrepancies between one's ideal and one's behavior may be obscured through indirect action (Ariely, 2008; Mazar et al., 2008). External incentives can also undermine intrinsic motivations to do good or to be good, resulting in reduced prosociality. In other instances, people who act for reputational credit may feel licensed to behave selfishly once they feel they have earned sufficient social credit (Monin & Miller,

2001; Sachdeva et al., 2009). Self-concept maintenance may therefore be in the service of reputation-building at the level of adaptive function (Mazar et al., 2008), but, again, these ultimate ends need not correspond with proximate motivations (Mayr, 1993; Von Hippel & Trivers, 2011).

SAINTS AND STRATEGISTS

Some people are nicer than others. This is obvious and also reflected in intersubject variation in prosociality documented in the studies reviewed above. But perhaps more interesting is that different people are nice for different reasons. Some people may act prosocially for reputational reasons (e.g., social credit) and others out of intrinsic motivations (e.g., to be good, to do good). There is variation in our dispositional "moral identity" (Aquino & Reed, 2002) and "social value orientation" (Van Lange, 1999), with consequences for base levels of prosociality and also for susceptibility to the reputational effects outlined above.

Gino et al. (2011) measured unethical behavior in participants who scored high or low on "moral identity" (Aquino & Reed, 2002), measured through agreement with statements such as "Being someone who is [generous, kind, fair, friendly] is an important part of who I am." Participants had an opportunity to cheat on an exam by falsely reporting their score. Additionally, some participants completed the exam after having completed a cognitively depleting task that reduces self-control capacity (cf. Baumeister, Bratslavsky, Muraven, & Tice, 1998). Participants with a low moral identity behaved more unethically and were also more affected by the self-control depletion manipulation. By contrast, there was no significant effect of self-control depletion on participants with high moral identity, suggesting that for "honest" participants, being honest was the default (and easy) response.

In a neuroimaging study, Greene and Paxton (2009) were able to sort participants into "honest" and "dishonest" groups based on cheating behavior. They then examined the neural responses to task trials featuring an opportunity to cheat, relative to trials in which there was no opportunity to cheat. For "dishonest" participants, refraining from cheating when provided the opportunity recruited the ACC (associated with conflict and negative affect) and the dorsal lateral PFC (associated with cognitive control). By contrast, for "honest" participants, refraining from cheating when given the opportunity looked no different from refraining from cheating when not given the opportunity. In other words, the brains of "honest" participants behaved as though there was never an opportunity to cheat.

Of course, refraining from antisocial behavior is not the same as engaging in prosocial behavior. Indeed, increased prosocial tendencies can sometimes track with *increased* antisocial tendencies (Hirsh, Galinsky, & Zhong, 2011). In a more direct test of individual differences in prosocial motivations, Simpson and Willer (2008) classified participants into "egoists," who report a desire to maximize their own rewards only, and "altruists," who report a desire to maximize rewards for themselves and others (Van Lange, 1999). Participants were given an opportunity to donate to an unknown other, either privately, or when watched by a third party who would later donate money to the participant. Participants did donate more under public than private conditions, but this effect was much larger for the "egoists" than "altruists," suggesting that "egoists" are more sensitive to public reputational concerns. In a second experiment (Simpson & Willer, 2008), participants played the role of a third party, watching a donation between two parties, and then donated to the former donor. Participants were told either that the donor knew he was being watched, or that he thought he acted anonymously. Participants donated more to an anonymous donor than to a public donor. However, this difference was also stronger for "egoists" than "altruists." As before, "altruists" would donate similarly large amounts to the former donor regardless of condition. Finally, Young et al. (2012) found that priming a positive moral self-concept leads to greater prosociality (see above). However, this effect was especially powerful for participants who did not mention reputational considerations (e.g., whether others appreciated their acts) in recounting their past good deeds (reflecting positive moral self-concept), suggesting that some individuals may be motivated to do good "for goodness' sake."

Consistent with the individual differences documented above, between honest and dishonest individuals, altruists and egoists, Rand, Greene, and Nowak (2012) demonstrated differences between participants who reported being generally trusting of others in their social environment versus untrusting. Priming trusting (but not untrusting) participants to rely on their gut intuitions led to higher donations in a public goods game, whereas priming them to rely on deliberate reflection led to lower contributions. In another experiment, comparing the amount of time trusting participants used to make their choice generated a similar behavioral profile—when responding quickly, trusting participants contributed more.

Finally, regardless of one's prosocial disposition, one may be motivated to act prosocially toward different agents for different reasons. One buys the first round of drinks for friends, expecting someone else to get the next round (e.g., direct reciprocity). But a parent may help her child without stipulation and in the absence of any direct social benefits. This may be because some find it intrinsically rewarding to help family. In a recent study (Telzer, Masten, Berkman, Lieberman, & Fulgini, 2011), participants made costly donations to family members while undergoing fMRI. Consistent with other work, donation was associated with activity in social cognitive brain regions such as the mPFC. Furthermore, for participants with strong stated family obligations, there was enhanced functional coupling between social cognitive and reward brain regions during donation.

Consistent behavioral findings come from Maner and Gailliot (2007), who found that the best predictors of prosocial behavior were moderated by the relationship between the prosocial agent and the recipient. Participants were presented with hypothetical opportunities to help a family member versus stranger (e.g., helping a family member versus stranger who has been evicted from their apartment). Participants rated their empathic concern for the person in need, as well as their feelings of "oneness" with that individual. While empathic concern best predicted willingness to help a family member, "oneness" best predicted willingness to help a stranger. Put another way, we may help strangers only to the extent that we feel similar or close to them, whereas we help family members out of unconditional empathic concern, regardless of similarity.

Conclusions

Prosocial behavior depends on numerous mental processes working in concert. We must first perceive an opportunity for acting prosocially and then we must motivate ourselves to act. If prosocial behavior is intended to benefit another, opportunities for prosocial behavior require the perception of another (agent or mind) who might benefit from such an act. We help those in need and we may assess need based on our perception of negative mental states in others. Finally, we find helping others rewarding and we will only act when sufficiently motivated by some kind of anticipated benefit.

The research reviewed here presents a rough outline of psychological and neurological underpinnings of prosocial behavior and also points to avenues for future research. For example, why do we help some more than others? The present data cannot distinguish between "empathetic" and "strategic" accounts. On an empathetic account, we find it easier to take the perspective of a similar other, leading to increased empathy and motivation to help. Activity in the mPFC may index psychological closeness, while activity in AI indexes perception of others' pain and perhaps our own empathic concern. By contrast, on a strategic account, we are motivated to help others when our actions will directly or indirectly help us at some point in the future. Cooperative or similar others may be more likely to reciprocate or to contribute toward our group's interests, which include our own interests. Likewise, the suffering of a group member may hurt the group as a whole (See Tomasello & Vaish, 2012). For example, a soccer player who sees a teammate fail may experience anguish and feel motivated to help him in order to ensure the team's (and his own) eventual success. On this account, mPFC activity may reflect the processing of group identity (e.g., is this my teammate?) or perspective taking in order to assess the likelihood of reciprocity (see Gilin, Carpenter, & Galinsky, in press).

Although prosocial behavior is rewarding, the reward may take the form of anticipated public benefits (i.e., knowing that one looks good in the eyes of others) or the private knowledge that one is a good and moral person (i.e., moral self-concept). We seem to act in order to appear good to others (Barclay & Willer, 2007; Hardy & Vugt, 2006) and also to ourselves (Mazar et al., 2008; Young et al., 2012). These motivational rewards may function differentially across prosocial agents (e.g., altruists versus egoists; Simpson & Willer, 2008) and also across the beneficiaries of prosocial behavior (e.g., family versus strangers; Maner & Gailliot,

2007). Similarly, empathetic and strategic motivations may not be mutually exclusive but could differ by person or by situation.

Future research should continue to resolve this ambiguity, perhaps by comparing prosocial behavior directed at different agents (e.g., family, friends, and strangers), under public versus private conditions. Indeed, prosocial behavior is multidimensional, encompassing diverse helpful acts directed at different people for multiple reasons. Understanding prosocial behavior across these dimensions will surely contribute to a richer account of when we do good, when we fail, and why.

References

Aknin, L. B., Sandstrom, G. M., Dunn, E. W., & Norton, M. I. (2011). It's the recipient that counts: Spending money on strong social ties leads to greater happiness than spending on weak social ties. *PloS One, 6*(2), e17018.

Amodio, D. M., & Frith, C. D. (2006). Meeting of minds: The medial frontal cortex and social cognition. *Nature Reviews Neuroscience, 7*(4), 268–277.

Andreoni, J., & Petrie, R. (2004). Public goods experiments without confidentiality: a glimpse into fund-raising. *Journal of Public Economics, 88*(7), 1605–1623.

Aquino, K., & Reed, A. II, (2002). The self-importance of moral identity. *Journal of Personality and Social Psychology, 83*, 1423–1440.

Ariely, D. (2008). *Predictably irrational.* New York: HarperCollins.

Axelrod, R., & Hamilton, W. D. (1981). The evolution of cooperation. *Science, 211*(4489), 1390–1396.

Barclay, P., Willer, R. (2007). Partner choice creates competitive altruism in humans. *Proceedings of the Royal Society B: Biological Sciences, 274*(1610), 749–753.

Bateson, M., Nettle, D., & Roberts, G. (2006). Cues of being watched enhance cooperation in a real-world setting. *Biology Letters, 2*(3), 412–414.

Batson, C. D. (2009). These things called empathy: Eight related but distinct phenomena. In J. Decety & W. Ickes (Eds.), *The social neuroscience of empathy* (pp. 3–15). Cambridge, MA: MIT Press.

Batson, C. D., Batson, J. G., Griffitt, C. A., Barrientos, S., Brandt, J. R., Sprengelmeyer, P., & Bayly, M. J. (1989). Negative-state relief and the empathy-altruism hypothesis. *Journal of Personality and Social Psychology, 56*(6), 922.

Baumeister, R. F., Bratslavsky, E., Muraven, M., & Tice, D. M. (1998). Ego depletion: Is the active self a limited resource? *Journal of Personality and Social Psychology, 74*(5), 1252–1265.

Bechara, A., Tranel, D., Damasio, H., & Damasio, A. R. (1996). Failure to respond autonomically to anticipated future outcomes following damage to prefrontal cortex. *Cerebral cortex, 6*(2), 215–225.

Bentin, S., Allison, T., Puce, A., Perez, E., & McCarthy, G. (1996). Electrophysiological studies of face perception in humans. *Journal of Cognitive Neuroscience, 8*(6), 551–565.

Bethlehem, R. A., van Honk, J., Auyeung, B., & Baron-Cohen, S. (2013). Oxytocin, brain physiology, and functional connectivity: A review of intranasal oxytocin fMRI studies. *Psychoneuroendocrinology, 38*(7), 962–974.

Bohnet, I., & Frey, B. S. (1999). Social distance and other-regarding behavior in dictator games: Comment. *The American Economic Review, 89*(1), 335–339.

Boyd, R., & Richerson, P. J. (2002). Group beneficial norms can spread rapidly in a structured population. *Journal of Theoretical Biology, 215*(3), 287–296.

Charness, G., & Gneezy, U. (2008). What's in a name? Anonymity and social distance in dictator and ultimatum games. *Journal of Economic Behavior and Organization, 68*(1), 29–35.

Cialdini, R. B. (2006). *Influence: The psychology of persuasion.* New York: Harper Business.

Cikara, M., Botvinick, M. M., & Fiske, S. T. (2011). Us versus them social identity shapes neural responses to intergroup competition and harm. *Psychological Science, 22*(3), 306–313.

Cikara, M., Bruneau, E. G., & Saxe, R. R. (2011). Us and them intergroup failures of empathy. *Current Directions in Psychological Science, 20*(3), 149–153.

Cloutier, J., Heatherton, T. F., Whalen, P. J., & Kelley, W. M. (2008). Are attractive people rewarding? Sex differences in the neural substrates of facial attractiveness. *Journal of Cognitive Neuroscience, 20*(6), 941–951.

Connolly, A. C., Guntupalli, J. S., Gors, J., Hanke, M., Halchenko, Y. O., … Haxby, J. V. (2012). The representation of biological classes in the human brain. *Journal of Neuroscience, 32*(8), 2608–2618.

Contreras, J. M., Banaji, M. R., & Mitchell, J. P. (2012). Dissociable neural correlates of stereotypes and other forms of semantic knowledge. *Social Cognitive and Affective Neuroscience, 7,* 764–770.

Cushman, F., Gray, K., Gaffey, A., & Mendes, W. B. (2012). Simulating murder: The aversion to harmful action. *Emotion, 12*(1), 2.

Damasio, A. R., Tranel, D., & Damasio, H. (1991). Somatic markers and the guidance of behavior: Theory and preliminary testing. In H. S. Levin, H. M. Eisenberg, A. L. Benton (Eds.), *Frontal Lobe Function and Dysfunction* (pp. 217–229). New York, NY: Oxford University Press.

Darley, J. M., & Latane, B. (1968). Bystander intervention in emergencies: diffusion of responsibility. *Journal of Personality and Social Psychology, 8*(4 part 1), 377.

De Dreu, C. K., Greer, L. L., Handgraaf, M. J., Shalvi, S., Van Kleef, G. A., Baas, M., … Feith, S. W. (2010). The neuropeptide oxytocin regulates parochial altruism in intergroup conflict among humans. *Science, 328*(5984), 1408–1411.

De Vignemont, F., & Singer, T. (2006). The empathic brain: How, when and why? *Trends in Cognitive Sciences, 10*(10), 435–441.

Decety, J., Echols, S., & Correll, J. (2010). The blame game: The effect of responsibility and social stigma on empathy for pain. *Journal of Cognitive Neuroscience, 22*(5), 985–997.

Decety, J., & Lamm, C. (2009). Empathy versus personal distress: Recent evidence from social neuroscience. In J. Decety & W. Ickes (Eds.), *The social neuroscience of* empathy (pp. 199–213). Cambridge, MA: MIT Press.

Eisenberg, N., & Eggum, N. D. (2009). Empathic responding: Sympathy and personal distress. In J. Decety & W. Ickes (Eds.), *The social neuroscience of empathy* (pp. 71–83). Cambridge: MIT Press.

Eisenberg, N. & Fabes, R. A. (1998). Prosocial development. In W. Damon & N. Eisengerb (Eds.), *Handbook of child psychology.* New York, NY: Wiley & Sons.

Ernest-Jones, M., Nettle, D., & Bateson, M. (2011). Effects of eye images on everyday cooperative behavior: A field experiment. *Evolution and Human Behavior, 32*(3), 172–178.

Fehr, E., & Camerer, C. F. (2007). Social neuroeconomics: The neural circuitry of social preferences. *Trends in Cognitive Sciences, 11*(10), 419–427.

Fiske, A. P., & Tetlock, P. E. (1997). Taboo trade-offs: Reactions to transactions that transgress the spheres of justice. *Political Psychology, 18*(2), 255–297.

Fiske, S. T., Cuddy, A. J., & Glick, P. (2007). Universal dimensions of social cognition: Warmth and competence. *Trends in Cognitive Sciences, 11*(2), 77–83.

Franzen, A., & Pointner, S. (2012). Anonymity in the dictator game revisited. *Journal of Economic Behavior and Organization, 81*, 74–81.

Frey, B. S., & Jegen, R. (2001). Motivation crowding theory. *Journal of Economic Surveys, 15*(5), 589–611.

Gallup, G (1999). *The Gallup Poll.* Wilmington, DE: Scholarly Resources. 248–249.

Gelman, S. A., & Gottfried, G. M. (1996). Children's causal explanations of animate and inanimate motion. *Child Development, 67*(5), 1970–1987.

Gervais, W. M., & Norenzayan, A. (2012). Like a camera in the sky? Thinking about God increases public self-awareness and socially desirable responding. *Journal of Experimental Social Psychology, 48*(1), 298–302.

Gilin, D., Maddux, W. W., Carpenter, J., & Galinsky, A. D. When to use your head and when to use your heart: The differential value of perspective-taking versus empathy in competitive interactions. *Personality and Social Psychological Bulletin 39*(1), 3–16.

Ginges, J., Atran, S., Medin, D., & Shikaki, K. (2007). Sacred bounds on rational resolution of violent political conflict. *Proceedings of the National Academy of Sciences, 104*(18), 7357–7360.

Gino, F., Schweitzer, M. E., Mead, N. L., & Ariely, D. (2011). Unable to resist temptation: How self-control depletion promotes unethical behavior. *Organizational Behavior and Human Decision Processes, 115*(2), 191–203.

Gneezy, U., & Rustichini, A. (2000a). Pay enough or don't pay at all. *Quarterly Journal of Economics, 115*(3), 791–810.

Gneezy, U., & Rustichini, A. (2000b). A fine is a price. *Journal of Legal Studies, 29*(1), 1–18.

Gray, H. (1918). *Anatomy of the human body.* Philadelphia, PA: Lea & Febiger.

Gray, H. M., Gray, K., & Wegner, D. M. (2007). Dimensions of mind perception. *Science, 315*(5812), 619–619.

Gray, K., & Wegner, D. M. (2009). Moral typecasting: Divergent perceptions of moral agents and moral patients. *Journal of Personality and Social Psychology, 96*(3), 505.

Greene, J. D., & Paxton, J. M. (2009). Patterns of neural activity associated with honest and dishonest moral decisions. *Proceedings of the National Academy of Sciences, 106*(30), 12506–12511.

Grossman, E., Donnelly, M., Price, R., Pickens, D., Morgan, V., Neighbor, G., & Blake, R. (2000). Brain areas involved in perception of biological motion. *Journal of Cognitive Neuroscience, 12*(5), 711–720.

Hadjikhani, N., Kveraga, K., Naik, P., & Ahlfors, S. P. (2009). Early (N170) activation of face-specific cortex by face-like objects. *Neuroreport, 20*(4), 403.

Haley, K. J., & Fessler, D. M. (2005). Nobody's watching? Subtle cues affect generosity in an anonymous economic game. *Evolution and Human Behavior, 26*(3), 245–256.

Hamann, K., Warneken, F., & Tomasello, M. (2012). Children's developing commitments to joint goals. *Child Development, 83*(1), 137–145.

Hamlin, J. K., & Wynn, K. (2011). Young infants prefer prosocial to antisocial others. *Cognitive Development, 26*(1), 30–39.

Harbaugh, W. T., Mayr, U., & Burghart, D. R. (2007). Neural responses to taxation and voluntary giving reveal motives for charitable donations. *Science, 316*(5831), 1622–1625.

Hardy, C. L., & Van Vugt, M. (2006). Nice guys finish first: The competitive altruism hypothesis. *Personality and Social Psychology Bulletin, 32*(10), 1402–1413.

Harris, L. T., & Fiske, S. T. (2006). Dehumanizing the lowest of the low: Neuroimaging responses to extreme out-groups. *Psychological Science, 17*(10), 847–853.

Heider, F., & Simmel, M. (1944). An experimental study of apparent behavior. *American Journal of Psychology*, 243–259.

Hirsh, J. B., Galinsky, A. D., & Zhong, C. B. (2011). Drunk, powerful, and in the dark: How general processes of disinhibition produce both prosocial and antisocial behavior. *Perspectives on Psychological Science, 6*(5), 415–427.

Israel, S., Lerer, E., Shalev, I., Uzefovsky, F., Reibold, M., Laiba, E.,...Ebstein, R. P. (2009). The oxytocin receptor (OXTR) contributes to prosocial fund allocations in the dictator game and the social value orientations task. *PLoS One, 4*(5), e5535.

Israel, S., Weisel, O., Ebstein, R. P., & Bornstein, G. (2012). Oxytocin, but not vasopressin, increases both parochial and universal altruism. *Psychoneuroendocrinology, 37*(8), 1341–1344.

Jackson, P. L., Meltzoff, A. N., & Decety, J. (2005). How do we perceive the pain of others? A window into the neural processes involved in empathy. *Neuroimage, 24*(3), 771–779.

Japan Center for International Exchange. (2012). US giving for Japan's 3/11 disaster exceeds $665 million. Retrieved from http://www.jcie.org/311recovery/usgiving-2.html

Jenkins, A. C., & Mitchell, J. P. (2011). Medial prefrontal cortex subserves diverse forms of self-reflection. *Social Neuroscience, 6*(3), 211–218.

Johnson, M. H., Dziurawiec, S., Ellis, H., & Morton, J. (1991). Newborns' preferential tracking of face-like stimuli and its subsequent decline. *Cognition, 40*, 1–19.

Kanwisher, N., McDermott, J., & Chun, M. M. (1997). The fusiform face area: A module in human extrastriate cortex specialized for face perception. *Journal of Neuroscience, 17*(11), 4302–4311.

Kelley, W. M., Macrae, C. N., Wyland, C. L., Caglar, S., Inati, S., & Heatherton, T. F. (2002). Finding the self? An event-related fMRI study. *Journal of Cognitive Neuroscience, 14*(5), 785–794.

Knafo, A., Israel, S., & Ebstein, R. P. (2011). Heritability of children's prosocial behavior and differential susceptibility to parenting by variation in the dopamine receptor D4 gene. *Development and Psychopathology, 23*(1), 53.

Knight, G. P., & Chao, C. C. (1991). Cooperative, competitive, and individualistic social values among 8- to 12-year-old siblings, friends, and acquaintances. *Personality and Social Psychology Bulletin, 17*(2), 201–211.

Knutson, B., & Cooper, J. C. (2005). Functional magnetic resonance imaging of reward prediction. *Current Opinion in Neurology, 18*(4), 411–417.

Krajbich, I., Adolphs, R., Tranel, D., Denburg, N. L., & Camerer, C. F. (2009). Economic games quantify diminished sense of guilt in patients with damage to the prefrontal cortex. *Journal of Neuroscience, 29*(7), 2188–2192.

Krienen, F. M., Tu, P. C., & Buckner, R. L. (2010). Clan mentality: Evidence that the medial prefrontal cortex responds to close others. *Journal of Neuroscience, 30*(41), 13906–13915.

Lah, K. (2011). Japanese seniors volunteer for Fukushima "suicide corps." *CNN World*. Retrieved from http://articles.cnn.com/2011-05-31/world/japan.nuclear.suicide_1_nuclear-plant-seniors-group-nuclear-crisis?_s=PM:WORLD

Lee, D. (2008). Game theory and neural basis of social decision-making. *Nature Neuroscience, 11*(4), 404–409.

Leimgruber, K. L., Shaw, A., Santos, L. R., & Olson, K. R. (2012). Young children are more generous when others are aware of their actions. *PLoS One, 7*(10), e48292.

Lieberman, M. D., Hariri, A., Jarcho, J. M., Eisenberger, N. I., & Bookheimer, S. Y. (2005). An fMRI investigation of race-related amygdala activity in African-American and Caucasian-American individuals. *Nature Neuroscience, 8*(6), 720–722.

Looser, C. E., Guntupalli, J. S., & Wheatley, T. (2012). Multivoxel patterns in face-sensitive temporal regions reveal an encoding schema based on detecting life in a face. *Social Cognitive and Affective Neuroscience*. Epub ahead of print, July 13, 2012. doi: 10.1093/scan/nss07

Luo, Y., & Baillargeon, R. (2005). Can a self-propelled box have a goal? Psychological reasoning in 5-month-old infants. *Psychological Science, 16*(8), 601–608.

Maner, J. K., & Gailliot, M. T. (2007). Altruism and egoism: Prosocial motivations for helping depend on relationship context. *European Journal of Social Psychology, 37*(2), 347–358.

Masten, C. L., Morelli, S. A., & Eisenberger, N. I. (2011). An fMRI investigation of empathy for "social pain" and subsequent prosocial behavior. *Neuroimage, 55*(1), 381–388.

Mayr, E. (1993). Proximate and ultimate causations. *Biology and Philosophy, 8*(1), 93–94.

Mazar, N., Amir, O., & Ariely, D. (2008). The dishonesty of honest people: A theory of self-concept maintenance. *Journal of Marketing Research, 45*(6), 633–644.

Mende-Siedlecki, P., Said, C. P., & Todorov, A. (2013). The social evaluation of faces: a meta-analysis of functional neuroimaging studies. *Social Cognitive and Affective Neuroscience, 8*(3), 285–299.

Mitchell, J. P., Ames, D. L., Jenkins, A. C., & Banaji, M. R. (2009). Neural correlates of stereotype application. *Journal of Cognitive Neuroscience, 21*(3), 594–604.

Mitchell, J. P., Macrae, C. N., & Banaji, M. R. (2006). Dissociable medial prefrontal contributions to judgments of similar and dissimilar others. *Neuron, 50*(4), 655–663.

Moll, J., Krueger, F., Zahn, R., Pardini, M., de Oliveira-Souza, R., & Grafman, J. (2006). Human fronto-mesolimbic networks guide decisions about charitable donation. *Proceedings of the National Academy of Sciences, 103*(42), 15623–15628.

Monin, B., & Miller, D. T. (2001). Moral credentials and the expression of prejudice. *Journal of Personality and Social Psychology, 81*(1), 33.

Moore, C. (2009). Fairness in children's resource allocation depends on the recipient. *Psychological Science, 20*(8), 944–948.

Morishima, Y., Schunk, D., Bruhin, A., Ruff, C. C., & Fehr, E. (2012). Linking brain structure and activation in temporoparietal junction to explain the neurobiology of human altruism. *Neuron, 75*(1), 73–79.

Morrison, S., Decety, J., & Molenberghs, P. (2012). The neuroscience of group membership. *Neuropsychologia, 50*(8), 2114–2120.

Nowak, M. A., & Sigmund, K. (2005). Evolution of indirect reciprocity. *Nature, 437*(7063), 1291–1298.

Panchanathan, K., & Boyd, R. (2004). Indirect reciprocity can stabilize cooperation without the second-order free rider problem. *Nature*, *432*(7016), 499–502.

Piazza, J., & Bering, J. M. (2008). Concerns about reputation via gossip promote generous allocations in an economic game. *Evolution and Human Behavior*, *29*(3), 172–178.

Piazza, J., Bering, J. M., & Ingram, G. (2011). "Princess Alice is watching you": Children's belief in an invisible person inhibits cheating. *Journal of Experimental Child Psychology*, *109*(3), 311–320.

Postmes, T., & Spears, R. (1998). Deindividuation and antinormative behavior: A meta-analysis. *Psychological Bulletin*, *123*(3), 238.

Rameson, L. T., Morelli, S. A., & Lieberman, M. D. (2012). The neural correlates of empathy: Experience, automaticity, and prosocial behavior. *Journal of Cognitive Neuroscience*, *24*(1), 235–245.

Rand, D. G., Greene, J. D., & Nowak, M. A. (2012). Spontaneous giving and calculated greed. *Nature*, *489*(7416), 427–430.

Rege, M., & Telle, K. (2004). The impact of social approval and framing on cooperation in public good situations. *Journal of Public Economics*, *88*(7), 1625–1644.

Rilling, J. K., Gutman, D. A., Zeh, T. R., Pagnoni, G., Berns, G. S., & Kilts, C. D. (2002). A neural basis for social cooperation. *Neuron*, *35*(2), 395–405.

Rilling, J. K., Sanfey, A. G., Aronson, J. A., Nystrom, L. E., & Cohen, J. D. (2004). Opposing BOLD responses to reciprocated and unreciprocated altruism in putative reward pathways. *Neuroreport*, *15*(16), 2539–2243.

Rozin, P., Millman, L., & Nemeroff, C. (1986). Operation of the laws of sympathetic magic in disgust and other domains. *Journal of Personality and Social Psychology*, *50*(4), 703.

Sachdeva, S., Iliev, R., & Medin, D. L. (2009). Sinning saints and saintly sinners: The paradox of moral self-regulation. *Psychological Science*, *20*(4), 523–528.

Satow, K. L. (1975). Social approval and helping. *Journal of Experimental Social Psychology*, *11*(6), 501–509.

Saxe, R., & Powell, L. J. (2006). It's the thought that counts: Specific brain regions for one component of theory of mind. *Psychological Science*, *17*(8), 692–699.

Scholl, B. J., & Tremoulet, P. D. (2000). Perceptual causality and animacy. *Trends in Cognitive Sciences*, *4*(8), 299–309.

Shariff, A. F., & Norenzayan, A. (2007). God is watching you: Priming God concepts increases prosocial behavior in an anonymous economic game. *Psychological Science*, *18*(9), 803–809.

Simpson, B., & Willer, R. (2008). Altruism and indirect reciprocity: The interaction of person and situation in prosocial behavior. *Social Psychology Quarterly*, *71*(1), 37–52.

Singer, J. E., Brush, C. A., & Lublin, S. C. (1965). Some aspects of deindividuation: Identification and conformity. *Journal of Experimental Social Psychology*, *1*(4), 356–378.

Singer, P. (1997). The drowning child and the expanding circle. *New Internationalist*, *289*, 28–30.

Singer, T., Seymour, B., O'Doherty, J. P., Stephan, K. E., Dolan, R. J., & Frith, C. D. (2006). Empathic neural responses are modulated by the perceived fairness of others. *Nature*, *439*(7075), 466–469.

Sober, E., & Wilson, D. S. (1998). *Unto others: The evolution and psychology of unselfish behavior* (No. 218). Cambridge, MA: Harvard University Press.

Stone, J., & Cooper, J. (2001). A self-standards model of cognitive dissonance. *Journal of Experimental Social Psychology, 37*(3), 228–243.

Tabibnia, G., Satpute, A. B., & Lieberman, M. D. (2008). The sunny side of fairness: Preference for fairness activates reward circuitry (and disregarding unfairness activates self-control circuitry). *Psychological Science, 19*(4), 339–347.

Telzer, E. H., Masten, C. L., Berkman, E. T., Lieberman, M. D., & Fuligni, A. J. (2011). Neural regions associated with self control and mentalizing are recruited during prosocial behaviors towards the family. *Neuroimage, 58*(1), 242–249.

Todorov, A., Gobbini, M. I., Evans, K. K., & Haxby, J. V. (2007). Spontaneous retrieval of affective person knowledge in face perception. *Neuropsychologia, 45*(1), 163–173.

Todorov, A., Said, C. P., Engell, A. D., & Oosterhof, N. N. (2008). Understanding evaluation of faces on social dimensions. *Trends in Cognitive Sciences, 12*(12), 455–460.

Tomasello, M., & Vaish, A. (2012). Origins of human cooperation and morality. *Annual Review of Psychology, 64*, 231–255.

Van Lange, P. A. (1999). The pursuit of joint outcomes and equality in outcomes: An integrative model of social value orientation. *Journal of Personality and Social Psychology, 77*(2), 337.

Von Hippel, W., & Trivers, R. (2011). The evolution and psychology of self-deception. *Behavioral and Brain Sciences, 34*(1), 1.

Waytz, A., Gray, K., Epley, N., & Wegner, D. M. (2010). Causes and consequences of mind perception. *Trends in Cognitive Sciences, 14*(8), 383–388.

Waytz, A., Zaki, J., & Mitchell, J. P. (2012). Response of dorsomedial prefrontal cortex predicts altruistic behavior. *The Journal of Neuroscience, 32*(22), 7646–7650.

West, S. A., El Mouden, C., & Gardner, A. (2011). Sixteen common misconceptions about the evolution of cooperation in humans. *Evolution and Human Behavior, 32*(4), 231–262.

Wheatley, T., Milleville, S. C., & Martin, A. (2007). Understanding animate agents: Distinct roles for the social network and mirror system. *Psychological Science, 18*, 469–474.

Wheatley, T., Weinberg, A., Looser, C., Moran, T., & Hajcak, G. (2011). Mind perception: Real but not artificial faces sustain neural activity beyond the N170/VPP. *PLoS One, 6*(3), e17960.

Xu, X., Zuo, X., Wang, X., & Han, S. (2009). Do you feel my pain? Racial group membership modulates empathic neural responses. *Journal of Neuroscience, 29*(26), 8525–8529.

Young, L., Chakroff, A., & Tom, J. (2012). Doing good leads to more good: The reinforcing power of a moral self-concept. *Review of Philosophy and Psychology, 3*(3), 325–334.

Young, L., & Saxe, R. (2009). Innocent intentions: A correlation between forgiveness for accidental harm and neural activity. *Neuropsychologia, 47*(10), 2065–2072.

Zak, P. J., Stanton, A. A., & Ahmadi, S. (2007). Oxytocin increases generosity in humans. *PLoS One, 2*(11), e1128.

Zhong, C. B., Bohns, V. K., & Gino, F. (2010). Good lamps are the best police: Darkness increases dishonesty and self-interested behavior. *Psychological Science, 21*(3), 311–314.

6

Autonomic Regulation, Polyvagal Theory, and Children's Prosocial Development

Paul D. Hastings and Jonas G. Miller

A team of linguists recently identified a small set of words, around two dozen, that have survived from their origins in an early Eurasiatic language that dates to some 15,000 years ago (Pagel, Atkinson, Calude, & Meade, 2013). That language might have given rise to more than 700 distinct known languages across the expanse of Asia and Europe. That these few "ultraconserved" words have weathered the millennia and appear in almost unchanged forms across disparate tongues in far-flung lands speaks to their essential, core function for the most enduring common elements of human communication.

Included in the list is the verb "to give."

Perhaps more than any other social mammalian species, the survival of humans has relied on our abilities to cooperate, trust, and help one another. Without question, humans can be selfish, untrustworthy, manipulative, and violent. Yet antisocial drives are not the sole motivators of human behavior, and in the history of our species these divisive impulses have been counteracted by prosocial motivations. We want to comfort and care for others, to share our efforts and belongings, and to know that others likewise will act prosocially toward us. To paraphrase Walt Whitman (1855, in Greenspan, 2005), "we are large, we contain multitudes." This complexity has bedeviled some evolutionary scientists who have focused singularly on the drive for survival of the individual organism, or individual gene. Yet, numerous sociobiologists have proposed models and presented data demonstrating that cooperative and altruistic acts can enhance the survival of social species (for review, see Hastings, Miller, Kahle, & Zahn-Waxler, 2014). In parents nurturing their young, in peers facilitating each other's play, and in neighbors sharing their tools, labor, and products, our ability to engage in harmonious social interactions has allowed us to endure and thrive.

Empathy is recognized as one of the primary, proximal motivations for engaging in cooperative, helpful, compassionate, and altruistic activities—in short, for giving of ourselves to benefit others. More than 200 years ago, Adam Smith (1759) proposed that our capacity to feel empathy for another's emotional circumstances was embodied in our own visceral responses. Modern evolutionary and functional theories of emotion continue this perspective, as emotional experiences involve changes in somatic and autonomic activity that prepare one to respond appropriately to the stimuli that evoke the emotions (Damasio, 2000; Hastings & Guyer, in press). Developmental scientists recognize that these approaches need to be ontological, accounting for the development of physiology, emotion, and behavior as children mature within the social spheres of their families, neighborhoods, and culture. Thus, an essential aspect of understanding the multidimensionality of prosocial development is examining how psychophysiological regulation underlies and contributes to children's emotional and behavioral responses to the needs and well-being of others.

Much of the research on the links between autonomic physiology and empathy or prosocial behavior in children and adults has been pursued outside of a particular theory or model. Yet, having such an overarching framework, based on current evolutionary and neurobiological knowledge, could provide structure and coherence for the complicated observations that have been made and could guide further efforts to understand the psychophysiology of prosocial development. In this chapter we propose that the polyvagal theory (Porges, 1985, 1995, 2007, 2011) can serve this purpose. Briefly, the polyvagal theory is a framework for understanding the evolution and regulatory functioning of the mammalian parasympathetic nervous system (PNS) through the influence of the 10th cranial nerve, or vagus nerve, on cardiac activity. Over more than 30 years of work, Porges has developed, refined, and validated his proposals that activity of the vagus nerve contributes to the self-regulation of attention, emotion, and social behavior. Empathy and prosocial behavior are included in—indeed, are central to—that set of adaptive competencies.

We begin by reviewing some of the basic neuroanatomy of the autonomic nervous system (ANS) and examine how this knowledge informed the early psychophysiological research on the development of empathy and prosocial behavior. We then expand on the polyvagal theory and how it places the vagus nerve at the center of a "social engagement system" that coordinates mammalian interactions and, in particular, supports the capacity for empathic, cooperative, and prosocial activities. The few recent studies on polyvagal theory and prosocial functioning are then considered, followed by our own recent research on parasympathetic regulation of emotion and children's empathic and prosocial development. We conclude with our reflections on the psychophysiological preparedness of children—and adults—to care, to help, and to give.

Autonomic Nervous System

The ANS is the rapid communication system between the central nervous system and the organs and smooth muscle tissues of the body, transmitting signals bidirectionally along its two primary branches, the sympathetic nervous system (SNS) and the parasympathetic nervous system (PNS) (Berntson, Quigley, & Lozano, 2007; Dawson, Schell, & Filion, 2007). The SNS and PNS differ structurally and neurochemically in their modes of activity, but jointly function to prepare the body for quick responses to salient stimuli. Antagonistic models of homeostatic regulation suggest that the SNS and PNS work as oppositional forces, with sympathetic activity eliciting increases in autonomic arousal and preparedness for active coping (excitatory; "fight-or-flight") and parasympathetic activity reducing arousal and supporting vegetative states (inhibitory; "rest-and-digest"). These opposing influences serve to return arousal to some optimal set-point after an evocative stimulus has perturbed the system.

The SNS is part of the sympathetic adrenomedullary system, one of the body's primary stress-response systems. In response to perceived threats or challenges, the SNS triggers the release of epinephrine and norepinephrine from the adrenal medulla, which contributes to the fight-or-flight response of many tissues. The activity of the PNS is principally "down-regulatory," serving to soothe or slow respiration, heart rate, and similar functions. Thus, a withdrawal or reduction of parasympathetic innervations in the presence of an evocative stimulus can help to release resources for active coping. After the challenge has been met, increased influence of the PNS terminates the sympathetically induced somatic arousal and facilitates recovery, returning the body to a calm state.

Although there are times at which the ANS functions according to the homeostatic principle, and homeostasis has served as the basis for a strong history of psychophysiological research, many researchers now regard this antagonistic model as too simplistic a portrayal of the complex and dynamic ways in which the SNS and PNS control somatic arousal. For example, the allodynamic control model (Berntson & Cacioppo, 2007) recognizes that we are constantly facing changing stimuli throughout our daily activities that require modifications to arousal levels. Hence, a system of autonomic regulation that continually exerted effort to return one toward a single set-point of arousal would be inefficient. From this perspective, the two branches of the ANS work in reciprocal, independent, and cooperative ways to continually adjust the activity levels of our physiological states in order to support adaptive functioning. In effect, being physiologically well regulated entails being flexible and responsive to both external cues and internal needs.

MEASURING AUTONOMIC NERVOUS SYSTEM ACTIVITY

Most organs are innervated by both branches of the ANS, which exert varying degrees of dominant influence. Some widely used measures of arousal do not allow researchers to draw precise inferences about the underlying causes of physiological change, because they are subject to both sympathetic and parasympathetic control. For example, general arousal can be assessed through increases in heart rate or blood pressure, but one cannot be certain of the extent to which these changes are due to greater sympathetic influence, to lessened parasympathetic influence, or to some interaction between the SNS and PNS. Fortunately, psychophysiologists have identified a set of noninvasive biological measures that can be attributed to the influence of one of the two branches.

More such measures exist for the SNS, and the first to be identified and still most widely used is the electrodermal response (EDR) or skin conductance levels (Dawson et al., 2007). The eccrine sweat glands are purely under the control of the SNS. Increased perspiration lowers the impedance of a weak electrical current between two electrodes applied to the skin, and measurement of that transmission provides an easy index of sympathetic arousal. Another measure gaining popularity is cardiac pre-ejection period (PEP), which is the duration of a brief component of a heartbeat called the electrical systole. Increases in sympathetic innervation shorten the PEP, which contributes to a faster beating of the heart (Berntson et al., 2007). Two more recently identified measures garnering the attention of developmental psychophysiologists are salivary levels of the enzyme alpha-amylase and pupillary dilation (changes in pupil size), although these are not exclusively influenced by the SNS.

To date, there is only one widely accepted, noninvasive measure of the PNS. The vagus nerve exerts a strong chronotropic influence on heart rate, affecting variations in the speed at which the heart beats, through its controlling influence on the sinoatrial node, the "pacemaker" of the heart (Berntson et al., 2007; Porges, 2011).[1] Although many factors affect heart rate variability (HRV), the specific component called *respiratory sinus arrhythmia* (RSA), or *cardiac vagal tone*, is recognized as an effective index of PNS influence on cardiac activity. Via the vagus nerve, the PNS establishes a coupling of the respiratory cycle and heart rate, with the interval between beats of the heart shortening slightly during inhalation and lengthening slightly during exhalation. Various statistical algorithms exist for isolating the specific frequency of HRV that corresponds to this coupled process, with the quantification of that frequency being called RSA. Increased parasympathetic influence is reflected in greater RSA, which usually (but not always) is associated with slower heart rate.

---

[1] Some developmental researchers have used a more global index of *heart rate variability* (HRV) as a measure of PNS regulation (e.g., Fabes et al., 1993, 1994). There are other contributors to HRV than the vagus nerve and coupling with the respiratory cycle, however, such that HRV cannot be treated as a precise and specific index of parasympathetic influence over cardiac activity. These studies have not been included in this review.

Activity of the ANS can be measured when people are in a quiescent state, in the absence of evocative stimuli. These basal or baseline measures often are characterized as individuals' typical levels of arousal, reflective of SNS and PNS activity in a calm waking state. Measures of reactive physiology consider arousal levels in response to salient cues or task demands. Usually, researchers are interested in knowing not only the level of SNS or PNS activity within the evocative context, but how the levels of activity have changed from the basal to the reactive state. Examining reactive change scores is thought to reveal how individuals are applying their sympathetic and parasympathetic regulation of arousal. Most developmental studies of reactive physiology have used fairly simple and static change scores, such as the arithmetic difference between measures of a given physiological index in the basal state and in an evocative context (Burt & Obradović, 2013). As we will discuss, these have increasingly been recognized as too simplistic for understanding the dynamic processes of physiological regulation (Hastings, Kahle, & Han, 2014).

Early Examinations of the Autonomic Nervous System and Prosocial Development

Because increased somatic arousal could support a motivation to withdraw from an aversive stimulus, some developmental researchers have argued that increased SNS activity in response to others' sadness, pain, or fear could reflect personal distress, which would interfere with other-oriented, prosocial engagement (Eisenberg, Fabes, Schaller, Carlo, & Miller, 1991). Conversely, it also has been proposed that orienting, attending, and responding to the needs of others could require mobilization of resources, such that increased SNS activity would support prosocial responding (Zahn-Waxler, Cole, Welsh, & Fox, 1995). There have been similarly opposing hypotheses put forward for the role of the PNS in empathic and prosocial responses (Hastings, Zahn-Waxler, Robinson, Usher, & Bridges, 2000). On the one hand, because effective prosocial behavior involves responding calmly to the needs of others, more "down-regulatory" parasympathetic activity, as indexed through higher RSA, could support such well-regulated, other-oriented actions. On the other hand, the distress or needs of another must be noticed for a prosocial response to be mounted, and reduced PNS activity, commonly called vagal suppression, might facilitate orienting or attending to those cues.

Findings reported in the developmental literature on the psychophysiology of empathy and prosocial behavior from the late 1980s through 2000 offered some support for all of these divergent predictions (Hastings, Zahn-Waxler, & McShane, 2006), though when considered collectively some patterns begin to emerge. A small majority of studies on heart rate and heart rate change suggested that more prosocial children had lower basal heart rates or more slowing of heart rate when observing sadness, distress, or pain in others (e.g., Eisenberg, Fabes, Miller, et al., 1989; Fabes, Eisenberg, & Miller, 1990). But higher basal heart rate (e.g., Zahn-Waxler et al., 1995) or heart rate acceleration in response to stimuli (e.g., Holmgren, Eisenberg, & Fabes, 1998) also were linked with prosocial indices in some studies. Conversely, studies of the specifically SNS index of skin conductance were more consistent in showing that stronger basal conductance and greater EDR were associated with more distressed responses or less prosocial behavior (e.g., Eisenberg et al., 1991; Fabes, Eisenberg, & Eisenbud, 1993). Considered together, then, these early studies provided moderately consistent evidence that strong SNS activity could interfere with children's empathic and prosocial responses to the needs of others.

With regard to parasympathetic regulation, between 1993 and 2000 there were four studies of children's empathy, sympathy, prosocial behavior and personal distress responses that included measures of basal RSA or RSA during exposure to emotional distress in others (Eisenberg, Fabes, Karbon, et al., 1996; Eisenberg, Fabes, Murphy, et al., 1996; Hastings et al., 2000; Zahn-Waxler et al., 1995). All of these included multiple measures of children's emotions and behaviors, and all found that the majority of relations between RSA and children's emotions and behaviors were nonsignificant. Of the significant associations, children with greater basal RSA were characterized as less empathic or prosocial in two studies (Eisenberg, Fabes, Karbon, et al., 1996; Zahn-Waxler et al., 1995). Children with greater RSA during exposure to evocative stimuli were sometimes found to be more empathic or prosocial (Eisenberg, Fabes, Murphy, et al., 1996) and sometimes found to be less so (Eisenberg, Fabes, Murphy, et al., 1996; Hastings et al., 2000). Overall, the early research provided little evidence that parasympathetic control of cardiac activity was an important contributor to children's prosocial development.

So why have we continued to study RSA?

Polyvagal Theory in Social Mammals

Porges (2007, 2011) has constructed the polyvagal theory around the evolutionary needs of mammals to both control their metabolically costly and sympathetically driven high heart rates, and, in response to nonthreatening cues from conspecifics, to inhibit fight-or-flight responses that would interfere with social cohesion and cooperative action. Let's unpack those tenets.

More primitive and evolutionarily older species, such as reptiles, do not show evidence of RSA (Porges, 2011). They have lower cardiac demands when at rest, and their behavioral responses to evocative cues are limited to orienting, freezing, defensive posturing, and fleeing. Reptiles do not prolong their attention to gather further information, express emotions, or attempt vocal communication.

Conversely, warm-blooded mammals have high-capacity cardiac muscles that, if left unchecked, would beat very quickly (Porges, 2011). This rapid heart rate is driven by the sinoatrial node, which functions as the heart's pacemaker and attempts to drive a level of cardiac activity that is considerably above what we would consider to be typical resting heart rates. Consequently, unregulated cardiac activity would rapidly consume energy stores. Despite this, mammals also have a broader and more flexible range of behavioral responses to evocative cues, including prolonged attention, affective expression, and vocalization.

The polyvagal theory accounts for these biological and behavioral differences between species by the fact that, in mammals, the vagus is actually a family of nerves that originate in adjacent but distinct parts of the brainstem and that serve different metabolic and behavioral functions (Porges, 2007). Shared across reptilian and mammalian species is the mostly unmyelinated vagus nerve that descends from the dorsal motor nucleus of the vagus (DMNX) and contributes to orienting and freezing responses. It is also responsible for involuntary vegetative functions, such as digestion. Unique to mammals is the myelinated vagus that descends from the nucleus ambiguus (NA) and persistently inhibits the sinoatrial node; hence, it is the "vagal brake" on cardiac activity. The quantification of that chronotropic control, RSA, is solely the product of the myelinated vagus (Porges, 2011). This branch of the vagus system also is associated with other cranial nerves that originate in the NA, such as the facial and trigeminal nerves, that control head orienting, facial expressions, and activity of the throat and larynx—in other words, muscles that are essential for emotional and vocal communication and over which mammals can exert voluntary control.

Thus, Porges (2011) has theorized that the regulatory activity of the myelinated vagus serves as both a check on cardiac activity that allows mammals to be in calm states and as part of the mechanism for expressing or communicating that calm and nonthreatening state to others. Further, because it is solely the product of the myelinated vagus that descends from the NA, RSA provides an index of both of those regulatory functions. When a salient or evocative stimulus is detected, orientation and attention are needed, and some suppression of RSA (or "release of the vagal brake") can be expected in support of that orienting response. If the stimulus is perceived to be threatening or challenging, such that resources might need to be mobilized in support of active coping responses, then greater or prolonged RSA suppression would be expected. If the stimulus is perceived to be nonthreatening or safe, however, then RSA augmentation (or "applying the vagal brake") would support calm engagement with this context.

These evaluations of threat or safety can occur extremely quickly and without conscious awareness. Porges (2007) has proposed the term "neuroception" for the activity of neural circuits in the primitive parts of the brain that rapidly distinguish safe versus threatening situations or people and then trigger prosocial versus defensive motor action patterns, respectively. Cooperative social species cannot rely only on fight, flight, or freeze responses. Porges (2011) argues that "to create relationships, humans must subdue these defensive reactions (in order) to engage, attach, and form lasting social bonds," and that " 'Playing nice' comes naturally when our neuroception detects safety and promotes physiological states that support social behavior" (p. 12).

IMPLICATIONS OF POLYVAGAL THEORY
FOR PROSOCIAL BEHAVIOR

Responding in caring and helpful ways toward another who is experiencing distress requires that one remain relatively calm rather than becoming distressed and focused on oneself. Calm and sociable engagement with others is supported by greater down-regulation of cardiac activity by the myelinated vagus. This parasympathetic regulation is reflected in higher RSA. Thus, maintaining relatively higher RSA when witnessing another in distress should be expected to support one's preparedness to respond to that distress in prosocial ways.

This is not to say that RSA suppression is reflective of poor parasympathetic self-regulation. Developmental studies have shown that children manifest RSA suppression in response to many stimuli and contexts, including films, puzzles, and social interaction tasks. Typically, RSA suppression has been measured using arithmetic or residualized change scores, and modest RSA suppression has been interpreted as a physiological index of effective emotion regulation (e.g., Katz & Rigterink, 2012). Indeed, a recent meta-analysis showed that children with more externalizing and internalizing problems tended to show less RSA suppression than children with fewer problems (Graziano & Derefinko, 2013). Intriguingly, though, the magnitude of RSA suppression was not reliably associated with indices of children's positive social functioning, such as peer relations, social competence, and prosocial behavior.

Inherent to the polyvagal theory is the proposal that there is not likely to be a simple linear association between emotion regulation and the magnitude of RSA change in response to stimuli (Beauchaine, 2012; Porges, 2011). Whether stronger RSA suppression, weaker RSA suppression, or RSA augmentation is reflective of effective parasympathetic regulation that supports adaptive behavior will depend on multiple factors (Hastings, Kahle, & Han, 2014). These include the nature of the social context or eliciting stimulus; different behavioral responses would be appropriate when encountering someone who is sad, versus scared, versus in pain, versus happy and friendly, and therefore different patterns of parasympathetic reactivity might be expected in these contexts. Analogously, distinct patterns of PNS regulation might be expected to support such prosocial behavioral responses as attentiveness and information processing, sympathy and compassion, or helpfulness and efforts to cheer someone up (Light & Zahn-Waxler, 2011). In addition, there are likely to be developmental changes in parasympathetic regulation; as children's emotional, cognitive, and social competencies mature, so too might there be changes in PNS activity that supports these competencies.

Finally, recognizing that emotional processes unfold over time, parasympathetic regulation needs to be considered as a dynamic process, rather than a simple difference between discrete states as suggested by static measures such as arithmetic or residual change scores (Brooker & Buss, 2010; Burt & Obradović, 2013). What is the shape of parasympathetic change over the course of an empathic episode? What is the magnitude of change at different points in time during empathy, rather than on average across an empathic experience? One might expect both RSA suppression and augmentation, perhaps occurring at different points during an empathic episode, to underlie children's ability to mount an appropriate prosocial response.

Our Recent Implementations of Polyvagal Theory

This perspective on the polyvagal theory grew out of our careful consideration of Porges's (2007, 2011) writings, but also from noticing in our own studies and in the wider literature findings that ran counter to the prevailing zeitgeist in developmental psychophysiology that more RSA suppression necessarily reflects better regulation (e.g., Marcovitch et al., 2010). Four recent studies of RSA change and displays of sympathy or prosocial behavior again produced divergent findings, but with a glimmer of a consistent pattern beginning to emerge (Hastings, Miller, et al., 2014). In two studies, more RSA augmentation (or less suppression) in response to empathy-eliciting stimuli was associated with greater sympathetic concern or compassion (Gill & Calkins, 2003; Oveis, Cohen et al., 2009). In two other studies, more RSA suppression (or less augmentation) to a challenging puzzle (Graziano, Keane, & Calkins, 2007) or an examiner feigning distress (Liew et al., 2011) predicted more prosocial behaviors like sharing and helping. Thus, mobilization of resources by the withdrawal of parasympathetic influence (RSA suppression) appeared to be associated with instrumental prosocial actions, whereas preparedness for calm social engagement by application of the vagal brake (RSA augmentation) was linked with positive, other-oriented emotional responses.

Our studies of RSA and emotion regulation also pointed to potentially beneficial roles of RSA augmentation. In an examination of the social engagement system, we examined preschoolers' parasympathetic activity during a brief play period with unfamiliar peers (Hastings, Nuselovici et al., 2008). Almost as many children displayed RSA augmentation relative to basal RSA as showed RSA suppression. In accord with Porges's (2007) concept of neuroception, we hypothesized that children who displayed RSA augmentation perceived the novel social context as safe for social engagement, whereas those who displayed RSA suppression saw it as an unsafe or intimidating situation. Supporting this, we found that RSA augmentation was associated with mothers' reports of children having better behavioral self-regulation and fewer internalizing and externalizing problems. Clearly, taking context into consideration is important for understanding how PNS activity is related to adjustment.

We next tackled the issue of timing: How could we examine the chronometry of parasympathetic regulation as it unfolded over an emotional event? We decided to use latent growth curve (LGC) modeling (Bollen & Curran, 2006) to examine the slope of RSA change in response to emotion inductions (Miller, Chochol, et al., 2013). Examining repeated measures of RSA over a 60-second anger story that involved four narrated pictures, each presented for 15 seconds, we found that children exhibited RSA suppression from (1) the neutral introduction to (2) the initiation of anger, followed by RSA augmentation (or recovery) in (3) the intensification of anger and stable RSA through (4) the mildly positive resolution. The LGC analysis showed that the latent slope of nonlinear change was a better fit to the RSA data than were linear or quadratic slope models, with the changes over time reflecting an initial "release of the vagal brake" (RSA suppression, perhaps in support of an orienting response) as the angry content of the story was presented, followed by "applying the vagal brake" (RSA augmentation, which could support calm attention) while children watched the story unfold. That this overall pattern reflected effective parasympathetic regulation of emotion was evident in the fact that the latent, nonlinear slope predicted children's behavioral self-control, as assessed through their reports of not responding aggressively to peer provocations. Conversely, neither the individual RSA suppression nor RSA augmentation components were uniquely associated with control of aggression (Miller et al., 2013). Therefore, children's effective self-regulation of anger was captured in their capacity to dynamically and flexibly modulate their levels of PNS activity.

To directly test whether this approach to measuring parasympathetic regulation might inform our understanding of children's empathy and prosocial behavior, we recently applied these techniques in an examination of children's RSA in a typical empathy-induction paradigm: while they watched a sad film (Miller, Nuselovici, Chochol, & Hastings, 2013). During the empathy-induction film, children saw two 90-second stories, which both progressed from affectively neutral to depicting sadness strongly and then were resolved and returned to neutral content (Zahn-Waxler et al., 1995). The normative pattern of RSA change was nonlinear in shape, and very similar to what we had observed for RSA response to the angry story (Miller, Chochol et al., 2013). On average, children showed RSA suppression during the initial introduction of sadness followed by RSA recovery and augmentation during the intensification of sadness, and RSA at the (affectively neutral) end of the stories was not different from what it had been at the (neutral) start. LGC modeling again showed that a latent slope of nonlinear change was an excellent fit to the data and provided a picture of parasympathetic regulation that is more closely analogous to theoretical depictions of emotions as dynamic processes that correspond with rapidly changing events in the environment (Cole, Martin, & Dennis, 2004; Dennis, Buss, & Hastings, 2012).

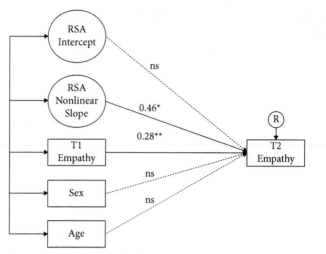

FIGURE 6.1 *Latent slope of nonlinear RSA change during an empathy induction video predicts the development of empathic concern two years later.*

Note: RSA = Respiratory Sinus Arrhythmia. *$p < .05$, **$p < .01$, two tailed. Standardized path coefficients.

   This was a longitudinal investigation. We observed children's behavior on the same day we measured their RSA and again 2 years later, when they returned to the lab. In both lab visits, the commonly used accident simulation paradigm (Van Hulle et al., 2013; Zahn-Waxler et al., 1995) was implemented to assess children's sympathetic and prosocial responses to distress in others, which were aggregated into a single measure of empathic concern (Hastings et al., 2000). Surprisingly, the latent slope of nonlinear RSA change was not associated with children's concurrent displays of empathic concern (nor were the separate measures of RSA suppression or augmentation). However, the latent slope significantly predicted the development of empathic concern over time. Controlling for children's initial empathic concern, children who showed more dynamic change in RSA (more suppression followed by more augmentation) displayed significantly more empathic concern in response to the accident simulations 2 years later (see Figure 6.1).

   This finding suggests that flexible disengagement and reengagement of the PNS during empathy supports children's development of prosocial and sympathetic responding to the distress of others. During empathic experiences, initial RSA suppression may support orienting to the distress of others as an emotionally salient event, as well as helping to initiate related coping efforts. Subsequent RSA augmentation then may be important for reinstating a calm but socially engaged state that supports other-oriented rather than self-oriented responding. Thus, this dynamic measure of RSA could help to resolve the discrepancies in the past literature by illustrating that both RSA suppression and RSA augmentation, albeit at different points during an emotional episode, are important for children's empathic concern.

As a final example, we examined the autonomic regulation of preschoolers' propensities for altruistic giving (Miller, Kahle, Lopez, & Hastings, 2013). Altruism is a form of prosocial behavior that requires sacrificing something of personal value for the benefit of others (Grusec, Hastings, & Almas, 2011). In this study, throughout a lab visit children were given tokens that could be traded in for a prize at the end. Before receiving the prize, children were given an opportunity to donate some, none, or all of their prize tokens to anonymous sick children so they also could get prizes. Children's PNS and SNS activity were assessed by recording RSA and PEP, respectively, while they received information about the opportunity to give to others in need, while they completed the altruism task, and afterward, while the examiner put away materials while chatting casually. There was, overall, very little change in sympathetic activity over the task, and children's PEP was unrelated to their altruistic giving. Conversely, children's parasympathetic activity was closely linked to altruism. Modeling analyses showed that children with greater parasympathetic activity (higher RSA) during the instruction period gave away significantly more of their tokens. While they were completing the altruism task itself, though, children who experienced greater RSA suppression also gave away more tokens. Finally, there was recovery of RSA during the concluding period, and children who had given away the most tokens also showed the most RSA augmentation.

This pattern closely parallels the aggregate picture from the four recent studies on RSA change and prosocial responding summarized at the start of this section (and see Hastings, Miller, et al., 2014), as well as the predictions of polyvagal theory (Porges, 2011). First, calm social engagement while learning about the opportunity to help others, as conferred by higher RSA, predicted more altruistic giving. Second, prosocial behavior was facilitated through preparedness for active but nondefensive coping, as RSA suppression released cardiac resources without requiring increased sympathetic activity (which would drive fight-or-flight responses). Third, having helped others in turn contributed to reestablishing a state of positive social connection, as reflected in RSA augmentation. Overall, children's willingness to give of themselves in order to help others was intricately linked to their capacity for flexible parasympathetic regulation.

Conclusions and Future Directions

The polyvagal theory is a powerful conceptual framework for organizing our observations of, and expectations for, the psychophysiological basis of prosocial development. An initial perception of inconsistency in the relations between PNS activity and children's empathy, sympathy, helpfulness, and altruism observed in past research belies a deeper pattern of complex yet meaningful parasympathetic regulation. Flexible increases and decreases in the inhibitory influence of the myelinated vagus nerve on cardiac activity, as revealed by augmentations and suppressions of cardiac RSA, support children's calm attentiveness toward the needs of others and their ability to act on this empathic engagement in order to provide assistance. The magnitude and timing of these dynamic changes in parasympathetic influence are likely to be dependent on context, social partners, and specific cues, but the social engagement system is finely tailored to be adaptive to our complex social and sociable world.

There is still, of course, much to be learned about the psychophysiology of empathy and prosocial behavior. As developmental scientists, we are very concerned with understanding the origins and maturational course of autonomic regulation of emotional and social processes. Although facial expressions of sympathy in response to others can be detected in infancy (Roth-Hanania, Davidov, & Zahn-Waxler, 2011), we do not yet know how early in development parasympathetic activity begins to influence young children's empathic engagement with others. As well, recognizing the multidimensionality of prosocial development, it will be important to examine how PNS regulation becomes involved in regulating the cognitive, affective, and behavioral aspects of children's positive responses to others. Although the research of Eisenberg and colleagues (e.g., Eisenberg, Fabes, Murphy, et al., 1996) and others (see Hastings, Miller, et al., 2014; Hastings et al., 2006) has identified links between RSA and sympathy and prosocial behavior in children of varying ages, there has not yet been a comprehensive, developmental investigation of how the PNS comes to regulate the multidimensional aspects of prosociality.

Neurobiological regulation also is complex and multidimensional. The PNS is one branch of the ANS, which itself is one system within our complex neurobiology. Although most affective and developmental psychophysiologists examine distinct systems in isolation, we know that our genes, brains, hormones, ANS, and other neurobiological processes must function in integrated and interactive ways to support our emotional, cognitive, behavioral, and social functioning (Hastings, Miller, et al., 2014). Further, our close relationships, surrounding community, and cultural structures both affect the development of these neurobiological systems and modulate how physiological activity contributes to psychosocial activity (Hastings, Kahle, & Han, 2014).

Scientists are beginning to embark on such integrative, multilevel examinations of empathy and prosocial behavior (e.g., Feldman, 2012), and this research holds great promise for our future understanding of our capacities to be compassionately engaged with others. The polyvagal theory can play a key role in guiding these investigations, because the PNS clearly is one of the systems that has been shaped by evolutionary forces to support our capacity to be a cooperative social species. When we give, our heart is in the right place.

References

Beauchaine, T. P. (2012). Physiological markers of emotion and behavior dysregulation in externalizing psychopathology. *Monographs of the Society for Research in Child Development, 77*(2), 79–86. doi: 10.1111/j.1540-5834.2011.00665.x

Berntson, G. G., & Cacioppo, J. T. (2007). Integrative physiology: Homeostasis, allostasis and the orchestration of systemic physiology. In J. T. Cacioppo, L. G. Tassinary, & G. G. Berntson (Eds.), *Handbook of psychophysiology* (3rd ed., pp. 433–452). Cambridge, UK: Cambridge University Press.

Berntson, G. G., Quigley, K. S., & Lozano, D. (2007). Cardiovascular psychophysiology. In J. T. Cacioppo, L. G. Tassinary, & G. G. Berntson (Eds.), *Handbook of psychophysiology* (3rd ed. pp. 182–210). Cambridge, UK: Cambridge University Press.

Bollen, K. A., & Curran, P. J. (2006). *Latent curve models: A structural equation approach.* New Jersey: John Wiley & Sons.

Brooker, R. J., & Buss, K. A. (2010). Dynamic measures of RSA predict distress and regulation in toddlers. *Developmental Psychobiology, 52*(4), 372–382. doi:10.1002/dev.20432

Burt, K. B., & Obradović, J. (2013). The construct of psychophysiological reactivity: Statistical and psychometric issues. *Developmental Review, 33*(1), 29–57. doi:10.1016/j.dr.2012.10.002

Cole, P. M., Martin, S. E., & Dennis, T. A. (2004). Emotion regulation as a scientific construct: Methodological challenges and directions for child development research. *Child Development, 75*(2), 317–333. doi:10.1111/j.1467-8624.2004.00673.x

Damasio, A. R. (2000). A second chance for emotion. In R. D. Lane & L. Nadel (Eds.), *Cognitive neuroscience of emotion: Series in affective science* (pp. 12–23). London: Oxford University Press.

Dawson, M. E., Schell, A. M., & Filion, D. L. (2007). The electrodermal system. In J. T. Cacioppo, L. G. Tassinary, & G. G. Berntson (Eds.), *Handbook of Psychophysiology* (3rd ed., pp. 159–181). Cambridge, UK: Cambridge University Press.

Dennis, T. A., Buss, K. A., & Hastings, P. D. (Eds.). (2012). Physiological measures of emotion from a developmental perspective: State of the science. *Monographs of the Society for Research in Child Development, 77*(2). doi: 10.1111/j.1540-5834.2011.00654.x

Eisenberg, N., Fabes, R. A., Miller, P. A., Fultz, J., Shell, R., Mathy, R. M., & Reno, R. (1989). Relation of sympathy and personal distress to prosocial behavior: A multimethod study. *Journal of Personality and Social Psychology, 57*, 55–66. doi: 10.1037/0022-3514.57.1.55

Eisenberg, N., Fabes, R. A., Murphy, B., Karbon, M., Smith, M., & Maszk, P. (1996). The relations of children's dispositional empathy-related responding to their emotionality, regulation, and social functioning. *Developmental Psychology, 32*, 195–209. doi: 10.1037/0012-1649.32.2.195

Eisenberg, N., Fabes, R. A., Schaller, M., Carlo, G., & Miller, P. A. (1991). The relations of parental characteristics and practices to children's vicarious emotional responding. *Child Development, 62*, 1393–1408. doi: 10.1111/j.1467-8624.1991.tb01613.x

Fabes, R. A., Eisenberg, N., & Eisenbud, L. (1993). Behavioral and physiological correlates of children's reactions to others in distress. *Developmental Psychology, 29*, 655–663. doi: 10.1037/0012-1649.29.4.655

Fabes, R. A., Eisenberg, N., Karbon, M., Troyer, D., & Switzer, G. (1994). The relations of children's emotion regulation to their vicarious emotional responses and comforting behaviors. *Child Development, 65*, 1678–1693. doi: 10.2307/1131287

Fabes, R. A., Eisenberg, N., & Miller, P. A. (1990). Maternal correlates of children's vicarious emotional responsiveness. *Developmental Psychology*, *26*, 639–648. doi: 10.1037/0012-1649.26.4.639

Feldman, R. (2012). Oxytocin and social affiliation in humans. *Hormones and Behavior*, *61*, 380–391. doi: 10.1016/j.yhbeh.2012.01.008

Gill, K. L., & Calkins, S. D. (2003). Do aggressive/destructive toddlers lack concern for others? Behavioral and physiological indicators of empathic responding in 2-year-old children. *Development and Psychopathology*, *15*(1), 55–71. doi: 10.1017/S095457940300004X

Graziano, P., & Derefinko, K. (2013). Cardiac vagal control and children's adaptive functioning: A meta-analysis. *Biological Psychology*, *94*, 22–37. doi: 10.1016/j.biopsycho.2013.04.011

Graziano, P. A, Keane, S. P., & Calkins, S. D. (2007). Cardiac vagal regulation and early peer status. *Child Development*, *78*(1), 264–278. doi: 10.1111/j.1467-8624.2007.00996.x

Greenspan, E. (2005). *Walt Whitman's "Song of Myself": A sourcebook and critical edition.* New York: Routledge.

Grusec, J. E., Hastings, P. D., Almas, A. (2011). Helping and prosocial behavior. In C. Hart & P. Smith (Eds.), *Handbook of childhood social development* (2nd ed., pp. 549–566). Malden, MA: Wiley-Blackwell.

Hastings, P. D., & Guyer, A. E. (in press). The physiological underpinnings of child psychopathology. In B. H. Schneider (Ed.), *Child and adolescent psychopathology*. Cambridge.

Hastings, P. D., Kahle, S., & Han, G. H. -P. (2014). Developmental affective psychophysiology: Using physiology to inform our understanding of emotional development. In K. H. Lagattuta (Ed.), *Children and emotion: New insights into developmental affective science* (pp. 13–28). Basel, Switzerland: Karger.

Hastings, P. D., Miller, J. G., Kahle, S., & Zahn-Waxler, C. (2014). The neurobiological basis of empathic concern for others. In M. Killen & J. Smetana (Eds.), *Handbook of moral development* (2nd ed.) (pp. 411–434). Mahwah, NJ: Erlbaum.

Hastings, P. D., Nuselovici, J. N., Utendale, W. T., Coutya, J., McShane, K. E., & Sullivan, C. (2008). Applying the polyvagal theory to children's emotion regulation: Social context, socialization, and adjustment. *Biological Psychology*, *79*(3), 299–306. doi:10.1016/j.biopsycho.2008.07.005

Hastings, P. D., Zahn-Waxler, C., & McShane, K. (2006). We are, by nature, moral creatures: Biological bases of concern for others. In M. Killen & J. Smetana (Eds.), *Handbook of moral development* (pp. 483– 516). Mahwah, NJ: Erlbaum.

Hastings, P. D., Zahn-Waxler, C., Robinson, J., Usher, B., & Bridges, D. (2000). The development of concern for others in children with behavior problems. *Developmental-Psychology*, *36*, 531–546. doi: 10.1037/0012-1649.36.5.531

Holmgren, R. A., Eisenberg, N., & Fabes, R. A. (1998). The relations of children's situational sympathy-related emotions to dispositional prosocial behaviour. *International Journal of Behavioural Development*, *22*, 169–293. doi: 10.1080/016502598384568

Katz, L. F., & Rigterink, T. (2012). Domestic violence and emotion socialization. *Monographs of the Society for Research in Child Development*, *77*, 52–60. doi: 10.1111/j.1540-5834.2011.00654.x

Liew, J., Eisenberg, N., Spinrad, T. L., Eggum, N. D., Haugen, R. G., Kupfer, A., Reiser, M. R., et al. (2011). Physiological regulation and fearfulness as predictors of young children's empathy-related reactions. *Social Development*, *20*(1), 111–134. doi: 10.1111/j.1467-9507.2010.00575.x

Light, S., & Zahn-Waxler, C. (2011). Nature and forms of empathy in the first years of life. In J. Decety (Ed.), *Empathy: From bench to bedside* (pp. 109–130). Cambridge, MA: MIT Press.

Marcovitch, S., Leigh, J., Calkins, S. D., Leerks, E. M., O'Brien, M., & Blankson, A. N. (2010). Moderate vagal withdrawal in 3.5-year-old children is associated with optimal performance on executive function tasks. *Developmental Psychobiology, 52*(6), 603–608. doi:10.1002/dev.20462

Miller, J. G., Chocol, C., Nuselovici, J. N., Utendale, W. T., Simard, M., & Hastings, P. D. (2013). Children's dynamic RSA change during anger and its relations with parenting, temperament, and control of aggression. *Biological Psychology, 92*(2), 417–425. doi:10.1016/j.biopsycho.2012.12.005

Miller, J. G., Kahle, S., Lopez, M., & Hastings, P. D. (2013, April). *Altruism, psychophysiology, and family socioeconomic status.* Poster presented at the biennial meeting of the Society for Research in Child Development, Seattle, WA.

Miller, J. G., Nuselovici, J. N., Chocol, C., & Hastings, P. D. (2013, April). *Dynamic parasympathetic regulation of sadness predicts the development of empathic concern over 2 years.* Paper presented at the biennial meeting of the Society for Research in Child Development, Seattle, WA.

Oveis, C., Cohen, A. B., Gruber, J., Shiota, M. N., Haidt, J., & Keltner, D. (2009). Resting respiratory sinus arrhythmia is associated with tonic positive emotionality. *Emotion, 9*(2), 265–270. doi: 10.1037/a0015383

Pagel, M., Atkinson, Q. D., Calude, A. S., & Meade, A. (2013). Ultraconserved words point to deep language ancestry across Eurasia. *Proceedings of the National Academy of Sciences, USA, 110,* 8471–8476. doi: 10.1073/pnas.1218726110

Porges, S. W. (1985). Respiratory sinus arrhythmia: An index of vagal tone. In J. F. Orlebeke, G. Mulder, & L. J. P. Van Dornen (Eds.), *Psychophysiology of cardiovascular control: Models, methods, and data* (pp. 437–450). New York: Plenum.

Porges, S. W. (1995). Orienting in a defensive world: Mammalian modifications of our evolutionary heritage; A polyvagal theory. *Psychophysiology, 32*(4), 301–318. doi: 10.1111/j.1469-8986.1995.tb01213.x

Porges, S. W. (2007). The polyvagal perspective. *Biological Psychology, 74*(2), 116–143. doi:10.1016/j.bbi.2008.05.010

Porges, S. W. (2011). *The polyvagal theory.* New York: Norton.

Roth-Hanania, R., Davidov, M., & Zahn-Waxler, C. (2011). Empathy development from 8 to 16 months: Early signs of concern for others. *Infant Behavior and Development, 34,* 447–458.

Smith, A. (1759). *The theory of moral sentiments.* London: A. Millar.

Van Hulle, C., Zahn-Waxler, C., Robinson, J. L., Rhee, S. H., P. D. Hastings, & Knafo, A. (2013). Autonomic correlates of children's concern and disregard for others. *Social Neuroscience, 8,* 275–290. doi: 10.1080/17470919.2013.791342

Zahn-Waxler, C., Cole, P. M., Welsh, J. D., & Fox, N. A. (1995). Psychophysiological correlates of empathy and prosocial behaviors in preschool children with behavior problems. *Development and Psychopathology, 7,* 27–48. doi: 10.1017/S0954579400006325

Socialization Perspectives

7

Parental Socialization of Prosocial Behavior

A MULTIDIMENSIONAL APPROACH

Laura M. Padilla-Walker

In a society where the news is dominated by coverage of continued war and conflict at home and overseas; mass murder in movie theaters, malls, and office buildings; and tragic school shootings; it would not be surprising if parents today were more concerned that their child not be the perpetrator or victim of such violence than whether or not their child was kind or helpful toward others. Indeed, the research community reflects similar priorities, with large portions of government funding being given to projects that address the avoidance of social problems such as teen pregnancy, delinquency, poverty, and violent crime. In addition, there are thousands of studies examining predictors and outcomes associated with childhood aggression, while there are relatively fewer examining positive outcomes in children. Perhaps the assumption is that "not being mean," or parental interventions aimed at reducing aggression and violence will, in turn, increase positive and prosocial behavior. As long as one's child is not the class bully or the queen bee, and is not being victimized by these people, parents and teachers may feel fairly satisfied that healthy outcomes are probable. However, the absence of negative behavior in children does not necessarily correlate with the presence of positive behavior, especially as children get older. Indeed, during adolescence studies have found antisocial or aggressive behavior and prosocial behavior to be either unrelated (Carlo, Roesch, & Melby, 1998; Padilla-Walker, 2007) or only moderately negatively associated with one another (Carlo, Mestre, et al., 2012; Carlo, McGinley, Hayes, & Martinez, 2012). It has been suggested that the main difference between socially rejected and socially controversial individuals is that the latter display advanced social skills, perhaps even displaying high levels of both antisocial and prosocial behavior (Newcomb, Bukowski, & Pattee, 1993). Thus, it is clearly not enough to focus on reducing negative behaviors in children unless those behaviors are actively replaced with positive alternatives.

While this perspective is certainly not as strongly endorsed or funded as are campaigns to reduce violence, there has been a renewed interest in the study of positive outcomes in the last 15 years or so, evidenced by movements such as the positive psychology movement (Seligman & Csikszentmihalyi, 2000), which focuses on the study of positive character traits in children and adolescents. In addition, renewed interest in prosocial development has occurred, with a call to better understand predictors of prosocial behavior and an emphasis on the need to pay more careful attention to the multidimensionality of prosocial development. While this volume highlights biological correlates and multiple socialization sources that influence prosocial development, the purpose of the current chapter is to focus specifically on parental socialization of prosocial behavior, as parents are often thought to be the earliest and most salient source of socialization in the lives of children (Grusec, 2006). The current chapter will go beyond examining the role of parenting on the avoidance of children's negative and aggressive behaviors and will systematically examine how parenting is associated with a variety of prosocial behaviors. As mentioned in the introduction to this volume (Padilla-Walker & Carlo, chapter 1, this volume), it is imperative that the field move beyond referring to prosocial behavior as a unidimensional construct, so in the current chapter I will examine the role of parental socialization on different types of prosocial behavior. First, I will discuss new minitheories and conceptual models of parental socialization that have important implications for prosocial development. Second, I will review the existing literature on parental socialization with an eye to highlighting different aspects of parenting as they relate to different types of prosocial behavior. And finally, I will discuss important future directions in the area of parental socialization of prosocial behavior.

Recent Theoretical Models of Parental Socialization

There are a number of existing chapters on the socialization of prosocial behavior that thoroughly cover classic theoretical approaches, including psychoanalytic and behavioral approaches, social learning theory, cognitive developmental theory (see Eisenberg, Fabes, & Spinrad, 2006; Eisenberg & Valiente, 2002; Grusec, 2006), and Hoffman's theory of moral internalization (Eisenberg & Valiente, 2002; Grusec, 2006; Hastings, Utendale, & Sullivan, 2007). While these theories all have value and application to the socialization of prosocial behavior, I will direct the reader to existing chapters for exhaustive theoretical reviews and in the current chapter I will briefly cover three relevant reconceptualizations of parental socialization, namely, Darling and Steinberg's (1993) integrative model, Grusec and Goodnow's (1994) reconceptualization of the role of parental discipline on children's internalization of values, and Grusec and Davidov's (2010) domain-specific approach to parental socialization. Although these models all have implications for diverse child outcomes, I will discuss them specifically as they relate to children's prosocial development.

INTEGRATIVE MODEL OF PARENTING

While there is fairly consistent evidence of the role of specific parenting practices on children's prosocial behavior, the role of parenting styles is less clear and seems to vary as a function of variables such as gender of the parent, culture, and socioeconomic status (Darling & Steinberg, 1993; Grusec & Goodnow, 1994). To address these inconsistencies, Darling and Steinberg proposed an integrative model of socialization by making a clear distinction between parenting styles (or global characteristics) and parenting practices. More specifically, parenting styles are defined as broad contextual variables representing the emotional climate of the parent-child relationship, while parenting practices are situational parental responses with specific socialization goals in mind. Conceptually, parenting styles are broad parenting behaviors that influence a child's responsiveness to socialization and make specific parenting practices more or less effective in promoting prosocial behavior. In other words, parenting styles moderate the relation between a given parenting practice and a child's subsequent prosocial behavior, primarily by influencing the child's responsiveness to parental discipline. For example, a mother who is consistently authoritative with her child increases the likelihood that the child will be accepting of maternal socialization attempts and also creates an environment where specific parenting practices (even power assertion) are more positively received by the child and more likely to promote prosocial outcomes.

PARENTAL DISCIPLINE AND CHILDREN'S INTERNALIZATION OF VALUES

Another minitheory of socialization that has implications for prosocial development is Grusec and Goodnow's (1994) reconceptualization of how parental discipline is associated with children's internalization of values and subsequent prosocial behavior (see also Grusec, Goodnow, & Kuczynski, 2000). Grusec and colleagues highlight the limitations to the current conceptualizations of socialization, including insufficient explanations for inconsistent relations between parenting and child outcomes, lack of attention to direction of effects, the treatment of parenting practices as unidimensional constructs, and the assumption that parents use one primary parenting practice rather than tailoring their response to the child's behavior. These limitations are addressed by the suggestion of a theoretical model that places the child at center stage in the socialization process and purports that before any parental message is internalized and expressed in prosocial outcomes, children must first accurately perceive parental socialization messages and choose to accept parental messages. Grusec and Goodnow highlight a number of parent and child characteristics that increase the likelihood of a child's accurate perception of parental messages, including clarity and redundancy of the parental message, the need to capture the child's attention, and the need to convey importance and positive intentions on the part of the parent. Three broad factors are also introduced that increase the likelihood of a child's acceptance of parental messages, including the child's perception of the appropriateness of the parental message, how motivating the message is to the child, and whether the parental message allows the child feelings of self-generation.

A DOMAIN-SPECIFIC APPROACH TO
PARENTAL SOCIALIZATION

Finally, a more recent reconceptualization of parenting that has potential implications for a multidimensional approach to prosocial development is Grusec and Davidov's (2010) domain approach to socialization. This approach attempts to organize disparate socialization research by suggesting that parenting behaviors can be organized into five distinct domains, each of which are associated with specific child outcomes and are thought to socialize prosocial development in different ways.

The first domain, *protection*, includes parental responses aimed at reducing the child's distress in the face of real or potential threat and should involve appropriate parental attempts to support and comfort the child. This domain includes commonly studied concepts such as parental attachment and oversolicitous parenting and should be associated with specific prosocial outcomes that are facilitated by the ability to regulate distress and anticipate support in threatening situations. For example, children whose parents display appropriate parenting behaviors in the protection domain should display higher levels of sympathy (as opposed to personal distress) because of their increased ability to regulate their own internal states and focus on the person in need. Alternatively, oversolicitous or helicopter parenting may result in a child who is less skilled at emotional regulation and who may become flooded when faced with the emotional distress of another and therefore be less able to respond prosocially.

The second domain, *reciprocity*, occurs in horizontal or equal-status interactions between parents and children when there is the opportunity for parents to be responsive to the desires of the child, such as during play for young children or during an increased number of interactions as the child transitions to adolescence and young adulthood. Appropriate parental responses in the reciprocity domain should be associated with children's compliant prosocial behavior and cooperation, because when parents listen and attend to children's reasonable demands, it often fosters reciprocal cooperation (e.g., Kochanska & Murray, 2000). Because of this process of receptive compliance, parenting in this domain may be particularly salient in increasing prosocial behavior toward specific family members rather than toward other family members, strangers, or friends.

The third domain, *control*, encompasses vertical interactions between parents and children where the power imbalance is more salient than in reciprocal interactions. Parenting in this domain should certainly decrease as children reach adolescence and young adulthood and may also be associated with fewer prosocial outcomes if it is used at later ages (e.g., Nelson, Padilla-Walker, Christensen, Evans, & Carroll, 2011). The hope of parental socialization is that early and appropriate control attempts (coupled with other adaptive parenting behaviors) should result in children's internalization of parental socialization messages so that direct parental control is no longer necessary. In the short term, parenting behaviors in the control domain may be associated with public or compliant prosocial behavior and low-cost prosocial behavior, especially if the child is motivated by praise or in order to avoid external punishment. However, the long-term socialization goal in this domain would likely be associated with internalization of parental standards and should be reflected in a variety of self-motivated prosocial behaviors that reflect minimized self-interest, such as sharing and being fair, as well as anonymous and altruistic prosocial behaviors.

The fourth domain, *guided learning*, includes parental scaffolding of children's skills, including cognitive, emotional, and social skills. Effective parenting in this domain includes teaching that is within a child's zone of proximal development and that becomes more child-directed with time and mastery. Although Vygotsky's theory focused on the role of guided learning on cognitive development (Vygotsky, 1978), which certainly has implications for children's moral and prosocial moral reasoning, Grusec and Davidov (2010) suggest that guided learning extends to emotional skills as well. Parental teaching and scaffolding of emotions likely results in children's ability to regulate, cope with, and understand emotions, which should in turn lead to higher levels of empathy and perspective taking. Research also suggests that guided learning is associated with children's perceived confidence in their abilities, which may be associated with higher cost helping (e.g., Staub, 1995), and taken together with emotional regulation, may result in a greater ability to help in highly emotional or dire situations, especially with strangers or unfamiliar peers.

The final domain, *group participation*, captures parents' attempts to define and shape children's in-group and encourage children's participation in socially appropriate behavior toward that group. Parenting in this domain often takes the form of family routines and rituals that communicate to children the shared identity of the family or group by modeling acceptable behavior and group norms rather than by purposeful and intentional teaching. Group participation should be more strongly associated with prosocial behavior toward those within children's in-group (e.g., family and friends) and may be reflected in specific behaviors such as voluntarily doing chores. In addition, families who have norms of engaging in high-cost helping behavior (e.g., extended volunteerism) and who help children to develop inclusive in-group boundaries may also promote high-cost or even exemplary helping in their children.

SUMMARY

Taken together, all three of these theoretical reconceptualizations have important implications for the role of parental socialization in children's prosocial development and highlight directions that will move the field forward in terms of multidimensionality of both parenting and prosocial behavior. First, parenting constructs should be carefully defined by making clear distinctions between parenting styles and practices and by attempting to use greater specificity within broader categories of parenting practices (e.g., examine specific behaviors such as yelling, grounding, and spanking instead of power assertion more broadly defined; Baumrind, 2012). Second, the role of the child should be much more central in the socialization process, considering a child's willingness to be socialized, as well as his or her accurate perception and acceptance of parental socialization messages regarding prosocial behavior. This is especially important as children get older and demand greater levels of autonomy (Collins, 1990) and as prosocial behavior becomes more stable (see Fortuna & Knafo, chapter 4, this volume). Finally, future research should carefully consider which domains of parenting influence different types of prosocial behavior. While parenting is complex and there is considerable interplay between parenting domains, it is likely that a more careful analysis of both parenting and prosocial behavior will reveal a clearer picture of how specific parental socialization attempts are associated with specific types of prosocial behavior.

Empirical Studies of Parental Socialization of Prosocial Behavior

PARENTAL WARMTH AND SUPPORT

There is a substantial body of research examining the link between parental warmth/support (and related constructs) and both children's and adolescents' prosocial behavior, although findings are somewhat mixed depending on the specific construct used, the method of measurement (e.g., observation vs. self-report), whether data are cross-sectional or longitudinal, and the age of the child. In younger children, maternal sensitivity (van der Mark et al., 2002) and responsiveness to distress have been associated with children's empathy and prosocial responding toward mixed targets (Davidov & Grusec, 2006); and a secure attachment with mother has been linked with increased helpfulness and sympathy toward peers (Kestenbaum, Farber, & Sroufe, 1989). Maternal warmth has been linked to 4- to 6-year-olds' helping, sharing, and comforting toward mixed targets (Yağmurlu & Sanson, 2009) and with representation of prosocial themes in story tasks completed by 6-year-olds (Laible, Carlo, Torquati, & Ontai, 2004). Maternal positively has also been linked to young children's global prosocial behavior toward peers (Knafo & Plomin, 2006), and when both maternal encouragement of connectedness and observed child connectedness with mother were high, children's voluntary helping and sharing increased (Liu, Chen, Zheng, Chen,

& Wang, 2009). That being said, other studies have found that maternal warmth is not associated with children's prosocial behavior (e.g., Davidov & Grusec, 2006; Iannotti, Cummings, Pierrehumbert, Milano, & Zahn-Waxler, 1992), highlighting the inconsistency of these relations and the possibility that the early attachment relationship and maternal responsiveness and sensitivity may be more important to the development of early prosocial behavior than is parental warmth.

In contrast, during adolescence, the majority of research suggests a link between parental warmth/support and adolescent outcomes, although these relations are dependent on the type and target of prosocial behavior. For example, one study examined a number of different prosocial tendencies and found that parental responsiveness was positively associated with compliant and negatively with altruistic prosocial behavior but was not associated with other types of prosocial behavior (Carlo, McGinley, Hayes, Batenhorst, & Wilkinson, 2007). Maternal warmth has also been linked to global prosocial behavior toward friends and strangers (Padilla-Walker & Christensen, 2011), and maternal attachment has been linked with self-reported defending behaviors toward peers who are victims (Nickerson, Mele, & Princiotta, 2008). In addition, a number of studies have examined parental warmth/support (or related constructs) as it relates to prosocial behavior specifically toward family members or parents. For example, parental attachment during adolescence was positively and directly associated with adolescents' helpfulness toward parents (Eberly & Montemayor, 1998) and was longitudinally associated with adolescent helpfulness and affection toward parents (Eberly & Montemayor, 1999). In addition, authoritative mothering (including maternal warmth/support) was associated with observed prosocial behavior toward mother (Padilla-Walker, Carlo, Christensen, Yorgason, 2012), and parental warmth was associated with global prosocial behavior toward family members (Padilla-Walker & Christensen, 2011).

Although these findings suggest that parental warmth/support might be particularly important in fostering prosocial behavior toward parents, additional research has found less consistent results when not specifying target. Namely, studies have found that maternal and paternal support did not have a direct effect on early adolescents' global prosocial behavior or sympathy toward unidentified targets (Carlo et al., 1998) and that mother-child relationship quality was not directly associated with prosocial tendencies (Barry, Padilla-Walker, Madsen, Nelson, 2008). Another study found that for families where parents were very involved in community service, parental reinforcement of children's interests (but not parental warmth), was associated positively with teens' community involvement (Fletcher, Elder, & Mekos, 2000).

Taken together, findings regarding parental warmth/support (and related constructs) present a somewhat complicated picture, suggesting that while attachment and responsiveness are consistently associated with prosocial behavior in childhood, associations may be somewhat more nuanced during adolescence, with potentially stronger relations between parental warmth/support and prosocial behavior toward parents or family members. In addition, this research highlights the importance of examining multiple aspects of parenting and prosocial behavior in a given study, as warmth may not be associated with prosocial outcomes when additional, more specific, aspects of parenting are considered; or may only be associated with certain types of prosocial behavior.

REACTIVE PARENTING

Reactive and proactive parenting behaviors differ meaningfully, and therefore it may be beneficial to consider them separately as they relate to prosocial behavior (Goodnow, 1997; Padilla-Walker & Thompson, 2005). More specifically, reactive parenting represents the way parents respond *after* or *in reaction to* a child's behavior and is most commonly conceptualized as parental discipline after transgression, but can also be parental responses after positive behavior. Thus, the current section will focus on reactive parenting that is associated with prosocial behavior, including parental discipline and control and parental praise and use of material rewards.

Parental Discipline and Control

Theory suggests that different parenting practices should be differentially related to children's prosocial behavior. More specifically, it is suggested that inductive parenting practices that focus on drawing the child's attention to the needs and feelings of others are associated with higher levels of prosocial behavior, while power assertive parenting is associated with lower levels of prosocial behavior (Hoffman, 2000). More specifically, inductive parenting tends to help the child focus on others, is guilt inducing, and encourages reparation; while power assertive parenting is often accompanied by negative emotions that lead to self-focus and result in the child attending to the way in which the parental message was delivered rather than on the message itself (Grusec & Goodnow, 1994; Hoffman, 2000).

Empirical research focusing on young to middle-aged children generally supports these theoretical tenets. More specifically, research suggests that authoritative discipline that includes inductive techniques (Janssens & Dekovic, 1997) and supportive, authoritative nonrestrictive parenting (Dekovic & Janssens, 1992) are positively associated with children's peer-nominated helpfulness and teacher-reported global prosocial behavior toward mixed targets. Parental induction was also positively associated with early adolescents' global prosocial behavior (combination of teacher-reported altruism, teacher-rated helpfulness, peer-nominated sharing and helping, and donating money) toward mixed targets (Krevans & Gibbs, 1996) and anonymous donating toward peers (Stewart & McBride-Chang, 2000). Although parental induction is often heralded as the most adaptive parenting practice, it has also been suggested that induction paired with power assertion (in the context of a positive parent-child relationship) may be effective, particularly for very young children's reparation attempts and altruistic behaviors (Zahn-Waxler, Radke-Yarrow, & King, 1979).

In contrast, a number of other studies suggest that power assertion and other forms of controlling parenting are not adaptive parenting practices in the promotion of prosocial behavior. Authoritarian or controlling parenting has been associated with lower levels of children's empathy and prosocial behavior toward peers (Hastings, Zahn-Waxler, Robinson, Usher, Bridges, 2000) and lower levels of peer-nominated helpfulness (Dekovic & Janssens, 1992). Although not directly assessing parenting practices, another study found that parents who valued compliance and obedience (as opposed to parents who valued prosocial behavior) had children with lower levels of prosocial behavior toward peers (Eisenberg, Wolchik, Goldberg, & Engel, 1992), suggesting that parental values and socialization goals are reflected in parenting practices (Grusec, Rudy, & Martini, 1997) and may therefore similarly impact children's behaviors.

While research is generally consistent in suggesting that power assertive and controlling parenting does not encourage children's prosocial behavior, it is even less likely to result in prosocial behavior from adolescents, as parental control is seen as less acceptable during the teen years compared with when children are younger (Barber, Stoltz, & Olsen, 2005). Research has found that power assertion is negatively associated with early adolescents' global prosocial behavior toward mixed targets (Krevans & Gibbs, 1996) and that parent-adolescent conflict is negatively associated with prosocial affection toward mothers (Eberly & Montemayor, 1999). However, it should be noted that the effectiveness of parenting practices during adolescence may be more complicated than during childhood because of adolescents' increased cognitive abilities and their understanding and perceptions of parental intent. Indeed, Grusec and Goodnow (1994) suggested that whether or not adolescents accept parental socialization messages and behave prosocially is associated not only with the discipline itself, but with the appropriateness of the specific parental discipline, or how well the parental response fits the child's misdeed. More specifically, parental use of yelling and punishment are perceived by adolescents as more appropriate in response to certain transgressions (e.g., moral transgressions) than others (e.g., conventional transgressions; Padilla-Walker & Carlo, 2004, 2006) and parental domain-appropriate discipline is positively (albeit indirectly) associated with global prosocial behavior toward unidentified targets (Hardy, Carlo, & Roesch, 2010; Padilla-Walker, 2007; Wyatt & Carlo, 2002). This body of research suggests that the impact of parental responses or discipline on adolescents' prosocial behavior is complex and includes the need to consider the context of parental discipline (e.g., is it in response to a child's positive or negative behavior?), the domain of the child's behavior, the child's perception of parental intent, and the child's own emotional response to the parental reaction (Padilla-Walker, 2008; Wyatt & Carlo, 2002).

Parental Praise and Material Rewards

While there is a substantial body of research examining parents' reactive responses to children's transgressions, there is a relatively smaller body of research that explores parents' responses to children's positive behaviors. This is surprising given that, especially for adolescents, research suggests that parental responses in positive contexts are strong predictors of adolescent behavior (Padilla-Walker & Carlo, 2006; Wyatt & Carlo, 2002). The two main parental responses that have been examined regarding prosocial behavior are parental praise and external or material rewards. In general, parental use of praise can be effective at improving internal motivation in children, especially when it focuses on autonomy and minimizes comparison (Henderlong & Lepper, 2002). In young children, maternal social approval and praise were associated with a combination of helping, sharing, and comforting prosocial behaviors in African American preschoolers (Garner, 2006). Furthermore, mothers' positive responses to their child's prosocial behavior resulted in high levels of gender specific prosocial behavior toward peers (Hastings, McShane, Parker, Ladha, 2007), but parental encouragement was not associated with increases in toddlers' helping toward strangers (Warneken & Tomasello, 2013), suggesting that the effectiveness of parental praise may differ as a function of the target of prosocial behavior. However, other studies have found that young children with the highest levels of prosocial behavior were those whose parents did not react to their spontaneous prosocial behavior (as opposed to parents who praised the behavior; Grusec, 1991), or that praise was only associated with helping in immediate situations (Fabes, Fultz, Eisenberg, May-Plumlee, & Christopher, 1989). In addition, children whose mothers felt positively about rewards were less likely to help in a nonreward situation and had lower mother-reported levels of prosocial behavior.

There have been relatively fewer studies examining parental praise during adolescence, but research suggests that parents praise their adolescent children more for actions that are seen as somewhat arbitrary (e.g., voluntarily clearing the table) than they do for moral or expected actions (e.g., telling the truth; Padilla-Walker & Carlo, 2006). In addition, one study found that parental praise during adolescence was positively associated with public prosocial behavior and negatively associated with altruistic prosocial behavior (Carlo et al., 2007), suggesting perhaps praise does more in promoting externally than internally motivated prosocial behavior. Taken together, these findings suggest a complicated association between praise and prosocial behavior in children, highlighting the need to consider developmental age, as well as how children and mothers perceive praise and how they use it in discipline situations (Fabes et al., 1989).

Research on the use of external or materials rewards as a means of rewarding prosocial behavior also has mixed findings, but generally suggests that parental use of external rewards is not effective. In young children, external reward was not associated with higher levels of prosocial behavior (Garner, 2006) and actually undermined toddlers' helping behavior toward strangers (Warneken &

Tomasello, 2008). Research on adolescents has found that allowance was not an effective motivator for helping family members or doing family chores (Klein, Graesch, & Izquierdo, 2009) and that parental use of material rewards was associated positively with public and emotional prosocial behavior but negatively with altruistic prosocial behavior (Carlo et al., 2007). Overall it seems that when children's behavior is already internally motivated, especially at young ages, the use of external reward, or overjustification (Warneken & Tomasello, 2008), may lead to extrinsic motivation and lower levels of helping. So although maternal praise and external rewards may result in desired behavior in the short term, long-term outcomes are not consistently favorable.

PROACTIVE PARENTING

In contrast to reactive parenting, proactive parenting is a parent's active attempts to socialize children *before* misbehavior (or positive behavior) occurs. In young children this may be as simple as a mother reminding her child to be kind to the other children at the park in the hopes of avoiding an altercation; or the somewhat more complicated approach that parents take to anticipating potentially conflicting values with which their adolescent child may come in contact in order to encourage family values and behavior. Proactive parenting may take the general form of parental monitoring attempts, parental teaching, and parent-child communication. Research has also highlighted proactive parenting efforts that focus on particular influences children may be exposed to, such as media (Nathanson, 1999; Padilla-Walker, Christensen, & Day, 2011) and peers (Mounts, 2002); and how parents manage these influences in an attempt to avoid any potentially negative impact on their children and to promote positive behavior. The effectiveness of proactive parenting is intuitive; for example, it is logical that talking with your teenager about the importance of kindness before they are engaging in bullying and relational aggression will be more effective than waiting until after they have been sent to the principal's office for fighting. Indeed, research suggests that proactive parenting may be particularly effective (as compared to reactive parenting) because these interactions generally are not as emotionally charged as are reactive interactions after transgression (Padilla-Walker & Thompson, 2005), thus the parental message may be more salient to children and adolescents during proactive socialization (Grusec & Goodnow, 1994). Therefore, the current section will focus on proactive parenting that is associated with prosocial behavior, including parental socialization of emotion, parental modeling and experiential learning, and parent-child communication and teaching.

Emotion Socialization

One way that parents may attempt to promote children's positive behavior is through the socialization of emotions. By helping children to label and understand their own emotions and those of others, parents often avoid negative interactions and promote positive interactions that may be motivated by emotional responses. This aspect of parental socialization seems most relevant for young children, and research suggests that parental socialization of emotions can take many forms, including using emotion language, teaching coping strategies, clarifying ambiguous emotional situations, modeling appropriate emotional responses, positively reinforcing children's appropriate emotions, or ignoring and/or punishing inappropriate emotions. In general, parental emotion socialization, especially nonpunitive socialization (Roberts, 1999), has been consistently associated with higher levels of social competence (positive peer relations, empathy, helping) among young children (Denham et al., 1997; Eisenberg, Cumberland, & Spinrad, 1998). More specifically, mothers' attempts to explain and label emotions were associated with children's attempts to understand and express concern for the emotions of others (Garner, 2003), and parental socialization of emotion- and problem-focused coping was associated with children's sympathy and comforting behavior (Eisenberg, Fabes, & Murphy, 1996; Eisenberg, Miller, Shell, McNalley, & Shea, 1991). In addition, the use of restriction during the display of inappropriate or hurtful displays of emotion was associated with children's sympathy, while the use of restriction during the display of nonhurtful emotional displays was associated with children's distress (Eisenberg et al., 1991). Further, mothers' encouragement of the expression of emotions was associated with children (especially boys) who displayed more comforting behavior (Eisenberg et al., 1996), while parental emphasis on emotional control (rather than the control of emotional expression) was associated with declines in friendly behavior (Roberts, 1999). The link between early emotion socialization and prosocial outcomes has also been found to have long-lasting positive effects, with mothers' positive emotion communication during childhood predicting adolescent girls' sympathy at age 15–16 (Eisenberg & McNally, 1993). Taken together, parents who help their children to understand and appropriately express emotions have children who are generally more socially competent and who display higher levels of prosocial behavior.

Experiential Learning

A diverse body of research has examined the role of experiential learning on children's prosocial behavior, with the assumption that parents who give children the opportunity to participate in helping behavior should promote future prosocial behavior. One way that research has examined parents' use of experiential learning is through the use of family chores or work. Indeed, parents encouraging children to participate in household work has long been thought to be an important precursor to more voluntary cooperative and helping behavior (Goodnow, 1988), although housework that is demanded or is seen as required merely in order to convenience parents may actually be detrimental to moral and prosocial development (Kohlberg, 1964). That being said, the six cultures study provides some of the most compelling evidence for the value of the experience of family chores in findings suggesting that those who were the most altruistic were also those who had the most frequent and meaningful helping roles within the family (e.g., caregiving, gathering firewood; Whiting & Whiting, 1975). More recent research on household chores as a training ground for future helping reveals a complex picture. Indeed, one study found that early adolescents who were expected to frequently be engaged in household work and helping were found to display higher levels of cooperative and compliant prosocial behavior (Baldwin, 2004). However, other research suggested that routine (as opposed to required) family-care housework (but not self-care housework) was associated with 12- to 14-year-old adolescents' mother-reported concern for family members, but was not associated with helpfulness toward a stranger (Grusec, Goodnow, & Cohen, 1996). Taken together these findings suggest that parents encouraging their children to do chores can be effective at promoting prosocial behavior but that it varies as a function of the parental approach to chores (e.g., encouraging vs. demanding) and the types of chores (family-care vs. self-care) and seems to be more consistently associated with helping behavior for older children. It should also be noted, however, that this is an area wherein culture seems to be particularly relevant, which is an important avenue for future research.

Another area where experiential learning has been found to be effective at promoting prosocial behavior is when parents encourage their children to be involved in volunteering, as having the opportunity to volunteer is an important predictor of volunteering behavior (Matsuba, Hart, & Atkins, 2007). Research suggests that encouraging teens to volunteer is associated positively with compliant and anonymous prosocial behaviors and with adolescent sympathy (Carlo et al., 2007) as well as with the extent of volunteering and one's intention to continue volunteering (McGinley, Lipperman-Kreda, Byrnes, & Carlo, 2010). Research also has found that volunteering during adolescence is associated with social responsibility (Cemalcilar, 2009) and continued volunteering during adulthood (Atkins, Hart, & Donnelly, 2005). These findings also highlight the potential importance of parents who participate in these behaviors with their children (i.e., parental modeling) rather than merely ordering or requiring their children to do so. There is not a large body of research on the impact of parental modeling as it relates to prosocial behavior, but research suggests that particularly in the case of consistent, extended, and high-cost prosocial behavior there is a link between children's helping and parents who also display high levels of prosocial behavior (e.g., legacy volunteering; Mustillo, Wilson, & Lynch 2004). One particularly salient example of this is the highly prosocial behaviors of the children of those individuals and families who sheltered Jews during World War II (Oliner & Oliner, 1988).

Taken together, these studies suggest that parents who structure informal or formal opportunities for their children to help may be promoting their children's prosocial behavior, although there are certainly many factors that complicate the nature of the relations between experiential learning and children's subsequent prosocial behavior. Generally it seems that parental use of experiential learning may be more effective in older children and adolescents, and that the manner in which parents approach the experience is important. Future examinations of family chores, parental encouragement of volunteering, and parental modeling should continue to consider a multidimensional perspective, as attention to type and target of prosocial behavior may greatly add to and potentially clarify current findings.

Prosocial Teaching

Another proactive strategy often used by parents to encourage prosocial behavior is prosocial teaching via parent-child discussion and conversation. This may occur in a variety of settings and has unfortunately received relatively little research attention, but is an important avenue for continued research. Indeed research with young children suggests that parents' discussion of prosocial behavior with their children is associated with observed giving toward peers and teacher-reported considerateness in young boys (Hastings et al., 2007). The same pattern holds true for adolescents, as suggested by one study that found parent-child conversations about moral issues were associated positively with dire, anonymous, and public prosocial behaviors and were associated indirectly with all types of prosocial behavior via adolescent sympathy (Carlo et al., 2007). Although parent-child conversations can be quite beneficial, especially when they are empathy-inducing and promote autonomy (McGrath, Wilson, & Frassetto, 1995), parents do run the risk of being perceived by children as preaching or lecturing, especially when teaching in prosocial (vs. antisocial) contexts (Padilla-Walker & Carlo, 2006). Indeed, research has found that parental preaching is not consistently related to children's prosocial behavior, donating in particular (Eisenberg et al., 2006), and is associated with negative emotions in adolescents, despite recognition that parents' intentions are to teach rather than control (Padilla-Walker & Carlo, 2006).

Another body of research that is relevant to parents' proactive attempts to discuss positive behavior with children in an attempt to promote future prosocial behavior is the literature on parental monitoring of media (Nathanson, 1999) and peers (Mounts, 2002). Indeed, one approach to parental monitoring that seems to be the most effective is referred to as prearming, or discussing potential negative influences and highlighting positive influences before the child's behavior is necessarily reflective. For example, parents might discuss the prosocial actions of a character on television or comment on the kind behaviors of a friend in an attempt to encourage that behavior to their child. Prearming has been found to be the most effective form of proactive monitoring (Padilla-Walker et al., 2011) and has been associated with lower levels of aggression (Nathanson, 1999), lower levels of drug use and delinquency (Mounts, 2002, 2004), more responsible media use (Padilla-Walker, Coyne, Fraser, Dyer, & Yorgason, 2012), and higher levels of friendship quality (Mounts, 2004). Relatively fewer studies have examined the role of parental prearming on prosocial outcomes, but those that have suggest a link between prearming and prosocial behavior in children (Horton & Santogrossi,

1978) and a recent study found higher value-congruent behavior between prosocial values and prosocial behaviors for parents who used prearming as opposed to other proactive strategies (Padilla-Walker, Fraser, & Harper, 2012). Clearly future research is warranted in this area.

Taken together, research suggests that parental teaching can be an effective way to promote prosocial behavior in children and adolescents, although additional research is needed. As with many other areas of parenting, the link between parental teaching and children's prosocial behavior is complex, may differ for children versus adolescents, and is most effective when it promotes autonomy and empathy. Future research should continue to examine how parents promote prosocial behavior by having conversations with children and adolescents in different contexts, such as with media or friends.

COMPLEXITIES TO CONSIDER

Indirect Effects of Parenting

It is important to note that parenting is not always directly associated with children's prosocial behavior, especially as children get older and their own characteristics are often a better predictor of their behavior than is current parenting. This is not to say that parents no longer matter, as it could be argued that it is a desirable outcome of appropriate socialization for children's behavior to become more self-generated and self-regulated than it might have been at earlier ages (Deci & Ryan, 1991; Grusec & Goodnow, 1994). Although studies often examine direct effects of parenting on children's behaviors, indirect effects are also important to examine in an attempt to more clearly understand the mechanisms through which parents continue to be a positive (or negative) influence on their children's prosocial development over time.

One of the most consistent predictors of prosocial behavior is a child's level of moral emotion, with particular emphasis placed on sympathy, or an other-oriented emotional response of sorrow or concern for the situation of another (Carlo et al., 2012; Eisenberg et al., 2006; Hoffman, 2000). In addition, a growing body of research supports the role of sympathy as a mediator between parenting and prosocial behavior, as moral emotion may be a motivating factor for children when parental directives are not enough to directly influence action. Research on young children has found sympathy to mediate the relations between parenting and children's prosocial behavior (e.g., Zhou et al., 2002), but these patterns have more often been examined during adolescence. For example, sympathy has been found to mediate the relation between parental discipline and adolescents' global prosocial behavior (Krevans & Gibbs, 1996), as well as the relation between positive parenting (warmth and involvement) and adolescents' prosocial behavior toward strangers and friends (Padilla-Walker & Christensen, 2011). Sympathy has also been found to mediate the relation between parental encouragement to volunteer and adolescents' volunteerism (McKinley et al., 2010).

Research has also highlighted the importance of effortful control or self-regulation as a predictor of early conscience development (Kochanska & Aksan, 2006) and prosocial behavior (Carlo et al., 2012; Eisenberg et al., 2006). It is assumed that one's ability to control impulses may be necessary in order to engage in prosocial behavior toward others, especially if the behavior is at a personal cost to the self. Given that parenting is a salient predictor of self-regulation, research has examined whether self-regulation is an important mediator between parenting and prosocial behavior. Studies have found that effortful control mediates the relation between parental warmth and negative behaviors in children (Eisenberg et al., 2005; see also Valiente et al., 2004), and between positive parenting and adolescents' prosocial behavior toward strangers, friends, and family (Padilla-Walker & Christensen, 2011; Padilla-Walker, Harper, & Jensen, 2010).

Finally, cognitions are commonly highlighted in the literature as important mechanisms through which parenting impacts prosocial behavior, with particular emphasis placed on the role of moral reasoning (Stewart & McBride-Chang, 2000), prosocial moral reasoning (Carlo, Knight, McGinley, & Hayes, 2011; Janssens & Dekovic, 1997), and perspective taking (Eisenberg et al., 2006). In addition, adolescents' personal prosocial values (Hardy et al., 2010; Padilla-Walker & Carlo, 2007), accurate perception and acceptance of parental values (Padilla-Walker, 2007), and internal regulation of values (Barry et al., 2008) have been consistently linked to prosocial behavior. One's own personal values are often associated with value-congruent behavior (Bardi & Shwartz, 2003), and a growing body of research suggests that parenting may help to facilitate these relations (Padilla-Walker, Fraser, et al., 2012).

Moderating Variables

In addition to the importance of considering indirect and mediated effects, research has suggested that parenting may not directly impact children's prosocial behavior, but may be more salient in the presence of certain moderators. One possible pattern is that raised by Darling and Steinberg (1993) suggesting that one, more global, form of parenting style may serve as a moderator for another, more specific, form of parenting practice; which may explain the somewhat inconsistent research on parenting styles as they relate to children's positive outcomes (Grusec & Goodnow, 1994). For example, research on young children suggests that attachment security moderates the relation between parenting and early conscience development (e.g., Kochanska, Aksan, Knaack, & Rhines 2004). Additionally, research has highlighted that certain aspects of parenting may be more salient for children with some temperamental profiles than others. For example, Hastings and colleagues found that protective parenting was a stronger predictor of concern toward mother for children (especially girls) who were highly inhibited (Hastings, Rubin, & DeRose, 2005) and that the association between parenting and children's emotion socialization was stronger for children with lower self-regulatory capacities (Hastings & De, 2008). In addition, research has found that early conscience development is promoted by gentle discipline for fearful children but by attachment security for fearless children (Fowles & Kochanska, 2000). Similar results have been found during adolescence, suggesting that maternal attachment is more important in promoting prosocial behavior for children (especially boys) who are relatively fearless than for those who are fearful (Padilla-Walker & Nelson, 2010). Research on adolescents has also examined aspects of temperament such as positive emotionality (Wills, Yeshiva, Sandy, Yaeger, & Shinar, 2001), anger and sociability (Carlo et al., 1998), and negative affectivity (Stice & Gonzales, 1998), although few of these studies examine prosocial outcomes. However, Carlo et al. (1998) found that adolescent sympathy was high when fathers' support was high, but adolescents' sociability and anger were low.

Taken together, this section highlights the complexities of relations between parenting and prosocial outcomes. First, there is an important body of research exploring the mechanisms through which parenting influences prosocial development, including moral emotions, self-regulation, and cognitions; with personal prosocial values being one of the most consistent mediators examined during adolescence. Numerous additional mediators have been examined as they relate to children's and adolescents' negative behavioral outcomes (e.g., persistence, hope, gratitude, perspective taking, personal distress), so further research should continue to explore the varied ways in which parenting influences prosocial development indirectly. In addition, research suggests that common moderators of parenting and prosocial behavior may include broad aspects of parenting (e.g., attachment, parenting style), child temperament, and child gender; and multiplicative associations with other child characteristics should continue to be explored. This research reveals complicated patterns between parenting and prosocial behavior that may help to explain sometimes weak and inconsistent relations and may suggest utility in continued research examining both mediators and moderators.

Future Directions

In the course of writing this chapter, a number of points became clear that provide fruitful avenues for future research, especially as they relate to the purpose of the current volume. First, the existing parenting literature is highly varied and somewhat difficult to organize meaningfully due to a general lack of consistency in measurement and conceptualization across studies, especially across childhood and adolescence. While some degree of this is to be expected, future research should consider theoretical justifications for measuring particular parenting dimensions so that an overall picture of parenting can be clearly delineated across studies and across time. While no one of the reconceptualizations of parenting mentioned at the beginning of this chapter is all encompassing enough to fully capture the diversity and complexity of parent-child interactions, each one provides important starting points for scholars who seek to meaningfully add to our understanding of how parenting influences children's prosocial development (Darling & Steinberg, 1993; Grusec & Davidov, 2010; Grusec & Goodnow, 1994).

Second and related to the above, future research should more carefully consider the type and target of prosocial behavior, as many studies did not differentiate by target and combined diverse types of prosocial behavior. Indeed, originally we had hoped to organize this chapter by the type of prosocial behavior in an attempt to highlight the multidimensionality of this outcome, but there were not enough studies that measured prosocial behavior similarly, or even comparably, to do so. It will be a valuable endeavor for future research to determine whether certain aspects of parenting are more or less likely to promote particular types of prosocial behavior than others and how this might change with the developmental age of the child, which will require the use of longitudinal study designs.

Third, future research should address parenting as it relates to prosocial behavior in different ethnic groups (see Carlo & Knight, chapter 12, this volume), in diverse cultures (see de Guzman, Do, & Kok, chapter 11, this volume), and among those of varying socioeconomic status. It is possible that different types of parenting promote different types of prosocial behavior or prosocial behavior toward different targets as a function of ethnicity or culture. Indeed, research suggests that children and adolescents from different ethnicities and cultures perceive parenting differently (Jackson-Newsome, Buchanan, & McDonald, 2008; Sorkhabi & Mandara, 2013), and while there may be consistencies between parenting and prosocial behavior regardless of culture, differences in the *meaning* of both parenting and prosocial behavior are as important to consider across diverse groups as are the relations between the two. It could be that parents from different cultures are using similar parenting styles or practices to communicate very different things to their children, which requires a much more detailed and nuanced approach to the study of parenting.

Fourth, future research should examine the role of the child in the socialization of prosocial behavior by examining interactions between biology and parenting as they relate to prosocial development; as well as bidirectional relations between the child's prosocial behavior and parenting. A growing body of research on genetics (see Fortuna & Knafo, chapter 4, this volume) and physiology (see Hastings & Miller, chapter 6, this volume) as they relate to prosocial development suggest a complicated process that includes multiplicative relations between biological factors and socialization influences (Knafo & Plomin, 2006). This is an area of research that is just developing and that is rich with ideas for future research. In addition, recent research suggests bidirectional relations between parenting and adolescents' prosocial behavior toward family (Padilla-Walker, Carlo, et al., 2012), with the most consistent longitudinal relations found between adolescents' prosocial behavior and later positive parenting. This suggests that although prosocial behavior may become relatively stable by adolescence, it does not cease to impact the quality of relationships, highlighting bidirectional relations that should continue to be examined longitudinally.

Finally, research should examine both fathering and mothering as they relate to different types and targets of prosocial behavior. While research examining limited types of prosocial behavior has found that mothers contribute more consistently to the development of prosocial behavior for both children (Hastings et al., 2007) and adolescents (Day & Padilla-Walker, 2009) than do fathers, it is possible that fathers' contributions to prosocial behavior are not as straightforward as mothers'. For example, research has found that mothers may be more salient in promoting sympathy in their children, while fathers are more salient in promoting self-regulation (Padilla-Walker & Christensen, 2011; Padilla-Walker, Day, Dyer, & Black, 2013), which may suggest that the mechanisms through which mothers and fathers influence children's prosocial development are different. In addition, mothers and fathers may promote different types of prosocial behavior, with mothers promoting compassion and cooperation and fathers promoting helpfulness (Eisenberg et al., 2006), which may vary based on gender stereotypes of helpfulness that are established in the home (Antill, Goodnow, Russell, & Cotton, 1996). While these are just a few potential ideas, clearly examining how fathers and mothers might be differentially important for prosocial development is a fruitful avenue for future research.

References

Antill, J. K., Goodnow, J. J., Russell, G., & Cotton, S. (1996). The influence of parents and family context on children's involvement in household tasks. *Sex Roles, 34*(3–4), 215–236.

Atkins, R., Hart, D., & Donnelly, T. M. (2005). The association of childhood personality type with volunteering during adolescence. *Merrill-Palmer Quarterly 51*(2), 145–162.

Baldwin, E. L. (2004). *The relationship of children's household work to measures of children's prosocial behaviors and positive self-perceptions.* Doctoral dissertation. College Park, Maryland: University of Maryland.

Barber, B. K., Stolz, H. E., & Olsen, J. A. (2005). Parental support, psychological control, and behavioral control: Assessing relevance across time, culture, and method. *Monographs of the Society for Research in Child Development, 70*, Serial No. 282.

Bardi, A., & Schwartz, S. H. (2003). Values and behavior: Strength and structure of relations. *Personality and Social Psychology Bulletin, 29*(10), 1207–1220.

Barry, C. M., Padilla-Walker, L., Madsen, S. D., & Nelson, L. J. (2008). The impact of maternal relationship quality on emerging adults' prosocial tendencies: Indirect effects via regulation of prosocial values. *Journal of Youth and Adolescence, 37*(5), 581–591.

Baumrind, D. (2012). Differentiating between confrontive and coercive kinds of parental power-assertive disciplinary practices. *Human Development, 55*, 35–51

Carlo, G., Crockett, L. J., Wolff, J. M., & Beal, S. J. (2012). The role of emotional reactivity, self-regulation, and puberty in adolescents' prosocial behaviors. *Social Development, 21*(4), 667–685.

Carlo, G., Knight, G. P., McGinley, M., & Hayes, R. (2011). The roles of parental inductions, moral emotions, and moral cognitions in prosocial tendencies among Mexican American and European American early adolescents. *Journal of Early Adolescence, 31*(6), 757–781.

Carlo, G., McGinley, M., Hayes, R., Batenhorst, C., & Wilkinson, J. (2007). Parenting styles or practices? Parenting, sympathy, and prosocial behaviors among adolescents. *Journal of Genetic Psychology*, 168(2), 147–176.

Carlo, G., McGinley, M., Hayes, R. C., & Martinez, M. M. (2012). Empathy as a mediator of the relations between parent and peer attachment and prosocial and physically aggressive behaviors in Mexican American college students. *Journal of Social and Personal Relationships*, 29(3), 337–357.

Carlo, G., Mestre, M., McGinley, M. M., Samper, P., Tur, A., & Sandman, D. (2012). The interplay of emotional instability, empathy, and coping on prosocial and aggressive behaviors. *Personality and Individual Differences*, 53(5), 675–680.

Carlo, G., Roesch, S. C., & Melby, J. (1998). The multiplicative relations of parenting and temperament to prosocial and antisocial behaviors in adolescence. *Journal of Early Adolescence*, 18(3), 266–290.

Cemalcilar, Z. (2009). Understanding individual characteristics of adolescents who volunteer. *Personality and Individual Differences*, 46(4), 432–436.

Collins, W. A. (1990). Parent-child relationships in the transition to adolescence: Continuity and change in interaction, affect, and cognition. In R. Montemayor, G. R. Adams, & T. G. Gullota (Eds.), *From childhood to adolescence: A transitional period?* (pp. 85–106). Newbury Park, CA: Sage.

Darling, N., & Steinberg, L. (1993). Parenting style as context: An integrative model. *Psychological Bulletin*, 113, 487–487.

Davidov, M., & Grusec, J. E. (2006). Untangling the links of parental responsiveness to distress and warmth to child outcomes. *Child Development*, 77, 44–58.

Day, R. D., & Padilla-Walker, L. M. (2009). Mother and father connectedness and involvement during early adolescence. *Journal of Family Psychology*, 23(6), 900–904.

Deci, E. L., & Ryan, R. M. (1991). A motivational approach to self: Integration in personality. In R. A. Dienstbier (Ed.), *Nebraska Symposium on Motivation, 1990: Perspectives on motivation* (pp. 237–288). Lincoln: University of Nebraska Press.

Dekovic, M., & Janssens, J. M. (1992). Parents' child-rearing style and child's sociometric status. *Developmental Psychology*, 28, 925–932.

Denham, S. A., Mitchell-Copeland, J., Strandberg, K., Auerbach, S., & Blair, K. (1997). Parental contributions to preschoolers' emotional competence: Direct and indirect effects. *Motivation and Emotion*, 21(1), 65–86.

Eberly, M. B., & Montemayor, R. (1998). Doing good deeds: An examination of adolescent prosocial behavior in the context of parent-adolescent relationships. *Journal of Adolescent Research*, 13(4), 403–432.

Eberly, M. B., & Montemayor, R. (1999). Adolescent affection and helpfulness toward parents: A 2-year follow-up. *Journal of Early Adolescence*, 19(2), 226–248.

Eisenberg, N., Cumberland, A., & Spinrad, T. L. (1998). Parental socialization of emotion. *Psychological Inquiry*, 9(4), 241–273.

Eisenberg, N., Fabes, R. A., & Murphy, B. C. (1996). Parents' reactions to children's negative emotions: Relations to children's social competence and comforting behavior. *Child Development*, 67, 2227–2247.

Eisenberg, N., Fabes, R., & Spinrad, T. L. (2006). Prosocial development. In N. Eisenberg, W. Damon, & R. M. Lerner (Eds.), *Handbook of child psychology: Vol. 3, Social, emotional, and personality development* (6th ed., pp. 646–718). Hoboken, NJ: Wiley.

Eisenberg, N., & McNally, S. (1993). Socialization and mothers' and adolescents' empathy-related characteristics. *Journal of Research on Adolescence, 3*(2), 171–191.

Eisenberg, N., Miller, P. A., Shell, R., McNalley, S., & Shea, C. (1991). Prosocial development in adolescence: A longitudinal study. *Developmental Psychology, 27*(5), 849.

Eisenberg, N., & Valiente, C. (2002). Parenting and children's prosocial and moral development. In M. H. Bornstein (Ed.), *Handbook of parenting: Vol. 5. Practical issues in parenting* (2nd ed., pp. 111–142). Mahwah, NJ: Erlbaum.

Eisenberg, N., Wolchik, S. A., Goldberg, L., & Engel, I. (1992). Parental values, reinforcement, and young children's prosocial behavior: A longitudinal study. *Journal of Genetic Psychology, 153*(1), 19–36.

Eisenberg, N., Zhou, Q., Spinrad, T. L., Valiente, C., Fabes, R. A., & Liew, J. (2005). Relations among positive parenting, children's effortful control, and externalizing problems: A three-wave longitudinal study. *Child Development, 76*(5), 1055–1071.

Fabes, R. A., Fultz, J., Eisenberg, N., May-Plumlee, T., & Christopher, F. (1989). Effects of rewards on children's prosocial motivation: A socialization study. *Developmental Psychology, 25*(4), 509–515.

Fletcher, A. C., Elder, G. H., & Mekos, D. (2000). Parental influences on adolescent involvement in community activities. *Journal of Research on Adolescence, 10*(1), 29–48.

Fowles, D. C., & Kochanska, G. (2000). Temperament as a moderator of pathways to conscience in children: The contribution of electrodermal activity. *Psychophysiology, 37*(6), 788–795.

Garner, P. W. (2003). Child and family correlates of toddlers' emotional and behavioral responses to a mishap. *Infant Mental Health Journal, 24*(6), 580–596.

Garner, P. W. (2006). Prediction of prosocial and emotional competence from maternal behavior in African American preschoolers. *Cultural Diversity and Ethnic Minority Psychology, 12*(2), 179–198.

Goodnow, J. J. (1988). Children's household work: Its nature and functions. *Psychological Bulletin, 103*(1), 5–26.

Goodnow, J. J. (1997). Parenting and the transmission and internalization of values: From social-cultural perspectives to within-family analyses. In J. E. Grusec & L. Kuczynski (Eds.), *Parenting and children's internalization of values: A handbook of contemporary theory* (pp. 333–361). New York: Wiley.

Grusec, J. E. (1991). Socializing concern for others in the home. *Developmental Psychology, 27*(2), 338–342.

Grusec, J. E. (2006). The development of moral behavior and conscience from a socialization perspective. In M. Killen & J. Smetana (Eds.), *Handbook of moral development* (pp. 243–266). Mahwah, NJ: Erlbaum.

Grusec, J. E., & Davidov, M. (2010). Integrating different perspectives on socialization theory and research: A domain-specific approach. *Child Development, 81*, 687–709.

Grusec, J. E., & Goodnow, J. J. (1994). Impact of parental discipline methods on the child's internalization of values: A reconceptualization of current points of view. *Developmental Psychology, 30*(1), 4.

Grusec, J. E., Goodnow, J. J., & Cohen, L. (1996). Household work and the development of concern for others. *Developmental Psychology, 32*(6), 999–1007.

Grusec, J. E., Goodnow, J. J., & Kuczynski, L. (2000). New directions in analyses of parenting contributions to children's acquisition of values. *Child Development, 71*(1), 205–211.

Grusec, J. E., Rudy, D., & Martini, T. (1997). Parenting cognitions and child outcomes: An overview and implications for children's internalization of values. In J. E. Grusec & L. E. Kuczynski (Eds.), *Parenting and children's internalization of values: A handbook of contemporary theory* (pp. 259–282). New York: Wiley.

Hardy, S. A., Carlo, G., & Roesch, S. C. (2010). Links between adolescents' expected parental reactions and prosocial behavioral tendencies: The mediating role of prosocial values. *Journal of Youth and Adolescence, 39*(1), 84–95.

Hastings, P. D., & De, I. (2008). Parasympathetic regulation and parental socialization of emotion: Biopsychosocial processes of adjustment in preschoolers. *Social Development, 17*(2), 211–238.

Hastings, P. D., McShane, K. E., Parker, R., & Ladha, F. (2007). Ready to make nice: Parental socialization of young sons' and daughters' prosocial behaviors with peers. *Journal of Genetic Psychology, 168*(2), 177–200.

Hastings, P. D., Rubin, K. H., & DeRose, L. (2005). Links among gender, inhibition, and parental socialization in the development of prosocial behavior. *Merrill-Palmer Quarterly, 51,* 501–527

Hastings, P. D., Utendale, W. T., & Sullivan, C. (2007). The socialization of prosocial development. In J. E. Grusec & P. D. Hastings (Eds.), *Handbook of socialization* (pp. 638–664). New York: Guilford Press.

Hastings, P. D., Zahn-Waxler, C., Robinson, J., Usher, B., & Bridges, D. (2000). The development of concern for others in children with behavior problems. *Developmental Psychology, 36,* 531–546.

Henderlong, J., & Lepper, M. R. (2002). The effects of praise on children's intrinsic motivation: a review and synthesis. *Psychological Bulletin, 128*(5), 774.

Hoffman, M. L. (2000). *Empathy and moral development: Implications for caring and justice.* Cambridge, UK, and New York: Cambridge University Press.

Horton, R.W., & Santogrossi, D.A. (1978). The effect of adult presence on reducing the influence of televised violence. *Personality and Social Psychology Bulletin, 4,* 337–340.

Iannotti, R. J., Cummings, E. M., Pierrehumbert, B., Milano, M. J., & Zahn-Waxler, C. (1992). Parental influences on prosocial behavior and empathy in early childhood. In J. Janssens & J. Gerris (Eds.), *Child rearing: Influences on prosocial and moral development* (pp. 77–100). Amsterdam: Swets & Zeitlinger.

Jackson-Newsom, J., Buchanan, C. M., & McDonald, R. M. (2008). Parenting and perceived maternal warmth in European American and African American adolescents. *Journal of Marriage and Family, 70*(1), 62–75.

Janssens, J. M., & Dekovic, M. (1997). Child rearing, prosocial moral reasoning, and prosocial behaviour. *International Journal of Behavioral Development, 20*(3), 509–527.

Kestenbaum, R., Farber, E. A., & Sroufe, L.A. (1989). Individual differences in empathy among preschoolers: Relation to attachment history. In N. Eisenberg (Ed.), *New directions for child development: Vol. 44. Empathy and related emotional responses* (pp. 51–64). San Francisco: Jossey-Bass.

Klein, W., Graesch, A. P., & Izquierdo, C. (2009). Children and chores: A mixed-methods study of children's household work in Los Angeles families. *Anthropology of Work Review, 30*(3), 98–109.

Knafo, A., & Plomin, R. (2006). Parental discipline and affection and children's prosocial behavior: Genetic and environmental links. *Journal of Personality and Social Psychology, 90*(1), 147.

Kochanska, G., & Aksan, N. (2006). Children's conscience and self-regulation. *Journal of Personality*, 74(6), 1587–1617.

Kochanska, G., Aksan, N., Knaack, A., & Rhines, H. M. (2004). Maternal parenting and children's conscience: Early security as moderator. *Child Development*, 75(4), 1229–1242.

Kochanska, G., & Murray, K. T. (2000). Mother–child mutually responsive orientation and conscience development: From toddler to early school age. *Child Development*, 71(2), 417–431.

Kohlberg, L. (1964). Development of moral character and moral ideology. *Review of Child Development Research*, 1, 381–431.

Krevans, J., & Gibbs, J. C. (1996). Parents' use of inductive discipline: Relations to children's empathy and prosocial behavior. *Child Development*, 67(6), 3263–3277.

Laible, D., Carlo, G., Torquati, J., & Ontai, L. (2004). Children's perceptions of family relationships as assessed in a doll story completion task: Links to parenting, social competence, and externalizing behavior. *Social Development*, 13(4), 551–569.

Liu, M., Chen, X., Zheng, S., Chen, H., & Wang, L. (2009). Maternal autonomy- and connectedness-oriented parenting behaviors as predictors of children's social behaviors in China. *Social Development*, 18(3), 671–689.

Matsuba, M. K., Hart, D., & Atkins, R. (2007). Psychological and social-structural influences on commitment to volunteering. *Journal of Research in Personality*, 41(4), 889–907.

McGinley, M., Lipperman-Kreda, S., Byrnes, H. F., & Carlo, G. (2010). Parental, social and dispositional pathways to Israeli adolescents' volunteering. *Journal of Applied Developmental Psychology*, 31(5), 386–394.

McGrath, M. P., Wilson, S. R., & Frassetto, S. J. (1995). Why some forms of inductive reasoning are better than others: Effects of cognitive focus, choice, and affect on children's prosocial behavior. *Merrill-Palmer Quarterly*, 41, 347–360.

Mounts, N. S. (2002). Parental management of adolescent peer relationships in context: The role of parenting style. *Journal of Family Psychology*, 16, 58–69.

Mounts, N. S. (2004). Adolescents' perceptions of parental management of peer relationships in an ethnically diverse sample. *Journal of Adolescent Research*, 19(4), 446–467.

Mustillo, S., Wilson, J., & Lynch, S. (2004). "Legacy volunteering": A test of two theories of intergenerational transmission. *Journal of Marriage and Family* 66:530–41.

Nathanson, A. I. (1999). Identifying and explaining the relationship between parental mediation and children's aggression. *Communication Research*, 26(2), 124–143.

Nelson, L. J., Padilla-Walker, L. M., Christensen, K. J., & Evans, C. A., Carroll, J. A. (2011). Parenting in emerging adulthood: An examination of parenting clusters and correlates. *Journal of Youth and Adolescence*, 40, 730–743.

Newcomb, A. F., Bukowski, W. M., & Pattee, L. (1993). Children's peer relations: A meta-analytic review of popular, rejected, neglected, controversial, and average sociometric status. *Psychological Bulletin*, 113, 99–128.

Nickerson, A. B., Mele, D., & Princiotta, D. (2008). Attachment and empathy as predictors of roles as defenders or outsiders in bullying interactions. *Journal of School Psychology*, 46(6), 687–703.

Oliner, S. P., & Oliner, P. M. (1988). *The altruistic personality: Rescuers of Jews in Nazi Europe*. New York: Free Press.

Padilla-Walker, L. M. (2007). Characteristics of mother-child interactions related to adolescents' positive values and behaviors. *Journal of Marriage and Family*, 69(3), 675–686.

Padilla-Walker, L. M. (2008). "My mom makes me so angry!" Adolescent perceptions of mother-child interactions as determinants of adolescent emotions. *Social Development*, *17*, 306–325.

Padilla-Walker, L. M., & Carlo, G. (2004). "It's not fair!": Adolescents' constructions of appropriateness of parental reactions. *Journal of Youth and Adolescence*, *33*(5), 389–401.

Padilla-Walker, L. M., & Carlo, G. (2006). Adolescent perceptions of appropriate parental reactions in moral and conventional social domains. *Social Development*, *15*(3), 480–500.

Padilla-Walker, L. M., & Carlo, G. (2007). Personal values as a mediator between parent and peer expectations and adolescent behaviors. *Journal of Family Psychology*, *21*, 538–541.

Padilla-Walker, L. M., Carlo, G., Christensen, K. J., & Yorgason, J. B. (2012). Bidirectional relations between authoritative parenting and adolescents' prosocial behaviors. *Journal of Research on Adolescence*, *22*(3), 400–408.

Padilla-Walker, L. M., & Christensen, K. J. (2011). Empathy and self-regulation as mediators between parenting and adolescents' prosocial behavior toward strangers, friends, and family. *Journal of Research on Adolescence*, *21*(3), 545–551.

Padilla-Walker, L. M., Christensen, K. J., & Day, R. D. (2011). Proactive parenting practices during early adolescence: A cluster approach. *Journal of Adolescence*, *34*, 203–214.

Padilla-Walker, L. M., Coyne, S. M., Fraser, A. M., Dyer, W. J., & Yorgason, J. B. (2012). Parents and adolescents growing up in the digital age: Latent growth curve analysis of proactive media monitoring. *Journal of Adolescence*, *35*, 1153–1165.

Padilla-Walker, L. M., Day, R. D., Dyer, W. J., & Black, B. C. (2013). "Keep on keeping on, even when it's hard!": Predictors and outcomes of adolescent persistence. *Journal of Early Adolescence*, *33*(4), 433–457.

Padilla-Walker, L. M., Fraser, A. M., & Harper, J. M. (2012). Walking the walk: The moderating role of proactive parenting on adolescents' value-congruent behaviors. *Journal of Adolescence*, *35*(5), 1141–1152.

Padilla-Walker, L. M., Harper, J. M., & Jensen, A. C. (2010). Self-regulation as a mediator between sibling relationship quality and early adolescents' positive and negative outcomes. *Journal of Family Psychology*, *24*(4), 419–428.

Padilla-Walker, L. M., & Nelson, L. J. (2010). Parenting and adolescents' values and behaviour: The moderating role of temperament. *Journal of Moral Education*, *39*(4), 491–509.

Padilla-Walker, L. M., & Thompson, R. A. (2005). Combating conflicting messages of values: A closer look at parental strategies. *Social Development*, *14*(2), 305–323.

Roberts, W. L. (1999). The socialization of emotional expression: Relations with prosocial behaviour and competence in five samples. *Canadian Journal of Behavioural Science*, *31*, 72–85.

Seligman, M. E. P., & Csikszentmihalyi, M. (2000). Positive psychology: An introduction. *American Psychologist*, *55*, 5–14.

Sorkhabi, N., & Mandara, J. (2013). Are the effects of Baumrind's parenting styles culturally specific or culturally equivalent? In R. E. Larzelere, A. Morris, A. W. Harrist (Eds.), *Authoritative parenting: Synthesizing nurturance and discipline for optimal child development* (pp. 113–135). Washington, DC: American Psychological Association.

Staub, E. (1995). The roots of prosocial and antisocial behavior in persons and groups: Environmental influence, personality, culture, and socialization. In W. M. Kurtines & J. L. Gewirtz (Eds.), *Moral development: An introduction* (pp. 431–453). Needham Heights, MA: Allyn & Bacon.

Stewart, S. M., & McBride-Chang, C. (2000). Influences on children's sharing in a multicultural setting. *Journal of Cross-Cultural Psychology, 31*(3), 333–348.

Stice, E., & Gonzales, N. (1998). Adolescent temperament moderates the relation of parenting to antisocial behavior and substance use. *Journal of Adolescent Research, 13*(1), 5–31.

Valiente, C., Eisenberg, N., Fabes, R. A., Shepard, S. A., Cumberland, A., & Losoya, S. H. (2004). Prediction of children's empathy-related responding from their effortful control and parents' expressivity. *Developmental Psychology, 40*(6), 911–926.

Vygotsky, L. S. (1978). *Mind in society: The development of higher psychological processes.* Cambridge, MA: Harvard University Press.

Warneken, F., & Tomasello, M. (2008). Extrinsic rewards undermine altruistic tendencies in 20-month-olds. *Developmental Psychology, 44*(6), 1785.

Warneken, F., & Tomasello, M. (2013). Parental presence and encouragement do not influence helping in young children. *Infancy, 18*, 345–368.

Whiting, B. B., & Whiting, J. W. M. (1975). *Children of six cultures: A psycho-cultural analysis.* Cambridge, MA: Harvard University Press.

Wills, T. A., Yeshiva, U., Sandy, J. M., Yaeger, A., & Shinar, O. (2001). Family risk factors and adolescent substance use: Moderation effects for temperament dimensions. *Developmental Psychology, 37*(3), 283–297.

Wyatt, J. M., & Carlo, G. (2002). What will my parents think? Relations among adolescents' expected parental reactions, prosocial moral reasoning, and prosocial and antisocial behaviors. *Journal of Adolescent Research, 17*(6), 646–666.

Yağmurlu, B., & Sanson, A. (2009). Parenting and temperament as predictors of prosocial behaviour in Australian and Turkish Australian children. *Australian Journal of Psychology, 61*, 77–88.

Zahn-Waxler, C., Radke-Yarrow, M., & King, R. A. (1979). Child rearing and children's prosocial initiations toward victims of distress. *Child Development, 50*, 319–330.

Zhou, Q., Eisenberg, N., Losoya, S. H., Fabes, R. A., Reiser, M., Guthrie, I. K., …Shepard, S. A. (2002). The relations of parental warmth and positive expressiveness to children's empathy-related responding and social functioning: A longitudinal study. *Child Development, 73*(3), 893–915.

{ 8 }

Sweetness on the Screen

A MULTIDIMENSIONAL VIEW OF PROSOCIAL BEHAVIOR IN MEDIA

Sarah M. Coyne and Nathan J. Smith

In *Curious George* (episode: "Sock Monkey Opera"), George's friend Betsy gets the chicken pox and is unable to attend her favorite opera, *Hansel and Gretel*. George attends the opera and enjoys the music, the actors, and the sets. However, he feels sad for Betsy. Upon coming home, George tries to think of something that he can do to cheer Betsy up. He decides to recreate the opera for Betsy and creates sock puppets of each character and an elaborate set that he can work himself. Later that day, George goes to Betsy's house, plays a CD of the opera, and performs his own version of *Hansel and Gretel* for his friend. Betsy is thrilled and exclaims that George's production was even better than the real thing.

This is one of many examples of prosocial behavior in the media where an individual voluntarily helps out another person or group of individuals. Such behavior is found in media aimed at children, adolescents, and adults. However, to date, there is little research focusing on portrayals and effects of viewing prosocial behavior in the media. Comparatively, there are dozens of content analyses (e.g., Bleakley, Jamieson, & Romer, 2012; Bridges et al., 2010; Coyne & Archer, 2004; National Television Violence Study, 1996, 1997, 1998) and over 1,000 studies conducted on violence in the media (Strasburger, 2009). Much of the research on prosocial behavior is limited in scope and is rather outdated. This chapter will review the research that has been conducted on prosocial behavior and will address avenues for future research. First, we will highlight the few content analyses that have been conducted on prosocial behavior in the media and will show that such behavior can be examined in a multidimensional fashion. We will then review prominent media theories, focusing both on media effects and on uses and gratifications. Next, we will examine the research on the effects of viewing prosocial media and will focus on television/movies, video games, and music. This section will examine these effects from a developmental perspective, focusing on

• children, adolescents, emerging adults, and adults. Finally, we will conclude with some suggestions for future research.

Content Analyses of Prosocial Behavior in the Media

Analyses examining the extent of prosocial content in modern media are rare. However, a few studies have examined the frequency and portrayal of prosocial behavior in television. Unfortunately, no recent research has examined the rate of prosocial content in video games or music, leaving plenty of room for future research to examine the incidence of prosocial media in those genres. This section will review the four content analyses that have been conducted on this topic and will end with a recent study showing how prosocial behavior can be examined from a multidimensional perspective in the media.

The first content analysis involving prosocial behavior in television considered a fairly broad notion of what constitutes prosocial television (Lee, 1988). The study defined prosocial behavior as models of "positive social relations," which were broken up into three categories: altruistic actions (e.g., sharing or helping others), socially approved affective behavior (e.g., expressions of love and caring), and control over negative predispositions (e.g., resisting temptation). The author analyzed 4 weeks of prime-time television in the 1985–1986 seasons. Of the programs analyzed, 97% included at least one prosocial incident; more than half (57%) of the incidents fell into the affective behavior category, 21% were altruistic, and 22% were control of negative predispositions. The author also considered the general prosocial themes of the television programs and concluded that about one-quarter contained prosocial themes.

Another content analysis involving prosocial behavior in television examined such behavior in regularly scheduled programs on three commercial television networks (Potter & Ware, 1989). Prosocial content was defined as "any attempt by one character to help another character." They measured both physical acts of helping (e.g., tangible aid to another) as well as symbolic acts (e.g., compliments). Of the prosocial content measured, 83.5% were considered to be symbolic and 16.5% were considered to be physical. The authors found that prosocial acts occurred in every type of television show watched, with the average number being just over 20 prosocial actions per hour.

In contrast, a more recent study analyzed the content of over 2,227 programs across 18 different television channels that aired between 6 a.m. and 11 p.m. (Smith et al., 2006). The authors used a more narrow definition of prosocial behavior, limiting its definition to instances of altruism, or "helping and/or sharing." Of the programs watched, 73% displayed altruistic behavior at some point during the program, at an average rate of 2.92 altruistic acts per hour. More specifically, children's programming had the highest percentage (78%) and average number of altruistic behaviors per hour (4.02), and public broadcast networks had the lowest percentage (58%) and average number of altruistic behaviors (2.36).

Recently, researchers have begun to examine the portrayal of prosocial behavior in the media from a multidimensional perspective. Padilla-Walker, Coyne, Fraser, and Stockdale (2013) analyzed the frequency and portrayal of prosocial behavior in animated Disney films. Unlike Smith et al. (2006), who examined only altruism, this study considered multiple motivations for prosocial behaviors, as well as numerous relevant contextual variables. For example, both verbal (e.g., complimenting) and physical (e.g., helping) types were examined. Additionally, prosocial behavior was further examined by motivation of the individual (e.g., public, dire, altruistic), as described previously in this volume (Padilla-Walker & Carlo, chapter 1, this volume; see also Carlo & Randall, 2002) and target of behavior (e.g., stranger, family). A number of other contextual features (e.g., gender, age) were also assessed.

Overall, using this multidimensional approach revealed one prosocial behavior portrayed every minute in the average Disney film (Padilla-Walker et al., 2013). This figure is much higher than the four acts per hour found by Smith et al. (2006). Accordingly, this research shows the importance of examining all types of prosocial behavior, and not simply altruism, when assessing overall levels of prosocial behavior in the media. The authors also found evidence for all motivations of prosocial behavior in the films: public (e.g., in *Robin Hood*, when Ka helps Prince John so he can gain approval), emotional (e.g., in *Tangled*, when Pascal comforts Rapunzel when she is upset), dire (e.g., in *The Lion King*, when Mufasa saves the lion cubs from the hyenas), anonymous (e.g., in *Robin Hood*, when Robin Hood anonymously gives money to the poor), altruism (e.g., in *The Little Mermaid*, when Prince Eric compliments Ariel), and compliant (e.g., in *The Incredibles*, when Mr. Incredible saves a citizen who is asking for help). Though altruism was the most common motivation portrayed for prosocial behavior in Disney films (at a rate of approximately 28 acts per hour), dire (20 acts per hour) and emotional motivations (9 acts per hour) were also very common. The targets of most prosocial behavior were friends, though there were a number of instances of such behavior aimed at family and strangers. Additionally, most prosocial behavior occurred without aggression, and most individuals helped targets that were similar to themselves in terms of gender, age, and attractiveness.

Collectively, this research reveals that prosocial behavior is portrayed in a complex and multidimensional way in the media. This certainly reflects how prosocial behavior occurs in real life (Carlo & Randall, 2002; Padilla-Walker & Christensen, 2011), and we hope that future content analyses on prosocial behavior in the media will take into account the multidimensionality of the behavior when examining both frequency and contextual features. Such an approach will provide us with a more accurate perspective of how prosocial behavior is actually portrayed in the media. Importantly, it may be that children learn better from viewing certain types or motivations of prosocial behavior than others, and such learning may be more easily transferable to real life. For example, a child might be more likely to imitate an emotional motivation, such as comforting a distressed friend, as opposed to behavior motivated by dire need, such as saving someone from an evil super-robot. As we understand more about how prosocial behavior is portrayed, we can begin to design studies to assess these possibilities.

Theories

There are a number of theories that might explain why viewing prosocial behavior in the media may influence attitudes and behaviors. *Social learning theory* suggests that viewers can experience vicarious learning from behaviors and attitudes expressed in the media (Bandura, Ross, & Ross, 1963). Importantly, social learning theory states that viewers will imitate behavior that is reinforced, but will avoid behavior that is punished in the media, at least in the short term. Unfortunately, little research has examined whether prosocial behavior is specifically rewarded or punished in various types of media. Padilla-Walker et al. (in press) did find that the vast majority (around 80%) of prosocial behavior in Disney films was portrayed without either a positive or a negative consequence. Additionally, Smith et al. (2006) found that public broadcast and children's networks were significantly more likely to show some type of reward/reinforcement for prosocial behavior compared to the other broadcast networks. Moreover, public broadcast networks were significantly less likely to display punishment after prosocial acts compared to the other networks. Though prosocial behavior is generally portrayed in a positive light, initiators rarely receive something directly from their behavior. However, lack of consequences likely is reflective of prosocial behavior in the real world. Though some prosocial behavior is rewarded (e.g., an individual who gets a medal of honor for saving someone's life), much prosocial behavior has no external consequence, especially if it is done anonymously. Accordingly, from a social learning perspective, future research could examine whether viewers are most likely to imitate prosocial behavior in the media that is overtly as opposed to intrinsically rewarded. In contrast, it may be that prosocial behavior that is rewarded in a recognizable way may somehow negate the power of the behavior as portrayed in the media. It may be that prosocial behavior portrayed in a truly altruistic matter will be more compelling and inspiring to viewers, and future research should certainly examine this possibility.

More recently, the general learning model (GLM) has been introduced to explain how viewing any type of behavior (including prosocial behavior) in the media might influence behaviors (Buckley & Anderson, 2006). This theory builds on social learning theory, but explains both short- and long-term effects of viewing media. According to the GLM, there are two types of input mechanisms that may be important when examining the effect of exposure to prosocial media. Personal inputs are everything the person brings to the current setting (e.g., temperament, personality, personal history, attitudes, etc.). Situational variables refer to environmental contexts (e.g., type of media content individuals are viewing, setting, medium, and whether other viewers are present). Both types of inputs interact and may influence an individual's current internal state in three main ways: affect, arousal, and cognition, which then influence behavioral decisions of the individual. In the short-term, this may influence prosocial and other behaviors. For example, an easygoing, conscientious individual (person input) might view prosocial content in the media (situational input). Viewing such material might influence their *affect*, by putting them in a happy mood; their *arousal*, by lowering blood pressure and stress response; and their *cognition*, by activating prosocial related scripts in memory. The individual then might get a phone call, for example, asking him/her to donate money to a charity. According to the GLM, the person's present internal state will guide the appraisal and decision-making process on whether to donate or not, and hypothetically, after viewing prosocial media, he/she would be more likely to be prosocial in this situation. The GLM also explains long-term effects of exposure to prosocial media. A long history of exposure to prosocial media may create cognitive scripts and normative beliefs regarding prosocial behavior, as opposed to activating such scripts and beliefs as in the short term. Additionally, the individual might be more likely to associate with prosocial individuals (who also view prosocial media) or visit places where prosocial themes are more relevant, thus changing the very situations an individual is likely to encounter. Unfortunately, little research has actually tested such assumptions in the long term, so we can only speculate on any long-term effects at this point.

The uses and gratifications approach might also be useful when discussing prosocial media (Katz, Blumler, & Gurevitch, 1973). Unlike effects theories, uses and gratifications theory states that each individual seeks out various media to fulfill certain needs. For example, an individual might view an action/adventure film to satiate feelings of sensation seeking. To our knowledge, research has not yet examined the uses and gratifications that viewers have for seeking out prosocial behavior in the media. This theory may speak to questions of why an individual would seek out kindness, caring, and helping behavior when they could view violence, hatred, and debauchery in the media. However, the theory provides some possibilities for speculation at this point. For example, viewers might seek out prosocial media as a coping mechanism, serving as almost an emotional "pick-me-up" when the person is angry, upset, or experiencing stress. Additionally, individuals may seek out prosocial media to maintain a positive mood or emotions. Individuals may also seek out prosocial media as a way to develop parasocial relationships with media characters who show positive characteristics that the individual values, including prosocial behavior (Branch, Wilson, & Agnew, 2013). Others may seek out prosocial behavior as a means of developing their identity; for example, if they hope that such behavior would become an important part of their own personal identity. Though these are just a few potential uses that prosocial media could fulfill, there are likely many reasons why people enjoy and seek out prosocial behavior in the media. Researchers have simply not examined such content from a uses and gratifications perspective.

Effects of Prosocial Media

This next section will examine the specific ways that exposure to prosocial media can influence behavior and attitudes. We have organized this section by medium and developmental period of viewer, as each seem to be important when examining this topic. Specifically, we have attempted to examine this topic across the life span including, childhood, adolescence, emerging adulthood, and adulthood. Unfortunately, there has been almost no research on effects of prosocial media during adolescence; accordingly, we have included the few studies that do exist with the childhood sections.

TELEVISION

Children and Adolescents

Research considering the effects of prosocial television date back to the 1970s, however, only one study after that time has considered what these effects are. Additionally, nearly every study to date has considered the effects of prosocial television only on young children, with the exception of one, which included some 7th and 12th graders in their sample. However, in spite of these limitations in the breadth of the literature, positive associations have been linked with children who view prosocial television compared with children who view neutral or aggressive television. For example, Rosenkoetter (1999) found that young children who viewed more prosocial sitcoms (e.g., *The Cosby Show*) tended to display more prosocial behaviors compared to children who watched fewer prosocial sitcoms. Similarly, children who watched a prosocial or constructive television program were significantly more helpful toward others in need compared with children who watched a neutral television program (Ahammer & Murray, 1979; Collins & Getz, 1976; Friedrich & Stein, 1975; Poulos, Rubinstein, & Liebert, 1975). Additionally, prosocial television viewing is associated with lower levels of aggression (both physical and verbal; see Bankart & Anderson, 1979; Collins & Getz, 1976; Friedrich-Cofer, Huston-Stein, Kipnis, Susman, & Clewett, 1979), although it appears that the effects may not hold over time. Moreover, it has been found that viewing prosocial television is associated with higher levels of constructive play (Bankart & Anderson, 1979; Drabman & Thomas, 1977) as well as an increase in rule obedience, tolerance of delay, and increased task persistence (Friedrich & Stein, 1973).

A more recent meta-analysis by Mares and Woodard (2005) revealed significant positive effects of viewing prosocial television versus a control, neutral, or aggressive television program on altruism, social interaction, aggression, and reducing stereotypes. The authors compared average effect sizes (across multiple studies/samples) of prosocial television viewing with the effect sizes of the control, neutral, or aggressive television viewing. The strongest effect sizes appeared when comparing prosocial television viewing with either a control or antisocial television viewing group, although most of these were medium-sized effects. Specifically, a medium to large effect was shown on altruism; medium effects were seen on social interaction; relatively small effect sizes were seen on aggression; and small to medium effect sizes were seen on reducing stereotypes. Most evident from this meta-analysis is that the effects of viewing prosocial television were stronger for the positive outcomes (altruism, social interaction, and reducing stereotypes) compared with the negative outcome (aggression). This suggests that viewing prosocial media may do more to promote prosocial behaviors and outcomes, rather than meaningfully reduce antisocial behaviors and outcomes. Additionally Mares and Woodard (2005) found stronger effects for girls compared with boys, for African Americans compared with Caucasians, and for children with higher socioeconomic status compared with those of lower socioeconomic status.

Interestingly, this same study found that the most harmful type of prosocial content to view was "aggressive prosocial behavior" (Mares & Woodard, 2005). This is behavior where the media character is attempting to help others, but does so in an aggressive manner. Such behavior is very common on television and is particularly rife in superhero programs, where such superheroes "save" civilization by hurting the "bad guys." Mares and Woodard's (2005) analysis found there were no positive effects of viewing aggressive prosocial content on subsequent prosocial behavior. Instead, such behavior was typically associated with increased aggressive behavior. Accordingly, it is important to examine the context of prosocial behavior on television, as some types will show more positive benefits than others.

Emerging Adults and Adults

In addition to the relative dearth of prosocial television research over the last 30 years, no research to date has considered the effects of viewing prosocial television or movies on emerging adults. The conclusion to draw from this is not that emerging adults don't watch television or movies, but rather that researchers have failed to consider the positive effects of prosocial television and movies on emerging adults. Considering the large amount of television and movie content distributed to emerging adults, it is important for future research to explore what effects prosocial content has on prosocial and antisocial outcomes. Emerging adults are still developing in a number of key ways, and several studies have examined how the media may influence key developmental tasks, such as identity, intimacy, and autonomy (for a review see Coyne, Padilla-Walker, & Howard, 2013). Given the wide range of development that is still occurring during this age (Arnett, 2006), it is imperative that research examine how prosocial behavior is being portrayed in television programs popular with this age group and what influence it has on prosocial and other behaviors. It is likely that similar positive associations as seen with children will be evident in this age group, though this is unknown.

Additionally, very little research to date has considered the effects of media (of any kind) on outcomes of older adults, and no research has considered the effects of prosocial television on older adults' behaviors and attitudes. Older adults are viewing relatively large amounts of television, with the average individual aged over 65 watching more than 4 hours of television per day (Grajczyk & Zöllner, 1998). Given what research has shown so far, it is likely that individuals of all ages who watch prosocial television and movies are positively influenced. However, given the differences in types of television that individuals of different age groups watch, it is possible that unique effects may be present in different cohorts.

VIDEO GAMES

Children and Adolescents

Research considering the effects of prosocial videogames on prosocial behavior is a relatively new field. Only recently have researchers begun considering positive influences that video games may have on the prosocial development of those playing them. A few key studies have measured the associations and effects of playing prosocial video games on behavior in early to late adolescence. Gentile et al. (2009) used a large sample of adolescents to measure the associations between reports of types of video game use and different types of prosocial behavior. Adolescents' reports of playing prosocial video games were positively associated with levels of helping behavior, cooperation and sharing, empathy, and emotional awareness. In contrast, reports of violent video game use were negatively associated with helping behavior and empathy, with no association linking violent video games to emotional awareness or cooperation and sharing. This is in contrast to an earlier study that found that playing an aggressive game tended to suppress donating behavior (Chambers & Ascione, 1987). In a separate study Gentile et al. (2009) found that adolescents who reported more prosocial video game exposure also reported more prosocial behavior 4 months later.

Other research with children or adolescents hasn't considered the prosocial content of video games as predictors of prosocial behavior. However, Ferguson and Garza (2011) found that adolescents who played violent video games reported more prosocial behavior (helping behavior) when they were online with other players, indicating that adolescents may be participating in prosocial behaviors, even when playing violent or aggressive video games. Additionally, one study has shown that early adolescent girls who reported playing video games together with their parents had higher levels of prosocial behavior and fewer internalizing problems and less aggression (Coyne, Padilla-Walker, Stockdale, & Day, 2011). Similar associations were not found for boys who played video games with their parents.

It will also be particularly important to examine whether aggressive prosocial content in video games has differential effects as compared to nonaggressive prosocial video games. Games that feature nonaggressive prosocial content are rare, though they do exist. For example, *Real Heroes: Firefighter* is a video game where the player acts as a firefighter to put out fires and rescue victims. However, many video games feature aggressive prosocial content, where the player is hurting others but for a prosocial reason, perhaps to save a civilization. Some of the more popular and lucrative video games feature this type of content. For example, both *Halo* and *Call of Duty* are first-person shooters where players defeat enemies to save one's own country from attacks from other countries or an alliance of aliens. Both are extremely violent and are rated M (suggested player age 17+), but both have underlying prosocial themes. Given the meta-analysis findings from Mares and Woodard (2005) discussed previously, it is likely that playing aggressive prosocial content will be more likely to lead to aggression as opposed to prosocial behavior. Though studies typically don't view such games as depicting prosocial behavior, a host of studies have found that exposure to media in which the violence is viewed as *justified* is particularly likely to lead to aggressive behavior (e.g., Berkowitz, Parke, Leyens, & West, 1974). Perhaps couching violence in a prosocial context may help players' justify violent behavior when played in the game. Though such games may influence behavior at any age, aggressive prosocial video games may be particularly influential during childhood and adolescence. First, children and adolescents tend to play more video games than in other developmental periods (e.g., Anderson, Gentile, & Buckley, 2007), and second, children and adolescents are still developing normative beliefs regarding both aggression and prosocial behavior (Huesmann & Guerra, 1997).

Emerging Adults and Adults

Compared with studies with children, significantly more research exists that shows the relationship between video games and prosocial behavior for emerging adults. One recent study considered the associations between violent video game play and prosocial behavior as it is directed toward a stranger, friend, or family. Specifically, the study revealed that exposure to violent video games was negatively associated with prosocial behavior toward family members, but this association did not hold for friends or strangers (Fraser, Padilla-Walker, Coyne, Nelson, & Stockdale, 2012). However, the authors suggest that exposure to violent video games is negatively related to prosocial behavior toward strangers, friends, and family via lowered empathic concern, which is associated with violent video game exposure.

While the deleterious effects of violent video games certainly exist, recent studies have found that cooperative play with others may dampen, and possibly extinguish, some of the negative effects of exposure to violent games (Ewoldsen et al., 2012; Greitemeyer, Traut-Mattausch, & Osswald, 2012). By assessing some of the effects associated with playing nonviolent prosocial video games, recent research has shown several positive effects associated with video game play. Playing prosocial video games is associated with reduced aggressive behaviors and feelings (Greitemeyer, Agthe, Turner, & Gschwendtner, 2012; Whitaker & Bushman, 2012). For example, Greitemeyer, Agthe, et al. (2012) found that individuals who had just played a prosocial video game were significantly less aggressive, both directly and indirectly, toward someone who they believed had poorly judged them, and emerging adults who play prosocial games are more helpful compared with those who play neutral or violent video games (Gentile et al., 2009; Greitemeyer & Osswald, 2010; Whitaker & Bushman, 2012). Similarly, playing prosocial video games is associated with fewer aggressive (Greitemeyer & Osswald, 2009) and more prosocial thoughts and cognitions (Greitemeyer & Osswald, 2011), and prosocial video game exposure is associated with decreased "schadenfreude," or feelings of pleasure at another's misfortune, as well as increased empathic concern for others compared to those who play neutral or violent video games (Greitemeyer, Osswald, & Brauer, 2010).

Though there are now a number of published studies examining prosocial video games in emerging adulthood, there is substantially less published that focuses on older adults. A few studies have found positive effects of playing video games in adulthood (such as decreasing loneliness: Goldstein et al., 1997; Kahlbaugh, Sperandio, Carlson, & Hauselt, 2011), but nothing has specifically been conducted on prosocial behavior. Accordingly, future research should examine prosocial video games in adulthood.

MUSIC

Research assessing the effects of prosocial music and lyrics on behavior and attitudes is limited to only a few studies within the last 10 years. Moreover, most studies of this nature have used samples of college students with the exception of two, which used samples of gym users and restaurant patrons. Knowledge concerning the effects of prosocial music exposure on children and early adolescents is virtually nonexistent, as is research with elderly participants. However, it is likely that the effects seen in different age groups are relevant to each other, but future research will need to study these effects in different aged populations.

Children and Adolescents

Of the existing research, no studies have considered the effects of prosocial music on the behaviors and attitudes of children or adolescents. However, a fairly large amount of literature exists which shows that music therapy has positive effects on individuals of all ages. Future research should consider differences between prosocial music and neutral music and their effects on behavior and attitudes.

Emerging Adults and Adults

In the existing research the effects of prosocial lyrics and music on behavior and attitudes are reported as positive. The most extensive research concerning the effects of prosocial music has been completed by Greitemeyer (2009a, 2009b).

The author has shown that participants who listen to prosocial music, relative to lyrically neutral music, tend to be more helpful, have increased access to prosocial thoughts, and have increased empathy toward others in need. Similarly, Greitemeyer (2011) added to this literature by showing that participants who listened to prosocial music, compared with those who listened to lyrically neutral songs, had lower aggressive affect (state hostility), more negative attitudes toward war and corporal punishment of children, and less aggression toward others.

Finally, a few studies have focused on the effects of lyrics compared with the tone of music. Warburton, Mohi, and Brummert-Lennings (2012) conducted a series of studies with emerging adults and constructed various versions of the same song, manipulating lyrics (aggressive: "Every time I see you, I want to hurt you"; prosocial: "Every time I see you, I want to help you") and tone (heavy metal and folk). Overall, content of lyrics appeared to be a better predictor than tone and consistently predicted aggressive behavior, hostility, and mood. Aggressive tone did predict physiological arousal and anger. Interestingly, the study also showed some interaction effects of tone and lyrics: those who listened to the prosocial lyrics with the light, positive tone were the least aggressive, hostile, and angry. Overall, this study has important implications when studying prosocial behavior and music and shows that though lyrics tend to show more robust effects, the tone of the music also has predictive value. This study did not specifically examine effects on prosocial behavior, though, and while it shows that aggressive behavior can be decreased by listening to prosocial lyrics and nonaggressive tone, future research could examine effects on prosocial behavior and attitudes.

Similar to other portions of prosocial media research, almost no research to date has considered whether prosocial music influences older adults. The two studies we identified were both conducted in nonlaboratory settings. North, Tarrant, and Hargreaves (2004) found that gym users who listened to positive mood music, as compared to users who listened to negative mood music, were much more willing to participate in helping and charitable behaviors. Research has also shown that patrons in a restaurant that played prosocial songs left greater tips compared to patrons who listened to lyrically neutral music (Jacob, Gueguen, & Boulbry, 2010). Though these are not specifically prosocial, other studies have found that listening to music can result in a number of positive behaviors, such as increased quality of life (Y. Lee, Chan, & Mok, 2010), positive health outcomes (Chan, Chan, Mok, & Tse, 2009; Chan, Wong, Onishi, & Thayala, 2012), and decreased stress (Mohammadi, Shahabi, & Panah, 2011), all of which may indirectly lead to prosocial behavior. Though none of these studies focused on prosocial music, they do indicate that music in general can promote positive behaviors, including prosocial behavior, in adulthood. Future research should certainly examine whether these outcomes are enhanced if the content of the music is specifically prosocial.

All Ages

Though most studies have focused on traditional media, some research has focused on prosocial behavior in newer types of media (e.g., cell phones and social networking sites). Because there is so little research, we have decided to combine such research in a section focusing on all developmental periods. For example, Coyne and colleagues have found that higher levels of cell phone use (Coyne, Padilla-Walker, Lambert, Coutts, & Fincham, 2013) and social networking (Coyne, Padilla-Walker, Harper, Day, & Stockdale, in press) in adolescence were both related to decreased connection with parents and subsequent lower levels of prosocial behavior. Such research seems to indicate that heightened media use might interfere with and possibly impede prosocial behavior during adolescence. Though notably, both these studies found that media use *with* parents (as opposed to use in general), was associated with increased feelings of connection with parents and positive outcomes, including prosocial behavior specifically directed toward the family. Accordingly, this highlights the importance of examining the context of media use, as the outcomes may differ depending on the target of prosocial behavior.

Other research has examined how new media can specifically induce prosocial behavior. Participating in social networking sites can induce a psychophysiological state indicative of strong positive valence and arousal (Mauri, Cipresso, Balgera, Villamira, & Riva, 2011). Other research shows that new media can be used to send prosocial messages or engage in prosocial behavior with other individuals. For example, Coyne, Stockdale, et al. (2011) found that romantic partners tended to send affectionate and kind messages more frequently than mean or hurtful messages, and such behavior was related to positive relationship outcomes. Social networking sites are also rife with opportunities to be prosocial. For example, Facebook users are able to post status updates, and their friends and relatives can comment positively on such updates. Simply "liking" a friends' status or picture could be construed as prosocial behavior, providing social network users with feelings of validation from their online friends, even though this likely represents a very low-cost, public form of behavior that would likely have few long-lasting positive effects. Indeed, it is possible that new media could be used as a tool to induce helping behavior. For example, Bond et al. (2012) showed that Facebook was used in positive ways to encourage people to vote during the 2010 U.S. congressional elections. Additionally, it is also possible that Facebook and other social networking sites could encourage individuals to help others, perhaps on national days of service. Certainly, new media represents a relatively novel mechanism for prosocial behavior to be seen and enacted, and researchers should be encouraged to focus on such media in the future.

OVERALL EFFECTS OF PROSOCIAL MEDIA

Overall, there is overwhelming evidence of the effects of using prosocial media to increase prosocial behavior and attitudes. Given what we know from the research with prosocial media, it is surprising that such large gaps still exist in the literature, and it is imperative to refortify our efforts to better understand the effects of prosocial media on individuals of all ages. Specifically, current research on the effects of prosocial television should be examined on participants of all ages. Additionally, effects of prosocial music and video games should be further studied, particularly with samples of children and adolescents, as well as older and elderly adults. Finally, future research should examine prosocial content in newer types of media, including cell phones, social networking sites, blogs, Internet sites, podcasts, and more.

Future Directions

Typically, prosocial behavior in the media has been measured as a unidimensional concept. However, as discussed heretofore, prosocial behavior is a complex and multidimensional construct. Accordingly, viewing different types of prosocial behavior may have differential effects depending on the motivation, target, or other contextual features. For example, when a child views prosocial behavior motivated by a dire need (e.g., saving someone's life), it may increase the chances that he/she would also help those in dire need. However, given that such life or death scenarios are rare in everyday life, it is more likely that the effects would be more generalized (i.e., viewing one type of prosocial behavior influencing multiple types). Therefore, the child who views dire prosocial behavior might be more likely to share or comfort a peer who is upset. Future research should examine each motivation of prosocial behavior and its unique effects on different types of prosocial behavior in the real world.

To date, almost all research on prosocial media has focused on strangers as the target of prosocial behavior. However, individuals behave in prosocial ways to a host of individuals in their lives, especially family and friends (Padilla-Walker & Christensen, 2011). Future research should examine whether exposure to prosocial behavior aimed toward different targets in the media differentially impacts prosocial behavior toward different targets in real life. For example, it may be that viewing prosocial behavior toward strangers has a greater impact on the viewer's own prosocial behavior toward strangers as compared to family or friends. Contrarily, it could also be argued that the effects would be generalizable toward any target. Additionally, there are examples in the media of characters being prosocial toward an enemy. For example, in *Harry Potter and the Deathly Hallows*, Harry saves his nemesis, Draco Malfoy, from being burned in a fire, even though he is prompted by his friends to leave Draco to his death. Such behavior represents a selfless act, and although children do not have "enemies" per se, there may be bullies or other individuals who are truly cruel to them. Harry's example (and others in the media) may motivate children to respond kindly to those who hurt them, perhaps enough to turn a cycle of bullying around (Gentile, Coyne, & Walsh, 2011). Although this is only speculation, it represents an interesting avenue for future research. Other research could examine whether viewing prosocial behavior in the media toward a perceived in-group member has a greater influence than behavior directed toward a perceived out-group member (see Eisenberg & Spinrad, chapter 2, this volume). Certainly, research has examined how media influences attitudes toward in-group and out-group members regarding ethnicity (e.g., Durkin, Nesdale, Dempsey, & McLean, 2012), so the target of prosocial behavior may particularly be important when viewed in this context.

Though we have taken a developmental approach in this chapter, there are some key gaps in the research literature. For example, almost all the research conducted on children was published in the 1970s or 1980s. Due to the Children's Educational Act (1990) requiring stations broadcasting children's programs to devote at least three hours to educational programing, much of which will likely be prosocial, media will have certainly changed since then. There are entire channels devoted to preschool-age children with many wonderful examples of prosocial media. Unfortunately, the research arena has not kept up with these changes. There is also almost no research on other media types aimed at children, such as video games, music, books, or new media. Though we know that exposure to prosocial content in such media has positive effects in emerging adults, almost no research has examined effects in childhood.

Furthermore, though adolescents spend over 7 hours a day viewing media content, with over 4 hours of that involving content on television (Kaiser Family Foundation, 2010), research has almost completely ignored this age group. Does prosocial behavior even exist in media aimed at adolescents? What is the effect of viewing such content in this age group? Prosocial behavior is extremely relevant during adolescence, as has been discussed in this volume, and parents (see Padilla-Walker, chapter 7, this volume) and peers (see Wentzel, chapter 9, this volume) are key socializing influences of such behavior. It is expected that media also acts as a key socializing influence for prosocial behavior during adolescence, though research has not examined this possibility. There is more research on prosocial media in emerging adulthood; however, this research has completely focused on video games and music. Indeed, there isn't a single study examining prosocial behavior on television or movies and its effects on prosocial behavior in either adolescence or emerging adulthood. Arguably, exposure to prosocial behavior in television and movies is substantially greater as compared to playing it in a game or hearing it in a song, which we note later is likely quite rare. Accordingly, future research should use a developmental approach when examining the portrayal and the effects of viewing prosocial behavior in the media to ensure that we have adequate research in each developmental period to fully understand the overall impact of viewing such behavior in the media.

In a developmental context, we might also ask whether prosocial media even has the power to influence individuals older than adolescence. Prosocial behavior is fairly stable by adolescence and emerging adulthood, and it may be that the media has very little power to influence behavior after a certain age. As in the media violence literature, it may be that prosocial content has a larger long-term effect in childhood and adolescence and a larger short-term effect later in life (Bushman & Huesmann, 2006). Longitudinal studies would certainly be important in answering this question, to examine at what age prosocial media has the greatest impact and whether it ever loses the ability to influence behavior and attitudes. One other developmental question concerns whether an individual can become "desensitized" to prosocial content in the media. This is certainly a concern with media violence, as heavy viewers of violent media tend to become emotionally and physiologically "numb" to the consequences of violence and are consequently less likely to help those in need (e.g., Krahé et al., 2011). Though the consequences are likely far less severe, it is possible that heavy viewers of prosocial content may similarly become "desensitized" to prosocial content in the media; accordingly, the positive benefits may be diminished over time.

There is also very little known about prosocial media from a cultural context. Most of the studies on prosocial media are conducted within the United States. Accordingly, we know very little about the frequency or portrayal of prosocial behavior in the media within other cultures. We know that prosocial behavior does have a cultural context (see Guzman, Do, & Kok, chapter 11, this volume); thus, it is possible that prosocial behavior is portrayed differently depending on the country of broadcast. Collectivist cultures which emphasize group cohesion, helping, and cooperation may be more likely to showcase prosocial behavior in their media as it may be more central to their culture. In contrast, individualistic cultures may be less likely to show prosocial behavior, or may be more likely to show it in ways that benefit the individual. The effects of viewing prosocial media may also be different depending on country of origin and future research should certainly examine this possibility.

This volume has also highlighted the role of parents in the socialization of prosocial behavior (see Padilla-Walker, chapter 7, this volume). Much media research has focused on parental media monitoring, though none in a prosocial context per se. Restrictive monitoring involves setting rules and regulation regarding media time and content. Certainly, parents can set rules that promote prosocial as opposed to aggressive media. Active monitoring involves discussion of media content and promotes critical thinking among viewers. Typically, active monitoring tends to offset the negative effects of media, such as exposure to violence, thin-ideal media, and advertising (e.g., Nathanson, 1999; Nathanson & Botta, 2003). Parents can use active monitoring to discuss prosocial media with their children. Media may also provide a particularly accessible jumping off point for discussions regarding civic activism, volunteering, sharing, donating, or any other type of prosocial behavior. Finally, coviewing (or coplaying) tends to enhance media effects, as parents are sending an implicit message of approval regarding media content (Nathanson, 2002). For example, Coyne, Padilla-Walker, et al. (2011) found that adolescent girls who played video games with their parents showed heightened feelings of connection and prosocial behavior. Importantly, some of these effects were diminished if they were playing age inappropriate games (M rated), which are more likely to include violence as opposed to prosocial behavior. Accordingly, if a parent views (or plays) prosocial media with children, this sends the message that the parent approves of such behavior and may encourage children to pay greater attention to such messages on screen. Almost all parental media monitoring research has focused on negative behaviors or messages in the media, such as sexualization of women, aggression, body image, racism, and fear (Clark, 2011). However, parental media monitoring likely influences how children and adolescents perceive prosocial content, as well, and future research should certainly examine this premise.

This volume also discusses prosocial exemplars during adolescence and adulthood (see Walker, chapter 21, this volume). Exemplars are individuals who have a highly moral identity and who do amazing prosocial acts at some point or throughout their lifetime. It would be fascinating to assess what types of media these individuals choose and whether such media influences their attitudes and behavior. For example, media is replete with moral exemplars (often based on true stories), such as Oskar Schindler from *Schindler's List* or Paul Rusesabagina from *Hotel Rwanda*. These are outstanding examples of prosocial behavior in media and they may inspire an individual to do great things.

Although content analyses have been conducted on prosocial media, they are few and far between. Indeed, we know that prosocial video games and prosocial music leads to positive outcomes, but we don't know exactly what proportion of video games and music have prosocial themes. Anecdotally, we would suspect that it is very low. In an industry where violence reigns supreme, there is very little room for purely prosocial games or music. We also suspect there is little demand for prosocial themed video games. For example, in the course or our own research, we have identified a number of prosocial games, such as *Firefighter* and *Zoo Vet*, however such titles pale in comparison in sales when compared with excessively violent video games such as *Call of Duty, Grand Theft Auto*, and *Halo*. One interesting recent trend is that we seem to be seeing more prosocial behavior in games on mobile devices and tablets, such as *Farmville*, where the game rewards players for helping other players. However, we need high-quality content analyses of prosocial behavior across *all* media types to assess whether the frequency is high enough to make any meaningful difference in a market dominated by violent themes. We also need research on understudied types of media, such as books. Though there are a number of content analyses involving aggression (Coyne, Callister, Pruett, et al., 2011), substance use (Coyne, Callister, & Phillips, 2011), sexual behavior (Callister et al., in press), and profanity (Coyne, Callister, et al., 2012) in books, research has not yet examined the frequency and portrayal of prosocial behavior in books. Likewise, while reading specific content, such as aggression, is associated with increased aggressive behavior (e.g., Bushman et al., 2007; Coyne, Ridge, et al., 2012; Kirsh & Olczak, 2002), we do not know whether reading prosocial behavior increases prosocial behavior.

Conclusion

Though some research has focused on prosocial media, we still have far to go in understanding how it influences behaviors and attitudes. Additionally, this research has merely scratched the surface in terms of understanding the multi-dimensionality of prosocial behavior. Accordingly, we hope that future research continues to examine prosocial media in its many different contexts.

In a closing note, we suspect that the overall lack of research on prosocial media, and perhaps the lack of prosocial media itself, sends a clear message regarding the level of importance our society and particularly our governmental leaders and media producers place on prosocial behavior in the media. As one example, PBS consistently struggles to maintain appropriations for funding (Grotticelli, 2012). However, PBS broadcasts a number of programs that have been shown to have positive outcomes for children. For example, *Sesame Street* is the television program that has received the most research attention of any television program currently or previously on the airwaves and has shown a number of positive outcomes for children (educational and behavioral), both in the short and long term (Mares & Woodard, 2005). Additionally, though prosocial behavior certainly is portrayed in all types of media, the levels are presumably low in several types of media, such as video games or music. Why are media producers slow to include prosocial content in their programs? And on a deeper level, why does the public have a thirst for the blood and violence spewed on today's television screens, as opposed to craving kindness, compassion, and a general regard for human life? Until society purposefully seeks out and desires such behavior in the media, media producers have no real motivation to include it in their products.

This chapter has shown that prosocial behavior does exist in the media and that exposure to such behavior is associated with subsequent prosocial behavior and attitudes in children, adolescents, and emerging adults. However, there is a real lack of research in a number of important areas as previously addressed. Though it is a continual fight to get prosocial content on the airwaves (Grotticelli, 2012), perhaps it is time for researchers to start taking this topic more seriously, if we really want the media to change in any way. Indeed, though violent media continues to be popular with viewers and media producers, it is not enough to focus on ways of decreasing violent media; rather we hope to find ways of supporting the addition of media that contain positive messages, including prosocial behavior. With continued research focusing on the multidimensionality of prosocial behavior, and media attention highlighting the positive findings, it is possible that we can force this issue into the spotlight and encourage portrayals of prosocial behavior to become increasingly common in today's media.

References

Ahammer, I. M., & Murray, J. P. (1979). Kindness in the kindergarten: The relative influence of role playing and prosocial television in facilitating altruism. *International Journal of Behavioral Development, 2,* 133–157.

Anderson, C. A., Gentile, D. A., & Buckley, K. A. (2007). *Violent video game effects on children and adolescents: Theory, research, and public policy.* New York: Oxford University Press.

Arnett, J. J. (2006). Emerging adulthood: Understanding the new way of coming of age. In J. J. Arnett and J. L. Tanner (Eds.), *Emerging adults in America: Coming of age in the 21st century.* (pp. 1–19). Washington DC: American Psychological Association.

Bandura, A., Ross, D., & Ross, S. A. (1963). Imitation of film-mediated aggressive models. *Journal of Abnormal and Social Psychology, 66,* 3–11.

Bankart, C., & Anderson, C. C. (1979). Short-term effects of prosocial television viewing on play of preschool boys and girls. *Psychological Reports, 44,* 935–941.

Berkowitz, L., Parke, R. D., Leyens, J., & West, S. G. (1974). Reactions of juvenile delinquents to "justified" and "less justified" movie violence. *Journal of Research in Crime and Delinquency,11,* 16–24.

Bleakley, A., Jamieson, P. E., & Romer, D. (2012). Trends of sexual and violent content by gender in top-grossing U.S. films, 1950–2006. *Journal of Adolescent Health, 51,* 73–79.

Bond, R. M., Fariss, C. J., Jones, J. J., Kramer, A. D. I., Marlow, C., Settle, J. E., & Fowler, J. H. (2012). A 6-million-person experiment in social influence and political mobilization. *Nature, 489,* 295–98.

Branch, S. E., Wilson, K. M., & Agnew, C. R. (2013). Committed to Oprah, Homer, or House: Using the investment model to understand parasocial relationships. *Psychology of Popular Media Culture, 2,* 96–109.

Bridges, A. J., Wosnitzer, R., Scharrer, E., Sun, C., & Liberman, R. (2010). Aggression and sexual behavior in best-selling pornography videos: A content analysis update. *Violence Against Women, 16,* 1065–1085.

Buckley, K. E., & Anderson, C. A. (2006). A theoretical model of the effects and consequences of playing video games. In P. Vorderer & Bryant (Eds.), *Playing video games: Motives, responses, and consequences* (pp. 363–378). Mahwah, NJ: Erlbaum.

Bushman, B. J., & Huesmann, L. R. (2006). Short-term and long-term effects of violent media on aggression in children and adults. *Archives of Pediatrics and Adolescent Medicine, 160,* 348–352.

Bushman, B. J., Ridge, R. D., Das, E., Key, C. W., & Busath, G. M. (2007). When God sanctions killing: Effect of scriptural violence on aggression. *Psychological Science, 18,* 204–207.

Callister, M., Coyne, S. M., Stern, L. A., Miller, M., Stockdale, L., Wells, B. M. (2012). Sexual content in adolescent literature. *Journal of Sex Research, 49,* 477–486.

Carlo, G., & Randall, B. A. (2002). The development of a measure of prosocial behaviors for late adolescents. *Journal of Youth and Adolescence, 31,* 31–44.

Chambers, J. H., & Ascione, F. R. (1987). The effects of prosocial and aggressive videogames on children's donating and helping. *Journal of Genetic Psychology, 148*, 499–505.

Chan, M., Chan, E., Mok, E., & Tse, F. (2009). Effect of music on depression levels and phys-iological responses in community-based older adults. *International Journal of Mental Health Nursing, 18*, 285–294.

Chan, M., Wong, Z., Onishi, H., & Thayala, N. (2012). Effects of music on depression in older people: A randomised controlled trial. *Journal of Clinical Nursing, 21*, 776–783.

Children's Television Act. (1990). Retrieved October 30, 2012, from http://thomas.loc.gov/cgi-bin/bdquery/z?d101:HR01677:@@@L&summ2=m&

Clark, L. S. (2011). Parental mediation theory for the digital age. *Communication Theory, 21*, 323–343.

Collins, W., & Getz, S. K. (1976). Children's social responses following modeled reactions to provocation: Prosocial effects of a television drama. *Journal of Personality, 44*, 488–500.

Coyne, S. M., & Archer, J. (2004). Indirect aggression in the media: A content analysis of British television programs. *Aggressive Behavior, 30*, 254–271.

Coyne, S. M., Callister, M., & Phillips, J. (2011). Getting boozy in books: Substance use in adolescent literature. *Health Communication, 26*, 512–515.

Coyne, S. M., Callister, M., Pruett, T., Nelson, D. A., Stockdale, L., & Wells, B. M. (2011). A Mean Read: Aggression in Adolescent English Literature. *Journal of Children and Media, 5*, 411–425.

Coyne, S. M., Callister, M., Stockdale, L., Nelson, D. A., & Wells, B. M. (2012). "A helluva read": Profanity in adolescent literature. *Mass Communication and Society, 15*, 360–383.

Coyne, S. M., Padilla-Walker, L. M., Harper, J., Day, R. D., & Stockdale, L. (in press). A friend request from dear old dad: Associations between parent/child social network-ing and adolescent outcomes. *Cyberpsychology, Behavior, and Social Networking.*

Coyne, S. M., Padilla-Walker, L. M., & Howard, E. (2013). Emerging in a digital world: A decade review of media use, effects, and gratifications in emerging adulthood. *Emerging Adulthood, 1*, 125–137.

Coyne, S. M., Padilla-Walker, L. M., Lambert, N., Coutts, H., & Fincham, F. (2013). A whole new reason to call mom: Cell phone use and associations with parental connection and aggression. Manuscript under review.

Coyne, S. M., Padilla-Walker, L. M., Stockdale, L., & Day, R. D. (2011). Game on... girls: Associations between co-playing video games and adolescent behavioral and family outcomes. *Journal of Adolescent Health, 49*, 160–165.

Coyne, S. M., Ridge, R., Stevens, M., Callister, M., & Stockdale, L. (2012). Backbiting and bloodshed in books: Short term effects of reading physical and relational aggression in literature. *British Journal of Social Psychology, 51*, 188–196.

Coyne, S. M., Stockdale, L., Busby, D., Iverson, B., & Grant, D. M. (2011). "I Luv U:)": A descrip-tive study on media use in individuals in romantic relationships. *Family Relations, 60*, 150–162.

Drabman, R. S., & Thomas, M. H. (1977). Children's imitation of aggressive and prosocial behavior when viewing alone and in pairs. *Journal of Communication, 27*, 199–205.

Durkin, K., Nesdale, D., Dempsey, G., & McLean, A. (2012). Young children's responses to media representations of intergroup threat and ethnicity. *British Journal of Developmental Psychology, 30*, 459–476.

Ewoldsen, D. R., Eno, C. A., Okdie, B. M., Velez, J. A., Guadagno, R. E., & DeCoster, J. (2012). Effect of playing violent video games cooperatively or competitively on subsequent cooperative behavior. *Cyberpsychology, Behavior, and Social Networking, 15,* 277–280.

Ferguson, C. J., & Garza, A. (2011). Call of (civic) duty: Action games and civic behavior in a large sample of youth. *Computers in Human Behavior, 27,* 770–775.

Fraser, A. M, Padilla-Walker, L. M., Coyne, S. M., Nelson, L. J., & Stockdale, L. A. (2012). Associations between violent video gaming, empathic concern, and prosocial behavior toward strangers, friends, and family members. *Journal of Youth and Adolescence, 41,* 636–649.

Friedrich, L. K., & Stein, A. H. (1973). Aggressive and prosocial television programs and the natural behavior of preschool children. *Monographs of the Society for Research in Child Development, 38.*

Friedrich, L. K., & Stein, A. H. (1975). Prosocial television and young children: The effects of verbal labeling and role playing on learning and behavior. *Child Development, 46,* 27–38.

Friedrich-Cofer, L. K., Huston-Stein, A., McBride Kipnis, D., Susman, E. J., & Clewett, A. S. (1979). Environmental enhancement of prosocial television content: Effects on interpersonal behavior, imaginative play, and self-regulation in a natural setting. *Developmental Psychology, 15,* 637–646.

Gentile, D. A., Anderson, C. A., Yukawa, S., Ihori, N., Saleem, M., Ming, L.,... Sakamoto, A. (2009). The effects of prosocial video games on prosocial behaviors: International evidence from correlational, longitudinal, and experimental studies. *Personality and Social Psychology Bulletin, 35,* 752–763.

Gentile, D. A., Coyne, S. M., & Walsh, D. A. (2011). Media violence, physical aggression and relational aggression in school age children: A short-term longitudinal study. *Aggressive Behavior, 37,* 193–206.

Goldstein, J. H., Cajko, L., Oosterbroek, M., Michielsen, M., van Houten, O., & Salverda, F. (1997). Video games and the elderly. *Social Behavior and Personality, 25,* 345–352.

Grajczyk, A., & Zöllner, O. (1998). How older people watch television: Telemetric data on the TV use in Germany in 1996. *Gerontology, 44,* 176–181.

Greitemeyer, T. (2009a). Effects of songs with prosocial lyrics on prosocial behavior: Further evidence and a mediating mechanism. *Personality and Social Psychology Bulletin, 35,* 1500–1511.

Greitemeyer, T. (2009b). Effects of songs with prosocial lyrics on prosocial thoughts, affect, and behavior. *Journal of Experimental Social Psychology, 45,* 186–190.

Greitemeyer, T. (2011). Exposure to music with prosocial lyrics reduces aggression: First evidence and test of the underlying mechanism. *Journal of Experimental Social Psychology, 47,* 28–36.

Greitemeyer, T., Agthe, M., Turner, R., & Gschwendtner, C. (2012). Acting prosocially reduces retaliation: Effects of prosocial video games on aggressive behavior. *European Journal of Social Psychology, 42,* 235–242.

Greitemeyer, T., & Osswald, S. (2009). Prosocial video games reduce aggressive cognitions. *Journal of Experimental Social Psychology, 45,* 896–900.

Greitemeyer, T., & Osswald, S. (2010). Effects of prosocial video games on prosocial behavior. *Journal of Personality and Social Psychology, 98,* 211–221.

Greitemeyer, T., & Osswald, S. (2011). Playing prosocial video games increases the accessibility of prosocial thoughts. *Journal of Social Psychology*, *151*, 121–128.

Greitemeyer, T., Osswald, S., & Brauer, M. (2010). Playing prosocial video games increases empathy and decreases schadenfreude. *Emotion*, *10*, 796–802.

Greitemeyer, T., Traut-Mattausch, E., & Osswald, S. (2012). How to ameliorate negative effects of violent video games on cooperation: Play it cooperatively in a team. *Computers in Human Behavior*, *28*, 1465–1470.

Grotticelli, M. (2012. July 20). Republicans in the House seek to cut PBS funding (again). Retrieved May 6, 2013, from http://broadcastengineering.com/blog/republicans-ho use-seek-cut-pbs-funding-again

Huesmann, L., & Guerra, N. G. (1997). Children's normative beliefs about aggression and aggressive behavior. *Journal of Personality and Social Psychology*, *72*, 408–419.

Jacob, C., Guéguen, N., & Boulbry, G. (2010). Effects of songs with prosocial lyrics on tipping behavior in a restaurant. *International Journal of Hospitality Management*, *29*, 761–763.

Kahlbaugh, P. E., Sperandio, A. J., Carlson, A. L., & Hauselt, J. (2011). Effects of playing Wii on well-being in the elderly: Physical activity, loneliness, and mood. *Activities, Adaptation and Aging*, *35*, 331–344.

Kaiser Family Foundation. (2010). *Generation M2: Media in the lives of 8- to 18-year-olds.* Menlo Park, CA: Author.

Katz, E., Blumler, J. G., & Gurevitch, M. (1973). Uses and gratification research. *Public Opinion Quarterly*, *37*, 509–523.

Kirsh, S. J., & Olczak, P.V. (2002). The effects of extremely violent comic books on social information processing. *Journal of Interpersonal Violence*, *17*, 1160–1178.

Krahé, B., Möller, I., Huesmann, L., Kirwil, L., Felber, J., & Berger, A. (2011). Desensitization to media violence: Links with habitual media violence exposure, aggressive cognitions, and aggressive behavior. *Journal of Personality and Social Psychology*, *100*, 630–646.

Lee, B. (1988). Prosocial content on prime-time television. *Applied Social Psychology Annual*, *8*, 238–246.

Lee, Y., Chan, M., & Mok, E. (2010). Effectiveness of music intervention on the quality of life of older people. *Journal of Advanced Nursing*, *66*, 2677–2687.

Mares, M., & Woodard, E. (2005). Positive effects of television on children's social interactions: A meta-analysis. *Media Psychology*, *7*, 301–322.

Mauri, M., Cipresso, P., Balgera, A., Villamira, M., & Riva, G. (2011). Why is Facebook so successful? Psychophysiological measures describe a core flow state while using Facebook. *Cyberpsychology, Behavior, and Social Networking*, *14*, 7236–731.

Mohammadi, A., Shahabi, T., & Panah, F. (2011). An evaluation of the effect of group music therapy on stress, anxiety, and depression levels in nursing home residents. *Canadian Journal of Music Therapy*, *17*, 55–68.

Nathanson, A. I., (1999). Identifying and explaining the relationship between parental mediation and children's aggression. *Communication Research*, *26*, 124–143.

Nathanson, A. I., (2002). The unintended effects of parental mediation of television on adolescents. *Media Psychology*, *4*, 207–230.

Nathanson, A. I., & Botta, R. A. (2003). Shaping the effects of television on adolescents' body image disturbance: The role of parental mediation. *Communication Research*, *30*, 304–331.

National Television Violence Study. (1996). *National television violence study* (Vol. 1). Thousand Oaks, CA: Sage.

National Television Violence Study. (1997). *National television violence study* (Vol. 2). Studio City, CA: Mediascope.

National Television Violence Study. (1998). *National television violence study* (Vol. 3). Santa Barbara: University of California, Santa Barbara, Center for Communication and Social Policy.

North, A. C., Tarrant, M., & Hargreaves, D. J. (2004). The effects of music on helping behavior: A field study. *Environment and Behavior, 36,* 266–275.

Padilla-Walker, L. M., & Christensen, K. J. (2011). Empathy and self-regulation as mediators between parenting and adolescents' prosocial behaviors toward strangers, friends, and family. *Journal of Research on Adolescence, 21,* 545–551.

Padilla-Walker, L. M., Coyne, S. M., Fraser, A., & Stockdale, L. (2013). Is Disney the nicest place on earth? Prosocial behavior in Disney films. *Journal of Communication, 63,* 393–412.

Potter, W., & Ware, W. (1989). The frequency and context of prosocial acts on primetime TV. *Journalism Quarterly, 66,* 359–66, 529.

Poulos, R. W., Rubinstein, E. A., & Liebert, R. M. (1975). Positive social learning. *Journal of Communication, 25,* 90–97.

Rosenkoetter, L. I. (1999). The television situation comedy and children's prosocial behavior. *Journal of Applied Social Psychology, 29,* 979–993.

Smith, S. W., Smith, S. L., Pieper, K. M., Yoo, J. H., Ferris, A. L., Downs, E., & Bowden, B. (2006). Altruism on American television: Examining the amount of, and context surrounding, acts of helping and sharing. *Journal of Communication, 56,* 707–727.

Strasburger, V. A. (2009). Why do adolescent health researchers ignore the impact of the media? *Journal of Adolescent Health, 44,* 203–205.

Warburton, W., Mohi, S., & Brummert-Lennings, H. (2012). *If Eminem did* Sound of Music: *The comparative effects of musical tone and lyrics on aggressive thoughts, feelings, and behaviours.* Paper presented at the International Society for Research on Aggression World Meeting (Luxembourg).

Whitaker, J. L., & Bushman, B. J. (2012). "Remain calm. Be kind." Effects of relaxing video games on aggressive and prosocial behavior. *Social Psychological and Personality Science, 3,* 88–92.

9

Prosocial Behavior and Peer Relations in Adolescence

Kathryn R. Wentzel

Prosocial behavior in the form of sharing, helping, and cooperating is a hallmark of social competence during adolescence. Prosocial behavior also has been related theoretically and empirically to other forms of social competence such as social acceptance and approval from peers (e.g., Bukowski & Sippola, 1996; Newcomb, Bukowski, & Patee, 1993; Wentzel, 2012) and to intellectual competencies such as academic performance (e.g., Feldhusen, Thurston, & Benning, 1970; Wentzel, 2012). In addition, researchers have identified a range of self-processes related to the development of prosocial behavior, including perspective taking, empathy, levels of moral reasoning, and affective functioning (Eisenberg & Fabes, 1998; Eisenberg, Morris, McDaniel, & Spinrad, 2009).

Although these important correlates of prosocial behavior have been well documented, less is known about social factors that motivate adolescents to display these positive forms of behavior. Of interest for the current chapter is that social interactions with peers have been linked to a range of prosocial actions. Researchers have focused on the role of peers in facilitating the development of cognitive structures that support prosocial behavior during early childhood (e.g., Eisenberg & Fabes, 1998). In contrast, work on adolescent prosocial behavior has focused more often on the motivational significance of social supports and resources afforded by peer relationships and interactions. Given that peer acceptance is tied to prosocial behavior (e.g., Wentzel, 1991; Wentzel & Caldwell, 1997; Wentzel & McNamara, 1999) and that adolescents are strongly oriented toward cultivating positive peer relationships, the role of peers in motivating prosocial behavior is likely to be especially important during this stage of development. A motivational perspective is further supported by the fact that displays of prosocial behavior tend to increase from childhood to adolescence (Eisenberg et al., 2009), even though the growth of cognitive skills that support prosocial behavior (e.g., moral reasoning, perspective taking) is relatively stable during adolescence (Eisenberg, Cumberland, Guthrie, Murphy, & Shepard, 2005).

The chapter is organized around three sections. To begin, the literature on peer relationships and prosocial behavior is reviewed, and mechanisms underlying peer influence are discussed. The multidimensional nature of prosocial development is apparent in this literature in several respects. First, multiple types of peer relationships have been related to prosocial behavior during adolescence. Second, multiple theoretical perspectives and processes have been proposed to explain these relations. Finally, the unique nature of peer contexts in promoting the development and displays of prosocial behavior stands in contrast to those provided by parents, teachers, schools, and communities described by others in this volume.

Next, a model for understanding adolescent prosocial behavior is presented. This explanatory model reflects the multidimensional nature of adolescent prosocial behavior and its motivational underpinnings in its integration of social cognitive models of prosocial behavior (Bandura, 1986), work on social motivation and social support (Wentzel, 2012), and self-determination theory (R. M. Ryan & Deci, 2000). Specifically, the model suggests that prosocial behavior is guided by motivational self-processes (e.g., goals, self-beliefs) and contextual supports (e.g., peer relationships) and that behavioral intent in the form of prosocial goal pursuit serves as a pathway that links these processes to prosocial behavior. Finally, remaining questions and future directions for research are discussed.

Prosocial Behavior and Peer Relationships

Researchers typically have studied adolescents' prosocial behavior and involvement with peers in two ways, within the context of relationships (e.g., degree of peer acceptance by the larger peer group, membership in specific peer groups, and dyadic friendships) and within structured learning activities (e.g., cooperative and collaborative learning). The focus of discussion in the present chapter is on prosocial behavior within the context of peer relationships (see Wentzel & Watkins, 2011, for a review of work on prosocial behavior and cooperative learning). Within the domain of peer relationships research, prosocial behavior is typically assessed using peer nomination procedures (teacher nominations or ratings are also used, but less frequently). This form of assessment requires students to identify classmates who typically display specific behaviors such as being helpful and supportive, showing concern (e.g., empathy), cooperating, and sharing; some procedures ask students to rate how often each of their classmates displays these types of behavior.

In this section, research on peer relationships and prosocial behavior during adolescence is briefly reviewed. Next, processes of influence are presented. Although influence is likely bidirectional, such that displays of prosocial behavior can result in the formation of positive relationships with peers, mechanisms that might explain the influence of peer relationships on prosocial behavior are the focus of discussion.

RESEARCH ON PEER RELATIONSHIPS
AND PROSOCIAL BEHAVIOR

Research on prosocial behavior and peers has focused on multiple aspects of peer relationships. For example, researchers have documented associations between peer sociometric status and prosocial behavioral outcomes. In general, when compared with their average-status peers, popular students tend to be more prosocial (e.g., helpful, cooperative, sharing), sociable, and less aggressive, and rejected students less compliant, less self-assured, less sociable, and more aggressive and withdrawn (Newcomb et al., 1993; Parkhurst & Asher, 1992; Wentzel, 1991; Wentzel & Asher, 1995). General levels of acceptance, or being liked by peers, also have been linked positively to these same types of prosocial behavior (Caprara, Barbaranelli, Pastorelli, Bandura, & Zimbardo, 2000; Eisenberg, Liew, & Pidada, 2004; Murphy, Shepard, Eisenberg, Fabes, & Guthrie, 1999; Wentzel & McNamara, 1999).

Of interest from a multidimensionality perspective is that prosocial behavior has been linked strongly and consistently to sociometric popularity (i.e., being liked) but not to popularity as indexed by peer centrality or social status (e.g., Ellis, Dumas, Mahdy, & Wolfe, 2012; Gorman, Schwartz, Nakamoto, & Mayeux, 2011; Poorthuis, Thomaes, Denissen, van Aken, & de Castro, 2012). Therefore, positive forms of behavior likely result in being liked and accepted by peers but are not central to defining social hierarchies and status among youth.

Adolescent peer relationships also are studied with respect to dyadic friendships. Although friendships have been described most often with respect to their functions (Furman, 1989) and their qualities (Parker & Asher, 1993), simply having a friend at school appears to be related to positive social behavior. Children with friends tend to be more sociable, cooperative, and self-confident when compared with their peers without friends (Coleman & Byrd, 2003; Newcomb & Bagwell, 1995; Wentzel, Barry, & Caldwell, 2004). Children with reciprocated friendships also tend to be more independent, emotionally supportive, altruistic and prosocial, and less aggressive than those who do not have such friendships (Aboud & Mendelson, 1996; Wentzel et al., 2004). Although speculative, the fact that having friendships that are reciprocated is related to more frequent displays of prosocial behavior implies that other qualities of friendships might be differentially related to prosocial behavior as well.

PROCESSES OF PEER INFLUENCE

For the most part, this evidence is based on correlational studies lacking strong bases for drawing causal inferences. Therefore, it is not clear whether positive behavioral outcomes are the result of social skill development emanating from peer interactions or from the motivational, social, and emotional benefits of having positive relationships with peers. However, it is reasonable to assume that for many children, peers have the power to influence the development and demonstrations of these competencies in a direct fashion. How then might these constructs be related to each other in theoretically meaningful ways? Is it some aspect of peer relationships that motivates social competencies, or do social competencies lead to positive social relationships and acceptance among peers?

Traditionally, theoretical explanations have focused on the broad notion that peer relationships provide opportunities for children to learn and practice cognitive skills that promote positive social outcomes. For example, Piaget (1965) argued that friendships afford a unique context for interaction and collaboration wherein children socially construct their morality of interpersonal responsibility and mutual concern. Presumably, these dyadic relationships provide a context in which conflicts can be resolved in a more egalitarian, reciprocal fashion than can be done in other relationship contexts with peers (e.g., peer groups) or with parents. In turn, these collaborative interactions motivate the development of cognitive skills such as perspective taking and moral reasoning that support prosocial forms of behavior (Kohlberg, 1986; Piaget, 1965). Youniss (1994) also has argued for a similar approach, whereby peers play a central role in the development of moral reasoning and the ability to engage in cooperative exchange.

These constructivist perspectives have provided a solid foundation for a large corpus of research on the cognitive underpinnings of prosocial behavior such as empathy and perspective taking (see Eisenberg & Fabes, 1998). Most of this work has focused on the development of intellectual skills during early and middle childhood, when cognitive structures are undergoing significant developmental changes. By adolescence, however, these skills are fairly stable (Eisenberg et al., 2005). Therefore, the impact of interactions with peers is more likely to take on motivational significance by providing social and emotional supports that promote engagement in prosocial forms of behavior. In this regard, Wentzel (2005) suggests that during adolescence peers can play a central role in motivating prosocial behavior by communicating norms and expectations for behavior valued by the peer group; providing help, advice, and instruction concerning how to accomplish these expectations; and creating interpersonal climates that afford the development of strong affective bonds and a sense of emotional security (see also Ford, 1992).

Several theoretical perspectives provide insights into how these supports might provide the motivational impetus to engage in prosocial behavior. At the simplest level, social cognitive theory (Bandura, 1986) suggests that direct communication and instruction provides students with valuable information about what is expected and how to accomplish various tasks. Therefore, peers who convey expectations that positive social interactions are important and enjoyable are likely to lead others to form similar positive attitudes (Bandura, 1986). Although this type of support is probably provided most frequently within dyadic or small peer group interactions, the larger peer group also can be a source of behavioral standards, with group pressures providing a mechanism whereby adherence to group standards and expectations is monitored and enforced (Berger & Rodkin, 2012; see also Brown, Bakken, Ameringer, & Mahon, 2008).

In addition, scholars have argued that adolescents provide straightforward social cues concerning what types of behavior are appropriate and desirable by modeling positive forms of social behavior on a regular basis (e.g., Wentzel et al., 2004). In this regard, it is reasonable to assume that prosocial behavior modeled by close friends should have a relatively strong influence during adolescence, in part because adolescents tend to interact with their friends more often than with adults, they report observing their friends' behavior with greater frequency than they do their nonfriends' behavior (Crokett, Losoff, & Peterson, 1984), and prosocial behavior occurs more frequently between friends than between peers who are not friends (Berndt & Keefe, 1995). To strengthen the effects of modeling further, friendships typically are characterized by strong emotional bonds (Berndt & Perry, 1986), thereby increasing the likelihood that friends will imitate each other's behavior (Bandura, 1986). This added benefit of emotional support should also lead to a sense of emotional well-being and subsequent prosocial behavior. Finally, as part of ongoing friendship interactions, a friend also is likely to reward a peer for behaving in ways that will affirm her personal qualities as well as promote the stability of the friendship.

Peers also can have a critical impact on adolescents' affective functioning; few would argue that the need to belong and to experience a sense of relatedness with peers is a powerful motivator of behavior (Baumeister & Leary, 1995). Theoretical perspectives propose that affectively close and supportive relationships can influence a wide range of competencies, primarily by promoting a positive sense of self and emotional well-being and a willingness to engage with the environment. Attachment theory principles (e.g., Bretherton, 1987) suggest that secure caregiver-child attachments result in a child's positive sense of self, curiosity and willingness to explore, and trust in others. In turn, these outcomes can be viewed as central precursors to children's beliefs about their efficacy to interact socially with others, beliefs about personal control, and intrinsic interest in social activities (e.g., Harter, 1978; Raider-Roth, 2005). Social support perspectives (Cohen & Wills, 1985; Sarason, Sarason, & Pierce, 1990) suggest that strong affective bonds and perceived support from others serve as buffers from stress and anxiety and contribute to a positive sense of emotional well-being. Finally, self-determination theory posits that a sense of positive well-being promotes efforts toward social integration and displays of socially desirable behavior (Connell & Wellborn, 1991; R. M. Ryan & Deci, 2000).

In support of these perspectives is evidence relating positive behavioral outcomes to perceived emotional support from peers. Specifically, adolescents report that their peer cliques and crowds provide them with a sense of emotional security and a sense of belonging. In contrast, children without friends or who are socially rejected are often lonely, emotionally distressed and depressed, and suffer from poor self-concepts (Wentzel & McNamara, 1999; Wentzel et al., 2004; Wentzel & Caldwell, 1997). In addition, perceived social and emotional support from peers has been associated positively with prosocial outcomes such as helping, sharing, and cooperating and related negatively to antisocial forms of behavior (e.g., Wentzel, 2012). In direct support of a stress-buffering hypothesis, Wentzel and McNamara (1999) documented pathways by which perceived emotional support from peers is related to prosocial behavior by way of emotional well-being. These findings were robust for perceived emotional support from classmates and acquaintances as well as from best friends. Conversely, depressive affect has been related negatively to students' prosocial behavior (Chen, Li, Li, Li, & Liu, 2000; Wentzel & McNamara, 1999) and pursuit of goals to help, share, and cooperate with others (Wentzel & Caldwell, 1997).

SUMMARY

Although not extensive, research on adolescent prosocial behavior underscores the multidimensionality of prosocial behavior at this age. Specifically, the research indicates significant and positive associations between various aspects of peer relationships and prosocial behavior. Assuming that peers have a meaningful impact on prosocial behavior, several social motivational processes were proposed to explain how peers exert such influence during adolescence. These involve communicating norms and expectations for behavior valued by the peer group; providing help, advice, and instruction concerning how to meet these expectations; and creating interpersonal climates that afford the development of strong affective bonds. In the following section, a more specific model that focuses on prosocial behavior as a form of context-specific social competence that is motivated by personal attributes as well as social and emotional supports provided by peers is described.

A Social Competence and Motivation Perspective on Prosocial Behavior

In the social developmental literature, social competence has been described from a variety of perspectives ranging from the development of individual skills to a more general adaptation within a particular setting. Ecologically based perspectives argue that both individual and contextual factors contribute to social competence, such that competence can only be understood in terms of context-specific effectiveness, being a product of personal attributes such as goals, values, self-regulatory skills, and cognitive abilities and of ways in which these attributes contribute to meeting situational requirements and demands (e.g., Bronfenbrenner, 1989). Central to many definitions of social competence is also the notion that contextual affordances and constraints contribute to and mold the development of these individual outcomes in ways that enable individuals to contribute to the social good (Barker, 1961; Bronfenbrenner, 1989). Social contexts are believed to play an integral role in providing opportunities for healthy social development as well as in defining the appropriate parameters of children's social accomplishments. In this chapter, therefore, social competence reflects this balance between the achievement of positive outcomes for the self and adherence to context-specific expectations for behavior.

Expanding on this notion of situated competence, Wentzel (2004) proposed a conceptual model of social motivation that incorporates self-processes and contextual supports to explain school-based competence, including prosocial behavior (see Wentzel, Filisetti, & Looney, 2007). In this model, students' prosocial behavior is in part a product of social reciprocity between themselves and their classmates. During adolescence, goals to demonstrate competence and to establish and maintain meaningful relationships with peers are especially important to youth as they confront the uncertainty and challenges of multiple cognitive, social, and school-related transitions.

Wentzel (2004, 2005) describes more specifically how peer interactions can promote the achievement of these outcomes, including positive social behavior. She suggests that students will come to value and subsequently pursue goals to behave in prosocial ways when their peers provide clear direction concerning norms and expectations for behavior valued by the peer group; help, advice, and instruction concerning how to accomplish these expectations; and interpersonal climates that afford the development of strong affective bonds and a sense of emotional security (see also Ford, 1992). Therefore, just as students must behave in ways that meet the expectations of their peers in order to be accepted and to experience emotional well-being and a sense of belongingness, so must their peers provide support for the achievement of students' goals.

In addition, Wentzel's model highlights the role of motivation in supporting prosocial behavior. Specifically, it depicts a pathway whereby contextual supports interact with motivational belief systems to influence goal pursuit, which in turn predicts behavior (see Wentzel, 2004; Wentzel et al., 2007). This pathway reflects the notion that people set goals for themselves and that these goals determine the direction of behavior and why people do what they do. In turn, the model also posits that goal pursuit is governed by self-processes and by concerns that emanate from social interactions and contextual cues. Self-processes take the form of beliefs that support decisions concerning goal pursuit, including underlying reasons for engaging in goal pursuits and beliefs about ability. In addition Wentzel recognizes the importance of beliefs about belongingness and emotional connectedness to others in supporting goal-directed behavior; engagement in socially valued activities at school is more likely to occur if students believe that others care about them. Finally, beliefs about moral and social obligations are believed to influence the outcomes that individuals choose to pursue in a given situation or setting. These typically derive from expectations for behavior communicated by others.

The model suggests that peers might influence motivation in multiple ways, not only by promoting goals to be prosocial but also by providing reasons for doing so and providing information concerning one's ability to behave in a prosocial manner. In the following sections, evidence that peers can contribute to motivational processes that support adolescent prosocial behavior is described.

MOTIVATIONAL PROCESSES AND PEER INFLUENCE

Goal-Directed Behavior

A basic tenet of motivational theories is that people set goals for themselves and that these goals can be powerful motivators of behavior (Austin & Vancouver, 1996; Bandura, 1986; Dweck, 1991). Of central interest for this chapter is that the pursuit of social goals has been studied as a process that provides direction to behavior that is situation specific. In this case, goals are defined as a cognitive representation of what it is that an individual is trying to achieve in a given situation (see also Ford, 1992; Wentzel, 2002); social goals can emanate from the individual or from external sources such as teachers or peers. Of relevance for a discussion of prosocial behavior would be goals to help, cooperate, and share. In addition, because this definition focuses only on desired outcomes, it includes the possibility that individuals can have multiple reasons (or subgoals) for their prosocial actions, such as intended benefits to the self (e.g., social approval) as well as intended benefits for others.

Research on students' prosocial goals has not been frequent. However, studies of social goal pursuit specific to classroom settings indicates that when asked to endorse social and academic goals to pursue at school, adolescent students typically indicate frequent attempts to achieve a range of social behavioral goals, including being dependable and responsible (e.g., following classroom rules, keeping promises with peers) and being helpful and cooperative (e.g., sharing information and resources, helping classmates with problems; Wentzel, 1989). The importance of these endorsements is reflected in findings across multiple studies that pursuit of goals to be prosocial and socially responsible is related significantly and positively to displays of prosocial behavior (Crocker & Canevello, 2008; A. Ryan & Shim, 2006; Salmivalli, Ojanen, Haenpaa, & Peets, 2005; Wentzel, 1991, 1994; Wentzel et al., 2007).

Peers and Prosocial Goal Pursuit

Of relevance for Wentzel's social competence approach is that students who endorse prosocial goals are also more likely to be accepted by their peers (Jarvinen & Nicholls, 1996; Wentzel, 1991, 1994). When compared with average-status children, popular children tend to report more frequent pursuit of prosocial goals. Students who are "neglected" (i.e., neither liked or disliked by their peers) also report more frequent pursuit of prosocial and social responsibility goals, whereas "controversial" students (i.e., either highly liked or disliked) report less frequent pursuit of responsibility goals (Wentzel, 1991). Therefore, it is reasonable to assume that students communicate to each other expectations concerning prosocial behavior. Limited evidence suggests that at least in some schools peers do actively promote the pursuit of prosocial outcomes: approximately 70% of adolescents from three predominantly middle-class middle schools reported that their peers expected them to be cooperative and helpful in class either sometimes or always (Wentzel, Batle, Russell, & Looney, 2010). Peer expectations for prosocial forms of behavior also have been related to students' pursuit of prosocial goals (Wentzel, Baker, & Russell, 2012; Wentzel et al., 2010; Wentzel et al., 2007). Of particular interest is that these relations between peer expectations and prosocial behavior are strongest when adolescents believe that their peers care about them and provide positive emotional supports (Wentzel et al., 2012).

Specific aspects of peer contexts that lead students to adopt these goals and values have not been studied. However, as noted earlier, the larger peer group can be a source of behavioral standards, and group pressures can provide a mechanism whereby adherence to group standards is monitored and enforced. Modeling of prosocial behavior can also promote the adoption of prosocial goals. In line with the basic tenets of social cognitive theory, Wentzel et al. (2004) argued further that although behavior can be learned by observing others, it is likely to be enacted to the extent that an individual is motivated to do so. Therefore, an adolescent's behavior might become more similar to a friend's behavior over time because they have adopted similar goals. Therefore, the most proximal target of a friend's influence should be an adolescent's pursuit of goals to behave in a prosocial manner. In support of this assertion is longitudinal evidence that the similarity in levels of prosocial intentions and prosocial behavior between friends increases over time and that pursuit of goals to be prosocial is associated positively with prosocial behavior (Wentzel et al., 2004). In addition, Barry and Wentzel (2006) found that a friend's prosocial behavior was most likely to be associated with an adolescent's goals to be helpful and cooperative when the individual had a strong, positive bond with that friend, and when interaction with that friend was frequent and cumulative over time.

Reasons for Engaging in Prosocial Behavior

Inherent in a definition of social goals based on content is a distinction between what a student is trying to achieve (i.e., goal content) and why they are trying to achieve it (i.e., their intent or reasons). In general, reasons *why* a student might want to pursue prosocial goals have been defined with respect to types of behavioral regulation (see Assor, 2012; R. M. Ryan & Connell, 1989), with external reasons reflecting fear of punishment or a desire to comply, introjected reasons reflecting desires to maintain a positive sense of self either through gaining social approval or avoiding negative feelings of guilt or shame, identified reasons that are based on acknowledgement that the behavior has value (e.g., it's the right thing to do), integrated reasons that reflect personal valuing of behavior that reflects a core aspect of one's identity (e.g., I want to do it because it's what I do), and intrinsic reasons based on the positive affect that prosocial behavior generates. These dimensions are useful for understanding prosocial behavior in that autonomous reasons (identified, integrated, and intrinsic) have been related positively to prosocial behavior to a greater extent that external and introjected reasons (R. M. Ryan & Connell, 1989; Weinstein & Ryan, 2010).

Self-determination theory suggests that (not unlike moral reasoning), these reasons reflect a developmental continuum from extrinsic to internalized regulation (R. M. Ryan & Deci, 2000). However, a simpler explanation that reflects the multidimensional nature of prosocial behavior is that adolescents can have multiple reasons (e.g., extrinsic as well as intrinsic) guiding their behavior (e.g., Batson, Ahmad, Powell, & Stocks, 2008; Staub, 1978). For example, Wentzel et al. (2007) confirmed that adolescents display prosocial behavior for intrinsically motivated reasons but also for reasons extrinsic to the self; adolescents were likely to pursue prosocial goals not only because they thought it was important to do so but also because of the social costs associated with *not* doing so. However, a comparison of students who reported primarily external reasons for pursuing prosocial goals with those who reported reasons based on personal values revealed that the external reason group also reported less frequent pursuit of prosocial goals than did the personal value group.

Peers and Reasons for Prosocial Behavior

In addition to communicating expectations for engaging in prosocial behavior, it is likely that peers also provide proximal input concerning reasons for doing so. This can happen in a number of ways. For example, students who see that their peers value and enjoy engaging in specific social tasks or interactions are likely to develop similar positive opinions and attitudes about those same tasks (Bandura, 1986). In support of this notion is indirect evidence that perceived expectations from peers for behaving prosocially were significant predictors of internalized reasons (e.g., "I want to make other people happy," "I think it's important to help others") for engaging in prosocial behavior (Wentzel et al., 2007). These findings were in contrast to those for teacher expectations for prosocial behavior, which were related to more external reasons.

Peers might also influence reasons for prosocial behavior by way of their influence on empathy and perspective-taking. For example, positive interactions with peers have been related to both of these outcomes (e.g., Carlo, McGinley, Hayes, & Martinez, 2012; Dekovic & Gerris, 1994; Fitzgerald & White, 2003). In turn, significant relations between empathy and introjected and internal reasons for prosocial behavior, but not between empathy and external reasons have been reported (R. M. Ryan & Connell, 1989). In our own work, empathy and perspective-taking were related most proximally to internal reasons for prosocial behavior and unrelated to external reasons (Wentzel et al., 2007). Finally, other emotional states related to the quality of peer relationships might also contribute to reasons for prosocial behavior. Depressive affect has been associated significantly and positively

to external and other-focused reasons for prosocial behavior but unrelated to internal reasons (Wentzel et al, 2007).

Finally, Assor (2012) argued that integrated reasons are most likely to emerge during adolescence when identity exploration and consolidation takes place. Therefore, it is likely that peers can also play an integral role in the development of integrated reasons for prosocial behavior by way of their impact on the development of moral identity (see also Hardy & Carlo, 2005). Indeed, within the context of peer crowds and friendships, peers provide unique opportunities for self-exploration, including the discovery of values that are important to self-definition. In this regard, adolescent peer crowds are believed to play a central role in facilitating the formation of students' identity and self-concept (Brown, Mory, & Kinney, 1994; Youniss, McLellan, & Mazer, 2001) by providing adolescents with values, norms, and interaction styles that are sanctioned and commonly displayed. Moral identity development might be especially supported within the context of peer group activities that focus on community service and civic engagement (Youniss, McLellan, Su, et al., 1999).

Perceived Competence

Perceived competence is believed to motivate efforts to achieve personal goals to the extent that the individual believes she has the ability to achieve them (Bandura, 1986). People's beliefs about their abilities influence what they choose to do and why they persist at certain activities and not others; the stronger someone's beliefs about ability, the more likely they are to engage in goal pursuit. Much research has focused on the role of beliefs about ability with respect to specific tasks (see Schunk & Pajares, 2005). Bandura (e.g., 2002, 2006) has also described personal agency more specifically with respect to moral behavior, highlighting the motivational properties of beliefs about one's ability to refrain from actions that will harm others and to engage in behavior than will benefit others. Bandura also notes that as children mature into adolescents and interact with each other more frequently than with adults, peers play an increasingly important role in promoting and sustaining displays of moral behavior (1986).

Studies have documented that adolescents' beliefs about their ability to be helpful are related to their displays of prosocial behavior (Chen et al., 2000; Midlarsky & Hannah, 1985; Thomas & McGarty, 2009; Wentzel et al., 2007). Studies of moral and empathic agency samples also have linked prosocial behavior to positive beliefs about one's ability to respond to the distress of others and to provide help in adolescent samples (e.g., Bandura, Caprara, Barbaranelli, Gerbino, & Pastorelli, 2003; Caprara et al., 2010; Caprara & Steca, 2005; 2007).

Peers and Perceived Competence

Peers can contribute to students' goals and expectations for performance by influencing perceptions of ability (Schunk & Pajares, 2009). Children utilize their peers for comparative purposes as early as four years of age (Butler, 2005). Although few studies have focused on efficacy and prosocial behavior, experimental work has shown that peers serve as powerful models that influence the development of academic self-efficacy (Schunk, 1987), especially when children observe similar peers who demonstrate successful ways to cope with failure. These modeling effects are especially likely to occur when peers are friends (Crockett et al., 1984).

Perhaps the most explicit and obvious way in which peers can have a direct influence on students' sense of competence is by way of help giving. Indeed, students who enjoy positive relationships with their peers will also have greater access to resources and information that can help them accomplish social tasks than those who do not. These resources can take the form of information and advice, modeled behavior, or specific experiences that facilitate learning specific skills (e.g., Cooper, Ayers-Lopez, & Marquis, 1982; Schunk, 1987). Developmental research on peer help giving is rare. However, findings on middle school students making the transition into high school suggest that receiving help from familiar peers tends to increase over the course of the transition (Wentzel et al., 2007).

SUMMARY

In this section, a model of social competence and motivation was described that is useful for understanding the multiple ways in which adolescents can motivate each other to engage in prosocial behavior. There is limited but convincing support for the notion that adolescent prosocial behavior is motivated by a complex, multidimensional set of self-processes, social supports, and contextual cues, with goal pursuit providing a pathway that links these processes to prosocial behavior. Research suggests that goals to behave in a prosocial manner can be motivated by multiple reasons, ranging from external (e.g., threats of punishment) to internalized (e.g., personal values) concerns. Beliefs about one's ability to engage in prosocial actions are also likely to motivate prosocial actions. Contextual supports in the form of friends and the broader peer group appear to play an additional, significant role by providing clear direction concerning norms and expectations for behavior; help, advice, and instruction concerning how to accomplish these expectations; and interpersonal climates that afford the development of strong affective bonds and a sense of emotional security. Much more work is needed to document the specific processes by which peers exert their influence on prosocial behavior. However, the model provides clear direction for future work in this area. In the following sections, remaining issues and directions for future work in this area are offered.

Remaining Issues and Future Directions

This chapter began by posing the question of how and why students' relationships with peers might be related to their prosocial behavior. In general, multiple aspects of peer relationships have been associated with adolescents' prosocial actions, as well as to underlying psychological processes that motivate such actions. Although many of these findings are based on concurrent assessments of peer relationships and adolescent behavior, some longitudinal findings indicate that these effects might persist over time. However, the significance of peer interactions and relationships as causal predictors of prosocial behavior is not yet clear. In addition, progress toward understanding the developmental significance of students' relationships with peers requires more systematic attention, conceptual frameworks of prosocial behavior could benefit from consideration of additional contextual influences that contribute to the nature and quality of peer relationships during adolescence, and research designs must take into account more diverse samples. In the following sections, I discuss each of these issues in greater depth.

DEVELOPMENTAL AND THEORETICAL ISSUES

The underlying premise of this chapter is that having friends and establishing positive interactions and relationships with the larger peer group have the potential to support and facilitate engagement in prosocial behavior in multiple ways. However, there are many unanswered questions concerning when and how peers exert their influence. From a developmental perspective, the role of peers in motivating positive forms of social behavior is likely to be especially critical during the middle and high school years. During this time, children exhibit increased interest in their peers, spend more time with them, and exhibit a growing psychological and emotional dependence on them for support and guidance as they make the transition into adolescence (Youniss & Smollar, 1989). Moreover, peer groups and crowds emerge primarily in the middle school years, peak at the beginning of high school, and then diminish in prevalence as well as influence by the end of high school (Brown, 1989). Therefore, efforts to understand the positive influence of peer relationships on prosocial outcomes must be sensitive to the multidimensional aspects of relationships, that is, the qualities and types of relationships that students form with each other at different points during middle school and high school.

Important differences that could impact motivation to behave prosocially within this age group also might exist. Initial findings indicate that younger adolescents (i.e., sixth graders) tend to experience stronger social influences on their prosocial behavior than do older students (Wentzel et al., 2007; Wentzel & McNamara, 1999). These findings are in line with explanations based on models of stage-environment fit, which highlight early adolescence as a critical period during which developmental needs and contextual affordances often conflict. For example, as children enter into early adolescence they tend to express stronger needs for autonomy and self-control than at other time points, while school contexts tend to provide fewer opportunities for young adolescents to fulfill these needs (Eccles & Midgley, 1989). Therefore, it is reasonable to expect that younger adolescents, who tend to experience fewer opportunities for autonomy and self-control in the classroom, might report more frequent use of external reasons for their classroom prosocial behavior than their older peers.

Further elaboration of Wentzel's model to include additional processes that might influence prosocial behavior in childhood would also provide impetus for longitudinal studies of children as they grow into the adolescent years. Inclusion of other social-cognitive and social-information processing variables (e.g., Crick & Dodge, 1994) and aspects of emotion and behavior regulation would add to the explanatory power of the model. In a related vein, the possibility that the positive social feedback from peers associated with prosocial behavior might influence the development of self-processes and the interpretation of contextual cues should not be discounted. To illustrate, it is likely that positive feedback in the form of social approval and acceptance from classmates is likely to increase the degree to which students are empathic toward peers, take their perspective, experience a positive sense of emotional well-being, and perceive positive expectations for continued prosocial behavior. Longitudinal and experimental work that can identify specific causal mechanisms is clearly needed in this regard.

In addition, research that follows individual students over the course of adolescence is needed to determine the extent to which the effects of contextual factors in early adolescence are fleeting or have a significant impact on later prosocial actions. Indeed, the multiple and multidimensional nature of contexts that adolescents experience has been ignored in this work. Moreover, scholars should explore factors that predict prosocial behavior among middle and late adolescents. This is particularly important given that older adolescents who display prosocial behavior appear to be on a positive developmental trajectory for competence as young adults. For instance, university students who report altruistic prosocial tendencies are more likely to have achieved a more consolidated sense of identity than are those reporting less prosocial tendencies (Padilla-Walker, Barry, Carroll, Madsen, & Nelson, 2008). This age group remains an important one to study, especially as adolescents transition into adulthood.

Several assumptions concerning the nature of prosocial behavior also warrant discussion. Specifically, most scholars assume that by adolescence students display prosocial behavior in fairly consistent fashion and therefore that it occurs in large part as a function of other fairly stable self-processes (Carlo, Crockett, Randall, & Roesch, 2007). However, the role of context-specific expectations for behavior that are likely to differ from classroom to classroom due to norms and values communicated by specific teachers and groups of peers are highlighted in this chapter. Empirical findings underscore the importance of these cues in predicting adolescents' behavior. Therefore, further investigations concerning the stability of prosocial behavior across settings and how peer expectations for prosocial behavior are communicated and enforced in multiple contexts are warranted. More in-depth examinations of how adolescents resolve conflicting expectations from peers and adults when making decisions about how to behave would also add to our understanding of these issues.

Finally, the impact of other social context factors such as gender, race, and culture also needs to be incorporated into the model. Continued research on classroom reward structures (Slavin, Hurley, & Chamberlain, 2003), organizational culture and climate (Roeser, Urdan, & Stephens, 2009), and person-environment fit (Eccles & Midgley, 1989) also can inform our understanding of how the social institutions and contexts within which adolescents interact can motivate them to behave in positive ways. Understanding ways in which teachers, classroom climates, and school-level policies contribute to these positive outcomes remains an important objective for future studies in this area. The roles of teachers and schools in promoting prosocial behavior are discussed in the following section.

THE ROLE OF TEACHERS AND SCHOOL CONTEXTS

In line with a context-specific approach, it also is important to consider ways in which teachers and schools can promote adolescent prosocial behavior and to incorporate these potential influences into behavioral and instructional interventions at school. In this regard, a growing body of work indicates that classroom teachers can have a powerful effect on students' relationships with peers (see also, Bergin, chapter 14, this volume). Teachers' expectations concerning students' aptitude and performance have been related to levels of peer acceptance and rejection (e.g., Donohue, Perry, & Weinstein, 2003; Farmer, Irvin, Sgammato, Dadisman, & Thompson, 2009; Mikami, Griggs, Reuland, & Gregory, 2012). Teachers' verbal and nonverbal behavior toward certain children, especially when critical, also has been related to how these children are treated by their peers (Harper & McCluskey, 2003).

The instructional approach that a teacher adopts also appears to have an impact on students' relationships with peers (Epstein, 1983; Farmer et al., 2009). For example, grouping practices have been associated with the quality of peer relationships (Gest & Rodkin, 2011); middle and high school students in classrooms where students are encouraged to talk to each other about class assignments, to work in small groups, and to move about while working on activities also are less likely to be socially isolated or rejected by their classmates, enjoy greater numbers of friends, and experience more diversity and stability in their friendships (e.g., Epstein, 1983; Gest & Rodkin, 2011). Classrooms that are homogeneous with respect to low levels of student ability and problem behavior can be deleterious to the formation and maintenance of positive, high quality, peer relationships over time (Barth, Dunlop, Dane, Lochman, & Wells, 2004).

Finally, the literature offers a range of practices that can facilitate the formation and maintenance of positive peer relationships at school. For example, school administrators can implement strategies to promote the development of positive peer interactions, such as frequent communication of prosocial values, use of inductive discipline to promote empathy and interpersonal understanding, use of collaborative and cooperative activities for instruction, and encouragement of students to help each other (Battistich, Solomon, Kim, Watson, & Schaps, 1995).

Students also can be taught a range of friendship-making strategies and other specific peer interaction skills (see Gresham, Van, & Cook, 2006).

RESEARCH DESIGN ISSUES

There are many issues concerning methodological and design issues in studies of adolescent prosocial behavior (see Eisenberg & Fabes, 1998). Different sources of information concerning behavior (e.g., peers, teachers, parents) are likely to have unique impressions of adolescents' behavior. Similarly, informants' race and gender also are likely to influence behavioral reports (Wentzel et al., 2007). Therefore, researchers need to be sensitive to the biases and limitations of behavioral ratings that various informants bring to their evaluations. The contexts within which behavior is displayed (e.g., classrooms, after-school activities) also need to be acknowledged when evaluating peer influence on behavior.

In addition to research on adolescents of different ages, researchers also need to focus on more diverse samples. Although it is likely that the underlying psychological processes that contribute to prosocial behavior are similar for all students regardless of race, ethnicity, gender, or other contextual and demographic variables, the degree to which these latter factors interact with psychological processes to influence adjustment outcomes is not known. For instance, definitions of what it means to help, cooperate, or share are likely to vary as a function of race, gender, neighborhood, or family background. Expanding our database to include the voices of underrepresented populations can only enrich our understanding of how and why adolescents behave in positive ways toward each other.

Finally, the multidimensional nature of prosocial behavior must be taken into account when designing future work in this area. For the most part, researchers have treated a range of prosocial outcomes as equivalent with respect to predictors, processes, and outcomes. However, it is not clear that the role of peers in motivating various aspects of prosocial behavior (e.g., cooperation vs. sharing vs. altruistic helping) is the same. Similarly, greater specification with respect to types of peer relationships (e.g., friendships vs. groups) and contexts (e.g., in school vs. out of school) is necessary to fully understand the role of peers in promoting displays of prosocial behavior. Therefore, greater attention to conceptual definitions of prosocial constructs that include more precise explanations of antecedents, outcomes, and developmental processes might prove extremely useful for moving the field forward.

Conclusions

Prosocial behavior in the form of sharing, helping, and cooperating is a hallmark of social competence during adolescence. However, although important correlates of prosocial behavior have been well documented, less is known about social factors that motivate adolescents to display these positive forms of behavior. This chapter has documented ways in which social interactions with peers have been linked to a range of prosocial actions, including interactions that facilitate the development of cognitive structures that support prosocial behavior and social supports and resources afforded by peer relationships and interactions that motivate displays of prosocial behavior. In addition, it proposed a more specific model of prosocial behavior that highlights motivational self-processes (e.g., goals, self-beliefs) and contextual supports (e.g., peer relationships) as antecedents of prosocial behavior and behavioral intent in the form of prosocial goal pursuit as a pathway that links these processes to prosocial behavior.

The multidimensional nature of prosocial behavior and its development is clearly apparent in this literature, especially as evidenced by the multiple types of peer relationships that have been related to prosocial behavior during adolescence, the multiple theoretical perspectives and processes that have been proposed to explain these relations and the unique affordances of peer contexts that promote the development and displays of prosocial behavior. Viewing the extant literature from a multidimensional perspective also has the potential to guide this area forward in new and important ways. Greater focus on delineating the unique aspects and effects of different types of peer relationships on various types of prosocial behavior can only enrich our understanding of ways in which social interactions with peers might facilitate the development of positive, prosocial actions of adolescents. Designing studies that utilize multiple methods and informants and performing research on more diverse samples that represent various ages within adolescence will also facilitate advancements in the field.

References

Aboud, F. E., & Mendelson, M. J. (1996). Determinants of friendship selection and quality: Developmental perspectives. In W. M. Bukowski, A. F. Newcomb, & W. W. Hartup (Eds.), *The company they keep: Friendship during childhood and adolescence* (pp. 87–112). New York: Cambridge University Press.

Assor, A. (2012). Autonomous moral motivation: Consequences, socializing antecedents, and the unique role of integrated moral principles. In M. Mikulincer & P. Shaver (Eds.), *The social psychology of morality* (pp. 239–255). Washington, DC: American Psychological Association.

Austin, J. T., & Vancouver, J. B. (1996). Goal constructs in psychology: Structure, process, and content. *Psychological Bulletin, 120,* 338–375.

Bandura, A. (1986). *Social foundations of thought and action: A social cognitive theory.* Englewood Cliffs, NJ: Prentice-Hall.

Bandura, A. (2002). Reflexive empathy: On predicting more than has ever been observed. *Behavioral and Brain Sciences, 25,* 24–25.

Bandura, A., Caprara, G. V., Barbaranelli, C., Gerbino, M., & Pastorelli, C. (2003). Role of affective self-regulatory efficacy in diverse spheres of psychosocial functioning. *Child Development, 74,* 769–782.

Barry, C., & Wentzel, K. R. (2006). The influence of middle school friendships on prosocial behavior: A longitudinal study. *Developmental Psychology, 42,* 153–163.

Barth, J., Dunlap, S., Dane, H., Lochman, J., & Wells, K. (2004). Classroom environment influences on aggression, peer relations, and academic focus. *Journal of School Psychology, 42,* 115–133.

Batson, C. D., Ahmad, N., Powell, A. A., & Stocks, E. L. (2008). Prosocial motivation. In J. Shah & W. Gardner (Eds.), *Handbook of motivation science* (pp. 135–149). New York: Guilford Press.

Battistich, V., Solomon, D., Kim, D., Watson, M., & Schaps, E. (1995). Schools as communities, poverty levels of student populations, and students' attitudes, motives, and performance: A multilevel analysis. *American Educational Research Journal, 32,* 627–658.

Baumeister, R. F., & Leary, M. R. (1995). The need to belong: Desire for interpersonal attachments as a fundamental human motivation. *Psychological Bulletin, 117,* 497–529.

Berger, C., & Rodkin, P. C. (2012). Group influences on individual aggression and prosociality: Early adolescents who change peer affiliations. *Social Development, 21,* 396–413.

Berndt, T. J., & Keefe, K. (1995). Friends' influence on adolescents' adjustment to school. *Child Development, 66,* 1312–1329.

Berndt, T. J., & Perry, T. B. (1986). Children's perceptions of friendships as supportive relationships. *Developmental Psychology, 22,* 640–648.

Bretherton, I. (1987). New perspectives on attachment relations: Security, communication and internal working models. In J. Osofsky (Ed.), *Handbook of infant development* (pp. 1061–1100). New York: Wiley.

Bronfenbrenner, U. (1989). Ecological systems theory. In R. Vasta (Ed.), *Annals of child development* (Vol. 6, pp. 187–250). Greenwich, CT: JAI.

Brown, B. B. (1989). The role of peer groups in adolescents' adjustment to secondary school. In T. J. Berndt & G. W. Ladd (Eds.), *Peer relationships in child development* (pp. 188–215). New York: Wiley.

Brown, B. B., Bakken, J. P., Ameringer, S. W., & Mahon, S. D. (2008). A comprehensive conceptualization of the peer influence process in adolescence. In M. Prinstein and K. Dodge (Eds.), *Understanding peer influence in children and adolescents* (pp. 17–44). New York: Guilford Press.

Brown, B. B., Mory, M. S., & Kinney, D. (1994). Casting adolescent crowds in a relational perspective: Caricature, channel, and context. In R. Montemayor, G. R. Adams, & T. P. Gullotta (Eds.), *Personal relationships during adolescence* (pp. 123–167). Newbury Park, CA: Sage.

Bukowski, W. M., & Sippola, L. K. (1996). Friendship and morality. In W. M. Bukowski & A. F. Newcomb (Eds.), *The company they keep: Friendship in childhood and adolescence* (pp. 238–261). Cambridge, UK: Cambridge University Press.

Butler, R. (2005). Competence assessment, competence, and motivation between early and middle childhood. In A. Elliot & C. Dweck (Eds.), *Handbook of competence and motivation* (pp. 202–221). New York: Guilford Press.

Caprara, G. V., Alessandri, G., DiGiunta, L., Panerai, L., & Eisenberg, N. (2010). The contribution of agreeableness and self-efficacy beliefs to prosociality. *European Journal of Personality, 24,* 36–55.

Caprara, G. V., Barbaranelli, C., Pastorelli, C., Bandura, A., & Zimbardo, P. (2000). Prosocial foundations of children's academic achievement. *Psychological Science, 11,* 302–306.

Caprara, G. V., & Steca, P. (2005). Self-efficacy beliefs as determinants of prosocial behavior conducive to life satisfaction across ages. *Journal of Social and Clinical Psychology, 24*, 191–217.

Caprara, G. V., & Steca, P. (2007). Prosocial agency: The contribution of values and self-efficacy beliefs to prosocial behavior across ages. *Journal of Social and Clinical Psychology, 26*, 218–239.

Carlo, G., Crockett, L., Randall, B., & Roesch, B. (2007). A latent growth curve analysis of prosocial behavior among rural adolescents. *Journal of Research on Adolescence, 17*, 301–324.

Carlo, G., McGinley, M., Hayes, R., & Martinez, M. M. (2012). Empathy as a mediator of the relations between parent and peer attachment and prosocial and physically aggressive behaviors in Mexican American college students. *Journal of Social and Personal Relationships, 29*, 337–357.

Chen, X., Li, D., Li, Z., Li, B., & Liu, M. (2000). Sociable and prosocial dimensions of social competence in Chinese children: Common and unique contributions to social, academic, and psychological adjustment. *Developmental Psychology, 36*, 302–314.

Cohen, S., & Wills, T. A. (1985). Stress, social support, and the buffering hypothesis. *Psychological Bulletin, 98*, 310–357.

Coleman, P. K., & Byrd, C. P. (2003). Interpersonal correlates of peer victimization among young adolescents. *Journal of Youth and Adolescence, 32*, 301–314.

Connell, J. P., & Wellborn, J. G. (1991). Competence, autonomy, and relatedness: A motivational analysis of self-system processes. In M. R. Gunnar & L. A. Sroufe (Eds.), *Self processes and development: The Minnesota symposia on child development* (Vol. 23; pp. 43–78). Hillsdale, NJ: Erlbaum.

Cooper, C. R., Ayers-Lopez, S., & Marquis, A. (1982). Children's discourse during peer learning in experimental and naturalistic situations. *Discourse Processes, 5*, 177–191.

Crick, N., & Dodge, K. A. (1994). A review and reformulation of social information-processing mechanisms in children's social adjustment. *Psychological Bulletin, 115*, 74–101.

Crocker, J., & Canevello, A. (2008). Creating and undermining social support in communal relationships: The role of compassionate and self-image goals. *Journal of Personality and Social Psychology, 95*, 555–575.

Crockett, L., Losoff, M., & Petersen, A. C. (1984). Perceptions of the peer group and friendship in early adolescence. *Journal of Early Adolescence, 4*, 155–181.

Dekovic, M., & Gerris, J. R. M. (1994). Developmental analysis of social cognitive and behavioral differences between popular and rejected children. *Journal of Applied Developmental Psychology, 15*, 367–386.

Donohue, K., Perry, K., & Weinstein, R. (2003). Teachers' classroom practices and children's rejection by their peers. *Journal of Applied Developmental Psychology, 24*, 91–118.

Dweck, C. S. (1991). Self-theories and goals: Their role in motivation, personality, and development. In R. Dienstbier (Ed.), *Nebraska symposium on motivation* (Vol. 38, pp. 199–236). Lincoln: University of Nebraska Press.

Eccles, J. S., & Midgley, C. (1989). Stage-environment fit: Developmentally appropriate classrooms for young adolescents. In C. Ames & R. Ames (Eds.), *Research on motivation in education* (Vol. 3, pp. 139–186). New York: Academic Press.

Eisenberg., N., Cumberland, A., Guthrie, I. K., Murphy, B. C., & Shepard, S. A. (2005). Age changes in prosocial responding and moral reasoning in adolescence and early adulthood. *Journal of Research on Adolescence, 15*, 235–260.

Eisenberg, N., & Fabes, R. A. (1998). Prosocial development. In W. Damon (Series Ed.) & N. Eisenberg (Vol. Ed.), *Handbook of child psychology: Vol. 3. Social, emotional, and personality development* (5th ed., pp. 701–778). New York: Wiley.

Eisenberg, N., Liew, J., & Pidada, S. U. (2004). The longitudinal relations of regulation and emotionality to quality of Indonesian children's socioemotional functioning. *Developmental Psychology, 40*, 790–804.

Eisenberg, N., Morris, A. S., McDaniel, B. & Spinrad, T. L. (2009). Moral cognitions and prosocial responding in adolescence. In R. M. Lerner & L. Steinberg (Eds), *Handbook of Adolescent Psychology, Vol 1, Individual bases of adolescent development, 3rd Edition* (pp. 229–265). Hoboken, NJ: Wiley.

Ellis, W. E., Dumas, T. M., Mahdy, J. C., & Wolfe, D. A. (2012). Observations of adolescent peer group interactions as a function of within- and between-group centrality status. *Journal of Research on Adolescence, 22*, 252–266.

Epstein, J. L. (1983). The influence of friends on achievement and affective outcomes. In J. L. Epstein & N. Karweit (Eds.), *Friends in school* (pp. 177–200). New York: Academic Press.

Farmer, T. W., Irvin, M. J., Sgammato, A. N., Dadisman, K., & Thompson, J. H. (2009). Interpersonal competence configurations in rural Appalachian fifth graders: Academic achievement and associated adjustment factors. *Elementary School Journal, 109*, 301–321.

Feldhusen, J. F., Thurston, J. R., & Benning, J. J. (1970). Longitudinal analyses of classroom behavior and school achievement. *Journal of Experimental Education, 38*, 4–10.

Fitzgerald, D. P., & White, K. J. (2003). Linking children's social worlds: Perspective-taking in parent-child and peer contexts. *Social Behavior and Personality, 31*, 509–522.

Ford, M. E. (1992). *Motivating humans: Goals, emotions, and personal agency beliefs.* Newbury Park, CA: Sage.

Furman, W. (1989). The development of children's social networks. In D. Belle (Ed.), *Children's social networks and social supports* (pp. 151–172). New York: Wiley.

Gest, S. D., & Rodkin, P. C. (2011). Teaching practices and elementary classroom peer ecologies. *Journal of Applied Developmental Psychology, 32*, 288–296.

Gorman, A. H., Schwartz, D., Nakamoto, J., & Mayeux, L. (2011). Unpopularity and disliking among peers: Partially distinct dimensions of adolescents' social experiences. *Journal of Applied Developmental Psychology, 32*, 208–217.

Gresham, F., Van, M., & Cook, C. (2006). Social-skills training for teaching replacement behaviors: Remediating acquisition in at-risk students. *Behavioral Disorders, 31*, 363–377.

Hardy, S. A., & Carlo, G. (2005). Identity as a source of moral motivation. *Human Development, 48*, 232–256.

Harper, L. V., & McCluskey, K. S. (2003). Teacher-child and child-child interactions in inclusive preschool settings: do adults inhibit peer interactions? *Early Childhood Research Quarterly, 18*, 163–184.

Harter, S. (1978). Effectance motivation reconsidered toward a developmental model. *Human Development, 21*, 34–64.

Jarvinen, D. W., & Nicholls, J. G. (1996). Adolescents' social goals, beliefs about the causes of social success, and satisfaction in peer relations. *Developmental Psychology, 3*, 435–441.

Kohlberg, L. (1986). A current statement on some theoretical issues. In S. Modgil & C. Modgil (Eds.), *Lawrence Kohlberg: Consensus and controversy* (pp. 485–546). Philadelphia: Falmer Press.

Midlarsky, E., & Hannah, M. E. (1985). Competence, reticence, and helping by children and adolescents. *Developmental Psychology, 23,* 534–541.

Mikami, A. Y., Griggs, M. S., Reuland, M. M., & Gregory, A. (2012). Teacher practices as predictors of children's classroom social preference *Journal of School Psychology, 50*(1), 95–111.

Murphy, B. C., Shepard, S. A., Eisenberg, N., Fabes, R. A., & Guthrie, I. (1999). Contemporaneous and longitudinal relations of dispositional sympathy to emotionality, regulation, and social functioning. *Journal of Early Adolescence, 19,* 66–97.

Newcomb, A. F., & Bagwell, C. L. (1995). Children's friendship relations: A meta-analytic review. *Psychological Bulletin, 117,* 306–347.

Newcomb, A. F., Bukowski, W. M., & Pattee, L. (1993). Children's peer relations: A meta-analytic review of popular, rejected, neglected, and controversial sociometric status. *Psychological Bulletin, 113,* 99–128.

Padilla-Walker, L. M., Barry, C. M., Carroll, J. S., Madsen, S. D., & Nelson, L. J. (2008). Looking on the bright side: The role of identity status and gender on positive orientations during emerging adulthood. *Journal of Adolescence, 31,* 451–467.

Parker, J. G., & Asher, S. R. (1993). Friendship and friendship quality in middle childhood: Links with peer group acceptance and feelings of loneliness and social dissatisfaction. *Developmental Psychology, 29,* 611–621.

Parkhurst, J. T., & Asher, S. R. (1992). Peer rejection in middle school—Subgroup differences in behavior, loneliness, and interpersonal concerns. *Developmental Psychology, 28,* 231–241.

Piaget, J. (1965). *The moral judgment of the child.* New York: The Free Press. (Originally published, 1932.)

Poorthuis, A. M. G., Thomaes, S., Dennissen, J. J. A., van Aken, M., & de Castro, B. O. (2012). Prosocial tendencies predict friendship quality, but not for popular children. *Journal of Experimental Child Psychology, 112,* 378–388.

Raider-Roth, M. B. (2005). Trusting what you know: Negotiating the relational context of classroom life. *Teachers College Record, 107,* 587–628.

Roeser, R., Urdan, T., & Stephens, J. (2009). School as a context of student motivation and achievement. In K. R. Wentzel & A. Wigfield (Eds.), *Handbook of motivation at school* (pp. 381–410). New York: Taylor Francis.

Ryan, A., & Shim, S. (2008). An exploration of young adolescents' social achievement goals and social adjustment in middle school. *Journal of Educational Psychology, 100,* 672–687.

Ryan, R. M., & Connell, J. P. (1989). Perceived locus of causality and internalization: Examining reasons for acting in two domains. *Journal of Personality and Social Psychology, 57,* 749–761.

Ryan, R. M., & Deci, E. L. (2000). Self-determination theory and the facilitation of intrinsic motivation, social development, and well-being. *American Psychologist, 55,* 68–78.

Salmivalli, C., Ojanen, T., Haanpaa, J., & Peets, K. (2005). "I'm ok but you're not" and other peer-relational schemas: Explaining individual differences in social goals. *Developmental Psychology, 41,* 363–375.

Sarason, B. R., Sarason, I. G., & Pierce, G. R. (1990). Traditional views of social support and their impact on assessment. In B. R. Sarason, I. G. Sarason, & G. R. Sarason (Eds.), *Social support: An interactional view* (pp. 9–25). New York: Wiley.

Schunk, D. H. (1987). Peer models and children's behavioral change. *Review of Educational Research*, *57*, 149–174.

Schunk, D. H., & Pajares, F. (2005). Competence perceptions and academic functioning. In A. Elliot & C. Dweck (Eds.), *Handbook of competence and motivation* (pp. 85–104). New York: Guilford Press.

Slavin, R. E., Hurley, E. A., & Chamberlain, A. (2003). Cooperative learning and achievement: Theory and research. In W. Reynolds & G. Miller (Eds.), *Handbook of psychology: Vol. 7. Educational psychology* (pp. 177–198). New York: Wiley.

Staub, F. (1978). *Positive social behavior and morality: Vol. 1. Social and personal influences.* New York: Academic.

Thomas, E. F., & McGarty, C. A. (2009). The role of efficacy and moral outrage norms in creating the potential for international development activism through group-based interaction. *British Journal of Social Psychology*, *48*, 115–134.

Weinstein, N., & Ryan, R. (2010). When helping helps: Autonomous motivation for prosocial behavior and its influence on well-being for the helper and recipient. *Journal of Personality and Social Psychology*, *98*, 222–244.

Wentzel, K. R. (1989). Adolescent classroom goals, standards for performance, and academic achievement: An interactionist perspective. *Journal of Educational Psychology*, *81*, 131–142.

Wentzel, K. R. (1991). Relations between social competence and academic achievement in early adolescence. *Child Development*, *62*, 1066–1078.

Wentzel, K. R. (1994). Relations of social goal pursuit to social acceptance, classroom behavior, and perceived social support. *Journal of Educational Psychology*, *86*, 173–182.

Wentzel, K. R. (2002). The contribution of social goal setting to children's school adjustment. In A. Wigfield & J. Eccles (Eds.), *Development of achievement motivation* (pp. 221–246). New York: Academic Press.

Wentzel, K. R. (2004). Understanding classroom competence: The role of social-motivational and self-processes. In R. Kail (Ed.), *Advances in child development and behavior* (Vol. 32, pp. 213–241). New York: Elsevier.

Wentzel, K. R. (2005). Peer relationships, motivation, and academic performance at school. In A. Elliot & C. Dweck (Eds.), *Handbook of competence and motivation* (pp. 279–296). New York: Guilford Press.

Wentzel, K. R. (2012). School adjustment. In W. Reynolds & G. Miller (Eds.), *Handbook of psychology: Vol. 7. Educational psychology.* New York: Wiley.

Wentzel, K. R., & Asher, S. R. (1995). Academic lives of neglected, rejected, popular, and controversial children. *Child Development*, *66*, 754–763.

Wentzel, K. R., Baker, S. A., & Russell, S. L. (2012). Young adolescents' perceptions of teachers' and peers' goals as predictors of social and academic goal pursuit. *Applied Psychology: An International Review*, *61*, 605–633.

Wentzel, K. R., Barry, C., & Caldwell, K. (2004). Friendships in middle school: Influences on motivation and school adjustment. *Journal of Educational Psychology*, *96*, 195–203.

Wentzel, K. R., Battle, A., Russell, S., & Looney, L. (2010). Social supports from teachers and peers as predictors of academic and social motivation. *Contemporary Educational Psychology*, *35*, 193–202.

Wentzel, K. R., & Caldwell, K. (1997). Friendships, peer acceptance, and group membership: Relations to academic achievement in middle school. *Child Development*, *68*, 1198–1209.

Wentzel, K. R., Filisetti, L., & Looney, L. (2007). Adolescent prosocial behavior: The role of self-processes and contextual cues. *Child Development, 78,* 895–910.

Wentzel, K. R., & McNamara, C. (1999). Interpersonal relationships, emotional distress, and prosocial behavior in middle school. *Journal of Early Adolescence, 19,* 114–125.

Wentzel, K. R., & Watkins, D. E. (2011). Peer relationships and learning: Implications for instruction. In R. Mayer and P. Alexander (Eds.), *Handbook of research on learning and instruction* (pp. 322–343). New York: Routledge.

Youniss, J. (1994). Children's friendship and peer culture: Implications for theories of networks and support. In F. Nestmann & K. Hurrelmann (Eds.), *Social networks and social support in childhood and adolescence* (pp. 75–88). Berlin, Germany: Degrader.

Youniss, J., McLellan, J. A., & Mazer, B. (2001). Voluntary service, peer group orientation, and civic engagement. *Journal of Adolescent Research, 5,* 456–468.

Youniss, J., McLellan, J. A., Su, Y., & Yates, M. (1999). The role of community service in identity development: Normative, unconventional, and deviant orientations. *Journal of Adolescent Research, 14,* 248–261.

Youniss, J., & Smollar, J. (1989). Adolescents' interpersonal relationships in social context. In T. J. Berndt & G. Ladd (Eds.), *Peer relationships in child development* (pp. 300–316). New York: Wiley.

10

Linking Grandparent Involvement with the Development of Prosocial Behavior in Adolescents

Jeremy B. Yorgason and Kathryn B. Gustafson

The development of prosocial behavior, or voluntary behavior meant to benefit another (Eisenberg, Fabes, & Spinrad, 2006), during adolescence is influenced by many factors. Although primary influences often reside with parents (see Padilla-Walker, chapter 7, this volume), role models outside the family of origin, such as grandparents, may also play an important role (Dunifon, 2013). Prosocial behavior is fundamentally important for the development of teens, as adolescence indicates a marked difference in the cognition and emotionality of individuals that leads to increased ability, intentionality, and consistency to behave prosocially (Eisenberg & Mussen, 1989). Although cognitive and emotional strides may result in an increased capacity for prosocial action during adolescence, this time period may also be characterized by increased risk behaviors. Quality relationships with nonparent figures can buffer against the negative aspects of adolescence (DuBois & Silverthorn, 2005), and grandparenting is an area of study that deserves more attention in adolescence. The importance of grandparents is highlighted most poignantly with children that are in high-risk situations, such as when grandparents buffer negative effects of economic, parenting, and child temperament risks (Barnett et al., 2010). Some have suggested that the influence of grandparents is mainly beneficial in such high-risk situations and that their influence is otherwise passive or redundant to parenting when risk is low or nonexistent (Lavers & Sonuga-Burke, 1997). In contrast, others have indicated that the influence of grandparents is substantive, even after controlling for parental influence (Yorgason, Padilla-Walker, & Jackson, 2011).

Indeed, a handful of studies have examined the influence that grandparent involvement has on grandchildren, as reported by grandchildren (e.g., Ruiz & Silverstein, 2007). Research in this area is important, as grandparents often invest various resources to benefit their grandchildren (Smith & Drew, 2002), yet little is known about related outcomes. In this chapter, we draw on family solidarity theory to provide a framework for research literature that examines adolescent benefits of grandparent involvement, specifically addressing ways that grandparents may influence the development of prosocial behaviors. We then review existing research on grandparenting and positive outcomes for adolescents, specifically focusing on prosocial behavior. Further, to add to the literature in this area, we present results from our own data illustrating longitudinal prosocial benefits of grandparent emotional involvement with their adolescent grandchildren and offer suggestions for future research.

Intergenerational Solidarity Theory: A Guiding Framework

Intergenerational solidarity theory considers ways that generations are linked across time by examining various interactions between generations. In essence, intergenerational solidarity theory describes social cohesion across generations (Bengtson & Roberts, 1991) and posits that different types of solidarity are linked or correlated with each other in important ways. As such, intergenerational solidarity theory provides a valuable framework for understanding ways that grandparents and grandchildren interact and how these interactions might foster prosocial behavior. Bengtson and Roberts (1991) proposed six different aspects of intergenerational solidarity or closeness, including (1) associational solidarity (frequency and patterns of interactions), (2) affectual solidarity (emotional closeness), (3) consensual solidarity (level of agreement on values and beliefs), (4) functional solidarity (helping and exchanges), (5) normative solidarity (commitment to familial roles), and (6) structural solidarity (opportunity structure for interaction such as proximity or number of family members). Each of these aspects of intergenerational solidarity may be linked to different dimensions of prosocial development in grandchildren.

Among the six types of solidarity, we focus on all but consensual solidarity. Associational solidarity is relevant in terms of how often, for how long, and in what capacities grandparents and their grandchildren interact. Interaction likely provides avenues for modeling, mentoring, supporting, and giving advice. Affectual solidarity focuses on grandchild reports of how close they feel toward a particular grandparent. Closeness provides a key measure of attachment. Functional solidarity is important when exploring how grandchildren respond to monetary gifts from grandparents to the family of the grandchild. Such interactions may facilitate better mental health, especially in high-risk situations. Normative solidarity is not measured directly in our research, yet may help to explain why grandchildren perform better in school or behave in certain ways when a grandparent is involved in their life. Specifically, grandchildren may be sensing expected family roles and obligations and responding to meet expectations (Eisenberg & Mussen, 1989; see also de Guzman, Do, & Kok, chapter 11, this volume; Kumru & Yağmurlu, chapter 16, this volume). Structural solidarity is considered in terms of geographic proximity between grandchild and the grandparent. Proximity is linked to increased interactions and closeness (Dunifon, 2013).

We consider the types of solidarity to be linked with each other as illustrated in Figure 10.1, where associational and structural solidarity contribute to functional and affectual solidarity. We extend intergenerational solidarity theory by expanding beyond the simple connections between solidarity constructs and instead link solidarity with the outcome of prosocial behavior in adolescents. Child development literature supports the idea that attachment may drive the links between affectual solidarity and prosocial behaviors. Specifically, parents have tended to influence levels of prosocial behavior in their children (Hastings, Utendale, & Sullivan, 2007). Mechanisms identified include attachment (Eberly & Montemayor, 1999), warmth from mothers (Carlo, Mestre, Samper, Tur, & Arment, 2011), and parent/child connectedness (Padilla-Walker & Christensen, 2011). Further, it has been suggested that through connections with their children, parents instill values that influence outward behaviors such as empathic concern and self-regulation (Grusec & Goodnow, 1994; Padilla-Walker & Carlo, 2007; Padilla-Walker & Christensen, 2011). Although we do not examine mechanisms of solidarity in this chapter with our own data, we do extend child development research to grandparent/grandchild attachment and potentially resulting prosocial behaviors.

In reference to grandparent/grandchild relations, higher frequency of contact and closer geographic proximity are linked to degree of helping from grandparents

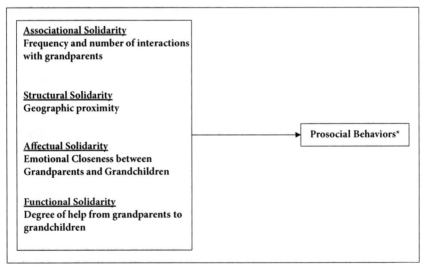

FIGURE 10.1 *Illustration of ways that intergenerational solidarity associates with prosocial development in adolescent grandchildren.*

*Prosocial behaviors may possibly represent *normative solidarity* through the maintaining of family roles and expectations by grandchildren.

and how close grandchildren feel to their grandparents (Dunifon & Bajracharya, 2012), which may be associated with the grandchildren forming attachments with grandparents. These attachments may influence grandchildren by their internalizing values that are expressed in prosocial ways to those around them. Grandparent involvement may also have indirect links with grandchildren through the parents, as parents may act as gatekeepers, and parents may benefit from grandparent support (Dunifon, 2013). Grandparent involvement may have direct links with grandchild outcomes through mutual interactions that model behavior or when direct support is given (Dunifon, 2013). Again, with data we have collected, we address the direct paths between grandparent involvement and grandchild outcomes, specifically in reference to prosocial behavior.

Grandparents and Their Grandchildren

The theoretical importance of grandparent-grandchild relations suggests utility in examining grandparenting from a multidimensional framework, and in this section we will briefly review the empirical literature that highlights these associations. More specifically, a broad assessment of the grandparent literature suggests four main veins of study that have been pursued in the current literature: (1) The grandparent's perspective of their role, such as through determining grandparent styles, meanings, and the benefits of grandparenthood (e.g., Cherlin & Furstenberg, 1985); (2) Experiences and suggestions for custodial grandparents, or those who provide full-time care for their grandchildren (e.g., Hayslip & Kaminski, 2005); (3) Predictors of grandparent involvement with their grandchildren (e.g., Sheehan & Petrovic, 2008); and (4) Grandchild benefits of grandparent involvement (e.g., Dunifon, 2013). The last of these themes is perhaps the least developed, yet crucial in understanding the prosocial development of grandchildren.

Grandparents hold a unique role in the lives of their grandchildren. As genetic progenitors they are generally invested in the well-being of their grandchildren (for an overview of grandparenting see Yorgason, LaPierre, & Hayter, 2013) and they carry out various roles and functions ranging from playmate, caregiver, friend, and mentor (King, Elder, & Conger, 2000) to family historian (Wiscott & Kopera-Fyre, 2000). Grandparent involvement can range from "no contact" to "surrogate parenting," with some grandparents playing a traditional or formal role, interacting with grandchildren infrequently such as on holidays and special occasions. Others act as part-time caregivers due to both parents of their grandchildren working or being unable to parent for other reasons such as divorce or incarceration. Caregiving grandparents are sometimes coresidents in their children's homes, yet a growing number of grandparents are full-time custodians who may have legal custody of and essentially raise their grandchildren.

Grandparents are important to the development of their grandchildren as they supplement parental care involving being role models; providing emotional, practical, and financial support; giving advice; and teaching and mentoring their grandchildren (Uhlenberg & Cheuk, 2010). Grandparents filling these roles may benefit their grandchild in various ways, as research supports links between grandparent involvement and more grandchild social and prosocial behaviors (e.g., Barnett, Scaramella, Neppl, Ontai, & Conger, 2010; Goodman, 2012; Mansson & Booth-Butterfield, 2011), improved education engagement (e.g., Mitchell, 2008), cultural learning (Thompson, Cameron, & Fuller-Thomson, 2013), and mental health (Botcheva & Feldman, 2004; Henderson, Hayslip, Sanders, & Louden, 2009), among other outcomes.

Few studies have examined links between grandparent involvement and the development of prosocial behaviors as they are defined in the current volume. Among such studies, grandparent-grandchild relationships historically have significant yet modest positive associations with beneficial grandchild outcomes. The relationship from grandparents to their grandchildren can be both direct (e.g., caregiving interactions) and indirect (e.g., financial or emotional support filtered through parent; Attar-Schwartz, Tan, & Buchanan, 2009). Some positive adolescent outcomes from grandparent involvement include an association with lower internalizing and externalizing behaviors (Lussier, Deater-Deckard, Dunn, & Davies, 2002), reduced adjustment difficulties related to parental divorce (Henderson et al., 2009), lower depressive symptoms in grandchildren in single-parent families (Ruiz & Silverstein, 2007), the buffering of various stressors (Barnett et al., 2010), and higher amounts of prosocial behavior in grandchildren (Attar-Schwartz, Tan, Buchanan, Flouri, & Griggs, 2009; Yorgason et al., 2011). Though these positive associations seem to contribute to the overall well-being of the grandchild, other research indicates no benefit from grandparent involvement (Dunifon & Bajracharya, 2012), suggesting the need for further study in this area. Few studies have directly addressed the role of grandparents in relation to the development of prosocial behavior in the grandchild across time.

Three studies have specifically addressed ways that grandparent involvement is linked with prosocial behavior in their grandchildren, with each suggesting a positive association. First, in a study of over 1,500 European youth between the ages of 11 and 16, Attar-Schwartz and colleagues (2009) found that increased grandparent involvement was linked with lower reports of emotional difficulties and higher reports of prosocial behaviors. Prosocial behaviors were measured by those authors using five items from the Strengths and Difficulties Questionnaire, which tapped behaviors including, "[being] helpful if someone is hurt, upset or feeling ill" (p. 69). Second, a study by Barnett and colleagues (2010) explored associations between grandmother involvement and prosocial behavior among 127 families with 3- to 4-year-old children. Prosocial behavior was measured using 10 items from the Social Competence Scale (LaFreniere & Dumas, 1996) that assessed behaviors such as "cooperates with others" and "accepts compromise" (Barnett et al., 2010, p. 638). Grandmother involvement did not have a direct main effect association with prosocial behavior, yet when interacting with negative emotional reactivity to frustration, grandmother involvement provided an important buffer.

Specifically, those with lower grandmother involvement and higher reactivity to frustration had lower prosocial behavior scores and vice versa. Last, Yorgason and colleagues (2011) examined longitudinal associations between prosocial behavior toward strangers and grandparent involvement among 408 adolescents between 11 and 14 years of age. Prosocial behavior was measured in that study using six items from the kindness and generosity subscale of the Values in Action Inventory of Strengths (Peterson & Seligman, 2004; e.g., "I help others even if it's not easy for me"; Yorgason et al., 2011, p. 554). Findings indicated that higher reports of closeness to a grandparent were linked with higher prosocial behavior toward strangers one year later, even after controlling for prior prosocial behavior and parent/child attachment levels. Further, these results held for grandchildren in single and two-parent families. In each of these studies, the standardized coefficients for grandparent involvement were statistically significant, yet modest (between 0.11 and 0.16), and associated r-square values were small, suggesting that grandparent involvement held an important yet minor association with prosocial behavior.

Prosocial Behavior: Complex Links with Grandparent Involvement

Although a growing number of studies have linked grandparenting to prosocial behavior, few of these studies have used a multidimensional framework in regard to either grandparenting or prosocial behavior. Above we have highlighted research suggesting the importance of considering multiple aspects of the grandparent relationship, but research also suggests that prosocial behavior is not a unidimensional construct (see Padilla-Walker & Carlo, chapter 1, this volume) and that grandparenting might be differentially associated with different types and targets of prosocial behavior. Thus, in this section we will discuss how grandparenting might be differentially associated with prosocial behavior toward three targets: family, friends, and strangers.

More specifically, Padilla-Walker and colleagues (in press) suggest that prosocial behavior may be directed at a number of different targets and different mechanisms may operate when youth interact with those closest to them (toward family), with familiar people in social situations (toward friends), and with people outside their known network (toward strangers). Some research would support the idea that grandparent influence may be linked with correlates of prosocial behavior toward all targets including family, friends, and strangers. For example, this could be evident in various studies indicating that grandparent involvement is linked with lower internalizing/externalizing behaviors, fewer emotional problems, increased self-confidence, better mental health, and fewer adjustment problems in response to stress (Barnett et al., 2010; Goodman, 2012; Henderson et al., 2009; Lussier et al., 2002; Ruiz & Silverstein, 2007). Although not directly tested in the grandparent literature just cited, if the primary benefit of grandparent involvement is indirect, via a mechanism such as secure attachment, then youth might accordingly act in prosocial ways toward all people around them.

Although prosocial behavior as an outcome has rarely been examined in the grandparenting literature, some studies generally suggest that grandparent involvement might be associated with prosocial behavior toward family, friends, and strangers. For example, extended kin, such as grandparents, may buffer negative decision-making in teens (Beam, Chen, & Greenberger, 2002), positively impact trust development in others (Meyer & Bouchey, 2010), and improve the cognitive, prosocial, and emotional development of young children (Gallagher, Abbott-Shim, & Vandewiele, 2011), all of which are important correlates of prosocial behavior. Also, Botcheva and Feldman (2004) found that grandparent involvement was linked to less harsh parenting and lower depression among youth during times of economic strain. Furthermore, Barnett and colleagues (2012) also suggested that conflict between grandparents and their adult children can have negative consequences on the grandchildren. Thus, grandparent involvement may be linked to grandchild prosocial behavior in family relationships through their interactions with the parents of their grandchildren, suggesting that if grandparenting can strengthen either parent-child relations or the child's prosocial behavior directly, there are likely to be increases in prosocial behavior toward family. In addition to positively influencing parent-child relations, grandparents are also often seen as a source of wisdom and they have been known to provide advice and social support to grandchildren in need (Dunifon, 2013). Acting in the role of mentor and emotional support, grandparents may specifically influence the development of prosocial behavior toward family, as well as toward friends and strangers.

In summary, prosocial behavior toward various targets illustrates the multidimensional nature of prosocial behavior and the complex way that grandparents may influence the development of different prosocial behaviors given different circumstances. Literature support of these associations is sparse, providing numerous directions for further study. To add to existing literature in this area, we did some further analyses using the Flourishing Families data to examine the contribution grandparents make to the prosocial development of their grandchildren.

Grandparent Involvement and Prosocial Behavior: Results from the Flourishing Families Study

The current analysis used structural equation modeling (SEM) to estimate three latent growth curve models in Mplus (Version 7, Muthen & Muthen, 2012) with data from 413 participants from the Flourishing Families Project. That is, 413 of the 500 original respondents reported on their relationship with their grandparent and so were included in the current analysis. We examined how reports of grandparent/grandchild intergenerational solidarity dimensions from Wave 2 of the study were linked to the development of prosocial behavior toward family members, friends, and strangers across Waves 2, 3, 4, and 5 (data were collected once a year). Grandparent emotional involvement, grandparent practical involvement (had taken care of grandchild, helped work on a family problem, and helped grandchild's family with money), distance between grandparent and grandchild residences, and relationship quality between grandparent and parents of the grandchild were all modeled as predictors of each prosocial growth curve. Each type of prosocial behavior (toward family, friends, and strangers) was modeled as a separate growth curve across four data points, and various aspects of grandparent/grandchild connections predicted the initial level (intercept) and trend across time (slope) of each type of prosocial behavior (see Figure 10.2 for graphic

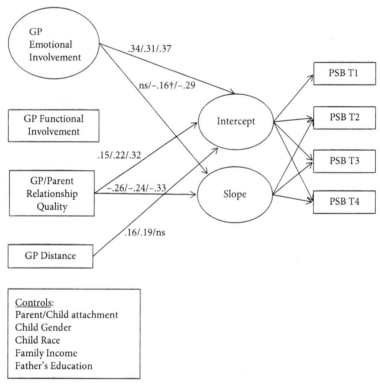

FIGURE 10.2 *Standardized coefficients of various forms of grandparent involvement as they predict variation in the initial levels (intercept) and change across time (slope) in prosocial behavior toward family/friends/strangers.*

Note: GP = Grandparent. All paths shown significant at p ≤ .05, except where noted by † indicating p ≤ .10. Coefficients are ordered as follows for each path: prosocial behavior toward family/toward friends/toward strangers. Model fit was as follows: Prosocial toward family model: Chi-square = 216.57, p ≤ .000; CFI = .94; RMSEA = .059 (lower CI = .049, upper CI = .069); SRMR = .052. Prosocial toward friends model: Chi-square = 192.94, p ≤ .000; CFI = .95; RMSEA = .053 (lower CI = .043, upper CI = .063); SRMR = .047. Prosocial toward strangers model: Chi-square = 175.45, p ≤ .000; CFI = .96; RMSEA = .048 (lower CI = .038, upper CI = .059); SRMR = .047.

representation of the SEM model). Goodness of model fit was examined using the Chi-square test of model fit, the comparative fit index (CFI), the root mean square error of approximation (RMSEA) and the standardized root mean square residual (SRMR). Each of the three models showed appropriate fit to the data (see note below Figure 10.2 for model fit statistics).

Findings from the three models showed interesting trends across time (see Table 10.1). First, each growth curve of prosocial behavior showed distinct initial levels, and each had a positive trend or increase across time. Prosocial behavior toward family had an initial unstandardized level of 1.74 (SE = .48, $p \leq$ .000), with a significant upward slope (B = .53, SE = .18, $p \leq$ .01). Prosocial behavior toward friends had an initial unstandardized level of 2.61 (SE = .36, $p \leq$ .000), with a significant upward slope (B = .41, SE = .13, $p \leq$ .01). Last, prosocial behavior toward strangers had an initial unstandardized level of 1.37 (SE = .41, $p \leq$ .01), with a significant upward slope (B = .36, SE = .14, $p \leq$ .01). In other words, adolescents reported the highest initial levels of prosocial behavior toward friends, followed by family, and reported the lowest initial levels of prosocial behavior toward strangers. Second, each type of prosocial behavior had a significant upward slope, suggesting that prosocial behavior toward all three targets was increasing over time.

Next, findings indicated that emotional closeness to a grandparent (a measure of affectual solidarity) was significantly associated with the initial levels of adolescent reports of prosocial behavior for family members (standardized β = .34,

TABLE 10.1 Unstandardized parameters from growth curve models predicting prosocial behavior toward family, friends, and strangers

| | Target of Prosocial Behavior | | | | | |
| | Family | | Friends | | Strangers | |
	Intercept	Slope	Intercept	Slope	Intercept	Slope
Mean Growth Estimate	1.74***	.53**	2.61***	.41**	1.37**	.36**
Variance of Growth Estimate	.36***	.03***	.18***	.02***	.27***	.02***
GP Emotional Involvement	.46***	-.03	.36***	-.05†	.49***	-.09***
GP Functional Involvement	.04	-.03	.02	.00	-.02	-.02
Parent/Child Relationship	.29***	-.03	.09	-.03	.20**	-.05†
GP Distance	.05**	-.01	.05***	-.01	.01	.00
Parent/Grandparent Relationship	.07*	-.03*	.08**	-.02*	.13***	-.03**
Covariates						
Race/Ethnicity	.02	-.03	-.14*	-.04†	-.00	.01
Income	-.01	-.01	-.04	.01	-.06†	.02
Gender	.27***	-.02	.52***	-.03	.29***	.00
Education	.00	-.01	.05*	-.01	.06	-.00

†$p \leq$ .10; *$p \leq$ .05; **$p \leq$ .01; ***$p \leq$ .001

Note: GP = Grandparent.

SE = .06, p ≤ .000), friends (standardized β = .31, SE = .06, p ≤ .000), and strangers (standardized β = .37, SE = .06, p ≤ .000). In other words, when adolescents reported higher closeness to a grandparent they also reported higher levels of prosocial behavior to all three targets at the first wave of our data. Closeness to a grandparent also was significantly associated with growth (slopes) of prosocial behavior with friends at a trend level (standardized β = -.16, SE = .08, p = .054) and with strangers (standardized β = -.29, SE = .09, p ≤ .001). The negative coefficients connecting grandparent involvement with the growth of prosocial behavior suggest that the upward slope in prosocial behavior toward friends and strangers across time was attenuated or lessened by closeness to a grandparent. This is not surprising as intercepts and growth trajectories are often negatively correlated in this type of analysis, indicating a possible ceiling effect (a higher initial level commonly associated with a less steep slope). This may be the case in the current analysis, as grandchildren with higher closeness to a grandparent started out at much higher initial levels of prosocial behavior. This finding could also be due to there being heterogeneity, or a significant amount of variance, in the growth trajectories of prosocial behavior.

Measures of structural solidarity (distance between grandparent and grandchild residences) and associational solidarity (measured by proxy from grandparent relationship quality with the parent of the grandchild) were also linked to initial levels of prosocial behavior and trends across time. Specifically, distance between where the grandparent and the grandchild lived was directly linked with initial levels of prosocial behavior toward family (standardized β = .16, SE = .06, p ≤ .01) and friends (standardized β = .19, SE = .06, p ≤ .001), but not toward strangers. These findings suggest that the further away grandparents live from their grandchild, the higher levels of prosocial behavior were reported toward family and friends.

Also, the grandparent's relationship with the their grandchild's parent was significantly associated with higher initial levels and less steep upward developmental trajectories of each type of prosocial behavior: Predicting intercepts for family (standardized β = .15, SE = .08, p ≤ .05), friends (standardized β = .22, SE = .07, p ≤ .01), and strangers (standardized β = .32, SE = .07, p ≤ .000); Predicting slopes for family (standardized β = -.26, SE = .11, p ≤ .05), friends, (standardized β = -.24, SE = .10, p ≤ .05), and strangers (standardized β = -.33, SE = .11, p ≤ .01). These findings suggest that the grandparent/parent relationship has an additive and similar association with prosocial behavior as does grandparent emotional involvement. In contrast, functional solidarity (as measured by grandparent functional or practical involvement) was not linked to significant changes in initial levels of prosocial behavior or development across time.

Some of the control variables had important associations with the initial levels and slopes of prosocial behaviors. As anticipated, parent/child attachment was significantly linked with the initial levels of prosocial behavior toward family (standardized β = .19, SE = .06, p ≤ .001) and strangers (standardized β = .14, SE = .05, p ≤ .01), but not toward friends. Female gender was associated with higher intercepts but not slopes of prosocial behavior toward family (standardized β = .20, SE = .05, p ≤ .001), friends (standardized β = .46, SE = .05, p ≤ .001), and strangers (standardized β = .23, SE = .05, p ≤ .001).

DISCUSSION

Findings from the literature and from our own data support the idea that grandparents play an important role in the development of prosocial behaviors for their grandchildren. Intergenerational solidarity, or various ways that grandparents stay connected with their grandchildren, likely plays an important role in the prosocial development of adolescents. Findings from our data analyses supported the theoretical idea that affectual solidarity (emotional closeness to a grandparent) and associational solidarity (as measured with relationship quality between a grandparent and parent) were linked to initial levels of all three types of prosocial behavior. These predictors were sometimes linked with less steep slopes in the increase of prosocial behavior across time. Also, structural solidarity (i.e., proximity) was associated in the opposite direction as anticipated in that a grandparent living farther away was linked with higher initial levels of prosocial behavior toward friends and strangers.

Grandparent emotional involvement, or intergenerational affectual solidarity, appears to give the development of prosocial behavior a jump-start. That is, grandchild reports of feeling close to a grandparent is related to higher initial levels of prosocial behavior toward family, friends, and strangers. This finding is consistent with other literature examining the associations of grandparent involvement and prosocial behaviors with others (Attar-Schwartz et al., 2009; Barnett et al., 2010; Yorgason et al., 2011). Grandparent emotional involvement represents a "direct" influence of grandparents. In contrast, better relationship quality between the grandparent and the child's parent was also linked with higher initial levels of each type of prosocial behavior, potentially representing an "indirect" influence of grandparent involvement. Each of these findings is present, even after controlling for parent/child attachment. These findings together support the theoretical perspective that "attachment" to a grandparent may be driving the links between grandparent involvement and higher prosocial behavior. From this perspective, when a child feels a stronger secure attachment to a loving adult outside the immediate family they may interact in more prosocial ways with all others—family, friends, and strangers.

It is not too surprising that higher grandparent emotional involvement is associated with a less steep upward slope in the development of prosocial behavior toward strangers and the same trend between relationship quality between grandparents and the grandchild's parent. This trend might be expected in that having higher initial levels of prosocial behavior would have some sort of a ceiling effect, with less room to grow. It is interesting that this trend is not consistent between emotional involvement and growth in prosocial behavior toward family and friends (friends was significant at the trend level). It may be that these two lower cost types of prosocial behavior receive less of a jump-start from grandparent involvement. Although standardized coefficients are similar in size, the means for prosocial behavior toward strangers are substantially lower, suggesting that the same size effect may have stronger meaning.

It was not anticipated that a higher distance between where grandparents and their grandchildren live would be linked to higher initial levels of prosocial behavior toward family and friends. Zero-order correlations confirmed that these associations were not suppressor effects (they were in the same direction and approximately the same magnitude). One possible interpretation of this result is that grandparents that live farther away spend less time in day-to-day care with grandchildren and they may spend more fun-seeking time together. Having a grandparent that lives farther away may be linked with more "intentional grandparenting," where grandparents place emphasis on meaningful interactions. Such emphasis could potentially be linked with prosocial behavior. Given recent advances in internet and cell phone communications across long-distances, perhaps distance is less of a factor in limiting grandparent involvement. Also, having an involved grandparent that lives farther away may give youth an opportunity to interact with grandparents in more formal settings.

It was also not anticipated that grandparent functional involvement (functional solidarity) would not be linked to any type of prosocial behavior. Some studies have noted similar findings, such as Dunifon and Bajracharya (2012), who indicated no association between grandparent involvement and adolescent grades and risky behavior. In contrast, Yorgason et al. (2011) found that when a grandchild's family had received financial help from grandparents in the past year the grandchild also reported higher school engagement. It is likely that functional involvement is most beneficial in situations of higher stress, such as economic stress, single-parent households, and stepfamilies (Henderson et al., 2009; Ruiz & Silverstein, 2007) and in relation to specific outcomes. It is also possible that grandparent functional involvement is associated with adolescents' prosocial behavior only indirectly, through the quality of parent-child interactions that may improve as a result of financial assistance. These and other potential mediators of grandparent involvement are important avenues for future research.

Directions for Further Study

Although some headway has been made to expand the current research on grandparent influences with adolescent prosocial behavior, there are seemingly endless possibilities for future study. Some of these are focused on various aspects of grandparenting, while others are centered on prosocial development. Various future directions are outlined below.

GRANDPARENT CHARACTERISTICS

In this chapter we used data from the Flourishing Families study, which examined trends across 4 years during adolescence. Future study is needed to see how grandparents may influence prosocial behavior during the preteen years and into adulthood (see Sheehan & Petrovic, 2008). Although the data analysis presented in this chapter controlled for both the parent/child relationship as well as the grandparent/parent relationship quality, rarely is this the case with other studies. Examinations of the role of grandparent influence especially need to consider this link as we know that grandparents influence their grandchildren directly, as well as indirectly (Dunifon, 2013), and without a control of the indirect influences, direct effects may be superficially inflated.

Although we have considered the importance of grandparent emotional closeness, functional involvement, proximity, and the grandparent/parent relations in association with prosocial behavior outcomes, other types of grandparent involvement beg further study. Other aspects of grandparent/grandchild relationships that warrant attention include benefits of gifts from grandparents, roles grandparents play in providing companionship, how they might buffer stress, benefits of their passing on family legacy/history/traditions, and specifically how they act as role models or socialization agents. Furthermore, it is important that researchers further explore the importance and mechanisms of geographic proximity (especially in light of the surprising findings in the current study), specifics about grandparent health, and divorce and step-parenting. These nuances highlight the multidimensionality of the grandparent relationship and call for research examining how different aspects of grandparenting might be associated with different types or targets of prosocial behavior.

ADVANCING UNDERSTANDING OF PROSOCIAL BEHAVIOR

The study of various targets of prosocial behavior is maturing, yet there does not seem to be a great deal of research on how grandchildren act in prosocial ways directly toward their grandparents (for an exception, see Kumru and Yağmurlu, chapter 16, this volume). It may be that prosocial behavior toward grandparents actually shapes grandparent involvement with their grandchildren, with interactions influencing each other in reciprocal ways. Some grandchildren become involved in caregiving for aging grandparents, especially when grandparents coreside with grandchildren. Caring for someone outside the immediate family in intensive ways may shape a prosocial template that spills over into other associations. Similar to emotional involvement with a grandparent, higher prosocial behavior with grandparents may be linked with other desirable prosocial outcomes concurrently and across time.

The mechanisms through which grandparent involvement influences prosocial behavior are not well understood. Research has indicated that predictors of

prosocial behavior include things such as empathy, self-regulation, family socialization, and moral reasoning (Eisenberg et al., 2006). It may be that grandparent
involvement is predictive of these or other mechanisms that may lead to increased
prosocial behavior. In addition, the current study raised the possibility of mediators such as attachment quality and the quality of the parent-child relationship.
Given that parenting is so often indirectly associated with prosocial outcomes,
especially during adolescence (see Padilla-Walker, chapter 7, this volume), it is
also likely that socialization from grandparents becomes more indirect over time,
which is an important avenue for future research.

   Grandparent involvement is often shaped and colored by cultural values.
Trends in published literature suggest higher rates of coresidency and parenting
involvement by African American grandparents (Hunter & Taylor, 1998). Hispanic
cultures often support *familismo* and close-knit extended families (Goodman &
Rao, 2007). Native American and Canadian First Nation grandparents often act as
cultural conservators (Fuller-Thomson & Minkler, 2005; Thompson, Cameron, &
Fuller-Thomson, 2013). Also, prosocial literature suggests that living with extended
family is influential in the development of prosocial behavior (de Guzman, Do, &
Kok, chapter 11, this volume; Eisenberg et al., 2006). In summary, each family has
cultural roots that shape expectations and patterns of grandparent involvement.
The influence of grandparent involvement on the development of prosocial values
and behaviors within and across cultures would enlighten the current literature. In
summary, there appears to be plenty of work that still needs to be accomplished in
better understanding the development of prosocial behavior in context of grandparent involvement.

Conclusion

The development of prosocial behaviors is desired for every child and adolescent in today's society. Although immediate family members (especially
parents) generally shape prosocial development, there is growing evidence
that grandparents often play a critical role. While this is especially true where
grandparents take on parenting or highly influential roles such as with custodial grandparenting, it appears as well that noncoresiding grandparent
involvement has both direct and indirect links with prosocial behavior in
grandchildren. Findings from analyses presented in the current chapter from
the Flourishing Families study indicated that grandparent emotional involvement (direct influence) and relationship quality between grandparents and
their grandchild's parent (indirect influence) are associated with higher initial
levels of prosocial behavior toward family, friends, and strangers. The importance of intergenerational family solidarity in relation to prosocial outcomes is
supported. Multiple avenues of further study are needed to better understand
the intricacies of grandparent involvement, mechanism linking grandparent

involvement with prosocial behaviors, and various developments in the study of prosocial behavior.

References

Attar-Schwartz, S., Tan, J., Buchanan, A. (2009). Adolescents' perspectives on relationships with grandparents: The contribution of adolescent, grandparent, and parent–grandparent relationship variables. *Children and Youth Services Review, 31*(9), p. 1057–1066. doi:10.1016/j.childyouth.2009.05.007

Attar-Schwartz, S., Tan, J. P., Buchanan, A., Flouri, E., & Griggs, J. (2009). Grandparenting and adolescent adjustment in two-parent biological, lone-parent, and stepfamilies. *Journal of Family Psychology, 23*, 67–75.

Barnett, M. A., Mills-Koonce, W. R., Gustafsson, H., Cox, M., & Family Life Project Key Investigators. (2012). Mother-grandmother conflict, negative parenting, and young children's social development in multigenerational families. *Family Relations, 61*, 864–877.

Barnett, M. A., Scaramella, L. V., Neppl, T. K., Ontai, L. L., & Conger, R. D. (2010). Grandmother involvement as a protective factor for early childhood social adjustment. *Journal of Family Psychology, 24*, 635–645.

Beam, M. R., Chen, C., & Greenberger, E. (2002). The nature of adolescents' relationships with their "very important" nonparental adults. *American Journal of Community Psychology, 30* (2), p. 305–325.

Bengtson, V. L., & Roberts, R. E. (1991). Intergenerational solidarity in aging families: An example of formal theory construction. *Journal of Marriage and the Family, 53*, 856–870.

Botcheva, L. B., & Feldman, S. S. (2004). Grandparents as family stabilizers during economic hardship in Bulgaria. *International Journal of Psychology, 39*, 157–168.

Carlo, G., Mestre, M. V., Samper, P., Tur, A., & Armenta, B. E. (2011). The longitudinal relations among dimensions of parenting styles, sympathy, prosocial moral reasoning, and prosocial behavior. *International Journal of Behavioral Development, 35*, 116–124.

Cherlin, A., & Furstenberg, F. (1985). Styles and strategies of grandparenting. In V. L. Bengtson & J. F. Robertson (Eds.), *Grandparenthood* (pp. 97–116). Beverly Hills, CA: Sage.

DuBois, D. L., & Silverthorn, N. (2005). Natural mentoring relationships and adolescent health: Evidence from a national study. *American Journal of Public Health, 95*(3), 518–524.

Dunifon, R. (2013). The influence of grandparents on the lives of children and adolescents. *Child Development Perspectives, 7*, 55–60.

Dunifon, R., & Bajracharya, A. (2012). The role of grandparents in the lives of youth. *Journal of Family Issues, 33*, 1168–1194.

Eberly, M. B., & Montemayor, R. (1999). Adolescent affection and helpfulness toward parents: A 2-year follow-up. *Journal of Early Adolescence, 19*, 226–248.

Eisenberg, N., Fabes, R. A., & Spinrad, T. L. (2006). Prosocial development. In W. Damon (Series Ed.), R. M. Lerner (Series Ed.), & N. Eisenberg (Vol. Ed.), *Handbook of child psychology: Vol. 3. Social, emotional, and personality development* (6th ed., pp. 646–718). New York: Wiley.

Eisenberg, N., & Mussen, P. H. (1989). *The roots of prosocial behavior in children*. Cambridge, UK: Cambridge University Press.

Fuller-Thomson, E., & Minkler, M. (2005). American Indian/Alaskan Native grandparents raising grandchildren: Findings from the Census 2000 Supplementary Survey. *Social Work, 50*, 131–139.

Gallagher, P. A., Abbott-Shim, M., & Vandewiele, L. (2011). Head Start mentor teachers impact child outcomes in protégé teachers' classrooms. *NHSA Dialog, 14*, p. 75–78.

Goodman, C. C. (2012). Caregiving grandmothers and their grandchildren: Well-being nine years later. *Children and Youth Services Review, 34*, 648–654.

Goodman, M. R., & Rao, S. P. (2007). Grandparents raising grandchildren in a US-Mexico border community. *Qualitative Health Research, 17*, 1117–1136.

Grusec, J. E., & Goodnow, J. J. (1994). Impact of parental discipline methods on the child's internalization of values: A reconceptualization of current points of view. *Developmental Psychology, 30*, 4–19.

Hastings, P. D., Utendale, W. T., & Sullivan, C. (2007). The socialization of prosocial development. In J. E. Grusec & P. D. Hastings (Eds.). *Handbook of socialization* (pp. 638–664). New York: Guilford Press.

Hayslip, B., Jr., Kaminski, P. (2005). Grandparents raising their grandchildren: A review of the literature and suggestions of practice. *Gerontologist, 45*, 262–269.

Henderson, C. E., Hayslip, B. R., Sanders, L. M., & Louden, L. (2009). Grandmother grandchild relationship quality predicts psychological adjustment among youth from divorced families. *Journal of Family Issues, 30*, 1245–1264.

Hunter, A. G., & Taylor, R. J. (1998). Grandparenthood in African American families. In M. E. Szinovacz (Ed.), *Handbook on grandparenthood* pp. 70—86).Westport, CT: Greenwood Press.

King, V., Elder, G. H., & Conger, R. D. (2000). Wisdom of the ages. In R. D. Conger & G. H. Elder (Eds.), *Children of the land: Adversity and success in rural America*. Chicago: University of Chicago Press.

Lavers, C. A., & Sonuga-Burke, E. J. (1997). Annotation: On the grandmothers' role in the adjustment and maladjustment of grandchildren. *Journal of Child Psychology and Psychiatry, 38*, 747–753.

Lussier, G., Deater-Deckard, K., Dunn, J., & Davies, L. (2002). Support across two generations: Children's closeness to grandparents following parental divorce and remarriage. *Journal of Family Psychology, 16*, 363–376.

Mansson, D., & Booth-Butterfield, M. (2011). Affectionate communication between grandparents and grandchildren: Examining grandchildren's relational attitudes and behaviors. *Southern States Communication Journal, 76*, 424–442.

Meyer, K. C., & Bouchey, H. A. (2010). Daring to DREAM: Results from a mentoring programme for at risk youth. *International Journal of Evidence Based Coaching and Mentoring, 18*, 67–84. doi: 10.1037/t05338-00

Mitchell, W. (2008). The role played by grandparents in family support and learning: Considerations for mainstream and special schools. *Support for Learning, 23*, 126–135.

Muthén, L. K., & Muthén, B. O. (1998–2012). *Mplus user's guide* (7th ed.). Los Angeles, CA: Muthén & Muthén.

Padilla-Walker, L. M., & Carlo, G. (2007). Personal values as a mediator between parent and peer expectations and adolescent behaviors. *Journal of Family Psychology, 21*, 538–541.

Padilla-Walker, L. M., & Christensen, K. J. (2011). Empathy and self-regulation as mediators between parenting and adolescents' prosocial behaviors toward strangers, friends, and family. *Journal of Research on Adolescence, 21,* 545–551.

Padilla-Walker, L. M., Dyer, W. J., Yorgason, J. B., Fraser, A. M., & Coyne, S. M. (in press). Adolescents' prosocial behavior toward family, friends, and strangers: A person-centered approach. *Journal of Research on Adolescence.*

Pallock, L. L., & Lamborn, S. D. (2006). Beyond parenting practices: Extended kinship support and the academic adjustment of African-American and European-American teens. *Journal of Adolescence, 29,* 813–828. doi: 10.1016/j.adolescence.2005.12.003

Peterson, C., & Seligman, M. E. P. (2004). *Character strengths and virtues: A handbook and classification.* Washington, DC: Oxford University Press.

Ruiz, S. A., & Silverstein, M. (2007). Relationships with grandparents and the emotional well-being of late adolescence and young adult grandchildren. *Journal of Social Issues, 63,* 793–808.

Sheehan, N. W., & Petrovic, K. (2008). Grandparents and their adult grandchildren: Recurring themes from the literature. *Marriage and Family Review, 44,* 99–124.

Smith, P. K., & Drew, L. M. (2002). Grandparenthood. In M. H. Bornstein (Ed.), *Handbook of parenting: Vol. 3. Being and becoming a parent* (2nd ed., pp. 141–172). Mahwah, NJ: Erlbaum.

Taylor, R. D. (1996). Adolescents' perceptions of kinship support and family management practices: Association with adolescent adjustment in African American families. *Developmental Psychology, 32*(4), 697–695.

Thompson, G. E., Cameron, R. E., & Fuller-Thomson, E. (2013). Walking the red road: The role of First Nations grandparents in promoting cultural well-being. *International Journal of Aging and Human Development, 76,* 55–78.

Uhlenberg, P., & Cheuk, M. (2010). The significance of grandparents to grandchildren: An international perspective. In D. Dannefer & C. Phillipson (Eds.), *The SAGE handbook of social gerontology.* Thousand Oaks, CA: Sage.

Wiscott, R., & Kopera-Fyre, K. (2000). Sharing of culture: Adult grandchildren's perceptions of intergenerational relations. *International Journal of Aging and Human Development, 51*(3), 199–215.

Yorgason, J. B., Padilla-Walker, L. M., & Jackson, J. (2011). Non-residential grandparents' financial and emotional involvement in relation to early adolescent grandchild outcomes. *Journal of Research on Adolescence, 21,* 552–558.

Yorgason, J. B., LaPierre, T. A., & Hayter, B. (in press). Grandparenting. In Alex C. Michalos (Ed.), *Encyclopedia of Quality of Life Research.* Springer.

Cultural and Contextual Perspectives

11

The Cultural Contexts of Children's Prosocial Behaviors

Maria Rosario T. de Guzman, Kieu Anh Do, and Car Mun Kok

In 1976 Beatrice Whiting famously urged researchers to "unpackage" the concept of culture and related constructs. She highlighted the need in social and behavioral research to tease out the complex and often interwoven factors that might underlie superficial culture group differences in child outcomes and suggested looking more closely at the child's learning environment, the details within which could provide important insight regarding children's behaviors that could better explain how culture might be manifested in the developmental landscape (Whiting, 1976). Almost 40 years later, the importance of culture in children's development is widely recognized, nonetheless researchers continue to wrestle with questions of what role culture plays in socialization, how it is manifested, and consequently how to measure its effects on child outcomes. In this chapter, we review current research on the interplay between culture and prosocial behavior and attempt to identify future directions toward this end.

The Challenge of Defining Culture

The challenge of defining "culture" and conceptualizing its manifestation has had a long history (Erickson, 2002; Super & Harkness, 2002). In 1952, Kroeber and Kluckohm identified 164 definitions and usages of the term (Munroe & Munroe, 1997), and these definitions and conceptualizations have evolved in many ways over the years (Erickson, 2002; Jahoda, 2012). E. B. Tylor's broad definition of culture in the late 1800s, for example, included the belief systems, knowledge, values, and all other practices developed by people participating in a particular community (Erickson, 2002). Culture was thus conceptualized as a somewhat static entity that was acquired in whole by people within a particular community.

Newer conceptualizations of culture vary (Jahoda, 2012). However, culture is generally viewed today as more dynamic, takes into account generational and historical change, emphasizes symbolic meanings, and depicts members of a community as acquiring the knowledge, habits, and norms through active participation in cultural practices throughout the lifetime. Moreover, culture is not viewed as a unitary entity acquired in whole. Instead, members participate in practices and gain cultural knowledge in various domains and to varying degrees, and can participate in multiple cultural communities (Cole & Tan, 2007; Erickson, 2002).

Cross-National and Cross-Ethnic Studies on Children's Prosocial Behaviors

Societies differ along many dimensions that have implications for prosocial behavior. John Whiting and Beatrice Whiting and their research associates conducted one of the earliest systematic culture-comparative studies in children's socialization in their groundbreaking Six Cultures study (1975; see also Whiting & Edwards, 1988). Using a standardized set of measures and data collection methods that drew from both psychology and anthropology (Whiting et al., 1966), they sought to document children's daily lives and learning environments to better understand how regularities and differences in their developmental landscape led to various outcomes. Among the many insights that emerged from this work were higher incidences of prosocial (e.g., nurturing, cooperative) behaviors in children from subsistence-based economies where both parents had high workloads (i.e., Kenya, Philippines, Mexico) compared with children from more complex and industrialized communities (i.e., Japan, United States, India).

More recently, the individualism-collectivism (I-C) dichotomy or some variation thereof (e.g., autonomy vs. relatedness) has been used frequently to frame and explain group differences. In broad terms, the individualism-collectivism distinction places nations or culture groups along a continuum based on the degree to which they espouse certain values—with some societies tending toward the valuation of independent and individual rights and goals and others valuing group goals and the perception of self as attached to the larger society (Triandis, 2001).

That broad culture-level variables might be reflected in children's prosocial behaviors has had some empirical support. Researchers suggest that children from societies that foster group orientation and a more collective sense of self (i.e., as opposed to individualistic norms) might be more inclined to express other-oriented behaviors such as those prosocial in nature in contrast to peers from more individualist oriented societies. For example, Israeli children from kibbutz communities, which typically emphasize communal living and high cooperation to meet shared goals, have been shown to display more prosocial, cooperative, and otherwise other-oriented behaviors compared with their urban-dwelling peers (Madsen & Shapira, 1977; Shapira & Madsen, 1969, 1974). Eisenberg and colleagues

(Eisenberg, Hertz-Lazarowitz, & Fuchs, 1990) also found that kibbutz children used more sophisticated modes of prosocial reasoning, particularly reciprocity- and needs-based thinking, compared with nonkibbutz peers, who reported more pragmatic and hedonistic modes of thinking. Partially supporting and partly contradicting these findings, Hollos (1980) found that among 6- to 8-year-old Hungarian children, those who were growing up in the context of farming communities where children are expected to contribute to household and farm chores collectively within their families scored lower on role- and perspective-taking measures compared to same-age peers who were in schools that espoused a collective ideology. However, children growing up in farms showed higher cooperative and lower competitive scores than schoolchildren, suggesting that cooperation, responsible action, and concern for others might be better fostered through exposure to actual experiences of collective participation and responsible work rather than direct teaching about group orientation.

More recent evidence for group differences in children's prosocial behaviors along the I-C dimension has been mixed. Stewart and McBride-Chang (2000) examined sharing behaviors of Western Caucasian (Australian, English, American, South African and Canadian) and Asian (Chinese, Thai, Indian, and Japanese) second grade students in Hong Kong. Asian children marginally shared more than Western peers, which appeared to be partly explained by the predominantly other-oriented parenting styles of their caregivers, which was in turn related to their levels of sharing. Yağmurlu and Sanson (2009), using teacher and parent reports as well as behavioral observations, found similar rates of prosocial behaviors in Turkish Australian and Australian preschoolers. Kärtner, Keller, and Chaudry (2010) found no differences between prosocial reactions of Indian and German toddlers to an experimentally manipulated stimulus of distress. Trommsdorff, Friedlmeier, and Mayer (2007), also exposing children to an experimentally manipulated stimulus of an adult in need and distress, found that German and Israeli preschoolers displayed more prosocial behaviors than Malaysian and Indonesian children in an experimental setting. They reasoned that children in collective-oriented societies are more sensitive to the hierarchical nature of relationships and in- versus out-group distinctions and thus might be hesitant to help the distressed adult in the experiment.

Asian societies are typically depicted as valuing collective norms and group orientation. To this end, Rao and Stewart (1999) did not directly test U.S. children in their study involving Chinese and Indian 4-year-olds and their sharing behaviors, but noted that their Asian samples displayed higher rates of sharing compared to U.S. children in other studies utilizing similar methodology (Birch & Billman, 1986). Somewhat relatedly, Asian American adolescents with lower levels of self-reported acculturation generally reported willingness to self-sacrifice in more domains (i.e., school work, money, giving up a date) and a higher willingness to sacrifice for their parents over friends compared with European American peers (Suzuki & Greenfield, 2002). In contrast, European Americans and highly acculturated Asian Americans were more willing to sacrifice for friends over their parents—supporting earlier researchers' contentions that Asians value collective norms and filial piety.

Within the same country, variability can be found among ethnic groups on the degree to which they espouse collective and family-oriented values as opposed to the fulfillment of individual goals (Garcia Coll, Meyer, & Brillon, 2002; McDade, 1995; Zayas & Solari, 1994). Consistent with these patterns, Spivak and Howes (2011) observed African American children as being more likely to engage in prosocial behavior compared with white or Latino children, and Latino children displaying more prosocial behavior than whites. The body of work by Knight and colleagues documents differences in cooperation and resource alloca- tion among Mexican American and European American children. Using game activities, they asked participants to distribute resources—allowing them to allo- cate more, the same as, or fewer resources to another person in relation to what they would receive (Knight & Kagan, 1977). Their findings showed that Mexican American children exhibited more cooperative resource allocation preferences than European American peers and that higher generational status was linked to lower preference for cooperative allocation. Those results are supported by their later work, which showed that children's sense of ethnic identity was related to patterns of resource allocation preference (Knight, Cota, & Bernal, 1993) and are consistent with recent research linking acculturation with lower levels of prosocial behavior (e.g., Armenta, Knight, Carlo, & Jacobson, 2011).

The Same Predictors in Different Cultural Contexts?

In addition to culture comparative studies, prosocial behavior research is also being conducted in an increasing number of societies around the world. Results of these studies are contributing to our understanding of the extent to which similar predictors operate across cultures. Research on parenting illustrates this point.

Parenting characterized by warmth, support, mutual respect, and nonpunitive punishment has long been linked to positive outcomes including those prosocial in nature. This pattern appears to be supported in several culture groups beyond majority populations in the United States. For example, Carlo and colleagues (Carlo, Knight, McGinley, & Hayes, 2011) found links between inductive parent- ing to six types of prosocial behaviors in both Mexican and European American youth. Whitside-Mansell and collaborators (2003) found that responsive par- enting was related to prosocial behaviors in both African American and white preschoolers. Haskett, Allaire, Kreig, and Hart (2008) found that parental sensi- tivity, characterized by warmth and responsiveness was a significant predictor of prosocial behavior in both African American and Caucasian children. Croatian youth's levels of prosociality have been linked to parental levels of warmth and support and negatively to parental levels of psychological control (Kerestes,

2006). Similarly, Deković and Janssens (1992) found in their study of children in the Netherlands that authoritative and democratic parenting was positively correlated with children's peer-nominated helpfulness as well as teacher-reported prosocial behavior.

Studies on other well-established predictors and correlates of prosocial behavior conducted in different societies are beginning to reveal the extent to which linkages are supported in various cultural contexts. For example, relations between sociocognitive factors and prosocial behavior has been shown in numerous studies, including those conducted outside the United States such as Spain, Brazil, India, Germany, Israel, and Malaysia (Carlo, Koller, Eisenberg, Da Silva, & Frohlich, 1996; Carlo, Mestre, Samper, Tur, & Armenta, 2010; Malti, Gummerum, Keller, & Buchmann, 2009; Trommsdorff et al., 2007). However, researchers have also noted that underlying cultural constructs could impact these relations. For instance, Kärtner and Keller (2012) challenge the universal applicability of the link between empathy and toddlers' understanding of others' mental states and consequently prosocial responding (e.g., Bischof-Köhler, 2012). They argue that empathically motivated prosocial responding necessitates both a sense of autonomy as an intentional agent and a sense of relatedness in order to sense others' distress; and that the development of autonomy and relatedness is impacted by cultural context. They found that toddlers' mirror recognition (representing the emergence of self-other recognition) was related to prosocial responding in Germany (autonomy-oriented) but not India (autonomy/related-oriented). They suggest alternative mechanisms surrounding prosocial behavior in children in relatedness-oriented cultures, for instance, emotional contagion, which is not contingent on children's ability to make self-other distinctions (Kärtner et al., 2010).

CROSS CULTURAL RESEARCH: REMAINING CHALLENGES

The near burgeoning of prosocial behavior research in various countries is allowing us to better understand the extent to which predictors and correlates operate similarly across culture groups, and findings from cross-cultural studies are beginning to shed light on the interplay between culture and prosocial behavior. Nonetheless, some challenges remain. First, the sampling of cultures is still somewhat limited. We still know little about the trajectory, correlates, and prosocial socialization experiences of children in less industrialized nations whose developmental landscape may be very different from children in North American samples more commonly represented in the literature. Second, what might account for cultural differences in prosocial behavior is lacking. Just as researchers examining societal-level differences in the I-C dimension highlight the need to examine within-culture variability (Kağitçibaşi, 1997; Leung & Brown, 1995; Oyserman et al., 2002), scholars in prosocial behavior also argue for the need to extend research beyond identifying group differences to include within-culture and intermediate factors to help account for group variation (Carlo, Roesch, Knight, & Koller, 2001; Eisenberg & Wang, 2003).

Certainly, there are numerous ways by which culture is instantiated in children's developmental context. One promising area relevant to prosocial behavior is that of parental beliefs. Also known as "ethno" or "folk theories," parental beliefs have important implications for children's socialization. While societal values and cultural syndromes represent broad dimensions, parental ethnotheories represent underlying motivations for parenting practices and adults' organization of children's early experiences. In many ways, parenting beliefs mirror the broader societal values and beliefs, while at the same time impacting parenting practices that shape children's outcomes (Harkness & Super, 2006; Parmar, Harkness, & Super, 2004), and thus might serve as an intermediate and more proximal predictor of prosocial behavior.

Parental beliefs differ across groups in ways consistent with broad cultural variables (e.g., Miller, Wang, Sandel, & Cho, 2002; Rosenthal & Roer-Strier, 2001; Wang & Tamis-LeMonda, 2003). For instance, Chinese American parents reported valuing benevolence and prosocial goals (valuing the welfare of people with whom one has frequent personal contact) in their children more than (and followed by) Mexican Americans, African Americans, and European Americans (Suizzo, 2007). And parental beliefs and values have been linked to parenting practices (Padmawidjaja & Chao, 2010) and child prosocial outcomes (Stewart & McBride-Chang, 2000). Linking broad culture values, parenting beliefs, parenting practices, and prosocial behaviors could be helpful in beginning to explain how cultural syndromes and broad societal orientations are manifested in children's socialization.

Finally, few studies incorporate potential culture-specific factors that might have important implications for prosocial behavior. Researchers examining Asian families have identified alternative conceptualizations of parenting styles, taking into account Confucian ideals and culture-specific notions of parenting roles (e.g., Chao & Tseng, 2002). Similarly, are there unique culture-specific constructs that impact prosocial behaviors? One exception to this gap is research on Latino values and prosocial behavior (see Carlo, Knight, Basilio, & Davis, chapter 12, this volume). Researchers suggest specific values that hold special relevance to this culture group, such as *familismo*, or the valuing of close relationships and interdependence within the family; *bien educado*, or proper behavior in all settings as this reflects on one's family; and finally *simpatia*, which is akin to smooth personal relations even in the face of conflict (Durand, 2011). In our recent study contrasting European American and first- and second-generation Latina mothers' beliefs about prosocial behaviors (de Guzman, Brown, Carlo & Knight, 2012), we found elements of those unique cultural factors in parents' definitions of prosocial behaviors—with beliefs around *bien educado, familismo,* and *simpatia* especially evident in first-generation respondents' conceptions of prosocial behaviors, and least evident in Caucasian American mothers' representations. Related to this, Calderon-Tena, Knight, and Carlo (2011) found that familism values mediated relations between prosocial parenting practices and prosocial behaviors of Mexican American youth. They concluded that prosocial parenting practices contribute to the internalization of familism values, which in turn promote prosocial behaviors. Research that identifies culture-specific values and factors is needed.

The Child in the Field: Anthropological Approach

Anthropological and field studies offer rich information about the daily lives, history, social structure, and beliefs and value orientations of societies in which children are reared (James, 2007; Tedlock, 2000). Studies of this nature are harder to mine for information on prosocial behaviors, as few, if any, specifically focus on this topic and most instead document prosocial behavior and its socialization within a broader discussion of the child's learning environment. Nonetheless, studies drawing from fieldwork are uniquely important for understanding the interplay between culture and prosocial behaviors for at least three reasons.

First, ethnographic and other field-based studies allow us to examine prosocial behaviors in natural settings. Experimental studies are important in that they can isolate the impact of specific variables. Nonetheless, naturalistic observations and ethnographic accounts are needed to provide contextual validity to findings from laboratory settings, as well as data drawn from surveys and self- or other-reported measures more typically used to study prosocial behavior (Gurven & Winking, 2008; Reyes-Garcia, Godoy, Vadez, Huanca, & Leonard, 2006). Studies conducted directly in natural settings help us understand prosocial behavior and their correlates as they occur in the real world—performed within the context of daily activities, in a wide range of settings, and with various social companions—the organization of which are reflective of the child's broader social and cultural ecology (e.g., Super & Harkness, 2002; Tietjen, 1989).

For example, studies on sibling caregiving provide some support for research on infant presence and prosocial behavior. Evidence suggests that the presence of infants can elicit nurturance and related prosocial, empathic, and related responding in children and adults because of their relative helplessness and high need for care (e.g., Bråten, 1996; Hay & Rheingold, 1983; Newman, 2000). Most of these studies, however, have been conducted within the confines of laboratory settings and have used highly controlled stimuli such as pictures or audio recordings of infant cries and vocalizations; and measured subsequent reactions through observations or self-reports (e.g., Catherine & Schonert-Reichl, 2011; Zahn-Waxler, Friedman, & Cummings, 1983). The cross-cultural generalizability of the power of infant presence and the extent to which this can be observed in settings outside the laboratory (e.g., in competition with a host of other powerful stimuli) has not been fully explored in mainstream psychological literature. However, there is ample support for the role that infant and toddler presence play in the expression and development of prosocial behavior in children through research on sibling caregiving.

In many places around the world, children are assigned to care for their younger siblings or relatives (Weisner & Gallimore, 1977). This appears to be more common in societies where both parents have a high workload, extended family are easily accessible, and families are situated in subsistence-based economies that involve cultivation of land (Hirasawa, 2005; Whiting & Edwards, 1988). Rich descriptions of the sibling caregiving experience can be found for children in Yucatec (Gaskins, 2000, 2003), Zinacatec (Raiban-Jamin, Maynard, & Greenfield, 2003), and Guatamala Mayan (Rogoff, 2003); East and Sub-Saharan African (LeVine, Dixon, LeVine, Richman, Leiderman, Keefer, & Brazelton, 1994); and Philippine (Nydegger & Nydegger, 1966) societies, among many others. In such contexts, children routinely comfort, entertain, clean, feed, and otherwise tend to the needs of young infants and toddlers. In some societies, children not only assist primary caregivers, they are sometimes even favored over fathers to take over caregiving duties when the mother is not available, as is the case among sedentarized hunter-gatherer Baka in Southern Cameroon (Hirasawa, 2005).

Sibling caregiving represents a rich opportunity for prosocial behavior. Raiban-Jami and colleagues (2003), in their observations of Zinacatec Mayan children in Mexico and Wolof children in Senegal noted that in both societies the caregiver is both the socializer and the socialized—scaffolding the development and learning of their younger sibling while themselves learning numerous skills in their active participation in caregiving. For children in these two cultural communities, sibling caregivers practice a myriad of prosocial and cooperative strategies to maintain harmony among the children, which is emphasized though not necessarily verbalized during sibling care and multiage play. For example, it is inevitable that in young children sometimes complain, behave in ways deemed inappropriate in a particular setting, or otherwise fail to comply with their older siblings' exhortations. In such incidences, the sibling caregiver finds ways to resolve the situation and might use multiple strategies such as comforting the child or temporarily changing the topic to distract the noncompliant, complaining, or otherwise misbehaving younger sibling.

Few studies have directly examined how sibling care might foster children's prosocial behaviors. Ember's (1973) early investigations found that Luo children who were assigned animal care duties showed higher levels of dominance than other children; and that those assigned childcare duties were more nurturing than their peers. Our reanalysis of subsets of the Six Cultures Study and related data showed that while Philippine children generally showed higher rates of prosocial behavior than their U.S. counterparts, U.S. and Philippine children both displayed higher rates of overall prosocial behavior when they were in the company of infants (de Guzman, Carlo, & Edwards, 2008); and that Kikuyu children displayed higher rates of nurturing behaviors, specifically when engaged in infant sibling care, and higher rates of prosocial dominant behavior when in the company of toddlers (de Guzman, Edwards, & Carlo, 2005). Together, these studies support and lend ecological validity to experimental findings that suggest that infant presence may encourage prosocial responding in children.

Related to the point of ecological validity, a second contribution of field-based studies is that they allow us to examine the interplay between prosocial behavior and a wide range of everyday activities and contexts, which vary substantially by cultural community. Cultural psychologists and anthropologists propose socialization models that focus on what they variously refer to as the "learning environment" (Whiting, 1980), "activity settings" (Farver, 1999), "ecocultural context" (Weisner, 2002), or the "developmental niche" (Super & Harkness, 1986) and how a child develops as a competent member of a given society and culture through her interactions therein. These researchers emphasize the importance of everyday settings in shaping children's behavior and suggest that regular participation in "mundane" daily activities is significant in the development of children as functioning members of their respective societies. Naturalistic and other forms of field research allow us to examine a broad range of contexts beyond the school or daycare setting, for example, children engaged in play, chores, rituals, and a host of other contexts—and how prosocial behavior might emerge in these different settings.

One example of an everyday activity where prosocial behavior may be evident is sibling care, as discussed earlier. Another example is children's participation in labor. Numerous ethnographic and other field-based studies document children's participation in house and economic work, which appear to also offer many opportunities for prosocial socialization. These experiences are particularly important because they serve as venues for the acquisition of practical skills and the socialization of cultural norms and serve as opportunities for apprenticeship for future roles (e.g., Rogoff, 2003; Maynard, 2005; see Padilla-Walker, chapter 7, this volume).

Lancy (2008) notes that while modern Western conceptualizations of childhood is that of a period of fragility and innocence, in fact, in many societies, children participate extensively in house and economic labor. Numerous ethnographic accounts corroborate this assertion, and culture comparative studies indicate differences in the amount of time children spend engaging in work across nations and socioeconomic groups (Ochs & Izquierdo, 2009; Tudge & Odero-Wanga, 2009).

Of course, for much of house and economic work, adults often innately scale down responsibilities to match children's developmental stage and capabilities (Lansy, 2008). Participation in work might begin by children's simply being in the vicinity of more capable workers, watching and observing those actors, and later participating in some capacity under adults' supervision or on their own (Paradise & Rogoff, 2009). Young children and toddlers might also perform simple tasks in close proximity to adults and later on their own (Ochs & Izquierdo, 2009). Alternatively, children might engage in work alongside adults, but are expected to produce less, as is the case of Mikea children in Madagascar who forage for edibles as part of adult groups but are not expected to accomplish the same level of success (Tucker & Young, 2005). They might, for instance, gather younger tubers that are easier to dig for, or gather and carry fewer nuts and fruits compared with more able-bodied adults.

In our own fieldwork, we return to Tarong, the Ilocos village examined by Nydegger and Nydegger (1966) as part of the Six Cultures study (Whiting & Whiting, 1975). Like the parents observed and interviewed in the 1950s, residents today (including some of the children in the original data set, now grandparents) expressed strong expectations for prosocial behaviors (e.g., to be "matulungin" or helpful) and expected young children of 3 or 4 years to contribute to household and wage labor, as well as childcare of their siblings. However, before they are considered "may isip" (i.e., literally, "having a mind" or sense at about age 7), these expectations included simply not being in the way of adults' work or to perform simple tasks such as pushing a baby's hammock, or helping string tobacco leaves. Older children of 6 or 7 are expected to participate in more sophisticated ways, for example, helping gather weeds, tending to animals, and helping prepare food or clean the home (de Guzman, Edwards, & Brown, 2011).

Certainly, play is an important context in which children learn social rules, gain skills, and practice competencies important within their particular cultural context; and this topic has been covered extensively by numerous other researchers (e.g., Fagen, 2011). Many examples of socialization for prosocial and related behaviors can be drawn from fieldwork in this area. For example, Corsaro (2005) describes toddlers' play in Italian preschools and details how a simple game of arranging chairs becomes a venue for children to practice cooperation and social inclusion skills. He also observed children engaging each other in the game and comforting each other when someone was hurt.

Goody (1991) describes Mbuti children of the Congo as having an area all to themselves for play—free of adult intervention and including a broad age range of children, between about 3 and 11 years old. Children play a wide range of games, including cooperative types that involve children working together. Moreover, there is a general emphasis on harmony among the children. They watch out for each other's well-being and among themselves foster positive relations and disallow such negative behaviors as severe teasing.

Socialization for prosocial behavior in the context of play does not only occur among age mates. Examining episodes of family interactions, Sirota (2010) documents middle-class U.S. mother-child pairs engaging in imaginative make-believe play, during which mothers enter the child-constructed make believe scenario to encourage compliance (e.g., coming to the dinner table). In so doing, mothers model cooperation and, perhaps unconsciously, expressed support for creativity and self-expression. Sirota (2010) describes this type of teaching as "fun morality," in which cultural norms and targeted behaviors are socialized through coconstructed play.

Finally, field-based studies allow us to look at prosocial behavior in light of the broader cultural system. Ethnographic research is particularly helpful in this regard because these studies typically draw from multiple sources of information (e.g., administrative data, interviews, observations) and document the daily lives of people as well as broader cultural constructs like societal values and beliefs (James, 2007). As such, when there is discussion of prosocial behavior and its socialization, we are able to examine these competencies in light of the broader cultural system. This is what is sometimes lacking in culture comparative work that might reveal interesting patterns of similarities or differences in frequency of performing prosocial behavior but do little to help us understand why such differences emerge.

For example, Jocano (1969) describes how, in a Philippine village in the Panay islands, expectations for sharing is especially high during mealtimes. Meals are highly regulated by parents, who monitor eating behaviors and communicate strong rules around propriety. For instance, children are not allowed to accept food from strangers, lest the family be thought of as being in need. Children are strongly expected to finish their food and are not allowed to express their dislike for what is served. Relevant to prosocial socialization, children as young as 1 year are urged to share their food, though the pressure is greatest for older children to share with younger siblings. These early experiences of sharing and prosocial expectations fit within the broader community norm of collective living; and high expectations for older siblings to share with younger ones is consistent with the age-based hierarchy found within the community.

In addition to broader cultural systems, ethnographic fieldwork data can potentially provide insight regarding prosocial socialization within changing social or ecological settings. Hirasawa (2005) conducted fieldwork among Baka pygmies in Southeastern Cameroon and noted that children from this community heavily engaged in infant care as secondary caregivers, much more than Aka and Efe pygmy children from neighboring Congo. Aka and Efe are also hunter-gatherers, are similarly involved in foraging, and have somewhat similar geographical terrain. Hirasawa (2005) posits that the introduction of land cultivation in the Baka community contributes to this difference—with mothers likely available nearby but working in the fields, thus both necessitating and allowing for some supervision of children as secondary caregivers. Moreover, with the introduction of land cultivation, there is less adult cosharing of food resources as is the case in purely hunting and gathering subsistence, thus, there are fewer adults around to share in childcare duties and a higher reliance on children to care for younger siblings.

Miles (1994) describes task assignment and the use of devil stories (i.e., fictional stories that include the devil in one form or another) as a way to socialize both gender roles and cooperative and other desired behaviors among rural to urban migrants in Ecuador. She suggests that the use of these traditional techniques fits within the broader context of rural to urban migration, for instance, as traditional Andean culture clashes or otherwise encounters Hispanic culture, where values and ways of life found in traditional rural environments meet with urban environments. The devil stories, sometimes ghoulish and gruesome, reflect underlying themes of "moral salvation" through work, dignity of labor, and other traditional values that parents fear are being threatened as they move to the city. The use of stories for socialization of moral and prosocial themes within the context of the broader culture has also been described by numerous other researchers describing a wide range of communities including Gikuyu in Kenya (Kenyatta, 1966), Southern Baltimore families in the United States (Miller & Moore, 1989), and young kindergarten classrooms in modern-day China (Stevenson, 1991).

Research using ethnographic and other field-based methods thus can be an important resource for understanding how prosocial behavior is manifest in children's daily lives in various cultures. These studies provide ecological validity to findings from laboratory and self-report studies, allow us to examine a wide range of contexts which themselves reflect the child's ecological and cultural milieu, and allow us to understand prosocial behavior and its socialization as they fit within the broader cultural system.

Future Directions in the Study of Prosocial Behavior in Cultural Context

As the studies reviewed in this chapter reflect, efforts to examine the interplay between culture and prosocial behavior represent a vast diversity in the conceptualizations of prosocial behavior, the methodological approaches taken, and the philosophical underpinnings guiding researchers' endeavors. Studies using the culture comparative approach—whether directly testing group differences (e.g., Kärtner et al., 2010) or testing factors and models in different cultural contexts (e.g., Rao & Stewart, 1999)—have contributed significantly to current understanding of systematic group variability in light of broad cultural factors, as well as the extent to which correlates of children's prosocial behavior operate similarly across cultures (e.g., Carlo et al., 2011). In-depth cultural explorations of children's learning environments, in contrast, have shed light (albeit, indirectly) on the sociocultural context of children's prosocial behaviors and contribute to our understanding of how different prosocial behaviors are socialized through everyday experiences, the role of various socialization agents, as well as its role in the broader social and cultural ecology of the child. Furthermore, both cultural and cross-cultural research have allowed for us to examine a broader range of contexts and a wider array of different types of prosocial behaviors (de Guzman et al., 2008).

Future studies can benefit from several research directions. First, while both field research and more traditional modes of psychological inquiry (e.g., laboratory experiments, surveys) have contributed substantially to our current understanding of prosocial behavior and culture, studies that blend both approaches are still lacking. Mixed-methods designs are particularly useful when the phenomenon under study is complex and one data source cannot sufficiently answer the research question (Creswell & Plano Clark, 2011); they combine not just methodologies but also paradigms that might include a culture comparative approach (Karasz & Singelis, 2009) and in-depth studies of issues within specific cultures (Bartholomew & Brown, 2012). One early example of this type of research was Whiting and Whiting's (1975; Whiting & Edwards, 1988) Six Cultures study, which used ethnographic fieldwork, systematic behavioral observations, and a host of quantitative methods such as standardized tests. Similar studies examining prosocial behavior and culture in more recent years are virtually nonexistent. Certainly, mixed methods research tends to be more resource-intensive and challenging for many reasons (e.g., lack of training in either qualitative or quantitative methods; the need to collect multiple types of data). However, as Bartholomew and Brown (2012) note in their review of mixed-methods studies in cultural research, this approach can provide multiple benefits, for example, allowing one to examine phenomena from multiple perspectives and to test theories systematically while still being sensitive to the "subtlety and uniqueness in cultures" (p. 188).

Similarly, in-depth within-culture studies that take on a more indigenous approach are lacking. Ethnographic and other field-based studies reviewed in this chapter suggest that prosocial behavior might hold variable meaning in different cultural contexts. Certainly, expectations for prosocial behavior and the types of prosocial behavior children display or have the opportunity to engage in, vary substantially by sociocultural context (de Guzman et al., 2008). We are also beginning to see that the very definition of "prosocial" is saturated with cultural meaning (de Guzman et al., 2012). An indigenous psychology lens (i.e., using perspectives and methodologies developed from within the culture group in which the study is conducted) has the potential to uncover unique concepts, develop theories and methods that are deeply rooted in cultural and social context, and generate information that is most relevant to the actual groups under study, as is the case of indigenous research endeavors in various cultural communities of such issues as values, parenting, and other topics (Allwood & Berry, 2006).

Another methodological gap, not unique to cultural or cross-cultural examinations of prosocial behavior, pertains to a dearth of studies using a longitudinal perspective. Few studies, even within mainstream psychology, examine prosocial behaviors longitudinally (e.g., Eisenberg, Guthrie, Murphy, & Shepard, 2002), and fewer still outside of the United States. One example is a longitudinal examination of the prosocial behaviors among Italian and Canadian children (Nantel-Vivier, Kokko, Caprara, Pastorelli, Paciello, et al., 2009). This study used a person-centered approach and identified various trajectories of prosocial behaviors between ages 10 and 15. Generally, children displayed stable or declining levels of prosocial behaviors as they moved from childhood to adolescence. Studies that examine prosocial behaviors longitudinally in other cultures would help not just in identifying age differences in children's performance of these acts but possibly also differences in the types of contexts and everyday experiences they access across age and time, changes in expectations, and their changing social relationships and the relative impact of socialization agents with age.

One final direction that might be useful to explore is the role of social change in the relations between culture and prosocial behavior. As we discussed earlier in this chapter, more recent conceptualizations of culture take into account its dynamic nature. Indeed, a growing body of work is beginning to identify various ways by which such trends as globalization, immigration patterns, access to technology, and other agents of rapid social change, are impacting on such cultural elements as "values" (Manago, 2012; Sun & Wang, 2010; van Oudenhoven & Ward, 2013), adults' perceptions regarding the value of children (Kağitçibaşi & Aataca, 2005; Kim, Park, Kwon, & Koo, 2005), and socialization goals (Ispa, 2002). As social change brings about shifts in the caregiving context and the child's learning environment, are there corresponding changes in expectations toward prosocial behavior, the types of contexts and learning environments that children access, or even in the role of social companions and socialization agents?

The interplay between culture and prosocial behavior is complicated and necessarily complex. While we might be a long way from fully "unpacking" the concept of culture as it pertains to prosocial behavior research, nonetheless our understanding of the many ways by which culture is manifested in the developmental context is steadily growing as researchers are approaching the issue from multiple perspectives and utilizing various methodologies and as prosocial behavior research is increasingly being conducted with a broader range of cultural communities.

References

Allwood, C. M., & Berry, J. W. (2006). Origins and development of indigenous psychologies: An international analysis. *International Journal of Psychology, 41*(4), 243–268. doi: 10.1080/00207590544000013

Armenta, B. E., Knight, G. P., Carlo, G., & Jacobson, R. P. (2011). The relation between ethnic group attachment and prosocial tendencies: The mediating role of cultural values. *European Journal of Social Psychology, 41*(1), 107–115. doi: 10.1002/ejsp.742

Bartholomew, T. T., & Brown, J. R. (2012). Mixed methods, culture, and psychology: A review of mixed methods in culture-specific psychological research. *International Perspectives in Psychology, 1*(3), 177–190. doi: 10.1037/a0029219

Birch, L. L., & Billman, J. (1986). Preschool children's food sharing with friends and acquaintances. *Child Development, 57*(2), 387–395. doi: 10.2307/1130594

Bischof-Köhler, D. (2012). Empathy and self-recognition in phylogenetic and ontogenetic perspective. *Emotion Review, 4*(1), 40–48. doi: 10.1177/1754073911421377

Bråten, S. (1996). When toddlers provide care: Infants' companion space. *Childhood, 3,* 449–465. doi: 10.1177/0907568296003004003

Calderón-Tena, C. O., Knight, G. P., & Carlo, G. (2011). The socialization of prosocial behavior tendencies among Mexican American adolescents: The role of familism values. *Cultural Diversity and Ethnic Minority Psychology, 17*(1), 98–106. doi: 10.1037/a0021825

Carlo, G., Knight, G. P., McGinley, M., & Hayes, R. (2011). The roles of parental inductions, moral emotions, and moral cognitions in prosocial tendencies among Mexican American and European American early adolescents. *Journal of Early Adolescence, 31*(6), 757–781. doi: 10.1177/0272431610373100

Carlo, G., Koller, S. H., Eisenberg, N., Da Silva, M. S., Frohlich, C. B. (1996). A cross-national study on the relations among prosocial moral reasoning, gender role orientations, and prosocial behaviors. *Developmental Psychology, 32*(2), 231–240. doi: 10.1037/0012-1649.32.2.231

Carlo, G., Mestre, M. V., Samper, P., Tur, A., & Armenta, Brian E. (2010). Feelings or cognitions? Moral cognitions and emotions as longitudinal predictors of prosocial and aggressive behaviors. *Personality and Individual Differences, 48*(8), 872–877. doi: 10.1016/j.paid.2010.02.010

Carlo, G., Roesch, S. C., Knight, G. P., & Koller, S. H. (2001). Between- or within-culture variation? Culture group as a mediator of the relations between individual differences and resource allocation preferences. *Journal of Applied Developmental Psychology, 22*(6), 559–579. doi: 10.1016/S0193-3973(01)00094-6

Catherine, N. L. A., & Schonert-Reichl, K. A. (2011). Children's perceptions and comforting strategies to infant crying: Relations to age, sex, and empathy-related responding. *British Journal of Developmental Psychology, 29*(3), 524–551. doi: 10.1348/026151010X521475

Chao, R., & Tseng, V. (2002). Parenting of Asians. In M. H. Bornstein (Series Ed.), *Handbook of parenting: Vol. 4. Social conditions and applied parenting* (2nd ed., pp. 59–93). Mahwah, NJ: Erlbaum.

Cole, P. M., & Tan, P. Z. (2007). Emotional socialization from a cultural perspective. In J. E. Grusec & P. D. Hastings (Eds.). *Handbook of socialization: Theory and research* (pp. 516–542). New York: Guilford Press.

Corsaro, W. A. (2005). Children's peer cultures and interpretive reproduction. In W. A. Corsaro (Ed.), *Sociology of childhood* (pp. 107–132). Thousand Oaks, CA: Sage.

Creswell, J. W., & Plano Clark, V. (2011). *Designing and conducting mixed methods research* (2nd ed.). Thousand Oaks, CA: Sage.

de Guzman, M. R. T., Brown, J., Carlo, G., & Knight, G. P. (2012). What does it mean to be prosocial? A cross-ethnic study of parental beliefs. *Psychology and Developing Societies, 24*(2), 239–268. doi: 10.1177/097133361202400207

de Guzman, M. R. T., Carlo, G., & Edwards, C. P. (2008). Prosocial behaviors in context: Examining the role of children's social companions. *International Journal of Behavioral Development, 32*(6), 522–530. doi 10.1177/0165025408095557

de Guzman, M. R. T., Edwards, C. P., & Brown, J. (2011, July). *The socialization of prosocial behaviors in a rural Philippine village*. Paper presented at the biennial meeting of the European Congress of Psychology, Istanbul, Turkey.

de Guzman, M. R. T., Edwards, C. P., & Carlo, G. (2005). Prosocial behaviors in context: A study of the Gikuyu children of Ngecha, Kenya. *Journal of Applied Developmental Psychology, 26*(5), 542–558. doi: 10.1016/j.appdev.2005.06.006

Deković, M., & Janssens, J. M. A. M. (1992). Parents' child-rearing style and child's sociometric status. *Developmental Psychology, 28*(5), 925–932. doi: 10.1037/0012-1649.28.5.925

Durand, T. M. (2011). Latina mothers' cultural beliefs about their children, parental roles, and education: Implications for effective and empowering home-school partnerships. *Urban Review, 43*(2), 255–278. doi: 10.1007/s11256-010-0167-5

Eisenberg, N., Guthrie, I. K., Cumberland, A., Murphy, B. C., Shepard, S. A., Zhou, Q., & Carlo, G. (2002). Prosocial development in early adulthood: A longitudinal study. *Journal of Personality and Social Psychology, 82*(6), 993–1006. doi: 10.1037/0022-3514.82.6.993

Eisenberg, N., Hertz-Lazarowitz, H., & Fuchs, I. (1990). Prosocial moral judgement in Israeli kibbutz and city children: A longitudinal study. *Merrill-Palmer Quarterly, 36*, 273–285.

Eisenberg, N., & Ota Wang, V. (2003). Toward a positive psychology: Social developmental and cultural contributions. In L. G. Aspinwall & U. M. Staudinger (Eds.), *A psychology of human strengths: Fundamental questions and future directions for a positive psychology* (pp. 117–229). Washington, DC: American Psychological Association.

Ember, C. R. (1973). Feminine task assignment and the social behavior of boys. *Ethos, 1*(4), 424–439. doi: 10.1525/eth.1973.1.4.02a00050

Erickson, F. (2002). Culture and human development. *Human Development, 45*(4), 299–306. doi: 10.1159/000064993

Fagen, R. M. (2011). Play and development. In A. D. Pellegrini (Ed.), *Oxford handbook of the development of play* (pp. 83–100). New York: Oxford University Press.

Farver, J. A. (1999). Activity setting analysis: A model for examining the role of culture in development. In A. Goncu (Ed.), *Children's engagement in the world: Sociocultural perspectives* (pp. 99–127). New York: Cambridge University Press.

Garcia Coll, C. T., Meyer, E. C., & Brillon, L. (2002). Ethnic and minority parenting. In M. H. Bornstein (Ed.), *Handbook of parenting: Vol. 2. Biology and ecology of parenting* (2nd ed., pp. 189–209). Mahwah, NJ: Erlbaum.

Gaskins, S. (2000). Children's daily activities in a Mayan village: A culturally grounded description. *Cross-Cultural Research, 34*(4), 375–389. doi: 0.1177/106939710003400405

Gaskins, S. (2003). From corn to cash: Change and continuity within Mayan families. *Ethos, 31*, 2. doi: 10.1525/eth.2003.31.2.248

Goody, E. (1991). The learning of prosocial behaviour in small-scale egalitarian societies: An anthropological view. In R. A. Hinde & J. Groebel (Eds.), *Cooperation and prosocial behavior* (pp. 106–128). New York: Cambridge University Press.

Gurven, M., & Winking, J. (2008). Collective action in action: Pro-social behavior in and out of the laboratory. *American Anthropologist, 110*(2), 179–190. doi: 10.1111/j.1548-1433.2008.00024.x

Harkness, S., & Super, C. M. (2006). Themes and variations: Parental ethnotheories in Western cultures. In K. Rubin & O. B. Chung (Eds.), *Parental beliefs, parenting, and child development in cross-cultural perspective* (pp. 61–79). New York: Psychology Press.

Haskett, M., Allaire, J., Kreig, S., & Hart, K. (2008). Protective and vulnerability factors for physically abused children: Effects of ethnicity and parenting context. *Child Abuse and Neglect, 32*(5), 567–576. doi: 10.1016/j.chiabu.2007.06.009

Hay, D. F., & Rheingold, H. L. (1983). The early appearance of some valued social behaviors. In H. Beilin (Series Ed.) & D. L. Bridgeman (Vol. Ed.), *Developmental Psychology Series: The nature of prosocial development: Interdisciplinary theories and strategies* (pp. 79–94). New York: Academic Press.

Hirasawa, A. (2005). Infant care among the sedentarized Baka hunter-gatherers in Southeastern Cameroon. In B. S. Hewlett & M. E. Lamb (Eds.), *Hunter-gatherer childhoods: Evolutionary, developmental and cultural perspectives* (pp. 365–384). New Brunswick, NJ: Transaction.

Hollos, M. (1980). Collective education in Hungary: The development of competitive, cooperative and role-taking behaviors. *Ethos, 8*(1), 3–23.

Ispa, J. (2002). Russian child care goals and values: From Perestroika to 2001. *Early Childhood Research Quarterly, 17*(3), 393–413. doi: 10.1016/S0885-2006(02)00171-0

Jahoda, G. (2012). Critical reflections on some recent definitions of "culture." *Culture and Psychology, 18*(3), 289–303. doi: 10.1177/1354067X12446229

James, A. (2007). Ethnography in the study of children and childhood. In P. A. Atkinson, S. Delamont, J. Lofland, & L. Lofland (Eds.), *Handbook of ethnography* (pp. 246–257). London: Sage.

Jocano, F. L. (1969). *Growing up in a Philippine barrio.* New York: Holt, Rinehart, & Winston.

Kağitçibaşi, C. (1997). Individualism and collectivism. In J. W. Berry, M. H. Segall, & C. Kagitcibasi (Eds.), *Handbook of cross-cultural psychology: Volume III. Social behavior and applications* (2nd ed., pp. 1–51). Needham Heights, MA: Allyn & Bacon.

Kağitçibaşi, C., & Ataca, B. (2005). Value of children and family change: A three-decade portrait from Turkey. *Applied Psychology, 54*(3), 317–337. doi: 10.1111/j.1464-0597.2005.0 0213.x

Karasz, A., & Singelis, T. M. (2009). Qualitative and mixed methods research in cross-cultural psychology. *Journal of Cross-Cultural Psychology, 40*(6), 909–916. doi: 10.1177/0022022109349172

Kärtner, J., & Keller, H. (2012). Comment: Culture-specific developmental pathways to prosocial behavior: A comment on Bischof-Köhler's universalist perspective. *Emotion Review, 4*(1), 49–50.

Kärtner, J., Keller, H., & Chaudhary, N. (2010). Cognitive and social influences on early prosocial behavior in two sociocultural contexts. *Developmental Psychology, 46*(4), 905–14. doi: 10.1037/a0019718.

Kenyatta, J. (1966). *Facing Mount Kenya: The tribal life of the Gikuyu.* New York: Random House.

Kerestes, G. (2006). Children's aggressive and prosocial behavior in relation to war exposure: Testing the role of perceived parenting and child's gender. *International Journal of Behavioral Development, 30*(3), 227–239.

Kim, U., Park, Y.-S., Kwon, Y.-E., & Koo, J. (2005). Values of children, parent-child relationship, and social change in Korea: Indigenous, cultural, and psychological analysis. *Applied Psychology, 54*(3), 338–354. doi: 10.1111/j.1464-0597.2005.00214.x

Knight, G. P., Cota, M. K., & Bernal, M. E. (1993). The socialization of cooperative, competitive, and individualistic preferences among Mexican American children: The mediating role of ethnic identity. *Hispanic Journal of Behavioral Sciences, 15*(3), 291–309. doi: 10.1177/07399863930153001

Knight, G. P., & Kagan, S. (1977). Acculturation of prosocial and competitive behaviors among second- and third-generation Mexican-American children. *Journal of Cross-Cultural Psychology, 8*(3), 273–284. doi: 10.1177/002202217783002

Lancy, D. F. (2008). *The anthropology of childhood: Cherubs, chattel, changelings.* Cambridge, UK: Cambridge University Press.

Leung, F. T. L., & Brown, M. (1995). Theoretical issues in cross-cultural career development: Cultural validity and cultural specificity. In W. B. Walsh & S. H. Osipow (Eds.), *Handbook of vocational psychology* (pp. 143–180). Hillsdale, NJ: Erlbaum.

LeVine, R. A., Dixon, S., LeVine, S., Richman, A., Leiderman, P. H., Keefer, C. H., & Brazelton, T. B. (1994). *Child care and culture: Lessons from Africa.* Cambridge, UK: Cambridge University Press.

Madsen, M. C., & Shapira, A. (1977). Cooperation and challenge in four cultures. *Journal of Social Psychology, 102*(2), 189–195.

Malti, T., Gummerum, M., Keller, M., & Buchmann, M. (2009). Children's moral motivation, sympathy, and prosocial behavior. *Child Development, 80*(2), 442–460. doi:10.1111/j.1467-8624.2009.01271.x

Manago, A. M. (2012). The new emerging adult in Chiapas, Mexico: Perceptions of traditional values and value change among first-generation Maya university students. *Journal of Adolescent Research, 27*(6), 663–713. doi: 10.1177/0743558411417863

Maynard, A. E. (2005). Introduction: Cultural learning in context. In A. E. Maynard & M. I. Martini (Eds.), *Learning in cultural context: Family, peers, and school* (pp.1–9). New York: Springer.

McDade, K. (1995). How we parent: Race and ethnic differences. In C. K. Jacobson (Ed.), *American families: Issues in race and ethnicity* (pp. 283–300). New York: Garland.

Miles, A. (1994). Helping out at home: Gender socialization, moral development, and devil stories in Cuenca, Ecuador. *Ethos, 22*(2), 132–157. doi: 10.1525/eth.1994.22.2.02a00010

Miller, P. J., & Moore, B. B. (1989). Narrative conjunctions of caregiver and child: A comparative perspective on socialization through stories. *Ethos, 17*(4), 428–449. doi: 10.1525/eth.1989.17.4.02a00020

Miller, P. J., Wang, S., Sandel, T., & Cho, G. E. (2002). Self-esteem as folk theory: A comparison of European American and Taiwanese mothers' beliefs. *Parenting: Science and Practice, 2*, 209–239. doi: 10.1207/S15327922PAR0203_02

Munroe, R. L., & Munroe, R. H. (1997). A comparative anthropological perspective. In J. W. Berry, Y. H. Poortinga, & J. Pandey (Eds.), *Handbook of cross-cultural psychology: Vol. I. Theory and method* (2nd ed., pp. 171–214). Boston: Allyn & Bacon.

Nantel-Vivier, A., Kokko, K., Caprara, G. V., Pastorelli, C., Gerbino, M. G., Paciello, M., …Tremblay, R. E. (2009). Prosocial development from childhood to adolescence: A multi-informant perspective with Canadian and Italian longitudinal studies. *Journal of Child Psychology and Psychiatry, 50*(5), 590–598. doi: doi:10.1111/j.1469-7610.2008.02039.x

Newman, R. S. (2000). Social influences on the development of children's adaptive help seeking: The role of parents, teachers, and peers. *Developmental Review, 20*(3), 350–404. doi:10.1006/drev.1999.0502

Nydegger, W. P., & Nydegger, C. (1966). *Tarong: An Ilocos barrio in the Philippines.* New York: Wiley.

Ochs, E., & Izquierdo, C. (2009). Responsibility in childhood: Three developmental trajectories. *Ethos, 37*(4), 391–413. doi: 10.1111/j.1548-1352.2009.01066.x

Oyserman, D., Coon, H. M., & Kemmelmeier, M. (2002). Rethinking individualism and collectivism: Evaluation of theoretical assumptions and meta-analysis. *Psychological Bulletin, 128*(1), 3–72. doi: 10.1037/0033-2909.128.1.3

Padmawidjaja, I. A., & Chao, R. K. (2010). Parental beliefs and their relation to the parental practices of immigrant Chinese Americans and European Americans. In S. T. Russell, L. J. Crockett, & R. K. Chao (Eds.), *Asian American parenting and parent-adolescent relationships* (pp. 37–60). New York: Springer. doi: 10.1007/978-1-4419-5728-3_3

Paradise, R., & Rogoff, B. (2009). Learning side by side: Learning by observing and pitching in. *Ethos, 37*(1), 102–138. doi: 10.1111/j.1548-1352.2009.01033.x

Parmar, P., Harkness, S., & Super, C. M. (2004). Asian and Euro-American parents' ethnotheories of play and learning: Effects on pre-school children's home routines and school behavior. *International Journal of Behavioral Development, 28*(2), 97–104. doi: 10.1080/01650250344000307.

Raiban-Jamin, J., Maynard, A. E., & Greenfield, P. (2003). Implications of sibling caregiving for sibling relations and teaching interactions in two cultures. *Ethos, 31*(2), 204–231. doi: 10.1525/eth.2003.31.2.204

Rao, N., & Stewart, S. M. (1999). Cultural influences on sharer and recipient behavior: Sharing in Chinese and Indian preschool children. *Journal of Cross-Cultural Psychology, 30*(2), 219–241. doi: 10.1177/0022022199030002005

Reyes-Garcia, V., Godoy, R., Vadez, V., Huanca, T., & Leonard, W. R. (2006). Personal and group incentives to invest in prosocial behavior: A study in the Bolivian Amazon. *Journal of Anthropological Research, 62*(1), 81–101.

Rogoff, B. (2003). *The cultural nature of human development*. New York: Oxford University.

Rosenthal, M. K., & Roer-Strier, D. (2001). Cultural differences in mothers' developmental goals and ethnotheories. *International Journal of Psychology, 36*(1), 20–31. doi: 10.1080/00207590042000029

Shapira, A., & Madsen, M. C. (1969). Cooperative and competitive behavior of kibbutz and urban children in Israel. *Child Development, 40*(2), 609–617.

Shapira, A., & Madsen, M. C. (1974). Between- and within-group cooperation and competition among kibbutz and non-kibbutz children. *Developmental Psychology, 10*, 140–145.

Sirota, K. G. (2010). Fun morality reconsidered: Mothering and the relational contours of maternal-child play in U.S. working family life. *Ethos, 38*(4), 388–405. doi: 10.1111/j.1548-1352.2010.01157.x.

Spivak, A. L., & Howes, C. (2011). Social and relational factors in early education and prosocial actions of children of diverse ethnocultural communities. *Merrill-Palmer Quarterly, 58*(1), 1–24.

Stevenson, H. W. (1991). The development of prosocial behavior in large-scale collective societies: China and Japan. In T. A. Hinde & J. Grobel (Eds.), *Cooperation and prosocial behaviour* (pp. 89–105). New York: Cambridge University Press.

Stewart, S. M., & McBride-Chang, C. (2000). Influences on children's sharing in a multicultural setting. *Journal of Cross Cultural Psychology, 31*(3), 333–348. doi: 10.1177/0022022100031003003

Suizzo, M. (2007). Parents' goals and values for children: Dimensions of independence and interdependence across four US ethnic groups. *Journal of Cross-Cultural Psychology, 38*(4), 506–530. doi: 10.1177/0022022107302365

Sun, J., & Wang, X. (2010). Value differences between generations in China: A study in Shanghai. *Journal of Youth Studies, 13*(1), 65–81. doi: 10.1080/13676260903173462

Super C. M., & Harkness, S. (1986). The developmental niche: A conceptualization at the interface of child and culture. *International Journal of Behavioral Development, 9*(4), 545–569. doi: 10.1177/016502548600900409

Super, C. M., & Harkness, S. (2002). Culture structures the environment for development. *Human Development, 45*(4), 270–274. doi: 10.1159/000064988

Suzuki, L. K., & Greenfield, P. M. (2002). The construction of everyday sacrifice in Asian Americans and European Americans: The roles of ethnicity and acculturation. *Cross-Cultural Research, 36*(3), 200–228. doi: 10.1177/10697102036003002

Tedlock, B. (2000). Ethnography and ethnographic representation. In N. K. Denzin & Y. S. Lincoln (Eds.), *Handbook of qualitative research* (2nd ed., pp. 455–486). Thousand Oaks, CA: Sage.

Tietjen, A. M. (1989). The ecology of children's social support networks. In D. Belle (Ed.), *Children's social networks and social supports* (pp. 37–69). New York: Wiley.

Triandis, H. (2001). Individualism-collectivism and personality. *Journal of Personality, 69,* 907–924. doi: 10.1111/1467-6494.696169

Trommsdorff, G., Friedlmeier, W., & Mayer, B. (2007). Sympathy, distress, and prosocial behavior of preschool children in four cultures. *International Journal of Behavioral Development, 31*(3), 284–293. doi: 10.1177/0165025407076441

Tucker, B., & Young, A. (2005). Growing up Mikea: Children's time allocation and tuber foraging in southwestern Madagascar. In B. S. Hewlett & M. E. Lamb (Eds.), *Hunter-gatherer childhoods: Evolutionary, developmental and cultural perspectives* (pp. 147–174). New Brunswick, NJ: Transaction.

Tudge, J. R. H., & Odero-Wanga, D. (2009). A cultural–ecological perspective on early childhood among the Luo of Kisumu, Kenya. In M. Fleer, M. Hedegaard, & J. R. H. Tudge (Eds.), *The world year book of education 2009: Childhood studies and the impact of globalization: Policies and practices at global and local levels* (pp. 142–160). New York: Routledge.

van Oudenhoven, J. P., & Ward, C. (2013). Fading majority cultures: The implications of transnationalism and demographic changes for immigrant acculturation. *Journal of Community and Applied Social Psychology, 23*(2), 81–97. doi: 10.1002/casp.2132

Wang, S., & Tamis-LeMonda, C. S. (2003). Do child-rearing values in Taiwan and the United States reflect cultural values of collectivism and individualism? *Journal of Cross-Cultural Psychology, 34,* 629–642. doi: 10.1177/0022022103255498

Weisner, T. S. (2002). Ecocultural understanding of children's developmental pathways. *Human Development, 45,* 275–281. doi: 10.1159/000064989

Weisner, T. S., & Gallimore, R. (1977). My brother's keeper: Child and sibling caretaking. *Current Anthropology, 18*(2), 169–190. doi: 10.1086/201883

Whiteside-Mansell, L., Bradley, R., Tresch Owen, M., Randolph, S., & Cauce, A. M. (2003). Parenting and children's behavior at 36 months: Equivalence between African American and European American mother-child dyads. *Parenting: Science and Practice, 3*(3), 197–234. doi: 10.1207/S15327922PAR0303_02

Whiting, B. B. (1976). The problem of the packaged variable. In K. Riegel & Meacham (Eds.), *The developing individual in a changing world: Historical and cultural issues* (Vol. 1, pp. 303–309). Chicago: Aldine.

Whiting, B. B. (1980). Culture and social behavior: A model for the development of social behavior. *Ethos, 8,* 95–115. doi: 10.1525/eth.1980.8.2.02a00010

Whiting, B. B., & Edwards, C. P. (1988). *Children of different worlds: The formation of social behavior.* Cambridge, MA: Harvard University Press.

Whiting, B. B., & Whiting, J. W. M. (1975). *Children of six cultures: A psycho-cultural analysis.* Cambridge, MA: Harvard University Press.

Whiting, J. W. M., Child, I. L., Lambert, W. W., Fischer, A. M., Fischer, J. L., Nydegger, C., … Romney, R. (1966). *Six cultures series: Vol. 1. Field guide for a study of socialization.* New York: Wiley.

Yağmurlu, B., & Sanson, A. (2009). Parenting and temperament as predictors of prosocial behavior in Australian and Turkish Australian children. *Australian Journal of Psychology*, *61*(2), 77–88. doi: 10.1080/00049530802001338

Zahn-Waxler, C., Friedman, S. L., & Cummings, E. M. (1983). Children's emotions and behaviors in response to infants' cries. *Child Development*, *54*(6), 1522–1528. doi:10.2307/1129815

Zayas, L. H., & Solari, F. (1994). Early childhood socialization in Hispanic families: Context, culture and practice implications. *Professional Psychology*, *25*, 200–206. doi: 10.1037/0735-7028.25.3.200

12

Predicting Prosocial Tendencies Among Mexican American Youth

THE INTERSECTION OF CULTURAL VALUES, SOCIAL COGNITIONS, AND SOCIAL EMOTIONS

Gustavo Carlo, George P. Knight, Camille D. Basilio, and Alexandra N. Davis

Prosocial behaviors refer to a wide range of actions intended to benefit others (Carlo, 2006; Eisenberg, Fabes, & Spinrad, 2006). Volunteerism, donating resources or goods, sharing with others, instrumentally assisting needy others, and providing emotional support for others are all considered prosocial behaviors. On one end of the spectrum, scholars acknowledge such actions that may be motivated by selfish goals, on the other end, scholars note behaviors that may be selflessly motivated (Batson, 1998; Staub, 2005). Most persons consider prosocial behaviors to be a generally desirable set of behaviors that can improve societal conditions, foster better interpersonal relationships, and contribute to more positive family and social dynamics. Moreover, prosocial behaviors have been linked positively to a number of indices of well-being and adjustment including lower aggression and delinquency, lower substance use, better physical health, higher levels of self-esteem and moral development, and improved academic performance (Carlo, 2006). At the broadest level of analysis, collective expressions of prosocial behaviors (including cooperative behaviors) may contribute significantly to global harmony and peace. Despite the relevance of prosocial behaviors to these important issues, the study of prosocial behaviors has waned, especially in the field of developmental psychology (c.f. Batson, 1998). In addition, the study of such behaviors among ethnic minority populations, including Latinos and Latinas, is rare. In the present chapter, we review prior theories and research on prosocial behaviors in Latino/a youth, present a framework and supporting recent research that integrates culture and traditional developmental models, and then discuss directions for future research.

Although much of the research on prosocial behaviors treats such actions as a homogeneous group, researchers have acknowledged the need to distinguish among different forms of prosocial behaviors (Carlo & Randall, 2001; Harthshone & May, 1930). Similar to research on aggression and other constructs, research in this field demonstrates that different forms of prosocial behaviors have unique sets of associated characteristics and correlates. Among the dimensions of prosocial behaviors to consider, scholars have investigated prosocial behaviors toward different target groups (Kumru & Yağmurlu, chapter 16, this volume; Padilla-Walker, chapter 7, this volume) or in specific social contexts (Carlo & Randall, 2002). Other scholars have been preoccupied with studying specific types of prosocial behaviors (e.g., sharing, blood donations, volunteerism; Penner, Dovidio, & Albrecht, 2000; Penner & Finkelstein, 1998) or distinct motives associated with specific prosocial behaviors (e.g., selfish, selfless; Batson, 1998; see Hawley, chapter 3, this volume). According to such scholars, there are possible unique patterns of age-trends, gender differences, and relations to theoretically relevant constructs associated with these different forms of prosocial behaviors.

Based on an extensive review of prior research, Carlo and his colleagues identified six relatively broad forms of prosocial behaviors (Carlo & Randall, 2001). The researchers focused primarily on prosocial behaviors that differed across contexts and motives (Carlo & Randall, 2001, 2002). Public prosocial behaviors referred to actions conducted in front of an audience. Prosocial behaviors that were expressed in emotionally evocative situations were deemed emotional. Emergency or crises conditions were labeled dire prosocial actions. Compliant prosocial behaviors were defined as behaviors in response to requests for assistance. Helping others without revealing one's identity was referred to as anonymous prosocial action. Altruistic prosocial behaviors included actions that benefit others without expectation for social or material rewards. These behaviors were not considered exhaustive of the different forms of possible prosocial behaviors but were forms that had been typically studied. Moreover, some forms of prosocial behaviors were expected to be significantly interrelated but others were not, and still others may be negatively interrelated. Finally, one would expect that, with age, such conceptual distinctions become stronger due to increases in sociocognitive and socioemotive functioning.

Based on this conceptual framework, the Prosocial Tendencies Measure (PTM) was developed and validated to use with late adolescents/young adults (Carlo & Randall, 2002) and early and middle adolescents (Carlo, Hausmann, Christiansen, & Randall, 2003). Since then, several studies have examined various psychometric properties of the PTM to use with different cultural populations (see Carlo, 2006 and Knight & Carlo, 2012, for reviews; see also McGinley, Opal, Richaud, & Mesurado, chapter 13, this volume). For example, among Mexican American early adolescents, investigators reported strong evidence for the six-factor model of the PTM (Carlo, Knight, McGinley, Zamboanga, & Jarvis, 2010). Further measurement tests yielded equivalent factor structures across gender and young versus middle-aged adolescents. Moreover, the PTM showed adequate functional equivalence and construct validity for this sample. Other research shows similar adequate psychometric qualities in the PTM in independent samples (e.g., Hardy & Carlo, 2005; McGinley & Carlo, 2007). Interestingly, the pattern of interrelations among the subscales yields evidence that some forms of prosocial behaviors are uncorrelated, others are negatively correlated, and others are modestly positively correlated; suggesting that prosocial tendencies are not a global construct.

Traditional Models of Prosocial Behavior: The Role of Social Cognitions

Traditional models of prosocial development have been guided mostly by cognitive-developmental (Eisenberg, 1986; Krebs & Van Hesteren, 1994) and socialization (Hoffman, 2001) theories. Children who act prosocial often engage in higher levels of moral reasoning (i.e., thinking about moral situations), which often reflects concern for others and values consistent with caring for others (Eisenberg & Fabes, 1998). Feshbach (1987) and others have suggested that individuals who are emotionally sensitive to the needs of others (i.e., sympathy) and who can understand needy others' situation (i.e., perspective taking) are more likely to engage in prosocial behaviors (and unlikely to engage in antisocial behaviors). Furthermore, children who engaged in prosocial behaviors are more likely to demonstrate optimal levels of emotion regulation (Eisenberg & Fabes, 1998). Taken together, these theories tend to emphasize the role of social cognitions and/ or emotions on prosocial and moral behaviors.

Consistent with these traditional theories, investigators have demonstrated generally reliable relations between sociocognitive and socioemotive traits and prosocial behaviors (Carlo, 2006; Eisenberg et al., 2006). For example, a meta-analytic review of the literature (Carlo, PytlikZillig, Roesch, & Dienstbier, 2009) reported that the overall relation between perspective taking and prosocial behavior was 0.28, across a wide range of methods and samples (see also Underwood & Moore, 1982). Although many cognitive developmentalists have focused on perspective taking (including theory of mind) as a primary correlate of prosocial behavior, other social cognitions (e.g., moral reasoning) and social emotions (e.g., empathy, sympathy) have been found to be linked to such behaviors (see Carlo, 2006; Eisenberg et al., 2006). Moreover, most scholars conceptualize these social cognitive and emotive processes as direct predictors of prosocial behaviors, but there is suggestive evidence that social cognitions (such as perspective taking) may actually place an upper limit on prosocial behaviors (Carlo et al., 2009; Eisenberg, 1986). That is, children may be less prone to engage in prosocial behaviors if they are limited in their perspective-taking skills. Furthermore, there is substantive evidence that specific forms of prosocial behaviors may require specific forms of perspective-taking skills (Carlo, Knight, Eisenberg, & Rotenberg, 1991; Knight, Johnson, Carlo, & Eisenberg, 1994; see Carlo et al., 2009). For example, emotional perspective taking is most relevant when helping requires decoding the emotional cues of need (Carlo et al., 1991). However, there is a relative lack of studies on this topic in ethnic minority samples including Latino/a samples. Therefore, tests of the generalizability of these traditional models of prosocial behaviors to Latino/a youth are sparse.

General Review of Prosocial Behaviors Among Mexican Americans

The early research on the prosocial development of Mexican American youth was focused primarily on documenting the prosocial nature of these youth, most often in direct comparison to European American youth. Several studies have indicated that Mexican American youth are generally more prosocial, compared with European American youth, in the sharing of resources (Knight & Kagan, 1977a, 1977b; Knight, Kagan, & Buriel, 1981; McClintock, 1974; Toda, Shinotsuka, McClintock, & Stech, 1978). There is also some evidence consistent with the idea that adaptation to the mainstream culture of the United States (i.e., acculturation) may be associated with reduced levels of some forms of prosocial behaviors among Mexican Americans. For example, the youth of immigrant Mexican parents are more prosocial and cooperative than the youth of Mexican American parents born in the United States or European American youth (Knight & Kagan, 1977b; see also de Guzman & Carlo, 2004). Furthermore, self-esteem is positively associated with cooperative preferences among the youth of immigrant Mexican parents but negatively associated with cooperative preferences among the youth of Mexican American parents born in the United States or European American youth (Kagan & Knight, 1979). In studies of predominantly Mexican American children, investigators reported that caregiving practices (helping the family) were positively associated with general social competence (e.g., Grau, Azmitia, & Quattlebaum, 2009; Kuperminc, Jurkovic, & Casey, 2009), suggesting that prosocial behaviors in the home might provide training for broader social competencies.

AGE- AND GENDER-RELATED DIFFERENCES IN PROSOCIAL BEHAVIORS

Although age-related changes in prosocial behaviors are well documented among European American and European children and adolescents (see Eisenberg & Fabes, 1998), such research is sparse among ethnic minority and Latino/a populations (Knight & Carlo, 2012). There are reported age differences in cooperative behaviors among Mexican American and Latino/a children such that older children exhibit more cooperative behaviors than younger children (see Knight, Bernal, & Carlo, 1995). However, there are no studies directly examining age differences or trends in PTM subscales in Latino/a youth. Moreover, the lack of

longitudinal studies of prosocial behaviors among Latino/as limits our understanding of developmental trends in such behaviors.

Although research on gender differences on the PTM among Latino/a youth
are lacking, findings with other ethnic youth suggest that gender differences in
prosocial behaviors might be dependent on the type of prosocial behavior and age.
Despite the commonly found gender differences in prosocial behaviors favoring
girls, research on European American youth examining specific forms of prosocial
behaviors demonstrates some gender differences favoring boys and other differences favoring girls (Carlo, 2006). For example, Carlo and Randall (2002) showed
that boys score higher on public prosocial behaviors than girls and that girls score
higher than boys on emotional prosocial behaviors (c.f., Eagly & Crowley, 1986).
In another study, girls scored higher than boys on altruistic prosocial behaviors
(Carlo et al., 2010). Furthermore, it is likely that such gender differences are associated with gender-specific socialization practices (as well as biological mechanisms) but there is no direct research on this issue.

THE SOCIALIZATION OF PROSOCIAL BEHAVIORS IN MEXICAN AMERICAN FAMILIES

Although substantial evidence exists on the genetic and biological substrates
of prosocial behaviors (see Fortuna & Knafo, chapter 4), research on prosocial
behaviors among Mexican Americans have focused on socialization mechanisms.
Specifically, the bulk of the research has emphasized the role of parents (especially
mothers) on children and adolescents' prosocial behaviors. Among children, scholars noted the relevance of parenting practices that foster tendencies (e.g., ethnic
identity) associated with a prosocial orientation. For example, Knight and his colleagues hypothesized (see Figure 12.1) that familial agents socialize their children
to acquire a strong identity with their cultural group via practices (e.g., assigning
familial duties and responsibilities) that orient their children toward caring for
family members. However, these scholars asserted that the acquisition and expression of ethnic identity is moderated by children's sociocognitive abilities (e.g., perspective taking) during the developmental period in which these sociocognitive
skills are emerging. As children's sociocognitive skills mature, children develop a
stronger sense of identity and this facilitates the expression of identity behaviors
consistent with their identity. These scholars focused on ethnic identity as a key
predictor of prosocial behaviors and that specific cultural values (e.g., familism)
were considered only one feature of that ethnic identity. That is, these authors
viewed ethnic identity as one component of self-concept, and this social identity
incorporated the behavioral expectations, attitudes, and values associated with
the ethnic group membership. However, as children mature and sociocognitive
capabilities become well established, such sociocognitive tendencies can directly
facilitate (rather than moderate) prosocial behaviors. Early research demonstrates
evidence consistent with the above proposed model. For example, in one study,

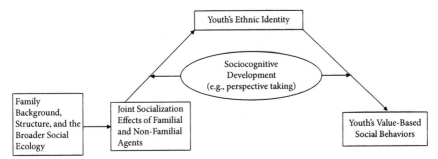

FIGURE 12.1 *Model depicting the moderating effect of sociocognitive traits on value based social behaviors (adapted from Knight et al., 1995).*

parental socialization practices predicted young children's ethnic identity that, in turn, predicted cooperative behaviors (Knight et al., 1993).

Carlo and de Guzman (2009) adapted the preceding model and explicitly hypothesized that both cultural values and sociocognitive tendencies directly predict Latino/a youth prosocial behaviors (see Figure 12.2). These latter scholars noted that there are an assortment of cultural values and sociocognitive tendencies capable of facilitating prosocial behaviors. For example, in addition to perspective taking, moral reasoning (i.e., thinking about care-based or justice-based dilemma situations) can also directly predict specific forms of prosocial behaviors. Furthermore, other cultural values such as respect for others, gender role values, and religiousness, can mediate the relations between sociocognitive skills and prosocial behaviors. Therefore, among older children and adolescents, strongly endorsed cultural

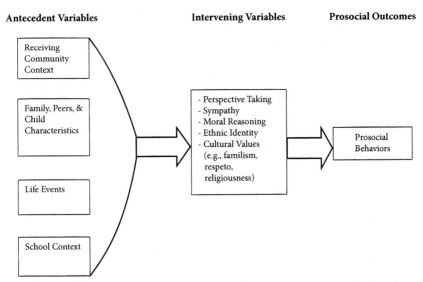

FIGURE 12.2 *Model depicting the mediating effects of sociocognitive traits and cultural values on prosocial behaviors (adapted from Carlo & de Guzman, 2009).*

values can provide the impetus to apply sociocognitive abilities to enact prosocial behaviors. One important implication of these theories is that age-related changes in prosocial behaviors among Latino/a youth can be explained by age-related changes in sociocognitive tendencies and in the acquisition of cultural values.

Other research has focused more on identifying the specific culturally related psychological constructs (e.g., familism, ethnic knowledge, religiousness) underlying the prosocial development of Mexican American youth. Knight, Cota, and Bernal (1993) reported empirical evidence that directly examined the cultural socialization that was associated with the sharing of resources with a peer. Mexican American mothers' ethnic knowledge and preferences were related positively to their teaching about Mexican culture, which was in turn related positively to their young child's ethnic identity (e.g., ethnic knowledge, ethnic self-identification, and ethnic preferences) and to sharing of resources. Other scholars asserted that the familism values embedded within the Mexican American culture would be particularly likely to foster compliant (i.e., helping when asked), emotional (i.e., helping in emotionally evocative situations), and dire (i.e., helping in emergency situations) prosocial tendencies (Armenta, Knight, Carlo, & Jacobsen, 2011; Calderón-Tena, Knight, & Carlo, 2011). These authors suggested that highly familistic-oriented mothers are more likely to ask and expect their young adolescents to do household chores, including caregiving of younger siblings. Engagement in these household chores and responsibilities, in turn, is likely to foster more compliance to authority figures and attunement to the needs of others in emotional and emergency situations. Thus, parental practices that strongly promote familism values may provide the impetus for greater prosocial behaviors when asked and in emotional and dire situations.

Consistent with this reasoning, Calderón-Tena et al. (2011) found that mothers' familism values were related positively to parenting behaviors that promote prosocial behavior, which in turn were related positively to their adolescent's perception of prosocial parenting. Further, adolescents' perceptions of prosocial parenting were related positively to their familism values and to compliant, emotional, and dire prosocial tendencies, and these relations were partially mediated by familism values. Armenta and colleagues (Armenta et al., 2011) demonstrated that a component of ethnic identity, ethnic affirmation, was associated with these specific forms of prosocial behaviors and that these associations were mediated through familism values but not mediated through values associated with the mainstream (U.S.) culture (personal achievement, self-reliance, material success). Specifically, ethnic affirmation and familism were associated with more compliant, emotional, dire, and anonymous (i.e., helping without other people's knowledge) prosocial tendencies; but mainstream individualist values were associated only with less altruistic (i.e., helping without expecting self-reward) and more public (i.e., helping in front of others) prosocial tendencies. Based on this value-specific pattern of relations, one might hypothesize that Mexican American youth who strongly endorse familism values might assist family and in-group members more so than youth who strongly endorse mainstream values. However, research on this specific issue is lacking.

Other research further demonstrates the role of parents and sociocognitive traits in the prosocial development of their children. Mexican American mothers (or primary caregivers) who used more induction-oriented discipline practices (i.e., the extent to which they use explanations to discipline their children) had children who felt more sympathy and concern for others and who in turn displayed more dire, compliant, anonymous, public, altruistic, and emotional prosocial behaviors (Carlo, Knight, McGinley, & Hayes, 2011). In contrast, prosocial moral reasoning (i.e., thinking about helping opportunities) was positively related to altruism, public, and anonymous prosocial behaviors but not dire, emotional, or compliant prosocial behaviors among Mexican American (or European American) youth.

In addition, in studies of Central and Mexican American youth, high levels of parental involvement were associated with high levels of prosocial behaviors (Carlo et al., 2010; Kerr, Beck, Shattuck, Kattar, & Uriburu, 2003). A recent study showed that parenting styles predicted social cognitions among Mexican American youth (Shen, Carlo, & Knight, in press). Although the studies directly examining the links between parental control and prosocial behaviors are limited (see Halgensuth, Ispa, & Rudy, 2006, and Livas-Dlott et al., 2010, for reviews of parental control among Latino/as), these studies show support for the applicability of traditional developmental models to Latino/a youth development.

Toward an Understanding of the Roles of Cultural Values, Social Cognitions, and Social Emotions in Prosocial Behaviors in Mexican American Youth

The Family CARE Project was designed to focus on the idea that the socialization of cultural values (e.g., familism values) fosters the use of social cognition skills (e.g., perspective taking), which in turn leads Mexican American youth to be relatively prosocial. That is, we envision that it is the transmission of cultural values to Mexican American youth, largely from family members, that sets the stage for these youth to be prosocial towards others, including persons outside the family. Thus, over time, a generalized prosocial orientation in many Mexican American youth results from the transmission of cultural values that espouse helping others, which promotes generalized social cognitive activities that facilitates prosocial actions.

Although other cultural values may be linked to prosocial behaviors, we have focused on familism in our early studies. Familism values incorporate three related sets of value constructs: familism-support, familism-obligations, and familism-referent. Familism-support includes a commitment to the family by providing for things such as a sense of unity, security, and emotional support. Familism-obligation includes a commitment to the family by being responsible for

behaviors designed to care for older adults or younger siblings and providing financial and living assistance to family members in times of need. Familism-referent
includes a commitment to thinking about oneself as a member of the family group
and understanding how one's behavior reflects on the family. At present, there is
relatively strong evidence of the transmission of these values from parents to youth
in Mexican American families. For example, Knight et al. (2011) used longitudinal
data to demonstrate that mothers' and fathers' Mexican American cultural values
(including familism values) were associated with their ethnic socialization and
that the mothers' ethnic socialization was prospectively associated with their adolescents' ethnic identity and endorsement of Mexican American cultural values.
Calderon et al. (2010) further showed that mothers' familism values are related to
parenting behaviors that promote prosocial behavioral tendencies, which in turn
are related to adolescents' perception of prosocial parenting practices. Further, adolescents' perception of prosocial parenting practices is related to their endorsement
of familism values and their emotional, compliant, and dire prosocial tendencies.

Other work yields evidence that supports the role of social cognition in predicting prosocial tendencies of Mexican American youth. For example, Carlo et al.
(2011) demonstrated that both prosocial moral reasoning and perspective taking are associated with greater prosocial tendencies among Mexican American
youth. In one unpublished study (Knight, Carlo, Basilio, & Davis, 2013) there is
further evidence supporting the theoretical position that familism values lead to
a relatively generalized tendency to engage in the social cognitive activities such
as perspective taking, which in turn leads to a relatively generalized prosocial orientation (Figure 12.3). This latter set of findings is consistent with the idea that

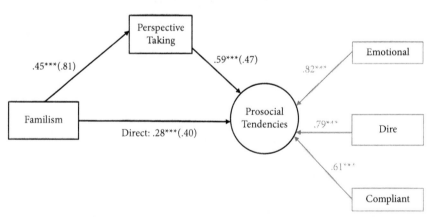

FIGURE 12.3 *Model of the direct and indirect path coefficients (unstandardized coefficients
in parentheses) of the association between adolescents' familism values and emotional,
compliant, and dire prosocial tendencies mediated through perspective taking.*

Note: Fit Statistics: $\chi2$ (4) = 5.47; CFI = .996; RMSEA = .04 (.00, .12); SRMR = .02; Indirect Effect = .27***
γ and λ reported are standardized (unstandardized) coefficients
***p < .001

familism values may encourage perspective taking, which in turn promotes certain types of prosocial tendencies.

This latter work and the findings from our research bring us full circle back toward integrating traditional and cultural socialization models of prosocial development. We believe this approach is essential to account for social cognitions and social emotions as well as culture-specific influences (such as cultural values and culture-specific parenting practices) of prosocial behaviors in Latino/a children and adolescents. Consideration of the roles of these predictors of prosocial behaviors provides a rich framework for understanding developmental and culture group differences, which will be necessary for more comprehensive models of prosocial development.

General Conclusions and Future Directions

In this chapter, we provide a brief review of the existing theories and research on prosocial development in Latino/a children and adolescents. As can be seen, there are relatively few studies, though the findings suggest a generally reliable pattern of findings in Latino/as: (1) there are some age and gender differences in prosocial behaviors; (2) family plays an important socializing role; and (3) perspective taking, ethnic identity, cultural values, moral reasoning, and sympathy are direct predictors of prosocial behaviors. We present preliminary findings that provide further support for the interplay of cultural values and social cognitions (i.e., perspective taking) in predicting prosocial behaviors among Mexican American youth. These findings are consistent with existing models of Latino/a youth prosocial development as well as with traditional models of prosocial development. The findings demonstrate the ability to better explain prosocial behaviors in Latino/a youth by accounting for the role of culture-specific variables such as familism, cultural values, and ethnic identity, in addition to considering sociocognitive predictors. These findings demonstrate the growing need for developmental models that incorporate culture-specific processes (e.g., cultural values) into traditional models of development (see also Raffaelli, Carlo, Carranza, & Gonzales-Kruger, 2005).

Advances in our understanding of prosocial development among Latino/as continue. Early research on prosocial behaviors among this population demonstrated consistent findings that cooperative and prosocial behaviors are frequently expressed. These early findings added an important balance to the almost exclusive focus by many social scientists on pathology and deficiencies in psychological and behavioral adjustment (see Garcia-Coll et al., 1996; Quintana et al., 2006; Raffaelli et al., 2005). However, more recent studies are showing a much more complex pattern of prosocial behavioral responding among Latino/as that is dependent on exposure to specific parenting practices, endorsement of specific cultural values, and expression of specific forms of prosocial behaviors. These new advances will undoubtedly result in more sophisticated intervention programs and policies to enhance prosocial development among Latino/as.

Despite the recent progress, there is still much to be done. For example, few longitudinal studies of prosocial behaviors among Latino/as exist. Such studies are important to better address questions about the direction of effects between predictors and outcomes. Moreover, longitudinal designs provide a rigorous approach to directly examine age-related changes in prosocial behaviors and associated correlates. In one of the few longitudinal studies of prosocial behaviors, Brittian et al. (2013) demonstrated that early exposure to discrimination experiences predicted later reduced levels of some forms of prosocial behaviors. Furthermore, the relations between discrimination experiences and prosocial behaviors were accounted for by individual differences in familism. Although the study cannot firmly rule out bidirectional effects nor strongly confirm cause-and-effect inferences, the findings provide evidence that is one important step closer to affirming the expected direction of causality as proposed by theorists.

The lack of longitudinal studies also limits our understanding of the developmental trajectories of different forms of prosocial behaviors and the mechanisms that might account for changes in such behaviors across time. For example, in general, some forms of prosocial behavior (e.g., compliant) might be expected to be more frequently expressed in childhood than in adolescence. However, among Latino/as, declines in compliant prosocial behaviors might not be as evident as in groups that value autonomy and independence (e.g., European American youth), given the importance of cultural values such as respeto and familism. Moreover, acculturative status might moderate such trends among Latino/a youth such that more acculturated youth may be more prone to declines in compliant prosocial behaviors similar to those found among European American youth. Longitudinal studies of specific forms of prosocial behaviors in Latino/a children and adolescents will need to include measures of the culture-specific mechanisms that might account for changes across time as well as the variables that might account for culture group differences.

Another limitation to our current understanding is the lack of studies that examine the role of other predictors of prosocial behaviors among Latino/as. For example, siblings, fathers, and extended family members (see Yorgason & Padilla-Walker, 2011) may play important socializing roles in Latino/a youth prosocial development, but their roles have yet to be researched (see Yorgason & Gustafson, chapter 10). Previous research on non-Latino/a samples suggests that siblings influence prosocial behaviors (Dunn & Munn, 1986; see also Padilla-Walker, Harper, & Jensen, 2010), and other research shows that siblings play an important socializing role in Mexican American youth (Killoren, Thayer, & Updegraff, 2008). Moreover, to date, most research has focused on familism, but other cultural values such as respect, religiousness, and traditional gender roles are much less studied. Because such values often form the basis for prosocial behaviors, the need for research on the associations between such values and prosocial actions is great. Finally, the extant evidence suggests that children from collectivist-oriented societies engage in high levels of help-ing toward kin but less so toward nonkin (de Guzman, Edwards, & Carlo, 2005). In contrast, this body of research suggests that European American youth may be more likely to engage in prosocial behaviors toward strangers (including altruistic behaviors) and nonkin than toward kin. Therefore, research that directly examines helping behaviors toward in-group and out-group members may uncover interesting patterns that may further our understanding of pro-social development.

We have not directly acknowledged the fact that most studies on prosocial behaviors in Latino/a samples have focused on families of Mexican heritage. The importance of research on this topic in other Latino/a subgroups cannot be understated. Although there are many commonalities among Latino/a fami-lies, the range of background and immigration histories, community character-istics, traditional rituals and customs, language dialects, socioeconomic status (SES), discriminatory experiences, and ethnocentric beliefs can be quite varied. Some research on cooperative behaviors suggests differences between Brazilian and European American children that parallel findings between Mexican and European American children (Carlo, Roesch, Knight, & Koller, 2001). However, one might expect relatively lower levels of prosocial behaviors (perhaps toward strangers) in Latino/a groups that experience higher levels of discrimination. Similarly, high-SES Latino/a youth may exhibit relatively lower levels of compli-ant prosocial behaviors, if independence is valued more in such families. The point is that we cannot assume homogeneity in prosocial behavior patterns across Latino/a groups and research on these behaviors in other Latino/a groups (e.g., Cubans, Puerto Ricans, Columbians, Nicaraguans) is necessary. Despite these limitations and gaps on our knowledge and understanding, the importance of continued research on prosocial behaviors in Latino/a populations cannot be understated in moving toward a more balanced understanding of Latino/a chil-dren and adolescents' well-being and health.

Acknowledgment

Funding for this project was provided by grants from the National Science Foundation to Gustavo Carlo (BNS-0132302) and George Knight (BNS-0132409).

References

Armenta, B. E., Knight, G. P., Carlo, G., & Jacobson, R. P. (2011). The relation between eth-nic group attachment and prosocial tendencies: The mediating role of cultural values. *European Journal of Social Psychology, 41,* 107–115.

Batson, C. D. (1998). The moral masquerade: Experimental exploration of the nature of moral motivation. *Phenomenology and the Cognitive Sciences*, 7(1), 51–66.

Brittian, A. S., O'Donnell, M., Knight, G. P., Carlo, G., Umaña-Taylor, A. J., & Roosa, M. W. (2013). Associations between adolescents' perceived discrimination and prosocial tendencies: The mediating role of Mexican American values. *Journal of Youth and Adolescence*, 42, 328–341.

Calderón-Tena, C. O., Knight, G. P., & Carlo, G. (2011). The socialization of prosocial behavior among Mexican American preadolescents: The role of familism. *Cultural Diversity and Ethnic Minority Psychology*, 17, 98–106.

Carlo, G. (2006). Care-based and altruistically-based morality. In M. Killen & J. G. Smetana (Eds.), *Handbook of moral development* (pp. 551–579). Mahwah, NJ: Erlbaum.

Carlo, G., & de Guzman, M. R. T. (2009). Theories and research on prosocial competencies among US Latinos/as. In F. Villaruel, G. Carlo, M. Azmitia, J. Grau, N. Cabrera, & J. Chahin (Eds.), *Handbook of U.S. Latino psychology* (pp. 191–211). Los Angeles, CA: Sage.

Carlo, G., Hausmann, A., Christiansen, S., & Randall, B. A. (2003). Sociocognitive and behavioral correlates of a measure of prosocial tendencies for adolescents. *Journal of Early Adolescence*, 23, 107–134.

Carlo, G., Knight, G. P., Eisenberg, N., & Rotenberg, K. J. (1991). Cognitive processes and prosocial behaviors among children: The role of affective attributions and reconciliations. *Developmental Psychology*, 27(3), 456–461.

Carlo, G., Knight, G. P., McGinley, M., & Hayes, R. (2011). The roles of parental inductions, moral emotions, and moral cognitions in prosocial tendencies among Mexican American and European American early adolescents. *Journal of Early Adolescence*, 31, 757–781.

Carlo, G., Knight, G. P., McGinley, M., Zamboanga, B. L., & Jarvis, L. H. (2010). The multidimensionality of prosocial behaviors and evidence of measurement equivalence in Mexican American and European American early adolescents. *Journal of Research on Adolescence*, 20, 334–358.

Carlo, G., PytlikZillig, L. M., Roesch, S. C., & Dienstbier, R. A. (2009). The elusive altruist: The psychological study of the altruistic personality. In D. Narvaez & D. K. Lapsley (Eds.), *Personality, identity, and character: Explorations in moral psychology*, (pp. 271–294). New York: Cambridge University Press.

Carlo, G., & Randall, B. A. (2001). Are all prosocial behaviors equal? A socioecological developmental conception of prosocial behavior. *Advances in Psychology Research*, 2, 151–170.

Carlo, G., & Randall, B. A. (2002). The development of a measure of prosocial behaviors for late adolescents. *Journal of Youth and Adolescence*, 31(1), 31–44.

Carlo, G., Roesch, S. C., Knight, G. P., & Koller, S. H. (2001). Between or within-culture variation? Culture group as a moderator of the relations between individual differences and resource allocation preferences. *Journal of Applied Developmental Psychology*, 22, 559–579.

de Guzman, M. R. T., & Carlo, G. (2004). Family, peer, and acculturative correlates of prosocial development among Latino youth in Nebraska. *Great Plains Research*, 14, 185–202.

de Guzman, M. R. T., Edwards, C. P., & Carlo, G. (2005). Prosocial behaviors in context: A study of the Gikuyu children of Ngecha, Kenya. *Journal of Applied Developmental Psychology*, 26(5), 542–558.

Dunn, J., & Munn, P. (1986). Siblings and the development of prosocial behaviour. *International Journal of Behavioral Development, 9*(3), 265–284.

Eagly, A. H., & Crowley, M. (1986). Gender and helping behavior: A meta-analytic review of the social psychological literature. *Psychological Bulletin, 100*(3), 283–308.

Eisenberg, N., & Fabes, R. A. (1998). Prosocial development. In N. Eisenberg, W. Damon, & R. M. Lerner (Eds.), *Handbook of child psychology: Vol. 3. Social, emotional and personality development* (6th ed., pp. 701–778). New York: Wiley.

Eisenberg, N., Fabes, R. A., & Spinrad, T. L. (2006). Prosocial development. In N. Eisenberg, W. Damon, & R. M. Lerner (Eds.), *Handbook of child psychology: Vol. 3. Social, emotional and personality development* (6th ed., pp. 646–718). New York: John Wiley.

Feshbach, N. D. (1987). Parental empathy and child adjustment/maladjustment. In N. Eisenberg & J. Strayer (Eds.), *Empathy and its development* (pp. 271–291). New York: Cambridge University Press.

García-Coll, C., Lamberty, G., Jenkins, R., Pipes McAdoo, H. P., Crnic, K., Wasik, B. H., & Garcia, H. V. (1996). An integrative model for the study of developmental competencies in minority children. *Child Development, 67*, 1891–1914.

Grau, J. M., Azmitia, M., & Quattlebaum, J. (2009). Latino families: Parenting, relational, and developmental processes. In F. A. Villarruel, G. Carlo, J. M. Grau, M. Azmitia, N. Cabrera, & T. J. Chahin (Eds.), *Handbook of US Latino psychology: Developmental and community based perspectives* (pp. 153–169). Thousand Oaks, CA: Sage.

Halgensuth, L., Ispa, J., & Rudy, D. (2006). Parental control in Latino families: An integrated review of the literature. *Child Development, 77*, 1282–1297.

Hardy, S. A., & Carlo, G. (2005). Religiosity and prosocial behaviours in adolescence: The mediating role of prosocial values. *Journal of Moral Education, 34*(2), 231–249.

Hoffman, M. L. (2001). *Empathy and moral development: Implications for caring and justice.* New York: Cambridge University Press.

Kagan, S., & Knight, G. P. (1979). Cooperation-competition and self-esteem: A case of cultural relativism. *Journal of Cross-Cultural Psychology, 10*, 457–467.

Kerr, M. H., Beck, K., Shattuck, T. D., Kattar, C., & Uriburu, D. (2003). Family involvement, problem and prosocial behavior outcomes of Latino youth. *American Journal of Health Behavior, 27*(Supplement 1), S55–S65.

Killoren, S. E., Thayer, S. M., & Updegraff, K. A. (2008). Conflict resolution between Mexican origin adolescent siblings. *Journal of Marriage and Family, 70*, 1200–1212.

Knight, G. P., Berkel, C., Umaña-Taylor, A. J., Gonzales, N. A., Ettekal, I., Jaconis, M., & Boyd, B. M. (2011). The familial socialization of culturally related values in Mexican American families. *Journal of Marriage and Family, 73*(5), 913–925.

Knight, G. P., Bernal, M. E., & Carlo, G. (1995). Socialization and the development of cooperative, competitive, and individualistic behaviors among Mexican American children. In E. E. Garcia and B. McLaughlin (Eds.), *Meeting the challenge of linguistic and cultural diversity in early childhood* (pp. 85–102). New York: Teachers College Press.

Knight, G. P., & Carlo, G. (2012). Prosocial development among Mexican American youth. *Child Development Perspectives, 6*(3), 258–263.

Knight, G. P., Carlo, G., Basilio, C., & Davis, A. (2013). Uncovering the links among cultural values, ethnic socialization practices, perspective taking, and prosocial behaviors in Mexican American youth. Unpublished manuscript.

Knight, G. P., Cota, M. K., & Bernal, M. E. (1993). The socialization of cooperative, competitive, and individualistic preferences among Mexican American children: The mediating role of ethnic identity. *Hispanic Journal of Behavioral Sciences, 15*, 291–309.

Knight, G. P., Johnson, L. G., Carlo, G., & Eisenberg, N. (1994). A multiplicative model of the dispositional antecedents of a prosocial behavior: Predicting more of the people more of the time. *Journal of Personality and Social Psychology, 66*(1), 178–183.

Knight, G. P., & Kagan, S. (1977a). Development of prosocial and competitive behaviors in Anglo-American and Mexican-American children. *Child Development, 48*, 1385–1394.

Knight, G. P., & Kagan, S. (1977b). Acculturation of prosocial and competitive behaviors among second- and third-generation Mexican-American children. *Journal of Cross-Cultural Psychology, 8*, 273–284.

Knight, G. P., Kagan, S., & Buriel, R. (1981). Confounding effects of individualism in children's cooperation-competition social motive measures. *Motivation and Emotion, 5*, 167–178.

Krebs, D. L., & Van Hesteren, F. (1994). The development of altruism: Toward an integrative model. *Developmental Review, 14*, 1–56.

Kuperminc, G. P., Jurkovic, G. J., & Casey, S. (2009). Relation of filial responsibility to the personal and social adjustment of Latino adolescents from immigrant families. *Journal of Family Psychology, 23*, 14–22.

Livas-Dlott, A., Fuller, B., Stein, G. L., Bridges, M., Figueroa, A. M., & Mireles, L. (2010). Commands, competence, and cariño: Maternal socialization practices in Mexican American families. *Developmental Psychology, 46*, 566–578.

McClintock, C. G. (1974). Development of social motives in Anglo-American and Mexican-American children. *Journal of Personality and Social Psychology, 29*, 348–354.

McGinley, M., & Carlo, G. (2007). Two sides of the same coin? The relations between prosocial and physically aggressive behaviors. *Journal of Youth and Adolescence, 36*(3), 337–349.

Padilla-Walker, L. M., Harper, J. M., & Jensen, A. C. (2010). Self-regulation as a mediator between sibling relationship quality and early adolescents' positive and negative outcomes. *Journal of Family Psychology, 24*, 419–428.

Penner, L. A., Dovidio, J. F., & Albrecht, T. L. (2000). Helping victims of loss and trauma: A social psychological perspective. In J. H. Harvey, E. D. Miller (Eds.), *Loss and trauma: General and close relationship perspectives* (pp. 62–85). New York: Brunner-Routledge.

Penner, L. A., & Finkelstein, M. A. (1998). Dispositional and structural determinants of volunteerism. *Journal of Personality and Social Psychology, 74*(2), 525.

Quintana, S. M., Aboud, F. E., Chao, R. K., Contreras-Grau, J., Cross, W. E., Jr., Hudley, C.,…Vietze, D. L. (2006). Race, ethnicity, and culture in child development: Contemporary research and future directions. *Child Development, 77*, 1129–1141.

Raffaelli, M., Carlo, G., Carranza, M. A., & Gonzales-Kruger, G. E. (2005). Understanding Latino children and adolescents in the mainstream: Placing culture at the center of developmental model. In R. Larson. Jensen (Eds.), *New horizons in developmental research: New directions for child and adolescent development* (pp. 23–32). San Francisco: Jossey-Bass.

Shen, Y.-L., Carlo, G., & Knight, G. P. (in press). Relations between parental discipline, empathy-related traits, and prosocial moral reasoning: A multicultural examination. *Journal of Early Adolescence.*

Staub, E. (2005). The roots of goodness: The fulfillment of basic human needs and the development of caring, helping and non-aggression, inclusive caring, moral courage, active bystandership, and altruism born of suffering. *Nebraska Symposium on Motivation, 51*, 33–72.

Toda, M., Shinotsuka, H., McClintock, C. G., & Stech, F. J. (1978). Development of competitive behavior as a function of culture, age, and social comparison. *Journal of Personality and Social Psychology, 36*, 825–839.

Underwood, B., & Moore, B. (1982). Perspective-taking and altruism. *Psychological Bulletin, 91*(1), 143.

Yorgason, J. B., & Padilla-Walker, L. M. (2011). Nonresidential grandparents' emotional and financial involvement in relation to early adolescent grandchild outcomes. *Journal of Research on Adolescence, 21*, 552–558.

13

Cross-Cultural Evidence of Multidimensional Prosocial Behaviors

AN EXAMINATION OF THE PROSOCIAL TENDENCIES MEASURE (PTM)

Meredith McGinley, Deanna Opal, María Cristina Richaud, and Belén Mesurado

Social behavior, whether intended to benefit others as prosocial behavior or otherwise, is inherently complex. Over many years researchers have accumulated mounting evidence of the complexity of prosocial behaviors in particular. This general term includes behaviors that may occur in a huge variety of contexts, motivated by anything from publicity to empathy, and the benefits of which may vary from nothing to money and accolades and can incur a cost to the self ranging from time or effort to one's own life. This chapter focuses on the importance of acknowledging the multiple layers enfolding prosocial behavior by highlighting over a decade of findings with one particular multidimensional measure. After reviewing the initial development, structure, reliability and validity of the Prosocial Tendencies Measure (PTM; Carlo, Hausmann, Christiansen, & Randall, 2003; Carlo & Randall, 2001, 2002), this chapter will highlight research using the PTM across other ethnicities and cultures and will ultimately present new evidence of the psychometric properties of this measure across European American and Argentinean adolescents.

Development, Structure, Reliability, and Validity of the Prosocial Tendencies Measure

DEVELOPMENT AND STRUCTURE

Developed by Carlo and his colleagues (Carlo et al., 2003; Carlo & Randall, 2001, 2002), the PTM assesses six types of prosocial behaviors based on either the situation or personal motives. Respondents are asked to rate on five-point Likert scale how various statements describe themselves (1 = *does not describe me at all*; 5 = *describes me greatly*). Altruistic prosocial behaviors (referred to as altruism for the remainder of the chapter) are defined by the personal motive of selfless helping in which there is no obvious direct reward for one's self (e.g., "*I feel that if I help someone, they should help me in the future*" is reverse-scored). Public prosocial behaviors (e.g., "*I can help others best when people are watching me*") are motivated by desires to help in front of an audience in order to gain approval or respect from others. Across situations, four other types of prosocial behaviors were identified. Compliant helping (e.g., "*When people ask me to help them, I don't hesitate*") is defined by helping in situations when another has specifically requested the individual's assistance. Anonymous prosocial behavior (e.g., "*I prefer to donate money without anyone knowing*") entails helping in situations in which the helper remains unknown to the recipient of the action. Emotional prosocial behaviors identify helping under emotionally evocative circumstances (e.g., "*I usually help others when they are very upset*"). Dire prosocial behaviors denote helping in emergency and crisis situations, such as when another is physically in danger or hurt in some manner (e.g., "*I tend to help people who are hurt badly*").

Originally, only four factors were conceptualized before the preliminary exploratory factor analyses of the PTM (Carlo & Randall, 2002). For example, emotional and dire prosocial behaviors, which initially were conceptualized to be the same type of helping, were found to be distinct during the development of the PTM (Carlo & Randall, 2002). Similarly, anonymous and public prosocial behaviors were found to load onto separate factors. Subsequent confirmatory factor analyses, in which the six-factor structure was identified a priori, has shown that this six-factor structure continues to best explain the relations among the items of the PTM, particularly when compared with alternative (e.g., one-, four-, and five-) factor structures (Carlo, Knight, McGinley, Zamboanga & Jarvis, 2010; McGinley & Carlo, 2007). However, Carlo et al. (2010) found that several items of the PTM-Revised (PTM-R) did not load well or were found by the analysis to load onto more than one factor; thus, these four items have been dropped from the PTM-R (two altruism items, one public item, and one anonymous item).

Regarding factor intercorrelations, emotional, dire, compliant, and anonymous situational factors tend to be positively related, whereas altruism and public (personally motivated) factors have typically been negatively correlated (Carlo & Randall, 2002; Carlo et al., 2003). However, relations between the motives and situations are less consistent. For example, in some studies public prosocial behaviors have been negatively related to anonymous and compliant prosocial behaviors (Carlo & Randall, 2002; Barry, Padilla-Walker, Madsen, & Nelson, 2008), while in others they are positively related to anonymous, compliant, dire, and emotional prosocial behaviors (Carlo et al., 2003; Carlo, McGinley, Hayes, Batenhorst, & Wilkinson, 2007; McGinley & Carlo, 2007; Padilla-Walker, Barry, Carroll, Madsen, & Nelson, 2008). Perhaps some adolescents, despite distinguishing these factors from one another, help in public forums because of strong societal expectations or because they frequently find themselves in situations in which helping others occurs in front of other people. Relations among situational factors with altruism are similarly divergent. Altruism is often positively related to emotional and compliant prosocial tendencies (Barry et al., 2008; Carlo et al., 2003; Carlo & Randall, 2002; McGinley & Carlo, 2007; Padilla-Walker et al., 2008) and, less often, positively linked to anonymous and dire prosocial tendencies (Hardy, 2006). However, altruism has also been negatively related with these four situational PTM subscales in studies of European and Mexican American early adolescents (Carlo et al., 2010; Carlo, McGinley, Hayes, & Martinez, 2012; Carlo, Knight, McGinley, & Hayes, 2011). Perhaps younger adolescents, who again distinguish these factors, simply do not engage in selfless acts of helping due to their current level of prosocial moral development (e.g., helping someone to gain approval from others; see below discussion).

RELIABILITY

Reliability for the PTM/PTM-R has been established across a number of studies. In its development, Carlo and Randall (2002) reported good test-retest reliability over a period of two weeks (r's ranged from .60 to .80). A number of other studies have found the internal reliability coefficients of the subscales to be at least acceptable, if not excellent, within European American majority samples (Barry et al., 2008; Carlo et al., 2003; Carlo et al., 2010, Carlo & Randall, 2002; Hardy, Carlo, & Roesch, 2010; McGinley & Carlo, 2007; Padilla-Walker et al., 2008). For example, reported alpha coefficients for the altruism subscales have been reported to range from .60 to .81 when self-reported, and .81 to .94 when reported by others (teacher, parent). For the public subscale, alphas ranged from .77 to .87 for the self-reported scale and .77 to .92 for other-report. The compliant subscale alphas ranged from .65 to .83 (self) and .65 to .91 (other-report). Alphas ranged from .77 to .84 for self-reported anonymous prosocial behavior and .77 to .91 for anonymous prosocial behavior reported by others. Internal reliability ranged from .80 to .88 (self) and .85 to .92 (other-report) for emotional prosocial behaviors and from .70 to .82 (self) and .82 to .86 (other-report) for dire prosocial behaviors.

CONVERGENT AND DISCRIMINANT VALIDITY

In initial studies, the factors related positively, but moderately, to global (i.e., motives and situations undifferentiated) prosocial behaviors. Public prosocial behavior was sometimes related to these global behaviors, but altruism was not related to global prosocial behaviors (Carlo et al., 2003; Carlo & Randall, 2002). Carlo et al. (2003) found that teacher-reported helping/generosity was not related to any of the six factors. There is a need for additional studies to explore how the PTM factors are related to reports by others and behavioral measures that distinguish various types of helping. Evidence for discriminant validity with the PTM is limited, but was reported by Carlo and colleagues (Carlo et al., 2003; Carlo &

Randall, 2002). The subscales of the PTM were generally not significantly correlated with participants' vocabulary, social desirability, and personal distress scores.

CONSTRUCT VALIDITY

Emotions, Traits/Values, and Self

Several studies over the last decade demonstrate that the subscales of the PTM
relate to other constructs in a hypothesized manner. For example, empathy and
perspective taking encourage prosocial behavior by motivating us to alleviate the
needs of others (Batson, Eklund, Chermok, Hoyt, & Ortiz, 2007). Numerous studies using the PTM have reported moderate and positive relations among these
constructs such that those with more empathy and perspective taking also tend
to be more prosocial (e.g., Carlo et al., 2003; Carlo et al., 2010; McGinley & Carlo,
2007). For example, Hardy (2006) found that empathy and perspective taking
(combined) positively correlated with all subscales of the PTM except for public
prosocial behavior.

Valuing the person in need is an antecedent of perspective taking and empathy, as
well as prosocial behavior (Batson et al., 2007). Barry et al. (2008) and Padilla-Walker
et al. (2008) reported that possessing more internalized prosocial values predicted
increased situational prosocial behaviors and altruism, whereas externally regulated
prosocial values predicted more public prosocial behaviors and less altruism. Another
value—ascription of responsibility (i.e., believing one is responsible for events)—has
been negatively linked to public prosocial behaviors and positively linked to all other
subscales, though these relations vary slightly by study. Adolescents with strong societal obligations were those who also reported helping across situations, but not publi-
cally or selflessly (Carlo et al., 2003; Carlo & Randall, 2002).

Prosocial behaviors as defined by the PTM have also been uniquely related
to religiosity. Three separate studies (Carlo et al., 2010; Hardy & Carlo, 2005,
Padilla-Walker et al., 2008) have reported that compliant and anonymous prosocial
behaviors and altruism were positively associated with religiosity, whereas the other
three factors were not related to religiosity. Hardy and Carlo (2005) demonstrated
that these relations are likely moderated by internalized values (e.g., kindness),
such that religiosity fosters prosocial values which then encourage certain prosocial
behaviors. Values also reflect an aspect of moral identity, which has been identified
as an important motivator of prosocial behaviors such as volunteering and donating
(Aquino & Reed, 2002; Hardy, 2006). Hardy (2006) found that moral identity—
valuing morality as an important aspect of one's self concept—was positively related
to all subscales of the PTM, with the exception of public prosocial behaviors.

Sociocognitive Correlates

Generally, the PTM subscales are uniquely related to increasingly more sophisticated (e.g., internalized) prosocial moral reasoning. For example, Carlo and

colleagues (Carlo et al., 2003; Carlo & Randall, 2002) reported that altruism, emotional, dire, compliant, and anonymous tendencies were positively related to internalized prosocial moral reasoning (versus lower levels of reasoning), whereas public was uniquely *positively* related to hedonistic (i.e., the lowest level of) prosocial moral reasoning. Subsequent studies appear to support that the motive-based tendencies are distinctively related to prosocial moral reasoning. Hardy (2006) found that mature, internalized prosocial moral reasoning was positively linked to altruism and negatively related to public prosocial tendencies. No relations were found with the remaining four prosocial scales. Taken together, these findings suggest that helping in front of an audience is more likely among those with externally oriented morals, and helping in other situations and with selfless motives is more likely among those with internalized moral values.

Gender and Aggression

Gender-role socialization from a young age includes encouraging different types of prosocial behavior in men and women; studies have found that men tend to engage in risky or chivalrous helping (which occur in public settings), whereas women participate through more nurturant roles (Eagly & Crowley, 1986; Hastings, Rubin, & DeRose, 2005). Gender differences therefore occur among the PTM subscales. Previous studies have reported that women and girls generally score higher on the emotional, compliant, and altruistic subscales, whereas men and boys score higher on public prosocial behaviors (Barry et al., 2008; Carlo et al., 2007; Carlo & Randall, 2002; Hardy, 2006; McGinley & Carlo, 2007; Padilla Walker et al., 2008).

Aggression has been found to be negatively related to compliant and altruistic prosocial behaviors and positively related to public prosocial behaviors (Carlo et al., 2003; McGinley & Carlo, 2007). Additionally, externalizing behaviors have shown to be negatively related to only compliant prosocial behaviors (Carlo et al., 2010). These findings emphasize the notion that the relations among helping dimensions and aggressive/externalizing behaviors is not straightforward nor does the presence of one dictate the absence of the other (see McGinley & Carlo, 2007).

Parenting

Parenting behaviors have been extensively studied in regard to the socialization of these six types of prosocial behaviors. Parental monitoring appears to be related to emotional, dire, and compliant prosocial behaviors (Carlo et al. 2010). Parental inductions, a type of discipline that orients children toward the needs of others using reasoning and explanations, was positively related to all factors of the PTM with the exception of altruism. Carlo et al. (2007) investigated how prosocial-oriented parenting practices predicted adolescents' reported prosocial behaviors (as assessed by the PTM). Social rewards, experiential prosocial parenting practices (e.g., parents and children volunteering together), conversations centered around helping others, and discursive (e.g., encouraging a shared mutual understanding) communication practices were generally positively related to all PTM subscales, though sometimes these relations were mediated by adolescents' self-reported sympathy. For example, conversations indirectly predicted emotional and compliant prosocial behaviors via adolescents' sympathy, whereas direct and indirect relations were evident for dire, public, and anonymous prosocial behaviors.

Social rewards, conversations, and discursive communication demonstrated negative relations with altruism, and similar results were found by Richaud, Mesurado, and Lemos (2012) in an Argentinean sample. On dimensions relating to parenting *styles*, however, they found that only responsiveness was weakly and positively related to compliant prosocial behaviors and that demandingness was weakly and positively related to anonymous and emotional prosocial behaviors; no indirect relations with sympathy were uncovered for these general styles. The study carried out in Argentina found that several measures of parenting styles more weakly contributed to the prediction of altruism and anonymous prosocial behaviors than these specific practices, although more intense styles (pathological control, extreme autonomy) seemed to account for more variance by positively predicting public and "responsive" (emotional, dire, and compliant; see below) prosocial behaviors (Richaud et al., 2012).

Similarly, Barry et al. (2008) found that general parent-child relationship qualities were not necessarily related to prosocial behaviors (support, companionship, aid, and intimacy), as reported by either parents or children, and did not strongly directly relate to the PTM. However, these relationship qualities predicted internal and external regulation, which in turn differentially predicted the six PTM factors. Hardy et al. (2010) reported that expected parental reactions to engaging in prosocial behaviors was not related to prosocial behaviors (reported by parents/teachers); mediational analyses revealed indirect paths predicting an *overall* measure of prosocial tendencies. Overall, the relations between parenting and prosocial behavior appeared to be mediated by the prosocial values that parents' socialization practices promote.

In sum, socialization that focuses on directly orienting youth toward the needs (physical or emotional) of others, or those that positively influence or monitor behavior, seem to be the most strongly related to other-oriented prosocial behaviors assessed by the PTM. Studies using more general measures of parenting tend to yield weaker relations, though indirect relations to PTM factors are found if this parenting promotes values or regulatory behaviors. Yet, the exact nature of these relations—direct and/or indirect relations, or the complete lack of relation, depends ultimately on the exact socialization method, internalization process, and prosocial behavior being assessed by the researcher. Thus, although our understanding of the relations among parenting and multidimensional behaviors is somewhat established, the complex nature of this socialization process requires continued and mindful replication and extension.

Research with Mexican Americans

The PTM has demonstrated sound psychometric properties across ethnic and cultural groups, even when translated into another language. Several studies have supported that the PTM-R is a reliable and valid measure to use with Mexican American youth (when administered in English). Carlo et al. (2010) reported that the six-factor structure of the PTM-R was upheld when compared against competing factor structures in a sample of Mexican American preadolescents (overall M age = 12.67). One-factor, four-factor, and five-factor alternative models did not explain the data as well as the six-factor model did, supporting the need to assess all six subscales separately in the overall sample. Moreover, the PTM-R displayed measurement invariance in this study suggesting that this measure analogously operates across these two ethnic groups, allowing for meaningful mean-level and associative comparisons. Additionally, these factors had adequate reliabilities and were uniquely related to externalizing behaviors (compliant only), parental monitoring (emotional, dire and compliant) and religiosity (altruism, compliant, and anonymous) in hypothesized directions.

Reliability and validity of the PTM-R in Mexican American youth samples was established by a series of studies by Carlo et al. (2010), Calderón-Tena, Knight, and Carlo (2011), and Armenta, Knight, Carlo, and Jacobson (2011). These scholars reported acceptable reliabilities for the PTM in a sample of younger Mexican American preadolescents (overall M age = 10.9). The six PTM-R factors were uniquely predicted by parental inductions, sympathy, and prosocial moral reasoning in hypothesized directions in the study conducted by Carlo et al. (2010). Armenta et al. (2011) reported that ethnic group attachment, familism, and mainstream values also predicted the six PTM-R factors in Mexican Americans, with greater attachment predicting emotional, dire, compliant, and anonymous prosocial behaviors; familism mediating these aforementioned relations; and mainstream American values predicting increased public prosocial behavior but decreased altruism. In an older sample of Mexican American college students (M age = 23.1 years), McGinley et al. (2010) also reported acceptable reliabilities of the PTM-R subscales. Additionally, sympathy was correlated positively with emotional, dire, and compliant prosocial behaviors for men and women and additionally with altruism for women and anonymous prosocial behaviors for men.

Carlo et al. (2011) examined a model of parental inductions, moral reasoning, empathy, and prosocial behavior in adolescents. Empathy mediated the relations between parental inductions and prosocial behaviors for both Mexican and European American adolescents. Empathy was related to all six prosocial behavior subscales, but prosocial moral reasoning was only related to altruistic, anonymous, and dire prosocial behaviors. Mexican Americans and European Americans had similar patterns of relations, but there were group mean differences. Compared to European Americans, Mexican Americans reported less altruistic prosocial behavior, but more public and anonymous prosocial behaviors. The authors theorized this was due to cultural differences in views and motivations surrounding different types of prosocial behaviors.

In a study of Mexican American college students, Carlo et al. (2012) examined a model explaining the relations among peer and parent attachment, empathy, and prosocial and aggressive behaviors. Attachment was positively related to empathy, which in turn was positively related to prosocial behavior (except for public, which was not related to empathy) and negatively related to aggressive behavior; empathy mediated the relationship between peer, but not parent, attachment and behavior. The mediation model was stronger for men than women in that more behaviors were predicted and empathy was a stronger mediator for them. Also, women reported higher levels of compliant prosocial behavior, empathy, and parent attachment, and men reported more aggression. Gender socialization that encourages empathy in women and discourages its expression in men may explain these findings.

The PTM Translated: Europe and Asia

The PTM has also been translated and administered to youth outside the United States. For example, the PTM has been translated into Turkish by Tuncel (2010). This study, examining the characteristics of Turkish undergraduate athletes, reported that the internal reliabilities of the six subscales were adequate. Additionally, women (vs. men) reported greater emotional prosocial behaviors, and team sports players (vs. sports players who play individually) reported greater anonymous prosocial behaviors. No mean differences in the six subscales were reported between athletes and nonathletes. Šukys (2010) reported adequate reliabilities for all six subscales for Lithuanian 10th-grade students in his study. Girls reported greater mean emotional, dire, altruistic, and compliant prosocial behaviors. Students who reported participation in extracurricular activities engaged in greater public, emotional, dire, and compliant prosocial behaviors than those who did not. Lin, Xiaoyi, Li, Liu, and Yang (2006) similarly reported adequate internal reliabilities for all subscales of the PTM for Chinese primary, secondary, and college students in the Yunnan province. Age differences across elementary, junior high, high school, and college were evident. Altruism, compliant, emotional, and dire prosocial behaviors increased across all age groups, whereas there was an overall increase in anonymous prosocial behavior but no difference between the two lowest age groups. High school students reported the lowest levels of public prosocial behaviors relative to the other three age groups. The three oldest groups of girls displayed lower mean levels of public prosocial behaviors than comparable boys. Chinese girls typically reported higher mean levels of altruism, emotional, dire, anonymous, and compliant prosocial behaviors than boys across most age groups. In stepwise regression analyses predicting other social behaviors, emotional prosocial behaviors was the strongest predictor of social competence and altruism was the strongest (negative) predictor of antisocial behaviors in elementary and high school students, whereas compliant prosocial behaviors was the strongest predictor of these outcomes in junior high students. College students were alternatively administered an age-appropriate measure of adaptability; altruism, dire, and compliant were roughly equally strong predictors in this regression model.

The PTM also has established validity in the Czech Republic. In a sample of Czech female college students, subscales of the PTM were distinctively related to sympathy and personality dimensions (Mlčák & Zaskodna 2008). Emotional, dire, and compliant prosocial behaviors were significantly correlated with empathic concern and perspective taking, and anonymous prosocial behaviors was only related to perspective taking. Subscales of the PTM were also associated with various dimensions of the NEO Five-Factor Inventory (NEO-FFI); students who were more compliant scored higher on extraversion, openness, agreeableness, and conscientiousness; students engaging in more altruistic and emotional prosocial behaviors scored higher on openness and agreeableness; and students who were engaged in greater dire prosocial behaviors scored higher on openness. Anonymous and public prosocial behaviors were not significantly associated with the NEO-FFI. In a second study, Mlčák (in press) reported several mean differences across distinct groups of students. Women reported greater altruistic but fewer public prosocial behaviors. Students pursuing helping professions reported greater anonymous, altruistic, and dire prosocial behaviors than students pursuing technical/economic professions. Students with volunteering experience reported greater dire, emotional, and anonymous helping behaviors than those without reported volunteering experience. In this study, similar relations with the NEO-FFI model were found, although differing patterns emerged with men being included in this study. Anonymous prosocial behavior was related to less extraversion but more openness and conscientiousness. Compliant prosocial behavior was related to increased extraversion, openness, agreeableness, and conscientiousness. Emotional, dire, and compliant prosocial behaviors were related to increased extraversion, openness, and conscientiousness, although only emotional was related to increased neuroticism and only compliant was related to increased agreeableness. Altruism was related to decreased neuroticism and increased openness and agreeableness, whereas public prosocial behavior was related to increased extraversion and decreased openness and agreeableness. Thus, across these two studies in the Czech Republic, each PTM subscale was linked to a unique combination of personality traits.

The Current Study

THE PTM IN ARGENTINA

A recent investigation of the factor structure of the PTM in children and adolescents in Argentina supported a four-factor structure of the PTM translated into Spanish. Richaud, Mesurado, and Kohan Cortada (2012) reported that dire, emotional, and compliant prosocial behaviors loaded onto a "responsive" latent factor, given the strong intercorrelations among these factors in the six-factor model. However, these findings could be a function of the age of children (*M* age = 12.4; youngest children age = 10), who may not be able to distinguish among the different situations these factors represent. In fact, other cross-cultural studies have supported a reduced PTM factor structure when examining children at this age (Shen, 2009). Thus, the question remains of how the factor structure of the PTM may look in a sample of older adolescents in Argentina. If the PTM is not established as a similarly multidimensional, reliable, and valid measure across cultures, it may not be appropriate to use this measure to compare various populations (Carlo et al., 2010; Knight & Hill, 1998; Knight, Tein, Prost, & Gonzales, 2002). Thus, the current study will review the structure and correlates of the translated PTM in an older adolescent sample from Argentina. A comparison adolescent sample from the United States will be simultaneously investigated in order to provide corroborating evidence of the multidimensionality of the PTM-R and to understand more fully how these subscales differentially relate to theoretically relevant measures.

PARTICIPANTS FROM THE UNITED STATES

Participants from the United States were 233 adolescents (*M* age = 16.70 years, *SD* = .87; 69% girls) from public high schools in the midwestern region of the United States who received class credit for their participation. Participants completed a survey packet consisting of several measures of their behaviors, beliefs, and attitudes about their parents. Although survey data also were obtained from parents, only 81 parents returned completed survey packets. According to the available data from these parent reports, the adolescents' ethnicity was typically European American and the average household income was reported as $45,000–$75,000.

ARGENTINEAN PARTICIPANTS

Participants from Argentina were 241 middle-class adolescents (*M* age = 16.32, *SD* = 1.18, 46% girls) from secondary schools in Buenos Aires, Argentina. In order to obtain permission to collect data, school principals were interviewed and the research was explained to them in a letter. Parents were asked for their permission through the school. The participants completed the questionnaire in the classroom during one session in groups of approximately 20 adolescents in the presence of a trained psychologist. Both parents had typically completed secondary school.

MEASURES

Students completed the PTM-R, a 21-item measure designed to assess how likely they are to engage in prosocial behaviors across a variety of situations (Carlo et al., 2003).

The PTM was translated using the backward translation strategy. First, the scale was translated independently into Spanish by two psychologists who were proficient in English and Spanish. Any differences in the resulting translations were discussed by the psychologists until they reached a final wording of the instrument. Subsequently, a different psychologist, who was not involved in this investigation, was asked to translate the instrument back into English. No major discrepancies were found between the original and the translated version.

Additionally, participants also completed the Expected Parental Reactions scale (Wyatt & Carlo, 2002), which is a 16-item measure that assesses adolescents' perceptions of how appropriately his or her parent would react to statements regarding acts of prosocial behavior. Respondents answered using a five-point Likert-type scale to indicate appropriateness. Finally, participants completed the Davis Interpersonal Reactivity Index (Davis, 1983). The Empathic Concern and Perspective Taking subscales were used in the current study and combined to form a 14-item sympathy index. Participants responded using a five-point Likert type scale with 1 = *Does not describe me*; 3 = *Sort of describes me*; and 5 = *Describes me very well*. All measures demonstrated adequate reliability for both U.S. and Argentinean samples.

DATA ANALYSIS PLAN

All analyses were conducted using Mplus 6.1 statistical software (Muthén & Muthén, 1998–2010). In order to establish the theorized six-factor model in the overall sample (see Figure 13.1), confirmatory factor analysis (CFA) was used. Alternative factor structures were also tested; first, the six-factor model was compared to a one-factor model. Next, since highly correlated factors can indicate construct overlap (Brown, 2006), factors having high correlations in the initial six-factor solution were combined and compared to the six-factor model. In all model examinations, fit is considered good if the comparative fit index (CFI) is greater than or equal to .95 (or .90 for adequate fit), the root mean square error of approximation (RMSEA) is less than or equal to .06 (or .08 for adequate fit), and the standardized root mean square residual (SRMR) is less than or equal to .08 (or .10 for adequate fit; Hu & Bentler, 1999; Kline, 1998; Weston & Gore, 2006). Since the above model comparisons do not represent true nested models, the Akaike information criterion (AIC) and the expected cross-validation index (ECVI) were used to assess relative fit. In general, the AIC and the ECVI correct model fit for model complexity, and lower values indicate better model fit (Brown, 2006).

ESTABLISHING THE SIX-FACTOR SOLUTION

United States

In the U.S. sample, the initial 21-item, six-factor model yielded a Heywood case (i.e., correlation higher than one). Upon inspection of the model, it was found that altruism and public exhibited multicollinearity ($r = .91$, $p < .001$). Inspection of the items revealed that a PTM-R item ("*I tend to help others when it makes me look good*") was highly correlated with another ("*I tend to help others when I am being watched*"). Therefore, we eliminated the former item from the six-factor model. The revised 20-item, six factor model yielded an acceptable solution and fit the data well ($\chi^2(155) = 304.633$, $p < .001$, CFI = .935, RMSEA = .064, SRMR = .054; see Figure 13.1). Factor loadings for this model were all positive and significant.

Competing models of the PTM-R were then tested. The one-factor model did not fit the data well ($\chi^2(170) = 1183.58$, $p < .001$, CFI = .556, RMSEA = .160, SRMR = .135). The AIC and ECVI values were lower for the theorized six-factor solution (AIC = 11371.14, ECVI = 2.65) than the one-factor solution (AIC = 12220.09, ECVI = 6.57), suggesting that the six-factor solution fit better. Next, a competing five-factor model was tested because the altruism and public latent factors remained highly correlated ($r = -.77$, $p < .001$). This five-factor solution had adequate fit ($\chi^2(160) = 368.842$, $p < .001$, CFI = .909, RMSEA = .075, SRMR = .062). Both the AIC and ECVI values were lower for the theorized six-factor solution (AIC = 11371.14, ECVI = 2.65) than this alternative five-factor solution (AIC = 11425.34, ECVI = 2.97), suggesting that the six-factor solution had better fit. Because the emotional, dire, and compliant latent factors were also highly correlated (r's ranged from = .68 to.81, p's < .001), a four-factor solution in which all emotional and dire items were loaded onto one latent factor was then tested. This model fit poorly according to fit indices ($\chi^2(164) = 467.569$, $p < .001$, CFI = .865, RMSEA = .091, SRMR = .071). Both the AIC and ECVI values were lower for the theorized six-factor solution (AIC = 11371.14, ECVI = 2.65) than this alternative four-factor solution (AIC = 11567.46, ECVI = 3.65), suggesting that the six-factor solution had better fit, and thus fit best compared with alternative solutions.

Argentina

In the Argentinean sample, the initial 21-item, 6-factor model yielded a Heywood case (i.e., correlation higher than one). Upon inspection of the model, it was found that the dire and emotional latent factors exhibited multicollinearity, such that the standardized correlation was greater than one. Inspection of the items revealed that a PTM-R question ("*Cuando alguien está en una mala situación es más fácil para mí ayudarlo*"/"*When I help someone in a bad situation it is easy for me to help them.*") was not worded correctly; thus we eliminated this item from the six-factor model. The revised 20-item, six factor model yielded an acceptable solution and fit the data adequately ($\chi^2(155) = 298.158$, $p < .001$, CFI = .910, RMSEA = .062, SRMR = .061; see Figure 13.1). Factor loadings for this model were all positive and significant.

Competing models of the PTM-R were then tested. The one-factor model did not fit the data well ($\chi^2(170) = 1231.62$, $p < .001$, CFI = .336, RMSEA = .162, SRMR = .193). The AIC and ECVI values were lower for the theorized six-factor

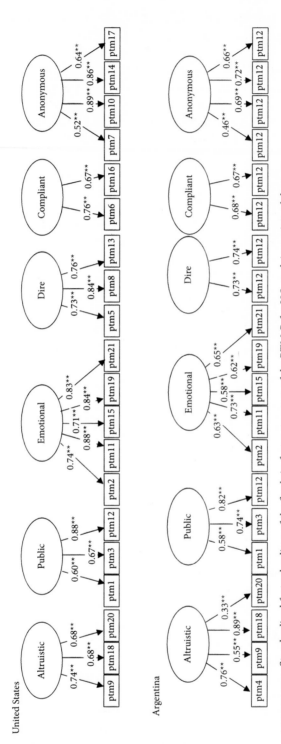

FIGURE 13.1 *Standardized factor loadings of the final six-factor structure of the PTM-R for U.S. and Argentine adolescents.*

$\chi 2(155) = 304.633, p < .001, CFI = .935, RMSEA = .064, SRMR = .054$

$\chi 2(155) = 298.158, p < .001, CFI = .910, RMSEA = .062, SRMR = .061$

solution (AIC = 13781.07, ECVI = 2.56) than the one-factor solution (AIC = 14684.53, ECVI = 6.60), suggesting that the six-factor solution fit better. Next, a competing five-factor model was tested because the altruism and public latent factors remained highly correlated (r = -.80, p < .001). This five-factor solution had a poorer fit to the data ($\chi^2(160)$ = 335.96, p < .001, CFI = .890, RMSEA = .068, SRMR = .064). Both the AIC and ECVI values were moreover lower for the theorized six-factor solution (AIC = 13781.07, ECVI = 2.56) than this alternative five-factor solution (AIC = 13808.88, ECVI = 2.76), suggesting that the six-factor solution had better fit. Because the emotional, dire, and compliant latent factors were also highly intercorrelated (r's ranged from = .81 to .94, p's < .001), a four-factor solution in which all emotional and dire items were loaded onto one latent factor was then tested. This model fit only adequately according to fit indices ($\chi^2(164)$ = 329.55, p < .001, CFI = .896, RMSEA = .065, SRMR = .068). Both the AIC and ECVI values were moreover lower for the theorized six-factor solution (AIC = 13781.07, ECVI = 2.56) than this alternative four-factor solution (AIC = 13794.46, ECVI = 2.76), suggesting that the six-factor solution had slightly better fit than the four-factor solution. Although the four-factor solution remains plausible, the six-factor solution is retained as it is moreover in agreement with previous theoretical and empirical findings of the PTM-R.

INTERCORRELATIONS AMONG MAIN STUDY FACTORS

United States

Intercorrelations among study scales can be found in Table 13.1. Altruism was negatively related to public and dire prosocial behaviors, as well as expected parental reactions. Public was positively related to emotional, dire, and compliant prosocial behaviors as well as expected parental reactions. Emotional, dire, compliant, and anonymous prosocial behaviors were positively intercorrelated with one another, and all four were additionally positively related to expected parental reactions and sympathy. Finally, girls endorsed greater emotional, dire, compliant, and anonymous prosocial behaviors, as well as expected parental reactions and sympathy.

Argentina

Altruism was negatively related to public and anonymous prosocial behavior but positively related to expected parental reactions, sympathy, and age. Public was positively related to emotional and anonymous prosocial behaviors but negatively related to expected parental reactions and age. Emotional, dire, compliant, and anonymous prosocial behaviors and sympathy were positively intercorrelated and were positively related to expected parental reactions (except for anonymous prosocial behaviors). Finally, girls endorsed greater altruism and sympathy, but less public prosocial behavior, than boys.

TABLE 13.1 Intercorrelations among the PTM latent factors, sympathy, expected parental reactions, gender, and age for U.S. (N = 233) and Argentine (N = 241) adolescents

	1	2	3	4	5	6	7	8	9	10
United States										
Altruism (1)	—									
Public (2)	$-.77^{**}$	—								
Emotional (3)	$-.08$	$.27^{**}$	—							
Dire (4)	$-.18^*$	$.18^*$	$.67^{**}$	—						
Compliant (5)	$.05$	$.28^{**}$	$.69^{**}$	$.82^{**}$	—					
Anonymous (6)	$-.12$	$.14+$	$.40^{**}$	$.61^{**}$	$.63^{**}$	—				
Parental Reactions (7)	-19^*	$.16^*$	$.27^{**}$	$.31^{**}$	$.44^{**}$	$.30^{**}$	—			
Sympathy (8)	$.12$	$.00$	$.55^{**}$	$.46^{**}$	$.62^{**}$	$.51^{**}$	$.24^{**}$	—		
Age (9)	$-.02$	$.04$	$-.03$	$.04$	$.04$	$.09$	$-.01$	$.08$	—	
Gender (10)	$.04$	$-.04$	$.29^{**}$	$.20^{**}$	$.17^*$	$.19^{**}$	$.20^{**}$	$.28^{**}$	$-.17^{**}$	—
Argentina										
Altruism (1)	—									
Public (2)	$-.81^{**}$	—								
Emotional (3)	$-.08$	$.17^*$	—							
Dire (4)	$.13$	$.00$	$.95^{**}$	—						
Compliant (5)	$.15+$	$-.07$	$.85^{**}$	$.82^{**}$	—					
Anonymous (6)	$-.25^{**}$	$.20^*$	$.38^{**}$	$.23^*$	$.38^{**}$	—				
Parental Reactions (7)	$.24^{**}$	$-.24^{**}$	$.20^*$	$.24^{**}$	$.33^{**}$	$.12$	—			
Sympathy (8)	$.20^{**}$	$-.08$	$.66^{**}$	$.63^{**}$	$.68^{**}$	$.30^{**}$	$.28^{**}$	—		
Age (9)	$.28^{**}$	$-.26^{**}$	$-.03$	$-.04$	$.10$	$-.01$	$.07$	$.03$	—	
Gender (10)	$.22^{**}$	$-.31^{**}$	$.12$	$.10$	$.06$	$-.13+$	$.17^{**}$	$.27^{**}$	$.09$	—

$^*p < .05$, $^{**}p < .01$

Discussion of Study Findings

As hypothesized, the six-factor structure of the PTM-R was upheld in adolescent samples in both the United States and Argentina. The six-factor structure displayed better fit than more parsimonious alternative models. For example, the one-factor model, in which all items of the PTM were modeled to load onto one latent prosocial factor, displayed extremely poor fit across both samples. This finding is similar to that by Carlo et al. (2010) in which the one-factor model did not converge mathematically, suggesting an extremely poor fit to the data. Additionally, the multiple factor alternative models, in which the factors that showed the most collinearity with one another were combined into a single factor, did not explain the relations among the data as well as the six-factor model. These findings again resonate with those of Carlo et al. (2010), in which similar competing models failed to explain the data as well as the six-factor model. Thus, it is important for researchers who use this measure, and possibly other measures that tap into multiple facets of prosocial behavior, not to collapse these subscales. Doing so may not adequately explain the data and constructs represented by them.

The intercorrelations of the PTM factors are similar to those reported by previous researchers. In the current study, the emotional, dire, compliant, and anonymous prosocial behaviors were positively intercorrelated in both samples (United States: r's = .40–.82; Argentina: r's = .23–.95). Altruism and public prosocial tendencies were negatively correlated in both samples as well. Public was positively related to emotional, dire, and compliant prosocial behaviors in the U.S. sample and emotional and anonymous in the Argentinean sample. In the U.S. sample, altruism was negatively related to dire, and in the Argentinean sample, altruism was negatively related to anonymous prosocial behaviors. Perhaps in both countries these adolescents believe that engaging in either type of prosocial behavior (dire or anonymous) is deservedly attached to some recognition that praises the individual for the positive social behavior.

Although some of these reported intercorrelations appear to be stronger than previously reported, this is a function of using the measurement aspect structural equation modeling (i.e., in which the unique error variance is estimated; typically, correlations tend to be attenuated when error is not estimated). However, the high intercorrelations among emotional, dire, and compliant subscales correspond with research conducted by Richaud et al. (2012) with a younger Argentinean sample, though the intercorrelations were somewhat weaker in the current study. Future research should continue to be mindful of participants' ages, as the PTM six-factor structure may not be appropriate for younger children (see also Shen, 2009).

As expected, self-reported sympathy was positively related to emotional, dire, compliant, and anonymous prosocial behaviors across adolescents. However, sympathy was not related to public prosocial behavior or altruism in the U.S. sample but it was positively related to altruism in the Argentinean sample. This may be a function of the value *simpatia* in this Latino culture. *Simpatia* refers not only to empathy or emotional sensitivity but also to moral character, such as maintaining harmony in relationships (Marin & Marin, 1991). Engaging in selfless acts may be necessary in maintaining this harmony, which is strongly related to emotional sensitivity via this value.

Expected parental reactions to adolescents' prosocial behaviors were positively related to public, emotional, dire, compliant, and anonymous prosocial behaviors in the U.S. sample. However, parental reactions were negatively related to altruism for U.S. adolescents. This relation was positive in the Argentinean adolescents, but the relation between public prosocial tendencies and expected parental reactions was negative. Notably, Latino parents tend to promote less independence (Domenech Rodriguez, Donovick, & Crowley, 2009) but strong familial interdependence via high levels of warmth and demandingness, as well as through the value of *familismo* (Ayón, Marsiglia, & Bermudez-Parsai, et al., 2010), which promotes strong obligation to the family. This strong family orientation, in addition to the encouraged value of simpatia, may lead adolescents in Argentina to be more receptive of socialization efforts intended to promote selfless helping behaviors toward others.

Gender and age differences were also found in the current study. U.S. adolescent girls reported higher mean levels of emotional, dire, compliant, and anonymous prosocial behaviors, whereas Argentinean adolescent girls reported greater altruistic, but fewer public, prosocial behaviors than their male counterparts. These findings are in accord with gender socialization theories and previous research with the PTM (see above). Additionally, older Argentinean adolescents reported higher levels of altruism but lower levels of public prosocial behaviors. This is in accord with cognitive developmental theory that suggests that greater cognitive skills (e.g., perspective taking) may be required for other-oriented behaviors whereas self-oriented behaviors do not require such skills (Carlo, 2006; Carlo et al., 2003). No age effects were found in the U.S. adolescent sample; this finding could be a function of the limited age range in the current study.

Although these findings further support the reliability and validity of the PTM-R subscales, several limitations associated with the nature of the data must be taken into consideration. Namely, measurement invariance tests and direct comparisons across the culture groups could not be conducted due to the slight difference in which exact items were included in the initial CFA for each group (i.e., configural invariance could not be established). Any conclusions regarding differences between cultures are tentative at best. Moreover, only two measures were available in order to establish validity (sympathy, expected parental reactions). Thus, construct validity with the PTM-R in this culture has yet to be fully established. Continued efforts to examine the relations between multidimensional prosocial behaviors and theorized constructs, such as values, prosocial moral reasoning, and risky behaviors are needed not only in Argentina, but other countries as well.

Despite the limitations, the current data provides corroborating evidence that the PTM-R is a psychometrically sound measure of multidimensional prosocial behaviors. Future research should continue to document its effectiveness by examining whether measurement properties of the multidimensional PTM are equivalent across ethnic or cultural groups, gender groups, age groups, and any other groups across which prosocial behaviors may be compared. In particular, conducting equivalence tests with other ethnicities (e.g., Asian Americans, African Americans) and cultures not yet examined (e.g., those in Europe, Asia, Middle East) would yield evidence of the universality of these dimensions of prosocial behavior. Limitations present in the current study also indicate that future studies should include large and balanced subgroups and ensure the complete initial congruency of the PTM's administration in order for tests of measurement invariance to be conducted.

Future studies should moreover attempt to understand possible between- and within-group processes that are related to each factor of the PTM as no studies to date have formally examined multidimensional prosocial behaviors in a multilevel model (Carlo, 2006). Additionally, no current studies have attempted to examine the development and correlates of prosocial behaviors over time. It is unknown what trajectories these various factors have, or what correlates best predict these individual trajectories. Finally, understanding multidimensional prosocial behaviors would also benefit from a person-level rather than variable-level study. Latent groups (either cross-sectional or over time, i.e., growth mixture modeling) comprising unique profiles of PTM subscales, for example, could display important differences regarding correlates. These methods could potentially give scholars the knowledge to help disentangle the somewhat complex and sometimes inconsistent relations found in previous studies of multidimensional prosocial behaviors.

More broadly speaking, examining the properties of the PTM as an example of a measure of multidimensional prosocial behaviors highlights the need for researchers in this field to be mindful of their measure of helping. Implementing global measures of helping may attenuate relations, direct and indirect, between prosocial behaviors and theoretically relevant constructs. Using a well-defined measure of helping behavior, whether defined by target, situation, or motive, provides researchers with additional information that helps make sense of differential relations that may arise when comparing groups of individuals (e.g., age, gender, ethnic or cultural groups). Similarly, using specific measures of prosocial behaviors may also orient researchers to the unique correlates that may promote these behaviors. For example, broader measures of parenting were found to be the least likely to relate to helping, whereas measures of specific parenting behaviors strongly correlated with specific types of prosocial behavior. This more complete, specific understanding of the links among prosocial behaviors and their correlates can lead to the most effective intervention practices among those wanting to promote helping behaviors in youth.

References

Aquino, K., & Reed, A., II. (2002). The self-importance of moral identity. *Journal of Personality and Social Psychology, 83*, 1423–1440.

Armenta, B. E., Knight, G. P., Carlo, G., & Jacobson, R. P. (2011). The relation between ethnic group attachment and prosocial tendencies: The mediating role of cultural values. *European Journal of Social Psychology, 41*, 107–115.

Ayón, C., Marsiglia, F. F., & Bermudez-Parsai, M. (2010). Latino family mental health: Exploring the role of discrimination and familismo. *Journal of Community Psychology, 38*, 742–756.

Barry, C. M., Padilla-Walker, L. M., Madsen, S. D., & Nelson, L. J. (2008). The impact of maternal relationship quality on emerging adults' prosocial tendencies: Indirect effects via regulation of prosocial values. *Journal of Youth and Adolescence, 37*, 581–591.

Batson, C. D., Eklund, J. H., Chermok, V. L., Hoyt, J. L., & Ortiz, B. G. (2007). An additional antecedent of empathic concern: Valuing the welfare of the person in need. *Journal of Personality and Social Psychology, 93*, 65–74.

Brown, T. A. (2006). *Confirmatory factor analysis for applied research*. New York: Guilford Press.

Calderón-Tena, C. O., Knight, G. P., & Carlo, G. (2011). The socialization of prosocial behavioral tendencies among Mexican American adolescents: The role of familism values. *Cultural Diversity and Ethnic Minority Psychology, 17*, 98–106.

Carlo, G. (2006). Care-based and altruistically-based morality. In M. Killen & J. G. Smetana (Eds.), *Handbook of moral development* (pp. 551–579). Mahwah, NJ: Erlbaum.

Carlo, G., Hausmann, A., Christiansen, S., & Randall, B. A. (2003). Sociocognitive and behavioral correlates of a measure of prosocial tendencies for adolescents. *Journal of Early Adolescence, 23*, 107–134.

Carlo, G., Knight, G. P., McGinley, M., & Hayes, R. (2011). The roles of parental inductions, moral emotions, and moral cognitions in prosocial tendencies among Mexican American and European American early adolescents. *Journal of Early Adolescence, 31*, 757–781.

Carlo, G., Knight, G. P., McGinley, M., Zamboanga, B. L., & Jarvis, L. H. (2010). Measurement and functional equivalence in prosocial behaviors among European and Mexican American early adolescents. *Journal of Research on Adolescence, 20*, 334–358.

Carlo, G., McGinley, M., Hayes, R., Batenhorst, C., & Wilkinson, J. (2007). Parenting styles or practices? Parenting, sympathy, and prosocial behaviors among adolescents. *Journal of Genetic Psychology, 168*, 147–176.

Carlo, G., McGinley, M., Hayes, R. C., & Martinez, M. (2012). Empathy as a mediator of the relations between parent and peer attachment and prosocial and physically aggressive behaviors in Mexican American college students. *Journal of Social and Personal Relationships, 29*, 337–357.

Carlo, G., & Randall, B. (2001). Are all prosocial behaviors equal? A socioecological developmental conception of prosocial behavior. In F. Columbus (Ed.), *Advances in psychology research* (Vol. 2, pp. 151–170). Huntington, NY: Nova Science.

Carlo, G., & Randall, B. A. (2002). The development of a measure of prosocial behaviors for late adolescents. *Journal of Youth and Adolescence, 31*, 31–44.

Davis, M. H. (1983). Measuring individual differences in empathy: Evidence for a multidimensional approach. *Journal of Personality and Social Psychology, 44*, 113–126.

Domenech Rodrigues, M. M., Donovick, M. R., & Crowley, S. L. (2009). Parenting styles in a cultural context: Observations of "protective parenting" in first-generation Latinos. *Family Process, 48*, 195–210.

Eagly, A. H., & Crowley, M. (1986). Gender and helping behavior: A meta-analytic review of the social psychological literature. *Psychological Bulletin, 100*, 283–308.

Hardy, S. A. (2006). Identity, reasoning, and emotion: An empirical comparison of three sources of moral motivation. *Motivation and Emotion, 30*, 207–215.

Hardy, S. A., & Carlo, G. (2005). Religiosity and prosocial behaviours in adolescence: The mediating role of prosocial values. *Journal of Moral Education, 34*, 231–249.

Hardy, S. A., Carlo, G., & Roesch, S. C. (2010). Links between adolescents' expected parental reactions and prosocial behavioral tendencies: The mediating role of prosocial values. *Journal of Youth and Adolescence, 39*, 84–95.

Hastings, P. D., Rubin, K. H., & DeRose, L. (2005). Links among gender, inhibition, and parental socialization in the development of prosocial behavior. *Merrill-Palmer Quarterly, 51*, 467–493.

Hu, L., & Bentler, P. M. (1999). Cutoff criteria for fit indexes in covariance structure analysis: Conventional criteria versus new alternatives. *Structural Equation Modeling, 6*, 1–55.

Kline, R. B. (1998). *Principals and practice of structural equation modeling.* New York: Guilford Press.

Knight, G. P., & Hill, N. E. (1998). Measurement equivalence in research involving minority adolescents. In V. McLoyd & L. Steinberg (Eds.), *Studying minority adolescents: Conceptual, methodological and theoretical issues* (pp. 183–210). Hillsdale, NJ: Erlbaum.

Knight, G. P., Tein, J.-Y., Prost, J. H., & Gonzales, N. A. (2002). Measurement equivalence and research on Latino children and families: The importance of culturally informed theory. In J. Contreras, K. Kears, & A. Neal-Barnett (Eds.), *Latino children and families in the United States: Current research and future directions* (pp. 181–201). Westport, CN: Praeger.

Lin, H., Xiaoyi, Li, H., Liu, C., Yang, S. (2006). Yunnan student prosocial tendencies trends and projections for school adjustment. *Psychological Development and Education, 22*, 44–51.

Marín, G., & Marín, B. (1991). *Research with Hispanic populations.* Thousand Oaks, CA: Sage.

McGinley, M., & Carlo, G. (2007). Two sides of the same coin? The relations between prosocial and physically aggressive behaviors. *Journal of Youth and Adolescence, 37*, 337–349.

McGinley, M., Carlo, G., Crockett, L. J., Raffaelli, M., Torres Stone, R. A., & Iturbide, M. I. (2010). Stressed and helping: The relations among acculturative stress, gender, and prosocial behaviors in Mexican Americans. *Journal of Social Psychology, 150*, 34–56.

Mlčák, Z. (in press). *The Big Five and prosocial personality aspects.* Paper presented in OEDM-SERM´12—The 2nd International e-Conference on Optimization, Education and Data Mining in Science, Engineering and Risk Management (November, 2012–January, 2013). Prag: Curriculum, 2013, p. 1–4, in press.

Mlčák, Z., & Záškodná, H. (2008). Analysis of relationships between prosocial tendencies, empathy, and the five factor personality model in students of helping professions. *Studia Psychologica, 50*, 201–216.

Muthén, L. K., & Muthén, B. O. (1998–2010). *Mplus user's guide* (6th ed.). Los Angeles, CA: Muthén & Muthén.

Padilla-Walker, L. M., Barry, C. M., Carroll, J. S., Madsen, S. D., & Nelson, L. J. (2008). Looking on the bright side: The role of identity status and gender on positive orientations during emerging adulthood. *Journal of Adolescence, 31*, 451–467.

Richaud, M. C., Mesurado, B., & Kohan Cortada, A. K. (2012). Analysis of dimensions of prosocial behavior in an Argentinean sample of children. *Psychological Reports: Mental and Physical Health, 111*, 1–10.

Richaud, M. C., Mesurado, B., & Lemos, V. (2012). Links between perception of parental actions and prosocial behavior in early adolescence. *Journal of Child and Family Studies, 22*, 637–646. doi: 10.1007/s10826-012-9617-x

Shen, Y. L. (2009, April). *Prosocial tendencies: An assessment of measure and the relationships to parental disciplines for Taiwanese children.* Poster presented at the Biennial Meeting of the Society for Research in Child Development, Denver, CO.

Šukys, S. (2010). Participation in after school activities and relationships with student expression of prosocial conduct. *Education, Physical Education, Sports, 79*, 77–85.

Tuncel, S. D. (2010). Comparing tendencies of athletes and nonathletes. *Journal of Physical Education and Sport, 29,* 81–85.

Weston, R., & Gore, P. A. (2006). A brief guide to structural equation modeling. *Counseling Psychologist, 34,* 719–751.

Wyatt, J. M., & Carlo, G. (2002). What will my parents think? Relations among adolescents' expected parental reactions, prosocial moral reasoning, and prosocial and antisocial behaviors. *Journal of Adolescent Research, 17,* 646–666.

14

Educating Students to Be Prosocial at School
Christi Bergin

> Shaunt'a has recently moved to a new high school. She is quiet
> and has few friends. In French class, a boy makes fun of her
> clothes. Shaunt'a acts as though she doesn't hear. However, another
> classmate, Dirk, knows she hears. Dirk says that he likes Shaunt'a's
> clothes, which silences the other boy. Dirk then tries to make
> Shaunt'a more comfortable by talking with her about whether she is
> going to try out for show choir.
>
> —ADAPTED FROM BERGIN AND BERGIN (2012, P. 313)

Is this example of prosocial behavior in school typical? Do students experience kindness from classmates on a daily basis? Does kindness in a classroom affect achievement? How can teachers create more kindly classrooms? This chapter will address each of these questions. It begins with descriptive research on the variety and frequency of prosocial behavior at school, then discusses the correlation between prosocial behavior and success at school, and concludes with a discussion of how educators can promote increased prosocial behavior at school. Children spend about a third of their waking hours in school, so it is important to understand their experience of prosocial behavior in this setting. This chapter is intended to be useful for educators as well as to raise awareness of the importance of studying prosocial behavior at school.

Prosocial behavior is part of the "soft skills" currently emphasized in PK-12 schools to better prepare youth for today's jobs. Soft skills refer to social and emotional skills, such as ability to get along with others. They are contrasted with "hard skills" such as core academic skills. The ability to work in a team and get along with classmates, customers, and coworkers, despite cultural differences, is considered an essential 21st-century skill for success in college or on the job. Indeed, such ability may be more important than academic skills in life success.

In the United States, at the district level, many schools now have mission statements that include promoting students' soft skills. At the state level, all 50 states have explicit standards for students' soft skills in preschool.[1] For example, Pennsylvania standards include "pro-social relationships with adults and peers." States are beginning to adopt similar standards for K-12 students. Currently, several states have such standards. For example, Illinois standards include "use...interpersonal skills to establish and maintain positive relationships" (Dusenbury, Zadrazil, Mart, & Weissberg, 2011). At the federal level, there is pending Congressional legislation to promote soft skills in schools, and in the 2012 Race to the Top grants, applicants were given bonus points if they made soft skills part of their improvement efforts. In addition, advocates are pushing to make students' social skills (1) a targeted area for research grants at the Institute of Education Sciences, (2) a focus of college coursework for aspiring teachers and principals, (3) an endorsed use of professional development funds in schools, and (4) part of the evaluation of teacher effectiveness (CASEL, 2013). For example, in Missouri, teachers' use of "strategies that promote social competence" in students is one of the indicators of effectiveness on which they may be evaluated.

This is a refreshingly positive direction. Schools have focused considerable resources on diminishing antisocial behavior, particularly bullying. However, they have paid scant attention to actively promoting prosocial behavior. While this shift in direction is welcome, it presents a challenge because most educators do not explicitly know how to promote prosocial behavior among students. This chapter makes a contribution to filling that void.

Prosocial Behaviors at School

Before addressing how educators might promote prosocial behavior among students, I will describe the prosocial behaviors students enact in school settings.

WHAT TYPES OF PROSOCIAL BEHAVIOR DO STUDENTS ENACT AT SCHOOL?

Prosocial behavior is voluntary behavior that benefits others or promotes harmonious relations with others (Radke-Yarrow, Zahn-Waxler, & Chapman, 1983). It encompasses a wide array of behaviors that occur at school. It includes obeying rules, whether they be social convention (e.g., saying "thank you") or obligatory

---

[1] Standards are explicit goals for what students should be able to know and do as a result of education, typically specified by grade level. Most states had standards for mathematics and language arts by 2000, but they varied in quality. To address this problem, in 2010 the Common Core standards in these domains were released, which most states have now adopted. The Common Core standards do not yet include soft skills.

moral laws (e.g., being honest, not hurting others). It includes kindnesses in which no rules are invoked (e.g., complimenting others). It requires a blend of self-assertion and domination (e.g., standing up for victims) and conceding to others (e.g., giving in to avoid fights). Thus, the construct of prosocial behavior is broad.

Just what kinds of prosocial behavior do students engage in at school? To address this question, colleagues and I conducted prototype studies of prosocial youth (Bergin, Bergin, & French, 1995; Bergin, Talley, & Hamer, 2003). A prototype study involves asking participants to nominate people they know who are prototypic in the construct and then give reasons for nominating them. The result is a collection of behaviors that are highly salient to participants, are authentic, and comprise the range commonly experienced.

In one study, we convened eight same-sex focus groups with 53 ethnically and socioeconomically diverse 6th graders. We asked them to identify the most prosocial peer they knew and to describe specific prosocial behaviors these exemplars engaged in (Bergin et al., 2003). The youth knew each other and were able to confirm or add to original comments about prosocial exemplars in their community. They generated 276 descriptions of specific prosocial behaviors that fell into 24 categories, as shown in Table 14.1.

Using a somewhat different approach, but still focused on students' perceptions, Greener and Crick (1999) asked 468 diverse 3rd to 6th graders to write a response to the question "What do boys/girls do when they want to be nice to someone?" Responses were placed into a priori categories, indicated in Table 14.1. Although responses were written briefly during class time and only one response per child was coded (which would limit the range of responses), their results are similar to our prototype study. Three categories—be friendly, be inclusive, and care/share—made up 90% of their responses. Similarly, Galliger, Tisak, and Tisak (2009) asked 3rd to 5th graders to describe prosocial behaviors they experienced on the school bus. They reported six prosocial behaviors that completely overlap with our prototype study, indicated in Table14.1.

In another set of prototype studies with younger children, we asked parents and teachers of 2- and 5-year-olds to name the most prosocial child they knew in this age group and describe specific prosocial behaviors these children enacted in their home and school settings (Bergin et al., 1995). Twenty attributes were nominated for 2-year-olds and 24 attributes were nominated for 5-year-olds, indicated in Table 14.1.

In summary, using different methods and involving different age groups and different samples, these studies together indicate that the behaviors of prosocial exemplars that are most salient to peers, teachers, and parents are remarkably similar. They are similar in both the type and the number of specific prosocial behaviors that were nominated. Thus, the behaviors in Table 14.1 likely form the core prosocial repertoire for school-age children.

TABLE 14.1 Behaviors of prosocial exemplars

1. Stands up for others (e.g., stops rumors or teasing, defends others)
2. ˙⁺#^Provides emotional support and comfort (e.g., cheers others up when they are down)
3. #*Helps others develop skills (e.g., explains things without cheating, gives classmates tips)
4. #*Compliments and encourages others (e.g., offers praise, says "try again" or "you're doing well")
5. ˙⁺#^Inclusive and friendly (e.g., makes sure no one is left out, befriends everyone)
6. ˙#^Provides physical assistance
7. ⁺^Humorous; makes others smile or turns put-downs into a joke
8. ⁺*Peacemaker (e.g., gets others to calm down or stop fighting, settles disagreements)
9. ˙⁺#^Shares (e.g., food, supplies)
10. ˙^Avoids fights; doesn't respond to taunts
11. Keeps confidences
12. ˙^Expresses happiness; cheerful
13. Confronts those who have done wrong
14. Provides community service
15. Honest
16. ⁺˙Avoids hurting others' feelings
17. Admits mistakes
18. ˙^Apologizes
19. Does not make fun of others; changes the subject when others are making fun of someone
20. *Coaches others in social skills; helps others work through social problems
21. Does not brag
22. Good sport
23. ˙^Willing to play
24. ^Calm—does not yell

Note: In order of frequency of mention by 6th graders in Bergin et al. (2003).
˙ behaviors mentioned by 3rd to 6th graders in Greener & Crick (1999).
behaviors mentioned by 3rd to 5th graders in Galliger et al. (2009).
* behaviors describing 5-year-olds in Bergin et al. (1995).
^ behaviors describing 2-year-olds in Bergin et al. (1995).

HOW COMMON IS PROSOCIAL BEHAVIOR AMONG STUDENTS AT SCHOOL?

It is difficult to answer this question. There is remarkably little research that addresses prevalence of prosocial behavior in authentic school settings. Recently, colleagues and I surveyed 3,661 4th to 12th graders in a small, midwestern city about prosocial experiences at school. We asked how often their classmates engaged in different prosocial behaviors in their classroom. The behaviors were the first eight listed in Table 14.1. Students responded on a scale of 1 (*never*) to 5 (*daily*). Almost all prosocial behaviors had a group mean between 3 (*monthly*) and 4 (*weekly*), with one exception. *Making others laugh* occurred more often, between weekly and daily (Bergin, Wang, & Bryant, 2011, March). Thus, prosocial behavior, as perceived by students, may not have a high frequency of occurrence in classrooms.

AGE TRENDS IN PROSOCIAL BEHAVIOR FROM PRESCHOOL TO
HIGH SCHOOL

As students progress from preschool through high school, does the substance or the frequency of their prosocial behavior change? There may be small age differences in the substance of prosocial behavior. For example, in the prototype studies discussed above, prosocial toddlers were described as being affectionate, whereas this was not mentioned by the older youth. It is common for teachers to emphasize expressions of affection with toddlers. A preschool teacher might tell a 3-year-old boy, "You hurt Luke's feelings. Give him a hug to make him feel better." At age 15, those same boys would find such an instruction from their high school teacher quite humorous. For another example, a cooperative 2-year-old was described as taking turns, while a cooperative 5-year-old was described as letting others have the best role in pretend play—each was described as successfully grappling with a key social challenge for their age group. Middle school students were described as engaging in a few more prosocial behaviors that were beyond toddler's developing skills, such as standing up for others who are wrongfully accused. Despite these differences in specific prosocial behaviors, the overall categories were largely consistent across age. In addition, Caldarella and Merrell (1997) reviewed 20 years of studies on children's social skills to identify empirically based categories of social skills. They found similar prosocial dimensions as those presented in Table 14.1 from ages 3 to 18. Thus, the specific details of prosocial behavior may change somewhat across age, as social skills develop, but the general substance may not.

Does the frequency of prosocial behavior increase with age? Common sense predicts it would, given that parents and teachers work hard to socialize children into behaving more prosocially. Cognitive-developmental theory also predicts it would because children become less egocentric with age and develop better moral reasoning and perspective-taking abilities (Piaget, 1983). However, two lines of research belie this prediction. First, prosocial behavior is present early in life. Indeed, as soon as infants are mobile they actively try to help others, suggesting that sophisticated moral reasoning or perspective-taking skills are not necessary for most prosocial behavior. Warneken and Tomasello (2009) argue that a predisposition toward altruism is innate in toddlers and is not driven by socialization, at least initially. Second, there is little evidence that prosocial behavior increases in natural settings (Eisenberg & Fabes, 1998; Radke-Yarrow et al., 1983).

Two studies that have addressed age trends in prosocial behavior at school find no evidence that it occurs more frequently with age. In one study, teachers rated whether five prosocial behaviors—considerate of other people's feelings; shares readily with other children; helpful if someone is hurt, upset, or feeling ill; kind to younger children; and often volunteers to help others—were characteristic of 5- to 17-year-old students. There was no correlation between ratings and age of student, suggesting teachers do not perceive older students as more prosocial than younger students (Scourfield, John, Martin, & McGuffin, 2004). In our study that

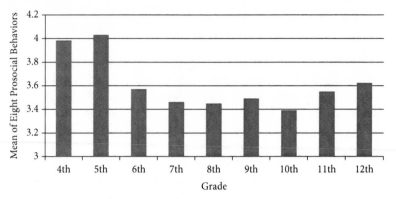

FIGURE 14.1 **Prosocial Behavior by Grade.**

Note: Scale is from 1 to 5 (never, hardly ever, monthly, weekly, and daily). School levels were elementary (4th–5th grades), middle school (6th–8th grades) and high school (9th–12th grades). The eight prosocial behaviors were: (1) stands up for others, (2) provides emotional support and comfort, (3) helps others develop skills, (4) compliments and encourages, (5) is inclusive and friendly, (6) provides physical assistance, (7) makes others smile or laugh, and (8) is a peacemaker.

asked over 3,000 4th to 12th graders how frequently their classmates engage in prosocial behavior, we found a decrease in mean reports from middle childhood to adolescence. Fourth and 5th graders reported the highest rates of prosocial behavior among classmates. The frequency diminished from 6th to 10th grade and then slightly increased again in 11th to 12th grade (Bergin et al., 2011, March). See Figure 14.1.

How is it possible that frequency of prosocial behavior may diminish in secondary school, given the effort adults put into teaching children to be kind and polite? There are a variety of reasons. First, adults sometimes train children to inhibit their natural prosocial impulses, such as telling them it is the teacher's job to take care of distressed classmates, not theirs. Second, children have many antisocial models that may counter their prosocial tendencies. Third, children become better able to regulate their own emotional response, so that they do not impulsively respond to others' distress or needs. Toddlers start out as indiscriminate altruists who become more selective with age, which may be driven by cognitive development that protects them from exploitation (Warneken & Tomasello, 2009). Prosocial behavior shifts from being a universal impulse of toddlers to a more controlled choice for older youth (Hay, 2009). Fourth, children become more aware of the costs of prosocial behavior and learn to protect their self-interests better. Hedonistic prosocial reasoning, which focuses on "what's in it for me?" may *increase* for some adolescents.

In this section I have addressed age trends across students. Yet, among students of the same age there are individual differences; some students are more prosocial than others. Prosocial behavior is almost universal in the first year of life, but by 2 to 3 years of age individual differences emerge. These very early individual differences remain fairly stable over time. That is, preschoolers who are more prosocial than their peers will likely be the most prosocial students in high school as well. These individual differences are important in school settings.

The Importance of Prosocial Behavior at School

Why should schools be interested in increasing prosocial behavior among students? Not only because such soft skills are linked to later adult success but also because prosocial behavior is also linked to social success and academic achievement in school.

PROSOCIAL BEHAVIOR PREDICTS SOCIAL SUCCESS AT SCHOOL

Students who are more prosocial are liked better by their peers and teachers. For example, in one study, 3- and 4-year-olds were asked to place pictures of their classmates into one of three boxes: liked a lot, kinda liked, and did not like (Denham, McKinley, Couchoud, & Holt, 1990). Children who were "liked a lot" were more prosocial. Similar effects have been found for elementary and secondary students (Bandura, Barbaranelli, Caprara, & Pastorelli, 1996; LaFontana & Cillessen, 2002; Warden & Mackinnon, 2003). This is important because students who are liked by their classmates and have friends at school enjoy school, feel bonded to school, actively participate, and have higher achievement (Thorkildsen, Reese, & Corsino, 2002; Véronneau, Vitaro, Brendgen, Dishion, & Tremblay, 2010; Witkow & Fuligni, 2010). Being liked by one's teacher is also important. The teacher-student relationship strongly predicts emotional well-being, academic motivation, grade point average (GPA), and test scores (Bergin & Bergin, 2009).

PROSOCIAL BEHAVIOR PREDICTS ACADEMIC ACHIEVEMENT

Academic achievement is as much a function of socioemotional well-being as it is of intelligence. Preschoolers intuitively know this. Their implicit view is that being smart and being nice go together. For example, when told about fictional children who are "smart and mean" or "not so smart and nice" preschoolers tend to remember the children as "smart and nice" (Heyman, Gee, & Giles, 2003). When asked, almost all will say it is possible to be both smart and mean, yet they do not pair meanness and smartness when they construct an image of someone. A similar, but smaller, effect was found for 9- to 10-year-olds. Being prosocial was more salient and important than being academically competent. The children were "more likely to misremember the intellectual ability information so as to match the valence of social trait information" (p. 531). They preferred to work with someone nice but not-so-smart rather than someone smart but mean, if a choice had to be made.

In our focus group study we also found that 6th graders described their exemplary prosocial peers using phrases such as "a good student" or "has a high vocabulary" (Bergin et al., 2003). We asked whether you have to be a good student to be prosocial. The youth unanimously said "no." We then asked if the particular prosocial exemplar they were thinking of was a good student. They unanimously said "yes." When these youth moved from the abstract to the particular, academic competence, in their experience, was clearly linked to prosocial behavior. Research supports their perspective.

Several studies have found that students who are more prosocial also tend to have higher academic achievement. Among preschoolers, prosocial behavior has been linked to higher scores on tests of intelligence, vocabulary, executive functions, emergent literacy, and mathematics (Bierman, Torres, Domitrovich, Welsh, & Gest, 2009; Galindo & Fuller, 2010). Among elementary students, prosocial behavior has been linked to tests of reading, mathematics, vocabulary, and nonverbal IQ (Adams, Snowling, Hennessy, & Kind, 1999; Miles & Stipek, 2006; Strayer & Roberts, 1989). Among secondary students, prosocial behavior has been linked to higher GPA, standardized test scores, and academic investment (Carlo, Crockett, Wilinson, & Beal, 2011; Wentzel, 1993).

Most of these studies use teacher or classmate report of prosocial behavior. It is possible that there is a halo effect in which academically talented children are perceived as more prosocial. However, a study using direct observation also found that prosocial behavior among preschoolers was linked to emergent literacy skills (Doctoroff, Greer, & Arnold, 2006).

Why Is Prosocial Behavior Linked to Academic Achievement?

The research described is correlational. It is possible that the relationship between prosocial behavior and higher academic achievement is due to a third variable (e.g., self-control) that causes them to covary. One study supports this possibility. Kindergarteners who were more prosocial had greater cognitive self-control, which in turn predicted better grades in language and mathematics in 1st grade (Normandeau & Guay, 1998). Prosocial children were better able to work toward long-term goals, stick to a task until finished, resist distractions, concentrate, and not give in to frustration.

However, it is also possible that prosocial behavior causes higher achievement. Such causality is suggested by longitudinal studies showing prosocial behavior at Time 1 predicts academic achievement at Time 2. For example, in one study kindergarteners who were more prosocial developed better reading and mathematics skills by 3rd grade (Romano et al., 2010). In another study, 3rd graders who were more prosocial had higher achievement in 8th grade, after controlling for initial achievement (Caprara, Barbaranelli, Pastorelli, Bandura, & Zimbardo, 2000).

There are at least three mechanisms through which prosocial behavior could cause higher achievement. One is by enhancing prosocial students' social success at school. As discussed above, positive peer and teacher relationships predict high achievement. The effect size of teacher-student relationships on achievement is quite large, suggesting it may be one of the most important aspects of effective teaching (Cornelius-White, 2007; Mashburn et al., 2008).

Another mechanism through which prosocial behavior could cause higher achievement is time on task. Students who are cooperative and follow class rules should be more academically successful than those who do not. This has been confirmed in multiple studies in early childhood. Prosocial preschoolers are more likely to show interest in schoolwork, work independently, take turns, listen, pay attention, persist, stay on task, and participate in class activities (Bierman, et al., 2009; Coolahan, Fantuzzo, Mendez, & McDermott, 2000; McClelland & Morrison, 2003). Research is needed to confirm these results in older students.

These two mechanisms are related. Both Bierman and colleagues (2009), whose work focuses on early childhood, and Wentzel (2006), whose work focuses on secondary students, have argued that students' prosocial behavior may cause higher achievement because the capacity to engage effectively with others is intertwined with the capacity to organize oneself for learning, such as focusing attention and complying with learning activities. They also both argue, in accord with developmental theories, that rich language and social exchanges with peers promote cognitive skills.

A third mechanism through which prosocial behavior could cause higher achievement is positive emotions. Prosocial children tend to be happy, cheerful individuals who help others to achieve a positive emotional state (see Table 14.1). Positive emotions promote learning and creativity because they broaden thought and motivate students to learn, be open to new information, and participate in activities (Fredrickson, 2001).

Thus far I have focused on research at the individual level. That is, highly prosocial *individuals* tend to have higher achievement. Research suggests there is a similar effect at the classroom level. That is, students achieve more if their *classmates* are prosocial. Students with caring, friendly, prosocial classmates tend to have higher grades (Griffith, 2002; Jia et al., 2009).

Why do students achieve more if their classmates are prosocial? Classmates and teachers are happier in classrooms filled with students who are kind, polite, and considerate—and positive emotions promote learning. In addition, Wentzel (2006) surmises that prosocial behavior creates a classroom context that is more conducive to learning and that feeling social support motivates students to pursue academic goals. Thus, students should have greater *engagement* in more prosocial classrooms. We addressed this in our survey of 4th–12th graders. In addition to reporting on the frequency of their classmates' prosocial behavior, students were asked to report on their own engagement in the same class. Their classmates' prosocial behavior accounted for a significant amount of variance (31%–44%) in different dimensions of engagement, such as being interested, thinking deeply, and participating during class (Bergin, Wang, & Bergin, 2013). Results confirm that classmates' prosocial behavior predicts student's own in-class engagement.

How Educators Can Promote Prosocial Behavior in Students

Children's prosocial behavior is learned and shaped by the adults around them including their teachers. This section discusses how educators can promote prosocial behavior at school and beyond.

School interventions are typically delivered at one of three levels, or tiers. Tier 1 *universal* (or primary) interventions are delivered by regular teachers in classrooms to all students. Tier 2 *targeted* (or secondary) interventions are delivered by specially trained staff, such as counselors, to students identified has having needs. Tier 3 *indicated* (or tertiary) interventions are delivered one-on-one by a specialized professional to students with intensive need. I will focus primarily on Tier 1 interventions because they apply to more students and can be implemented in any school. In addition, according to a meta-analysis discussed below, social skills interventions may be most effective when delivered by classroom teachers (Durlak, Weissberg, Dymnicki, Taylor, & Schellinger, 2011).

Tier 1 interventions for prosocial behavior can be implemented in one of two ways:

1. Teachers behave in ways that promote prosocial behavior in their daily, routine interactions with students as they enact their regular academic curriculum.
2. Formal programs are implemented that supplement the regular academic curriculum with an additional curriculum designed to teach prosocial behavior.

TEACHER PRACTICES THAT PROMOTE PROSOCIAL BEHAVIOR IN STUDENTS

In this section I will introduce seven teacher practices that should promote prosocial behavior in their students. Any teacher, from preschool to high school, can immediately initiate these behaviors in their own classrooms. The following discussion extrapolates generously from the research on parent practices because there is remarkably little research on teacher practices. These seven practices are not necessarily exhaustive; there may be other important practices that have not yet been researched.

Forming Positive Student-Teacher Relationships

Teachers form positive relationships with students when teachers are sensitive, responsive, warm, use noncoercive discipline, support students' autonomy, and come to class well prepared (Bergin & Bergin, 2009). Research robustly links sensitive, responsive parenting and secure parent-child relationships with prosocial behavior in children, including their prosocial behavior at school. Thus, it is not surprising that the few studies addressing this have also found that teacher warmth and positive student-teacher relationships are associated with greater prosocial behavior (Howes & Ritchie, 1999; Kienbaum, 2001; Mitchell-Copeland, Denham, & DeMulder, 1997) and that conflicted student-teacher relationships are associated with decreased prosocial behavior (Birch & Ladd, 1998). This research has been conducted primarily in early childhood settings. Research is needed to confirm these effects with older students.

Promoting Emotional Competence in Students

Teachers help students develop emotional competence when they are sensitive to students' emotions, directly teach constructive coping strategies, create a positive climate in the classroom, and seize opportunities to talk about emotions, which helps students label, describe, and understand emotions. One experiment found that when 5th–6th grade teachers asked "feeling" questions (e.g., how would you feel if…) as they taught literature, rather than just critical thinking questions, their students were more supportive of one another and felt the classroom was a friendlier place compared with a control group (Shechtman & Yaman, 2012). They also learned more content. Emotional competence refers to both the ability to regulate one's own emotions and the ability to read others' emotions. Both abilities predict prosocial behavior (Eisenberg & Fabes, 2006). Students with good emotion regulation feel more positive than negative emotions, such as gratitude, affection, and joy, which promotes prosocial behavior. Students who read others' emotions better, such as Dirk in the opening vignette, are more likely to engage in empathy-motivated prosocial behavior.

Modeling Prosocial Behavior

Teachers can model prosocial behavior themselves, or point out the virtuous acts of others in the news, literature, or within the classroom. According to social cognitive theory, such modeling should increase students' prosocial behavior (Bandura, 1986). In a study of college students, witnessing or learning of others' virtuous acts inspired and motivated more prosocial behavior (Schnall, Roper, & Fessler, 2010). In another study, a preschool teacher varied how much prosocial behavior she modeled and how warm she was (Yarrow, Scott, & Waxler, 1973). Only under conditions of *both* warmth and modeling did the children increase their prosocial behavior. Warmth from an adult makes imitation of the adult more likely.

Espousing Prosocial Values

Teachers can tell their students to respect others, be kind, stand up for others, share, and help each other. They can communicate to students that they are responsible for each other. However, teachers often convey the opposite; that it is only the teachers' responsibility to take care of students. They may scold students for being "out of their seats" if they go to the aid of another. When asked why they do not help, students indicate that they are not supposed to do anything when adults are available (Caplan & Hay, 1989). Yet, effective classroom management stresses shared responsibility for a positive classroom.

The parenting research suggests that parents who espouse prosocial values have more prosocial children if they respond supportively when their child behaves prosocially (Eisenberg, Wolchik, Goldberg, & Engle, 1992; Hoffman, 1975) and are warm (Bergin, 1987). Thus, merely telling students to be nice is not likely to be as effective as telling them to be nice in the context of a warm student-teacher relationship in which the teacher graciously supports prosocial overtures.

Using Inductive Discipline

Teachers can use "victim-centered induction" when students misbehave. This refers to (1) pointing out how a student's misbehavior affects others, (2) asking the student to imagine being in the others' place, and (3) suggesting concrete acts of reparation. This approach teaches students to focus on others' well-being. It also provides practice of prosocial behavior as students make reparation. In a study with preschoolers, when teachers were trained to use victim-centered induction, students' prosocial behavior increased dramatically (Ramaswamy & Bergin, 2009).

Reinforcing Prosocial Behavior

Teachers can contingently praise prosocial acts among their students. Praise that comes from a loved or respected adult and is directed at the child rather than the act, such as "*You are a good boy*" rather than "*That was a good thing to do*," predicts increased prosocial behavior (Mills & Grusec, 1989). However, tangible rewards are different; they may undermine intrinsically motivated prosocial behavior. For example, in one study tangible rewards undermined 3rd graders' later willingness to tutor 1st graders and made their tutoring more tense and hostile (Szynal-Brown & Morgan, 1983).

Providing Opportunities for Practice

Teachers can provide opportunities for students to practice prosocial behavior in day-to-day events that spontaneously arise, such as helping a classmate clean up a spill, or in a formal program, such as tutoring or community service. Frequent practice results in well-worn scripts or habits that increase prosocial behavior over time. Many daily, mundane situations in classrooms that call for sharing, helping, or cooperating do not require empathy or sophisticated moral reasoning as much as they require habitual responses. Research with parents finds that having children help with tasks that benefit others, is linked to increased prosocial behavior in toddlers to teenagers (Bergin, 1987; Grusec, Goodnow, & Cohen, 1997).

Training Teachers to Use These Practices: An Experimental Study

The research discussed in this section is primarily correlational. Experimental studies are needed to investigate whether these teacher practices cause increased prosocial behavior in students, and whether teachers can be trained to use these practices more frequently. We conducted an experimental study in eight Head Start classrooms (Ramaswamy & Bergin, 2009). Teachers were matched for experience and then randomly assigned to one of four groups; (1) induction only, (2) reinforcement only, (3) induction and reinforcement, and (4) a control group. Using peer coaching, teachers were trained to use induction when a child misbehaved, and/or to use verbal or physical reinforcement (hug, pat, compliment) when a child engaged in prosocial behavior. Teacher behaviors were observed. Prosocial acts in the classroom were counted before training and again two months after training, with observers blind to group status.

Results suggested that teachers only modestly changed their behavior. However, the children's prosocial behavior increased dramatically in the induction group (144%), less dramatically in the reinforcement group (84%) and reinforcement-and-induction group (39%), and insignificantly (5%) in the control group. Teachers in the induction group remarked on obvious changes in individual children. Teachers reported that using reinforcement was easier and more enjoyable than using induction and that learning to use both reinforcement and induction at the same time was overwhelming. Implications are that increases in these two teacher practices may have caused increased students' prosocial behavior, that induction may be more powerful than reinforcement, and that simple interventions that change just one behavior at a time may be most easily implemented. Similar experiments are needed to address other teaching practices and in other classroom contexts.

In summary, this section outlines seven teacher practices that may promote prosocial behavior in students. These behaviors can be readily incorporated into any teacher's classroom without expense or change to school structure or curriculum. They simply require understanding and a will to enact them. In contrast, there are formal interventions with supplemental curriculum designed to increase prosocial behavior. I will discuss those next.

FORMAL PROGRAMS DESIGNED TO PROMOTE PROSOCIAL BEHAVIOR IN STUDENTS

As states are increasingly adopting standards for students' soft skills, schools are scrambling to adopt programs to help them meet these standards. In a survey of 800 teachers in 84 schools, many reported that they had received training in the past 12 months in character education (41%) and social and emotional development (28%) of students (Social and Character Development Research Consortium, 2010).

A smorgasbord of programs is now available for schools to purchase that claim to promote positive development of students. These programs typically are Tier 1; they are delivered to all students by regular classroom teachers rather than specialized staff. They have curriculum accompanied by professional development trainings, manuals, and materials for students. They may be modular where a single teacher (or small group of teachers) implements the program in a classroom or they may be comprehensive where the schoolwide staff (e.g., teachers, administrators, counselors, and others) shares responsibility for consistent practices across the school community. There is not room to discuss all the programs currently available, but I will discuss one widely used exemplary program and then summarize two reviews of key movements in this field—character development and social and emotional learning (SEL)—that investigate whether such programs are generally effective.

Exemplary Program: The Caring School Community.

The Caring School Community (CSC) began in the early 1980s as the Child Development Project, to promote prosocial behavior and caring communities at school. Over time, the name changed and the goals expanded to include cognitive development and reduction of risk factors for delinquency. It has been implemented in thousands of classrooms. The U.S. Department of Health and Human Services has recognized it as an exemplary program.

The CSC is a Tier 1 multiyear, schoolwide program for elementary and middle schools. There are four components:

1. Scripted lessons on prosocial values (fairness, helpfulness, caring, respect, personal responsibility).
2. Pairing classes of older students with younger students to build relationships and promote learning.
3. Social activities for the school community.
4. Activities to do at home with family members.

Teachers use inductive discipline, read "values-rich" literature, and provide students with opportunities to engage in collaboration, give and receive help, discuss others' perspectives, and practice social skills. The classroom management and literature components were later dropped because they were too difficult to implement (IES, 2007).

How effective is it? A report by the What Works Clearinghouse[2] (WWC) finds CSC to have moderate to large positive effects on behavior, but not on values or achievement (IES, 2007). Two studies meet the WWC standards with reservations; a randomized controlled study conducted in San Ramon in grades K-4, and a quasi-experimental study conducted in six districts in grades 3-6. The San Ramon study found that spontaneous prosocial behavior and supportive friendly, helpful behavior increased, but there was no effect on two other behaviors (Battistich, 2003). In contrast, the six-district study did not conclusively find

---

[2] The WWC is a service of the U.S. Department of Education's Institute of Education Science (IES). Staff conducts reviews of widely used programs to determine the level of scientific rigor of the research conducted on the program. Reviews are readily available at the IES website.

significant effects on prosocial behavior—even when they focused only on the five schools that implemented it well. Only schools that successfully established a caring community promoted prosocial behavior. Students' perceptions of how much their classmates cared for one another was correlated with spontaneous prosocial behavior (e.g., concern, inclusiveness, cooperation, friendliness) and school bonding (Solomon, Battistich, Watson, Schaps, & Lewis, 2000).

Social and Character Development Programs

A social and character development (SACD) program is designed to promote the social and character development of students. Character refers to moral and ethical behaviors and virtues, such as honesty, fairness, trustworthiness, and caring. These programs actively instill core values and teach students to enact those values. The voluntary enactment of any virtue that results in benefit to others is, by definition, prosocial behavior.

To investigate the effectiveness of SACD programs, the Institute of Education Sciences and the Centers for Disease Control and Prevention awarded competitive grants to researchers to conduct rigorous randomized controlled trials of seven evidence-based SACD programs:

1. Academic and Behavioral Competencies Program (ABC)
2. Competence Support Program (CSP)
3. Love in a Big World (LBW)
4. Positive Action (PA)
5. Promoting Alternative Thinking Strategies (PATHS)
6. The 4Rs Program (Reading, Writing, Respect, and Resolution)
7. Second Step (SS)

All programs are Tier 1 and aim to promote positive behavior, reduce negative behavior, and improve academic performance. Three programs specifically address prosocial behavior: LBW addresses kindness and caring, PA addresses honesty, and PATHS addresses peer relations.

Before implementing programs, teachers receive between one-half and three full days of training and up to weekly consultations through the school year. Common components are role playing, direct instruction, story reading, journaling, cooperative learning, punishment (time out) for negative behavior, and rewards for positive behavior. Programs provide curriculum guides for teachers and accompanying activities for students (e.g., software, videos, worksheets, and literature). Love in a Big World involves teacher-led lessons with story reading for 10–15 minutes daily over 30 weeks and intentional reinforcement of good behavior. Promoting Alternative Thinking Strategies uses direct instruction, role playing, and modeling of skills in 20–30 minute lessons, 3 to 5 days per week. Positive Action also uses direct instruction, story reading, and role-playing in 15- to 20-minute lessons, 4 days per week, and teacher modeling of positive behavior.

Programs were implemented for 3 years, from the beginning of 3rd grade to the end of 5th grade. Each program was implemented in 5 to 7 schools, with a comparable number of control schools, and involved several hundred children. At least 20 outcomes were measured across programs, one of which assessed prosocial behavior (e.g., cheer someone up who is feeling sad, or help someone who is being picked on) based on self, parent, and teacher report.

Overall results for prosocial behavior were discouraging (Social and Character Development Research Consortium, 2010). Two programs showed no effects. Two programs showed nonsignificant but potentially substantive effects for teacher report only and in only one year; one was positive and one was detrimental. Three programs showed improvement for only one reporter (self, parent, or teacher) in only one year, followed by detrimental effects reported by only one reporter in a subsequent year.

The authors provide four possibilities for the failure to find effects. (1) The programs are not powerful enough to be effective. (2) They are weakly implemented. However, fidelity of implementation was not associated with more beneficial outcomes (although there was some suggestion that low fidelity was linked to detrimental outcomes). (3) Control schools were engaging in similar practices. However, teachers in the intervention group reported significantly greater use of materials and methods to promote social and character development in their classrooms than control group teachers. (4) The evaluation methods were problematic, such as poor alignment between the program and the outcome measure of prosocial behavior. Most programs focused more on global social skills than on prosocial behavior. The null effects in this cross-site, multiprogram study are different from the next review.

Social and Emotional Learning Programs

Social and emotional learning (SEL) programs aim to teach children discrete social or emotional skills while also creating a more positive social climate in the classroom and throughout the school. The term "SEL" has been popularized by the Collaborative for Academic, Social, and Emotional Learning (CASEL). The mission of CASEL is to establish SEL programs as part of regular school programming, in preschools through high schools, by conducting research, promoting legislation, and disseminating information to educators. This work is important because most schools use programs that lack research on their effectiveness.

CASEL only recognizes SEL programs delivered universally (Tier 1) in school settings with sequenced series of lessons. This does not include programs that merely seek to improve teacher practices. According to CASEL, there are five key goals of SEL programs: (1) self-awareness, (2) social awareness, (3) self-management, (4) relationship skills, and (5) responsible decision-making. None of these skills are prosocial behavior per se, although they include both antecedents (e.g., emotion regulation, affective perspective taking, self-confidence) and consequences (e.g., having healthy relationships) of prosocial behavior. Thus, promoting some of these skills should lead to greater prosocial behavior, and greater prosocial behavior should lead to some of these goals. Of the many dozens of SEL programs, few measure prosocial behavior explicitly, but most use measures with at least some items addressing prosocial behavior.

To investigate the effectiveness of SEL programs, CASEL researchers conducted a meta-analysis of 213 SEL programs (Durlak et al., 2011). They organized dependent variables across all the studies into six categories: (1) academic performance, (2) attitudes toward self and others, (3) social and emotional skills, (4) conduct problems, (5) emotional distress, and (6) positive social behavior. This last category includes prosocial behavior, but it is not clear just how broad this category is or how many studies actually measured prosocial behavior. Across 59 studies that addressed this category, they found an effect size of 0.26 (confidence interval 0.15 to 0.38). For the 12 studies that included follow-up assessment at least 6 months later, the effect size at follow-up was 0.17.

It is not clear how to reconcile the small but positive results of this SEL meta-analysis with the null effects of the rigorous, well-conducted SACD cross-site evaluation. Both SACD and SEL programs have similar approaches and goals. Indeed, at least three of the seven programs in the SACD consortium report are also part of the CASEL meta-analysis. One likely explanation for the disparate findings is scientific rigor. The meta-analysis included a variety of research designs and included studies implemented by developer-researchers delivered at maximum strength, like the two CSC studies discussed above. In contrast, the SACD report used only rigorous randomized controlled trials (RCT) implemented in community settings by regular teachers. Such RCTs tend to underestimate true effects, while less rigorous designs tend to overestimate true effects (Staines & Cleland, 2012). Thus, true effects may lie somewhere between the two sets of results.

Despite their positive monikers, in practice SEL and SACD programs emphasize preventing misbehavior more than promoting prosocial behavior, because schools have pushed this emphasis. However, two studies suggest that if schools want to increase achievement, they should shift emphasis to promoting prosocial behavior. In a study of 3rd and 4th graders, positive behaviors more strongly predicted academic achievement over the school year than negative behaviors (Malecki & Elliot, 2002). Similarly in a study of poor, minority preschoolers, prosocial deficits were more predictive of poor cognitive outcomes than antisocial behavior was (Bierman et al., 2009). Some practices and programs may both reduce problem behavior and increase prosocial behavior, but not all will have this dual effect because antisocial and prosocial behavior can be orthogonal.

In summary, students, from preschool to high school, enact a wide variety of prosocial behavior at school. Prosocial behavior occurs infrequently in classrooms, with frequency dropping after elementary grades. Students who are more prosocial than their peers tend to have greater social and academic success in school. In addition, students have higher achievement when they have more classmates who are prosocial. Thus, increasing prosocial behavior should be of interest to educators. Indeed, the few studies that address this suggest that promoting prosocial behavior may be more predictive of achievement than reducing problem behavior. There are several teaching practices that should increase prosocial behavior in the classroom. In addition, there are formal curriculum-based programs to promote prosocial behavior, but the evidence suggests these programs have small effects.

Future Directions

Prosocial behavior in schools has not received the same degree of research attention as antisocial behavior, despite the evidence that it predicts academic success. More research on prosocial behavior in schools would contribute to basic understanding of prosocial behavior in authentic contexts and prepare educators to create classrooms more conducive to learning. Currently, there is a huge gap between research and practice, with many schools implementing interventions with small or unknown effects. Future research should focus on three areas.

First, research should address which dimensions of prosocial behavior matter in classrooms. Prosocial behavior is a multidimensional construct. It is likely that some prosocial behaviors are more closely aligned to school success than others. For example, cooperating with classmates on learning tasks is an obvious candidate for promoting achievement, whereas it is less obvious how comforting others may promote achievement. Unfortunately almost all studies reported herein use summary measures, rather than reporting on specific dimensions of prosocial behavior. These measures include a wide array of prosocial behaviors, such as kindness, consideration, sharing, helping, comforting, stopping quarrels, inviting others to join activities, praising others' work, and volunteering. More careful measurement is needed to determine which prosocial behaviors are most important for promoting school success.

Second, research should address which teacher practices or intervention components have the largest effect size on specific, important dimensions of prosocial behavior. In discussing teacher practices that are likely to influence prosocial behavior, I extrapolated from parenting research because there is so little research on teaching. Given that the studies of teacher practices that do exist support the parenting research, this is an appropriate place to begin, but it is time to move forward. In the Ramaswamy and Bergin (2009) intervention, we found that use of inductive discipline was more effective than reinforcement. More such experimental studies are needed to investigate effect size and causality.

Which teaching practice or intervention component is most effective may depend on the prosocial behavior in question. This concern was raised in an early study in which I measured multiple parenting practices and multiple prosocial behaviors among toddlers (Bergin, 1987). I found that different prosocial behaviors were predicted by different parenting practices. A few parenting practices were strongly linked to multiple prosocial behaviors: use of victim-centered induction, providing opportunities to practice, and praise for prosocial acts. Other practices were linked to only some prosocial behaviors; affectionate warmth, avoiding use of power assertive discipline, and modeling cooperation with the child.

Small scale, very targeted interventions that address specific prosocial behaviors may be most effective in classrooms. Because the research literature on formal intervention programs is somewhat discouraging, there has been a tendency to add more components to programs. Yet, in the SEL meta-analysis, multicomponent programs were *less* effective (Durlak et al., 2011). They were more likely to have implementation problems, and programs with implementation problems had no effect. In the Ramaswamy & Bergin (2009) intervention, we found that a single change in practice was more powerful than changing two teacher practices. Teachers found it difficult to implement two new practices compared with one.

Third, research should address how we can effectively train teachers to enact promising practice. Durlak and colleagues (2011) found that the effect of SEL programs varied significantly by teacher. Jennings and Greenberg (2009) argue that SEL programs are more effective when implemented by teachers who themselves have social and emotional competence. Such teachers may benefit most from training (Webster-Stratton, Reid, & Stoolmiller, 2008). Research that addresses these three questions—which dimensions of prosocial behavior are critical to success at school, which teaching practices have the greatest effect on these dimensions, and how to best train teachers—would contribute substantially to basic understanding of prosocial development, as well as help children and teachers flourish at school.

References

Adams, J. W., Snowling, M. J., Hennessy, S. M., & Kind, P. (1999). Problems of behaviour, reading and arithmetic: Assessments of comorbidity using the Strengths and Difficulties Questionnaire. *British Journal of Educational Psychology, 69*, 571–585.

Bandura, A. (1986). *Social foundations of thought and action: A social cognitive theory.* Englewood Cliffs, NJ: Prentice-Hall.

Bandura, A., Barbaranelli, C., Caprara, G., & Pastorelli, C. (1996). Multifaceted impact of self-efficacy beliefs on academic functioning. *Child Development, 67*, 1206–1222.

Battistich, V. (2003). Effects of a school-based program to enhance prosocial development on children's peer relations and social adjustment. *Journal of Research in Character Education, 1*(1), 1–16.

Bergin, C. (1987). Prosocial development in toddlers: The patterning of mother-infant interactions. In M. E. Ford & D. H. Ford (Eds.), *Humans as self-constructing living systems: Putting the framework to work* (pp. 121–143). Hillsdale, NJ: Erlbaum.

Bergin, C., & Bergin, D. A. (2009). Attachment in the classroom. *Educational Psychology Review, 21*, 141–170.

Bergin, C., & Bergin, D. A. (2012). *Child and adolescent development in your classroom.* Belmont, CA: Wadsworth Cengage.

Bergin, C., Bergin, D. A., & French, E. (1995). Preschoolers' prosocial repertoires: Parents' perspectives. *Early Childhood Research Quarterly, 10*, 81–103.

Bergin, C., Talley, S., & Hamer, L. (2003). Prosocial behaviours of young adolescents: A focus group study. *Journal of Adolescence, 26*, 13–32.

Bergin, C., Wang, Z., & Bergin, D. (2013, April). *Prosocial behavior and engagement in fourth to twelfth grade classrooms.* Paper presented at the American Educational Research Association, San Francisco.

Bergin, C., Wang, Z., & Bryant, R. (2011, March). *Prosocial behavior in fourth to twelfth grade classrooms.* Paper presented at the Society for Research in Child Development, Montreal.

Bierman, K. L., Torres, M. M., Domitrovich, C. E., Welsh, J. A., & Gest, S. D. (2009). Behavioral and cognitive readiness for school: Cross-domain associations for children attending Head Start. *Social Development, 18*(2), 305–323.

Birch, S., & Ladd, G. (1998). Children's interpersonal behaviors and the teacher-child relationship. *Developmental Psychology, 34*(5), 934–946.

Caldarella, P., & Merrell, K. W. (1997). Common dimensions of social skills of children and adolescents: A taxonomy of positive behaviors. *School Psychology Review, 26*(2), 264–278.

Caplan, M., & Hay, D. F. (1989). Preschoolers' responses to peers' distress and beliefs about bystander intervention. *Journal of Child Psychology and Psychiatry and Allied Disciplines, 30*(2), 231–242.

Caprara, G., Barbaranelli, C., Pastorelli, C., Bandura, A., & Zimbardo, P. (2000). Prosocial foundations of children's academic achievement. *Psychological Science, 11*(4), 302–306.

Carlo, G., Crockett, L. S., Wilkinson, J. L., & Beal, S. J. (2011). The longitudinal relationships between rural adolescents' prosocial behaviors and young adult substance use. *Journal of Youth and Adolescence, 40*, 1192–1202.

CASEL. (2013). *Social and emotional learning policy agenda.* Report retrieved from CASEL. org 5/23/2013.

Coolahan, K., Fantuzzo, J., Mendez, J., & McDermott, P. (2000). Preschool peer interactions and readiness to learn: Relationships between classroom peer play and learning behaviors and conduct. *Journal of Educational Psychology, 92*(3), 458–465.

Cornelius-White, J. (2007). Learner-centered teacher-student relationships are effective: A meta-analysis. *Review of Educational Research, 77*(1), 113–143.

Denham, S. A., McKinley, M., Couchoud, E. A., & Holt, R. (1990). Emotional and behavioral predictors of preschool peer ratings. *Child Development, 61*, 1145–1152.

Doctoroff, G. L., Greer, J. A., & Arnold, D. H. (2006). The relationship between social behavior and emergent literacy among preschool boys and girls. *Journal of Applied Developmental Psychology, 27*(1), 1–13.

Durlak, J. A., Weissberg, R. P., Dymnicki, A. B., Taylor, R. D., & Schellinger, K. B. (2011). The impact of enhancing students' social and emotional learning: A meta-analysis of school-based universal interventions. *Child Development, 82*(1), 405–432.

Dusenbury, L., Zadrazil, J., Mart, A., & Weissberg, R. P. (2011). *State learning standards to advance social and emotional learning. Chicago: University of Illinois at Chicago,* Social and Emotional Learning Research Group.

Eisenberg, N., & Fabes, R. A. (1998). Prosocial development. In W. Damon & N. Eisenberg (Eds.), *Handbook of child development: Social, emotional, and personality development* (5th ed., Vol. 3, pp. 701–778). New York: Wiley.

Eisenberg, N., Wolchik, S., Goldberg, L., & Engle, I. (1992). Parental values, reinforcement, and young children's prosocial behavior: A longitudinal study. *Journal of Genetic Psychology, 153*(1), 19–36.

Fredrickson, B. L. (2001). The role of positive emotions in positive psychology: The broaden-and-build theory of positive emotions. *American Psychologist, 56*(3), 218–226.

Galindo, C., & Fuller, B. (2010). The social competence of Latino kindergartners and growth in mathematical understanding. *Developmental Psychology, 46*(3), 579–592.

Galliger, C., Tisak, M., & Tisak, J. (2009). When the wheels on the bus go round: Social interactions on the school bus. *Social Psychology of Education, 12*(1), 43–62. doi: 10.1007/s11218-008-9072-0

Greener, S., & Crick, N. R. (1999). Normative beliefs about prosocial behavior in middle childhood: What does it mean to be nice? *Social Development, 8*(3), 349–363. doi: 10.1111/1467-9507.00100

Griffith, J. (2002). A multilevel analysis of the relation of school learning and social environments to minority achievement in public elementary schools. *Elementary School Journal, 102,* 349–366.

Grusec, J., Goodnow, J. J., & Cohen, L. (1997). Household work and the development of concern for others. *Developmental Psychology, 32*(6), 999–1007.

Hay, D. (2009). The roots and branches of human altruism. *British Journal of Psychology, 100,* 473–479.

Heyman, G., Gee, C., & Giles, J. (2003). Preschool children's reasoning about ability. *Child Development, 74*(2), 516–534.

Hoffman, M. L. (1975). Altruistic behavior and the parent-child relationship. *Journal of Personality and Social Psychology, 31,* 937–943.

Howes, C., & Ritchie, S. (1999). Attachment organizations in children with difficult life circumstances. *Development and Psychopathology, 11,* 251–268.

Institute of Education Sciences (IES). (2007). *The Caring School Community WWC intervention report.* Washington DC: U.S. Department of Education, Institute of Education Sciences, National Center for Education Evaluation and Regional Assistance.

Jennings, P. A., & Greenberg, M. T. (2009). The prosocial classroom: Teacher social and emotional competence in relation to student and classroom outcomes. *Review of Educational Research, 79*(1), 491–525.

Jia, Y., Way, N., Ling, G., Yoskihawa, H., Chen, X., Hughes, D., . . . Lu, Z. (2009). The influence of student perceptions of school climate on socioemotional and academic adjustment: A comparison of Chinese and American adolescents. *Child Development, 80*(5), 1514–1530.

Kienbaum, J. (2001). The socialization of compassionate behavior by child care teachers. *Early Education and Development, 12*(1), 139–153.

LaFontana, K., & Cillessen, A. (2002). Children's perceptions of popular and unpopular peers: A multimethod assessment. *Developmental Psychology, 38*(5), 635–647.

Malecki, C., & Elliot, S. (2002). Children's social behaviors as predictors of academic achievement: A longitudinal analysis. *School Psychology Quarterly, 17*(1), 1–23.

Mashburn, A. J., Pianta, R. C., Hamre, B., Downer, J. T., Barbarin, O. A., Bryant, D., Howes, C. (2008). Measures of classroom quality in prekindergarten and children's development of academic, language, and social skills. *Child Development, 79*(3), 732–749.

McClelland, M., & Morrison, F. (2003). The emergence of learning-related social skills in preschool children. *Early Childhood Research Quarterly, 18*, 206–224.

Miles, S., & Stipek, D. (2006). Contemporaneous and longitudinal associations between social behavior and literacy achievement in a sample of low-income elementary school children. *Child Development, 77*(1), 103–117.

Mills, R. S. L., & Grusec, J. E. (1989). Cognitive, affective, and behavioral consequences of praising altruism. *Merrill-Palmer Quarterly, 35*(3), 299–326.

Mitchell-Copeland, J., Denham, S., & DeMulder, E. (1997). Q-sort assessment of child-teacher attachment relationships and social competence in the preschool. *Early Education and Development, 8*(1), 27–39.

Normandeau, S., & Guay, F. (1998). Preschool behavior and first-grade school achievement: The mediational role of cognitive self-control. *Journal of Educational Psychology, 90*(1), 111–121.

Piaget, J. (1983). Piaget's theory. In P. Mussen, (Series Ed.) & W. Kessen (Volume Ed.), *Handbook of child psychology* (4th ed., Vol. 1, pp. 103–128). New York: Wiley.

Radke-Yarrow, M., Zahn-Waxler, C., & Chapman, M. (1983). Children's prosocial dispositions and behavior. In P. Mussen (Ed.), *Handbook of child psychology* (4th ed., Vol. 4, pp. 469–545). New York: Wiley.

Ramaswamy, V., & Bergin, C. C. (2009). Do reinforcement and induction increase prosocial behavior? Results of a teacher-based intervention in preschools. *Journal of Research in Childhood Education, 23*(4), 525–536.

Romano, E., Babchishin, L., Pagani, L. S., & Kohen, D. (2010). School readiness and later achievement: Replication and extension using a nationwide Canadian survey. *Developmental Psychology, 46*(5), 995–1007.

Schnall, S., Roper, J., & Fessler, D. M. T. (2010). Elevation leads to altruistic behavior. *Psychological Science, 21*(3), 315–320.

Scourfield, J., John, B., Martin, N., & McGuffin, P. (2004). The development of prosocial behavior in children and adolescents: A twin study. *Journal of Child Psychology and Psychiatry, 45*(5), 927–935.

Shechtman, Z., & Yaman, M. A. (2012). SEL as a component of a literature class to improve relationships, behavior, motivation and content knowledge. *American Educational Research Journal, 49*(3), 546–567.

Social and Character Development Research Consortium. (2010). *Efficacy of schoolwide programs to promote social and character development and reduce problem behavior in elementary school children (NCER 2011–2001)*. Washington, DC: National Center for Education Research, Institute of Education Sciences.

Solomon, D., Battistich, V., Watson, M., Schaps, E., & Lewis, C. (2000). A six-district study of educational change: Direct and mediated effects of the Child Development Project. *Social Psychology of Education, 41*(1), 3–51.

Staines, G. L., & Cleland, C. M. (2012). Observational studies versus randomized controlled trials of behavioral interventions in field settings. *Review of General Psychology, 16*(1), 37–58. doi: 10.1037/a0026493

Strayer, J., & Roberts, W. (1989). Children's empathy and role-taking: Child and parental factors and relations to prosocial behavior. *Journal of Applied Developmental Psychology, 10*, 227–239.

Szynal-Brown, C., & Morgan, R. (1983). The effects of reward on tutor's behavior in a cross-age tutoring context. *Journal of Experimental Child Psychology, 36*(2), 196–208.

Thorkildsen, T., Reese, D., & Corsino, A. (2002). School ecologies and attitudes about exclusionary behavior among adolescents and young adults. *Merrill-Palmer Quarterly, 48*(1), 25–51.

Véronneau, M.-H., Vitaro, F., Brendgen, M., Dishion, T. J., & Tremblay, R. E. (2010). Transactional analysis of the reciprocal links between peer experiences and academic achievement from middle childhood to early adolescence. *Developmental Psychology, 46*(4), 773–790.

Warden, D., & Mackinnon, S. (2003). Prosocial children, bullies and victims: An investigation of their sociometric status, empathy and social problem-solving strategies. *British Journal of Developmental Psychology, 21,* 367–385.

Warneken, F., & Tomasello, M. (2009). The roots of human altruism. *British Journal of Psychology, 100*(455–471).

Webster-Stratton, C., Reid, M. J., & Stoolmiller, M. (2008). Preventing conduct problems and improving school readiness: Evaluation of the Incredible Years Teacher and Child Training Programs in high-risk schools. *Journal of Child Psychology and Psychiatry, 49*(5), 471–488.

Wentzel, K. R. (1993). Does being good make the grade? Social behavior and academic competence in middle school. *Journal of Educational Psychology, 85,* 357–364.

Wentzel, K. R. (2006). A social motivation perspective for classroom management. In C. M. Evertson & C. S. Weinstein (Eds.), *Handbook of classroom management* (pp. 619–643). Mahwah, NJ: Erlbaum.

Witkow, M. R., & Fuligni, A. J. (2010). In-school versus out-of-school friendships and academic achievement among an ethnically diverse sample of adolescents. *Journal of Research on Adolescence, 20*(3), 631–650.

Yarrow, M., Scott, P., & Waxler, C. (1973). Learning concern for others. *Developmental Psychology, 8,* 240–260.

Specific Targets and Types of Prosocial Behavior

15

Parents as Recipients of Adolescent Prosocial Behavior

Mary B. Eberly Lewis

The socialization processes by which children and adolescents become kind, considerate, concerned, and helpful toward others have been a focus of inquiry and debate for parents, researchers, and philosophers alike (Carlo, 2006). Behaving prosocially toward others is fundamental for healthy functioning within dyads, groups, and society at large and reflects social and moral competencies (Carlo, 2006; Carlo, Knight, McGinley, Goodvin, & Roesch, 2010). The significance of adolescents' prosocial actions toward their parents is no exception. Few studies exist, however, investigating the ways that adolescents behave prosocially toward their parents, perhaps because theory and research has emphasized behaviors and processes associated with distancing or renegotiation in parent and adolescent relationships, rather than on those behaviors and qualities that maintain bonds and socioemotional connections (Collins & Laursen, 2004; Steinberg & Silk, 2002). The relational quality associated with adolescents acting in prosocial ways *toward* parents is important because prosocial behaviors occur within an ongoing relationship with a history, diverse and frequent interactions, symbolic representations, sets of expectations, and an anticipated future (Hinde, 1979; Kuczynski, 2003). Being prosocial relationally incorporates those qualities that go beyond traditionally studied dispositional qualities or immediate situational demands. This chapter focuses on the ways in which adolescents' prosocial behavior toward parents emulate those relational dynamics.

Studying adolescent prosocial behavior toward parents in a relational context is important for several reasons. First, a relational context implies that socialization is bidirectional (Grusec & Goodnow, 1994; Kuczynski, 2003); therefore, adolescents' prosocial behavior toward parents both influences and is influenced by interactions with parents. In three recent studies, researchers found that adolescents' empathy-related qualities and prosocial behavior longitudinally predicted positive, need-support parenting 1 and 2 years later, respectively, as well as finding that parenting predicted adolescent prosocial behavior and empathy over time (Miklikowska, Duriez, & Soenens, 2011; Padilla-Walker, Carlo, Christensen, & Yorgason, 2012; Padilla-Walker, Dyer, Yorgason, Fraser, & Coyne, in press). Second, adolescents' helpful, considerate, and kind behavior toward parents reflects socialization goals (Goodnow, 1988; Goodnow & Warton, 1991). Helping in the home and other forms of household work tap pragmatic concerns, such as skills necessary for independent living; relational concerns, such as ways to negotiate shared tasks or show concern and support for another family member; and moral concerns, such as respecting a family members' rights or sacrificing self-interests to promote another's well-being (Goodnow, 1988; Goodnow & Warton, 1991; Grusec, Goodnow, & Cohen, 1996). Third, the nature and quality of parent-adolescent relationships may be revealed by the ways in which adolescents behave prosocially toward parents (Collins & Steinberg, 2006; Eberly & Montemayor, 1998, 1999; Kuczynski, 2003; Kumru, 2002; Padilla-Walker & Christensen, 2011). Several authors have identified a positive link between adolescent prosocial behavior toward parents and attachment quality, positive parenting, closeness and familial cohesion, interdependency and filial identity (Eberly & Montemayor, 1998, 1999; Kumru, 2002; Padilla-Walker & Christensen, 2011; Padilla-Walker et al., in press). Fourth, adolescent prosocial behavior might reflect age-related changes in adolescents, parents, and their shared relationships. Eberly, Montemayor, and Flannery (1993) found that adolescent helpfulness and affection toward parents declined as a function of pubertal maturation. A relational approach is warranted in order to better understand the nature and function of the many ways that adolescents behave prosocially toward their parents.

The present chapter is divided into four main sections. The first section frames prosocial behavior in a relational context recognizing it as multidimensional and multifaceted. The second section introduces a relational approach demonstrating how adolescents' prosocial behavior is embedded in interactions with parents. The third section discusses adolescent prosocial behavior toward parents as a function of conflict, autonomy, and harmony, highlighting change and transformation across adolescence. The final section presents a brief overview of individual differences that might be associated with variation in adolescent prosocial behavior toward mothers and fathers.

Defining Prosocial Behavior: Issues of Multidimensionality in Relationships

A commonly accepted and often cited definition of prosocial behavior is "any voluntary behavior intended to benefit another" (Eisenberg, Fabes, & Spinrad, 2006, p. 646). The strength of this definition is in its ability to account for behavior that might be either planned (formal) or spontaneous (informal; Amato, 1990). It includes behavior motivated by hedonistic, instrumental, or self-beneficent reasons as well as other-oriented, moral, or altruistic intentions (Batson & Shaw, 1991; Eisenberg et al., 2006, Hawley, chapter 3, this volume). This definition allows for actions characterized by immediate and agreeable compliance to requests, adherence to obedience, and demonstration of respect (Carlo & Randall, 2002; Kumru, 2002). It provides parameters for behavior that occurs in different contexts or under various circumstances, such as acting in public, anonymously, in response to an emotionally distressed other, or in a dire emergency (Carlo & Randall, 2002). Moreover, the definition allows for breadth, recognizing that prosocial behavior can manifest in different actions, such as helping, being considerate, demonstrating affection, sharing, giving/donating, and providing emotional support (Eberly & Montemayor, 1998; Padilla-Walker & Carlo, chapter 1, this volume). Within relationships, prosocial behavior taps all such dimensions and contexts, requiring a multidimensional view to better account for variation in behavior.

In parent-adolescent relationships, adolescents' voluntary actions intended to benefit mothers and fathers encompass various underlying motives, circumstances, and forms. The same form of behavior might have several underlying motives in different contexts or situations. A daughter giving a hug to her mother might be motivated by a desire to elicit an affectionate response and feel comforted (self-beneficent) or be a way to show support or concern for her mother if her mother was upset (other-oriented). Alternatively, a similar motive or intention might be displayed in different forms of behavior. A son might demonstrate altruistic concern when his father is ill or injured by sacrificing his time to keep his father company rather than going on an outing with friends or by quitting extracurricular activities in order to get a job to help with family finances. Although discerning motivations and intentions is complex (Eisenberg et al., 2006), identifying the nature, frequency, and diversity of adolescents' prosocial behavior toward parents and their underlying motives in differing contexts certainly warrants future investigation. Adolescent prosocial behavior toward parents must be viewed through a multidimensional, multifaceted lens, resulting in predictive and explanatory power (Padilla-Walker & Carlo, chapter 1, this volume).

ADOLESCENT PROSOCIAL BEHAVIOR: A RELATIONAL APPROACH

According to Amato (1990), relationships with family members "are guided by a communal orientation in which frequent helping is expected, regardless of the partner's ability to 'repay' the helper in the short-term" (p. 31). There is a sense of obligation to respond to and be cognizant of the other person in the relationship (Clark & Mills, 2012; Goodnow, 1988). A communal orientation implies that members wish to maintain social ties and affirm personal investment in one another (Amato, 1990). Prosocial behavior within relationships is one form of behavior that aids in maintaining relational quality (Clark & Mills, 2013). Its presence is pivotal to keeping relationships harmonious and functional. Behavioral norms, such as norms of reciprocity, norms of personal responsibility, and kinship, dictate the nature by which members engage in prosocial behavior with one another over time (Hamilton, 1971; Staub, 1972; Trivers, 1971). Thus, a relational framework integrates communal qualities intrinsic to prosocial behavior within an ongoing interpersonal relationship that has a past, present, and future with the dispositional propensities and situational parameters placed on its enactment (Amato, 1990).

Parents' and children's behavior are linked inextricably in recurrent reciprocal interchanges, which give rise to a relational context in which members are entrenched (Kuczynski, 2003). The influence between parents and children is bidirectional and ongoing (Kuczynski, 2003; Maccoby & Martin, 1983). Their shared relationship has systemic properties, such that changes internal to or external to the relationship prompt evolution within the relationship and, by extension, in the ways that they behave toward one another (Kuczynski, 2003). Regardless of her dispositional propensity to be prosocial, a daughter's willingness to comfort her mother might depend on the degree to which she has provided comfort in the past, how it was received, whether she feels empathy for her mother, the fact that her mother is female (i.e., gender role adherence), and the degree to which conflicted or harmonious interactions characterize their relationship. Therefore, adolescents' kind and helpful actions toward parents cannot be viewed as isolated events or prosocial dispositions because the patterned ways that each dyad interacts, characteristics inherent to the relationship, and qualities of each individual (mother, father, and adolescent), moderate and or mediate the expression of adolescents' prosocial behavior.

Several fundamental qualities of relationships elucidate ways to understand prosocial behavior from a relational perspective (Collins & Laursen, 2004). First, relationships occur over time and have measurable duration resulting in a shared history (Berscheid, Snyder, & Omoto, 1989; Hinde & Stevenson-Hinde, 1987; Kuczynski; 2003). Second, content of past interactions as well as the patterning and distribution of positive, negative, and neutral interchanges contribute to memory and expectations of members' behavior (Collins & Laursen, 2004). Third, members derive meaning and global characterizations from patterns of past interchanges. The meaning and global attributes attached to the dynamics of the relationship, such as perceptions of emotional climate or experience of warmth, becomes the filter through which members interpret the cognitive, emotional, and behavioral responsiveness of one to another (Collins & Laursen, 2004). Fourth, adolescents and parents also acquire roles that govern the degree of influence, expected behavior, and means by which actions from another are discouraged or encouraged (Collins & Laursen, 2004). These qualities set the stage for the anticipation of the future course of the relationship. Thus, the various ways that adolescents behave prosocially toward parents would reflect the embedded patterns of interactions, their shared history, how that history is represented, the role that each member is assigned within that relationship, as well as the anticipation of future interactions. In the present chapter, two aspects of the relational approach will be discussed in association with adolescents' prosocial behavior toward parents, namely, content and quality of interaction patterns and three global attributes that are considered to be central to transformation in parent and adolescent relationships (Steinberg & Silk, 2002).

CONTENT AND QUALITY OF SOCIAL INTERACTION PATTERNS

Adolescents have the ability to demonstrate affection, be considerate and respectful, find ways to be helpful, provide emotional support, and make self-sacrifices to benefit parents (Eberly & Montemayor, 1998, 1999; Grusec et al., 1996; Kumru, 2002). The question for research is to determine how each of these types of prosocial actions manifests in the interchanges between adolescents and their parents. Perhaps some forms are tied to specific aspects of their shared relationship, such as helping one another with household tasks. Other forms of behavior might be linked to personal preferences or competencies, and still others might be tied to characteristic ways of behaving toward a particular beneficiary. Based on gender role norms, a son might offer emotional comfort to his mother who is distressed but leave his father alone (Goodnow, Bowes, Warton, Dawes, & Taylor, 1991). Moreover, prosocial actions most likely represent a form of communal reciprocation across time rather than an immediate momentary exchange (Clark & Mills, 2013). Thus, discerning whether adolescents' prosocial behavior toward parents is contingent on an immediately preceding parent behavior, a response to parent behavior at an earlier time, a symbolic representation of the relationship, or any combination of these factors is difficult. Regardless, an examination of exchange patterns might explicate the ebb and flow of prosocial interchanges between parents and adolescents.

The concept of exchange patterns has received attention in research on intergenerational support between adult children and elderly parents (Gouldner, 1960; Hollstien & Bria, 1998). In this framework, a distinction is made between short-term reciprocity, which focuses on concurrent patterns of giving and receiving, and long-term reciprocity, which is the idea that adult children repay elderly parents who supported them earlier in life. The currency of short-term and long-term exchange is the form that behavior takes. Concurrent patterns of exchange include homomorphic reciprocity (transfers of the same currency: adolescent affection for parent affection) and heteromorphic reciprocity (exchange of different currencies: adolescent respectful behavior for parent permission to extend curfew; Gouldner, 1960). Concurrent patterns might be more sensitive to the existing perturbations in parent and adolescent dynamics. Long-term reciprocity is based on the anticipation that most adolescents have lifelong relationships with parents; thus, acting prosocially is a means by which contributions can be made to their potential future support from parents, in effect, a "support bank" (see Antonucci & Jackson, 1990). Adolescents might show stability in their prosocial actions toward parents with the long-term expectation that parents will provide support in the distant future. A long-term view, however, requires mature systemic perspective-taking, a skill that appears later in adolescence (Davis & Franzoi, 1991; Roberts & Strayer, 1996), and the belief that parents will have the means and desire to provide future assistance. For those adolescents who are not yet cognizant of potential parental support or do not foresee future support, acting prosocially toward caregivers might be lessened. Speculative at best, perhaps the diversity and fluctuation of adolescents' prosocial behaviors represents responses to recent occurrences or anticipation of future parental behavior.

Parents' reactions to their adolescents' prosocial behaviors also may be important to consider. Some reactions might reward while others might discourage adolescents' initiatives. In addition, whether adolescents choose to act prosocially may be tied to their anticipation of parents' responses. In research with young children, Grusec (1991) asked mothers to keep a record of the ways in which they responded to their 4- and 7-year-old children's spontaneous prosocial behaviors at home. Findings revealed that mothers rarely used material reward; rather, they used social reinforcement and acknowledgment. Interestingly, children who were least prosocial were those who often received social approval/praise and acknowledgment. No response from mothers was associated with 4-year-old children being ranked as most prosocial. Curious as to why social reinforcement would undermine children's prosociality, Henderlong and Lepper (2002) focused on factors contributing to the effectiveness of praise. They suggested that the effectiveness of praise depends on performance attributions (praise for controllable features of a task versus praise for an easy task), autonomy promotion (praise focused on endogenous attributions versus praise used to control or overjustify), effect on self-efficacy and competence (praise that emphasizes personal competence versus praise derived from social comparison), and expectations for standards of behavior (descriptive praise versus praise that conveys meeting impossible standards). What remains to be determined is the nature of parental responses and to what prosocial behaviors they respond as well as how often, how consistently, and in what context. Additionally, anticipation of parental response should also be considered. Wyatt and Carlo (2002) found that adolescents' anticipation of the appropriateness of parents' reactions to prosocial behavior was linked to the likelihood of adolescents actually being more prosocial toward others (peers and strangers). By extension, the reaction that adolescents anticipate receiving from parents might be associated with whether or not they choose to behave prosocially toward parents. Whether these ideas hold true in parent-adolescent relationships is a question for future research, and research employing a social interactional approach that focuses on the dynamics of giving and receiving might be fruitful.

In summary, the shared relational history between parents and adolescents offers a chronological context for understanding the propensity, diversity, and frequency of adolescents' prosocial behavior toward their mothers and fathers. From a social-interactional point of view, contingency or exchange patterns that epitomize what adolescents do and how those prosocial actions are responded to within parent-adolescent relationships may shed light on the interactional mechanisms underlying their presence. Longitudinal work is needed that looks at an overall inclination toward behaving prosocially toward parents including examination of trends in different types of adolescent prosocial behavior and parents' responses to those actions.

REPRESENTATIONS AND MEANING
OF RELATIONSHIP ATTRIBUTES

Variation in adolescent prosocial behavior toward parents might also be linked to the attributions and portrayals of parenting and parent-adolescent relationships. Representations are constructed from an amalgamation of the patterns and associated meaning of interactions over time (Collins & Laursen, 2004). They become the filter through which adolescents and parents interpret and anticipate one another's emotional and behavioral responsiveness, and they affect the quality of relationships. According to Steinberg and Silk (2002), three dimensions of parent-adolescent relationships have been the primary focus of the majority of research, namely, conflict, autonomy, and harmony. Conflict represents the degree to which parent-adolescent relationships are characterized by hostility and disagreement. Autonomy reflects the degree to which adolescents assume independence from parents behaviorally, emotionally, and cognitively, or the degree to which parents maintain control over their youth. Harmony refers to warmth, involvement, and closeness between parents and adolescents. These dimensions are interdependent, yet considered individually, each has the potential to be linked in different ways and to different forms of adolescents' prosocial actions toward parents.

Changes in qualitative dimensions between parents and adolescents reveal that parent-adolescent relationships transform from being asymmetrical, where children are dependent on parents, to becoming more egalitarian during early adulthood. The transformation process is witnessed in perturbations associated with conflict, negotiation of autonomy, and harmony (Steinberg & Silk, 2002). Catalysts include normative developmental change in adolescents (puberty, self-definition, cognition, affiliation with peers), changes in social contexts (school, unsupervised time, media exposure), and changes in parents at midlife. Given that adolescents' prosocial actions toward parents are linked to those relational dimensions, variation in adolescent prosocial actions should parallel relationship fluctuations.

Conflict

Most likely, conflict within the parent-child relationship and adolescents' prosocial behavior are cyclically linked over time. Most conflicts between parents and adolescents are resolved and enhance understanding in interpersonal relationships. Rarely are conflicts characterized by angry, hostile fighting resulting in disengagement and severe disturbance (Adams & Laursen, 2007) or result in long-term negative effects (Smetana, 1996). Parent-adolescent conflict and adolescent prosocial behavior would be expected to be inversely related. The absence of some forms of prosocial behavior, such as helping within the home, often is a conflict catalyst (Smetana, 1988). Eberly and Montemayor (1999) found that the frequency of helpfulness toward parents declined between the eighth and tenth grades, which they proposed was tied to the increase in conflict often reported between parents and adolescents. Affectively, frequent and intense arguments might diminish how often adolescents act in caring, affectionate, and considerate ways. Alternatively, arguments also provide opportunities to learn constructive conflict resolution strategies and reparation (Adams & Laursen, 2007; Cooper, 1988). The link between adolescent prosocial behavior and parent-adolescent conflict, consequently, would depend on the content and nature of the conflict.

Conflicts arise for many reasons and are a normative part of relationships (Collins & Laursen, 2004). Content of parent-adolescent arguments usually consists of mundane, everyday issues, such as asking adolescents to have tidy bedrooms or complete assigned household tasks in a timely fashion (Laursen, Coy, & Collins, 1998). Certainly an element of obedience exists, but parents, especially mothers, often regard adolescents doing chores agreeably on request, without a reminder, or helping spontaneously as helpful and acts of caring (Goodnow, 1988; Goodnow & Delaney, 1989; Goodnow & Warton, 1991). However, forgotten, delayed, resisted, abandoned, or poorly done chores often become fodder for conflict. Some research has shown that the contention surrounding household work lies in the understanding of ownership or jurisdiction of the task or the circumstance, that is, the distinction between conventional (familial) and personal responsibility (Smetana, 1988). If parents view helping around the home as a way that adolescents show concern and care for the parents, then disregard for helping may be interpreted as a lack of caring. Parents may also feel personally rejected when requests are ignored or dismissed because they might feel taken for granted, unimportant, unappreciated, or demoted to the role of a servant, contributing the likelihood of conflict (Goodnow & Warton, 1991). Violating norms regarding expectations of cooperation, helping, and expression of gratitude for household work could be associated with conflict between parents and adolescents.

The frequency and the affective quality of parent-adolescent disagreements may also be associated with adolescents' prosocial behavior toward their parents because of their contribution to the emotional climate of the relationship. The frequency of conflicted interchanges peaks in early adolescence, rivaling that of distressed marriages, declines during midadolescence, and declines again in late adolescence (Adams & Laursen, 2001). The intensity and frequency of expressed negative affectivity, however, increases from early adolescence to midadolescence with little change thereafter. Although almost no research exists regarding the association between adolescents' prosocial actions toward parents and parent-adolescent arguments, it could be expected that as more heated and more frequent coercive conflicts occur, adolescents are less likely to be affectionate, considerate, and helpful toward their parents. For example, families characterized by a dominant, negative, hostile emotional climate are associated with preschoolers and children who are more antisocial—a dispositional characteristic associated with less empathy and concern for others, low levels of sympathy, high levels of personal distress, and less prosocial responsiveness toward peers (Eisenberg et al., 1992; Hastings, Zahn-Waxler, Robinson, Usher, & Bridges, 2000). Moreover, Carlo, Roesch, and Melby (1998) found that adolescents' reports of anger were inversely related to prosocial behavior and sympathy toward peers, and Eberly and Montemayor (1999) found that the more adolescents reported conflict with mothers, the less affection mothers reported receiving concurrently and after two years. Adolescents' prosocial feelings, such as empathy and sympathy, and corresponding actions, such as being affectionate and considerate, toward their mothers and fathers might be diminished by frequent and highly negative parent-adolescent conflicts, as those particular forms of prosocial behavior are considered integral to expressions of affiliation or cohesion in relationships.

Conversely, the aftermath of conflict often leads to resolution, which includes acts of reparation or prosocial behavior. To date, however, research has focused on adolescents' angry and neutral reactions after conflicts, finding that emotional responses are more coercive between parents and adolescents than between adolescents and peers (Adams & Laursen, 2001). Other research on young adults found that self-conscious emotions, which include guilt, shame, and remorse, were important for coping with interpersonal conflict and engaging in amendatory behaviors (Barrett, 1995; Baumeister, Stillwell, & Heatherton, 1994). More specifically, guilt proneness has been associated with empathy and perspective taking and consequent reparative action, whereas shame was linked to personal distress often resulting in blame or increased aggression toward the other person (Behrendt & Ben-Ari, 2012; Carlson & Miller, 1987; Tangney, Stuewig, & Mashek, 2007). Similar connections could be hypothesized for adolescents' responses to conflicts with parents; however, youths' empathic and perspective-taking abilities are developing throughout adolescence (Davis & Franzoi, 1991; Miklikowska et al., 2011; Roberts & Strayer, 1996). Younger adolescents would be less able to hold a systemic view of their actions and reactions after conflicts than would older adolescents. Perhaps guilt-prone adolescents, especially those who are more advanced in their development of empathy and perspective-taking, might find ways to reestablish their connection with parents through prosocial actions, such as displays of affection, gift giving, and helping, that is, prosocial actions that indicate a desire to reestablish a sense of relational closeness. In contrast, shame-prone youth or youth who have less mature empathic and perspective-taking abilities, would have greater self-concern and personal distress and be less likely to act prosocially toward parents after conflicts. For future studies, identifying forms of adolescent prosocial behavior that constitute reparative actions after conflict or, more broadly, prosocial actions engaged in to enhance affiliation and cohesiveness is warranted. Specific to parent-adolescent conflict, the moderational role of self-conscious emotions in the link between parent-adolescent conflict and reparative adolescent behavior toward parents also warrants study.

Autonomy

Although autonomy is often thought of as an intrapersonal quality, its development occurs in an interpersonal context (Collins & Steinberg, 2006). For adolescents, autonomy encompasses a shift from greater dependency on parents for behavioral and emotional regulation toward becoming individuals who are volitional, personally responsible, competent, and independent (Bugental & Grusec, 2006; Collins & Steinberg, 2006; Steinberg & Silk, 2002). For parents, adolescents' emergent autonomy requires a willingness to relinquish parental control, ascribe greater responsibility to their adolescent children, and encourage independent decision-making and self-regulation (Collins, Gleason, & Sesma, 1997; Collins & Steinberg, 2006). According to Douvan and Adelson (1966), autonomy may be classified in three ways: "*emotional autonomy*, which refers to the subjective feelings of independence, especially from parents; *behavioral autonomy*, which refers to the capacity for independent decision making and self governance, and *value autonomy*, which refers to the development of an independent world view [based on] overarching principles and beliefs" (as cited in Collins & Steinberg, 2006, p. 1033). All three types of autonomy are likely involved in adolescents' ability to identify opportunities to be kind and helpful toward parents as well as act on those opportunities.

The connection between adolescents' prosocial behavior toward parents and adolescents' emotional autonomy from parents might be witnessed in the degree to which adolescents are capable of seeing parents as individuals who can be helped and cared for, and that adolescents, themselves, believe they are capable of such caregiving. Children and early adolescents view their parents as omnipotent authority figures whose primary role is that of resource holder, caregiver, protector, and disciplinarian while concurrently viewing themselves as recipients of care and protection (Laursen & Collins, 1988; Steinberg & Silverberg, 1986). In their review, Laursen and Collins (1988) propose that adolescents' ability to achieve emotional autonomy from parents is prompted by a change in self-conceptions toward establishing a unique identity distinct from that of parents. Conceptions of parents also change from that of individuals who serve an authoritative role to that of people with unique characteristics, vulnerabilities, and strengths. Increasing cognitive complexity and greater perspective-taking skills facilitates transformation in perceptions (Selman, 1980; Youniss & Smollar, 1985), both of which increase from early through late adolescence and are linked to youths' prosocial behavior toward non-family members (Davis & Franzoi, 1991; Miklikowska et al., 2011; Strayer & Roberts, 1997). With increasing emotional autonomy, adolescents are more likely to experience empathy and sympathy for parents that would allow them to view parents as people toward whom youth can demonstrate concern, to appreciate why being helpful around the home is meaningful to parents, and to offer emotional support when parents are distressed rather than viewing parents in the role of caregiver, disciplinarian, and protector.

Adolescents' prosocial actions toward parents might also reflect changes in behavioral and value autonomy. For adolescents, both forms of autonomy require an internalization of personal behavioral standards that guide the ability to act volitionally, responsibly, and ethically (Collins & Steinberg, 2006). Maturation in adolescents' behavioral autonomy is witnessed in the personal standards about contributions to and attitude toward household maintenance. Typically, household work is divided into family-care activities (those that contribute to the communal family well-being and maintenance, such as doing laundry or vacuuming) and self-care activities (those that exclusively involve the self, such as cleaning up one's own mess or brushing one's teeth). Although parental intent in assigning chores to youth might be to instill a sense of responsibility and learn tasks necessary for adolescents' future independent living, household work also contributes to the development of showing care toward others (Goodnow, 1988). Choosing to voluntarily help a parent with household tasks independent of requests or prompts, providing child care for younger siblings, taking on increasing responsibility for home management, and engaging in self-care without parental reminders might be considered beneficial and prosocial from mothers' and fathers' perspectives. In order to recognize the significance of such assistance to parents requires that adolescents achieve maturity in behavioral autonomy such that actions are intrinsically volitional. Adolescents' participation in household tasks that help parents provides opportunities to develop personal, internalized standards of behavior that are associated with the attainment of behavioral autonomy.

Internalization and adherence to a personal and ideological set of standards is the teleological goal of value autonomy. Value autonomy often is equated with moral development, including both prosocial moral reasoning and prohibitive moral reasoning (Eisenberg et al., 2006). The development of value autonomy also includes establishing the content of moral values, and integrating that content as components of moral identity (Hardy & Carlo, 2011). Perhaps, then, the link between adolescents' prosocial behavior toward parents and the maturation of value autonomy is revealed through the indoctrination of prosocial conventions and expression of values important for parent-adolescent relationships (Kuczynski & Navara, 2006), such as being respectful and honoring parents (familism). In her study of Turkish adolescents, Kumru (2002) found that respect for parents was viewed as prosocial by youth and parents alike. Moreover, she found that midadolescents (approximately age 14) were less respectful than early adolescents (approximately age 12), a finding that parallels transformational trends in conflict with autonomy seeking from parents. The value of familism, which is defined by its emphasis on providing emotional and instrumental family support, obligation and duty toward family, and viewing the self in relation to family (Carlo & Knight, chapter 12, this volume; Knight, et al., 2010), has been linked to adolescent prosocial behavior toward others and toward family members in Mexican American youth (Calderon-Tena, Knight, & Carlo, 2011; Knight & Carlo, 2012). Although familism and its link to prosocial behavior toward parents has not yet been studied, fluctuations might occur as a function of value autonomy, as well as issues surrounding acculturation and ethnic identity development (Knight & Carlo, 2012).

Adolescents' reasons for making sacrifices for family members instead of satisfying personal interests also illustrates the development of value autonomy. Personal sacrifices require perspective taking, empathy, and adherence to an internalized set of standards regarding family and close, significant relationships. Two studies, which employed hypothetical dilemmas, revealed that adolescents' reasoning about prosocial obligations toward close others, including parents, showed clear preferences for making sacrifices for close others over pursuing personal desires (Killen & Turiel, 1998; Smetana et al., 2009). Early adolescents and midadolescents cited concern for others and a desire to maintain relationships as primary reasons for making those sacrifices. Moreover, youth and parents, alike, believed that helping in high-need situations was imperative, in contrast to helping in low-need situations, where adolescents believed that helping was necessary but parents did not (Smetana et al., 2009). Three dimensions of prosociality are made evident by these studies. One dimension is the type of behavior, itself, and whether actions are perceived as pragmatic, prudential, or moral (Smetana et al., 2009). Discerning the type of behavior is a necessary component in deciding a course of action. Relatedly, a second dimension highlights the need of the other juxtaposed with the cost involved in the self-sacrificial situation. Perhaps with maturation, the development of value autonomy contributes to this discernment. Adolescents become more capable of making distinctions between situations where acting prosocially is required and those circumstances where taking prosocial action is unnecessary or perhaps inappropriate. A third dimension illuminates maturational differences in motives or reasons for choosing a particular course of action. Perhaps in early adolescence, due to a stereotyped notion of appropriate behavior, adolescents make personal concessions for mothers' and fathers' benefits because that is what a "good child would do." In later adolescence, as moral standards become internalized, youth become sensitive to the parental circumstances and engage in behavior consistent with internalized values. The transformation in value autonomy is not realized in the particular action per se; rather it is reflected in underlying reasons and motives.

Parents, too, are involved in this developmental process by encouraging youths' individuality, supporting youth in independent decision-making and behavioral efficacy, assigning responsibility, and acknowledging and supporting adolescents' moral points of view (Collins & Steinberg, 2006). Parents who recognize their adolescent children as emotionally autonomous and competent individuals might expect to be recipients of their adolescents' age-appropriate compassion and emotional or instrumental support. Central to behavioral autonomy, many parents increase the amount of responsibility for family-care household work and expect adolescents to willingly follow through with household assignments across adolescence (Collins et al., 1997). When and if adolescents perform family-care and self-care activities of their own accord, the burden of household care on mothers and fathers is alleviated. Goodnow (1988; Goodnow & Delaney, 1989; Goodnow & Warton, 1991) proposed that children and adolescents' participation in household work reflects the socialization of showing concern and care for others, distinguishing between helping and taking responsibility, a shift in goal-setting and supervision, meaningful contributions to the family or to a relationship, and the acquisition of values regarding norms and rules underlying caring relationships. Thus, household work and self-governance might be linked to parents' encouragement of adolescent behavioral autonomy.

Recognition of adolescents' developing value autonomy might be witnessed in parents' solicitation of moral advice and opinions or in their willingness to discuss moral events with their adolescent children. Whether parents ask for advice or elicit adolescents' opinions regarding moral situations as a function of maturation requires future investigation, but would demonstrate some benefits parents might gain from adolescents' increasing value autonomy. Parents' increasing expectations to receive care, concern, and assistance from their adolescent children over time are inextricably linked to adolescents' developing autonomy.

Harmony

Interestingly, the transformation in harmony and closeness between adolescents and parents is given the least consideration in contemporary research on parent and adolescent relations (Steinberg & Silk, 2002). Constructs representing harmony and closeness include subjective emotional qualities, such as attachment security, warmth and connectedness, and trust as well as behavioral indicators, such as communication patterns, expression of positive affect, interdependence, and time spent together (involvement; Collins & Laursen, 2004; Steinberg & Silk, 2002). From early to late adolescence, the ordinal level of emotional closeness across parent-adolescent dyads does not appear to change, but, within dyads, the frequency of expression of affection and positive affect, subjective feelings of closeness, and number of shared activities fluctuates (Larson, Richards, Moneta, Holmbeck, & Duckett, 1996; Steinberg & Silk, 2002). The ways in which adolescents act prosocially toward parents might be another means by which to study closeness and harmony. Prosocial behavior within ongoing relationships, in general, has been associated with harmonious communal bonds and relationship maintenance strategies (Clark & Mills, 2012). From a relational perspective, adolescents' kind, considerate, and helpful actions toward parents would be both consequences and antecedents of closeness and harmony (Eberly & Montemayor, 1998). As consequences, adolescents' prosocial actions toward parents might transpire naturally indicating parent and youth connectedness. Prosocial actions are a regular and integral part of some dyads but less so for other dyads. As antecedents, adolescent prosocial actions toward parents, such as being affectionate, giving gifts, recognizing and acting on opportunities to help, and being respectful, would contribute to a positive emotional climate and harmonious interactions.

Adolescents' prosocial behavior would be expected to demonstrate a degree of overall stability across dyads yet also reveal fluctuation within dyads as harmony and perceptions of closeness waxes and wanes across adolescence.

An extensive body of work shows that positive relationship characteristics and parenting are linked to children's and adolescents' prosocial values, empathy, sympathy, perspective-taking, and behavior toward non-family members (see Eisenberg et al., 2006 for a review). Within parent-adolescent relationships, "emotional ties to parents may be indicated in subtle and very private ways, including friendly teasing and small acts of concern, as well as more obvious forms of interdependence such as shared activities with fathers and self-disclosure to mothers" (Collins & Laursen, 2004, p. 333). Eberly and Montemayor (1998) found that daughters' and sons' reports of attachment were linked directly and indirectly through interdependence to the frequency of adolescents' affection toward parents. In a follow-up study, adolescent reports of attachment quality also predicted adolescent reports of affection and helpfulness toward mothers and fathers after two years (Eberly & Montemayor, 1999). More recently, Padilla-Walker and Christensen (2011) found that positive parenting, as assessed through reports of involvement and connectedness, predicted adolescents' prosocial behavior toward family via adolescents' empathy and self-regulation. In other analyses, Padilla-Walker et al. (in press) found that youth classified as having consistently high levels of prosocial behavior also reported the greater connection with mothers; whereas youth with the lowest levels of prosocial behavior reported less connection to mothers as well as having the lowest levels of empathic concern and self-regulation. These studies imply that relational attributes representing connection and closeness in parent-adolescent relationships give rise to adolescent prosocial behavior toward parents.

Adolescents' interpersonal trust of parents holds promise as a factor predicting adolescents' prosocial behavior toward parents. According to Rotenberg (2010), interpersonal trust is based on the degree to which one views a partner as reliable, emotionally available, and honest. Taking action, consequently, is rooted in the belief that the person in need is sincere and genuine in their need-based circumstance and that the relationship partner would reciprocate in kind should a similar situation arise in the future (Carlo, Randall, Rotenberg, & Armenta, 2010). Some support for the association between prosocial behavior and trust can be derived from research in social psychology that has revealed significant links among commitment, prorelationship behavior, and trust in romantic and marital relationships (Rusbult & Agnew, 2010; Wieselquist, Rusbult, Foster & Agnew, 1999). Other research revealed that dimensions of trust, such as honesty and trustworthiness, were most relevant to predicting altruism, behaving prosocially in public, and responding to an emotionally laden situation in late adolescents (Carlo et al., 2010). Future research is warranted to look at adolescents' prosocial behaviors toward parents and its link with the degree to which adolescents perceive their parents as trustworthy.

In many ways, adolescents' prosocial activities would be expected to contribute to closeness and harmony with parents. Padilla-Walker et al. (2012) found that adolescents' prosocial behavior toward parents predicted authoritative parenting 1 year later, again demonstrating that the prosocial ways that adolescents behave toward their parents affect the relational quality. Although need support and authoritative parenting do not directly assess the construct of closeness and harmony per se, those parenting attributes include warmth, regulation, and autonomy support, all of which are associated with cohesive family relations (Maccoby & Martin, 1983). As would be predicted using a relational approach, the importance of adolescents' behavior in building and maintaining parent-adolescent relations is evident. Most likely, however, the association between parent-adolescent connectedness and prosocial behavior toward parents is bidirectional. In a 2-year longitudinal study, Miklikowska and colleagues (2011) found support for a reciprocal effects model in which fathers' need support (i.e., provision of warmth and support for autonomy) at baseline predicted sons' and daughters' perspective-taking skills and mothers' need support at baseline predicted daughters' empathy one year later. After a subsequent year, sons' and daughters' perspective-taking skills, but not empathic concern, predicted increases in paternal need support. What is important to highlight is the finding that adolescents' perspective taking—an important dimension of prosocial actions—contributed to future harmonious forms of parental behaviors. Several recommendations for future research can be ascertained from these findings. Longitudinal research is necessary to accurately examine the bidirectional and reciprocal nature of adolescent prosocial behavior and relational connectedness. Future research might work to discern types of adolescent prosocial behavior toward parents that contribute to feelings of closeness and connectedness. The diversity of adolescents' acts of kindness, willingness to share, or make personal sacrifices to benefit parents might be the catalyst that generates harmony in parent-adolescent relationships.

In summary, three aspects of parents' and adolescents' relations contribute to transformation and change in their shared relationship, each of which might be tied to the degree to which parents are recipients of adolescents' prosocial behavior. Conflict was tied to willingness to take on household work, expression of affection, showing concern, and enacting acts of prosocial reparation. Emotional autonomy also was linked to perspective taking, empathy, and displays of care and concern. Behavioral and value autonomy were hypothesized to be linked to taking personal responsibility for household work, being respectful, and endorsement of making personal sacrifices for parents rather than satisfying personal desires. Harmony and closeness were linked to displays of affection, helpfulness, and global measures of prosocial actions toward parents and family. Other forms of prosocial behavior might also be relevant to understanding the link between dynamics between parents and adolescents and adolescent prosocial behavior toward parents, but what those forms might be are the substance of future research endeavors.

Individual Differences—Contributions of Each Member

The focus of the present chapter has concerned itself with qualities of parent-adolescent relationships to which both parents and adolescents contribute. However, a relational approach requires that individual differences associated with each member of the relationship also be taken into consideration as factors that moderate the nature of relationship qualities and resultant behavior (Hinde & Stevenson-Hinde, 1987), such as gender, adolescent age, family constellation, parent employment status, and adolescent and parent mental and physical health. Due to space limitations, several potential individual factors that might affect the ways that adolescents act prosocially toward parents will be presented here but not explored in full. Parent gender and adolescent gender affect variation in adolescents' prosocial behavior toward parents (Eberly & Montemayor, 1998, 1999). Research on helpfulness and housework indicate that mothers receive more assistance than fathers, and daughters tend to be more helpful than sons (Coltrane, 2000; Eberly & Montemayor, 1998, 1999; Goodnow, 1988). Miklikowska et al. (2011) found that parent gender was important for socializing empathy and perspective-taking skills in sons and daughters. Mothers' nurturance and support for autonomy predicted daughters' affectively based empathy, whereas fathers' nurturance and support for autonomy was linked to sons' and daughters' cognitively based perspective taking over time. Adolescent age is another factor to consider. The socioemotional skills and competencies of early adolescents are less mature than those of older adolescents; thus, differences in adolescent prosocial behavior toward parents would be expected with maturity. Family constellation might also be a key consideration. Adolescents in two-parent intact families might have a different set of responsibilities and expectations than youth in single-headed households (Barber & Eccles, 1992). Additionally, adolescents from recently divorced families often pull away from parents as a means to cope with separation and interparental conflict (for a review, see Hetherington & Stanley-Hagan, 2002), thereby reducing time and opportunity to demonstrate affection or other prosocial and affiliative behaviors toward parents. Yet, other types of prosocial behaviors might increase after divorce. Greater household responsibility often is placed on adolescent daughters more so than on sons in post-divorce, single-headed households (Hilton & Haldeman, 1991). Differences in adolescents' helpfulness also vary depending on parent employment status. Daughters of dual-earner families were found to do more of the household work than sons, whereas daughters and sons of mothers who worked part-time with husbands who worked full-time helped the least (Benin & Edwards, 1990). Sons and daughters with mothers who stayed at home helped equally around the house and significantly more often than youth whose mothers worked part-time. How parent employment status affects other forms of prosocial behavior is unknown.

Parent and adolescent mental health and physical health also could be a factor contributing to variation in adolescent prosocial behavior toward parents. Recently, the notion of parentification or adultification has drawn attention in the literature. Parentification occurs when adolescents and parents reverse roles such that adolescents become the caretakers of parents, often providing developmentally inappropriate instrumental and emotional support for their parents (Earley & Cushway, 2002). Examples of parents who might look to their adolescent children are those who have severe mental illness, are recently divorced, have a history of sexual abuse, and are of low income status (for further discussion, see Earley & Cushway, 2002). Adolescent mental health also would affect their propensity to be prosocial toward parents. For example, in one meta-analysis of aggression (Card, Stucky, Sawalani, & Little, 2008), direct aggression was associated with externalizing behavior problems and low levels of prosocial behavior. In contrast, the authors found that internalizing problems were associated with indirect aggression and higher levels of prosocial behavior. Whether such results would be generally true of parent-adolescent relationships requires future research; however, this meta-analysis provides some guidance. Taken together, parent and adolescent gender, age, family constellation, employment status, and parent and adolescent mental health are individual differences that might be associated with the nature and frequency of adolescents' prosocial behavior toward parents.

Conclusion

Accounting for the different ways that adolescents behave prosocially toward their parents requires a framework that incorporates the dynamics within the parent-adolescent relationship as well as the individual characteristics of each member (Eisenberg et al., 2006; Padilla-Walker et al., in press). Conceptually, the present chapter proposes that the multidimensional nature of prosocial behavior toward parents can best be understood from the context of close relationships (Collins & Laursen, 2004; Hinde & Stevenson-Hinde, 1987). Because of the communal nature of prosocial behavior within significant long-term close relationships (Amato, 1990), adolescents' basic, everyday acts of kindness, helpfulness, consideration, and self-sacrifice not only reflect how they experience their relationships with each parent but also contribute to that same dynamic. The transactional nature of the interplay between relational qualities and prosocial actions may be studied at a micro level of interactional interchanges, immediate and reciprocal reactions, and short-term and long-term exchange mechanisms. Global attributes of parent-adolescent relationships, that is, those that reveal perturbations and transformation, also highlight the degree to which adolescent prosocial behavior is embedded in their relationships. Adolescents' prosocial behavior toward their mothers and fathers takes different forms and is enacted for different reasons within the relationship. Gaining a better understanding of the ways that adolescents' prosocial actions function in parent-adolescent relationships may be a key means by which youth and their parents can develop and maintain rewarding, long-term relationships.

References

Adams, R., & Laursen, B. (2001). The organization and dynamics of adolescent conflict with parents and friends. *Journal of Marriage and Family, 63,* 97–110.

Adams, R. E., & Laursen, B. (2007). The correlates of conflict: Disagreement is not necessarily detrimental. *Journal of Family Psychology, 21,* 445–458.

Amato, P. R. (1990). Personality and social network involvement as predictors of helping behavior in everyday life. *Social Psychology Quarterly, 53,* 31–43.

Antonucci, T. C., & Jackson, J. S. (1990). The role of reciprocity in social support. In B. R. Sarason, I. G. Sarason, & G. R. Pierce, *Social support: An interactional view* (pp. 173–198). New York: John Wiley.

Barber, B., & Eccles, J. S. (1992). A developmental view of the impact of divorce and single parenting on children and adolescents. *Psychological Bulletin, 111,* 108–126.

Barrett, K. C. (1995). A functionalist approach to shame and guilt. In J. P. Tangney & K. W. Fischer (Eds.), *Self-conscious emotions: Shame, guilt, embarrassment, and pride* (pp. 25–63). New York: Guilford Press.

Batson, D. C., & Shaw, L. L. (1991). Evidence for altruism: Toward a pluralism of prosocial motives. *Psychological Inquiry, 2,* 107–122.

Baumeister, R. F., Stillwell, A. M., & Heatherton, T, F. (1994). Guilt: An interpersonal approach. *Psychological Bulletin, 115,* 243–267.

Behrendt, H., & Ben-Ari, R. (2012). The positive side of negative emotion: The role of guilt and shame in coping with interpersonal conflict. *Journal of Conflict Resolution, 56,* 1116–1138.

Benin, M. H., & Edwards, D. A. (1990). Adolescent's chores: The difference between dual— and single—earner families. *Journal of Marriage and the Family, 55,* 361–373.

Berscheid, E., Snyder, M., & Omoto, A. M. (1989). The relationship closeness inventory: Assessing the closeness of interpersonal relationships. *Journal of Personality and Social Psychology, 57,* 792–807.

Bugental, D. B., & Grusec, J. E. (2006). Socialization processes, In N. Eisenberg (Vol. Ed.). *Handbook of child psychology: Vol. 3. Social, emotional, and personality development* (6th ed., pp. 389–428). New York: Wiley.

Calderon-Tena, C. O., Knight, G. P., & Carlo, G. (2011). The socialization of prosocial behavior tendencies among Mexican American adolescents: The role of familism values. *Cultural Diversity an Ethnic Minority Psychology, 17,* 98–106.

Card, N. A., Stucky, B. D., Sawalani, G. M., & Little, T. D. (2008). Direct and indirect aggression during childhood and adolescence: A meta-analytic review of gender differences, intercorrelations, and relations to maladjustment. *Child Development, 79,* 1185–1229.

Carlo, G. (2006). Care-based and altruistically based morality. In M. Killen & J. Smetana (Eds.), *Handbook of moral development* (pp. 551–579). Mahwah, NJ: Erlbaum.

Carlo, G., Knight, G. P., McGinley, M., Goodvin, R., & Roesch, S. C. (2010). Understanding the developmental relations between perspective taking and prosocial behaviors: A meta-analytic examination of the task-specificity hypothesis. In J. Carpendale, G. Iarocci, U. Muller, B. Sokol, & A. Young (Eds.), Self- and social-regulation: Exploring the relations between social interaction, social cognition, and the development of executive functions (pp. 234–269). Oxford, UK: Oxford University Press.

Carlo, G., & Randall, B. A. (2002). The development of a measure of prosocial behaviors for late adolescents. *Journal of Youth and Adolescence, 31*, 31–44.

Carlo, G., Randall, B. A., Rotenberg, K. J., & Armenta, B. E. (2010). *A friend in need is a friend indeed: Exploring the relations among trust beliefs, prosocial tendencies, and friendships.* (pp. 270–294). New York: Cambridge University Press.

Carlo, G., Roesch, S. C., & Melby, J. (1998). The multiplicative relations of parenting and temperament to prosocial and antisocial behaviors in adolescence. *Journal of Early Adolescence, 18*, 266–290.

Carlson, M., & Miller, N. (1987). Explanation of the relation between negative mood and helping. *Psychological Bulletin, 102*, 91–108.

Clark, M. S., & Mills, J. R. (2012). A theory of communal (and exchange) relationships. Thousand Oaks, CA: Sage.

Collins, W. A., Gleason, T., & Sesma, A. (1997). Internalization, autonomy, and relationships: Development during adolescence. In J. E. Grusec & L. Kuczynski (Eds.), *Parenting and children's internalization of values: A handbook of contemporary theory* (pp. 78–99). New York: John Wiley.

Collins, A. W., & Laursen, B. (2004). Changing relationships, changing youth: Interpersonal contexts of adolescent development. *Journal of Early Adolescence, 24*, 55–62.

Collins, W. A., & Steinberg, L. (2006). Adolescent development in interpersonal context. In W. Damon & R. M. Lerner (Series Eds.) & N. Eisenberg (Vol. Ed.), *Handbook of child psychology: Vol. 3. Social, emotional, and personality development 6th edition* (6th ed., pp. 1003–1067). Hoboken, NJ: Wiley.

Coltrane, S. (2000). Research on household labor: Modeling and measuring the social embeddedness of routine family work. *Journal of Marriage and the Family, 62*, 1208–1233.

Cooper, C. R. (1988). The role of conflict in parent-adolescent relationships. In M. R. Gunnar & W. A. Collins (Eds.), *The Minnesota Symposia on Child Psychology: Vol. 21. Development during the transition to adolescence* (pp. 181–197). Hillsdale, NJ: Erlbaum.

Davis, M. H., & Franzoi, S. L. (1991). Stability and change in adolescent self-consciousness and empathy. *Journal of Research in Personality, 25*, 70–87.

Douvan, E., & Adelson, J. (1966). *The adolescent experience.* New York: Norton.

Earley, L., & Cushway, D. (2002). The parentified child. *Clinical Child Psychology and Psychiatry, 7*, 163–178.

Eberly, M. B., & Montemayor, R. (1998). Doing good deeds: An examination of adolescent prosocial behavior in the context of parent-adolescent relationships. *Journal of Adolescent Research, 13*, 403–432.

Eberly, M. B., & Montemayor, R. (1999). Adolescent affection and helpfulness toward parents: A 2-year follow-up. *Journal of Early Adolescence, 19*, 226–248.

Eberly, M. B., Montemayor, R., & Flannery, D. J. (1993). Variation in adolescent helpfulness toward parents in a family context. *Journal of Early Adolescence, 13*, 228–244.

Eisenberg, N., Fabes, R. A., Carlo, G., Troyer, D., Speer, A. L., Karbon, M., & Switzer, G. (1992). The relations of maternal practices and characteristics to children's vicarious emotional responsiveness. *Child Development, 63,* 583–602.

Eisenberg, N., Fabes, R. A., & Spinrad, T. L. (2006). Prosocial development. In: W. Damon (Series Ed.) N. Eisenberg (Vol. Ed.), *Handbook of child psychology. Vol. 3. Social, emotional, and personality development* (6th ed., pp. 646–718). New York: Wiley.

Goodnow, J. J. (1988). Children's household work: Its nature and functions. *Psychological Bulletin, 103,* 5–26.

Goodnow, J. J., Bowes, J. M., Warton, P. M., Dawes, L. J., & Taylor, A. J. (1991). Would you ask someone else to do this task? Parents' and children's ideas about household work requests. *Developmental Psychology, 27,* 817–828.

Goodnow, J. J., & Delaney, S. (1989). Children's household work: Task differences, styles of assignment, and links to family relationships. *Journal of Applied Developmental Psychology, 10,* 209–226.

Goodnow, J. J., & Warton, P. M. (1991). The social bases of cognition: Interactions about work and their implications. *Merrill-Palmer Quarterly, 37,* 27–58.

Gouldner, A. W. (1960). The norm of reciprocity: A preliminary statement. *American Sociological Review, 25,* 161–178.

Grusec, J. E. (1991). Socializing concern for others in the home. *Developmental Psychology, 27,* 338–342.

Grusec, J. E., & Goodnow, J. J. (1994). Impact of parental discipline methods on child's internalization of values: A reconceptualization of current points of view. *Developmental Psychology, 30,* 4–19.

Grusec, J. E., Goodnow, J. J., & Cohen, L. (1996). Household work and the development of concern for others. *Developmental Psychology, 32,* 999–1007.

Hamilton, W. D. (1971). Selection of selfish and altruistic behavior in some extreme models. In J. G. Eisenberg & W. S. Dillon (Eds.), *Man and beast: Comparative social behavior* (pp. 59–91). Washington, DC: Smithsonian Institute.

Hardy, S. A., & Carlo, G. (2011). *Moral identity.* New York: Springer Science + Business Media.

Hastings, P. D., Zahn-Waxler, C., Robinson, J., Usher, B., & Bridges, D. (2000). The development of concern for others in children with behavior problems. *Developmental Psychology, 36,* 531–546.

Henderlong, J., & Lepper, M. R. (2002). The effects of praise on children's intrinsic motivation: A review and synthesis. *Psychological Bulletin, 128,* 774–795.

Hetherington, E. M., & Stanley-Hagan, M. (2002). Parenting in divorced and remarried families. In M. Bornstein (Ed.), *Handbook of Parenting* (2nd ed., pp. 287–316). Mahwah, NJ: Erlbaum.

Hilton, J. M., & Haldeman, V. A. (1991). Gender differences in the performance of household tasks by adults and children in single-parent and two-parent, two-earner families. *Journal of Family Issues, 12,* 114–130.

Hinde, R. A. (1979). *Towards understanding relationships.* New York: Academic Press.

Hinde, R. A., & Stevenson-Hinde, J. (1987). Interpersonal relationships and child development. *Developmental Review, 7,* 1–21.

Killen, M., & Turiel, E. (1998). Adolescents' and young adults' evaluations of helping and sacrificing for others. *Journal of Research on Adolescence, 8,* 355–375.

Knight, G. P., & Carlo, G. (2012). Prosocial development among Mexican American youth. *Child Development Perspectives, 6,* 258–263.

Knight, G. P., Gonzales, N. A., Saenz, D. S., Bonds, D. D., German, M., Deardorff, J., Roosav, M. W., & Updegraff, K. A. (2010). The Mexican American cultural values scale for adolescents and adults. *Journal of Early Adolescence, 30,* 444–481.

Kuczynski, L. (Ed.). (2003). *Handbook of dynamics in parent-child relations.* Thousand Oaks, California: Sage.

Kuczynski, L., & Navara, G. S. (2006). Sources of innovation and change in socialization, internalization, and acculturation. In M. Killen & J. Smetana (Eds.), *Handbook of moral development* (pp. 551–579). Mahwah, NJ: Erlbaum.

Kumru, A. (2002). Prosocial behavior within the family context and its correlates among Turkish early adolescents. *ETD collection for University of Nebraska—Lincoln.* Paper AAI3074086. Lincoln: University of Nebraska.

Larson, R. W., Richards, M. H., Moneta, G., Holmbeck, G., & Duckett, E. (1996). Changes in adolescents' daily interactions with their families from ages 10 to 18: Disengagement and transformation. *Developmental Psychology, 32,* 744–754.

Laursen, B., & Collins, W. A. (1988).Conceptual changes during adolescence and effects upon parent-child relationships. *Journal of Adolescent Research, 3,* 119–139.

Laursen, B., Coy, K. C., & Collins, W. A. (1998). Reconsidering changes in parent-child conflict across adolescence: A meta-analysis. *Child Development, 69,* 817–832.

Maccoby, E. E., & Martin, J. A. (1983). Socialization in the context of the family: Parent-child interaction. In P. H. Mussen (Series Ed.) and E. M. Hetherington (Vol. Ed.), *Handbook of child psychology. Vol. 4: Socialization, personality, and social development* (4th ed., pp. 1–101). New York: Wiley.

Miklikowska, M., Duriez, B., & Soenens, B. (2011). Family roots of empathy-related characteristics: The role of perceived maternal and paternal need support in adolescence. *Developmental Psychology, 47,* 1342–1352.

Padilla-Walker, L. M., Carlo, G., Christensen, K. J., & Yorgason J. B. (2012). Bidirectional relations between authoritative parenting and adolescents' prosocial behaviors. *Journal of Research on Adolescence, 22,* 400–408.

Padilla-Walker, L. M., & Christensen, K. J. (2011). Empathy and self-regulation as mediators between parenting and adolescents' prosocial behavior toward strangers, friends, and family. *Journal of Research on Adolescence, 21,* 545–551.

Padilla-Walker, L. M., Dyer, W. J., Yorgason, J. B., Fraser, A. M., & Coyne, S. M. (in press). Adolescents' prosocial behavior toward family, friends, and strangers: A person-centered approach. *Journal of Research on Adolescence.*

Roberts, W., & Strayer, J. (1996). Empathy, emotional expressiveness, and prosocial behavior. *Child Development, 67,* 449–470.

Rotenberg, K. J. (2010). Introduction. In K J. Rotenberg (Ed). *Interpersonal trust during childhood and adolescence.* (pp. 3–7). New York: Cambridge University Press.

Rusbult, C. E., & Agnew, C. R. (2010). *Prosocial motivation and behavior in close relationships* (pp. 327–345). Washington, DC: American Psychological Association.

Selman, R. L. (1980). *The growth of interpersonal understanding: Developmental and clinical analyses.* San Diego, CA: Academic Press.

Smetana, J. G. (1988). Adolescents' and parents' conceptions of parental authority. *Child Development, 59,* 321–335.

Smetana, J. G. (1996). Adolescent-parent conflict: Implications for adaptive and maladaptive development. In D. Cicchetti & S. L. Toth (Eds.), *Rochester Symposium on Developmental Psychopathology. Adolescence: Opportunities and challenge* (pp.1–46). Rochester, New York: University of Rochester Press.

Smetana, J. G., Tasopoulos-Chan, M., Gettman, D. C., Villalobos, M., Campione-Barr, N., & Metzger, A. (2009). Adolescents' and parents' evaluations of helping versus fulfilling personal desires in family situations. *Child Development, 80*, 280–294.

Smollar, J., & Youniss, J. (1985). Parent-adolescent relations in adolescents whose parents are divorced. *Journal of Early Adolescence, 5*, 129–144.

Staub, E. (1972). Instigation to goodness: The role of social norms and interpersonal influence. *Journal of Social Issues, 28*, 131–150.

Steinberg, L., & Silk, J. S. (2002). Parenting adolescents. In M. H. Bornstein (Ed.), *Handbook of parenting: Vol. 1. Children and parenting* (pp. 103–133). Mahwah, NJ: Erlbaum.

Steinberg, L., & Silverberg, S. B. (1986). The vicissitudes of autonomy in early adolescence. *Child Development, 57*, 841–851.

Tangney, J. P., Stuewig, J., & Mashek, D. J. (2007). Moral emotions and behavior. *Annual Review of Psychology, 58*, 345–372.

Trivers, R. L. (1971). The evolution of reciprocal altruism. *Quarterly Review of Biology, 46*, 35–57.

Wieselquist, J., Rusbult, C. E., Foster, C. A., & Agnew, C. R. (1999). Commitment, pro-relationship behavior, and trust in close relationships. *Journal of Personality and Social Psychology, 77*(5), 942–966.

Wyatt, J. M., & Carlo, G. (2002). What will my parents think? Relations among adolescents' expected parental reactions, prosocial moral reasoning, and prosocial and antisocial behaviors. *Journal of Adolescent Research, 17*, 646–666.

Youniss, J., & Smollar, J. (1985). *Adolescent relations with mothers, fathers, and friends.* Chicago: University of Chicago Press.

16

Prosocial Behaviors Toward Siblings and Grandparents

Asiye Kumru and Bilge Yağmurlu

Prosocial behavior (i.e., behavior primarily intended to benefit others; Eisenberg, 1986) has received much attention from developmental and social psychologists (see Batson, 1998; Eisenberg, Fabes, & Spinrad, 2006; for review). However, most of these studies have examined children helping nonrelatives such as strangers and friends. With the exception of evolutionary biologists, who have focused more on prosocial behavior within families in the natural world than toward strangers, comparatively little research has been undertaken on prosocial behavior toward family members. As Webster (2003) stated, the tendency to focus on prosocial behavior toward strangers could be because choosing to help strangers is thought to be a rare and noble human quality, whereas helping one's own kin is thought of as commonplace and occasionally nepotistic. However, a great deal of helping, support, caring, and altruistic behavior occurs toward multiple family members, and children and adolescents learn and develop many important prosocial skills within these close relationships.

In this chapter, we review studies that investigated prosocial behaviors displayed toward siblings and grandparents and, while doing so, we try to focus our review on research that includes adolescents. There has been a small, yet significant body of research examining prosocial behavior toward those with whom adolescents have a relationship, namely friends (Bergin, chapter 14, this volume; Wentzel, chapter 9, this volume) and family (Lewis, chapter 15, this volume). However, as many researchers and readers of developmental psychology are aware, very few studies in the prosocial development literature focus solely on siblings or grandparents; and few of them include adolescents only. Thus, in this chapter we focus on the prosocial behaviors of adolescents toward siblings and grandparents, while reviewing some relevant research conducted on younger age groups.

We begin by briefly explaining the nature of prosocial behaviors toward family members, as well as motivational factors (selfish, moral) and definitional issues related to those behaviors. Evolutionary (kin selection, reciprocal altruism) and relational perspectives on the origins of prosocial behaviors are reviewed. Finally, we present the literature about the predictors of prosocial behavior toward siblings and grandparents and the role of social and cultural context, and provide suggestions for future research.

Definitional Issues of Prosocial Behavior

Prosocial behavior can be defined as acts that serve to protect or enhance the welfare of others (Carlo & Randall, 2001; Eisenberg et al., 2006). This is a very general description of the construct, which represents a broad category of acts including, but not limited to, helping, sharing, caring, comforting, cooperating, defending, rescuing, and volunteering (Bryant & Croskenberg, 1980). Any of these behaviors may serve different functions, so there is a need for careful distinctions between the various types of prosocial behaviors and underlying motives for those behaviors.

People may act prosocially for several reasons. For instance, why do we help or why do we do a favor for a friend? We help or do a favor because it is in our own best interest, because we have no choice, because we expect to see the help or favor reciprocated, or because we have truly genuine concern for the welfare of another. In other words, people can act prosocially for selfish reasons, to get rewards, or to avoid punishment. One might want to avoid negative consequences that follow from not doing what social norms prescribe (Berkowitz, 1972) or might also try to get benefits, expecting that those whom they have helped will reciprocate as a result of powerful and seemingly universal norms of reciprocity (Mauss, 1954). One might act to maintain his or her positive mood or help to alleviate one's own distress as well (Carlson & Miller, 1987). Alternatively, an individual might just act prosocially for moral reasons guided by values and principles that lead them to promote others' welfare (Staub, 2005). As can be seen, the motivations for displays of concern for others are diverse, and those motivations may comprise important distinctions for understanding prosocial behavior, but relatively little research has addressed this issue (see also Eisenberg & Spinrad, chapter 2, this volume).

It is also important to note that motivational factors might be different for prosocial behaviors in different contexts. In the family context the relationship is more related to duties, obligations, and responsibilities, and close relationships require more commitment and resource allocation than any other type of relationship. In close relationships (e.g., kinship relationships), people often share communally with one another or give aid to another based on a less self-serving desire (Fiske, 1992; Haslam & Fiske, 1999). On the other hand, although prosocial behavior is not always done for selfish reasons among strangers, people might act based on a relatively more self-centered desire to maximize the ratio of their benefits over their costs when interacting with strangers (Cialdini, Brown, Lewis,

Luce, & Neuberg, 1997). However, unlike distant social relationships, people usually experience relatively higher levels of empathic concern and genuine concern for another person's welfare in close relationships (Aron, Aron, & Smallon, 1992; Clark & Reis, 1988). Maner and Gailliot (2006) found that when controlled for egoistic motivators (negative affect, oneness); empathic concern was linked to participants' willingness to help a kin member but not a stranger. Indeed, a body of research suggests that different motives can drive affiliative behaviors in different relationship contexts (Reis, Collins, & Berscheid, 2000). Thus, in this sense, it seems that motives that underlie prosocial acts are multidimensional and may differ depending on whether the target is a stranger or a close family member.

Another reason it is important to make distinctions between potential recipients of aid is because identity and characteristics of the potential recipient of prosocial behavior seem to be an important factor in children's concern for others' welfare (de Guzman, Carlo, & Edwards, 2008). Children's prosocial behaviors are influenced by the nature of the ongoing social interactions between a potential recipient and the benefactor (Staub & Noerenberg, 1981). Although data pertaining to this issue are relatively scarce, it is obvious that children do not help all persons equally (Eisenberg, 1983). The recipient of prosocial behavior tends to change with the child's age. Even at very young ages (i.e., 14 months old), infants were found to have motivation to help other adults, even if they were not familiar peers or family members (Warneken & Tomasello, 2007). As children grow older, the overall rate of prosocial behaviors increase and also the recipients of the prosocial behaviors become more exclusive (Hay, 2009). In the early childhood years, children start to direct their prosocial behaviors more toward family members and friends than other people (Hay & Cook, 2007). Studies show that children are more likely to comfort their mothers than a stranger (Young, Fox, & Zahn-Waxler, 1999) and that they prefer to help people who are relatively important in their life such as family members (Killen & Truiel, 1998; van der Mark, van IJzendoorn, Bakermans-Kranenburg, 2002; Young et al., 1999).

However, in a study with 3- to 11-year-old children living in the United States and the Philippines, de Guzman et al. (2008) found frequency of prosocial behaviors varied as a function of kinship, but differently for the community groups. They observed that children in the Filipino sample were generally more prosocial toward relatives, while children in the U.S. sample showed more prosocial behaviors toward nonrelatives. Also, they found that frequency of children's prosocial behavior varied as a function of the age of social companion for young (3- to 5-year-old) and older (6- to 10-year-old) children. In comparison to three different age groups as a recipient of prosocial behaviors (infants/toddlers, children, and adults), young children (3–5 years old) directed more prosocial behaviors toward adults (in the case of relatives) and infant/toddlers (in the case of nonrelatives) in both samples. For relatives older children displayed more prosocial behaviors toward infants/toddlers in both samples; however, for nonrelatives prosocial behavior was directed the most toward other children in the U.S. sample while it was directed toward other children the least in the Filipino sample. In another U.S. sample, a similar pattern was observed, with teens reporting the highest level of prosocial behavior toward friends and then family members (Padilla-Walker & Christensen, 2010). Thus, serious attention should be given to examine the potential effects of recipients' characteristics as well as contextual and cultural factors on children's prosocial responding.

Finally, it is also vital to differentiate different types or forms of prosocial behaviors. Studies suggest that there are different types of prosocial behaviors and that these types are related differently to theoretically related constructs (Carlo & Randall, 2001). In fact, there is ample empirical evidence on task-specific forms of cognitive, emotive, and personality correlates of prosocial behaviors (e.g., Carlo, Knight, Eisenberg, & Rotenberg, 1991). Also, some prosocial behaviors are evident in childhood, while others are not frequently observed until later childhood or adolescence (see Eisenberg et al., 2006). This suggests different developmental trajectories and correlates of different types of prosocial behaviors.

Classification of Prosocial Behaviors within the Family Context

On a daily basis, varieties of prosocial acts can be observed in all families across cultures. However, we know little about the extent to which mechanisms and factors relate to different prosocial behaviors toward different family members. Thus, this chapter examines different types of prosocial behaviors, specifically helping, affection, and sharing toward siblings and grandparents. Helping can be defined as offering physical assistance, emotional support, tangible assistance, supervision, teaching, nurturance, or general aid to another person (Midlarsky & Hannah, 1995). This instrumental behavior is viewed as an aspect of socialization that is a response to family needs (Eberly & Montemayor, 1998). Unlike altruism, which requires the actor to be primarily motivated by other-serving goals, helping has fewer constraints with respect to intention or outcome of prosocial behavior.

Affection is defined as a volunteered anticipation of family members' feelings and desires such as "giving a compliment" or saying "I love you." This considerate action has affectional value (Goodnow & Warton, 1991) that contributes to the quality of relationships, but affection may be subtle and go overtly unrecognized during adolescence. Eberly and Montemayor (1998) suggest that the presence or absence of this behavior might reflect rapport and cohesiveness in adolescent-parent relationships. Thus, these affectionate behaviors are not expected to be required or part of a daily routine, rather they are voluntary. Eberly and Montemayor (1998) also found that adolescent helpfulness and affection were related but separate dimensions. They suggest that helpfulness might serve functional purposes for the family, but it can be perceived as emotional support by the adolescent, especially when family members are distressed. However, in many cases, helping behavior does not directly address the emotional needs of the family member.

Sharing is an another type of prosocial behavior that exemplifies the willing-ness to take the welfare of others into account but it is a special case of a more gen-eral dilemma in terms of demanding the sacrifice of material possessions by the sharer for the benefit of others. For a child, sharing requires the ability to recog-nize the inequality between the resources of oneself and another and to overcome the desire to keep the resources for oneself (Hay, 2009). For that reason, sharing is relatively rare in comparison with helping at younger ages (Eisenberg, 2005; Grusec, 1991). Studies have shown that preschool children are less likely to share than to exhibit other forms of prosocial behavior such as cooperating (Dunfield, Kuhlmeier, O'Connell, & Kelley, 2011) or helping (Birch & Billman, 1986; Grusec, 1991). Also, it is recognized that sharing occurs at low rates in very young children (Hay, Caplan, Castle, & Stimson, 1991). A recent experiment examining sharing has shown that 18-month-old children share toys with adult playmates much less often, require substantial scaffolding from the partner to behave prosocially, and are less generous than 24-month-olds (Brownell, Iesue, Nichols, & Svetlova, 2013). Sharing (i.e., resource allocations with friends and acquaintances) increases from early to middle childhood (Malti, Gummerum, Keller, Chaparro, & Buchmann, 2012). As children move from middle to late childhood, prosocial decisions increasingly incorporate more differentiated concerns including fairness, moral-ity, reciprocity, need, merit, and social reputation (Almas, Alexander, Sorensen, & Tungodden, 2010). In fact, being accepted by others at the kindergarten age leads to an increased willingness to share valuable resources with others on the part of the elementary school-age child (Malti et al., 2012). There is also some empirical data on sharing behavior suggesting that with increasing age sharing varies as a function of context (Benenson, Markovits, Roy, & Denko, 2003). Researchers who examine food-sharing behavior in several species believe that certain basic contex-tual factors, such as biological relatedness, survival value of resources, hunger, and sex modulate food-sharing behaviors. Indeed, sharing is greater among relatives than among nonrelatives (Ma & Leung, 1993). Similarly, Markovits, Benenson, and Kramer (2003) found that sharing was higher between siblings than classmates and strangers. They also found that the quality of the relationship has a greater impact on expected sharing with classmates than with siblings. Taken together, these studies indicate that beginning in toddlerhood, sharing behavior increases over middle to later childhood, but further longitudinal studies should assess dif-ferent types of sharing behaviors among kin versus nonkin with a comparable instrument from toddlerhood to adolescence.

Theoretical Perspectives

Approaches to explain prosocial acts are numerous and span different disciplines (Hawley, chapter 3, this volume; Padilla-Walker, chapter 7, this volume). For that reason we limit ourselves to two approaches, including evolutionary and relational perspectives that are more relevant to understanding prosocial responding toward family members. First we will review evolutionary perspectives that focus on explaining ultimate reasons for the occurrence of prosocial behavior and then introduce relational perspectives that stress more proximate mechanisms of how prosocial behaviors emerge.

EVOLUTIONARY THEORIES OF PROSOCIAL BEHAVIORS

Evolutionary theories help us understand whether, how, and why a strong prosocial orientation may have evolved through natural selection processes (see Hawley, chapter 3, this volume). The evolutionary perspective on prosocial acts proposes that these behaviors depend on genetic relatedness and the reproductive value of the recipient (Burnstein, Crandall, & Kitayama, 1994). In the literature, two evolutionary processes in particular have received extensive attention: kin selection or inclusive fitness (Hamilton, 1964) and reciprocal altruism (Trivers, 1971). From the evolutionary perspective, some researchers have tested gene-centered theories of evolution claiming that when an individual sacrifices his or her own life to protect the lives of kin, this is acting in the interest of one's own genes, while others go beyond that to explain why organisms that have selfish genes at times tend to behave in a cooperative manner with certain nonkin.

Inclusive fitness theory proposes that people should be biased to distribute more assistance and resources to kin than to nonkin. To explain altruism (see Hawley, chapter 3, this volume, for clarification on the difference between psychological and biological altruism) and cooperation in evolutionary theory, Hamilton (1964) applied the Mendelian particulate inheritance theory, stating that since genes are inherited relatives will share more genes than do nonrelatives. Studies have consistently shown that resources are almost always distributed preferentially to closer biological relatives (Berte, 1988; Judge, 1995). Also, individuals seem to be more willing to take greater risks to help close biological relatives (Korchmaros & Kenny, 2001), provide assistance to kin more readily than to nonkin, and are more likely to help close kin rather than distant kin, especially in life-or-death situations (Burnstein et al., 1994; Neyer & Lang, 2003). According to Hamilton (1964), the likelihood of altruistic behavior could be predicted accurately on the basis of the degree of genetic closeness, the cost of the behavior to the actor, and the amount of benefit to the recipient. However, this does not explain prosocial behavior that takes place between nonkin.

Trivers (1971) introduced *reciprocal altruism theory* to explain why organisms who have selfish genes at times tend to behave in a cooperative manner with certain nonkin. This theory suggests that individuals who cooperate and help others in need would increase the possibility to benefit from reciprocation when they need help. This reception of aid is likely to facilitate individual survival and reproductive output. In support of the hypothesis of evolutionary selection for reciprocal altruism, examples of behavioral reciprocity were found in most social mammals, including bats, primates, and humans (de Waal, 1996). Later on, de Waal and Brosnan (2006) also observed some aspects of human reciprocity in other primates, especially chimpanzees.

However, some social scientists explicitly state that evolutionary processes cannot explain altruistic behaviors toward unrelated strangers (e.g., McAndrew, 2002). In fact, in the literature many researchers focus almost entirely on discrete proximate predictors of prosocial behavior without paying much attention to the conceptual relations between these predictors and the deeper origins of the human capacity for prosocial behavior. Although these evolutionary theories do not replace existing social psychological models of prosocial behaviors, they may help unify these models by locating their explanatory mechanisms within a broader conceptual framework. In other words, evolutionary approaches can be very useful in gaining a more complete understanding of deeper conceptual relations between the many different proximal predictors of prosocial behavior and its origin within human beings.

RELATIONAL PERSPECTIVE TO PROSOCIAL BEHAVIORS

The relational perspective seeks to understand the dynamics of social interaction that occur within the enduring context of relationships. It describes relationships generally as a series of interactions over time between individuals who are known to each other (Lollis & Kuczynski, 1997). A relational perspective begins with two primary premises to understand an individual's behavior: psychological experience always implies a connection or a relationship with another person and it is always dynamic and changing. The relational perspective proposes that since people are oriented to relationships, social life can be defined as a process of seeking, making, maintaining, adjusting, repairing construing, and sanctioning relationships. It claims that people generally want to relate to each other and feel committed to the basic types of relationships such as kinship and friendship (Fiske, 1992). According to Fiske (1992), people's intentions with regard to other people are essentially sociable, and their social goals inherently relational. Fiske's (1992) theory of relational models proposes that there are four fundamental ways for people to relate to one another and that each relational model has its own moral rules. These four models are communal sharing (i.e., people treat all members of a category as equivalent and undifferentiated as in close kinship ties), authority ranking (i.e., people attend to their positions in a linear ordering like relations across generations and between genders in many traditional societies), equality matching (i.e., each person is entitled to the same amount as each other person in the relationship, like acquaintances or colleagues), and market pricing (i.e., people orient to ratio values). Fiske (1992) argued that in order to generate, understand, coordinate, and evaluate social relationships people rarely use any one of these models alone, rather they use two or more models in different phases of an inter-action or at different, hierarchically nested levels.

Furthermore, the relational perspective emphasizes that close relation-ships have a history from which their qualities derive. According to Hinde and Stevenson-Hinde (1987), a relationship consists of a series of interactions over time. The behavior manifested in interactions relies on relationship qualities and individual characteristics of both members. Also, the strength and quality of the relationship to a potential recipient might be related to the likelihood of expe-riencing empathy for the recipient and of adopting the recipient's perspective (Batson & Shaw, 1991).

Eberly and Montemayor (1998) have described the occurrence of prosocial behavior as a function of relationship quality. They suggest that the recipients of the behavior are important since research and theory in social psychology have advocated that when the beneficiary is considered, the probability of prosocial behavior is affected through norms of reciprocity and social responsibility, kin-ship, and anticipation of social rewards including receiving help in the future (Fiske, 1992; Hamilton, 1971; Staub, 1972). Scholars have noted that a great deal of everyday helping originates from the relationship between the helper and the recipient. For example, when family members are in need, help is typically pro-vided because the role in the relationship itself demands such behavior. Helping is simply a part of what it means to occupy certain roles in relation to others. It has been shown that expectations of giving and receiving aid are part of the role defini-tions of "family members" (see Amato, 1990) and there is cross-cultural supportive evidence from anthropological research for this notion (Essock-Vitale & McGuire, 1980; see also de Guzman, Do, & kok, chapter 11, this volume).

Prosocial Behaviors Toward Multiple Family Members

PROSOCIAL BEHAVIORS TOWARD SIBLINGS

The existence (or absence) of siblings has an impact on individual development (see Bjorklund & Pellegrini, 2002). For almost all children (except those who are reared in institutions), the developmental context is constituted by the family. This is sometimes in the form of nuclear family, comprising mother, father, and siblings; and sometimes in the form of extended family, also including other second-degree and sometimes third-degree relatives of the parents (especially for those who live in rural regions and tribal societies). Within families, researchers have identified diverse patterns of interaction (Moos & Moos, 1986). Vertical relationships are those that a child has with a person who has greater knowledge and social power (i.e., child-adult relationship). Horizontal relationships are characterized by indi-viduals with the same amount of social power (i.e., child-child relationship). These two kinds of relationships serve different functions. More specifically, vertical rela-tionships are primarily characterized by protection and security. Basic social skills are also first observed within vertical relationships. However, these skills later develop in the context of horizontal relationships as the child engages in cooperative and competitive behavior with peers (Hartup, 1989). While the peer relationship is a horizontal relationship characterized by reciprocity and the parent-child relationship is characterized by complementarity, sibling interaction requires special attention, as it is mainly associated with reciprocal features. However, differential effects of age, birth interval, and sex on sibling development, also point to the complementary side of the relationship (Dunn, 1983).

Researchers have identified four independent dimensions of sibling relationships: warmth/closeness, relative power/status, conflict, and rivalry. The warmth/closeness dimension includes helping nurturance, intimacy, companionship, and admiration (Midlarsky, Hannah, & Corley, 1995). Caretaking behavior, which is another aspect of warmth/closeness, may contain challenge and punishment as well as concern (Bryant, 1989). Researchers believe that sibling relationships provide one of the most stable and powerful developmental contexts for the transmission of social behaviors, including both prosocial and antisocial behavior (Stormshak, Bullock, & Falkenstein, 2009). Siblings are a source of support and skill development; relationships among siblings help the development of self-regulation and emotional understanding (Padilla-Walker, Harper, & Jensen, 2010).

As we review the literature on prosocial behavior, we see that findings indicate a general age-related increase in the level of prosocial behavior displayed by children. This is partly due to the considerable improvement in empathy, self-regulation, and sociocognitive skills in the preschool years (Knafo, Zahn-Waxler, Van Hulle, Robinson, & Rhee, 2008). Studies that examined prosocial behaviors among *siblings* have also revealed an increase in prosocial behavior both in the preschool years (Pepler, Abramovitch, & Corter, 1981) and in late childhood (ages 8 to 11; Tucker, Updegraff, McHale, & Crouter, 1999).

The findings with regard to the effect of birth interval on positive social development are not clear-cut. While the literature shows that older children are more likely to display prosocial acts toward their younger siblings, it also appears that having an older sibling is more advantageous for the development of empathic responding in younger siblings, rather than vice versa (Tucker et al., 1999). Nevertheless, these studies usually assess the role of having siblings, or having younger versus older siblings in prosocial acts of children in general, and do not specifically assess sibling-oriented prosocial behavior.

Gender composition also appears to have some role in the prosocial behavior of sibling dyads. It has been found that in siblings, boy/boy dyads report lower levels of positive relationship qualities like caring, intimacy, and conflict resolution than the boy/girl or girl/girl dyads (Cole & Kerns, 2001). Older girl siblings are also reported to be more prosocial than older boy siblings (Abramovich, Corter, & Lando, 1979). In different studies Wenger (1983, 1989) found that by age 5–8, girls showed more nurturance and prosocial responsibility to their 2- to 3-year-old siblings than did boys. Furthermore, studies have also revealed that having a sister is associated with displaying more prosocial acts (contrary to competitive behaviors) than having a brother (Van Lange, Otten, De Bruin, & Joireman, 1997). It must be noted that, in general, the influence of gender composition of the siblings is more significant for older age groups, while its role is negligible in siblings' prosocial behaviors in preschool years (Pepler et al., 1981).

There are few studies that examine how parenting and parent-child interaction are related with prosocial behaviors among siblings. It is usually reported that affectionate parenting increases prosocial sibling interaction in young children (Volling & Belsky, 1992). Bryant and Crockenberg (1980) focused on prosocial behaviors (comforting, sharing, helping) among preschool-age daughters and found that for both older and younger siblings, parenting behavior was a more significant predictor of sibling prosocial behavior than was child behavior. Sensitive maternal responding to children's expressed needs have a facilitating role in children's comforting and sharing behaviors. A similar pattern has been reported for adolescents. Studies conducted with youth reveal that their prosocial acts toward family members were predicted by positive mothering, showing that the quality of parent-child relationship is very important for positive social behaviors displayed toward family members (Kumru, 2002).

Experiencing sensitive parenting may increase prosocial behavior through modeling and may also increase sympathy and empathy of the child by decreasing self-concern (Hoffman, 1975). Findings have also revealed that attachment between the child and mother predicts early adolescents' prosocial behavior by increasing interdependency (Eberly & Montemayor, 1998). On the other hand, negative maternal child-rearing behaviors like high maternal control increase sibling conflict (Volling & Belsky, 1992), and high maternal disapproval (unsolicited negative behavior) is associated with less comforting and sharing among siblings (Bryant & Crockenberg, 1980). According to Hoffman (1975), power assertion and restrictive control evoke fear and anger in the child, which increases personal distress (a self-focused, aversive emotional reaction; Eisenberg, 1986). Self-concern then impedes the child from focusing on the needy party's distress or harm, and decreases the likelihood of displaying prosocial behavior.

Although it may sound contradictory, studies have also revealed that maternal ignoring is positively correlated with prosocial behavior among siblings. In a study by Bryant and Crockenberg (1980), when mothers ignored frequently, both older and younger children were more likely to request prosocial behavior and ask their siblings for help. It appears that when mothers are unavailable for their children, the siblings may turn to each other for help and comforting. So, such an adverse condition has the potential to stimulate prosocial interaction between siblings, despite the possible detrimental impact of such an environment. In such situations, an older child may be especially likely to actively engage with their sibling. A similar result was reported by Whiting and Whiting (1975), who found that children who were responsible for caretaking in the family were also more prosocial in different ways. These findings suggest that the roles of the child and expectations from him/her in the family might have a facilitating role in the development of prosocial behavior, especially toward siblings. This may directly increase the prosocial behavior of older siblings through forcing them to be the substitute care providers and may also indirectly increase prosocial behavior of the younger child through modeling; the younger sibling may learn positive social acts by observing and imitating the older sibling (Pepler et al., 1981). In summary, studies suggest that there is an age-related increase in the level of prosocial behavior toward siblings in preschool years and late childhood. However, further studies are needed to examine differential effects of age, birth interval, and sex composition in the levels and types of sibling-oriented prosocial behavior during childhood as well as adolescence. Family relationship features, particularly affectionate and sensitive parenting, increase prosocial sibling interaction in children and adolescents. Again, more research is needed to explore how parenting styles, parent's child-rearing behaviors, and quality of the child's relationships with his/her mother and father as well as grandparents are related with prosocial behaviors among siblings. Now, we will explore the characteristics of the grandparent-grandchild relationship and review the literature about children's and adolescents' prosocial behaviors within this relationship context.

PROSOCIAL BEHAVIORS TOWARD GRANDPARENTS

Adolescence involves various transitions that may modify a youth's relationship with grandparents as well as parents. The quality and the meaning of grandparent-child relationships are transformed during early adolescence, but it is not clear how extensive these changes are for most families. Nor is it understood how the transformations are shaped by the interaction of many factors, including adolescents' and grandparents' characteristics and the contexts in which these dyadic relationship are embedded, such as culture, socioeconomic status of the family, and the nature of the relationship between parents and grandparents (see Monserud, 2008). The literature indicates that the modification of children's relationships with grandparents during adolescence is mixed (Creasey & Koblewski, 1991). While some studies have shown that contact with grandparents tends to lessen during the transition from childhood to adolescence (Roberto & Stoes, 1992), others have displayed that the significance of grandparents and the desire for contact with them does not decrease in adolescence (Kornhaber & Woodward, 1981). It seems that older children may tend to spend less time with grandparents, but they still report high levels of affection and respect for their grandparents (Van Ranst, Verschueren, & Macroen, 1995). In a study with Turkish early adolescents, Kumru (2002) found that for both boys and girls, younger age groups showed more prosocial behaviors toward grandparents than older age (adolescence) groups, as reported by mothers.

Previous studies have shown that parents mediate the relationship between grandparents and the grandchild (Attar-Schwartz, Tan, Buchanan, Flouri, &

Griggs, 2009). Indeed, parents can bridge the generation gap between grandparents and grandchildren by acting as "gatekeepers." The literature provides supporting evidence for the parent-as-mediator theory by showing that parents affect these relationships by setting examples and providing opportunities for interaction between grandparents and their grandchildren (Block, 2000; Fergusson, Maughan, & Golding, 2008). It has been shown that when the parents and grandparents have a high quality relationship, the grandparents are more likely to be important figures in the lives of children (Mueller & Elder, 2003). However, there is no research examining the mediating effects of parents on their children's prosocial responding toward their grandparents within the family context.

Parental behavior associated with the promotion of attachment quality may encourage children's and adolescents' prosocial and sympathetic responsiveness toward family members. One would expect that higher quality of attachment to parents should also predict more frequent prosocial acts toward grandparents. In attempts to explain individual differences in prosocial responding, research has highlighted the contributions of parent-child relationship qualities (e.g., warmth and responsiveness; Barnet, 1987; Eisenberg & McNally, 1993) and parenting characteristics (e.g., parenting styles; Eisenberg & Valiente, 2002; see also Padilla-Walker, chapter 7, this volume). There is evidence that parental warmth and closeness as well as authoritative parenting practices promote early adolescents' prosocial acts toward grandparents (Kumru, 2002). Nevertheless, again, the existing literature on how parental as well as grandparental characteristics influence children's and adolescents' prosocial responding toward their grandparents is lacking.

Finally, researchers have examined several important variables linked to prosocial responding toward mostly strangers (see Eisenberg et al., 2006, for a review), among which personal dispositional variables, such as sociocognitive and emotive factors, appear to play a particularly important role. This body of work suggests that there are certain cognitive necessities and prerequisites involved in helping others (Carlo et al., 1991). Indeed, more sophisticated types of reasoning have been linked to higher prosocial responding (Batson, 1991; Carlo, Koller, Eisenberg, DaSilva, & Frohlich, 1996; Eisenberg, 1986; Knight, Johnson, Carlo, & Eisenberg, 1994). Furthermore, while there are some inconsistencies in the literature (Eisenberg, 1986; Feshbach, 1987), generally, studies have also indicated significant positive links between prosocial behaviors and perspective-taking (Eisenberg, Miller, Shell, McNalley, & Shea, 1991; Wentzel, Filisetti, & Looney, 2007). Similarly, emotional variables such as empathy, or the experience of emotions congruent with those of others, have been linked to the performance of prosocial acts (Batson et al., 1989; Betancourt, 1990; Carlo et al., 1991; Eisenberg, Guthrie, Murphy, Shepard, Cumberland, & Carlo, 1999; Iannotti, 1985; Roberts & Strayer, 1996).

However, studies examining prosocial acts toward grandparents provide inconsistent evidence. In one study adolescents who had high levels of sympathy and concern for unfortunate others displayed more prosocial behaviors toward their grandparents (Kumru, 2002). However, Padilla-Walker and Christensen (2011) found that empathy did not predict prosocial behavior displayed by adolescents toward the family members, but only toward strangers and friends (however, this study did not include grandparents explicitly). Similarly contrary to existing literature, Kumru (2002) found that prosocial moral reasoning did not significantly predict prosocial behaviors toward grandparents for either adolescent or parent reports of adolescents' behavior. At first glance, this is rather surprising. Yet, prior research has shown evidence that prosocial moral reasoning is more likely to be associated with prosocial actions that are high in cost (e.g., donating money) rather than low in cost (e.g., helping pick up dropped paper clips; see Eisenberg et al., 2006, for review). Eisenberg and Shell (1986) proposed that low-cost prosocial behavior might be performed automatically without much moral consideration. Indeed, prosocial moral reasoning reflects an orientation to the needs of self or others in conflict situations where issues of justice, fairness, or caring are prevalent. Helping, sharing, and showing affection to others within the family may require little cost and may be performed automatically without moral considerations. As mentioned previously, prosocial behaviors toward family members, such as grandparents, are often motivated by social norms and role expectations rather than moral principles.

Taken together, existing research suggests there is much to be done in the area of prosocial behavior within the grandparent-grandchild relationship. Although research has found grandparent involvement to be associated with adolescents' prosocial behavior, this has mostly been prosocial behavior toward those outside the family (see Yorgason & Gustafson, chapter 10, this volume). Thus, it will be important for future research to continue to examine aspects of the grandparent-grandchild relationship, as well as the mediating role of the grandparent-parent relationship, that might foster adolescents' prosocial behavior toward their grandparents. In the following section, we will discuss the important contextual factors modulating prosocial acts within the family.

The Role of Social and Cultural Context in Prosocial Behaviors Toward Multiple Family Members

Studies show that in many species greater relatedness is associated with higher levels of prosocial behaviors, and humans are no exception (see Steward-Williams, 2007). It is plausible to suggest that such prosocial behaviors that arise from a need situation in the family are more prevalent in social and cultural contexts that endorse interdependence. Many studies indicate that genetic relatedness increases prosocial behaviors (Smith, Kish, & Crawford, 1987; Webster, 2003). However, to understand how or why prosociality could have evolved, we also need to have an understanding of the physical and social conditions in which people live (Simpson & Beckes, 2010). In general, interdependence is valued more in underdeveloped societies, where the social system does not provide extensive institutions to take responsibility for its dependent people, such as the elderly and sick, the orphans, and the disabled. Hence, valuing needs of family members over personal needs, interdependence, and self-sacrifice are reinforced over values such as self-reliance and autonomy. Kağıtçıbaşı (2007) calls this a "functionally extended family" and suggests that an important duty of the family members in these societies is to take care of their elderly and vulnerable members.

Consistent with the assumption that economic difficulties influence mutual support among family members in traditional societies, the Value of Children study (Kağıtçıbaşı, 1984) indicated that interdependence, or "being close, loyal and faithful to parents," was highly valued in adult children in Indonesia, the Philippines, Turkey, and Thailand. Old-age security values (being seen as a source of economic and psychological security in old age) were highly endorsed in Singapore, the Republic of Korea, Turkey, and Taiwan. This value was not endorsed by people in industrialized countries such as Germany, showing that children were raised to become independently functioning adults and were not expected to support their elderly parents. Lower education, income level, and social security were related to the old-age security values. In less developed countries where parents expect to be taken care of by their children, they have more children (Kağıtçıbaşı, 1982). It is also plausible that in such a sociocultural context, children and adolescents display more prosocial behaviors toward family members, including their siblings and grandparents.

This viewpoint is also supported by the studies that suggest that prosocial behaviors directed toward family might be different from the prosocial behaviors directed toward friends and strangers. The finding that empathy did not predict prosocial behavior displayed by adolescents toward the family members but only toward strangers and friends (Padilla-Walker & Christensen, 2011) suggested that planned helping is displayed more as part of the child's responsibilities in the family and may not require empathizing with the recipient of the prosocial act. A study conducted with university undergraduate students (Stewart-Williams, 2007) showed that as the cost of helping increased, kin (siblings and cousins) received a larger share of the help given and acquaintances or friends received a smaller share. Cultural studies suggest that identification with one's group is related to higher levels of in-group prosocial behaviors, and this might be especially relevant in collectivistic cultures, where people may tend to enact high levels of positive behaviors to in-group but not to out-group members (Triandis, 1994). Thus, the context and recipient of prosocial behavior may be a particularly important consideration. These findings show that prosocial behaviors are influenced by people's beliefs, which are related to their cultural values. Hence, it is important to understand the cultural context in order to explain the processes underlying differences in prosocial behaviors. This requires investigating the role of context and avoiding making generalizations from one context to another (Harkness, 2002). Within-culture differences must of course also be taken into account, as these can sometimes be bigger than between-culture differences (Betancourt, Hardin, & Manzi, 1992).

Conclusions and Future Directions

The study of prosocial behavior toward multiple family members is progressing, yet incomplete. Describing a behavior as "prosocial" focuses on the consequences of the behavior (e.g., benefiting another person or group) but avoids any implicit or explicit assumptions about whether the behavior is motivated by altruistic or egoistic concerns. The question of which motivation underlies prosocial actions is an important one if we want to understand what facilitates prosocial development in different relationship contexts.

There is ample evidence that prosocial behavior is a multidimensional construct (Carlo & Randall, 2001; Padilla-Walker & Carlo, chapter 1, this volume). In this line of research, studies suggest that there are different types of prosocial behaviors and that these types are related differently to theoretically related constructs. There is ample empirical evidence on task-specific forms of cognitive, emotive, and personality correlates of prosocial behaviors (e.g., Carlo et al., 1991). From this point, it is important to ask: In the course of prosocial development do different types of prosocial acts take different form or function in kin versus nonkin contexts, depending on the recipient of prosocial behavior? Analysis of contextual factors will help to better understand which settings are most appropriate for interventions to promote different types of prosocial behaviors. Also, examining of prosocial behaviors toward multiple family members in different ethnic and cultural groups may reveal both cultural specificity and universality. Understanding that positive aspects of human functioning are subject to external influence, and that as a society we can act to reduce violence and aggression by supporting kindness and compassion, we can provide an opportunity to translate social science into effective social family policy and practice.

We are building a body of knowledge about human prosociality across fields, including psychology, sociology, anthropology, biology, even economics. The interest in the development of concern for welfare of family members is not limited to examination by research psychologists. Because of its breadth, research on prosocial behavior can facilitate the development of interdisciplinary and multidisciplinary collaborations and perspectives for both theory and application. Researchers with different approaches have used various measures. Diversity of measurement is appropriate for studying prosociality across disciplines, but at some point we must be able to compare the findings of different research groups. Also, it is important to note that self-reports (i.e., narratives, interviews) in the assessment of prosocial behavior have some limitations regarding prosocial acts in the real world. We need to include direct observations, physiological measures, and other-report (e.g., peers, teachers, parents) measures more frequently. It is obvious that progress in this area of research depends on using more sophisticated research designs (e.g., longitudinal studies and multivariate approaches) and developing culturally valid measures of prosocial behavior—including studies that assess the ethnic measurement equivalence of such measures (for an example, see McGinley, Opal, Richaud, & Mesurado, chapter 13, this volume).

In closing, researchers have documented that adolescents are prosocial toward their siblings and grandparents, but some questions remain to be answered. For instance, how does the temporary increase in conflict for adolescent relationships with extended family members influence adolescent prosocial behavior toward multiple family members, and how might age and gender serve as moderators of this process? Does positive relationship interaction co-occur with adolescent-siblings and -grandparent conflict? The role of realignment of the child's relationship with extended family members on an early adolescent's prosocial behaviors within the family context remains a virtually unexplored area. In fact, it is important to note that childhood is a critical period when the family first exerts its influence on a child's prosocial development. Family is the first context where children express their prosociality and becomes the training ground for future prosocial behaviors. Thus, there is a need for longitudinal studies examining prosocial behaviors toward different family members across childhood and adolescence and even across the life span, given the opportunities for children to express prosocial behaviors toward their siblings, parents, and grandparents well into older adulthood.

We know little regarding the links between sociocognitive/socioemotive skills and all sorts of prosocial behaviors including helping, sharing, and caring in families. Evolutionary theories suggest that one of the driving forces behind prosocial behavior is sympathy, especially if members of one's immediate social groups are involved (de Waal, 2008). Human infants may be born as "natural altruists" (e.g., Hoffman, 1975), may be especially responsive to socialization influences, or may possess experience-expectant predispositions that are readily shaped by intensely caring, reciprocal, and prosocial human social environments (Dunn, 2006; Hastings, Utendale, & Sullivan, 2007). In either case, to understand the origins of prosocial behavior and what drives its growth, we must examine the effects of family socialization agents like siblings and grandparents as well as parents in the development of such emotions and social and moral cognitions related to prosocial behavior.

References

Abramovitch, R., Corter, C., & Lando, B. (1979). Sibling interaction in the home. *Child Development, 50,* 997–1003.

Almas I., Alexander W., Sørensen C. E. Ø., & Tungodden, B. (2010). Fairness and the development of inequality acceptance. *Science, 328,* 1176–1178.

Amato, P. (1990). Personality and social network involvement as predictors of helping behavior in everyday life. *Social Psychology Quarterly, 53*, 31–43.

Aron, A., Aron, E. N., & Smollan, D. (1992). Inclusion of other in the Self Scale and the structure of interpersonal closeness. *Journal of Personality and Social Psychology, 63*, 596–612.

Attar-Schwartz, S., Tan, J. P., Buchanan, A., Flouri, E., & Griggs, J. (2009). Grandparenting and adolescent adjustment in two-parent biological, lone-parent, and stepfamilies. *Journal of Family Psychology, 23*, 67–75.

Batson, C. D. (1991). *The altruism question: Toward a social-psychological answer*. Hillsdale, NJ: Erlbaum.

Batson, C. D. (1998). Altruism and prosocial behavior. In D. T. Gilbert, S. T. Fiske, & G. Lindzey (Eds.), *The handbook of social psychology* (4th ed., Vol. 2, pp. 317–356). New York: McGraw-Hill.

Batson, C. D., Batson, J. G., Griffitt, C. A., Barrientos, S., Brandt, R., Sprengelmeyer, P., & Bayly, M. J. (1989). Negative-state relief and the empathy-altruism hypothesis. *Journal of Personality and Social Psychology, 56*, 922–933.

Batson C. D., & Shaw, L. L. (1991). Evidence for altruism: Toward a pluralism of prosocial motives. *Psychological Inquiry, 2*, 107–122.

Benenson, J., Markovits, H., Roy, R., & Denko, P. (2003). Behavioral rules underlying learning to share: Effects of development and context. *International Journal of Behavioral Development, 27*, 116–121.

Berkowitz, L. (1972). Social norms, feelings, and other factors affecting helping behavior and altruism. In L. Berkowitz (Ed.), *Advances in experimental social psychology* (Vol. 6, pp. 63–108). New York: Academic Press.

Berte, N. A. (1988). K'ekchi horticulture labor exchange: Productive and reproductive implications. In L. Betzig, M. Borgerhoff Mulder, & P. Turke (Eds.), *Human reproductive behavior: A Darwinian perspective* (pp. 83–96). Cambridge, UK: Cambridge University Press.

Betancourt, H. (1990). An attribution-empathy model of helping behavior: Behavioral intentions and judgements of help-giving. *Personality and Social Psychological Bulletin, 16*, 573–591.

Betancourt, H., Hardin, C., & Manzi, J. (1992). Beliefs, value orientation, and culture in attribution processes and helping behavior. *Journal of Cross-Cultural Psychology, 23*, 179–195.

Birch, L., & Billman, J. (1986). Preschool children's food sharing with friends and acquaintances. *Child Development, 57*, 387–395. doi:10.2307/1130594

Bjorklund, D. F., & Pellegrini, A. D. (2002). *The origins of human nature: Evolutionary developmental psychology*. Washington, DC: American Psychological Association

Block, C. E. (2000). Dyadic and gender differences in perceptions of the grandparent-grandchild relationship. *International Journal of Aging and Human Development, 51*, 85–104.

Brownell, C. A., Iesue, S. S., Nichols, S. R., & Svetlova, M. (2013). Mine or yours? Development of sharing in toddlers in relation to ownership understanding. *Child Development, 84*, 906–920. doi: 10.1111/cdev.12009

Bryant, B. K. (1989). The child's perspective of sibling caretaking and its relevance to understanding social-emotional functioning and development. In P.G. Zuckow (Ed.),

Sibling interaction across cultures: Theoretical and methodological issues (pp. 143–164). New York: Springer-Verlag.

Bryant, B. K., & Crockenberg, S. B. (1980). Correlates and dimensions of prosocial behavior: A study of female siblings with their mothers. *Child Development, 51*(2), 529–544.

Burnstein, E., Crandall, C., & Kitayama, S. (1994). Some neo-Darwinian decision rules for altruism: Weighing cues for inclusive fitness as a function of the biological importance of the decision. *Journal of Personality and Social Psychology, 67*, 773–789.

Carlo, G., Knight, G. P., Eisenberg, N., & Rotenberg, K. (1991). Cognitive processes and prosocial behavior among children: The role of affective attributions and reconciliations. *Developmental Psychology, 27*, 456–461.

Carlo, G., Koller, S. H., Eisenberg, N., DaSilva, M., & Frohlich, C. (1996). A cross-national study on the relations among prosocial moral reasoning, gender role orientations, and prosocial behaviors. *Developmental Psychology, 32*, 231–240.

Carlo, G., & Randall, B.A. (2001). Are all prosocial behaviors equal? A socioecological developmental conception of prosocial behavior. In F. Columbus (Ed.), *Advances in psychology research* (Vol. 2, pp. 151–170). New York: Nova Science.

Carlson, M., & Miller, N. (1987). Explanation of the relation between negative mood and helping: *Psychological Bulletin, 102*, 91–108.

Cialdini, R. B., Brown, S. L., Lewis, B. P., Luce, C., & Neuberg, S. L. (1997). Reinterpreting the empathy-altruism relationship: When one into one equals oneness. *Journal of Personality and Social Psychology, 73*, 481–494.

Clark, M. S., & Reis, H. T. (1988). Interpersonal processes in close relationships. *Annual Review of Psychology, 39*, 609–672.

Cole, A., & Kerns, K. A. (2001). Perceptions of sibling qualities and activities of early adolescents. *Journal of Early Adolescence, 21*(2), 204–226. doi:10.1177/0272431601021002004

Creasey, G. L., & Koblewski, P. J. (1991). Adolescent grandchildren's relationships with maternal and paternal grandmothers and grandfathers. *Journal of Adolescence, 14*, 373–387.

de Guzman, M. R. T., Carlo, G., & Edwards, C. P. (2008). Prosocial behaviors in context: Examining the role of children's social companions. *International Journal of Behavioral Development, 36*, 538–546.

de Waal, F. B. M. (1996). *Good natured: The origins of right and wrong in humans and other animals*. Cambridge, MA: Harvard University Press.

de Waal, F. B. M. (2008). Putting the altruism back into altruism: The evolution of empathy. *Annual Review of Psychology, 59*, 279–300.

de Waal, F. B. M., & Brosnan S. F. (2006). Simple and complex reciprocity in primates. In P. M. Kappeler & C. P. van Schaik (Eds.), *Cooperation in primates and humans: Mechanisms and evolution* (pp. 85–105). Berlin: Springer.

Dunfield, K., Kuhlmeier, V., O'Connell, L., & Kelley, E. (2011). Examining the diversity of prosocial behavior: Helping, sharing, and comforting in infancy. *Infancy, 16*, 227–247. doi:10.1111/j.1532-7078.2010.00041.x

Dunn, J. (2006). Moral development in early childhood and social interaction in the family. In M. Killen & J. G. Smetana (Eds.), *Handbook of moral development* (pp. 331–350). Mahwah, NJ: Erlbaum.

Eberly, M. B., & Montemayor, R. (1998). Doing good deeds: An examination of adolescent prosocial behavior in the context of parent–adolescent relationships. *Journal of Adolescent Research, 13*(4), 403–432. doi:10.1177/0743554898134003

Eberly, M. B., & Montemayor, R. (1999). Adolescent affection and helpfulness toward parents: A 2-year follow-up. *Journal of Early Adolescence, 19*(2), 226–248. doi:10.1177/0272431699019002005

Eisenberg, N. (1983). Children's differentiations among potential recipients of aid. *Child Development, 54*, 594–602.

Eisenberg, N. (1986). *Altruistic emotion, cognition, and behavior.* Hillsdale, NJ: Erlbaum.

Eisenberg, N. (2005). The development of empathy-related responding. *Nebraska Symposium on Motivation, 51*, 71–117.

Eisenberg, N., Fabes, R. A., & Spinrad, T. L. (2006). Prosocial development. In W. Damon (Series Ed.) & N. Eisenberg (Vol. Ed.), *Handbook of child psychology: Vol. 3. Social, emotional, and personality development* (6th ed., pp. 646–718). New York: Wiley.

Eisenberg, N., Guthrie, I. K., Murphy, B. C., Shepard, S. A., Cumberland, A., & Carlo, G. (1999). Consistency and development of prosocial dispositions: A longitudinal study. *Child Development, 70*, 1360–1372.

Eisenberg, N., & McNally, S. (1993). Socialization and mothers' and adolescents' empathy-related characteristics. *Journal of Research on Adolescence, 3*, 171–191.

Eisenberg, N., Miller, P. A., Shell, R., McNalley, S., & Shea, C. (1991). Prosocial development in adolescence: A longitudinal study. *Developmental Psychology, 27*, 849–857.

Eisenberg, N., & Shell, R. (1986). The relation of prosocial moral judgment and behavior in children: The mediating role of cost. *Personality and Social Psychology Bulletin, 12*, 426–433.

Eisenberg, N., & Valiente, C. (2002). Parenting and children's prosocial and moral development. In M. H. Bornstein (Ed.), *Handbook of parenting: Vol. 5. Practical issues in parenting* (2nd ed., pp. 111–142). Mahwah, NJ: Erlbaum.

Essock-Vitale, S. M., & McGuire, M. T. (1980). Predictions derived from the theories of kin selection and reciprocation assessed by Anthropological data. *Ethology and Sociobiology, 1*, 233–243.

Fergusson, E., Maughan, B., & Golding, J. (2008). Which children receive grandparental care and what effect does it have? *Journal of Child Psychology and Psychiatry, 49*, 161–169.

Feshbach, N. D. (1987). Parental empathy and child adjustment/maladjustment. In N. Eisenberg & J. Strayer (Eds.), *Empathy and its development* (pp. 271–291). New York: Cambridge University Press.

Fiske, A. P. (1992). The four elementary forms of sociality: Framework for a unified theory of social relations. *Psychological Review, 99*, 689–723.

Goodnow, J. J., & Warton, P. M. (1991). The social bases of social cognition: Interactions about work and their implications. *Merrill-Palmer Quarterly, 37*, 27–58.

Grusec, J. (1991). Socializing concern for others in the home. *Developmental Psychology, 27*, 338–342.

Hamilton, W. D. (1964). The genetical evolution of social behaviour I and II. *Journal of Theoretical Biology, 7*, 1–52.

Hamilton, W. D. (1971). Geometry for the selfish herd. *Journal of Theoretical Biology, 31*, 295–311.

Harkness, S. (2002). Culture and social development: Explanations and evidence. In P. K. Smith & C. H. Hart (Eds.), *Blackwell handbook of childhood social development* (pp. 60–77). Oxford: Blackwell Publishing.

Haslam, N., & Fiske, A. P. (1999). Relational models theory: A confirmatory factor analysis. *Personal Relationships, 6*, 241–250.

Hastings, P. D., Utendale, W. T., & Sullivan, C. (2007).The socialization of prosocial development. In J. E. Grusec & P. D. Hastings (Ed.), *Handbook of socialization: Theory and research* (pp. 638–664). New York: Guilford Press.

Hay, D. F. (2009). The roots and branches of human altruism. *British Journal of Psychology, 100*, 473–479.

Hay, D. F., Caplan, M., Castle, J., & Stimson, C. A. (1991). Does sharing become increasingly "rational" in the second year of life? *Developmental Psychology, 27*, 987–993. doi:10.1037/0012-1649.27.6.987

Hay, D. F, & Cook, K. V. (2007). The transformation of prosocial behaviour from infancy to childhood. In C. A. Brownell & C. B. Kopp (Eds.), *Socioemotional development in the toddler years: Transitions and transformations.* New York: Guilford.

Hinde, R. A., & Stevenson-Hinde, J. (1987). Interpersonal relationships and child development. *Developmental Review, 7*, 1–21.

Hoffman, M. L. (1975). Moral internalization, parental power, and the nature of parent-child interaction. *Developmental Psychology, 11*(2), 228–239.

Iannotti, R. J. (1985). Naturalistic and structured assessments of prosocial behavior in preschool children: The influence of empathy and perspective taking. *Developmental Psychology, 21*, 46–55.

Judge, D. S. (1995). American legacies and the variable life histories of women and men. *Human Nature, 6*, 291–324.

Kağıtçıbaşı, Ç. (1982). Old-age security value of children. *Journal of Cross-Cultural Psychology, 13*(1), 29–42.

Kağıtçıbaşı, Ç. (1984). Socialization in traditional society: A challenge to psychology. *International Journal of Psychology, 19*, 145–157.

Kağıtçıbaşı, Ç. (2007). *Family, self, and human development across cultures: Theory and applications* (2nd ed.). Mahwah, NJ: Erlbaum.

Killen, M., & Turiel, E. (1998). Adolescents' and young adults' evaluations of helping and sacrificing for others. *Journal of Research on Adolescence, 8*, 355–375.

Knafo, A., Zahn-Waxler, C., Van Hulle, C., Robinson, J. L., & Rhee, S. (2008). The developmental origins of a disposition toward empathy: Genetic and environmental contributions. *Emotion, 8*(6), 737–752. doi:10.1037/a0014179

Knight, G. P., Johnson, L. G., Carlo, G., & Eisenberg, N. (1994). A multiplicative model of the dispositional antecedents of a prosocial behavior: Predicting more of the people more of the time. *Journal of Personality and Social Psychology, 66*, 178–183.

Korchmaros, J. D., & Kenny, D. A. (2001). Emotional closeness as a mediator of the effect of genetic relatedness on altruism. *Psychological Science, 12*, 262–265.

Kornhaber, A., & Woodward, K. L. (1981). *Grandparent/grandchild: The vital connection.* Garden City: NY: Anchor Press.

Kumru, A. (2002). *Prosocial behaviors within the family context and its correlates among Turkish early adolescents.* Unpublished doctoral dissertation, University of Nebraska-Lincoln.

Lollis, S., & Kuczynski, L. (1997). Beyond one hand clapping: Seeing bidirectionality in parent-child relations. *Journal of Social and Personal Relationships, 14*, 441–461.

Ma, H. K., & Leung, M. C. (1993). Effects of age, sex, and social relationships on the altruistic behavior of Chinese children. *Journal of Genetic Psychology, 153*, 293–303.

Malti, T., Gummerum, M., Keller, M., Chaparro, M. P., & Buchmann, M. (2012). Early sympathy and social acceptance predict the development of sharing in children. *PloS One, 7*, 1–7. doi:10.1371/journal.pone.0052017

Maner, J. K., & Gailliot, M. T. (2006). Altruism and egoism: Prosocial motivations for helping depend on relationship context. *European Journal of Social Psychology, 37*, 347–358. doi: 10.1002/ejsp.364

Markovits, H., Benenson, J. F., & Kramer, D. L. (2003). Children and adolescents' internal models of food-sharing behavior include complex evaluations of contextual factors. *Child Development, 74*, 1697–1708

Mauss, M. (1954). *The gift: Forms and functions of exchange in archaic societies*. Glencoe, IL: Free Press.

McAndrew, F. T. (2002). New evolutionary perspectives on altruism: Multilevel-selection and costly-signaling theories. *Current Directions in Psychological Science, 11*, 79–82.

Midlarsky, E., & Hannah, M. E., & Corley, R. (1995). Assessing adolescents' prosocial behavior: The family helping inventory. *Adolescence, 30*, 141–156.

Monserud, M. A. (2008). Intergenerational relationships and affectual solidarity between grandparents and young adults. *Journal of Marriage and the Family, 70*, 182–195.

Moos, R. H., & Moos, B. S. (1986). *The Family Environment Scale manual* (2nd ed.). Palo Alto, CA: Consulting Psychologist Press.

Mueller, M. M., & Elder, G. H. (2003). Family contingencies across the generations: Grandparent–grandchild relationships in holistic perspective. *Journal of Marriage and Family, 65*, 404–417.

Neyer, F. J., & Lang, F. R. (2003). Blood is thicker than water: Kinship orientation across adulthood. *Journal of Personality and Social Psychology, 84*, 310–321.

Padilla-Walker, L. M., & Christensen, K. J. (2010). Empathy and self-regulation as mediators between parenting and adolescents' prosocial behavior toward strangers, friends, and family. *Journal of Research on Adolescence, 21*(3), 545–551. doi:10.1111/j.1532-7795.2010.00695.x

Padilla-Walker, L. M., Harper, J. M., & Jensen, A. C. (2010). Self-regulation as a mediator between sibling relationship quality and early adolescents' positive and negative outcomes. *Journal of Family Psychology, 24*, 419–428.

Pepler, D. J., Abramovitch, R., & Corter, C. (1981). Sibling interaction in the home: A longitudinal study. *Child Development, 52*(4), 1344–1347. doi:10.2307/1129530

Reis, H. T., Collins, W., & Berscheid, E. (2000). The relationship context of human behavior and development. *Psychological Bulletin, 126*, 844–872.

Roberto, K. A., & Stroes, J. (1992). Grandchildren and grandparents: Roles, influences, and relationships. *Journal of International Aging and Human Development, 34*, 227–239.

Roberts, W., & Strayer, J. (1996). Empathy, emotional expressiveness, and prosocial behavior. *Child Development, 67*, 449–470.

Simpson, J. A., & Beckes, L. (2010). Evolutionary perspectives on prosocial behavior. In M. Mikulincer, P. R. Shaver (Eds.), *Prosocial motives, emotions, and behavior: The better angels of our nature* (pp. 35–53). Washington, DC: American Psychological Association. doi:10.1037/12061-002

Smith, M. S., Kish, B. L., & Crawford, C. B. (1987). Inheritance of wealth as human kin investment. *Ethology and Sociobiology, 8*, 171–182.

Staub, E. (1972). Instigation to goodness: The role of social norms and interpersonal influence. *Journal of Social Issues, 28*, 131–150.

Staub, E. (2005). The roots of goodness: The fulfillment of basic human needs and the development of caring, helping and nonaggression, inclusive caring, moral courage, active bystandership, and altruism born of suffering. In G. Carlo & C. Edwards (Eds.), *Nebraska Symposium on Motivation: Vol. 51. Moral motivation through the life span: Theory, research, applications* (pp. 33–72). Lincoln: University of Nebraska Press.

Staub, E., & Noerenberg, H. (1981). Property rights, deservingness, reciprocity, friendship: The transactional character of children's sharing behavior. *Journal of Personality and Social Psychology, 40*, 271–289.

Stewart-Williams, S. (2007). Altruism among kin vs. nonkin: Effects of cost of help and reciprocal exchange. *Evolution and Human Behavior, 28*, 193–198.

Stormshak, E. A., Bullock, B. M., & Falkenstein, C. A. (2009). Harnessing the power of sibling relationships as a tool for optimizing social-emotional development. *New Directions for Child and Adolescent Development, 126*, 61–77. doi: 10.1002/cd.257

Triandis, H. C. (1994). *Culture and social behavior*. New York: McGraw-Hill.

Trivers R. (1971). The evolution of reciprocal altruism. *Quarterly Review of Biology, 46*, 35–57.

Tucker, C., Updegraff, K. A., McHale, S. M., & Crouter, A. C. (1999). Older siblings as socializers of younger siblings' empathy. *Journal of Early Adolescence, 19*(2), 176–198. doi:10.1177/0272431699019002003

van der Mark, I. L., van IJzendoorn, M. H., & Bakermans-Kranenburg, M. J. (2002). Development of empathy in girls during the second year of life: Associations with parenting, attachment, and temperament. *Social Development, 11*, 451–468.

Van Lange, P. A. M., Otten, W., De Bruin, E. M. N., & Joireman, J. A. (1997). Development of prosocial, individualistic, and competitive orientations: Theory and preliminary evidence. *Journal of Personality and Social Psychology, 73*, 733–746. doi:10.1037/0022-3514.73.4.733

Van Ranst, N., Verschueren, K., & Macroen, A. (1995). The meaning of grandparents as viewed by adolescent grandchildren: An empirical study in Belgium. *International Journal of Human Development, 41*, 311–324.

Volling, B. L., & Belsky, J. (1992). The contribution of mother-child and father-child relationships to the quality of sibling interaction: A longitudinal study. *Child Development, 63*(5), 1209–1222. doi:10.2307/1131528

Warneken, F., & Tomasello, M. (2007). Helping and cooperation at 14 months of age. *Infancy, 11*, 271–294.

Webster, G. D. (2003). Prosocial behavior in families: Moderators of resource sharing. *Journal of Experimental Social Psychology, 39*, 644–652. doi:10.1016/S0022-1031(03)00055-6

Wenger, M. (1983). *Gender role socialization in an East African community: Social interaction between 2- to 3-year-olds and older children in social ecological perspective*. Ed.D. dissertation. Harvard Graduate School of Education.

Wenger, M. (1989). Work, play, and social relationships among children in a Giriama community. In D. Belle (Ed.), *Children's social networks and social supports* (pp. 91–118). New York: Wiley.

Wentzel, K. R., Filisetti, L, & Looney, L. (2007). Adolescent prosocial behavior: The role of self-processes and contextual cues. *Child Development, 78*, 895–910.

Whiting, B., & Whiting, J. (1975). *Children of six cultures: A psycho-cultural analysis.* Cambridge, MA: Harvard University Press.

Young, S. K., Fox, N. A., & Zahn-Waxler, C. (1999). The relations between temperament and empathy in 2-year-olds. *Developmental Psychology, 35*, 1189–1197.

17

Prosocial Behaviors in Early Childhood

HELPING OTHERS, RESPONDING TO THE DISTRESS OF OTHERS, AND WORKING WITH OTHERS

Deborah Laible and Erin Karahuta

Prosocial behavior consists of a wide range of cooperative, helpful, and supportive actions that are focused on benefiting others, especially (although not limited to) when others are in need or in distress (Eisenberg & Fabes, 1998), and includes behaviors such as "assisting, sharing, being kind and considerate, comforting, cooperating, protecting someone from harm, rescuing someone from danger, and feeling empathy and sympathy" (Radke-Yarrow & Zahn-Waxler, 1986, p. 208). Surprisingly, the propensity to engage in prosocial behavior emerges relatively early in childhood, perhaps by the end of the first year of life, when children begin to engage in sharing, cooperative behavior, and instrumental helping behavior (such as informing an experimenter about the location of a moved object; see Hay & Cook, 2007, for a review). Children's empathic concern and comforting behavior emerges soon after, sometime early during the second year of life (Zahn-Waxler, Radke-Yarrow, Wagner, & Chapman, 1992; Zahn-Waxler, Robinson & Emde, 1992). Thus, well before children's third birthdays, young children are already displaying a rich diversity of prosocial behaviors.

The goal of our chapter is to review the different types of prosocial behaviors that are present during infancy, the toddler years, and early preschool years and, if possible, to map their developmental course. We focus on three broad types of prosocial behavior that seem to emerge during infancy and toddlerhood. The first is *responsiveness to the distress of others*, which includes children's empathic concern and comforting behavior. The second involves children's *helping behavior*, which has mostly been studied with regard to children's informing behavior, instrumental helping, and helping with housework. Finally, we discuss children's *ability to work with others*, including their ability to share resources with others, cooperate with others to meet goals, and comply with the requests of others. It seems likely that these are orthogonal dimensions of prosocial behavior that have different developmental timelines and different correlates. However, this point has not been well addressed by researchers. Much of the work that has been done on early prosocial behaviors is cross-sectional in design and involves relatively small and select samples (see Hay & Cook, 2007). Longitudinal investigations examining the developmental trajectory of prosocial behaviors in early childhood have been rare and have tended to focus on only a single type of prosocial behavior (e.g., comforting; see Zahn-Waxler, Radke-Yarrow, et al., 1992). As a result, it is not particularly clear how the different types of prosocial behaviors unfold in concert across early childhood and how they are interrelated.

Following our discussion of the three types of prosocial behavior that have been studied in early childhood, we also speculate more broadly about the developmental course of prosocial behavior across the first three years of life. Although a number of researchers have argued for the idea that prosocial behavior becomes increasingly frequent across early childhood due to children's growing social cognitive sophistication coupled with increasing socialization from parents (see e.g., Eisenberg & Fabes, 1998), others have speculated that prosocial behavior becomes increasingly selective and therefore decreases across early childhood (see Hay & Cook, 2007; see also Werneken & Tomasello, 2009). We review the arguments and evidence on both sides of the debate.

In addition, we discuss the possible explanations for why prosocial behaviors are such an early emerging developmental phenomenon. Prosocial behaviors in older children are assumed to be a direct result of children's social cognitive skills (e.g., perspective taking) combined with their motivations to act on behalf of others (e.g., empathy; Batson, Ahmad, Powell, & Stocks, 2008). Given that these processes are assumed to be primitive in infancy and toddlerhood, the motivations for early prosocial behavior might be different (although not necessarily so). Therefore, we highlight a couple of possible explanations for the early ontogeny of prosocial behavior. We end with a discussion of future directions for researchers doing work in this area.

Responsiveness to the Distress of Others: Feeling for and Comforting Others

A small body of work has explored how young children respond to the distress of others, focusing on their empathic responses and comforting behavior. Generally, this work suggests that young children are surprisingly responsive to the distress of others.

EMPATHY

Empathy involves "sharing the perceived emotion of another" (Eisenberg & Strayer, 1990, p. 5) and can involve either sympathy, that is, feeling concern for the distressed other, or personal distress, a more self-focused reaction to another's distress (Eisenberg et al., 2006). In early childhood, it is often impossible to distinguish between the types of empathic responses. It seems likely that empathic responses that appear during the first year of life involve high levels of personal or self-distress, although even this point has been debated (see below). At some point, however, probably during the second and third years of life, more other-oriented concern seems to be more clearly part of the toddlers' repertoire of emotional skills.

Children's responsiveness to the distress of others appears remarkably early in development. Newborn babies will cry in response to the sound of another baby's cry within several days after birth (Dondi, Simion, & Caltran, 1999; Martin & Clark, 1982; Sagi & Hoffman, 1976). Interestingly, babies show more distress to the cry of another baby than to their own cry (Dondi et al., 1999) or to other aversive noises (such as nonhuman or synthetic cries), which lends support to the idea that such responsiveness is more than just a response to an aversive noise. Moreover, Dondi et al. (1999) demonstrated increased facial expressions of distress on infants in response to the cries of unfamiliar infants. Because infants' distress was demonstrated in a different modality (facial expressions instead of vocal expressions), it is clear that infants were not just imitating the distress of the other infant but actually reacting to its meaning (Saarni, Campos, Camras, & Witherington, 2006). Although it seems likely that this reactive crying is the result of processes like emotional contagion (Moore, 1990) rather than true empathy, this early affective sharing, or emotional resonance, is still an important element of empathy that appears early during ontogeny (de Waal, 2006).

Recent work also suggests that infants' distress reactions to the cries of others is not limited to the first couple of months of life, but extends across the first year of life (Geangu, Benga, Stahl, & Striano, 2010). Geangu et al. (2010) studied 1-, 3-, 6-, and 9-month-old infants and found no age differences in the amount of distress (vocal or facial) that infants experienced when exposed to the cry of another child. Similar work has found that older infants are responsive to both the positive and negative emotional states of mothers. For example, Termine and Izard (1988) found that 9-month-old infants expressed more negative affect when exposed to their mothers' negative emotional expressions (and more joy when mothers expressed joy), supporting the idea that infants are demonstrating congruent emotional reactions to caregivers that are similar to empathic reactions. Of course, it is not clear from this work whether such responses stem from emotional contagion, imitation, or some comprehension of the mother's emotional state. However, there is work that suggests by the end of the first year of life, infants are somewhat sophisticated consumers of emotional information. For example, the rich literature on social referencing suggests that infants not only respond to the emotions of others, but are using that information to guide their behavior in uncertain or ambiguous situations (Saarni, Mumme, & Campos, 1998). These studies support the idea that infants have some primitive understanding of the meaning of emotional expressions by the end of the first year of life.

It is unclear as to whether this early empathy is self-focused, other-focused, or a combination of the two. Hoffman (2000) argued that this early empathy, which he referred to as egocentric empathic distress, is not transformed into more other-oriented empathic distress until the second year of life, when infants become capable of distinguishing the self from others (Hoffman, 2000). However, some work has questioned the assumption that the infant's distress to the negative affect of others is entirely self-focused (see e.g., Hay, Nash, & Pederson, 1981; Roth-Hanania, Davidov, & Zahn-Waxler, 2011). For example, Hay et al. (1981) found that infants often directed their attention to and oriented toward a fussing peer in a laboratory playroom, but seldom cried in response to the distress of the peer. Moreover, close to half of the infants in the Hay et al. (1981) study sought contact (through leaning, touching, or gesturing) with a distressed peer. Similarly, Roth-Hanania et al. (2011) found that infants as young as 8 months were capable of directing looks of concern toward distressed others and made attempts to comprehend the distress of both mothers and peers (e.g., through inquiry or exploration) and that these tendencies increased across the second year of life. Both studies (i.e., Hay et al., 1981; Roth-Hanania et al., 2011) raise the possibility that this early empathy may not be entirely self-focused.

Although it is not entirely clear whether the infant's responsiveness to the distress of others involves some degree of other-oriented concern, a variety of studies have demonstrated that children do possess empathic (or other-oriented) responsiveness to the distress of others by their second year of life (Demetriou & Hay, 2004; Knafo, Zahn-Waxler, Van Hulle, Robinson, & Rhee, 2008; Zahn-Waxler, Radke-Yarrow, et al., 1992; Zahn-Waxler, Robinson, et al., 1992). These studies have examined both cognitive and affective components of empathy and have found that both are present in toddlers as young as 12–14 months. Thus, toddlers demonstrate clear attempts to actively understand, inquire, or comprehend another's distress (often referred to as hypothesis testing; Knafo et al., 2008; Zahn-Waxler, Radke-Yarrow, et al., 1992; Zahn-Waxler, Robinson, et al., 1992). In addition, toddlers also demonstrate affective concern for others in distress as demonstrated through facial expressions, vocalizations, and gestures (Knafo et al., 2008; Zahn-Waxler, Radke-Yarrow, et al., 1992; Zahn-Waxler, Robinson, et al., 1992). The empathic responsiveness of toddlers has been demonstrated in laboratory settings, naturalistic settings, and through maternal reports (Demetriou & Hay, 2004; Knafo et al., 2008; Zahn-Waxler, Radke-Yarrow, et al., 1992; Zahn-Waxler, Robinson, et al., 1992).

Hoffman (1975, 1984, 2000) argued empathic distress during the first half of the second year of life still involves some degree of egocentrism, because of the limited ability of young toddlers to engage in role taking and limited ability of toddlers to separate themselves from others. More mature empathy emerges later in the second year of life, when children begin to recognize that other people's emotional states are different from their own and children can engage in some primitive role taking. Recent work, however, has suggested sophisticated role-taking abilities may be in place as early as 18-months (see Vaish, Carpenter, & Tomasello, 2009). For example, in Vaish et al. (2009) 18- and 25-month-old children observed an adult either harming another adult (e.g., destroying a possession) or doing something similar that did not involve harm (i.e., a control condition). In both conditions, the adult displayed no emotional cues. In the study, both 18- and 25-month-olds showed more concern for and engaged in more prosocial behavior toward the victim in the harm condition versus the control condition, which suggests that young children were potentially able to sympathize with and take the emotional perspective of the victim even in the absence of emotional cues (Vaish et al., 2009).

EMPATHIC HELPING

Also during the second year of life, toddlers begin to demonstrate prosocial behaviors toward victims who are in distress. Thus, there is evidence that these children may intervene with victims in distress by patting, hugging, offering physical assistance, or fetching adults to help (Zahn-Waxler & Radke-Yarrow, 1982). Initial attempts to alleviate the distress of others by toddlers may involve attempts to give the other person something that they themselves find comforting, but as children become better at separating their own emotional states from those of others, children begin to engage in more appropriate comforting strategies (Hoffman, 2000). Research supports the idea that young children's attempts to alleviate the distress of others increases in frequency across early childhood (see Knafo et al., 2008; Lamb & Zakhireh, 1997; Volbrecht, Lemery-Chalfant, Aksan, Zahn-Waxler, & Goldsmith, 2007; Zahn-Waxler & Radke-Yarrow, 1982; Zahn-Waxler, Radke-Yarrow et al., 1992).

Young children, however, do not always respond to the distress of others with prosocial interventions; unsympathetic responses (such as aggression or laughing) are also frequent during early childhood (see Radke-Yarrow & Zahn-Waxler, 1984; Zahn-Waxler & Radke-Yarrow, 1982; Zahn-Waxler, Radke-Yarrow, et al., 1992). Moreover, prosocial actions to peer distress, especially in daycare settings, may be relatively rare. Lamb and Zakrireh (1997) found in one of the few observational studies conducted in a daycare setting that toddlers (between the ages of 9 and 27 months) responded prosocially to only 11 of 345 peer distress episodes. However, these rates are unusually low compared with other studies (see e.g., Zahn-Waxler, Radke-Yarrow, et al., 1992) and may be in part due to the fact that young children believe that they are not supposed to help when adults are present (see Caplan & Hay, 1989).

SUMMARY

Both infants and toddlers demonstrate remarkable responsiveness to the distress of others in the form of empathic distress. It remains unclear, however, as to exactly when this empathic distress becomes other focused, rather than self-focused. Nonetheless, the affective, cognitive, and behavioral (e.g., comforting) components of empathy increase across early childhood.

Helping Others

Researchers have also explored young children's ability to provide instrumental assistance to adults, including informing them about missing objects and providing help to achieve goals. This work suggests that infants as young as 12 months show some ability to instrumentally help adults when assistance is needed.

INFORMING

One of the earliest forms of instrumental helping to emerge involves informing adults about missing objects through pointing (see Liszkowski, Carpenter, Striano, & Tomasello, 2006; Liszkowski, Carpenter, & Tomasello, 2008). Both 12- and 18-month-old infants have been shown to helpfully inform an adult of an object's location when an object went missing due to accidental circumstances (e.g., accidentally pushing an object off a table), distraction (e.g., forgetting the location of an object after attending to something else), or removal by a third party unbeknownst to the adult (e.g., a second experimenter moves the item while the first adult is away; Liszkowski et al., 2006). Moreover, both the 12- and 18-month-old children were just as likely to point to missing adult-related objects (such as staplers) as toys, suggesting that this informing was more about helping the experimenter locate the missing object and less about the child pointing to an attractive object that he or she wanted to possess (Liszkowski et al., 2006). Follow-up studies indicate that infants are more likely to point to inform adults of an object's location when the adult clearly had no knowledge of where the displaced object was (e.g., she did not see the object fall down), as opposed to situations where the adult possessed information about where the object was located (e.g., the adult clearly saw the object fall down; Liszkowski et al., 2008). This suggests that this early pointing behavior is based on the desire to communicate knowledge to the experimenter about the missing object and may indicate that young children possess some understanding of the ignorance or knowledge of the adult (Liszkowski et al., 2008).

INSTRUMENTAL HELPING

In addition, in a series of elegant experiments, Warneken and Tomasello (2006, 2007, 2008) demonstrated that children between 14 and 18 months of age will reliably provide instrumental help to an adult experimenter who cannot achieve his or her goals. The help that toddlers provided to the experimenter in these studies was spontaneous, flexible, and varied (Warneken & Tomasello, 2006, 2007, 2008). Children assisted with both relatively simple tasks (e.g., reaching for objects that were out of reach) and more complex ones as well (e.g., helping open a cabinet because the hands of the experimenter are full). It is important to point out, however, that the youngest children (i.e., the 14-month-olds) helped solely with simple tasks (Warneken & Tomasello, 2007) and not in the more complex situations. Also, both age groups were sensitive to the experimenter's goals in the situation and helped when the experimenter was in need (e.g., he accidently dropped a clothes pin and could not reach it) but not when the experimenter was not in need (e.g., he intentionally threw the clothes pin onto the ground).

Interestingly, the children who helped the adult experimenter in Warneken and Tomasello's studies (2006, 2007) helped in the total absence of encouragement or praise by either the mother or the experimenter. A follow-up study with 18-month-olds indicated that young children were not more likely to help when presented with material rewards for helping (Warneken, Hare, Melis, Hanus, & Tomasello, 2007). In fact, there is evidence with slightly older children (i.e., 20-month-olds) that rewarding children's early instrumental helping behavior may undermine their intrinsic motivation to help others (Warneken & Tomasello, 2008). Children who were given a material reward for helping were less likely to subsequently help the experimenter as compared with those children who received no reward or who received social praise.

This early instrumental helping that emerges in young children may be linked with children's understanding of the goals and intentions of others. Thus, in order to help another achieve a goal, a young child must first recognize what the goal entails, and this emerges by the second year of life, if not sooner. There is pretty strong evidence from multiple studies that children between the ages of 12 and 18 months demonstrate an understanding of the behavior of others in terms of underlying intentions and goals (see Tomasello, Carpenter, Call, Behne, & Moll, 2005, for a review). For example, by 15 months, children in imitation studies can represent the goals of others and can reproduce the adult's intended result, rather than the action that the adults was observed doing (Bellagamba & Tomasello, 1999; Johnson, Booth, & O'Hearn, 2001). It is important to point out, however, that research increasingly suggests that some underlying understanding of intentionality and goals may be present in even younger children, perhaps even as soon as 8–12 months (e.g., Brandone & Wellman, 2009; Phillips & Wellman, 2005; Woodward, 1998).

Although instrumental helping is relatively frequent among toddlers, it depends to some extent on the type of helping involved (see Svetlova, Nichols, & Brownell 2010). Svetlova et al. (2010) examined a variety of situations in which children could instrumentally help an adult, including a series of tasks that were action based (e.g., picking up a clothespin dropped out of reach), emotion based (e.g., handing a distressed experimenter her favorite teddy bear), or altruism based (e.g., giving the experimenter the child's *own* blanket to alleviate her distress).

Both 18-month-old and 30-month-old children were more likely to help in the action-based conditions than in the emotion- or altruism-based conditions, and both groups of children were less likely to help when the behavior was costly (i.e., in the altruism condition, where children had to surrender their own possession to aid the experimenter). Unsurprisingly, there was also evidence that 18-month-olds required substantially more verbal scaffolding (e.g., requests for help) than 30-month-olds to support their helping behavior, especially in the more complex emotion-based helping tasks.

HELPING WITH HOUSEWORK

Anecdotal evidence also suggested that toddlers will provide parents with spontaneous help with household tasks and chores (Church, 1966), an observation that was also backed up in an early laboratory study. Rheingold (1982) examined the frequency with which children between the ages of 18–30 months spontaneously helped both parents and an unknown experimenter complete a series of household tasks in the lab (e.g., sweeping up bits of paper or putting away groceries). Without any prompting from either parents or the unknown experimenter, all of the toddlers helped the adults with at least some of their household tasks and did so relatively quickly. Surprisingly, the toddlers were just as likely to help an unfamiliar adult as a parent. Moreover, the older children assisted with a higher percentage of household tasks than younger children, also suggesting that children's instrumental helping in the home might increase with age.

SUMMARY

As early as 12 months, children demonstrate instrumental helping; they will inform an experimenter (through pointing) about the location of a missing object. By 14 months, children also will help an experimenter (and presumably parents) achieve relatively simple goals (e.g., by picking up a clothespin that has fallen out of reach), and by 18 months, children will help across a number of complex tasks in the lab and at home. Researchers have speculated that children's instrumental helping is likely linked with their understanding of the goals and intentions of others, which develops at the end of the first year of life.

Working with Others: Sharing, Cooperation, and Compliance

The ability to work with others to share resources or attain joint goals also emerges relatively early in development. By the end of the first year of life, infants begin to share resources, engage in cooperative activities, and accede to the wishes of others.

SHARING

Early research on sharing suggests that children begin to engage in this type of prosocial behavior in infancy, and in fact, it may be the first type of prosocial behavior that emerges in childhood. Children begin to spontaneously offer food and toys to others, especially parents, as early as 8 months (Hay, 1979; Hay & Murray, 1982), and this behavior is well developed by 12 to 18 months. Whereas sharing spontaneously may occur with relative ease in the first year of life, sharing at the request of others may be more challenging for infants, especially since relinquishing requires inhibitory processes that are later developing (Hay & Cook, 2007). However, shortly after their first birthday, children will also relinquish objects when requested to do so by either verbal or nonverbal (e.g., outstretched hands) requests (Hay & Murray, 1982; Hay et al., 1991).

This early sharing in infancy may be motivated by children's early attempts to affiliate with, communicate with, and sustain interactions with others (Hay, 1979; Hay & Cook, 2007). Thus, researchers have speculated that these early sharing behaviors are important both for creating and sustaining joint attention (Woodward, Sommerville, & Guajardo, 2001), and therefore, form the basis for learning skills that are critical for human interaction (Hay & Cook, 2007). Sharing is so normative among infants around their first birthday, that the absence of this behavior may be an early sign of autism (Sigman, Mundy, Sherman, & Ungerer, 1986).

The developmental course of sharing, however, is less clear than the other types of prosocial behaviors because limited research has been done on this topic (Brownell, Svetlova, & Nichols, 2009). By 24 months, children will offer each other toys in naturally occurring play situations, but when not engaged in joint play, sharing is often limited unless requested by an adult (Hay, Castle, Davies, Demetriou, & Stimson, 1999; Levitt, Weber, Clark, & McDonnell, 1985). Toddlers tend to be possessive of their own belongings (Hay, 2006) and are often hesitant to relinquish play objects spontaneously, even when it is clear that the resources of their partner are limited (Levitt et al., 1985). Even in the preschool years, sharing does not necessarily occur with the same frequency as other types of prosocial behaviors, such as helping (Eisenberg, 2005; Grusec, 1991). Thus, for example, Birch and Billman (1986) found that preschool children were particularly ungenerous in sharing food with peers (reserving only 1 piece for their peers versus 10 pieces for themselves).

It is not entirely clear why young children are not motivated to share. Part of the explanation may be that sharing is cognitively complex and involves children monitoring the resources of others, understanding the units of shared resources or time, and making a cost-benefit analysis. Thus, the cognitive demands of sharing may limit children's ability to share resources with others. For example, Knight and colleagues (Knight, Bohlmeyer, Schneider, & Harris, 1993) found that temporal monitoring was partially responsible for the link between age and the equal sharing of limited resources (e.g., a crayon to color a picture). When the cognitive demands involved in monitoring time were reduced experimentally, young children were more likely to share the resource equally. It may also be that sharing is often more costly than comforting behavior or helping (in that it involves giving up a material good that one possesses) and this may be why the behavior has a low base rate in toddlerhood and the preschool years. Thus, during this period, costly prosocial behavior, such as sharing, may decrease when children begin to understand issues of ownership and the cost of sharing (Fasig, 2000; Hay, Caplan, Castle, & Stimson, 1991). Once children learn rules regarding norms of equity and fairness in later childhood (e.g., around 6 or 7), children may share more readily and divide resources more equitably (see Melis, Altrichter, & Tomasello, 2013).

Experimental work with young children does suggest that there are circumstances under which young children are more likely to share resources, however. Early work by Levitt et al. (1985) found that toddlers between 29 and 36 months were more likely to share with a toy-deprived child if the other child had shared when the roles were previously reversed. These findings suggest that young children might be sensitive to the reciprocity involved in relationships. Brownell et al. (2009) found evidence that 25-month-old children (but not 18-month-olds) were more likely to share food when the experimenter made their needs explicit (as opposed to remaining silent about their needs), suggesting that young children may need adult scaffolding to engage in sharing with unfamiliar adults. Finally, recent work suggests that 3-year-old children are likely to distribute resources equitably if both partners collaborated to achieve some spoils, even when it would have been easy for one partner to monopolize the resources (Warneken, Lohse, Melis, & Tomasello, 2011). However, when one partner does not collaborate to achieve resources (and freeloads), 3-year-old children do not distribute the resources gained through collaboration equally. Instead, they reward those who contribute to the collaborative effort. These findings suggest young children are also aware of the contributions made by parties in collaborative endeavors.

COMPLIANCE

The ability to comply with the requests of caregivers (and others) is considered to be an important developmental milestone that emerges relatively early. By the end of the first year, infants will often comply with the requests of others (Gralinski & Kopp, 1993). Children's compliance has been recognized as an important aspect of early conscience development (Kochanska & Aksan, 1995; Kochanska, Aksan, & Koenig, 1995). Less attention, however, has been paid to the idea that it might also indicate an early type of prosocial behavior. Nonetheless, there are good reasons to believe that it does. The ability to comply with another's requests and wishes fosters harmony in relationships and allows for dyads or group members to respond more constructively to problems (see Hay & Cook, 2007). Moreover, the willingness to embrace the agenda of others can involve self-sacrificing that is similar to sharing or other types of prosocial behavior.

It seems important to realize that compliance does not always involve obedience, or a more begrudging bending to the will of others, but can and often does involve children's enthusiastic responsiveness to the requests of others (see Hay & Cook, 2007; Rheingold, Cook, & Kowlowitz, 1987). Committed compliance, an internally motivated, eager, self-sustaining type of compliance has been well studied in the literature (although almost exclusively with regard to parents; see e.g., Kochanska & Aksan, 1995; Kochanska et al., 1995, Kochanska, Tjebkes, & Forman, 1998; Kochanska et al., 2010; Spinrad et al., 2012). Researchers have argued that committed compliance is the first step in children's internalization of parental values (see Gralinski & Kopp, 1993; Kochanska et al., 1995) and that it indicates a readiness to be socialized (Kochanska et al., 1995; Kochanska et al., 2010). Moreover, children's eagerness to embrace and cooperate with the agenda of parents has been closely linked with relationship qualities such as mutually positive affect (Kochanska & Aksan, 1995). Researchers have argued that this desire to cooperate with the parental agenda is fostered by a positive emotional climate in the family that creates a willingness for the child to comply with and cooperate with parental requests (Maccoby & Martin, 1983; Kochanska & Aksan, 1995).

COOPERATION AND COLLABORATION

Children also show some evidence of cooperative and collaborative play relatively early. During the first year of life, infants engage in dyadic play that involves turn-taking, defined roles, and adjusting their behavior to be responsive to others (e.g., peek-a-boo), but this occurs mostly when they are scaffolded and supported by an adult partner (Eckerman & Peterman, 2001; Hay, Payne, & Chadwick, 2004). Cooperation with peers, however, is much slower to develop. Before 18 months, peer interactions are primitive, involving little coordination and sharing of goals (see Brownell & Brown, 1992, and Eckerman & Peterman, 2001, for reviews). After 18 months, however, children become more sophisticated in terms of engaging partners in joint play and problem solving and are capable of engaging in successful coordination to solve problems (Brownell & Carriger, 1990, 1991; Eckerman, Davis, & Didow, 1989). Brownell and Carriger (1991), for example, examined the ability of toddlers to coordinate actions to solve a cooperative problem-solving task. The tasks required one child to coordinate actions on a transparent box with another (e.g., one child needed to push a handle while the other retrieved the toys). Twelve-month-olds were unable to solve the problem cooperatively, but one-half of the 18-month-olds and most of the 24- and 30-month-old dyads solved the problem.

More recent studies have examined the explanation for children's early cooperative behavior. Are young children able to understand their own and their partner's actions as involving collaborative activity with joint goals and intentions? To address this issue, Warneken and colleagues (Warneken, Chen, & Tomasello, 2006; Warneken, Gräfenhain, & Tomasello, 2012) examined children's responses to the interruption of collaborative activity by adult partners. In the first study, Warneken et al. (2006) found that both 18- and 24-month-olds would attempt to reengage an adult collaborative partner who stopped working toward the joint goals. The second study (Warneken et al., 2011) demonstrated that children did not just react to the partner's cessation of activity in the first study, but instead understood something about the partner's behavior as involving a violation of their collaborative activity. Young children in the second study were more likely to attempt to reengage a recalcitrant partner when the partner stopped collaborating because she was unable to continue rather than when a partner was unwilling to continue, suggesting that children were sensitive to the partner's intentions with regard to collaboration. Moreover, young children were equally likely to attempt to reengage a partner in a situation where the adult's engagement was necessary for the child to perform his/her actions versus in a situation involving a social goal for which the dyads did not have to coordinate actions but could do so if they so wished. Thus, Warneken et al. (2011) argued that children do not just see cooperative activity as involving their own goal fulfillment but also see partners as collaborative agents. Young children seemed to understand that the goal of the activity was to act jointly and they were willing to encourage their partners when this joint endeavor ceased.

SUMMARY

Children begin to cooperate, comply, and share with others before their first birthdays, making these behaviors some of the earliest types of prosocial behaviors to emerge. Sharing of resources, particularly with peers, is difficult for toddlers and develops slowly, likely because sharing is cognitively complex and is costly. Children's initial cooperative behavior requires scaffolding by an adult partner, and children do not coordinate goals with peers until the end of their second year of life. Children's compliant behavior may also be an early form of prosocial behavior and it has been linked with children's early conscience development.

Broader Issues

INTERRELATIONS BETWEEN TYPES OF PROSOCIAL BEHAVIORS AND STABILITY

Researchers have speculated about when and how soon prosocial tendencies consolidate into a prosocial disposition (see e.g., Dunfield, Kuhlmeier, O'Connell, & Kelly, 2011). The question of whether there are individual differences in prosocial behavior that remain stable across infancy, toddlerhood, and the preschool years, however, has not been well examined in the literature. Dunn and Munn (1986) found some stability in the cooperative, sharing, helping, and comforting behavior of toddler siblings toward each other (across a 6-month period), as well as some interrelations between the different types of prosocial behaviors, but the pattern of findings was not particularly consistent or strong. Dunfield et al. (2011) more recently found no interrelationships between three types of prosocial behaviors (i.e., helping, sharing, and comforting) in a group of 18- and 24-month-old toddlers. Work on empathy and children's empathic helping (i.e., comforting) supports the idea that there is modest consistency in empathic and comforting responses across contexts (e.g., mother versus strangers; see e.g., Spinrad & Stifter, 2006) and across time (Zahn-Waxler, Radke-Yarrow, et al., 1992; Zahn-Waxler, Robinson et al., 1992). However, longitudinal work on early sharing found little evidence of the stability of sharing behavior across the first couple of years of life (Hay et al., 1999). Thus, although there is evidence for some short-term stability in prosocial dispositions (see e.g., Koestner, Franz, & Weinberger, 1990), evidence that these dispositions have consolidated in early childhood is lacking. It is important to point out, however, that there is some indication that early prosocial behavior does predict later prosocial behavior, lending support to the idea that there is some consistency in prosocial behavior across childhood more broadly. For example, Eisenberg et al. (1999) did find that sharing during the preschool years predicted prosocial behavior in adolescence. Similarly, cooperation at age 4 has been found to predict subsequent compliance at the end of middle childhood (Hay & Pawlby, 2003).

DEVELOPMENTAL TRENDS

Most theories of prosocial behavior assume increases in children's empathic and prosocial behaviors across infancy, toddlerhood, and the preschool years (see Eisenberg et al., 2006, for a review; see Hay & Cook, 2007, for an alternative theory). Cognitive theories, for example, assume that improvements in children's social cognition, especially perspective taking, moral reasoning, and theory of mind, make prosocial behaviors more likely as children get older (see e.g., Miller, Eisenberg, Fabes, & Shell, 1996). Along the same lines, improvements in children's emotional skills, especially emotional understanding and regulation, are also assumed to increase children's prosocial tendencies (e.g., Denham, 1998; Eisenberg et al., 1996; Eisenberg et al., 2006). Finally, socialization theorists also predict increases in prosocial behaviors across early childhood as a result of increases in socialization attempts by parents aimed at fostering this behavior (e.g., inductive discipline; Hoffman, 2000).

Not all theorists, however, have argued for increases in prosocial behaviors across early childhood. Hay and her colleagues (Hay & Cook, 2007; Hay et al., 1999) have argued for the idea that prosocial behaviors emerge during the first and second year of life but decline thereafter, as children become more selective in their application of prosocial behaviors. Hay (1994) argues that although initially children direct prosocial behaviors at a broad section of individuals, children become increasingly selective in their targets of prosocial behaviors, especially as they become familiar with the norms about when and to whom it is appropriate to express prosocial behavior. Children also become increasingly aware of the costs of prosocial behaviors, which makes prosocial behaviors less likely (Hay et al., 1991). Thus, across early childhood, children begin to direct prosocial behavior toward people that are similar to them and with whom they have reciprocal relationships. Gender, in particular, begins to play a role in this selectivity as same-sex peer preferences lead to children sharing, cooperating, and helping more with same-sex peers over opposite-sex peers (e.g., Hay et al., 1999). Research supporting Hay's ideas, however, has been relatively mixed. For example, Hay et al. (1991) found no differences in sharing between 1- and 2-year-old children. In a similar study, Hay et al. (1999) found that the predicted decline in sharing was qualified by cohort and gender differences. Thus, the developmental pattern of sharing was not particularly clear in the Hay et al. (1999) study. There was some indication, in fact, that older girls (e.g., 30-month-olds) were increasing their rates of sharing across time (although girls were more likely to share with other girls).

To examine the issue of age-related increases in prosocial behavior more concretely, Eisenberg and Fabes (1998) conducted a meta-analysis of prosocial behavior and age. There were age-related increases in prosocial behaviors for children under the age of three (with an effect size of .24) and during the preschool years (with an effect size of .36), but there were no differences between the two time periods (infancy/ toddlerhood and the preschool years) in terms of prosocial behaviors. Eisenberg et al. (2006) speculate that is because there were so few studies that compared these two age groups. Thus, clearly more work (especially with longitudinal designs) is needed to examine how prosocial behaviors change across early childhood.

Although it is not clear that there is a decrease in the overall rates of prosocial behaviors in early childhood, there is good evidence that children are selective in their choice of targets with regard to prosocial behaviors. Research has supported that in general, toddlers' prosocial behaviors are more frequent with familiar than unfamiliar people. Thus, for example, toddlers are more likely to express empathy toward, comfort, share resources with, and help mothers over unfamiliar experimenters (Robinson, Zahn-Waxler, & Emde, 2001; van der Mark, van IJzendoorn, & Bakermans-Kranenburg, 2002; Rheingold, Hay, & West, 1976; for an exception see Rheingold, 1982). Young preschool children also express a preference for sharing resources with siblings and close friends over strangers (Olson & Spelke, 2008), and work with older children suggests that children are more likely to allocate resources to siblings and friends over acquaintances (Knight & Chao, 1991). A number of researchers have speculated that stranger weariness and fear proneness might prevent toddlers from engaging in prosocial behavior with strangers (Stanhope, Bell, & Parker-Cohen, 1987; Young, Fox, & Zahn-Waxler (1999). Despite this idea, however, there is still a wealth of evidence that suggests that young children engage in instrumental helping, comforting, and cooperative behavior with unfamiliar experimenters (e.g., Rheingold, 1982; Warneken & Tomasello, 2006; Zahn-Waxler, Radke-Yarrow, et al., 1992), even if this behavior less frequent than with familiar individuals.

EXPLANATIONS FOR THIS EARLY PROSOCIAL BEHAVIOR

In conclusion, a growing body of work suggests that young children, even infants, are capable of engaging in a variety of prosocial behaviors. The question that has been posed, therefore, is how do we explain the presence of prosocial behavior in young children, given that children are not yet sophisticated in terms of the social cognition? Several possible explanations arise to explain this. First, there is growing evidence that young children's social cognition might be more advanced than originally believed. For example, as discussed earlier, there is growing evidence that children may be able to reason about the goals and intentions of others well before their first birthdays (see e.g., Brandone & Wellman, 2009; Kamewari, Kato, Kanda, Ishiguro, & Hiraki, 2005; Woodward, 1998). There is also some preliminary evidence that infants begin to differentiate themselves from others during the first year of life (see Thompson, 2006, for a review). Finally, there is evidence that even infants as young as 6 months might have the ability to distinguish between prosocial versus antisocial acts and may prefer prosocial protagonists over antisocial ones (Hamlin, Wynn, & Bloom, 2007). All of these lines of work suggest that infants may have some of the prerequisite social cognitive skills necessary to facilitate this early prosocial behavior.

Second and more likely, however, is that early prosocial behavior may have different motivations than later prosocial behavior. Infants may share with and cooperate with others initially because they are motivated to engage with and affiliate with others, especially parents, peers, and siblings. Thus, early prosocial behaviors (especially object-related prosocial behaviors such as sharing) may be more motivated by communicative and social functions than later prosocial behaviors, which may be motivated more by the concern for others (Eisenberg, Wolchick, Goldberg, & Engel, 1992; Hay & Cook, 2007; Rheingold, 1982). Thus, it is not necessary to assume that advanced social cognition is necessary to explain the prosocial behavior that has been demonstrated during infancy and the toddler years.

Third, and finally, early empathic and prosocial behavior may also be the result of a biological substrate (Hoffman, 1981; Tomasello, 2008; Zahn-Waxler, Robinson, et al., 1992). Researchers have pointed to a number of sources of support for this idea. First, a number of theorists have argued for the idea that the reactive or empathic crying discussed earlier indicates that young children are biologically predisposed to be responsive to the distress of others (Hoffman, 1981). Moreover, researchers have also suggested that prosocial behaviors are present prior to adult's attempts to socialize the behavior (Warneken & Tomasello, 2009), and work suggests that infants are motivated to help with or without parental encouragement and experimenter rewards, suggesting that socialization is not necessary for the emergence of these early types of prosocial behaviors (Warneken & Tomasello, 2008). Biomedical and genetic research has also implicated a number of hormones and neurotransmitters (including dopamine, serotonin, vasopressin, and oxytocin) that provide a biological basis for prosocial behavior (see Carlo, 2013, for a review). Finally, there is some evidence of helpful behavior among chimpanzees (see Tomasello, 2009 for a review), suggesting that helpful behavior is not just an artifact of human culture, and its presence among related species lends support for the idea that it is part of the human behavioral repertoire.

SUMMARY

There is some limited evidence of short-term stability in prosocial dispositions across time, although it is not clear that there are strong interrelations between the different types of prosocial behaviors in early childhood. In general, there is some evidence that prosocial behavior increases across early childhood. At the same time, there is evidence that children are selective in who is the target of their prosocial behavior, and some researchers have argued that this selectivity may increase across time. Finally, researchers have made a number of arguments to try and explain the presence of prosocial behavior in early childhood. For example, researchers have argued for the idea that children's early prosocial behaviors have social and affiliative motivations or are the result of a biological substrate.

Conclusions and Future Directions

In conclusion, it is clear that the overwhelming majority of young children engage in helpful or empathic behavior and do so relatively early in development (Hay et al., 1999; Warneken & Tomasello, 2006; Zahn-Waxler, Radke-Yarrow, et al., 1992). The rates of prosocial behavior in early childhood may not be high, given that young children spend a lot of their time involved in independent play, which affords relatively few opportunities to be responsive to the needs of others (Hay & Cook, 2007), and because in early childhood children spend a lot of time in adult-supervised and structured activities. Nonetheless, prosocial behavior among young children seems to be equally as frequent (if not more so) as their aggressive behavior. For example, Hay et al. (1999; Hay, Castle, & Davies, 2000) found that toddlers were just as likely to share objects as to grab them and that across time children's prosocial sharing initiations become more frequent than their antisocial taking of toys.

Despite the recent impressive research that has documented the remarkable altruistic nature of young infants and toddlers, many questions remained unanswered by research. In general, children's empathic helping behavior has received the most attention by researchers and includes a number of longitudinal studies and a number of studies that have explored the temperamental, genetic, and parental factors that relate to these skills (see e.g., Knafo et al., 2008; Murphy & Laible, 2013; Spinrad & Stifter, 2006). As a result, it is time for research in this area to begin to explore the complex interplay that genetic (and other biological) factors have with environmental factors (e.g., parental responsiveness) in predicting empathic behavior. There is growing evidence, for example, that some children have genetic (or temperamental) profiles that make them more susceptible to the influence of rearing environments (see Belsky & Pluess, 2009; see Fortuna & Knafo, chapter 4, this volume). For example, children with a dopamine receptor D4 7-repeat allele benefited more from positive maternal parenting (with regard to prosocial behavior) than did children without this gene (Knafo, Israel, & Ebstein, 2011). More work along these lines is needed in early childhood. There is also a need for more research, especially with creative methodology, to explore the links between children's early social cognitive skills (e.g., perspective taking) and their empathic distress and comforting behavior (see Vaish et al., 2009, for an example of a creative design).

Children's sharing behavior has not been well studied in the literature, and as a result, there is need for more research on the normative developmental course of this behavior. Moreover, it would be important for researchers to understand why sharing behavior is particularly infrequent among toddlers. Thus, laboratory work is needed to understand the barriers to sharing. Studies that manipulate the cost of sharing, the cognitive load needed to share, and characteristics of the person in need (e.g., the relationship of the person to the child) could not only address the barriers that prohibit sharing, but illuminate the contexts under which sharing might be more likely. Similarly, work is needed that explores the peer contexts in which children are likely to collaborate and/or comply with the wishes of others, especially to achieve cooperative goals. In addition, relatively little work has examined the developmental processes (e.g., self-regulation) that make young children's cooperative behavior possible (for an exception see Brownell & Carriger, 1990).

Although elegant experimental designs have shown that young children are proficient instrumental helpers, there remain a number of unaddressed questions about this behavior. First, if instrumental helping has its roots in evolution (see Hawley, chapter 3, this volume; Warneken & Tomasello, 2009), young children should show a bias toward helping kin. Despite this, the bulk of the laboratory research on instrumental helping has focused on children's instrumental helping of an unrelated experimenter. Rates of helping might be higher if the targets of the helping behavior are family members and this could be easily addressed in laboratory paradigms. Second, although it is clear that there are remarkable individual differences in the amount of instrumental helping that children engage in during laboratory paradigms (see Warneken & Tomasello, 2007), relatively little is known about what factors contribute to individual differences in this type of helping. This is a rich avenue for future researchers, who could examine genetic, temperamental, social cognitive, and parental influences that relate to instrumental helping.

Finally, it is not clear whether prosocial behaviors of all types increase across early childhood or become more selective as others have argued (see e.g., Hay & Cook, 2007). Ultimately, there are reasons to believe that the developmental trajectories may vary depending on the type of prosocial behavior examined. For example, whereas research has documented increases in children's comforting behavior across the toddler years (see Zahn-Waxler, Robinson, et al., 1992), rates of sharing do not seem to increase and may remain steady or even decline (see Hay et al., 1991; Hay et al., 1999). Longitudinal work on more than one type of prosocial behavior is needed in order to sort out the developmental trajectories of different types of prosocial behaviors across time. It also seems important to examine the interconnections between the types of prosocial behaviors in order to understand the degree to which these behaviors are related or separate constructs. Ultimately, there is growing evidence that the different types of prosocial behavior are separate constructs with different developmental trajectories and correlates (see Dunfield et al., 2011; Hay & Cook, 2007).

References

Batson, C. D., Ahmad, N., Powell, A., Stocks, E., Shah, J., & Gardner, W. L. (2008). Prosocial motivation. In J. Y. Shah, & W. L. Gardner (Eds.), *Handbook of motivation science* (pp. 135–149). New York: Guilford Press.

Bellagamba, F., & Tomasello, M. (1999). Re-enacting intended acts: Comparing 12- and 18-month-olds. *Infant Behavior and Development, 22*, 277–282. doi: 10.1016/S0163-6383(99)00002-8

Belsky, J., & Pluess, M. (2009). Beyond diathesis-stress: Differential susceptibility to environmental influences. *Psychological Bulletin, 135*, 885–908. doi: 10.1037/a0017376

Birch, L. L., & Billman, J. (1986). Preschool children's food sharing with friends and acquaintances. *Child Development, 57*, 387–395. doi: 10.2307/1130594

Brandone, A. C., & Wellman, H. M. (2009). You can't always get what you want: Infants understand failed goal-directed actions. *Psychological Science, 20*, 85–91. doi: 10.1111/j.1467-9280.2008.02246.x

Brownell, C., & Brown, E. (1992). Peers and play in infants and toddlers. In J. Van Hasselt & M. Herson (Eds.), *Handbook of social development* (pp. 183–200). New York: Plenum Press.

Brownell, C. A., & Carriger, M. S. (1990). Changes in cooperation and self-other differentiation during the second year. *Child Development, 61*, 1164–1174. doi: 10.2307/1130884

Brownell, C. A., & Carriger, M. S. (1991). Collaborations among toddler peers: Individual contributions to social contexts. In L. B. Resnick & J. M. Levine (Eds.), *Perspectives on socially shared cognition* (pp. 365–383). Washington, DC: American Psychological Association. doi: 10.1037/10096-016

Brownell, C. A., Svetlova, M., & Nichols, S. (2009). To share or not to share: When do toddlers respond to another's needs? *Infancy, 14*, 117–130. doi: 10.1080/15250000802569868

Caplan, M. Z., & Hay, D. F. (1989). Preschoolers' responses to peers' distress and beliefs about bystander intervention. *Journal of Child Psychology and Psychiatry, 30*, 231–243. doi: 10.1111/j.1469-7610.1989.tb00237.x

Carlo, G. (2014). The development and correlates of prosocial moral behaviors. In M. Killen & J. G. Smetana (Eds.), *Handbook of moral development* (2nd ed.) (pp. 208–235). New York: Psychology Press.

Church, J. (1966). *Three babies: Biographies of cognitive development*. New York: Random House.

Demetriou, H., & Hay, D. F. (2004). Toddlers' reactions to the distress of familiar peers: The importance of context. *Infancy, 6*, 299–318. doi: 10.1207/s15327078in0602_9

Denham, S. A. (1998). *Emotional development in young children*. New York: Guilford.

Dondi, M., Simion, F., & Caltran, G. (1999). Can newborns discriminate between their own cry and the cry of another newborn infant? *Developmental Psychology, 35*, 418. doi: 10.1037/0012-1649.35.2.418

Dunfield, K., Kuhlmeier, V.A., O'Connell, L., & Kelley, E. (2011). Examining the diversity of prosocial behavior: Helping, sharing, and comforting in infancy. *Infancy, 16*, 227–247. doi: 10.1111/j.1532-7078.2010.00041.x

Dunn, J., & Munn, P. (1986). Siblings and the development of prosocial behavior. *International Journal of Behavioural Development, 9*, 265–284.

Eckerman, C. O., Davis, C. C., & Didow, S. M. (1989). Toddlers' emerging ways of achieving social coordinations with a peer. *Child Development, 60*, 440–453. doi: 10.2307/1130988

Eckerman, C. O., & Peterman, K. (2001). Peers and infant social/communicative development. In G. Bremner & A. Fogel (Eds.), *The Blackwell handbook of infant development* (pp. 427–464). Malden, MA: Blackwell.

Eisenberg, N. (2005). The development of empathy-related responding. In G. Carlo & C. P. Edwards (Eds.), *Moral motivation through the life span (pp. 73–117)*. Lincoln: University of Nebraska Press.

Eisenberg, N., & Fabes, R. A. (1998). Prosocial development. In W. Damon & N. Eisenberg (Eds.), *Handbook of child psychology: Vol. 3. Social, emotional, and personality development* (pp. 701–778). New York: Wiley.

Eisenberg, N., Fabes, R. A., Karbon, M., Murphy, B. C., Wosinski, M., Polazzi, L., Carlo, G., Juhnke, C. (1996). The relations of children's dispositional prosocial behavior to emotionality, regulation, and social functioning. *Child Development, 67*, 974–992. doi: 10.2307/1131874

Eisenberg, N., Fabes, R. A., & Spinrad, T. L. (2006). Prosocial development. In N. Eisenberg (Vol. Ed.), W. Damon & R. M. Lerner (Series Eds.), *Handbook of child psychology: Vol. 3. Social, emotional, and personality development* (pp. 646–718). New York: Wiley.

Eisenberg, N., & Strayer, J. (1990). Critical issues in the study of empathy. In N. Eisenberg & J. Strayer (Eds.), *Empathy and its development* (pp. 3–16). New York: Cambridge University Press.

Eisenberg, N., Wolchik, S., Goldberg, L., Engel, I. (1992). Parental values, reinforcement, and young children's prosocial behavior: A longitudinal study. *Journal of Genetic Psychology, 153*, 19–36.

Fasig, L. G. (2000). Toddlers' understanding of ownership: Implications for self-concept development. *Social Development, 9*, 370–382. doi: 10.1111/1467-9507.00131

Geangu, E., Benga, O., Stahl, D. & Striano, T. (2010). Contagious crying beyond the first days of life. *Infant Behavior and Development, 33*, 279–288. doi: 10.1016/j.infbeh.2010.03.004

Gralinski, J. H., & Kopp, C. B. (1993). Everyday rules for behavior: Mothers' requests to young children. *Developmental Psychology, 29*, 573–584. doi: 10.1037/0012-1649.29.3.573

Grusec, J. (1991), Socializing concern for others in the home. *Developmental Psychology, 27*, 338–342. doi: 10.1037/0012-1649.27.2.338

Hamlin, J. K., Wynn, K., & Bloom, P. (2007). Social evaluation by preverbal infants. *Nature, 450*, 557–559. doi: 10.1038/nature06288

Hay, D. F. (1979). Cooperative interactions and sharing between very young children and their parents. *Developmental Psychology, 15*, 647–653. doi: 10.1037/0012-1649.15.6.647

Hay, D. F. (1994). Prosocial development. *Journal of Child Psychology and Psychiatry, 35*, 29–71. doi: 10.1111/j.1469-7610.1994.tb01132.x

Hay, D. F. (2006). Yours and mine: Toddlers talk about possessions with familiar peers. *British Journal of Developmental Psychology, 24*, 39–52. doi: 10.1348/026151005X68880

Hay, D. F., Caplan, M., Castle, J., & Stimson, C. A. (1991). Does sharing become increasingly more "rational" in the second year of life? *Developmental Psychology, 27*, 987–993. doi: 10.1037/0012-1649.27.6.987

Hay, D. F., Castle, J., & Davies, L. (2000). Toddlers' use of force against familiar peers: A precursor of serious aggression? *Child Development, 71*, 457–467. doi: 10.1111/1467-8624.00157

Hay, D. F., Castle, J., Davies, L., Demetriou, H., & Stimson, C. (1999). Prosocial action in very early childhood. *Journal of Child Psychology and Psychiatry, 40*, 905–916. doi: 10.1111/1469-7610.00508

Hay, D. F., & Cook, K. V. (2007). The transformation of prosocial behaviour from infancy to childhood. In C. Brownell C. B. Kopp (Eds.), *Socioemotional development in the toddler years* (pp. 100–131). New York: Guilford Press.

Hay, D. F., & Murray, P. (1982). Giving and requesting: Social facilitation of infants' offers to adults. *Infant Behavior and Development, 5*, 301–310. doi: 10.1016/S0163-6383(82)80039-8

Hay, D. F., Nash, A., & Pedersen, J. (1981). Responses of six-month-olds to the distress of their peers. *Child Development*, 1071–1075. doi: 10.2307/1129114

Hay, D. F., Payne, A., & Chadwick, A. (2004). Peer relations in childhood. *Journal of Child Psychology and Psychiatry, 45*, 84–108. doi: 10.1046/j.0021-9630.2003.00308.x

Hay, D. F., & Pawlby, S. (2003). Prosocial development in relation to children's and mothers' psychological problems. *Child Development, 74*, 1295–1308. doi: 10.1111/1467-8624.00609

Hoffman, M. L. (1975). Developmental synthesis of affect and cognition and its implications for altruistic motivation. *Developmental Psychology, 11*, 607–22. doi: 10.1037/0012-1649.11.5.607

Hoffman, M. L. (1981). Is altruism part of human nature? *Human Development, 40*, 121–137. doi: 10.1037/0022-3514.40.1.121

Hoffman, M. L. (1984). Interaction of affect and cognition in empathy. In C. E. Izard & R. B. Kagan (Eds.), *Emotions, cognition, and behavior* (pp. 103–131). Cambridge, UK: Cambridge University Press.

Hoffman, M. L. (2000). *Empathy and Moral Development: Implications for Caring and Justice.* Cambridge University Press, Cambridge, UK.

Johnson, S. C., Booth, A., & O'Hearn, K. (2001). Inferring the goal of a non-human agent. *Cognitive Development, 16*, 637–656. doi: 10.1016/S0885-2014(01)00043-0

Kamewari, K., Kato, M., Kanda, T., Ishiguro, H., & Hiraki, K. (2005). Six-and-a-half-month-old children positively attribute goals to human action and to humanoid-robot motion. *Cognitive Development, 20*, 303–320. doi: 10.1016/j.cogdev.2005.04.004

Knafo, A., Israel, S., & Ebstein, R. P. (2011). Heritability of children's prosocial behavior and differential susceptibility to parenting by variation in the dopamine receptor D4 gene. *Development and Psychopathology, 23*, 53–67. doi: 10.1017/S0954579410000647

Knafo, A., Zahn-Waxler, C., Van Hulle, C., Robinson, J. L., & Rhee, S. H. (2008). The developmental origins of a disposition toward empathy: Genetic and environmental contributions. *Emotion, 8,* 737. doi: 10.1037/a0014179

Knight, G. P. Bohlmeyer, E. M. Stewart, H. S. Harris, J. D. (1993). Age differences in temporal monitoring and equal sharing in a fixed-duration sharing task. *British Journal of Developmental Psychology, 11,* 143–158. doi: 10.1111/j.2044-835X.1993.tb00594.x

Knight, G. P., & Chao, C. (1991). Cooperative, competitive, and individualistic social values among 8- to 12-year-old siblings, friends and acquaintances. *Personality and Social Psychology Bulletin, 7,* 201–211. doi: 10.1177/014616729101700213

Kochanska, G. (1994). Beyond cognition: Expanding the search for the early roots of internalization and conscience. *Developmental Psychology, 30,* 20–23. doi: 10.1037/0012-1649.30.1.20

Kochanska, G., & Aksan, N. (1995). Mother-child mutually positive affect, the quality of child compliance to requests and prohibitions, and maternal controls as correlates of early internalization. *Child Development, 66,* 236–254. doi: 10.2307/1131203

Kochanska, G., Aksan, N., & Koenig, A. L. (1995). A longitudinal study of the roots of preschoolers' conscience: Committed compliance and emerging internalization. *Child Development, 66,* 1752–1769. doi: 10.2307/1131908

Kochanska, G., Tjebkes, T. L., & Forman, D. R. (1998). Children's emerging regulation of conduct: Restraint, compliance, and internalization from infancy to the second year. *Child Development, 69,* 1378–1389. doi: 10.2307/1132272

Kochanska, G., Woodward, J., Kim, S., Koenig, J., Yoon, J., & Barry, R. (2010). Positive socialization mechanisms in secure and insecure parent-child dyads: Two longitudinal studies. *Journal of Child Psychology and Psychiatry, 51,* 998–1009. Doi:10.111/j.1469-7610:2010.02238.x

Koestner, R., Franz, C., & Weinberger, J. (1990). The family origins of empathic concern: A 26-year longitudinal study. *Journal of Personality and Social Psychology, 58,* 709–717. doi: 10.1037/0022-3514.58.4.709

Lamb, S., & Zakhireh, B. (1997). Toddlers' attention to the distress of peers in a daycare setting, *Early Education and Development, 8,* 105–118. doi: 10.1207/s15566935eed0802_1

Levitt, M. J., Weber, R. A., Clark, M. C., & McDonnell, P. (1985). Reciprocity of exchange in toddler sharing behavior. *Developmental Psychology, 21,* 122–123. doi: 10.1037/0012-1649.21.1.122

Liszkowski, U., Carpenter, M., Striano, T., & Tomasello, M. (2006). Twelve- and 18-month-olds point to provide information for others. *Journal of Cognition and Development, 7,* 173–187. doi: 10.1207/s15327647jcd0702_2

Liszkowski, U., Carpenter, M., & Tomasello, M. (2008). Twelve-month-olds communicate helpfully and appropriately for knowledgeable and ignorant partners. *Cognition, 108,* 732–739. doi: 10.1016/j.cognition.2008.06.013

Maccoby, E. E., & Martin, J. A. (1983). Socialization in the context of the family: Parent-child interaction. In P. H. Mussen & E. M. Hetherington (Eds.), *Handbook of child psychology: Vol. 4. Socialization, personality, and social development* (4th ed., pp. 1–101). New York: Wiley.

Martin, G. B., & Clark, R. D. (1982). Distress crying in neonates: Species and peer specificity. *Developmental Psychology, 18,* 3–9. doi: 10.1037/0012-1649.18.1.3

Melis, A., Altrichter, K., & Tomasello, M. (2013). Allocation of resources to collaborators and free-riders in 3-year-olds. *Journal of Experimental Child Psychology, 114*, 364–370.

Miller, P. A., Eisenberg, N., Fabes, R. A., & Shell, R. (1996). Relations of moral reasoning and vicarious emotion to young children's prosocial behaviour toward peers and adults. *Developmental Psychology, 32*, 210–219. doi: 10.1037/0012-1649.32.2.210

Olson, K. R., & Spelke, E. S. (2008). Foundations of cooperation in preschool children. *Cognition, 108*, 222–231. doi: 10.1016/j.cognition.2007.12.003

Murphy, T. M., & Laible, D. J. (2013). The influence of attachment on preschool children's empathic responding, *International Journal of Behavioral Development, 37*, 436–440.

Phillips, A. T., & Wellman, H. M. (2005). Infants' understanding of object-directed action. *Cognition, 98*, 137–155. doi: 10.1016/j.cognition.2004.11.005

Radke-Yarrow, M., & Zahn-Waxler, C. (1984). Roots, motives, and patterns in children's prosocial behavior. In E. Staub, D. Bar-Tal, J. Karylowski, & J. Reykowski (Eds.), *Development and maintenance of prosocial behavior: International perspectives on positive behavior* (pp. 81–99). New York: Plenum.

Rheingold, H. L. (1982). Little children's participation in the work of adults, a nascent prosocial behavior. *Child Development, 53*, 114–121 doi: 10.2307/1129643

Rheingold, H. L., Cook, K. V., & Kolowitz, V. (1987). Commands activate the behavior and pleasure of 2-year old children. *Developmental Psychology, 23*, 146–151. doi: 10.1037/0012-1649.23.1.146

Rheingold, H. L., Hay, D. F., & West, M. J. (1976). Sharing in the second year of life. *Child Development, 47*, 1148–1158. doi: 10.2307/1128454

Robinson, J., Zahn-Waxler, C., & Emde, R. N. (2001). Relationship context as a moderator of sources of individual differences in empathic development. In R. N. Emde & J. K. Hewitt (Eds.), *Infancy to early childhood: Genetic and environmental influences on developmental change* (pp. 257–268). New York: Oxford University Press.

Roth-Hanania, R., Davidov, M., & Zahn-Waxler, C. (2011). Empathy development from 8 to 16 months: Early signs of concern for others. *Infant Behavior and Development, 34*, 447–458. doi: 10.1016/j.infbeh.2011.04.007

Saarni, C., Campos, J. J., Camras, L. A., & Witherington, D. (2006). Emotional development: action, communication, and understanding. In N. Einsenberg (Ed.), *Handbook of child psychology.* Vol. 3. Social, emotional, and personality development (6th ed.) (pp. 226–299). New York: John Wiley & Sons.

Saarni, C., Mumme, D., & Campos, J. (1998). Emotional development: Action, communication, and understanding. In N. Eisenberg (Vol. Ed.), *Social, emotional, and personality development* (pp. 237–311). Vol. 3 of W. Damon (Series Ed.), Handbook of child psychology. New York: John Wiley.

Sagi, A., & Hoffman, M. L. (1976). Empathic distress in the newborn. *Developmental Psychology, 12*, 175. doi: 10.1037/0012-1649.12.2.175

Sigman, M., Mundy, P., Sherman, T., & Ungerer, J. A. (1986). Social interactions of autistic, mentally retarded, and normal children and their caregivers. *Journal of Child Psychology and Psychiatry, 27*, 647–656. doi: 10.1111/j.1469-7610.1986.tb00189.x

Spinrad, T., Eisenberg, N., Silva, K., Eggum, N., Reiser, M., Edwards, A., … Gaertner, B. (2012). Longitudinal relations among maternal behaviors, effortful control, and young children's committed compliance. *Developmental Psychology, 48*, 552–566.

Spinrad, T. L., & Stifter, C. A. (2006). Toddlers' empathy-related responding to distress: Predictions from negative emotionality and maternal behavior in infancy. *Infancy* *10*, 97–121. doi: 10.1207/s15327078in1002_1

Stanhope, P., Bell, R., & Parker-Cohen, N. (1987). Temperament and helping behavior in preschool children. *Developmental Psychology*, *23*, 347–353. doi: 10.1037/0012-1649.23.3.347

Svetlova, M., Nichols, S., & Brownell, C. (2010). Toddlers' prosocial behavior: From instrumental to empathic to altruistic helping. *Child Development*, *81*, 1814–1827. doi: 10.1111/j.1467-8624.2010.01512.x

Termine, N. T. & Izard, C. E. (1988). Infants' responses to their mothers' expressions of joy and sadness. *Developmental Psychology*, *24*, 223–229. doi: 10.1037/0012-1649.24.2.223

Tomasello, M. Carpenter, M., Call, J., Behne, T., & Moll, H. (2005). Understanding and sharing intentions: The origins of cultural cognition. *The Behavioral and Brain Sciences*, *28*, 675–691. doi: 10.1017/S0140525X05000129

Thompson, R. A. (2006). The development of the person: Social understanding, relationships, conscience, self. In W. Damon, R. M. Lerner, & N. Eisenberg (Eds.), *Handbook of child psychology: Vol. 3. Social, emotional and personality development* (6th ed., pp. 24–98). New York: Wiley.

Tomasello, M. (2008). *Origins of human communication*. Cambridge, MA: MIT Press.

Tomasello, M. (2009). *Why we cooperate*. Cambridge, MA: MIT Press.

Vaish, A., Carpenter, M., & Tomasello, M. (2009). Sympathy through affective perspective taking and its relation to prosocial behavior in toddlers. *Developmental Psychology*, *45*, 534–543. doi: 10.1037/a0014322

van der Mark, I., IJzendoorn, M., & Bakermans-Kranenburg, M. (2002). Development of empathy in girls during the second year of life: Associations with parenting, attachment, and temperament. *Social Development*, *11*, 451–468. doi: 10.1111/1467-9507.00210

Volbrecht, M. M., Lemery-Chalfant, K., Aksan, N., Zahn-Waxler, C., & Goldsmith, H. H. (2007). Examining the familial link between positive affect and empathy development in the second year. *Journal of Genetic Psychology*, *168*, 105–129. doi: 10.3200/GNTP.168.2.105-130

Warneken, F., Chen, R., & Tomasello, M. (2006). Cooperative activities in young children and chimpanzees. *Child Development*, *77*, 640–663. doi: 10.1111/j.1467-8624.2006.00895.x

Warneken, F., Gräfenhain, M., & Tomasello, M. (2012), Collaborative partner or social tool? New evidence for young children's understanding of joint intentions in collaborative activities. *Developmental Science*, *15*, 54–61. doi: 10.1111/j.1467-7687.2011.01107.x

Warneken, F., Hare, B., Melis, A. P., Hanus, D., & Tomasello, M. (2007). Spontaneous altruism by chimpanzees and young children. *PLoS Biology*, *5*, e184. 10.1371/journal.pbio.0050184.

Warneken, F., Lohse, K., Melis, A. P., & Tomasello, M. (2011). Young children share the spoils after collaboration. *Psychological Science*, *22*, 267–273. doi: 10.1177/0956797610395392

Warneken, F., & Tomasello, M. (2008). Extrinsic rewards undermine altruistic tendencies in 20-month-olds. *Developmental Psychology*, *44*, 1785–1788. doi: 10.1037/a0013860

Warneken, F., & Tomasello, M. (2009). The roots of human altruism. *British Journal of Psychology*, *100*, 455–471. doi: 10.1348/000712608X379061

Warneken, F., & Tomasello, M. (2006). Altruistic helping in human infants and young chimpanzees. *Science*, *311*, 1301–1303. doi: 10.1126/science.1121448

Warneken, F., & Tomasello, M. (2007). Helping and cooperation at 14 months of age. *Infancy, 11*, 271–294. doi: 10.1111/j.1532-7078.2007.tb00227.x

Woodward, A. L. (1998). Infants selectively encode the goal object of an actor's reach, *Cognition, 69*, 1–34. doi: 10.1016/S0010-0277(98)00058-4

Woodward, A. L., Sommerville, J. A., & Guajardo, J. J. (2001). How infants make sense of intentional action. In B. Malle, L. Moses, & D. Baldwin (Eds.), *Intentions and intentionality: Foundations of social cognition (pp. 149–169)*. Cambridge, MA: MIT Press.

Young, S. K., Fox, N. A., & Zahn-Waxler, C. (1999). The relations between temperament and empathy in 2-year-olds. *Developmental Psychology, 35*, 1189–1197. doi: 10.1037/0012-1 649.35.5.1189

Zahn-Waxler, C., & Radke-Yarrow, M. (1982). The development of altruism: Alternative research strategies. In N. Eisenberg (Ed.), *The development of prosocial behavior* (pp. 109–137). New York: Academic Press.

Zahn-Waxler, C., Radke-Yarrow, M., Wagner, E., & Chapman, M. (1992). Development of concern for others. *Developmental Psychology, 28*, 126–136. doi: 10.1037/0012-1649.28.1.126

Zahn-Waxler, C., Robinson, J. L., & Emde, R. (1992). The development of empathy in twins. *Developmental Psychology, 28*, 1038–1047. doi: 10.1037/0012-1649.28.6.1038

18

Adopting a Multidimensional Perspective on College Students' Prosocial Behaviors

Brandy A. Randall and Jennifer R. Wenner

March 2009 was a tumultuous time in Fargo, North Dakota, and Moorhead, Minnesota (FM), two relatively small cities in the upper midwestern United States, separated by the Red River of the North. The Red River flows from south to north, creating some level of flooding each spring as the ice thaws in the warmer south and the water has nowhere to go in the still frozen north. Most years see only minor flooding; however, 2009 set a new flood record and was designated a 100-year flood. Residents were frantically sandbagging as the flood forecasts crept higher and higher each day. The city of Grand Forks to the north had been inundated with flood waters slightly more than 10 years before, and most of the city had to be rebuilt. The FM community was fighting against this very real possibility, desperately trying to keep the river from flooding the cities. The river was fighting back, with the crest predictions suddenly higher and a week earlier than had been expected. Almost certain devastation was imminent. Thousands feared the loss of their homes, their livelihoods, and maybe their lives.

The administrations of the three local universities decided to cancel classes for a week. This was the week prior to spring break for many of the students. The universities, the mayor, and others appealed to the students to stay and help save the cities, rather than go home. Amazingly enough, even though they could have just gone home and started their break early, as most of them were not local residents, the majority stayed. And helped. The universities organized bussing from campus to the sandbagging sites. Prakash Matthews, North Dakota State University (NDSU) vice-president for student affairs, reported that 1,000 people volunteered within the first hour, stating, "This is what NDSU is all about. This is what is special about our students" ("Students Help," 2009). Actual numbers of volunteers are difficult to come by, as many students just showed up at the sites. NDSU's numbers show that over 2,000 students checked in to be bussed to the flood-fighting locations. Overall, local university students contributed thousands of volunteer hours in the wet and cold that FM was experiencing at the time to build the dikes that saved the city. Afterward, everyone agreed that the communities would have likely been lost if the college students had not helped. Jim Gilmour, director of Fargo Planning, said, "The college students are very important to the city of Fargo. They worked around the clock to fight the flood.... They played an unparalleled role in saving the community" (Hough, 2009). Concordia University student Todd Reynolds said, "We're a part of this community. It's our responsibility to do this" ("Flood 2009," 2009).

This picture of college students as engaged in their communities, willing to sacrifice fun, free time, and comfort while engaging in a physically demanding task in the brutal cold is in marked contrast to recent studies indicating that college students are not as nice as they used to be. Specifically, Twenge and Foster (2010) found that American college students' levels of narcissism increased between 1982 and 2009. Konrath, O'Brien, and Hsing (2011) found that levels of both empathic concern and perspective taking declined among college students between 1979 and 2009. Such results are seemingly at odds with college student behavior during the 2009 FM flood. Discrepancies such as these highlight the need for a deep understanding of prosocial behaviors (i.e., voluntary behavior intended to benefit another; Eisenberg, Fabes, & Spinrad, 2006) among young adults, including young adults attending college.

Young adulthood (or emerging adulthood) is an important developmental period, during which individuals tend to have more responsibility and freedom than they did as adolescents, yet often still are not fully engaged in the adult world of jobs, partner commitments, and children (Arnett, 2000). Individuals are making a multitude of choices during this period that set the stage for the direction their lives will take. Understanding young adult prosocial behaviors and their associations with other constructs that are important during this developmental period can help us more fully understand the trajectories that positive behaviors may follow from this point forward.

On the face of it, there have been many investigations of prosocial behavior that focused on a young adult population. Specifically, social psychologists, who in many ways were responsible for a new emphasis on understanding prosocial behaviors with their investigations of bystander intervention beginning in the late 1960s, have been criticized for an overreliance on college students in their experimental studies (Sears, 1986). The research coming out of social psychological laboratories has played a key role in understanding situational and personality influences on prosocial behaviors. However, even though many of these studies have used young adult samples, they have been of limited value in understanding young adults' prosocial behaviors from a developmental standpoint (e.g., Bizman, Yinon, Ronco, & Shachar, 1980; Stocks, Lishner, & Decker, 2009).

Scholars have utilized various approaches to measure prosocial behavior. Studies in the broader field run the gamut from lab-based experiments to observations to self-report surveys. However, studies that examine young adult prosocial behavior from a developmental perspective almost exclusively rely on self-report measures that provide information about the individual's ongoing behavioral tendencies across multiple contexts. Popular self-report measures historically have tended to focus on a global set of behaviors and resulted in a scale score indicating whether people were generally more or less frequently prosocial (e.g., Rushton, Chrisjohn, & Fekken, 1981). However, as Carlo and Randall (2002) discuss (and as is noted elsewhere in this volume), there are multiple types of prosocial behaviors enacted for multiple motives. Prosocial behaviors performed for different reasons are differentially related to other constructs of interest. This is an important consideration for fully understanding young adult prosocial behavior, as examining young adult prosocial behavior from a multidimensional perspective can yield insights into the developmental precursors of different prosocial tendencies, as well as their possible consequences.

This chapter will review literature relevant to understanding young adult prosocial behavior, present new data that examines correlates of young adult prosocial behavior from a multidimensional perspective, and then discuss implications of the findings as well as the limitations in our knowledge base and potential future directions. Primary attention will focus on the correlates that have been the most commonly investigated at multiple points of the life span, most notably emotional and cognitive variables. Attention will also be given to the social context of prosocial behaviors and to the ways in which prosocial behaviors link to antisocial behaviors.

Emotional and Cognitive Correlates of Prosocial Behavior

Substantial empirical and theoretical evidence supports the key role that emotion and cognition play in prosocial behavior, particularly empathic responding, personal distress, and perspective taking. Although a thorough review is beyond the scope of this chapter (see Eisenberg, Wentzel, & Harris, 1998, for a review), generally scholars find that sympathy (also termed empathic concern), that is, care and concern for the needs of another, contributes to prosocial behavior across the life span (e.g., Laible, Carlo, & Roesch, 2004; Stiff, Dillard, Somera, Kim, & Sleight 1988). Further, gender differences are frequently observed, such that girls and women tend to be higher in empathic concern than do boys and men. However, gender differences in empathy are impacted by the methodology used, with the most pronounced gender differences found using self-report empathy measures (Eisenberg et al., 2006). Perspective taking, the ability to see another's point of view, has also been associated with an increased likelihood of prosocial behavior, in part through the influence on empathic concern. Specially, seeing another's point of view makes it more likely to respond with increased level of empathic concern, facilitating a prosocial response. This pattern has been found across the life span, including in studies with college students (e.g., Stiff et al., 1988). Empathic concern particularly seems to promote an altruistic response (Stocks et al., 2009). In contrast, personal distress (a negative emotional reaction to the experience of another's emotional state; Eisenberg et al., 2006) has typically been linked with a reduced likelihood of enacting prosocial behavior (and altruism), especially when escape from the situation is simple. For example, Carlo, Allen, and Buhman (1999) found significant associations between trait perspective taking and college students' intent to volunteer. Personal distress increases the focus on the self and reduces the capacity for empathic concern for the needs of the other, thereby reducing prosocial behavior.

Self-esteem, a general feeling of self-worth, has been theoretically linked with prosocial behavior, as both a cause and an outcome. However, empirical evidence for this linkage is mixed. For example, Laible et al. (2004) found a positive relation between adolescents' prosocial behavior (assessed using a global measure) and self-esteem, although this was stronger for girls. Self-report data shows a positive link between self-esteem and volunteering in college students (Brown, Hoye, & Nicholson, 2012). In contrast, Schwartz, Zamboanga, and Jarvis (2007) found no relation between self-esteem and a multidimensional measure of prosocial behavior among Hispanic college students. One limitation of the Schwartz et al. (2007) study is that they scored the prosocial measure by summing all the items so that any variation between prosocial behavior subtypes and self-esteem was lost. Thus, the relation between self-esteem and different aspects of prosocial behavior for adolescents and young adults remains an unanswered question.

Emotional states have also been linked with prosocial behavior. Positive emotional tone, or a general tendency to experience positive affect, has been linked to higher levels of prosocial behavior. For example, individuals in a positive mood are more likely to engage in prosocial behavior (George, 1991). Focusing more on emotional regulation, Eisenberg and her colleagues have consistently found that individuals who are prone to negative emotionality are less likely to engage in prosocial behavior (see Eisenberg et al., 2006). Interestingly, there is some evidence that positive mood may enhance an individual's unconscious mirroring of another's actions (Kuhbandner, Pekrun, & Maier, 2010), which may then lead to an empathic response that might, in turn, lead to empathic concern/sympathy with further processing. People may also engage in prosocial behavior when in a positive mood in order to maintain their positive state (Eisenberg, 2000).

Prosocial Behaviors and Relationships

Substantial evidence indicates that parents play a key role in setting the stage for their offsprings' prosocial behavior development (Eisenberg & Murphy, 1995; Padilla-Walker, chapter 7, this volume). Although Western young adults typically are seen as interacting less with their parents on a day-to-day basis than adolescents or children, parents are still important to this age group, though perhaps in a less direct way than earlier in the life span. Barry, Padilla-Walker, Madsen, and Nelson (2008) found that mother-child relationship quality was associated with

young adults' prosocial values, which in turn linked to their prosocial tendencies. Specifically, young adults with higher quality relationships with their mothers
reported greater internal regulation of and less external regulation of prosocial
values. Internal regulation of prosocial values linked to higher levels of compliant,
anonymous, and altruistic helping, while external regulation was associated with
higher levels of public helping. Thus, parents continue to exert an indirect influence on their offsprings' prosocial tendencies, even into the college years.

Peers are also an important influence on prosocial behavior. Relations between
prosocial behavior and multiple aspects of the peer social context have been shown
across childhood, adolescence, and into adulthood. Quality of the peer relationship, acceptance by peers, loneliness, and peers' prosocial behaviors have been
linked with the individual's prosocial behavior. For example, prosocial behavior
measured using peer nominations predicted peer acceptance among early adolescents (Wentzel & Erdley, 1993) and college students (Lansu & Cillessen, 2012).
Self- and peer reports of prosocial behavior are positively associated with indices
of friendship quality among adolescents, including high levels of closeness and
low levels of conflict (Cillessen, Jiang, West, & Laszkowski, 2005). Global measures of prosocial behavior are associated with lower levels of loneliness in adolescence (Woodhouse, Dykas, & Cassidy, 2011). Friends' prosocial behavior predicted
middle adolescents' prosocial behavior (measured using a global peer report) one
year later and related both concurrently and longitudinally to adolescents' prosocial goal pursuit, although this relation was moderated by the affective quality of
the friendship (Barry & Wentzel, 2006). A longitudinal study using Gallup Poll
data from adults found that people with more friends were more likely to engage
in prosocial behavior (assessed with a global self-report measure; O'Malley,
Arbesman, Steiger, Fowler, & Christakis, 2012). Furthermore, this data showed
that behaving in a more prosocial manner was associated with the development
of closer interpersonal relationships, but that the reverse was not true. Finally, a
series of studies with college students demonstrated that experimentally created
social rejection has the power to reduce prosocial behavior (Twenge, Baumeister,
DeWall, Ciarocco, & Bartels, 2007). Thus, prosocial behavior appears to support
the development and maintenance of peer relationships; furthermore, the number
and quality of the relationships and the prosocial behaviors of individuals in the
peer network can influence prosocial behaviors across a range of ages.

Links Between Prosocial Behaviors and Problem Behaviors

Global measures of prosocial behavior have been linked to several different forms
of problem behaviors in both adolescence and young adulthood. Prosocial behavior is negatively correlated with antisocial behavior in early adolescence (Wentzel
& Erdley, 1993). Peer-reported prosocial behaviors have also been associated with
both aggression and delinquency in early adolescence, although this link was

mediated by agreeableness and conscientiousness among girls (Pursell, Laursen, Rubin, Booth-LaForce, & Rose-Krasnor, 2008). Adolescents with lower prosocial orientation (a composite measure of behavior and orientation) demonstrated higher levels of misconduct (a composite of delinquency and substance use; Lim, Khoo, & Wong, 2007). However, Nguyen, Clark, and Belgrave (2011) found no relation between drug use and prosocial behavior for African American adolescents. Interestingly, prosocial behaviors during adolescence appear to have ramifications into adulthood. Specifically, adolescents who volunteered during the latter part of high school were significantly less likely to have been arrested by young adulthood (Uggen & Janikula, 1999). Additionally, increased prosocial behavior during adolescence (assessed with a global measure) was associated concurrently and longitudinally with deviance and substance use (Carlo, Crockett, Wilkinson, & Beal, 2011). Thus, prosocial behavior appears to play a protective role in regard to problem behaviors; however, the extent that this is true across different types of prosocial behaviors remains unexplored.

In sum, prior research has consistently demonstrated that prosocial behaviors are associated with emotional and cognitive response tendencies. Furthermore, prosocial behaviors are linked with higher quality parent-child relationships, higher quality friendships, more friendships, and having more prosocial friends. Finally, prosocial behaviors may serve to reduce the likelihood that adolescents and young adults will engage in problem behaviors such as substance use and delinquency. Although some of the studies mentioned in this review have used multifaceted measures of prosocial behavior, such a nuanced view of prosocial behavior is really in its infancy. For example, most of the studies that link aspects of peer relationships with prosocial behavior use global measures of behaviors that are centered in the peer social world (e.g., helps, shares, and cooperates with other kids).

A summary of a study with college students will be presented to highlight the advantages of adopting a multidimensional perspective. This data provides an opportunity to examine the correlates in college students of a multidimensional measure of prosocial behaviors across a range of variables that have previously been highlighted in the prosocial behavior literature and to contrast the pattern of correlations with those found using a global measure of prosocial behavior. Given the substantial literature demonstrating gender differences in prosocial behavior, as well as in the link of prosocial behavior to other variables, the pattern of correlations is examined separately for women and men. As this study will show, adopting a multidimensional perspective has the potential to provide a deeper understanding of prosocial behavior in young adults.

A STUDY OF PROSOCIAL BEHAVIOR IN COLLEGE STUDENTS

Participants were 18- to 22-year-old undergraduate students (N = 247) attending a university in the upper Midwest (177 women, M age = 19.38) who completed an anonymous survey assessing their prosocial behaviors, emotional and cognitive variables, peer variables, and problem behaviors.

Prosocial behaviors were evaluated using both a global measure of prosocial behavior that is typical of assessments of prosocial behavior in previous research, as well as a multidimensional measure. This provides us the opportunity to directly compare the results one obtains with each approach. The multidimensional measure used was the Prosocial Tendencies Measure (PTM; Carlo & Randall, 2001), which assesses six forms of prosocial behavior including altruism (voluntary helping behavior motivated primarily by concern for the needs and welfare of another), anonymous (helping performed without others being aware of who helped), compliant (helping in response to a verbal or nonverbal request), dire (helping in crisis or emergency situations), emotional (helping in situations that contain emotionally evocative cues), and public (helping performed in front of others).

Global prosocial behavior was measured using questions from the Primary Prevention Awareness, Attitudes and Usage Scale (PPAAUS; Swisher, Shute, & Bibeau, 1985) that assess volunteering, helping, raising or donating money, sharing, and doing favors for others.

Emotional and cognitive variables that were evaluated included empathic concern, perspective taking and personal distress (Davis, 1983), self-esteem (Rosenberg, 1965), positive emotional tone (Petersen, Schulenberg, Abramowitz, Offer, & Jarcho, 1984), and loneliness (Russell, Peplau, & Cutrona, 1980). Peer variables assessed were peer relationship quality (Petersen et al., 1984), having prosocial friends (Tilton-Weaver & Galambos, 2003), and having antisocial friends (constructed by first author).

Participants' problem behaviors that were examined included deviant behavior (Swisher et al., 1985) and substance use (drugs, alcohol, and cigarettes; Swisher et al., 1985). Correlations between the prosocial behavior measures and the prosocial behavior correlates are shown separately for men and women in Table 18.1.

GENDER AND PROSOCIAL BEHAVIORS

For the overall sample, women reported significantly more altruism ($r = .27$; $p < .001$) and a trend toward more emotional prosocial behavior ($r = .13$; $p < .10$) than men. Men reported significantly more anonymous ($r = -.15$; $p < .05$) and public prosocial behavior ($r = -.21$; $p < .01$) and show a trend toward more dire prosocial behavior ($r = -.13$; $p < .10$) than women. Gender was not significantly correlated with compliant prosocial behavior, or with the global measure of prosocial behavior.

CORRELATES OF MULTIDIMENSIONAL AND GLOBAL PROSOCIAL BEHAVIOR

Correlations were calculated separately for women and men to examine gender-related patterns (see Table 18.1 for correlations and means). R-to-z

TABLE 18.1 Correlations between types of prosocial behavior and demographic, emotional, cognitive, social, and behavioral variables by gender

Variable	M	Altruism	Anonymous	Compliant	Dire	Emotional	Public	Global
1. Age	19.51 (19.13)	.14 (.19)	-.16+ (.17)	-.03 (.00)	-.32*** (-.11)	-.22* (-.01)	-.22* (-.08)	-.01 (.02)
2. Perspective Taking	3.45 (3.40)	.03 (.03)	.23* (.29*)	.37*** (.32*)	.48*** (.33**)	.40*** (.28*)	-.08 (-.01)	.27** (.01)
3. Personal Distress	2.54 (2.29)	-.11 (-.28*)	.05 (.23+)	-.22* (-.00)	-.22* (-.01)	-.02 (.15)	.24** (.20)	-.01 (-.27*)
4. Empathic Concern	3.99 (3.58)	.34*** (.23+)	.24** (.37***)	.45*** (.32*)	.38*** (.38**)	.46*** (.49***)	-.24** (-.23+)	.35*** (.25*)
5. Emotional Tone	4.39 (4.12)	.09 (.05)	.10 (-.25*)	.20* (.11)	.21* (.04)	.13 (-.17)	-.11 (.07)	.13 (.25*)
6. Self-Esteem	3.14 (3.08)	.06 (-.06)	.06 (-.15)	.22* (.12)	.10 (.09)	.17+ (-.07)	-.11 (.07)	.14 (.34**)
7. Loneliness	2.20 (2.36)	-.19* (.02)	-.00 (.09)	-.20* (-.22+)	-.19* (-.23+)	-.24** (-.01)	.09 (-.19)	-.14 (-.18)
8. Peer Relationship Quality	4.32 (3.99)	-.01 (-.09)	-.09 (-.33**)	.14 (.15)	.22* (.01)	.24** (-.12)	-.06 (.25*)	.15 (.25*)
9. Prosocial Friends	4.59 (4.31)	.32*** (.07)	.09 (.24+)	.20* (.21)	.21* (.28*)	.06 (.19)	-.14 (.06)	.10 (.05)
10. Antisocial Friends	1.63 (1.76)	-.33*** (-.14)	-.04 (-.17)	-.14 (.11)	.07 (-.06)	.17+ (-.15)	.19* (.18)	.03 (.07)
11. Substance Use	2.25 (2.13)	-.33*** (-.12)	-.06 (-.26*)	-.24** (-.05)	-.01 (-.21+)	.03 (-.23+)	.16+ (.15)	.10 (.11)
12. Deviance	1.74 (1.99)	-.53*** (-.25*)	.03 (-.17)	-.24** (-.21+)	.04 (-.34**)	.13 (-.15)	.42*** (.20)	.16+ (.08)
13. Prosocial Behavior M		4.30 (3.86)	2.79 (3.07)	3.79 (3.65)	3.12 (3.33)	2.99 (2.77)	1.83 (2.17)	3.94 (3.83)

Note: Men's statistics are in parentheses. Significant and trend correlations are bolded. Significant gender differences are underlined.
+ p < .10; * p < .05; ** p < .01; *** p < .001.

transformations were calculated to compare the magnitude of the correlations for men and women. Z scores greater than 1.96 were significant at the $p < .05$ level and are underlined in Table 18.1. No other pairs of correlates were significantly different for men and women. First, we present the correlates of prosocial behavior that were significant for both women and men. Then we present correlates that were significant for only women and only men.

PROSOCIAL BEHAVIOR CORRELATES FOR WOMEN AND MEN

Higher levels of perspective taking were significantly correlated with higher levels of anonymous, compliant, dire, and emotional prosocial behavior in both men and women. Empathic concern was related to global prosocial behaviors and all subtypes of prosocial behavior for both men and women, though some relations were at a trend level. Higher loneliness was significantly associated with lower levels of compliant and dire prosocial behavior in women, with a similar pattern for men at the trend level. More deviance was significantly associated with less compliant prosocial behavior in women, with a similar relation for men at the trend level. Having more prosocial friends was significantly associated with higher levels of dire prosocial behavior in men and women. For both men and women, a higher level of deviance was significantly associated with lower altruism, however, the association for women was significantly stronger than for men ($z = 2.08$). There were no other similarities in the pattern of significant correlations for men and women.

PROSOCIAL BEHAVIOR CORRELATES FOR WOMEN ONLY

Several correlations were significant only for women. Older women college students and those reporting more personal distress reported significantly lower levels of dire prosocial behavior. A positive emotional tone and more positive peer relationship quality were associated with significantly higher levels of dire prosocial behaviors. Older women college students also reported lower levels of emotional and public prosocial behaviors (a pattern seen at the trend level with anonymous prosocial behavior). This finding for age is interesting, given that the age range spanned only 4 years. Further, the correlation between age and anonymous prosocial behavior was significantly different for women and for men ($z = 2.12$). Higher levels of perspective taking were associated with more frequent global prosocial behavior. Higher levels of personal distress in women were significantly associated with lower levels of compliant prosocial behavior and higher levels of public prosocial behavior. Women reporting a more positive emotional tone and higher self-esteem and those with more prosocial friends reported significantly higher levels of compliant prosocial behavior. Women reporting higher peer relationship quality reported significantly higher levels of emotional prosocial behavior (seen at a trend level with self-esteem), with the correlations for women significantly different from men's (z = 2.34). Higher levels of loneliness, more frequent substance use, and having more antisocial friends were significantly associated with lower levels of altruism, while having more prosocial friends was significantly associated with higher levels of altruism. Increased loneliness was also associated with lower levels of emotional prosocial behaviors. Those with more antisocial friends and those reporting higher levels of deviance reported significantly higher levels of public prosocial behavior (seen at a trend level with substance use). Having more antisocial friends was associated with higher levels of emotional prosocial behavior at a trend level and was significantly different from men (z = 2.03). Higher deviance was also associated with more frequent global prosocial behavior at a trend level.

PROSOCIAL BEHAVIOR CORRELATES FOR MEN ONLY

As with women, several correlations were significant for men only. Men with more prosocial friends and those reporting more personal distress reported more anonymous prosocial behavior at the trend level. Men who reported higher levels of personal distress reported significantly lower levels of altruism and more frequent global prosocial behaviors. Men who reported more positive emotional tone and positive peer relationship quality reported significantly lower levels of anonymous prosocial behavior and more frequent global prosocial behaviors. The correlation between emotional tone and anonymous prosocial behavior for men was significantly different from women (z = 2.25). Higher peer relationship quality was also significantly associated with more public prosocial behavior, and this correlation was significantly different from that found in women (z = 1.97). Men reporting higher levels of self-esteem reported participating in significantly more global prosocial behaviors. Men reporting more substance use reported significantly lower levels of anonymous prosocial behavior (a pattern seen at the trend level with dire and emotional prosocial behavior). Men reporting more deviant behavior reported significantly lower levels of dire prosocial behavior, and this association in men was significantly different from women (z = 2.52).

Discussion of Study Findings

The data presented here suggest that there is substantial utility in considering young adult prosocial behavior from a multidimensional perspective. The relations between different dimensions of prosocial behavior tendencies and a range of potential correlates yielded a pattern considerably different from the pattern shown when looking only at a global measure of prosocial behavior. The picture is further complicated when looking at the patterns separately by gender. Although only a handful of correlations between prosocial tendencies and other variables were significantly different from each other for men and women, this may have been in part because of the relatively small number of men in the sample. There were a number of correlations that were significant for one gender and not the other. Research that has examined links between the PTM and other constructs has not shown gender differences (e.g., Barry et al., 2008; Padilla-Walker, Barry, Carroll, Madsen, & Nelson, 2008), though this may be a function of the constructs that were examined. Thus, gender appears to lead to differential relations between prosocial behavior tendencies and some constructs but not others. Additionally, it is important to keep in mind that the young adults included in this sample were college attending. Prosocial behavior tendencies may play out differently in the lives of young adults with other life circumstances.

Substantial development continues to happen during the young adult period. Young adults are seeking to establish their place in the world, to determine the trajectories their lives will take from that point forward. Some are taking on adult roles, such as parenting and childbearing; others are exploring their career options; others have entered into military service or full-time employment. Even though we have been considering young adulthood as a single phase of the life span, this does not negate the possibility that there is variability in prosocial tendencies within that period. The data presented here suggests that in fact there may be age-related changes in prosocial tendencies, although this may only be the case for women. Specifically, older women college students reported greater levels of altruism and lower levels of dire and public prosocial tendencies. This pattern makes sense when considering the college context. Younger women college students may be enacting prosocial behavior in part as a way to attract potential friends and potential mates, while older women college students would be more established in their relationships. Additionally, dire prosocial tendencies may decline with age in women as they may include an element of risk, and risk taking declines across this period of the life span (Steinberg et al., 2008). Additional evidence that prosocial tendencies need to be examined with attention to changes related to development within the young adult period comes from a study by Padilla-Walker et al. (2008) that linked prosocial tendencies with identity status. Young adults with a diffused identity status reported more public and less compliant, altruistic, dire, and emotional prosocial tendencies than respondents with any other identity status. Young adults with an achieved identity status reported more altruistic prosocial tendencies than young adults with a foreclosed or diffused identity status. These two cross-sectional studies taken together highlight the need for longitudinal studies across the young adult period to examine changes as well as stability in prosocial tendencies for men and women.

The importance of empathic concern in the study of prosocial behavior is demonstrated by this study in that all types of prosocial behavior were associated with empathic concern for both men and women. Despite this fact, empathic concern does not always necessarily promote prosocial behavior. In fact, public prosocial behavior and empathic concern were negatively related for both men and women. This may be because public prosocial behavior is the only type of prosocial behavior included in the PTM that is likely to be primarily egoistically motivated, and substantial literature indicates that empathy is linked to selflessly motivated helping (e.g. Batson, 1998). Results of this study suggest that empathic concern may actually discourage egoistically motivated helping, as it was negatively related to public prosocial behavior. Perspective taking was also related to all subtypes of prosocial behavior, except altruistic and public prosocial behavior, as well as to global prosocial behavior for women only. Perspective taking was likely unrelated to public prosocial behavior because public prosocial behavior is unrelated to others and their needs, thus, perspective taking ability would not facilitate public prosocial behavior. However, the result was unexpected for altruism. Previous research examining the association between altruism as measured by the PTM and perspective taking has had mixed results. Carlo, Hausmann, Christiansen, and Randall (2003) found no relation between altruism and perspective taking among early or middle adolescents. However, Carlo and Randall (2002) found that perspective taking was significantly positively related to the PTM measure of altruism in college students. Thus, further research is warranted to establish whether the finding in this study was an anomaly, and the extent to which particular sample characteristics may affect the relation between perspective taking and the PTM's measure of altruism.

The young adult social context appears to matter for their prosocial tendencies, though in some cases this varied by gender. Lonely men and women report engaging in significantly less compliant and dire prosocial behaviors, while lonely women college students report engaging in fewer altruistic and emotional prosocial behaviors. Loneliness was unrelated to anonymous, public, and global prosocial behaviors. This pattern of relations makes sense when one considers the types of prosocial behaviors that increase the likelihood of affiliating with others, which would reduce loneliness. Interestingly, all prosocial behaviors may not enhance peer relationship quality. Only dire and emotional prosocial behaviors were associated with peer relationship quality for women. It is likely that for women, prosocial behaviors that fit with gender role norms of being a source of support for one's friends when they need it (Eagly & Crowley, 1986) would enhance the quality of those relationships. Interestingly, for men, higher quality peer relationships were associated with higher levels of public and global prosocial behavior and lower levels of anonymous prosocial behavior. Perhaps gender role norms for men provide social rewards to men who publicly behave in prosocial ways and a cost for men who do not take credit for their actions. These findings may serve to enhance our understanding of links between multidimensional prosocial tendencies and the affective side of peer relationships in young adulthood, particularly when considering gender.

Young adults' perceptions of their friends' antisocial and prosocial behaviors is linked to their own prosocial behaviors. For example, women with antisocial friends reported lower levels of altruism and higher levels of public prosocial behaviors, where those with prosocial friends reported higher levels of altruistic, compliant, and dire prosocial behavior. The links between young adults' own problem behaviors and their prosocial behaviors are similar to the links with their friends' problem behaviors. Specifically, young adults' deviant behaviors are associated with lower levels of altruism and compliance, lower levels of dire prosocial behavior in men, and higher levels of public prosocial behavior for women. Substance use was also linked with lower levels of anonymous, emotional, and dire prosocial behavior in men and lower levels of compliant and altruistic and higher levels of public prosocial behavior in women. Though the pattern varies by gender, it appears that the behavioral choices of young adults and their friends provide an important context that either supports or detracts from the more positively focused prosocial behaviors. This pattern of relations is consistent with problem-behavior theory, which suggests that conventional behaviors and friends will cluster together, whereas unconventional behaviors and friends will also cluster together (e.g., Donovan, Jessor, & Costa, 1991).

Particularly for women, certain forms of prosocial behavior were associated with many of the variables drawn from the peer relationship realm. Specifically, higher levels of both altruism and compliant prosocial behavior were associated with more positive and fewer negative friend behaviors and experiences. This may again be due to gender role norms and the expectation that women should be helpful (Eagly & Crowley, 1986), on their own or if asked, allowing those who have more helpful tendencies to have more positive friend-related experiences.

It is also interesting to note that compliant prosocial behavior was significantly associated with almost every cognitive, emotional, and social variable. However, when the patterns are examined, a distinct picture emerges. Perspective taking and empathic concern were both positively associated with compliant prosocial behavior for both men and women. These variables help individuals determine when others need assistance and motivate them to act by creating an emotional link between the individual and the person in need. This occurs despite the helper's gender and so there is no surprise that a lack of gender differences exists in these variables.

Emotional tone, self-esteem, and having prosocial friends were significantly positively related to compliant prosocial behavior but only in women. This may be because compliant prosocial behavior assesses helping when asked, which is consistent with female gender role norms (Eagly & Crowley, 1986), especially for these variables. The relation may not be significant for men because this type of prosocial behavior is not an aspect of their typical gender role norms, and thus does not have an effect on variables such as men's self-esteem. Loneliness was negatively associated with compliant prosocial behavior in men and women. Despite gender norm differences, helping is likely to still support affiliation with others. Thus, even though compliant prosocial behavior is not part of masculine gender role norms, it may still be an important social factor for all individuals regardless of gender. Deviance was also negatively associated with compliant prosocial behavior in men and women. Helping when asked is part of conventional social expectations for all people. Therefore the same kinds of characteristics that promote helping when asked may also be likely to discourage deviant behavior and make gender a nonfactor in this instance.

Far more pairs of correlations were significant either for men or for women than were significant for both, indicating the importance of the overall gender picture. This finding suggests that gender role socialization likely has a substantial influence on prosocial behavior development and on the meaning and consequences of prosocial behavior in young adult lives. Although there were fairly consistent findings for men and women on perspective taking and empathic concern as linked with prosocial behavior, a much different pattern emerged when examining correlates that are not typically considered in assessments of prosocial behavior. Although this study is correlational in nature and the direction of effects cannot be determined, it is likely that prosocial behaviors are more of a cause than a consequence of variables such as having prosocial friends or engaging in deviant acts, although the possibility that there are bidirectional effects cannot be discounted. However, this study does support the notion that to truly understand the roles of different types of prosocial behavior for different aspects of young adult lives, it is imperative to consider the role of gender.

General Discussion and Future Directions

Continued research is needed on the unique contexts of young adults' lives. More focused attention on the role of media and technology as influences on young adult prosocial behavior tendencies is one example of an important area of future study. Pervasive forms of technology, such as video games, computers, and cell phones, provide opportunities to enhance or detract from prosocial behavior. For example, Fraser, Padilla-Walker, Coyne, Nelson, and Stockdale (2012) found using self-report data that playing violent video games was associated with lower empathic concern and lower levels of prosocial behavior among college students. Attention to the role of social media as it links to prosocial tendencies is also needed (Coyne & Smith, chapter 8, this volume).

As noted previously, the vast majority of the literature on prosocial behaviors in young adulthood uses college student samples. This is true both of the research coming from a social psychological perspective and the research that takes a developmental perspective. As many scholars have noted (e.g. Sears, 1986), college students are unique in many ways. Prosocial behaviors may look very different for young adults whose lives are primarily centered in noncollege contexts. For example, what do we know about prosocial behavior development for young adults serving in the military? Is their military service itself a form of prosocial behavior? How does the specific role they play in the military affect their prosocial behavior? What are the effects of serving in combat? Similarly, young adults who are engaging in caregiving of family members (of various ages), even if they are college attending, may follow unique trajectories of prosocial behavior development because of their caregiving experiences. Young adults who are engaged in full-time employment are likely to spend their day with other adults from a much broader spectrum of the age range than college-attending young adults. What are the implications of this for their prosocial behavior development? Finally, as has been noted by Henrich, Heine, and Norenzayan (2010) and by Arnett (2008), the most psychological research focuses on WEIRD populations (Western, educated, industrialized, rich, democratic) that are not representative of about 95% of the world. We know almost nothing about young adults' prosocial behavior development in non-WEIRD societies.

As the research discussed in this chapter highlights, there is a clear need to study multiple forms of prosocial behaviors in young adulthood. Different forms of prosocial behavior differ in their precursors, correlates, and consequences. Developing a deeper understanding of what this looks like in different young adult populations is essential to advance theories about prosocial behavior development. This examination must include a more systematic look at the role of gender in these patterns. However, gender is likely not the only social identity variable that plays a role, and identifying the influence of other important factors will require a concerted effort by prosocial behavior scholars.

In sum, there are many questions that need to be addressed in order to have a comprehensive understanding of young adult prosocial behaviors, with just a few addressed here. We are in great need of a better understanding, as the young adult period sets the stage for the rest of adulthood. As a society, we are deeply reliant on the prosocial activities of our adult populations. Communities depend on volunteer services to fulfill basic community needs. Many organizations that fill important needs for people (e.g., the poor, the hungry, the sick, the disenfranchised) could not exist without volunteer service and donations. Schools rely on the prosocial activities of parents to meet the needs that paid staff cannot meet. If our young adult population is, in fact, becoming more narcissistic and less helpful than previous generations (Twenge & Foster, 2010), this does not bode well for our future. However, as exemplified by the tremendous level of engagement that was demonstrated by the flood-fighting young adults who were discussed at the outset of this chapter, there appears to be a good foundation from which to build prosocial adults if we have a better understanding of what leads to such efforts.

References

Arnett, J. J. (2000). Emerging adulthood: A theory of development from the late teens through the twenties. *American Psychologist*, 55(5), 469–480. doi:10.1037/0003-066X.55.5.469

Arnett, J. J. (2008). The neglected 95%: Why American psychology needs to become less American. *American Psychologist*, *63*(7), 602–614. doi:10.1037/0003-066X.63.7.602

Barry, C. M., Padilla-Walker, L. M., Madsen, S. D., & Nelson, L. J. (2008). The impact of maternal relationship quality on emerging adults' prosocial tendencies: Indirect effects via regulation of prosocial values. *Journal of Youth and Adolescence*, *37*(5), 581–591. doi:10.1007/s10964-007-9238-7

Barry, C. M., & Wentzel, K. R. (2006). Friend influence on prosocial behavior: The role of motivational factors and friendship characteristics. *Developmental Psychology*, *42*(1), 153–163. doi:10.1037/0012-1649.42.1.153

Batson, C. D. (1998). Altruism and prosocial behavior. In D. T. Gilbert, S. T. Fiske, & G. Lindzey (Eds.), *The handbook of social psychology* (4th ed., Vol. 2, pp. 282–316). New York: McGraw-Hill.

Bizman, A., Yinon, Y., Ronco, B., & Shachar, T. (1980). Regaining self-esteem through helping behavior. *Journal of Psychology*, *105*, 203–209.

Brown, K. M., Hoye, R., & Nicholson, M. (2012). Self-esteem, self-efficacy, and social connectedness as mediators of the relationship between volunteering and well-being. *Journal of Social Service Research*, *38*(4), 468–483. doi:10.1080/0148837 6.20212.687706

Carlo, G., Allen, J. B., & Buhman, D. C. (1999). Facilitating and disinhibiting prosocial behaviors: The nonlinear interaction of trait perspective taking and trait personal distress and volunteering. *Basic and Applied Social Psychology*, *21*(3), 189–197.

Carlo, G., Crockett, L. J., Wilkinson, J. L., & Beal, S. J. (2011). The longitudinal relationships between rural adolescents' prosocial behaviors and young adult substance use. *Journal of Youth and Adolescence*, *40*, 1192–1202. doi:10.1007/s10964-010-9588-4

Carlo, G., Hausmann, A., Christiansen, S., & Randall, B. A. (2003). Sociocognitive and behavioral correlates of a measure of prosocial tendencies for adolescents. *Journal of Early Adolescence*, *23*(1), 107–134. doi: 10.1177/0272431602239132

Carlo, G., & Randall, B. A. (2001). Are all prosocial behaviors equal? A socioecological developmental conception of prosocial behavior. In F. Columbus (Ed.), *Advances in psychology research* (Vol. 3, pp. 151–170). Huntington, NY: Nova Sciences.

Carlo, G., & Randall, B. A. (2002). The development of a measure of prosocial behaviors for late adolescents. *Journal of Youth and Adolescence*, *31*(1), 31–44.

Cillessen, A. H. N., Jiang, X. L., West, T. V., & Laszkowski, D. K. (2005). Predictors of dyadic friendship quality in adolescence. *International Journal of Behavioral Development*, *29*(2), 165–172. doi: 10.1080/01650250444000360

Davis, M. H. (1983). Measuring individual differences in empathy: Evidence for a multidimensional approach. *Journal of Personality and Social Psychology*, *44*(1), 113–126.

Donovan, J. E., Jessor, R., & Costa, F. M. (1991). Adolescent health behavior and conventionality-unconventionality: An extension of problem-behavior theory. *Health Psychology*, *10*(1), 52–61.

Eagly, A. H., & Crowley, M. (1986). Gender and helping behavior: A meta-analytic review of the social psychological literature. *Psychological Bulletin*, *100*(3), 283–308.

Eisenberg, N. (2000). Emotion, regulation, and moral development. *Annual Review of Psychology*, *51*, 665–697.

Eisenberg, N., Fabes, R. A., & Spinrad, T. L. (2006). Prosocial development. In N. Eisenberg (Vol. Ed.), W. Damon & R. M. Lerner (Series Eds.), *Handbook of child psychology: Social, emotional, and personality development* (Vol. 3, pp. 646–718). Hoboken, NJ: Wiley.

Eisenberg, N., & Murphy, B. (1995). Parenting and children's moral development. In M. H. Bornstein (Ed.), *Handbook of parenting: Vol. 4. Applied and practical parenting* (pp. 227–257). Mahwah, NJ: Erlbaum.

Eisenberg, N., Wentzel, N., & Harris, J. D. (1998). The role of emotionality and regulation in empathy- related responding. *School Psychology Review, 27*(4), 506–522.

Flood 2009: First responders. (2009). *Concordia Magazine.* Retrieved from http://www.cord.edu/Magazine/2009/summer/feature/feature2.php

Fraser, A. M., Padilla-Walker, L. M., Coyne, S. M., Nelson, L. J., & Stockdale, L. A. (2012). Associations between violent video gaming, empathic concern, and prosocial behavior toward strangers, friends, and family members. *Journal of Youth and Adolescence, 41,* 636–649. doi:10.1007/s10964-012-9742-2

George, J. M. (1991). State or trait: Effects of positive mood on prosocial behaviors at work. *Journal of Applied Psychology, 76*(2), 299–307.

Henrich, J., Steven, H., & Norenzayan, A. (2010). The weirdest people in the world? *Behavioral and Brain Sciences, 33,* 61–175. doi:10.1017/S01452X0999152X

Hough, J. (April, 2009). Partnerships that save a community: Universities and public transportation. *Passenger Transport.* Retrieved from http://newsmanager.commpartners.com/aptapt/issues/2009-04-13/5.html#top

Konrath, S. H., O'Brien, E. H., & Hsing, C. (2011). Changes in dispositional empathy in American college students over time: A meta-analysis. *Personality and Social Psychology Review, 15*(2), 180–198. doi: 10.1177/1088868310377395

Kuhbandner, C., Pekrun, R., & Maier, M. A. (2010). The role of positive and negative affect in the "mirroring" of other persons' actions. *Cognition and Emotion, 24*(7), 1182–1190. doi:10.1080/02699930903119196

Laible, D. J., Carlo, G., & Roesch, S. C. (2004). Pathways to self-esteem in late adolescence: The role of parent and peer attachment, empathy, and social behaviors. *Journal of Adolescence, 27*(6), 703–716. doi:10.1016/j.adolescence.2004.05.005

Lansu, A. M., & Cillessen, A. H. N. (2012). Peer status in emerging adulthood: Associations of popularity and preference with social roles and behavior. *Journal of Adolescent Research, 27*(1), 132–150. doi:10.1177/07435584

Lim, K. M., Khoo, A., & Wong, M. Y. (2007). Relationship of delinquent behaviors to prosocial orientations of adolescents. *North American Journal of Psychology, 9*(1), 183–188.

Nguyen, A. B., Clark, T.T., & Belgrave, F. Z. (2011). Empathy and drug use behaviors among African-American adolescents. *Journal of Drug Education, 41*(3), 289–308. doi:10.2190/DE.41.3.d

O'Malley, J. A., Arbesman, S., Steiger, D. M., Fowler, J. H., & Christakis, N. A. (2012). Egocentric social network structure, health, and prosocial behaviors in a national panel study of Americans. *PLoS ONE, 7*(5), 1–9. doi:10.1371/journal.pone.0032650

Padilla-Walker, L. M., Barry, C. M., Carroll, J. S., Madsen, S. D., & Nelson, L. J. (2008). Looking on the bright side: The role of identity status and gender on positive orientations during emerging adulthood. *Journal of Adolescence, 31,* 451–467. doi: 10.1016/j.adolescence.2007.09.001

Petersen, A.C., Schulenberg, J. E., Abramowitz, R. H., Offer, D., & Jarcho, H. D. (1984). A self-image questionnaire for young adolescents (SIQYA): Reliability and validity studies. *Journal of Youth and Adolescence, 13*(2), 93–111.

Pursell, G. R., Laursen, B., Rubin, K. H., Booth-LaForce, C., & Rose-Krasnor, L. (2008). Gender differences in patterns of association between prosocial behavior, personality, and externalizing problems. *Journal of Research in Personality, 42,* 472–481. doi:10.1016/j.jrp.2007.06.003

Rosenberg, M. (1965). *Society and the adolescent self-image.* Princeton, NJ: Princeton University Press.

Rushton, J. P., Chrisjohn, R. D., & Fekken, G. C. (1981). The altruistic personality and the self-report altruism scale. *Personal Development Differences, 2,* 1–11.

Russell, D., Peplau, L. A., & Cutrona, C. E. (1980). The revised UCLA loneliness scale: Concurrent and discriminant validity evidence. *Journal of Personality and Social Psychology, 39*(3), 472–480.

Schwartz, S. J., Zamboanga, B. L., & Jarvis, L. H. (2007). Ethnic identity and acculturation in Hispanic early adolescents: Mediated relationships to academic grades, prosocial behaviors, and externalizing symptoms. *Cultural Diversity and Ethnic Minority Psychology, 13*(4), 364–373. doi:10.1037/1099-9809.13.4.364

Sears, D. O. (1986). College sophomores in the laboratory: Influences of a narrow data base on social psychology's view of human nature. *Journal of Personality and Social Psychology, 51*(3), 515–530.

Steinberg, L., Albert, D., Cauffman, E., Banich, M., Graham, S., & Woolard, J. (2008). Age differences in sensation seeking and impulsivity as indexed by behavior and self-report: Evidence for a dual systems model. *Developmental Psychology, 44*(6), 1764–1778. doi:10.1037/a0012955

Stiff, J. B., Price Dillard, J., Somera, L., Kim, H., & Sleight, C. (1988). Empathy, communication, and prosocial behavior. *Communication Monographs, 55,* 198–213.

Stocks, E. L., Lishner, D. A., & Decker, S. K. (2009). Altruism or psychological escape: Why does empathy promote prosocial behavior? *European Journal of Social Psychology, 39,* 649–665. doi:10.1002/ejsp.561

Students help with sandbagging efforts. (2009, March). *It's Happening at State, 1*(6). Retrieved from http://www.ndsu.edu /fileadmin/ihas/IHAS_Schedule/2009_Archive/ihas.03252009.pdf

Swisher, J. D., Shute, R. E., & Bibeau, D. (1985). Assessing drug and alcohol abuse: An instrument for planning and evaluation. *Measurement and Evaluation in Counseling and Development, 17,* 91–97.

Tilton-Weaver, L. C., & Galambos, N. L. (2003). Adolescents' characteristics and parents' beliefs as predictors of parents' peer management behaviors. *Journal of Research on Adolescence, 13,* 269–300.

Twenge, J. M., Baumeister, R. F., DeWall, C. N., Ciarocco, N. J., & Bartels, J. M. (2007). Social exclusion decreases prosocial behavior. *Journal of Personality and Social Psychology, 92*(1), 56–66. doi:10.1037/0022-3514.92.1.56

Twenge, J. M., & Foster, J. D. (2010). Birth cohort increases in narcissistic personality traits among American college students: 1982–2009. *Social Psychological and Personality Science, 1*(1), 99–106. doi: 10.1177/1948550609355719

Uggen, C., & Janikula, J. (1999). Volunteerism and arrest in the transition to adulthood. *Social Forces, 78*(1), 331–362.

Wentzel, K. R., & Erdley, C. A. (1993). Strategies for making friends: Relations to social behavior and peer acceptance in early adolescence. *Developmental Psychology, 29*(5), 819–826.

Woodhouse, S. S., Dykas, M. J., & Cassidy, J. (2011). Loneliness and peer relations in adolescence. *Social Development, 21*(2), 273–293. doi:10.1111/j.1467-9507.2011.00611.x

19

The Social Construction of Volunteering

Daniel Hart and Michael J. Sulik

There may be no better window onto the terrain of prosocial life than volunteering. Through volunteering, researchers can see the operation and interaction of the full range of influences on prosocial behavior, including genes (e.g., Gregory, Light-Häusermann, Rijsdijk, & Eley, 2009), emotions (Hart & Matsuba, 2007), personality traits (e.g., Atkins, Hart, & Donnelly, 2005, Matsuba, Hart, & Atkins, 2007), families (e.g., Hart, Atkins, Markey, & Youniss, 2004), and social institutions (Wilson, 2000). Volunteering is unusually visible because it often occurs in public spaces at scheduled times and places and consequently is available to researchers for inspection.

Because we ascribe great value to voluntary labor on behalf of others, research on volunteering is also of social and economic importance. Volunteering is usually perceived as admirable and deserving of moral recognition. Those who donate large blocks of time on behalf of others are considered to be moral exemplars and are studied intensively for the insights their personalities offer into moral functioning (Colby & Damon, 1994, Hart & Fegley, 1995). Furthermore, volunteering is associated with greater well-being (Thoits & Hewitt, 2001) and may have benefits for an individual as well as the wider community. Moreover, volunteering is important economically. The annual monetary value of this donated labor is calculated to be more than 280 billion dollars (Independent Sector, 2005).

Our goal in this chapter is to highlight the *socially constructed* nature of volunteering. Volunteering is a complex of motives, commitments, and actions often occurring in settings shaped by public institutions (churches, schools, community groups). The salience of different motives within an individual, the types of actions that are performed as a volunteer, and the institutions that scaffold the activity vary, and as they do so too does the meaning of what it means to be a volunteer. In this chapter, we explore lines of work that highlight the social factors that influence the meaning (the social construction) of volunteering. We then offer an example of how the appreciation of the social construction of volunteering allows for the identification of cohort effects in developmental research on volunteering. Our point is that fully characterizing the personality, social, and demographic influences on volunteering requires an appreciation of the *meaning* of volunteering to those involved in it.

Societal and Historical Influences

INTERNATIONAL COMPARISONS

In 1999, adults in the United States and a number of other countries responded to the World Value Survey (WVS). Participants were asked to answer a variety of questions about their attitudes, values, and behaviors. Of particular interest here were participants' responses to 18 items about volunteering. These items asked whether participants had contributed any "unpaid work" in a variety of contexts (e.g., "social welfare service for the elderly," "political action groups," "youth work"). We considered any individual who reported providing unpaid work in any one of these 18 contexts to be a volunteer; individuals who had not provided unpaid work in any of these contexts were judged to be nonvolunteers. We then calculated the proportion of participants in each country who were volunteers.

Figure 19.1 presents these averages. Two trends are evident. The first is that, relative to other countries, the United States has extraordinarily high rates of volunteering. Residents of the United States reported volunteering at rates two to ten times higher than other countries. Figure 19.1 also makes evident the wide variability in volunteering rates across nations.

What factors explain the differences among countries in volunteering rates? One possible explanation is that individual characteristics that promote entry into volunteering are more prevalent in countries with high levels of volunteering than in countries where volunteering is relatively uncommon. For example, on average, volunteers are better educated and happier than are nonvolunteers. Perhaps the difference between the United States and Russia in volunteering evident in Figure 19.1 is a reflection of greater educational attainment and life satisfaction among Americans than among Russians.

In fact, there is some evidence that differences among countries in individual-level characteristics such as life satisfaction and educational attainment may explain some of the variation between countries. Plagnol and Huppert (2010) used European survey data and found that differences in volunteering rates among European countries were related to differences in educational attainment and happiness. However, Plagnol and Huppert concluded that their findings were most important in demonstrating that differences between countries in individuals' characteristics such as education and happiness *did not* account for the bulk of international variability in volunteering rates. Perhaps not surprisingly, Plagnol and Huppert concluded that there are important cultural differences, not reflective

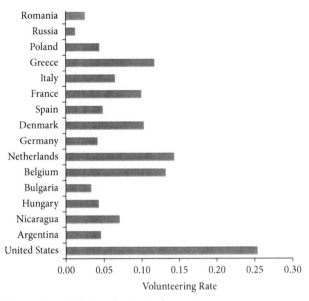

FIGURE 19.1 *Proportion of adults volunteering by country.*

of individuals' educational levels and personality, that must be responsible for variation in volunteering among European countries.

There is also evidence that differences between countries in human, social, and cultural capital predict whether or not an individual will volunteer, even while accounting for personal characteristics. For example, Parboteeah, Cullen, and Lim (2004) used data from the WVS to demonstrate that both within- and between-country education independently predict whether an individual will volunteer; other cultural values such as religiosity, collectivism, and degree of liberal democracy also predicted volunteering while controlling for individual characteristics.

Interactions between individual characteristics and broader cultural variables have also been documented. Ruiter and De Graaf (2006) focused on one facet of culture, religiosity, and its consequences for international variability in volunteering rates. They found that very religious countries—in their study, a large fraction of the population practicing a Christian religion—had higher rates of volunteering than did relatively secular countries. Importantly, Ruiter and De Graaf found that nonreligious adults living in a religious country were more likely to volunteer than were nonreligious adults living in secular societies. The implication is that differences among societies in religious participation shape cultural norms and values that in turn affect the behavior of everyone in those societies.

Cultural norms and values do more than depress or elevate the expression of volunteering behavior; it is simplistic (and wrong) to imagine that the social structures of some countries increase the likelihood of the "good" behavior of volunteering while others, less successful, have social structures that undermine prosocial behavior. It is more accurate to imagine that the *meaning* of volunteering is affected by culture and that as a consequence the motivations to engage in it shift as well.

Some evidence for variation in meaning of volunteering from country to country can be drawn from the WVS, the source of data for Figure 19.1. In addition to responding to questions about volunteering, participants in the WVS were asked to judge how important six roles/activities (family, friends, leisure, politics, work, religion) were in their lives. These judgments can help frame the meaning of volunteering in a society. Consider as an example one type of volunteering assessed in the WVS, "unpaid work [with] an organization concerned with health." In the United States, adults who reported unpaid work for a health-related organization were *more* likely to judge "friends" to be important in their lives than were nonvolunteers, while in Portugal health-related volunteers were *less* likely than nonvolunteers to believe that friends were central to their lives. Lithuanians who believed that "leisure" was important in their lives volunteered *more* often than Lithuanians less concerned about recreation; the situation was reversed in the Netherlands, where those volunteering in health-related organizations were *less* likely to judge leisure to be important in their lives than Dutch nonvolunteers.

Most readers, drawing on cultural knowledge and stereotypes, could offer interpretations for why valuing friends is positively associated with volunteering in the United States but apparently deters volunteering in Portugal, or why leisure and volunteering in Lithuania are linked but appear opposed in the Netherlands. Unfortunately, the data available in the WVS are not sufficiently rich to determine what kind of interpretation of links between culture and volunteering is correct (Hodgkinson, 2003). In our opinion, this is because the data in the WVS do not reveal clearly the meaning—the social construction—of volunteering.

IDENTIFYING HISTORICAL TRANSFORMATIONS IN THE MEANING OF VOLUNTEERING

Meaning and Word Co-Occurrence

In the previous section, we suggested that the patterns of attitudes associated with volunteering varied from country to country and that shifts in these patterns suggest differences in the meaning of volunteering. Here we present a line of research that examines more directly the meaning of volunteering and in so doing demonstrates quite powerfully the social construction of volunteering. Our work on this topic focuses on the evolving meaning of volunteering in the United States between 1800 and 2008.

To assess the meaning of volunteering in the United States, we made use of millions of scanned books published since 1800 (this data set is described in the next section). This corpus of words has already been demonstrated to reveal important cultural trends (Michel et al., 2011). For example, Kesebir and Kesebir (2012) have used these data to illuminate trends in moral language over the course of the twentieth century, Klein (2013) has demonstrated that rapid increases in institutionalization and bureaucratization of American society at the end of the 19th century are revealed through analysis of the word corpus collected by Google, and Twenge, Campbell, and Gentile (2012) have found considerable evidence in this data source for their hypothesis that narcissism has increased in American society between 1960 and the end of the century. For each year between 1800 and 2008 we calculated the proximity of classes of words previously identified as corresponding to categories of moral values or moral foundations (Graham, Haidt, & Nosek, 2009) to the word "volunteer." These categories, which have emerged as empirically distinct aspects of moral concern across many different cultures (Graham et al., 2011), are authority, fairness, harm, in-group/out-group, and purity. Proximity between words in texts is known to reveal semantic similarity (e.g., "hot," "warm") rather than sequential information (e.g., "hot," "dog"; see Lund & Burgess, 1996, and Netzer, Feldman, Goldenberg, & Moshe-Fresko, 2012, for recent demonstrations). High proximity of words linked to a moral foundation and the word "volunteer" suggests that the two are linked semantically. For example, if "volunteer" commonly co-occurs with words representative of the authority moral foundation, this suggests that volunteering is understood as embedded in a network of values linked to respect for authority. Conversely, low proximity between "volunteer" and "in-group/out-group" words would indicate that connotations of "volunteer" do not reference local communities and groups.

Google Ngram Data

Using optical character recognition (OCR), Google has digitized over 15 million books, of which over 5 million were selected for inclusion in a database based on the high quality of the OCR data and the presence of metadata such as location and year of publication (Michel et al., 2011). Data for this study come from all books in this database published in the United States between 1900 and 2008. These data are publicly available and can be downloaded from http://books.google.com/ngrams/datasets.

In this data set, a string of characters that is uninterrupted by a space or punctuation is called a 1-gram. With some exceptions (e.g., numbers, punctuation, hyphenated words), a 1-gram corresponds to an English word; a sequence of five consecutive 1-grams is called a 5-gram. To prevent copyright infringement, the books have been divided into 5-grams, which makes it difficult (if not impossible) to reconstruct the full text of each book.

To identify 5-grams locating the word "volunteer" in moral space, we used dictionaries developed by Graham et al. (2009). These dictionaries contain words and word stems representative of virtue and vice for Haidt's (2007) five moral foundations. We matched our modified dictionaries (see the Appendix) to the 5-gram data. For each 5-gram, we created dummy codes (0 = absent; 1 = present) for the word "volunteer" and for the words in each of the dictionaries. We cross-tabulated these dummy codes and calculated the Jaccard proximity score—the intersection of two sets divided by the union of those sets—for each year from 1850 to 2008 for each of the types of morality. This procedure results in a proximity coefficient representing the semantic similarity of volunteering with each moral foundation. An important limitation to this approach is that the Ngram data are correlational, so changes in proximity between different sets of words may potentially be due to confounding variables such as changes in the publishing industry or changes in language use over time (e.g., changes in the frequency or meaning of words).

Trends in the Moral Meaning of Volunteering

Figure 19.2 depicts one set of initial findings from our investigation into the moral meaning of volunteering. Generally, since 1800 volunteering has increasingly been linked to words corresponding to the moral foundation of harm. This means that, over the past two centuries, Americans have gradually come to understand volunteering as an activity that aims to help others and arises from sympathy for those in need. Within the broad trend toward increasing alignment of volunteering with the moral foundation of harm since 1800 are peaks and valleys. For example, the proximity of volunteer with harm words peaked at the end of the 19th century and then declined through the middle of the 20th century. Figure 19.2 indicates that the proximity of volunteering with harm moral foundation words increased at an astounding rate from 1960 through 2008. The graph suggests, then, that sympathy-induced helping of others was much less common a notion in 1960 than

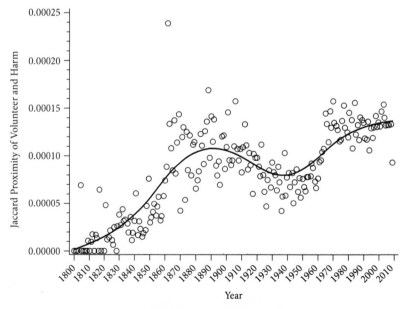

FIGURE 19.2 *Proximity of volunteer with harm moral foundation words by year.*

it was in 2008. In other words, volunteering had a different *meaning* in 1960 than it does in 2008.

How did Americans understand volunteering in 1960 when the proximity of volunteering and moral foundation words related to harm were at their 20th-century low point? Figure 19.3 suggests that for a short period in American history, centered in the 1950s and 1960s, volunteer had meanings suggestive of the moral foundation of purity. This means that in mid-20th-century America, people understood volunteering to have connotations of duty and religious obligation. We do not have a simple explanation for the rapid waxing and waning of volunteering as duty and obligation; it is possible that Protestantism peaked at that point in American history (it has been declining since; Pew, 2013). If true, then perhaps during the 1950s and 1960s Protestant America saw volunteering as a Christian responsibility. In other words, volunteering may have been construed as a set of actions motivated by religious duty rather than by the desire to alleviate suffering in another.

Social Construction, Development, and Historical Cohorts

The contemporary American framing of volunteering as sympathy-induced helping of others has important implications for understanding the precursors of volunteer behavior, such as personality. Atkins et al. (2005) demonstrated that early

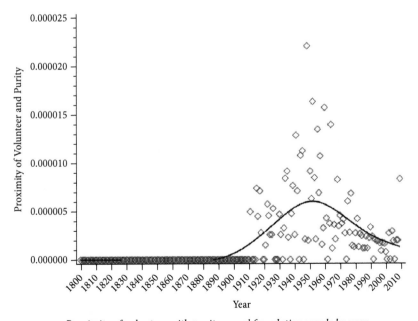

FIGURE 19.3 *Proximity of volunteer with purity moral foundation words by year.*

childhood personality differentiated those who volunteered in adolescence from those who did not. Specifically, Atkins and his colleagues found that those who would become volunteers in adolescence were characterized as resilient in childhood, with good social skills and an ability to regulate emotion.

To identify more precisely the facets of personality linked to volunteering, many researchers have used the Five Factor model of personality, according to which personality has five broad traits: neuroticism (a tendency toward negative emotions), extraversion (gregariousness, positive emotions), openness (curiosity), conscientiousness (achievement motivation, organization), and agreeableness (sympathy, social cooperation). Not surprisingly, many researchers (e.g., Ozer & Benet-Martinez, 2006) have proposed that persons for whom the dimension of agreeableness is very characteristic—individuals who are sympathetic and work well with others—are more likely to volunteer than individuals who are very unsympathetic. In general, research is generally consonant with the expectation that the personality dimension of agreeableness and volunteering are associated. For example, Carlo, Okun, Knight, and de Guzman (2005) tested the association of personality traits and volunteering in a large sample of college students and found that, as predicted, those who scored high on the dimension of agreeableness were more likely to report having volunteered. The implication is that sympathy and kindness predispose individuals to entry into volunteering. One possibility to be examined in future work is whether personality is differentially related to different types of, or motivations for, volunteering.

Note, however, that the association of agreeableness and volunteering may reflect to some extent the cultural construal of volunteering as sympathy-induced helping behavior. People seek confirmation of the elements of their personalities and identities; this axiom is the basis of self-verification theory (for a review, see Swann, 2011), for which much evidence has accumulated. Individuals who judge themselves to be high in agreeableness are consequently likely to behave in ways that confirm for themselves and reveal to others their sympathetic natures. Volunteering, in late 20th-century America, is understood to be exactly the kind of behavior that reflects a sympathetic disposition.

The association between agreeableness and volunteering ought to be particularly strong for Americans born in the last third of the 20th century. This is because this cohort grew up in a culture in which volunteering has always connoted behavior linked to sympathy and the alleviation of suffering in others, as indicated in Figure 19.2. Adults born since 1970 high in agreeableness understand volunteering to be a form of action that expresses to others and confirms for themselves one facet of their personalities.

Agreeableness and volunteering ought to be associated in older adults as well, though perhaps not as closely as in younger adults. On the one hand, like young adults, older adults live in a culture that construes volunteering in such a way that participation as a volunteer confirms for oneself and others the personality qualities of sympathy, cooperation, and so on. Consequently, older adults who judge themselves to be high in agreeableness ought to be more likely to volunteer than older adults who perceive themselves to low in agreeableness. On the other hand, older Americans, say those born in the 1940s and before, grew into adulthood in the pre-1970s culture, a culture in which volunteering was not embedded in a moral network associated with sympathy and the prevention of harm to others. As Figure 19.2 indicates, those who became adults prior to 1970 acquired an understanding of volunteering that was subtly different from that of late 20th-century America. Adults born in the 1940s and earlier grew up in a culture that understood volunteering to be less expressive of sympathetic tendencies than is true of contemporary construals of volunteering and are likely to retain some residue of their notions of volunteering acquired during childhood, adolescence, and early adulthood. In other words, Americans born in the 1940s and earlier are likely to view volunteering as less expressive of sympathy, cooperation, and care for others than are younger Americans. The consequence is an attenuated association between agreeableness and volunteering; if older Americans understand volunteering to be only weakly expressive of sympathetic helping, then volunteering is not a pattern of behavior expressive to self and others of one's personality traits linked to agreeableness. One prediction, then, is that the association of agreeableness with volunteering ought to be positive and particularly robust among young adults and positive, but less so, among older adults.

Recall that Americans born in the 1940s and earlier came of age in a culture that associated volunteering with words connoting duty, sacredness, and religious responsibility (Figure 19.3). One possibility is that for these Americans, religion and volunteering are more correlated than for Americans born since the 1970s; the latter never experienced a culture in which volunteering was connotatively embedded in the purity moral foundation and consequently may be less likely to see religion and volunteering as bound together. Framed as a hypothesis, this line of reasoning predicts that religious participation will be more diagnostic of volunteering for older adults (who lived in a culture that prized volunteering as a reflection of moral purity and religious obligation) than among younger adults (who have experienced only a culture in which volunteering is framed as sympathy-induced aid to others).

To examine these hypotheses, we used data from the *Mid*life in the United States (MIDUS) survey. The sample of the MIDUS survey was representative in 1995 of American adults between the ages of 25 and 74. Agreeableness was assessed by asking participants to rate themselves on a set of adjectives (e.g., "sympathetic," "caring") on a four-point scale ranging from "not at all" to "a lot." The personality dimensions of neuroticism, extraversion, openness, and conscientiousness were similarly assessed. Judgments were averaged, forming summary scores for each of the five personality dimensions for each participant.

Two questions on the survey are directly relevant to religious participation. The first asked participants to report how many times, during an average month, they attended religious services. Participants responded with a number. In a different part of the survey, participants were asked to report using a five-point scale (with items "more than once a week," about once a week," "one to three times a month," "less than once a month," "never") how often they usually attended religious or spiritual services. We assigned participants who reported that they attended religious services four or more times a month (in response to the first question) and that they attended religious services at least once a week (to the second question) to the *regular church attendance group*. All others were in the irregular church attendance group.

Participants also responded to the question "On average, about how many hours per month do you spend doing formal volunteer work of any of the following types?" These types included "Hospital, nursing home, or other health-care-oriented volunteer work," "School or other youth-related volunteer work," "Volunteer work for political organizations or causes," and "Volunteer work for any other organization, cause or charity." We selected the health-care oriented type for analysis, because it seemed more relevant for a wide age range than "school or youth-related work" (older adults without children in schools are less likely to volunteer in schools), more related to agreeableness than volunteer work for political organizations, and clearer in meaning than volunteering "for any other organization." Participants who reported one or more hours a month volunteered were assigned to the health-care volunteer category; all others were assigned to the nonvolunteer category.

The MIDUS also solicited demographic (age, race/ethnicity, educational attainment, family income) information from participants.

Using logistic regression, to predict healthcare volunteer status, we tested the interaction between age and each of the five personality dimensions and between age and regular church attendance. In all models, we controlled for income, gender, and educational attainment. The hypotheses outlined earlier were supported by significant interactions between age and agreeableness and age and between age and regular church attendance (the details are available from the authors). The significant findings are reported in Figures 19.4 and 19.5. Together, the two figures suggest that older adults are more likely than younger adults to be healthcare volunteers.

More relevant for the purposes of this chapter, Figure 19.4 illustrates the significant interaction between agreeableness and age in the prediction of healthcare volunteering. As hypothesized, agreeableness is a better predictor (the slope is steeper) for younger adults than for older adults. We argued that this result is to be expected, given that younger adults—unlike older adults—have grown up in a culture in which volunteering has always been intertwined with sympathetic helping. The consequence is that volunteering is aligned with the personality dispositions constituting agreeableness; those high in agreeableness perceive volunteering as a context in which to verify for themselves and others their tendencies toward agreeableness. Because older Americans grew into adulthood in an era of American history in which volunteering was less tightly wound with concern with others, we have argued that volunteering is less likely to be valued as a means

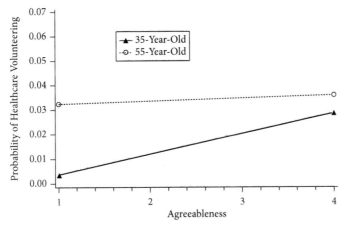

FIGURE 19.4 *Association of the probability of healthcare volunteering with agreeableness as a function of age, predicted from parameter estimates from logistic regression.*

of confirming corresponding personality traits. This is the reason that agreeableness is less predictive of healthcare volunteer status for older adults than it is for younger adults.

Figure 19.5 illustrates the significant interaction between age and regular church attendance in the prediction of healthcare volunteering. Consistent with our argument earlier, church attendance is more predictive of volunteer status for older adults than it is for younger adults. We suggested earlier that this trend could arise from differences in meaning of volunteering between older and younger adults. Older American adults, Figure 19.5 suggests, acquired an understanding of volunteering during youth and early adulthood that made salient the relation

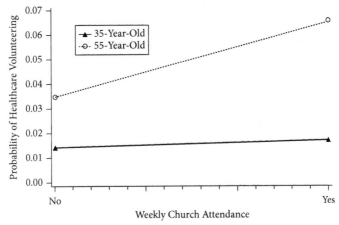

FIGURE 19.5 *Association of the probability of healthcare volunteering with regular church attendance as a function of age, predicted from parameter estimates from logistic regression.*

of volunteering and religious obligations. Accordingly, volunteering is expected of religious individuals, while those without or with weak religious inclinations may lack this source of motivation for volunteering. This is the reason why religious participation, indexed by regular church attendance, differentiates volunteers from nonvolunteers so clearly for older adults. Because younger Americans never experienced the cultural phase in the United States during which volunteering and the purity moral foundation were connected, we suggested that their understanding of volunteering as connected to religious life is weaker, relative to that of older Americans. As a consequence, regular church attendance matters little for younger adults for the prediction of volunteer status.

Meaning and Action

HISTORY AND MEANING

One of our goals for the chapter is to highlight the importance of meaning for understanding prosocial behavior. Behavior intended to help others depends, in part, on inferences concerning what others need and how best to provide aid. In many contexts the needs of others are clear, as are the kinds of actions appropriate for aid. For example, Warneken and Tomasello (2009) have demonstrated that chimpanzees are able to infer the intentions of human experimenters repeatedly grasping for objects slightly more than an arm's length away and are able to respond by moving the objects into the reach of the experimenters. This kind of prosocial activity requires an ability to infer the intentions of other minds and a disposition to help others. The fact that chimpanzees—biologically similar to humans, but without language and sophisticated theory-of-mind capacities—can and do provide aid in this context suggests that the context provides strong affordances for prosocial behavior. Pushing an object closer to a person straining to reach it is, in other words, nearly automatic, as are many other sorts of prosocial behavior.

Volunteering is altogether different from helping another by pushing an object closer. Volunteering, in contrast to pushing an object closer, is saturated with cultural meaning. The clearest evidence for the cultural saturation of volunteering emerges from our analyses of books published in the United States over the past two centuries. We found that the location of volunteering in moral space has changed fairly substantially over the course of American history. In the United States today, volunteering is understood as a form of behavior arising from benevolence and sympathy and reflects a desire to provide assistance to those in need. An American volunteer is a caring person and views herself as such.

Our findings, however, suggested that this conception of volunteering has reached its apogee only in the last 40 years. In the United States in the 1950s and 1960s, the connections between volunteering and words connoting sympathy and benevolence were much weaker than is true today. Indeed, during the post–World

War II era in the United States, the framing of volunteering in terms of duty and religious responsibility peaked.

Others have made arguments loosely consistent with our thesis that the meaning of volunteering can change over the course of history. For example, Friedland and Morimoto (2005, p. 4) have suggested that volunteering for young people today has become a "zombie" category of activity, by which they mean that the moral value that once characterized adolescent volunteering, as a context that both reveals and trains prosocial dispositions, has been displaced by instrumental goals. Although youthful volunteering once was motivated by the desire to help others, Friedland and Morimoto argue that at least some of contemporary volunteering today is oriented toward acquiring experiences that are valued in admission to selective colleges and entry into the job market. Adolescent volunteering in the 21st century is a zombie activity, then, because it looks like volunteering of forty years ago but lacks the core moral content.

Volunteering has many potential motivations, including instrumental and moral goals. It is, however, difficult to determine whether egoistic motives are more strongly related to volunteering today than in years past. Figure 19.2 suggests that the connections of volunteering with the moral vocabulary related to care, sympathy, and concern for others grew stronger over the last half of the 20th century, so the notion of zombie volunteering apparently escaped popular culture reflected in published books. Nonetheless, we agree with Friedland and Morimoto that the historical evolution of meaning of volunteering has important implications for understanding how and why people donate time on a regular basis to help others.

AGE AND COHORT DIFFERENCES

Figures 19.4 and 19.5 indicate that the value of personality and religious participation for predicting one type of volunteering vary as a function of age. Some might interpret these findings as a reflection of internal development. For example, perhaps agreeableness is a better predictor of volunteering for younger adults than it is for older adults—as depicted in Figure 19.4—because younger adults are in greater need of aligning their personality traits with behavior than are older adults. This interpretation is bolstered by findings that younger adults are more likely to engage in self-monitoring than are older adults (Reifman, Klein, & Murphy, 1989).

Our argument instead highlights historical influences, rather than internal development, for the age-varying associations of religion and agreeableness with personality. The value of personality for predicting volunteering differs for younger and older adults because the *meaning* of volunteering underwent historical change. Because older adults grew up in a time in America in which volunteering had associations with moral purity and younger adults experienced only a later cultural milieu in which volunteering was prized for reducing suffering in others, older and younger adults likely have subtly different conceptions of volunteering. These differences shade the motivational landscape for volunteering, highlighting for older adults the opportunities for fulfilling duties in volunteering and for younger adults the value of volunteering for expressing sympathy and aiding others. These are not *developmental* changes; we do not expect young adults understanding of volunteering to evolve as they age. Instead, differences in the understanding of volunteering reflect the effects of history in shaping the interpretations people make of the worlds in which they live.

Conclusions

Researchers study volunteering because it is easy to do so (due to its public and predictable occurrence), because of its importance for the well-being of some societies, and because volunteering reveals relations of prosocial behavior to a variety of social processes and psychological characteristics. Our point in this chapter is that volunteering is also socially constructed; it is an activity with moral meaning that varies from country to country and from era to era within a country. These variations matter; surely the reason that rates of volunteering are dramatically different around the globe (Figure 19.1) is that different cultures provide different meanings, and consequently different motivations and values, for volunteering. Similarly the evolving meaning of volunteering in the last half of the 20th century in America affected the reasons younger and older Americans became volunteers.

We hope that our argument for the social construction of volunteering is a useful reminder that cultural context matters. This conclusion has multiple implications for contemporary research. The first of these is that efforts to characterize volunteering in terms of types (e.g., Metz, McLellan & Youniss, 2003) or dimensions of underlying motivations (Snyder & Omoto, 1992) are culturally embedded. This means that the alignment of a typology of volunteering with the outcomes of participation, or the decomposition of motivations in order to understand paths of entry into volunteering, need to be augmented by attention to cultural context.

The findings we presented in this chapter lead to the conclusion that it may make little sense to imagine that a meta-analysis of studies from different nations will converge on a clear set of precursors to volunteering, or that findings concerning volunteering in the 1950s in the United States would be replicated with contemporary data. This is because the cultural meaning of volunteering varies across countries and historical periods and in so doing transforms the foundations for volunteering.

We have also demonstrated in this chapter one way in which cultural trends and their evolution can be assessed, using newly available large data sets. Consequently, while integrating cultural influences into theoretical accounts of volunteering adds considerable complexity, this complexity can now be investigated using the information available in the increasingly digitized world. There are many opportunities for enriching psychological and sociological research by drawing on the new sources of information available in the niches of the Internet.

New sources of information allow old problems to become empirically tractable. But the old problem—the interpenetration of culture and behavior—remains at the heart of work by psychologists and sociologists. Volunteering may be more shaped by culture than many forms of prosocial behavior, as we have suggested. Nonetheless, a full account of human prosocial life will be incomplete without an account integrating biological, psychological, sociological, and cultural influences.

Appendix

Harm (Virtue): safe*, peace*, compassion*, help*, empath*, sympath*, care, caring, protect*, shield, shelter, amity, secur*, benefit*, defen*, guard*

Harm (Vice), harm*, suffer*, war, wars, warl*, warring, fight*, violen*, hurt*, kill, kills, killer*, killed, killing, endanger*, cruel*, brutal*, abuse*, damag*, ravage, detriment*, crush*, attack*, annihilate*, destroy, stomp, spurn, impair, wound*

Fairness (Virtue): fair, fairly, fairness, fair-*, fairmind*, fairplay, equal*, justice, justness, justifi*, reciproc*, impartial*, egalitar*, rights, equity, evenness, equivalent, unbias*, tolerant, equable, balance*, homologous, unprejudice*, reasonable, constant

Fairness (Vice): unfair*, unequal*, bias*, unjust*, injust*, bigot*, discriminat*, disproportion*, inequitable, prejud*, dishonest, unscrupulous, dissociate, preference, favoritism, exclusion, exclud*

In-group (Virtue): together, nation*, homeland*, family, families, familial, group, patriot*, communal, commune*, communit*, communis*, comrad*, cadre, collectiv*, joint, unison, unite*, fellow*, guild, solidarity, devot*, member, cliqu*, cohort, ally, insider

In-group (Vice): foreign*, enem*, individual*, deceiv*, jilt*, imposter, miscreant, spy, sequester, renegade, terroris*, immigra*

Authority (Virtue): obey*, obedien*, duty, law, duti*, honor*, respect, respectful*, respected, respects, order*, father*, mother, motherl*, mothering, mothers, tradition*, hierarch*, authorit*, permit, permission, status*, rank*, leader*, class, bourgeoisie, caste*, position, complian*, command, supremacy, control, submi*, allegian*, serve, abide, defere*, defer, revere*, venerat*, comply

Authority (Vice): defian*, rebel*, dissent*, subver*, disrespect*, disobe*, sediti*, agitat*, insubordinat*, illegal*, lawless*, insurgent, mutinous, defy*, dissident, unfaithful, alienate, defector, nonconformist, oppose, protest, refuse, denounce, remonstrate, riot*, obstruct

Purity (Virtue): purity, pure*, clean*, steril*, sacred*, chast*, holy, holiness, saint*, celiba*, abstention, virgin, virgins, virginity, virginal, austerity, modesty, abstinen*, abstemiousness, limpid, unadulterated, maiden, virtuous, refined, immaculate, innocent, pristine, church*

Purity (Vice): disgust*, deprav*, disease*, unclean*, contagio*, sin, sinful*, sinner*, sins, sinned, sinning, slut*, whore, dirt*, impiety, impious, profan*, gross, repuls*, sick*, promiscu*, lewd*, adulter*, debauche*, defile*, tramp, prostitut*, unchaste, intemperate, wanton, profligate, filth*, trashy, obscen*, lax, taint*, stain*, tarnish*, debase*, desecrat*, blemish, exploitat*, pervert

References

Atkins, R., Hart, D., & Donnelly, T. M. (2005). The association of childhood personality type with volunteering during adolescence. *Merrill-Palmer Quarterly, 51*(2), 145–162.

Carlo, G., Okun, M. A., Knight, G. P., & De Guzman, M. R. T. (2005). The interplay of traits and motives on volunteering: agreeableness, extraversion and prosocial value motivation. *Personality and Individual Differences, 38*(6), 1293–1305.

Colby, A., & Damon, W. (1994). *Some do care*. New York, NY: Free Press.

Friedland, L., & Morimoto, S. (2005). The changing lifeworld of young people: Risk, resume-padding, and civic engagement. *The Center for Information and Research on Civic Learning and Engagement (CIRCLE). Working Paper, 40.*

Graham, J., Haidt, J., & Nosek, B. A. (2009). Liberals and conservatives rely on different sets of moral foundations. *Journal of Personality and Social Psychology, 96*(5), 1029.

Graham, J., Nosek, B. A., Haidt, J., Iyer, R., Kovela, S., & Ditto, P. H. (2011). Mapping the moral domain. *Journal of Personality and Social Psychology, 101*(2), 366–385.

Gregory, A. M., Light-Häusermann, J. H., Rijsdijk, F., & Eley, T. C. (2009). Behavioral genetic analyses of prosocial behavior in adolescents. *Developmental Science, 12*(1), 165–174.

Haidt, J. (2007). The new synthesis in moral psychology. *Science, 316*(5827), 998–1002.

Hart, D., Atkins, R., Markey, P., & Youniss, J. (2004). Youth bulges in communities: The effects of age structure on adolescent civic knowledge and civic participation. *Psychological Science, 15*(9), 591–597.

Hart, D., & Fegley, S. (1995). Prosocial behavior and caring in adolescence: Relations to self-understanding and social judgment. *Child Development, 66*(5), 1346–1359.

Hart, D., & Matsuba, M. K. (2007). The development of pride in moral life. In In J. L. Tracy, R. W. Robins, & J. P. Tangney (Eds.), *The self-conscious emotions: Theory and research* (pp. 114–133). New York, NY: Guilford.

Independent Sector (2005, November). Dollar Value of a Volunteer Hour. Retrieved from http://www.independentsector.org/programs/research/volunteer_time.html

Kesebir, P., & Kesebir, S. (2012). The cultural salience of moral character and virtue declined in twentieth century America. *Journal of Positive Psychology, 7*(6), 471–480.

Klein, D. B. (2013, April 22). *Ngrams of the great transformations*. SSRN Scholarly Paper. Rochester, NY: Social Science Research Network. http://papers.ssrn.com/abstract=2255246

Lund, K., & Burgess, C. (1996). Producing high-dimensional semantic spaces from lexical co-occurrence. *Behavior Research Methods, 28*(2), 203–208.

Matsuba, M. K., Hart, D., & Atkins, R. (2007). Psychological and social-structural influences on commitment to volunteering. *Journal of Research in Personality, 41*(4), 889–907.

Metz, E., McLellan, J., & Youniss, J. (2003). Types of voluntary service and adolescents' civic development. *Journal of Adolescent Research, 18*(2), 188–203. doi:10.1177/0743558402250350.

Michel, J., Shen, Y. K., Aiden, A. P., Veres, A., Gray, M. K., The Google Books Team, Pickett, J. P., et al. (2011). Quantitative analysis of culture using millions of digitized books. *Science, 331*(6014), 176–182.

Netzer, O., Feldman, R., Goldenberg, J., & Fresko, M. (2012). Mine your own business: Market-structure surveillance through text mining. *Marketing Science, 31*(3), 521–543.

Ozer, D. J., & Benet-Martinez, V. (2006). Personality and the prediction of consequential outcomes. *Annual Review of Psychology, 57*, 401–421.

Parboteeah, K. O., Cullen, J. B., & Lim, L. (2004). Formal volunteering: A cross-national test. *Journal of World Business, 39*, 431–441. doi:10.1016/j.jwb.2004.08.007

Pew Forum. (2012). *"Nones" on the Rise: One-in-five adults have no religious affiliation.* Retrieved from http://www.pewforum.org/Unaffiliated/nones-on-the-rise.aspx

Plagnol, A. C., & Huppert, F. A. (2010). Happy to help? Exploring the factors associated with variations in rates of volunteering across Europe. *Social Indicators Research, 97*(2), 157–176.

Reifman, A., Klein, J. G., & Murphy, S. T. (1989). Self-monitoring and age. *Psychology and Aging, 4*(2), 245.

Ruiter, S., & De Graaf, N. D. (2006). National context, religiosity, and volunteering: Results from 53 countries. *American Sociological Review, 71*(2), 191–210.

Snyder, M., & Omoto, A. M. (1992). Volunteerism and society's response to the HIV epidemic. *Current Directions in Psychological Science 1*(4), 113–116.

Swann, W. B., Jr., (2011). Self-verification theory. In P. A. M. Van Lange, A. W. Kruglanski, & E. T. Higgins (Eds.), *Handbook of theories of social psychology* (Vol. 2, pp. 23–42). Thousand Oaks, CA: Sage.

Thoits, P. A., & Hewitt, L. N. (2001). Volunteer work and well-being. *Journal of Health and Social Behavior, 42*, 115. doi:10.2307/3090173

Twenge, J. M., Campbell, W. K., & Gentile, B. (2012, July 10). Increases in individualistic words and phrases in American books, 1960–2008. *PLoS ONE, 7*(7): e40181. doi:10.1371/journal.pone.0040181

Warneken, F., & Tomasello, M. (2009). Varieties of altruism in children and chimpanzees. *Trends in Cognitive Sciences, 13*(9), 397.

Wilson, J. (2000). Volunteering. *Annual Review of Sociology, 26*, 215–240.

20

Early Generativity and Types of Civic Engagement in Adolescence and Emerging Adulthood

Michael W. Pratt and Heather L. Lawford

Introduction

A mother volunteers weekly at her son's school. A supervisor spends personal time helping a junior colleague at work to learn new skills. A teacher stays late to coach hockey for his high school's team. A group of people demonstrate at a rally against environmental damage to a rainforest. All these activities appear to share an altruistic, prosocial quality of helping others at some cost to the self. They also seem to involve the orientation of that help toward future generations and their needs, a specific focus Erik Erikson (1950) described using the term "generativity." In this chapter, drawing on longitudinal research, we explore the commonalities, differences, and development of generative motives and actions in young people. We begin by introducing the idea of generativity, then review its early predictors and later correlates across four different domains of civic life in emerging adulthood (Arnett, 2012), and end with a discussion of prospects for future research in this field.

What Is Generativity and How Does It Develop?

"Generativity," a term coined by Erikson (1968), is a personality construct defined as care and concern for future generations as a legacy of the self and is commonly expressed through parenting as well as teaching, mentoring, creating, and maintaining the values of a culture or society. It was first identified in Erikson's model of personality as a construct central to midlife, the seventh of his eight stages. The motives of generativity are both self-serving (wanting to live on through one's works) and giving of the self (wanting something better, or just as good, for the next generation). Generativity provides a way of linking the generations together and passing on key values and behaviors that are the foundation of any viable society (Erikson, 1968). Generativity thus may be seen to have both communal components of caring for future generations and agentic components of leaving a legacy of the self after death (McAdams, 2001a).

Kotre (1984) described four forms of generativity that unfold across the life course: biological, parental, technical, and societal. Biological and parental generativity refer to having and rearing children. Technical generativity focuses on the passing on of skills and knowledge. Societal generativity is focused on civic and political involvement in the wider society to care for the future. Snarey's (1993) research on men showed that greater involvement in biological and parenting roles in early adulthood predicted to more engagement in technical and societal caring later in midlife. In this chapter, we do not focus on biological or parental generativity, but explore generativity in technical (e.g., work) and societal (e.g., civic and political) forms in emerging adulthood. Such role contexts involve engagement in prosocial forms of behavior to pass on skills, values, and traditions to youth.

McAdams and de St. Aubin (1992) developed a complex model of generativity that is used widely in psychological research. Their model consists of seven different components. The first four are somewhat motivational features, including a desire to be needed, cultural pressure to behave in a generative way, an optimistic outlook on humanity, and a sense of caring about leaving a legacy that will positively impact future generations. The last three components are more action based, including commitment, behavior, and narrative. The narrative component is a weaving of generativity into one's identity, as the life story becomes what McAdams (2001a) called a "commitment script."

Most of the research to date on this construct, following the Erikson life span framework, has been focused on midlife adults. Nevertheless, several researchers have argued that generativity may be manifested in earlier forms during adolescence (Lawford, Pratt, Hunsberger, & Pancer, 2005; Pratt, Arnold, & Lawford, 2009). Stewart and Vandewater (1998) suggested that development of generativity across the life span is also complex, involving the early development of concern and desire in youth, but with later development of generative action and accomplishment only in midlife and beyond. In this chapter, we discuss the possible role of generativity in youth and its relation to civic engagement in adolescence and emerging adulthood.

It also seems important to distinguish the construct of generativity from other, related constructs. These include altruism, the care for others as opposed to the self, prosocial moral values such as benevolence and universalism (Schwartz, 1994), and youth purpose (Damon et al., 2003). We expect that these other measures will show overlap with generativity, given their similar emphasis on care for others (in the case of altruism), as well as the self's purpose and sense of meaning. However, generativity is a distinctive, complex construct, that combines a communal, caring focus which has an altruistic, other-oriented orientation with, and in the service of, a purposive, agentic component—a desire to leave a legacy of the self as an underlying goal. In this sense, generativity is a hybrid notion that integrates these two broad principles of altruism and self-focus. It overlaps considerably with some of the ideas of moral development and integration articulated by Frimer and Walker (2009), and indeed there is evidence that moral development and generativity may be substantively linked in development (Pratt et al., 2009). It also overlaps somewhat with the construct of "youth purpose" (Damon, Menon, & Bronk, 2003), but is more specific in its focus on care for future generations.

ASSESSING GENERATIVITY IN ADOLESCENTS AND EMERGING ADULTS

In this section, we briefly review some important measures of generativity and provide evidence about their reliability and validity among younger samples. The most commonly used measure from the McAdams and de St. Aubin (1992) model is the Loyola Generativity Scale (LGS), which is a 20-item measure of generative concern, a conscious focus on the next generation. Sample items include "I think that I would like the work of a teacher," and "I think that I will be remembered for a long time after I die." As these examples show, the measure assesses both concern for future generations and the idea of leaving a legacy. The LGS has shown good internal and test-retest reliability with adults and is a consistent positive predictor of greater prosocial action and civic engagement (McAdams & de St. Aubin, 1992).

We have assessed generativity extensively over the period from late adolescence to early adulthood in a longitudinal study that has followed a sample of several hundred Canadian high school students from ages 17 to 32. This sample has been assessed five times. In the first three rounds (ages 17, 19, and 23), most data collection consisted of questionnaires on personality, adjustment and life satisfaction, family, and civic involvement (e.g., Pancer, Pratt, Hunsberger, & Alisat, 2007). At ages 26 and 32, a life story interview protocol, similar to that developed by McAdams (2001b) was also administered. We call this longitudinal project the Futures Study.

In our studies of the Futures sample, we measured generative concern, using the LGS, at ages 19, 23, 26, and 32. We also used the generative strivings procedure of Emmons at age 26. And we used a measure of community and social engagement (the Youth Inventory of Involvement, YII; Pancer et al., 2007), as an index of prosocial and generative action, at ages 17, 19, 23, 26, and 32. Reliability analyses indicated similar findings to adult samples, and our results for youth replicated for the most part the findings for adults discussed above. At age 26 in the Futures Study, we examined the intercorrelations of the LGS and the YII. We also correlated these measures with generative motivations expressed in a measure of personal strivings (using a procedure developed by Emmons, 1989). These were positive and significant in all cases, resembling the results from adults (McAdams & de St. Aubin, 1992). Consistency of individual variations on the LGS in the Futures Sample was also strong across the age range 19 to 32 (in the .65 range). The age 19

LGS measure was more moderately correlated with later scores from age 23 on (*r*s ranged from.45 to .52), but still substantial. It may be that the LGS was less valid at age 19 than later, but it was also the case that we used a shorter version of the LGS at this age, and so the explanation of these lower correlations is difficult to interpret clearly.

A number of studies with adults have shown that generativity is positively associated with measures of well-being (e.g., McAdams, Reynolds, Lewis, Patten, & Bowman, 2001). Similarly, generative concern on the LGS has been associated with better adjustment and lower depression and loneliness scores among both adolescents and emerging adults (Lawford et al., 2005; Pratt, Alisat, Bisson, & Norris, 2013). These findings provide additional construct validity for this measure in samples of youth. We also had data on a subsample of participants in the Futures Study at age 23, who were administered both the LGS and a scale of altruism (Rushton, Chrisjohn, & Fekken, 1981). Correlations between these two measures showed that they were moderately positively associated (*r* = .42). In addition, the LGS was somewhat better correlated with the Youth Involvement Inventory than was the altruism scale.

Predictors of Generativity in Adolescents and Emerging Adults

Multiple studies now suggest that the LGS is a reliable and valid measure of generativity within adolescent and emerging adult age groups. In earlier work, we found that young people (aged 17) who were more engaged in the community were more likely to report increases in generative motivation later (Lawford et al., 2005). Similarly, Frensch and colleagues found evidence of generative themes in narratives told by late adolescents and emerging adults in a different sample (Frensch, Pratt, & Norris, 2007). Based on Erikson's developmental stage model, higher levels of generativity should be attained more readily by those who solve the earlier issues of identity and intimacy more effectively. Indeed, the evidence for this among youth is quite consistent. Busch and Hofer (2011) found that adolescents with a more achieved identity reported higher rates of generativity on the LGS across two different cultures. Mackinnon, Nosko, Pratt, and Norris (2011) reported that generative concern was associated with narratives that expressed higher levels of intimacy in both friendship and romantic contexts among emerging adults (age 26) in the Futures sample. Similarly, but in a different sample, Lawford, Doyle, and Markiewitz (2013) found that younger adolescents who reported demonstrating more care for their close friends were also more likely to report higher levels of generativity on the LGS one year later.

Research on generativity in youth is still relatively new, and questions remain about whether such studies represent evidence for mature generativity as is typically studied in midlife adults. Most research on youth has focused on motivations

to be generative rather than on the later components of McAdams's model mentioned earlier. Moreover, it may be that young people are less concerned with ideas
of leaving a legacy compared with midlife counterparts, although concerns for
future generations or the state of things beyond their lifetime are evident. For
example, as discussed below, youth seem to have genuine concerns for issues such
as the environment, because of consequences that could occur beyond their own
lifetimes.

Early findings from the Futures sample showed that generative concern on
the LGS at 23 was predicted uniquely by higher levels of authoritative family parenting and by greater community involvement at age 17 (Lawford et al.,
2005). We can now extend these analyses to the prediction of generative concern at age 32 in the Futures data set, drawing on two further rounds in this
study (waves at ages 26 and 32). Do the findings at age 23 continue to hold up?
Indeed, they do (see Figure 20.1). In our more recent studies, we have assessed
a broad, multicomponent model of positive family parenting at age 17, which
included: (1) higher levels of adolescent-parent interaction, (2) more authoritative parenting expressing both greater warmth and guidance, and (3) stronger
family cohesion and communication (Dumas, Lawford, Tieu, & Pratt, 2009).
Using a simultaneous regression analysis, reports of this composite model of
positive family parenting at 17 and of higher involvement in social and community activities at 17 both continued to predict scores on the LGS positively and
significantly into young adulthood at age 32, controlling for sex and for father's
education levels (see Figure 20.1). Even when scores on the LGS at age 23 were
entered in this equation, effects of early positive family parenting and community engagement remained uniquely significant. This model predicted about
50% of the variance in generative concern at 32 over 15 years of development.
Family and community experiences of adolescence appear to play a substantial
role in the development of generativity by young adulthood.

Generativity Across Four Contexts of Civic
Engagement Among Youth

In an important book, *Caring and Doing for Others: Social Responsibility in the
Domains of Family, Work and Community*, Alice Rossi (2001) examined prosocial engagement in midlife, drawing on a large, representative study of midlife
adults in the United States (the MIDUS Study). Chapters in the Rossi volume covered various life domains, including family, community, and work, as
the subtitle of the book indicates. In conducting research for this chapter, we
explored a range of the various nonfamily domains discussed by Rossi in her
volume as a way of organizing and investigating what we know of how these
domains might be related to generative concern in young people. Most research
on civic engagement in youth to date has focused on community volunteering

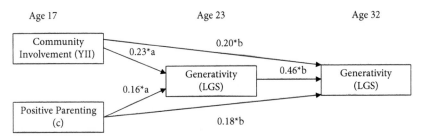

FIGURE 20.1 *Longitudinal predictors (standardized betas) of age 32 generative concern from adolescent and emerging adulthood measures, controlled for sex and parent education level.*

LGS = Loyola Generativity Scale, YII = Youth Involvement Inventory $p < .05$
(a) N = 260, regression on LGS at 23, R^2 = .14, $F(4,256) = 10.78$, $p < .001$
(b) N = 87, regression on LGS at 32, R^2 = .50, $F(5,82) = 16.53$, $p < .001$
(c) Summary index of parent authoritativeness, family cohesion, and parent interaction ratings as reported by adolescents at 17

and political citizenship (e.g., Flanagan, 2005; Hart, Donnelly, Youniss, & Atkins, 2007). However, following Rossi's book, and our own interests as well, we have added sections on environmental engagement and on work. In each section of the reviews, we first briefly cover the relevant literature and then discuss our own longitudinal evidence on each topic, mostly from our Futures sample.

Research by Larson, Hansen, and Moneta (2006) has suggested that different contexts of youth activity engagement might provide different types of opportunities for development to the youth who participate in them. Six different types of activities were surveyed, including sports, arts, academic clubs, community organizations, service activities, and faith-based organizations. Experiences in the classroom, job, and peer group were also studied as comparisons. Faith-based and service-oriented contexts stood out particularly as providing high levels of opportunities for interpersonal gains in teamwork, positive social relations and adult network connections, and social capital. Comparing these organizational experiences to job, classroom, and friendship contexts showed that the classroom was lower than all youth organizations in positive interpersonal development, whereas experiences in the peer group and on the job generally were not so different from other youth activity contexts.

These data suggest that activity domains vary in their opportunities for growth of prosocial concern in individuals. Generativity as a construct thus may be more relevant to some of these domains than others. Furthermore, people do not invest equally in all such domains in their lives. Famous exemplars of caring in public life, such as Gandhi, were often not as dedicated to care in their private, family lives (Erikson, 1969). If this is true of exemplars, it seems almost certain to be true of more ordinary individuals. Indeed, Rossi (2001) reported that, although *norms* of helping were positively correlated for individuals across the domains of family, work, and community in the MIDUS midlife sample, levels of actual helping behaviors themselves were largely unrelated across these domains. Similarly, the four domains of civic engagement we report on below showed quite low levels of positive correlations among each other in our Futures Sample at ages 26 and 32 (all $rs < .24$). Perhaps the most interesting of these was a low, but significant, positive relation between work satisfaction and community involvement at age 32. Nevertheless, generativity in youth may be more likely to be important in predicting civic engagement in certain domains, perhaps where personal investment and identity commitment are established early, than in those where identity commitment is weaker and later developing (e.g., in vocational versus political domains, see Fadjukoff, Kokko, & Pulkkinen, 2010). Next, we review the evidence on generativity in relation to four contexts of extra-family civic engagement: community activity, pro-environmental action and concern, work and vocational choices, and political engagement.

COMMUNITY ENGAGEMENT AS A CONTEXT FOR EXPRESSING GENERATIVITY IN YOUTH

I'd say probably about three years ago, I was volunteering with a drop-in centre for homeless and street youth. There was this one particular youth that I got pretty close with, we had really good chemistry. I looked at him as a little brother really. He got in a little trouble with the law and ended up in jail, and I never once judged him . . . So the last time I talked to him, I found out that he actually applied himself and went back to school, 'cause he was really good at working on cars. I really encouraged him that he should probably look into getting into a trade working with cars. He went from being a bad kid to doing something, so that brought a lot of positive things to me. I wasn't there to change every kid that went through that door, but if I could have impact on one kid then that just makes me want to volunteer more and just give something to the community. It was a really good life experience for me and a positive thing to do to return back to the community. (Brian, a 26-year-old in the Futures Study on a volunteer experience)

Despite the traditional focus in psychology on family, school, and peers as the major socializing forces of adolescence, there has been recent interest in the role of civic organizations, clubs, and volunteer opportunities as another key setting for growth in young people (e.g., Flanagan, 2005; Larson, 2000). A number of authors have decried the lack of such involvement in North American society in general (e.g., see *Bowling Alone*, Putnam, 2000) and its negative implications for overall civic health. Recent research on positive youth development has begun to explore the potential benefits of community and volunteer involvement specifically in adolescence and emerging adulthood (Smetana, Campione-Barr, & Metzger, 2006).

Several longitudinal studies have shown that community involvement in adolescence seems to predict higher levels of community service and engagement in later life (e.g., Hart et al., 2007). These authors used a U.S. national sample of high school seniors who were followed up 8 years later to examine predictors of community volunteer activity, as well as of voting behavior. Hart et al. found that civic engagement at 26 was positively predicted by civic engagement at 18. It was also predicted by extracurricular activities at school, especially involving leadership roles in instrumental groups, like student government or yearbook, and so on. It was not, however, predicted by civic knowledge at Grade 12, which was also measured. The authors suggested that these patterns of prediction might be accounted for at least partly by the development of a sense of civic identity through these experiences, as well as by the acquisition of skills and a sense of capability through working with the support and guidance of adults (Hart et al., 2007). Larson (2000) indeed suggested that the supportive role of adult involvement in these voluntary groups for youth is a very important one.

Flanagan (2005), in the context of research on political and civic engagement, has also reviewed the role of community involvement and civic programs in youth development. She noted several important outcomes of such experiences, including a subsequent ethic of service, which was linked conceptually to the development of a sense of civic and collective social identity. Students involved in these programs were also shown to have a higher degree of trust and social attachment within their wider society, surely an important outcome (Flanagan, 2005).

In an earlier study, a group of exceptional teenage volunteers from an impoverished urban community in the United States were interviewed and compared to a matched sample of less engaged teenagers to see if these exemplars think about themselves and their lives differently (Hart & Fegley, 1995). This research suggested that a sense of moral or civic identity may be fostered by these helping roles. For example, the exemplar youth, who spent extensive amounts of time caring for others, were more likely to describe themselves using prosocial, positive moral terms (like kind or helpful) than matched comparison teenagers.

Walker and Frimer (2007) studied Canadian adults who received public recognition for two different types of admirable behavior (caring vs. bravery). These authors found that those who received national awards for sustained caring and helping activities were distinctive from those who received awards for specific heroic acts of bravery in terms of several factors, including showing personality profiles with substantially higher levels of generative concern. Greater generativity was clearly linked to sustained patterns of positive social engagement among these award-winning adults. But what leads to what in these profile differences? Longitudinal data can help us begin to address this question.

Using data from our Futures Sample, Lawford et al. (2005) reported that community involvement at age 17, as assessed on the YII, was a positive predictor of generativity at age 23, as assessed on the LGS, as we discussed previously. While we cannot tell what causes what in these correlational data either, some internal analyses suggested that generative concern and community engagement were likely mutually influential across this developmental period (Lawford et al., 2005). Busch and Hofer (2011) recently reported cross-sectional data on midadolescents in two different cultures which replicated the positive association of the LGS and community involvement in both countries. We similarly found a significant association between community involvement and generativity among 15-year-olds in a family study of parents and their adolescent children (Pratt et al., 2013). These studies suggest that prosocial engagement in youth may indeed encourage greater levels of generativity of personality. But generativity may also foster increased community involvement (Jia, Pratt, & Alisat, 2013).

We have now extended our work on the Futures sample into young adulthood, so we can examine these patterns more comprehensively from 17 to 32, using multiple regression analyses. These analyses indicated that: (1) community involvement at 17 continues to be an important predictor of community engagement at age 32 (paralleling findings by Hart et al., 2007) and (2) generativity at age 23 in our data set, which was predicted positively by community involvement at 17, also contributed uniquely and independently to the prediction of community engagement at 32, after age 17 community engagement had been entered. Positive parenting at age 17 was only a marginal predictor of community engagement at 32, though it significantly predicted the LGS at 23 (Lawford et al., 2005) and at age 32 (as shown in Figure 20.1).

We also tested the narrative data on community experiences in the Futures Study using a parallel model. Community scenes, such as Brian's above, which were narrated at age 26, were coded for their level of enthusiasm and impact on a 0–3 scale, by a rater who was unaware of other data (Sleightholm, Alisat, Norris, & Pratt, 2012). These ratings were substantially positively correlated with questionnaire evidence on level of community engagement reported on the YII, as expected ($r = .53$), and so were analyzed using the same general conceptual model used to test the questionnaire data—assessing generativity at age 23 and positive family parenting at age 17 as predictors of enthusiasm ratings of community engagement in the stories told at age 26. Both of these factors (positive parenting and generativity) were unique positive predictors of participants' level of enthusiasm in community scenes. As Brian says above, "that (impact on one kid) *just made me want to volunteer more and give back something to the community.*"

So generativity in emerging adulthood (age 23) was a predictor of later community involvement, even after adolescent community involvement and family parenting at age 17 had been taken into account. Feelings of generative concern appear to have been strengthened by these early experiences in the family and community and in turn then may act as amplifiers of further civic and community involvement into young adulthood, just as Brian's story suggests. This finding certainly fits with the previous research evidence on early community involvement (e.g., Hart et al., 2007), but additionally supports the idea that feelings of generative concern and "giving back" may act as proximal influences in the development of civic responsibility. Next we turn to work on a specific area of civic engagement, environmental activism among youth.

ENVIRONMENTALISM AS A CONTEXT FOR EXPRESSING GENERATIVITY IN YOUTH

Frank, a 27-year-old from our Canadian environmental activist study described below, focused on the preservation of biodiversity, discusses a major turning point in his life story:

> I think, probably the big first thing with the campaign was I got my school involved by writing letters. Collected over 700 letters and I mailed them away, and I thought, you know, 700 letters? Damn, we're going to get that animal saved and move on to the next thing. And we got a letter back from the government and it said, basically "we don't give a xxxx"...So the issue was now we had to find what we were going to do. So the next big thing was probably having the chance to go up and see the animal in person. And, obviously, it's one thing to campaign for something you see in a photograph and another to see it in person, and having the chance to go up and see this animal living in this dark forested backdrop, it was really an inspiring moment. The guy who took us out to see the animal, his wife had just given birth to a child. I remember he made me promise to his daughter that the animal would be still there when she grew up and she has children. And so I made her a promise and I'm pretty damned determined to keep it. So that was a big thing.

Calls for concern and urgent action on the issues of climate change, sustainability and preservation of biodiversity for the Earth have grown louder over the past two decades (e.g., Lovelock, 2009). While many are involved in these causes, very modest actual headway on these portentous issues has been made to date. The public is concerned, but often not enough to change our poor stewardship of the natural world. Alarmingly, some recent research suggests that the level of engagement and concern with environmental causes among youth in the U.S. has actually declined over the past several decades (Twenge, Campbell, & Freeman, 2012; Wray-Lake, Flanagan, & Osgood, 2010). Given that these are the future decision-makers of society, this is discouraging.

Some psychological research has sought to explore the role of various attitude and behavior change processes in altering environmental behavior (Gifford, 2008), but much more needs to be done. Very little of this research has focused on generativity and environmentalism, despite suggestions that concern for future generations is an important moral force toward caring for the Earth (Moore & Nelson,

2010). As Frank says in his story about preserving the wild for his guide's infant daughter, investment in future generations and their opportunities to experience nature, can be a generative backdrop to difficult struggles for the natural world.

In some recent research, we have explored how generativity may be important in parents' socialization of their adolescent children (aged 14–16) toward greater involvement with environmental actions and causes (Pratt et al., 2013). In this study, both parents and their teenagers responded to questionnaires on generativity and the environment. We found that more generative parents on the LGS reported greater concerns about teaching their child to be environmentally conscious and also described a greater number of environmental activities in which the child participated in the home. Furthermore, young adolescents' own levels of generativity on this measure predicted positively to self-reports of environmental activities. These findings support the idea that generative concern may provide a motive structure that can encourage both parents and their adolescents toward everyday involvement in activities of care for the earth.

But how about more serious long-term engagement with the environment, such as the commitment seen in our activist Frank's story above? Several qualitative studies have focused on the life experiences of environmental activists, mostly midlife, highly engaged adults (e.g., Horwitz, 1996). Horwitz collected written responses from midlife environmentalists in the United States. Their sense of identity, according to Horwitz, was often shaped by a strong identification with nature and the environment and also often encouraged by identification with early mentors or guides who were strongly committed to nature as well. Protecting and caring for nature became strongly linked to the sense of self. Generativity, involving care and concern for the next generations, was also mentioned as a motivator by a number of these individuals as helping them commit to a moral concern for the future of the earth and all of nature.

Extending this work, over the past several years, we have been engaged in a study of both youth and midlife adult environmental activists in Canada. About half of these activists were between the ages of 18 and 27 (M age = 23), while the rest were between 28 and 59 (M age = 43). A comparison sample of youth and midlife individuals, not involved in environmental activism, was also included (Matsuba & Pratt, in press; Matsuba et al., 2012). Our activists were drawn from several organizations, such as the Sierra Club, Greenpeace, the Green Party of Canada, and from youth environmental coalitions. Their interests included climate change, biodiversity and habitat preservation, social justice, pollution/health issues, and education.

How did people respond on the various questionnaire tasks? The activists scored much more highly than nonactivists on various measures of generative concern and action regarding future generations (Matsuba et al., 2012). These quantitative findings fit well with the qualitative evidence of Horwitz (1996) on generative motivation as a factor in people becoming more involved in environmental issues. Further, we found these relations between generativity and environmentalism were just as strong for our emerging adult group in this study as for our midlife activists. Generative concern was as salient for young people as for adults.

What did participants have to say in the interviews about their life experiences as related to the environment? We rated each of the environmental stories told by the activists and nonactivists on some key general dimensions of narrative, including meaningfulness, impact on the person's life, and vividness (Alisat, Norris, Pratt, Matsuba, & McAdams, 2013). The results of these general analyses of people's environmental stories about their lives were quite parallel to the findings described earlier for the questionnaire data. First, those individuals who were higher on a sense of environmental identity were more likely to tell meaningful and important, as well as vivid, stories. More engaged youth, and those with stronger environmental identities, had stronger narrative identities as reflected in the longer and better articulated stories they told, like Frank's story above. More generative people also told more meaningful and thoughtful stories about the environment. This finding parallels what Matsuba et al. (2012) reported regarding generativity and environmental attitudes and behaviors in this sample. The new wrinkle here is that generative concern was linked to a more sophisticated and thoughtful *life story*, told more convincingly. Finally, when the person's level of generative concern was entered to predict story quality, the effects of environmental identity measured by questionnaire were weakened (Alisat et al., 2013). This reflects the fact that the relation of people's sense of identity to the life story was partly mediated through the presence of stronger generative motivation in this domain.

Longitudinal data from the Futures Study support and extend findings from the Canadian Activist Study. At age 32, individuals in the Futures sample were given several standard questionnaire measures of environmental behaviors, attitudes, and identity. Controlling for gender and for a separate measure of prosocial motivation at 23, we found that higher generative concern at 23 predicted prospectively to this environmental engagement index at 32 (Pratt, Norris, Alisat, & Matsuba, 2012). These results support the interpretation of the findings of the Activist Study, within a more "ordinary" sample that was not selected for activism. They also suggest that generativity may lead environmentalism in terms of causal ordering. However, we think it most plausible that these two variables, as in the generativity-community involvement context discussed above, are mutually influential across this period of development.

Results from these studies, then, compare closely with earlier, qualitative data collected from older, midlife activists (Horwitz, 1996). Generativity appears to predict greater environmental investment, among both youth and midlife adults. Despite legitimate worries that concerns regarding the environment have become less salient among young people in recent decades (Twenge et al., 2012; Wray-Lake et al., 2010), our youthful activists, like Frank, told a different tale. Their version of the life story in emerging adulthood showed a generative conviction that change is possible in this important domain of civic engagement.

WORK AND CAREER AS A CONTEXT FOR EXPRESSING
GENERATIVITY IN YOUTH

Sue, a 25-year-old in the Futures Sample:

> I am a child and youth counselor and that's what I went to school for, and
> I love it. It's important to me, I want to help kids. I want them to know
> they're not alone, and they have someone they can trust, someone that's
> gonna advocate for them. And I want to give them some of the opportuni-
> ties and skills that I didn't have as a teenager so they're not gonna make the
> same mistakes." (Interviewer: How does your work relate to your sense of
> who you are as a person?) "I'm definitely a care taker and someone who likes
> to do things for others. It's a big part of who I am in my personal and my
> professional life.

Work, paid or otherwise and with its many pleasures and sorrows, occupies much
of our adult lives (de Botton, 2009). Most young people in North America begin at
least part-time work in adolescence by emerging adulthood, most of us are regularly employed or at least on the way to a job or career (Arnett, 2012). As Erikson
(1968) emphasized, deciding on a vocation is a key part of the identity work of
adolescence and emerging adulthood for both men and women in contemporary society and all the more challenging due to the fluid dynamics of modern
economies (Hendry & Kloep,2007). Research in midlife has shown that the social
responsibility aspects of work can have much relevance to the way in which adults
make sense of their work lives (Colby, Sippola, & Phelps, 2001). Work is often
highly interwoven with the individual's engagement in the wider society as well,
shaping volunteering patterns and roles within the wider community. And many
jobs, as in Sue's description above, are clearly more geared to the expression of the
prosocial impulses and feelings of their occupants than are others. In this section,
we briefly review what is known about the ways in which such vocational choices
and experiences may be related to generativity in adults and then discuss some
evidence on these relations in youth from the Futures sample.

Research by Colby et al. (2001) on an interview subsample from the large
MIDUS midlife sample of adults in the United States explored the relations of generative concern on a version of the LGS among these adults to their descriptions of
their work lives. Findings suggested both that social responsibility considerations
were a key theme that many adults described as important in their interviews
about work, and that this concern was related positively to levels of generative concern as measured by questionnaire in the MIDUS data set. Furthermore, more use
of themes of social responsibility in the interviews was associated with greater satisfaction levels in the work role (Colby et al., 2001). Longitudinal work by Stewart
and her colleagues on women (e.g., Peterson & Stewart, 1996) has indicated that
the relations between generativity and work engagement may be somewhat complex, with those women in careers showing more likelihood of investing their

generative qualities in the work domain, whereas those in less career-oriented jobs demonstrated more associations between family roles and generativity (and few such associations with their work roles). Recent research on midlife men has also shown relations between generative predispositions and mentoring/leadership and interpersonal care in the work context, as well as positive links between generativity and level of work satisfaction (Clark & Arnold, 2008). Although only a modest body of research to date, these studies suggest generative caring for the needs of others and for younger colleagues finds expression in adults' vocational roles in midlife and can be vocationally satisfying among both men and women.

In the Futures Study, we explored the relations between work and career satisfaction during emerging adulthood and their links to earlier assessments of generativity in our sample (Pratt, Norris, & Alisat, 2012). At age 26, participants were interviewed using a somewhat shortened version of the interview on social responsibility and work developed by Colby et al. (2001). These interviews were rated reliably for levels of meaning and satisfaction with work, as well as for themes of social responsibility and extrinsic motivation (following Colby et al.'s thematic coding). The pattern of longitudinal correlations suggested that generativity on the LGS at 23 was a modest positive predictor of ratings of interviews for social responsibility and of work meaningfulness ratings at 26. The LGS at 23 did not predict rated work satisfaction or extrinsic work motivation at 26, however. But what about satisfaction in young adulthood at age 32? Compellingly, a work scale based on a composite of self-ratings of enjoyment, importance, and satisfaction at age 32 was substantially predicted by the LGS at age 23 ($r_{partial} = .33, p < .01$).

We also examined the **type** of occupation reported at ages 26 and 32, sorting jobs into work that emphasized more prosocial or caring roles (e.g., teaching, social work) versus work that did not (e.g., sales, financial advising, manufacturing). Between 30% and 35% of occupations in our sample were judged to embody specifically care-focused work. Those who were higher on generativity at age 23 in our sample were more likely to be engaged in such prosocial work roles at 26 and 32. Controlling for educational attainment (a well-established predictor of occupation) and sex, the partial correlations between the LGS at age 23 and caring occupational status at 26 and 32 were positive and significant, $r = .21$, and $r = .26$ (both $ps < .05$).

These findings suggested that generativity at 23 was a significant marker of choice of future vocational role in young adulthood. In turn, work satisfaction was higher among those in such caring roles at 26 and 32, supporting the findings of Colby et al. (2001) among midlife adults that feelings of social responsibility and care for others may provide one of the key satisfactions in work life. Nonetheless, work type and generative concern, though positively linked to each other as discussed, contributed independently to people's self-ratings of overall work satisfaction at 32. In fact, those in noncare occupations showed similar positive associations between earlier scores on the LGS at 23 and job satisfaction at 32 as did those in care-oriented jobs. Some jobs may afford more opportunities for social responsibility and care than others, as the quote from Sue earlier suggests, and these jobs may be sought out by more generative emerging adults. Yet those who were more generative at 23 in our sample found ways to invest these concerns in work of all types, as our findings also suggest, perhaps through activities such as mentoring and supporting clients or coworkers, and this predicted their level of job satisfaction. These findings clearly suggest that generativity in emerging adulthood can play some role in shaping work lives and experiences, which in turn may impact social and civic engagement across the life course.

POLITICAL INVOLVEMENT AS A CONTEXT FOR EXPRESSING GENERATIVITY IN YOUTH

As in some other areas of civic engagement discussed above, there has been concern over declines in political participation by North American youth over the past 30 years (e.g., Syvertsen, Wray-Lake, Flanagan, Osgood, & Briddell, 2011). In particular, both traditional political activities such as voting or campaigning and alternative activities such as protesting have shown uneven but general downward trends among samples of youth from the 1970s to the 2000s. These patterns have seemed to go hand in hand with declines in other measures like trust in government (Syvertsen et al., 2011). As noted above, however, volunteering rates have actually shown an increase since the 1990s (Twenge et al., 2012), suggesting that youth have shifted their patterns of civic engagement, rather than simply curtailing such activities across the board.

As in many identity-relevant domains, the levels and types of engagement shown during the period of emerging adulthood may be especially noteworthy, because they tend to set the pattern for subsequent levels of engagement and political orientation in adulthood. For example, McAdam's (1988) work on the "Freedom Summer" cohort in the 1960s civil rights movement in the U.S. South showed that individuals who participated in this challenging and risky work (vs. those who volunteered to go but then did not) were much more left-leaning politically and more engaged in political issues 20 years later. Other work (Alwin & Krosnick, 1991), too, suggests that early political orientation has important long-term implications for adulthood, perhaps through identity processes that are prominent during late adolescence and emerging adulthood.

As we noted above, some longitudinal studies have found that more civic engagement among youth has been shown to predict more political activity in maturity (e.g., voting behavior, Hart et al., 2007). Understanding the patterns of these changes would be enhanced by a specific framework for thinking about the development of political engagement. Finlay, Flanagan, and Wray-Lake (2011) reported on a longitudinal study of a U.S. sample of AmeriCorps volunteers and a comparison group that followed civic and political activity in these individuals from adolescence to young adulthood. Latent transition analysis was used to describe the patterns of change in the sample, and three statuses were identified: less engaged, voting-engaged, and highly committed. Transitions over time were from the less engaged to the voting-engaged status and, for a smaller sample of the AmeriCorps group, from less engaged to highly committed. Several factors were predictive of these statuses, notably university attendance, which also predicted higher political engagement across the sample.

Using this general framework, we conducted analyses of political engagement in the Futures Sample based on self-report measures of political interest and voting behaviors, as well as reports on a standard set of political activities (such as attending a demonstration, working on a campaign, or contacting a public official). These various measures in the political domain were modestly positively correlated at age 32, though not consistently so before this in the data set. In order to investigate the role of generativity as a predictor in this domain, we first examined the correlations between the LGS measured at age 23, with ratings of political interest and frequency of voting at 32. Unfortunately we did not collect these voting and interest measures in the age 26 wave, but we did measure political activity at both 26 and 32. Partial correlations controlled for completed education level (as suggested by Finlay et al.). The longitudinal correlation for the LGS at 23 and political activity at 26 was positive and significant, $r_{partial} = .27$, $p < .05$, though it was only marginally significant by age 32, $r_{partial} = .17$, $p = .10$. Correlations of age 23 generativity and political interest and voting at 32 were positive, but not significant.

Though these effects were consistent with expectations, they were clearly weak compared with the results in the previous three domains described above. Why might this be? It is helpful to consider the life course model of Finlay et al. (2011) in thinking about these results. In this study, most individuals in late adolescence and emerging adulthood were found at the first two levels over this period: little engaged or voting-engaged. However, a small subset of individuals in their sample had reached the committed status. It seems possible that generative concern may have its most meaningful impact only on the attainment of this level and that high levels of generative concern may not be particularly important for the developmental transition from the " little engaged" level to the "voting-engaged" level. If so, it would not be surprising that our longitudinal analyses did not detect much predictability from generative concern at 23 to later interest and voting and only modest levels of prediction to political activity. Political identity is a slowly developing domain for many, in contrast to the vocational and volunteer engagement domains, so it may be that low levels of engagement explain the weak relations in these data.

Summary: The Role of Generativity in Civic Engagement in Youth

In this chapter, drawing mainly on longitudinal data from a Canadian youth sample (the Futures Study) spanning age 17 to age 32, we have presented evidence on four domains of engagement outside of the family and personal relationships: community volunteering, environmentalism, work, and political involvement. In three of these domains (community, environmentalism, and work), we found quite clear evidence that generative concern, as assessed at the age 23 wave in our sample by the Loyola Generativity Scale of McAdams and de St. Aubin (1992), was predictive of higher levels of subsequent civic involvement in early adulthood. This pattern was much weaker for the political domain in our data. Nevertheless, the findings for adolescents and emerging adults in the first three domains were similar to results among midlife adults that we reviewed, strengthening our interpretation that these results on early generativity are meaningful. It was also noteworthy that we found quite parallel data on the LGS as a predictor of measures of the life stories told by youth in the community and environmental domains. These converging findings across quantitative and narrative methodologies lend further support to the potential role of generative concern in enhancing and deepening civic engagement.

We argued in the introduction that generative concern, while related to general altruism, is a distinctive measure focused more specifically on care for youth as a legacy of the self for the future. In the Futures data set, we had standard measures at age 23 of endorsement of personal values (benevolence and universalism), which represent the prosocial quadrant in the circumplex model of personal values of Schwartz (1994). In Table 20.1, we show the evidence from a composite measure of these two value scales in comparison to the LGS at age 23. We provide partial correlations of our major civic engagement measures at ages 26 and 32 with the LGS and the Schwartz value indices, as well as partial correlations for the LGS and these engagement measures after *controlling* for the Schwartz value composite. As indicated in the table, these various domains of engagement were positively related to prosocial values, as expected if they are indeed measures of

TABLE 20.1 Partial correlations of the LGS at 23 and 26, the Schwartz Altruistic Values Composite at age 23 and later measures of civic engagement in the Futures Sample (a)

Measure	LGS at 23	Schwartz Composite Index at 23	LGS at 23, Controlling for Schwartz Index	LGS at 26
Community Involvement 32	.44***	.31**	.36**	.53***
Environmental Involvement 32	.27**	.20	.22*	.24*
Work Satisfaction 32	.33**	.07	.36**	.39**
Work Type 26	.28*	.26*	.17	.11
Work Type 32	.28**	.20*	.22*	.11
Political Interest 32	.19*	.10	.13	.02
Voting 32	.11	.03	.09	.08
Political Action 26	.32**	.24*	.25*	.24*
Political Action 32	.17*	.19*	.11	.34**

(a) partial correlations, controlling for sex and family social class background
* $p < .05$
** $p < .01$
*** $p < .001$

prosocial activities. However, most measures were more strongly correlated with the LGS than with the Schwartz index, and the LGS remained significant as a predictor after the Schwartz index was controlled, as shown in the fourth column of Table 20.1. This supports discriminant validity for the generativity measure from altruistic values, particularly in the community and work domains.

These data support the argument that generative concern is meaningful and important as an aspect of personality differences by emerging adulthood (at least by age 23) and does not wait until midlife for its substantive emergence (Lawford et al., 2013; Lawford et al., 2005; Matsuba et al., 2012; Pratt et al., 2009). No doubt, other aspects of generativity, such as generative accomplishment or narration, unfold in complex ways and at later times across the life course, as argued by others (Stewart & Vandewater, 1998). But by age 23, the measure of generative concern was reasonably stable and comparable to the same measure at age 26. Furthermore, our findings for the domain of community engagement suggested that generativity at 23 was a *unique* contributor to the development of these activities at 32, above and beyond variations in earlier levels of the activities in adolescence (we could not analyze this for the other domains in the Futures data set, since we did not have measures in adolescence of work satisfaction or of environmentalism). Nevertheless, this finding suggests that generativity may be part of a positive feedback loop, through which initial engagement in a domain leads to consolidation of generative concern, which in turn leads to further engagement in that domain. Our findings in the domain of work, too, suggested that generativity may contribute to strengthening youth goals of social responsibility, which in turn were linked to greater subsequent job satisfaction, consistent with the Colby et al. (2001) evidence from midlife. In sum, positive bidirectional influences between generativity and engagement seem likely in many of these civic domains.

What about the theme of this volume, the complexity of development in the prosocial domain? Our results showed that there were only weak relations between forms of civic engagement across the various domains we studied, consistent with evidence from midlife (Rossi, 2001). This was particularly clear for the political domain, which was not much related to activities in the other domains, and also very weakly related to early generativity compared to the other three civic domains. This finding supports the complexity of variation in development across domains of civic engagement, which we suggested above might be partly attributed to the slowly developing level of identity commitment in the political sphere (e.g., Fadjukoff et al., 2010).

Future Research Questions and Directions

Several important implications for future research are suggested by this review. First, of course, this research shows the value of systematic longitudinal study on the sorts of questions raised by early generativity as a potential factor in civic development. There is a need for more such work exploring the family and extra-familial role of youth development in this area. Family socialization may indeed foster positive development in youth, perhaps in conjunction with parental encouragement of civic volunteering and engagement, as we suggested for the domain of environmentalism above, but more work is needed to understand the coordination of family and extra-family processes better (Pratt et al., 2013). Second, efforts should be undertaken to link the development of different forms of generativity (e.g., biological, parental, technical, and societal, as suggested by Kotre, 1984) with specific domains of prosocial actions. For example, as suggested above, these forms can be readily mapped onto distinct domains of engagement such as family, work, and civic volunteering, and exploring these specific links may help to generate more detailed models. Third, traditional family-based studies of socialization do not account for the possibility of genetic pathways. Studies examining this alternative pathway would be informative, as the biological emphasis in the present volume highlights (e.g., Fortuna & Knafo, chapter 4, this volume). Fourth, systematic work should be undertaken to follow up evidence that successful adaptation with regard to earlier developmental tasks in the Erikson framework—such as identity and intimacy—shows evidence of fostering better resolution of the issues of generativity and, in turn, higher levels of prosocial and civic engagement among youth.

Fifth, links between identity development and generativity deserve special attention, in particular because the findings so far suggest that investment in particular domains as a part of one's emerging sense of identity may serve to consolidate and build stronger investment in that domain as a source of generative accomplishment and engagement as well. It seems likely that such an outcome depends on youth experiencing opportunities to engage in reflection and meaning-making around these civic experiences (Yates & Youniss, 1996). Finally, the parallels between results using both traditional and narrative measures in the Futures data set suggest the potential for using these two methodologies in a synergistic way, to deepen our understanding of development across this period of life, when the life story itself is emerging and consolidating (McAdams, 2001b). Narrative methods can guide our approach to new phenomena in useful ways and may suggest more complex and interesting questions for future research using quantitative methodologies. Such a mixed-method approach offers opportunities for studying the processes and complexities of prosocial development as it unfolds in adolescence and emerging adulthood. In particular, such work may help us to understand better how the construct of generativity is related to, but also perhaps different from, other aspects of prosocial and altruistic motivation in young people.

ACKNOWLEDGMENT

The authors thank Shmuel Shulman for his comments on an earlier draft of this manuscript. The research reported in this chapter was supported by grants from the Social Sciences and Humanities Research Council of Canada.

References

Alisat, S., Norris, J. E., Pratt, M. W., Matsuba, M. K., & McAdams, D. P. (2013). *Caring for the future of the Earth: Generativity as a mediator for the prediction of environmental narratives from identity among Canadian activists and nonactivists.* Manuscript submitted for publication.

Alwin, D., & Krosnick, J. (1991). Aging, cohorts and the stability of sociopolitical orientations over the lifespan. *American Journal of Sociology, 97*(1), 169–195.

Arnett, J. J. (2012). *Adolescence and emerging adulthood: A cultural approach* (5th ed.). Saddle River, NJ: Pearson/Prentice-Hall.

Busch, H., & Hofer, J. (2011). Identity, prosocial behavior, and generative concern in German and Cameroonian Nso adolescents. *Journal of Adolescence, 34,* 629–638.

Clark, M., & Arnold, J. (2008). The nature, prevalence and correlates of generativity among men in middle career. *Journal of Vocational Behavior, 73*(3), 473–484.

Colby, A., Sippola, L., & Phelps, E. (2001). Social responsibility and paid work in contemporary American life. In A. Rossi (Ed.), *Caring and doing for others* (pp. 463–504). Chicago: Chicago University Press.

Damon, W., Menon, J., & Bronk, K. C. (2003). The development of purpose during adolescence. *Applied Developmental Science, 7,* 119–128.

de Botton, A. (2009). *The pleasures and sorrows of work.* Toronto: McClelland & Stewart.

Dumas, T. M., Lawford, H. L., Tieu, T., & Pratt, M. W. (2009). Positive parenting in adolescence and its relation to low point life story narration and identity status in emerging adulthood: A longitudinal analysis. *Developmental Psychology, 45,* 1531–1544.

Emmons, R. A. (1989). The personal striving approach to personality. In L. A. Pervin (Ed.), *Goal concepts in personality and social psychology* (pp. 87–126). Hillsdale, NJ: Erlbaum.

Erikson, E. H. (1968). *Identity, youth, and crisis.* New York: Norton.

Erikson, E. H. (1969). *Gandhi's truth.* New York: Norton.

Fadjukoff, P., Kokko, K., & Pulkkinen, L.(2010). Changing economic conditions and identity formation in adulthood. *European Psychologist, 15,* 293–307.

Finlay, A., Flanagan, C., & Wray-Lake, L. (2011). Civic engagement patterns and transitions over eight years: The AmeriCorps National Study. *Developmental Psychology, 47,* 1728–1743.

Flanagan, C. A. (2005). Voluteerism, leadership, political socialization and civic engagement. In R. Lerner & L. Steinberg (Eds.), *Handbook of adolescent psychology.* New York: Wiley.

Frensch, K. M., Pratt, M. W., & Norris, J. E. (2007). Foundations of generativity: Personal and family correlates of adolescents' generative life story themes. *Journal of Research in Personality, 41,* 45–62.

Frimer, J. A., & Walker, L. J. (2009). Reconciling the self and morality: An empirical model of moral centrality development. *Developmental Psychology, 45*, 1669–1681.

Gifford, R. (2008). Psychology's essential role in alleviating the impacts of climate change. *Canadian Psychology, 49*, 273–280.

Hart, D., Donnelly, T., Youniss, J., & Atkins, R. (2007). High school community service as a predictor of adult voting and volunteering. *American Educational Research Journal, 44*, 197–219.

Hart, D., & Fegley, S. (1995). Prosocial behavior and caring in adolescence: Relations to self-understanding and social judgment. *Child Development, 66*, 1346–1359.

Hendry, L., & Kloep, M. (2007). Conceptualizing emerging adulthood: Inspecting the emperor's new clothes? *Child Development Perspectives, 1*(2), 74–79.

Horwitz, W. A. (1996). Developmental origins of environmental ethics: The life experiences of activists. *Ethics and Behavior, 6*, 29–54.

Jia, F., Pratt, M. W., & Alisat, S. (2013, April). *Identity and community involvement predict generativity in emerging adults: A longitudinal study using multilevel modeling.* Poster presented at the Society for Research in Child Development Meeting, Seattle, Washington.

Kotre, J. (1984). *Outliving the self: Generativity and the interpretation of lives.* Baltimore, MD: Johns Hopkins University Press.

Larson R. W. (2000). Toward a psychology of positive youth development. *American Psychologist, 55*, 170–183.

Larson, R. W., Hansen, D. M., & Moneta, G. (2006). Differing profiles of developmental experiences across organized youth activities. *Developmental Psychology, 42*, 849–863.

Lawford, H. L., Doyle, A. B., & Markiewitz, D. (2013). The association between early generative concern and caregiving with friends from early to middle adolescence. *Journal of Youth and Adolescence.* doi 10.1007/s10964-012-9888-y

Lawford, H., Pratt, M. W., Hunsberger, B., & Pancer, S. M. (2005). Adolescent generativity: A longitudinal study of two possible contexts for learning concern for future generations. *Journal of Research on Adolescence, 15*, 261–273.

Mackinnon, S. P., Nosko, A., Pratt, M. W., & Norris, J. (2011). Intimacy and thematic patterns in young adults' narratives of romantic and friendship domains predict levels of Eriksonian generativity: A mixed method analysis. *Journal of Personality, 79*, 587–618.

Matsuba, M. K., & Pratt, M. W. (in press). The making of an environmentalist: A developmental psychological perspective. *New Directions in Child and Adolescent Development.*

Matsuba, M. K., Pratt, M. W., Norris, J. E., Mohle, E., Alisat, S., & McAdams, D. P. (2012). Environmentalism as a context for expressing generativity and identity: Patterns among activist and uninvolved youth and midlife adults. *Journal of Personality, 80*, 1091–1115.

McAdam, D. (1989). Consequences of activism. *American Sociological Review, 54*, 744–760.

McAdams, D. P. (2001a). Generativity at midlife. In M. Lachman (Ed.), *Handbook of midlife development* (pp. 395–443). New York: Wiley.

McAdams, D. P. (2001b). The psychology of life stories. *Review of General Psychology, 5*(2), 100–122.

McAdams, D. P., & de St. Aubin, E. (1992). A theory of generativity and its assessment through self-report, behavioral acts, and narrative themes in autobiography. *Journal of Personality and Social Psychology, 62*, 1003–1015.

McAdams, D. P., Reynolds, J., Lewis, M., Patten, A., & Bowman, P. J. (2001). When bad things turn good and good things turn bad: Sequences of redemption and contamination in life narrative, and their relation to psychosocial adaptation in midlife adults and in students. *Personality and Social Psychology Bulletin, 27,* 472–483.

Moore, K. D., & Nelson, M. P. (2010). *Moral ground: Ethical action for a planet in peril.* San Antonio, TX: Trinity University Press.

Pancer, S. M., Pratt, M. W., Hunsberger, B., & Alisat, S. (2007). Community and political involvement in adolescence: What distinguishes the activists from the uninvolved? *Journal of Community Psychology, 35,* 741–759.

Peterson, B. E., & Stewart, A. J. (1996). Antecedents and contexts of generativity motivation at midlife. *Psychology and Aging, 11*(1), 21–33.

Pratt, M. W., Alisat, S., Bisson, E., & Norris, J. E. (2013). Earth mothers: Generativity and environmental concerns in adolescents and their parents. *Journal of Moral Education, 42*(1), 12–27.

Pratt, M. W., Arnold, M. L., & Lawford, H. L. (2009). Growing towards care: A narrative approach to prosocial moral identity and generativity of personality in emerging adulthood. In D. Narvaez & D. Lapsley (Eds.), *Moral self, identity and character: Prospects for a new field of study* (pp. 295–315). New York: Cambridge University Press.

Pratt, M. W., Norris, J. E., & Alisat, S. A. (2012, March). *Caring about work: A longitudinal analysis of adolescent personality predictors of young adult work engagement.* Paper presented at the Society for Research on Adolescence Meetings, Vancouver, British Columbia, Canada.

Pratt, M. W., Norris, J. E., Alisat, S., & Matsuba, M. K. (2012, July). *Generativity in emerging adulthood as a predictor of environmental engagement in young adults: A Canadian longitudinal study.* Paper presented at the International Society for the Study of Behavioral Development Meetings, Edmonton, Alberta, Canada.

Putnam, R. D. (2000). *Bowling alone.* New York: Simon & Schuster.

Rossi, A. (2001). Domains and dilemmas of social responsibility. In A Rossi (Ed.), *Caring and doing for others* (pp. 97–134). Chicago: Chicago University Press.

Rushton, J. P., Chrisjohn, R. D., & Fekken, G. C. (1981). The altruistic personality and self-report scale. *Personality and Individual Differences, 2,* 293–302.

Schwartz, S. H. (1994). Are there universal aspects in the structure and content of human values? *Journal of Social Issues, 50,* 19–45.

Sleightholm, M., Alisat, S., Norris, J. E., & Pratt, M. W. (2012, March). *Getting involved: Predictors of community commitment across adolescence and emerging adulthood.* Poster presented at the Society for Research on Adolescence Meetings, Vancouver, British Columbia, Canada.

Smetana, J., Campione-Barr, J., & Metzger, A. (2006). Adolescent development in interpersonal and societal context. *Annual Review of Psychology, 57,* 355–284.

Snarey, J. (1993). *How fathers care for the next generation.* Cambridge, MA: Harvard University Press.

Stewart, A. J., & Vandewater, E. A. (1998). The course of generativity. In D. P. McAdams & E. de St. Aubin (Eds.), *Generativity and adult development* (pp. 75–100). Washington, DC: American Psychological Association Press.

Syvertsen, A. K., Wray-Lake, L., Flanagan, C. A., Osgood D. W., & Briddell, L. (2011). Thirty-year trends in U.S. adolescents' civic engagement: Changing participation and educational differences. *Journal of Research on Adolescence, 21,* 586–594.

Twenge, J. M., Campbell, W. K., & Freeman, E. C. (2012). Generational differences in young adults' life goals, concern for others and civic orientation, 1966–2009. *Journal of Personality and Social Psychology, 102*(5), 1045–1062.

Walker, L. J., & Frimer, J. A. (2007). Moral personality of brave and caring exemplars. *Journal of Personality and Social Psychology, 93*(5), 845–860.

Wray-Lake, L., Flanagan, C. A., & Osgood, D. W. (2010). Examining trends in adolescent environmental attitudes, beliefs, and behaviours across three decades. *Environment and Behavior, 42*, 61–85.

Yates, M., & Youniss, J. (1996). Community service and political-moral identity in adolescents. *Journal of Research on Adolescence, 6*, 271–284.

21

Prosocial Exemplarity in Adolescence and Adulthood

Lawrence J. Walker

How can we explain the behavior of people who dedicate decades of their lives in volunteer service to those who are disadvantaged? What about those who tirelessly support social justice, humanitarian, or environmental causes? And then there are those who risk their lives in rescuing others in dire emergency situations. What motivates them? These extraordinary actions, committed by otherwise ordinary people, intrigue and inspire us precisely because they don't make any good sense—they are clearly intended to promote others' welfare but seemingly have no benefit for oneself; indeed, they inevitably entail considerable cost, risk, and trouble. So, why be prosocial? Why do good? Wherein is the motivation to be moral?

Such questions have been a persistent conundrum for thinkers across the centuries (Richter, 2007) and are particularly salient in the shadow of the Enlightenment because of its influence on our understanding of human nature and our definition of morality. Its dualistic conception of human nature bifurcated reason and personality; its formalist conception of morality emphasized duties and rights in regard to justice and welfare concerns. Together, these notions imparted the received wisdom—now reflected in many contemporary psychological theories— that individuals should (and could be motivated to) set aside personal interests and instead follow the dictates of reason or higher values to engage in the varied prosocial actions that are essential for social living in a civil society.

Note that implicit in such arguments is the contention that morality should not be self-regarding, that there is no moral credit in advancing one's own interests; rather, moral credit accrues when one manages to suppress one's own wants, desires, and projects in order to do the right thing. Morality, in that conception, entails acting out of drear duty, onerous obligation, and selfless sacrifice—and against one's natural inclinations and personal interests. Thus, others' interests are held to be ethically prior to one's own. So wherein is the motivation to act morally, to behave prosocially? Such a conception of moral motivation is inert and, quite frankly, psychologically unrealistic.

The contention that I advance in this chapter is that prosocial morality can and should be self-regarding, advancing one's own interests. As moral agents, we can "have our cake and eat it too," reflecting in many regards Hillel's aphorism, "If I am not for myself, who will be for me? Yet, if I am for myself only, what am I? And if not now, when?" (Pirkei Avot 1:14). Similarly, in contemporary psychology, Perloff (1987) and Staub (2005) contend that self-interest can be enlightened in inducing altruism-like behaviors and Hawley (chapter 3, this volume) explicates aspects of prosociality that can be instrumental to the self.

The argument that morality can be self-regarding is informed by Flanagan's (1991, 2009) insights on the issue. He acknowledges—and holds that our theories of morality and moral functioning must do the same—that people are rightly partial to their personal interests, projects, and commitments that fundamentally give meaning to life and that such meaning is constitutive of morality (obviously reflecting a more eudaimonic view of the moral domain). And he contends that our theories, to be taken as credible and viable, must specify the motivational mechanism for the actualization of their posited ideals and that such a mechanism must be psychologically feasible "for creatures like us" (Flanagan, 1991, p. 48). My aim is to do just that. The aspect of morality that is my focus here is the prosocial or the supererogatory—behavior that goes beyond what is strictly required.

The mechanism for prosocial morality explored in this chapter is the developing appropriation of morality as core to individuals' identity and personality. Notions of motivation and personality have frequently been disparaged as explanatory concepts in moral psychology, as evidenced by Kohlberg's (1981) denigration of notions of character (the so-called bag of virtues) and elevation of notions of moral rationality and by Turiel's (1983) segregation of the personal from the moral domain. However, the mechanism advanced here transforms the duality between self-interest and morality by explaining how one's (self-enhancing) personal interests can be accomplished through the enactment of (self-transcending) prosocial behaviors that promote the needs and interests of others.

Dual Foci

FOCUS ON ADOLESCENCE AND ADULTHOOD

This chapter focuses on prosocial morality in adolescence and adulthood—and not just because other authors in this volume have staked out the earlier part of the life span. Obviously, the foundations set for moral development in infancy, toddlerhood, and childhood are hugely significant, but there are good reasons for my focus on adolescence and adulthood, especially in light of the purported mechanism of the appropriation of morality to the self.

It has long been recognized that adolescence is a time for identity formation (Erikson, 1968) and of accentuated awareness of intrapsychic and interpersonal functioning (Selman, 1980). In late adolescence and early adulthood, some people seemingly embark on what we could call a "moral career," engaging in consistent and long-term patterns of prosocial behavior, whereas others take a more self-interested path in life. So there often seems to be something of a turning-point at that juncture in the life span.

A further justification for a research focus on adulthood is that we can examine moral functioning in its more mature, full-blown form. This represents a strategy of "reverse engineering" in which we start with an analysis of the finished product and then work backward—in this case, developmentally—to figure out the age-related trajectories and operative mechanisms.

FOCUS ON EXEMPLARITY

As the chapter title harkens, my focus is not only on adolescence and adulthood but additionally through the perspective of exemplarity—behavior that is regarded as commendable and worthy of imitation. Much (but not all) of the research to be featured here has examined aspects of the psychological functioning of people who have demonstrated inordinate prosocial behavior—as exemplars of morality. This perspective of exemplarity has considerable heuristic value (see Walker, 2002, for a further discussion).

One advantage of this approach is that it allows an empirical comparison between prosocial exemplars and ordinary folk (or some other similar contrast group). The use of such "extreme" groups has the potential to magnify differences on the variables of interest. This strategy thus allows operative processes of psychological functioning to be more readily discerned.

Of course, prosocial exemplars are identified precisely because they have engaged in meaningful real-world behaviors that have had considerable impact. These behaviors have true significance and ecological validity. Contrast such behaviors (e.g., caring for the homeless, saving a stranger from a car fire) with what often passes for a proxy of prosocial behavior in the lab (e.g., contrived donations, transitory expressions of empathy, self-reports). Of course, laboratory studies of prosocial behavior do have their empirical value, particularly in facilitating the testing of causal mechanisms in the context of a highly controlled experimental situation, but often that level of control forces compromises in the real-world significance of the prosocial behaviors assessed.

In many instances, research with exemplars has entailed a rather broadband assessment of their psychological functioning (the rarity of such exemplars seems to evoke extensive data collection by researchers). This facilitates within-person analyses of the often complex relationships among various aspects of exemplars' functioning, which would not be possible with the traditional variable-level analytic approach. Person-level analyses have greater potential to yield holistic understandings of these phenomenologically real behaviors.

Finally, research on exemplars can inform the viability of the ethical ideals that mark the assumed endpoint of our models of prosociality. For example, is there evidence that people can actually attain and sustain the type of motivation and prosocial behavior that our theories demand? Is there one such endpoint or might we need to accommodate multiple ideals of moral excellence?

Appropriation of Morality to the Self

An emerging theme in thinking about moral motivation over the last couple of decades has been the alignment of morality with the self, such that moral concerns and commitments become endemic to identity and personality. Blasi (1983, 1984) and Damon (1984) both can be credited with introducing the notion of the moral self as a core explanatory concept in moral functioning. Note that this selfhood notion ran counter to the then-prevailing view that rationality was the defining feature of the moral domain and its fundamental psychological manifestation.

A variety of motivational mechanisms related to the moral self were proffered (Blasi, 1983, 1984, 2005; Damon, 1984), including the need for psychological self-consistency or coherence, a sense of personal responsibility (viz., that what was morally good was also obligatory for the self), integrity of identity, willpower, and moral desires. Unfortunately, these notions were never adequately operationalized and so have not yet gained much traction.

However, one concept pertaining to the moral self has had staying power—moral centrality. This motivational mechanism refers to the extent to which morality is central to one's identity or sense of self, which, of course, may vary considerably across individuals (both in the content of the moral concerns and in their salience). Erikson (1968) had largely framed identity formation in terms of occupational choice and political ideology; what Blasi and Damon did was to explicitly add morality to the identity mix, arguing that self-identity could also be framed by morality, which would explain, to a considerable extent, moral motivation and subsequent behavior. Thus, once morality has been appropriated to the self, then acting in that regard would obviously be self-enhancing whereas failing to do so would be self-defeating.

Despite the appeal of a moral self model, there are a couple of cautions to note. One is that moral centrality as a motivational mechanism is apparently not activated until identity formation begins in adolescence, leaving moral motivation in the earlier part of the life span and the patterns and processes of its development largely unexplained. As Blasi (1993) acknowledged, genuine morality is clearly evident in childhood, in children's evaluations (Hamlin, Wynn, & Bloom, 2007), conversations (Wright & Bartsch, 2008), and self-referential emotions and other aspects of conscience (Kochanska & Thompson, 1997). The other caution is that, until recently, the supportive empirical evidence for this mechanism of moral motivation has been thin on the ground.

The first suggestive evidence for this notion of moral centrality came from the monumental study of Holocaust rescuers conducted by Oliner and Oliner (1988). Although they explored a wide range of factors presumed to contribute to altruistic action, their focus was more on situational and demographic variables than personological ones. However, their surveys did indicate stronger internalization of the values of prosociality and personal integrity among rescuers than nonrescuers, suggesting the moral centrality of these motives.

Colby and Damon's (1992) qualitative study of moral exemplars more explicitly focused on aspects of moral self-understanding. To identify these moral exemplars they assembled a diverse panel of ethical experts who derived a set of criteria for moral exemplarity and then nominated people who met those criteria. Colby and Damon proceeded to do a case-study analysis of a small sample of these identified exemplars (who were largely social activists pursing prosocial causes) and, in so doing, ascertained several features of mature moral development.

Perhaps the feature that most impressed Colby and Damon was that these moral exemplars had an identity that meaningfully fused the personal and moral aspects of their lives (see their chapter 11, this volume). Various aspects of their lives were not compartmentalized and uncoordinated, as is more typical in adult development (Damon & Hart, 1988). Morality occupied a central place in the exemplars' sense of self; and moral action was not regarded as an exercise in self-sacrifice nor the result of heady deliberative adjudication of competing options. Indeed, their appropriation of morality to the self instead meant that these exemplars derived considerable personal fulfillment from pursuing their prosocial projects. This is the psychological mechanism that holds promise for explaining prosocial motivation.

By definition, exemplars are uncommon and their rarity means that they are often studied using qualitative methodology. Interestingly, with other groups of exemplars such as Holocaust rescuers, Carnegie medalists, philanthropists, emergency response personnel, military heroes, hospice volunteers, and L'Arche assistants (Monroe, 2002; Oliner, 2003; Reimer, 2009), similar impressions were drawn by researchers along the lines that, frequently, personal and moral concerns were integrated in the psychological functioning of prosocial exemplars. Despite the many virtues of qualitative research designs, their lack of objective methodology and appropriate comparison groups pose challenges for drawing valid and reliable inferences about psychological mechanisms. We now turn our attention to research using the quantitative methods of psychological science to address these issues.

The research enterprise examining the appropriation of morality to the self has proceeded along two largely parallel but complementary tracks representing different levels of personality description (McAdams, 1995). One track has focused on the appropriation of moral traits to identity; the other has focused on the integration of moral and personal concerns in broader aspects of personality (such as goal motivation, developmental achievements, and integrative life narratives). First up in our discussion is the line of research on the possession of moral traits.

Moral Identity

Trait-based models have come to be the dominant perspective in the field of personality research, based on the assumption that behavioral dispositions are meaningfully tapped by trait terms. This implies that the possession of moral traits in identity should be predictive of prosocial behavior. But which personality traits are particularly morally relevant and thus constitutive of a moral identity? McCrae and John (1992) suggested that agreeableness and conscientiousness (two of the Big Five personality factors) are "the classic dimensions of character, describing 'good' versus 'evil' and 'strong-willed' versus 'weak-willed' individuals" (p. 197), and McAdams (2009) suggested the addition of the openness-to-experience factor to the mix, but such global personality dimensions are not sufficiently informative for our purposes.

To empirically address the question of which traits are morally relevant, one fruitful approach has been to examine notions of moral excellence that are extant in common, everyday understandings. This approach, of course, differs from those that are philosophically driven, but perhaps better represents what is actually operative in everyday life. Once traits descriptive of a mature moral identity have been derived, then the process of exploring developmental patterns can be undertaken.

CONCEPTIONS OF MORAL TRAITS

A taxonomy of moral character traits in people's implicit conceptions was derived by Walker and Pitts (1998). This was accomplished in a series of studies wherein samples of adults were first asked to generate the traits of a highly moral person, then to rate the prototypicality of a distilled list of these traits, and finally to organize these traits into meaningful groups. Analyses of these data revealed six clusters of moral traits in ordinary individuals' conceptions of moral excellence (what is regarded as highly moral), embodying themes of: principles/ideals, dependability/loyalty, integrity, care/trustworthiness, fairness, and confidence. These are the sort of traits that should be characteristic of a moral identity. In a follow-up study, Smith, Türk Smith, and Christopher (2007) found similar conceptions of moral traits across various cross-cultural samples.

Walker and Pitts (1998) further derived the underlying dimensions characterizing people's conceptions of moral excellence: a *self/other* dimension was the primary one and reflects the tension in moral functioning between personal agency at one pole and more interpersonal concerns at the other; the secondary dimension was *external/internal* and reflects the tension between adherence to external norms and internal aspects of conscience. Reassuringly, in a later study of conceptions of moral traits characteristic of different types of moral excellence (just, brave, and caring), Walker and Hennig (2004) found that these disparate types all exemplified the same tension between agentic and communal traits in moral functioning. These findings, based on naturalistic conceptions of moral excellence, reinforce the framing of this chapter in that they reference the significance of the fundamental motivational duality of self and other, of agency and communion.

Walker's studies examined conceptions of moral traits among adults only and did not assess developmental patterns. This limitation was addressed in a series of studies by Hardy, Walker, Olsen, Skalski, and Basinger (2011) that derived, using similar procedures, adolescents' taxonomy of moral traits. Although analyses revealed that similar clusters and dimensions of moral traits were found in adolescents' conceptions here as were found in adults' conceptions in Walker's prior studies, some developmental patterns were evident. For example, older adolescents in Hardy et al.'s free-listing procedure generated more moral trait terms than did younger adolescents, indicating the increased accessibility of the concept with age. Further, the relationship between the accessibility of these traits and their perceived importance was stronger for older than for younger adolescents, suggesting a more coherent conceptual framing with development. And more clusters were derived from older adolescents' organization of these traits than from the younger adolescents, indicating greater differentiation in their understandings. Research has yet to examine moral-trait conceptions earlier in childhood, but more concrete and less nuanced patterns might be anticipated.

So we now have some sense of the moral-trait conceptions of adolescents and adults. The question naturally arises as to whether the self-attribution of such moral traits is predictive of actual prosocial behavior.

SELF-ATTRIBUTION OF MORAL TRAITS

Initial indications that possession of moral traits was associated with meaningful behavior came from Hart and Fegley's (1995) study of adolescent moral exemplars, from a disadvantaged context, who were identified because of their extraordinary care for, and service to, others. Along with a matched comparison group of adolescents, they completed various personality measures including an open-ended description of the self. Analyses of these self-ascribed attributes revealed that the adolescent care exemplars included more moral traits and goals than did the comparison adolescents, indicating that self-understanding, framed by moral traits, may be in some sense implicated in moral action.

Our discussion so far has focused on conceptions of moral traits because they inform the content of a moral identity. So we now shift to the assessment of moral identity and its validity. Reimer, DeWitt Goudelock, and Walker (2009) used the moral traits derived in Walker and Pitts's (1998) study of naturalistic conceptions to develop a measure of moral identity. A subset of these traits was formulated into a 44-item self-attribution scale, which was then administered to a large sample of high school students. Responses were subjected to factor analysis, which yielded five factors, largely aligning with the clusters derived from Walker and Pitts's data. Then Reimer et al. assessed the predictive validity of their moral identity scale and found that the principled–idealistic and caring–dependable moral-trait self-attribution factors were predictive of volunteer involvement and service motivation.

Reimer et al.'s (2009) moral identity scale relied on moral-trait terms generated by adults in Walker and Pitts's (1998) study, but those trait terms may not well represent the aspects of moral functioning that are most relevant and salient for adolescents. This limitation prompted Hardy, Walker, Olsen, Woodbury, and Hickman (in press) to develop another measure of moral identity, based on adolescents' conceptions of moral traits and tapping the moral ideal self. With this measure, attributions of moral traits are not for the actual self, rather attributions are for the ideal self, the person one aspires to be. The moral ideal self can serve as a motivational guide for behavior by focusing on terminal values and goals and by triggering affect (e.g., when there is a disparity between the actual and ideal self).

So in the Hardy et al. (in press) study, adolescents themselves generated the moral-trait terms (adapting the procedures discussed earlier in studies of naturalistic conceptions), which were then formulated into a 20-item measure of moral identity. A sample of adolescents then rated these moral traits for the ideal self. It was found that the moral ideal self was positively associated with parent-reported adolescent altruism and moral traits and was negatively associated with parent-reported adolescent aggression and adolescent-reported cheating, providing rather convincing evidence of the predictive validity of this measure of moral identity wherein moral traits are appropriated to the self.

What has become the most widely used measure of moral identity was earlier developed by Aquino and Reed (2002). Their measure taps the centrality or self-relevant importance of moral traits for identity. The measure first presents a set of nine traits that are considered to be characteristic of a moral person (essentially activating the concept) and then respondents are asked to rate, on a 10-item scale, the extent to which they identify with those characteristics. The measure has two subscales: the internalization subscale taps the personal importance of possessing these traits, whereas the symbolization subscale taps the public aspects of moral identity in communicating one's morality to others (which seems to focus more on impression management). Thus, in general, this measure of moral identity assesses the self-perceived importance (or centrality) of moral traits.

Some evidence has been reported indicating that moral centrality in identity is predictive of prosocial behavior. For example, Aquino and Reed (2002) found that the internalization subscale of their measure predicted actual food-drive donations among high-school students. Reed and Aquino (2003) examined the relationship between the self-importance of moral identity and expressions of out-group hostility, based on the presumption that lower levels of hostility reflected an expanded perspective of moral concern. In a series of studies with university students, they found that the internalization subscale predicted a sense of moral obligations toward out-groups, the worthiness of humanitarian aid to out-groups, donation of money for humanitarian aid to an out-group, and less willingness to accept civilian deaths as "collateral damage" of a retaliatory military action against an out-group. Thus, the internalization of moral traits seems to be a significant predictor of prosocial attitudes and behavior.

One of the conceptual issues that characterizes the study of moral identity is the interaction between dispositional versus situational perspectives (see Walker, 2014, for an extended discussion). A trait-based dispositional perspective assumes considerable cross-situational consistency and temporal stability in behavioral dispositions (Penner & Orom, 2010) and so focuses on the "possession" of moral traits. Research reviewed in this chapter so far has fallen within the purview of the dispositional perspective. In contrast, a state-based situational perspective recognizes the role of contextual factors in both moral identity and behavior and so focuses on the cognitive and affective mechanisms in the activation (or deactivation) of aspects of moral identity.

The relevance of the situational perspective has often involved experimentally manipulating moral identity by priming its salience in some way, often implicitly. This can be accomplished, for example, by having participants compose a story using moral trait terms or doing a crossword search for moral terms. The effect of priming moral identity was examined by Reed, Aquino, and Levy (2007). University students and adults were assigned to either a moral-identity or a neutral priming condition. They found that priming moral identity increased participants' professed willingness to donate time to a charitable organization (relative to a business marketing association), in comparison to the neutral priming.

In a subsequent study with undergraduate business students, Aquino, Freeman, Reed, Lim, and Felps (2009) examined the joint influence of a dispositional factor (moral centrality) and a situational factor (moral priming) on moral behavior. They assessed the trait-based extent of moral centrality using Aquino and Reed's (2002) measure of moral identity and then manipulated the salience of moral identity (using either a moral or a neutral prime). In a lab session, students were then involved in a virtual task making investment decisions wherein individual interests competed with the collective good. Aquino et al. (2009) found that sustained cooperative behavior in the face of the apparent self-interested behaviors of others was only evidenced by participants who had a highly central moral identity that had also been primed, indicating the joint influence of both dispositional and situational factors.

It should be realized that the dispositional and situational perspectives are not fundamentally antithetical (Hardy & Carlo, 2011) and instead should be regarded as complementary. One would be hard pressed to find a researcher who did not acknowledge that moral identity is an individual-differences variable that reflects at least some element of intrapersonal consistency across contexts and over time. But, it also seems widely recognized that the exercise of virtues should be appropriate to the situation; that is, traits should have some contextual specificity. And, of course, it is assumed that the development of moral traits is, at least in part, an outcome of socialization influences. So the pitting of character versus context seems to be a false dichotomy (Penner & Orom, 2010).

The moral motivational mechanism that frames this chapter is the appropriation of morality to the self. I noted earlier that research in this regard has proceeded along two tracks. One track—and the one that has been my focus so far—has dealt with the self-attribution of moral traits to identity. The other track—to which I will turn shortly—has explored the integration of personal and moral concerns in other aspects of personality. The limitation of the trait-based focus is that it reflects but a single level of personality description (behavioral traits). This level entails description that is somewhat broad, nonspecific, and superficial. To get a more adequate handle on moral motivation, we need to explore other morally relevant aspects of personality that have the potential to explain how morality gets appropriated to the self. Such will be my focus for the remainder of the chapter.

Moral Personality

LEVELS OF PERSONALITY DESCRIPTION

Although behavioral traits have more recently been at the forefront of the study of personality, other aspects of functioning should be considered if one is to really know the person. McAdams (1995, 2009) has advanced a typology that references three levels of personality description and that has garnered increased acceptance as a framing for the field.

The first level is that of *dispositional traits*—broad, nonconditional, decontextualized, and implicitly comparative dimensions—of the sort that have been the focus so far in this chapter.

The second level entails *characteristic adaptations*—the motivational, strategic, and developmental features of personality that are typically more contextualized in role, place, and time. These characteristically adaptive strategies may be particularly revelatory of individuals' goal motivation, more so than are generic traits.

The third level references *integrative life narratives*—the psychosocial construction of an identity that confers a sense of purpose, meaning, continuity, and coherence in life. In providing such accounts of their lives, people either explicitly or implicitly assume a moral stance regarding both self and society and thereby impart to their identity some moral valence.

McAdams and Cox (2010) helpfully illustrate the three levels of personality description (dispositional traits, characteristic adaptations, and integrative life narratives) in terms of three roles that people commonly adopt in life: actor, agent, and author, respectively. The enhanced value in going beyond the (mere) consideration of dispositional traits in understanding moral motivation has been examined in a couple of studies of moral exemplars in which personality has been tapped at all three levels of description. In both Matsuba and Walker's (2004, 2005) and Walker and Frimer's (2007) studies minimal differences were found between moral exemplars and matched comparison participants in terms of dispositional traits, but marked differences between these groups were evident in terms of personality variables reflecting the levels of characteristic adaptations and integrative life narratives.

Among the myriad personality variables that fall under the scope of characteristic adaptations and integrative life narratives, a basic issue involves identifying which ones are especially relevant to the issue of moral motivation. It is to that challenging question that we now turn.

CORE VARIABLES OF MORAL PERSONALITY

In attempting to identify the core variables of the moral personality, the research strategy necessitates the casting of a wide net, with a comprehensive and broadband assessment, ideally across all levels of personality description and involving multiple types of measures. We have conducted a series of studies of this type which, I will argue, yield a coherent pattern of findings that lay the groundwork for a better understanding of prosocial motivation.

Among the first studies to undertake a broadband assessment of morally relevant aspects of personality across the three levels was a study conducted with a local sample of young adults who had been identified for their extraordinary involvement with a range of social service agencies (Matsuba & Walker, 2004, 2005). These prosocial exemplars, along with a group of matched comparison participants, responded to several personality inventories and measures and participated in a life-review interview, which was then analyzed for various features of personality. In total, this personality assessment tapped traits, adaptations, and narratives.

As intimated earlier, at the level of dispositional traits, the young adult exemplars were not particularly distinguished from their comparisons, with no significant differences on four of the Big-Five personality factors. They did, however, evidence stronger traits of agreeableness (which is certainly consistent with their prosociality). At the level of characteristic adaptations, differences were more robust. For example, exemplars evidenced an accentuated other-model of adult attachment (an obvious communal theme), advanced ego-identity status, more developed moral reasoning, and a higher level of epistemic (or faith) development reflecting a broader and more inclusive worldview. The latter finding resonates with Colby and Damon's (1992) observation that most of their exemplars evidenced a religiosity, spirituality, or faith that transcended the self (see Walker & Frimer, 2008, for an extended discussion of this aspect).

And, finally, at the level of integrative life narratives, Matsuba and Walker (2005) found that exemplars expressed more prosocial goals for their future, had greater ideological depth in the expression of their values and beliefs, had more recollections from their childhood of others' suffering, and expressed stronger themes of agency in their life stories. Noteworthy, at this point, are the indications that elements of both agency and communion are strongly operative in exemplars' motivation.

In Matsuba and Walker's (2004, 2005) study, the prosocial exemplars were young adults who were just embarking on a "moral career." In a subsequent study, Walker and Frimer (2007) examined older and perhaps more notable exemplars who had received Canadian national recognition for their actions. Here two different types of exemplars (caring and brave) were included: some had received the Caring Canadian Award for years of extraordinary volunteer service to groups, communities, or humanitarian causes; others had received the Medal of Bravery for risking their lives to save another. Despite the dramatically different nature of the actions that garnered these awards, both types are unequivocally prosocial.

Along with these exemplars, a group of individually matched comparison participants responded to a comprehensive set of measures assessing all three levels of personality description. Interestingly, no differences between exemplars and comparisons were found at the level of dispositional traits, whereas differences were extensive and robust at the level of integrative life narratives. For example, in their life stories, exemplars more frequently spontaneously recalled formative, prosocial relationships in childhood than did comparisons, including secure attachments, the benefit of "helpers" who fostered development, and exposure to the needs of others. Exemplars' accounts also more frequently entailed instances of what McAdams (2006) calls "redemption," wherein negative life events were construed positively so that some benefit or meaning was derived from them. Exemplars' life stories were also coded as reflecting a more positive affective tone, indicating the pervasive optimism that was also noted by Colby and Damon (1992). Such optimism and the tendency to redeem critical life events are adaptive in sustaining prosocial action in the face of obstacles and disappointments.

Walker and Frimer (2007) also found that exemplars, more so than comparison participants, had stronger themes of both agency and communion in their life stories. This finding is especially important to highlight because these two fundamental motives are often conceptualized as competing: "getting ahead" versus "getting along" (Hogan, 1982). I will shortly return to this finding and its significance for understanding moral motivation.

Implicit so far in our discussion of both moral identity and moral personality has been the assumption that moral motivation takes but a singular form. Flanagan's (1991) philosophical analysis has challenged that assumption, suggesting that there legitimately may be different varieties of moral personality. He contends that moral excellence can take different manifestations, implicating the multidimensional nature of moral motivation. Is there any evidence for moral modularity?

Walker, Frimer, and Dunlop (2010) examined that question by conducting a cluster analysis of the Canadian moral exemplars in Walker and Frimer's (2007) study, based on a large collection of personality variables. Three distinct clusters of moral exemplars were revealed, suggesting that, indeed, different modes of moral motivation may be operative in prosocial action.

One cluster was pervasively *communal*, across the various levels of personality description, with behavioral traits of nurturance, goal motivation expressed in terms of interpersonal relationships and generativity, and evident themes of communion running through their life stories. These exemplars were clearly characterized by prosocial emotionality and social interdependence. The attributes of this cluster of exemplars resonate with the prosocial personality orientation described by Penner in his program of research, particularly the factor of other-oriented empathy (Penner & Orom, 2010). Although agency was not a particularly defining feature of this cluster, these exemplars were not only more communal than their comparisons but were also more agentic.

The second cluster of exemplars was characterized by variables somewhat more "in the head," to use colloquial parlance. These included behavioral traits of openness to experience, goal motivation in terms of self-understanding and personal growth, and advanced epistemic and moral reasoning. This was labeled the *deliberative* cluster because it entailed the prosocial motivation imparted by a reflective and perhaps principled approach to meaning-making, an enhanced social awareness, and an openness to divergent perspectives. The expanded worldview characterizing these exemplars illustrates Staub's (2005) notion of the development of inclusive caring—the humanizing of all people—that can motivate altruistic action. This cluster of exemplars also provides some solace to the cognitive-developmental perspective of the auto-motivating power of moral rationality (Kohlberg, 1984).

The third cluster was unequivocally ordinary in terms of moral motivation, characterized by banal personality functioning in comparison to other exemplars and indistinguishable from their comparisons. By default (given the absence of distinguishing aspects of personality), the existence of this *ordinary* cluster lends support to the situational perspective (Doris, 2002; Zimbardo, 2007), which contends that contextual forces are primary in instigating moral behavior. This cluster of personologically ordinary people, who have engaged in extraordinary action, challenges the framing of this chapter, which has assumed the causally operative mechanism of moral motivation, and so this bids some further reflection.

What sense can we make of these findings? As it turns out, this ordinary cluster was composed primarily of bravery award recipients, whereas the other two clusters were composed primarily of caring exemplars or were more balanced in their membership. This pattern suggests that one-off heroic action may often be instigated by powerful situational factors operative in such emergency (or strong) situations, whereas a prosocial career more likely is sustained by dispositional factors of moral motivation. Fleeson (2004) offers a resolution of the competing person × situation perspectives, claiming that both have applicability: The situational perspective seems to better explain the enactment of single, momentary behaviors, whereas the dispositional perspective better accounts for longer-term behavioral patterns. Regardless, these findings illustrate the multidimensional character of prosocial exemplarity and strongly suggest a multifaceted search for the processes underlying moral functioning and development.

INTEGRATION OF AGENCY AND COMMUNION IN MOTIVATION

This chapter is framed by the notion that the appropriation of morality to the self is critical to understanding prosocial motivation. In the first half of the chapter, the discussion focused on the possession and significance of moral traits in identity. In the second half, the focus has been the integration of personal and moral aspects of life in aspects of personality functioning beyond traits. All of this suggests the psychological mechanism of aligning and reconciling the interests of self and others.

As was noted earlier, the fundamental dimension underlying naturalistic conceptions of morality (Hardy et al., 2011; Walker & Hennig, 2004; Walker & Pitts, 1998) references the tension between self- and other-focused traits, between agency and communion. Likewise, in the field of motivation, the fundamental themes are agency and communion (Bakan, 1966; Hogan, 1982; McAdams, 1988). Agency captures the self-enhancing aspects of motivation, the disposition to individuate and to advance the self ("getting ahead"). Communion reflects the other-enhancing aspects, the disposition to promote social cohesion and the welfare of others ("getting along"). These motives are typically conceptualized as conflicting and antithetical (e.g., Schwartz, 1992, locates them on opposite sides of his values circumplex; also see Schwartz et al., 2012).

In contrast, Frimer and Walker's (2009) reconciliation model proposes that, in moral maturity, these two motivations can become effectively integrated; and there is some theorizing that speaks to the adaptive aspects of such integration (Blasi, 2004; Colby & Damon, 1992; Damon, 1984; McAdams, 1993; Wiggins, 1991). But Frimer and Walker add a developmental framing, arguing that the two motives develop mostly in segregation in childhood and adolescence until beginning to butt into each other as they strengthen, provoking some resolution in late adolescence or early adulthood. The typical resolution entails the dominance of one motive and the diminution of the other, as in unmitigated agency (the unfettered pursuit of wealth and power for its own sake). However, the model predicts that moral exemplars resolve the motivational tension differently by appropriating prosocial communal concerns to the self. The motives are transformed from being independent and competing to being interdependent and synergistic. In other words, moral exemplars largely fulfill their personal interests by investing in prosocial action advancing the cause of others.

Recall the consistent pattern of findings of accentuated levels of both agentic and communal motivation in the personality functioning of exemplars across a range of manifestations (Matsuba & Walker, 2004, 2005; Walker & Frimer, 2007). Note that these exemplars were not just prosocially communal, but were also strongly agentic, striving for influence, power, competence, and achievement. They were highly motivated in general. But the crux question is whether or not there is any evidence of a synergistic interaction between them—a total effect that is more than the mere sum of its parts.

Walker and Frimer (2007) addressed this issue by subsequently conducting a logistic regression analysis, predicting group classification (as exemplar or comparison). In the first step, agency and communion were entered as baseline control variables, both making strong independent contributions. In the second step, the statistical interaction term was entered; however, it did not significantly add to the predictive power of the regression equation. There was no evidence of synergy between these two motives.

Intrigued by this null finding, Frimer, Walker, Dunlop, Lee, and Riches (2011) returned to the issue, conducting a reanalysis that involved two notable refinements, one conceptual and the other analytical. The conceptual refinement was to more precisely define agency and communion as promoting the interests of self and others, respectively; a conceptualization that is more germane to the motivational reconciliation envisaged by the model. In Walker and Frimer's (2007) prior analysis, agency and communion had been coded by a collection of themes extant in the literature (including constructs such as empowerment and self-mastery to tap agency, dialogue and unity/togetherness to tap communion), and that admixture may have been obscuring the synergistic effect.

The analytical refinement was to replace the traditional variable-level approach to assessing interactions (statistically) with a person-level approach (Magnusson, 1999) which assesses them with greater phenomenological validity. In the variable approach, interactions are merely assessed on the basis of the overall strength of the variables when there may actually be minimal integration (as when individuals vacillate between two strong motives that are compartmentalized). In contrast, in the within-person approach, the interaction between agency and communion is tapped by the observable extent of meaningful co-occurrence of these motives within the same thought structure.

When Frimer et al. (2011) implemented both refinements (conceptual and analytical), they found the first evidence of a synergistic interaction between agency and communion. Exemplars had both motivational themes frequently coordinated in their narratives, whereas comparison participants did not deviate from chance co-occurrence. This finding reinforces the contention that promoting the interests of others is also psychologically self-enhancing in moral maturity.

However, there is an ambiguity in Frimer et al.'s (2011) evidence of the integration of agency and communion in moral maturity: Their coding of the interaction of these motives was merely assessed by their co-occurrence within the same thought structure, but that does not differentiate the directionality between them. The co-occurrence could be of the type of agency promoting communion (e.g., "I'm using my influence to help the poor") or of the type of communion promoting agency (e.g., "I'm helping the poor to increase my status"). These types obviously warrant different moral evaluations. To address this ambiguity, Frimer, Walker, Lee, Riches, and Dunlop (2012) revised their coding procedures to tap the directionality between motives, adapting Rokeach's (1973) notion of instrumental and terminal values. An instrumental value serves, or is a means to, something else; a terminal value is an end it itself.

In Frimer et al. (2012) study, subjects were widely known, influential figures of the past century, as identified by *Time* magazine. These are people of both positive and negative renown who have had, regardless, incredible impact. A large sample of social-science experts rated these figures on various dimensions of moral exemplarity. The top-ranking target figures (e.g., Nelson Mandela, Aung San Suu Kyi, Mother Teresa) were classified as moral exemplars, and the bottom-ranking (e.g., Vladmir Putin, Kim Jong Il, George W. Bush) were classified as comparison figures of comparable influence.

Since these figures were not available for direct participation in research, their personality functioning could only be studied "at a distance" through the content analysis of archival materials such as speeches and interviews. These archival materials were first coded for agency and communion and then subsequently coded for the hierarchical directionality between these two modes of motivation.

Comparison figures clearly displayed a pattern of unmitigated agency—considerably more agency than communion at both the instrumental and terminal levels of motivation—agency as instrumental to more agency. Moral exemplars also displayed considerably more agency than communion at the instrumental level; they were influential people, after all. But at the terminal level, they were unequivocally communal. Both groups were similarly equipped (with instrumental agency), but were engaged in vastly different projects. Exemplars displayed instrumental agency for the cause of terminal communion, the embodiment of enlightened self-interest. For the morally mature, personal influence, achievement, and fulfillment are actualized in an integrated mode of motivation by promoting others' welfare. This is fundamentally what it means to appropriate morality to the self.

Some Concluding Challenges

This chapter has faced the challenge of explaining prosocial behavior, behavior that is ostensibly intended to benefit others but that entails considerable cost and risk to the self. So why do good? Many existing theories disregard or denigrate the role of the self in moral motivation, arguing explicitly or implicitly that the moral agent's task is to somehow overcome self-interest to do the right thing (Haidt, 2008). Those perspectives lack motivational oomph and are psychologically unrealistic.

My contention is that prosocial morality can and should be self-regarding. The psychological maneuver is to capitalize on self-interest by refocusing it so that morality is integral to one's identity and that agency and personal fulfillment are accomplished through prosocial objectives. This simply means appropriating prosocial moral concerns to the self, which can be keenly motivating "for creatures like us" (Flanagan, 1991, p. 32).

In this chapter I reviewed two tracks of research in that regard. One track where there has been productive research over the last decade has focused on the possession of moral traits as central to identity. The other track has focused on broader aspects of moral personality, particularly the integration of agency and communion in moral motivation in such a way that self-interested agentic concerns are channeled into prosocial communal action. The findings of these different programs of research provide different but converging lenses for understanding the appropriation of morality to different aspects of the self's functioning.

The investigative process adopted here was largely one of reverse engineering, with a focus on the relatively mature manifestations of moral motivation in adolescence and in emerging and later adulthood. This process is one of studying the end product or, in this case, the developmental endpoint, and then engaging in deconstruction to figure out the functional mechanisms.

Now having some sense what exemplary prosociality consists of, developmental questions rise to the fore as directions for future research. For example, what are the early socialization experiences that lay the groundwork for later development of a prosocial moral identity and integrated motivation? What about the requisite sociocognitive understandings? What are the various trajectories of moral identity and motivation through adolescence and adulthood, and how can these various paths in life be explained? How can the adaptive aspects of moral traits and motivation be fostered in personality while inoculating against their shadow-side that sometimes surfaces, at cost to both self and others?

The complexity in understanding prosocial behavior also lies in the many varied forms it can take and, presumably, the differing pathways that lead to their development. While there may be some core and widely shared features of prosocial morality—as I have argued is the case for agency and communion—its manifestation can arise from different personality profiles (as has been shown by Dunlop & Walker, 2013, for brave exemplars, and by Dunlop, Walker, & Matsuba, 2012, for care exemplars). Future research should more systematically explore the core and the distinctive aspects of different forms of prosocial morality, reflecting its multidimensional nature.

References

Aquino, K., Freeman, D., Reed, A., II, Lim, V. K. G., & Felps, W. (2009). Testing a social cognitive model of moral behavior: The interactive influence of situations and moral identity centrality. *Journal of Personality and Social Psychology, 97*, 123–141. doi:10.1037/a0015406

Aquino, K., & Reed, A., II. (2002). The self-importance of moral identity. *Journal of Personality and Social Psychology, 83*, 1423–1440. doi:10.1037/0022-3514.83.6.1423

Bakan, D. (1966). *The duality of human existence: An essay on psychology and religion.* Chicago: Rand McNally.

Blasi, A. (1983). Moral cognition and moral action: A theoretical perspective. *Developmental Review, 3*, 178–210. doi:10.1016/0273-2297(83)90029-1

Blasi, A. (1984). Moral identity: Its role in moral functioning. In W. M. Kurtines & J. L. Gewirtz (Eds.), *Morality, moral behavior, and moral development* (pp. 128–139). New York: Wiley.

Blasi, A. (1993). The development of identity: Some implications for moral functioning. In G. G. Noam & T. E. Wren (Eds.), *The moral self* (pp. 99–122). Cambridge, MA: MIT Press.

Blasi, A. (2004). Moral functioning: Moral understanding and personality. In D. K. Lapsley & D. Narvaez (Eds.), *Moral development, self, and identity* (pp. 335–347). Mahwah, NJ: Erlbaum.

Blasi, A. (2005). Moral character: A psychological approach. In D. K. Lapsley & F. C. Power (Eds.), *Character psychology and character education* (pp. 67–100). Notre Dame, IN: University of Notre Dame Press.

Colby, A., & Damon, W. (1992). *Some do care: Contemporary lives of moral commitment.* New York: Free Press.

Damon, W. (1984). Self-understanding and moral development from childhood to adolescence. In W. M. Kurtines & J. L. Gewirtz (Eds.), *Morality, moral behavior, and moral development* (pp. 109–127). New York: Wiley.

Damon, W., & Hart, D. (1988). *Self-understanding in childhood and adolescence.* Cambridge, UK: Cambridge University Press.

Doris, J. M. (2002). *Lack of character: Personality and moral behavior.* Cambridge, UK: Cambridge University Press.

Dunlop, W. L., & Walker, L. J. (2013). The personality profile of brave exemplars: A person-centered analysis. *Journal of Research in Personality, 47*, 380–384. doi:10.1016/j.jrp.2013.03.004

Dunlop, W. L., Walker, L. J., & Matsuba, M. K. (2012). The distinctive moral personality of care exemplars. *Journal of Positive Psychology, 7*, 131–143. doi:10.1080/17439760.2012.662994

Erikson, E. H. (1968). *Identity, youth, and crisis.* New York: Norton.

Flanagan, O. (1991). *Varieties of moral personality: Ethics and psychological realism.* Cambridge, MA: Harvard University Press.

Flanagan, O. (2009). Moral science? Still metaphysical after all these years. In D. Narvaez & D. K. Lapsley (Eds.), *Personality, identity, and character: Explorations in moral psychology* (pp. 52–78). New York: Cambridge University Press.

Fleeson, W. (2004). Moving personality beyond the person–situation debate: The challenge and the opportunity of within-person variability. *Current Directions in Psychological Science, 13*, 83–87. doi:10.1111/j.0963-7214.2004.00280.x

Frimer, J. A., & Walker, L. J. (2009). Reconciling the self and morality: An empirical model of moral centrality development. *Developmental Psychology, 45,* 1669–1681. doi:10.1037/a0017418

Frimer, J. A., Walker, L. J., Dunlop, W. L., Lee, B. H., & Riches, A. (2011). The integration of agency and communion in moral personality: Evidence of enlightened self-interest. *Journal of Personality and Social Psychology, 101,* 149–163. doi:10.1037/a0023780

Frimer, J. A., Walker, L. J., Lee, B. H., Riches, A., & Dunlop, W. L. (2012). Hierarchical integration of agency and communion: A study of influential moral figures. *Journal of Personality, 80,* 1117–1145. doi:10.1111/j.1467-6494.2012.00764.x

Haidt, J. (2008). Morality. *Perspectives on Psychological Science, 3,* 65–72. doi:10.1111/j.1745-6916.2008.00063.x

Hamlin, J., Wynn, K., & Bloom, P. (2007). Social evaluation in preverbal infants. *Nature, 450*(7169), 557–559. doi:10.1038/nature06288

Hardy, S. A., & Carlo, G. (2011). Moral identity: Where identity formation and moral development converge. In S. J. Schwartz, K. Luyckx, & V. L. Vignoles (Eds.), *Handbook of identity theory and research* (pp. 495–514). New York: Springer.

Hardy, S. A., Walker, L. J., Olsen, J. A., Skalski, J. E., & Basinger, J. C. (2011). Adolescent naturalistic conceptions of moral maturity. *Social Development, 20,* 562–586. doi:10.1111/j.1467-9507.2010.00590.x

Hardy, S. A., Walker, L. J., Olsen, J. A., Woodbury, R. D., & Hickman, J. R. (in press). Moral identity as moral ideal self: Links to adolescent outcomes. *Developmental Psychology.* doi:10.1037/a0033598

Hart, D., & Fegley, S. (1995). Prosocial behavior and caring in adolescence: Relations to self-understanding and social judgment. *Child Development, 66,* 1346–1359. doi:10.2307/1131651

Hogan, R. (1982). A socioanalytic theory of personality. In M. M. Page (Ed.), *Nebraska Symposium on Motivation: Vol. 30. Personality: Current theory and research* (pp. 55–89). Lincoln: University of Nebraska Press.

Kochanska, G., & Thompson, R. A. (1997). The emergence and development of conscience in toddlerhood and early childhood. In J. E. Grusec & L. Kuczynski (Eds.), *Parenting and children's internalization of values: A handbook of contemporary theory* (pp. 53–77). Hoboken, NJ: Wiley.

Kohlberg, L. (1981). *Essays on moral development: Vol. 1. The philosophy of moral development.* San Francisco: Harper & Row.

Kohlberg, L. (1984). *Essays on moral development: Vol. 2. The psychology of moral development.* San Francisco: Harper & Row.

Magnusson, D. (1999). Holistic interactionism: A perspective for research on personality development. In L. A. Pervin & O. P. John (Eds.), *Handbook of personality: Theory and research* (2nd ed., pp. 219–247). New York: Guilford Press.

Matsuba, M. K., & Walker, L. J. (2004). Extraordinary moral commitment: Young adults working for social organizations. *Journal of Personality, 72,* 413–436. doi:10.1111/j.0022-3506.2004.00267.x

Matsuba, M. K., & Walker, L. J. (2005). Young adult moral exemplars: The making of self through stories. *Journal of Research on Adolescence, 15,* 275–297. doi:10.1111/j.1532-7795.2005.00097.x

McAdams, D. P. (1988). *Power, intimacy, and the life story: Personological inquiries into identity.* New York: Guilford Press.

McAdams, D. P. (1993). *The stories we live by: Personal myths and the making of the self.* New York: Guilford Press.

McAdams, D. P. (1995). What do we know when we know a person? *Journal of Personality, 63,* 365–396. doi:10.1111/j.1467-6494.1995.tb00500.x

McAdams, D. P. (2006). *The redemptive self: Stories Americans live by.* New York: Oxford University Press.

McAdams, D. P. (2009). The moral personality. In D. Narvaez & D. K. Lapsley (Eds.), *Personality, identity, and character: Explorations in moral psychology* (pp. 11–29). New York: Cambridge University Press.

McAdams, D. P., & Cox, K. S. (2010). Self and identity across the life span. In M. E. Lamb, A. M. Freund, & R. M. Lerner (Eds.), *Handbook of life-span development, Vol. 2: Social and emotional development* (pp. 158–207). Hoboken, NJ: Wiley. doi:10.1002/9780470880166.hlsd002006

McCrae, R. R., & John, O. P. (1992). An introduction to the five-factor model and its applications. *Journal of Personality, 60,* 175–215. doi:10.1111/j.1467-6494.1992.tb00970.x

Monroe, K. R. (2002). Explicating altruism. In S. G. Post, L. G. Underwood, J. P. Schloss, & W. B. Hurlbut (Eds.), *Altruism and altruistic love: Science, philosophy, and religion in dialogue* (pp. 106–122). New York: Oxford University Press.

Oliner, S. P. (2003). *Do unto others: Extraordinary acts of ordinary people.* Boulder, CO: Westview.

Oliner, S. P., & Oliner, P. M. (1988). *The altruistic personality: Rescuers of Jews in Nazi Europe.* New York: Free Press.

Penner, L. A., & Orom, H. (2010). Enduring goodness: A person-by-situation perspective on prosocial behavior. In M. Mikulincer & P. R. Shaver (Eds.), *Prosocial motives, emotions, and behavior: The better angels of our nature* (pp. 55–72). Washington, DC: American Psychological Association. doi:10.1037/12061-003

Perloff, R. (1987). Self-interest and personal responsibility redux. *American Psychologist, 42,* 3–11. doi:10.1037/0003-066X.42.1.3

Reed, A., II, & Aquino, K. (2003). Moral identity and the expanding circle of moral regard toward out-groups. *Journal of Personality and Social Psychology, 84,* 1270–1286. doi:10.1037/0022-3514.84.6.1270

Reed, A., II, Aquino, K., & Levy, E. (2007). Moral identity and judgments of charitable behaviors. *Journal of Marketing, 71,* 178–193. doi:10.1509/jmkg.71.1.178

Reimer, K. S. (2009). *Living L'Arche: Stories of compassion, love, and disability.* London: Continuum.

Reimer, K. S., DeWitt Goudelock, B. M., & Walker, L. J. (2009). Developing conceptions of moral maturity: Traits and identity in adolescent personality. *Journal of Positive Psychology, 4,* 372–388. doi:10.1080/17439760902992431

Richter, D. (2007). *Why be good? A historical introduction to ethics.* New York: Oxford University Press.

Rokeach, M. (1973). *The nature of human values.* New York: Free Press.

Schwartz, S. H. (1992). Universals in the content and structure of values: Theoretical advances and empirical tests in 20 countries. *Advances in Experimental Social Psychology, 25,* 1–65. doi:10.1016/S0065-2601(08)60281-6

Schwartz, S. H., Cieciuch, J., Vecchione, M., Davidov, E., Fischer, R., Beierlein, C., ... Konty, M. (2012). Refining the theory of basic individual values. *Journal of Personality and Social Psychology, 103,* 663–668. doi:10.1037/a0029393

Selman, R. L. (1980). *Growth of interpersonal understanding: Developmental and clinical analyses*. New York: Academic Press.

Smith, K. D., Türk Smith, S., & Christopher, J. C. (2007). What defines the good person? Cross-cultural comparisons of experts' models with lay prototypes. *Journal of Cross-Cultural Psychology, 38*, 333–360. doi:10.1177/0022022107300279

Staub, E. (2005). The roots of goodness: The fulfillment of basic human needs and the development of caring, helping and non-aggression, inclusive caring, moral courage, active bystandership, and altruism born of suffering. In G. Carlo & C. P. Edwards (Eds.), *Nebraska Symposium on Motivation: Vol. 51. Moral motivation through the life span* (pp. 33–72). Lincoln: University of Nebraska Press.

Turiel, E. (1983). *The development of social knowledge: Morality and convention*. Cambridge, UK: Cambridge University Press.

Walker, L. J. (2002). Moral exemplarity. In W. Damon (Ed.), *Bringing in a new era in character education* (pp. 65–83). Stanford, CA: Hoover Institution Press.

Walker, L. J. (2014). Moral personality, motivation, and identity. In M. Killen & J. G. Smetana (Eds.), *Handbook of moral development* (2nd ed., pp. 497–519). New York: Taylor & Francis.

Walker, L. J., & Frimer, J. A. (2007). Moral personality of brave and caring exemplars. *Journal of Personality and Social Psychology, 93*, 845–860. doi:10.1037/0022-3514.93.5.845

Walker, L. J., & Frimer, J. A. (2008). Being good for goodness' sake: Transcendence in the lives of moral heroes. In F. Oser & W. Veugelers (Eds.), *Getting involved: Global citizenship development and sources of moral values* (pp. 309–326). Rotterdam, The Netherlands: Sense.

Walker, L. J., Frimer, J. A., & Dunlop, W. L. (2010). Varieties of moral personality: Beyond the banality of heroism. *Journal of Personality, 78*, 907–942. doi:10.1111/j.1467-6494.2010.00637.x

Walker, L. J., & Hennig, K. H. (2004). Differing conceptions of moral exemplarity: Just, brave, and caring. *Journal of Personality and Social Psychology, 86*, 629–647. doi:10.1037/0022-3514.86.4.629

Walker, L. J., & Pitts, R. C. (1998). Naturalistic conceptions of moral maturity. *Developmental Psychology, 34*, 403–419. doi:10.1037/0012-1649.34.3.403

Wiggins, J. S. (1991). Agency and communion as conceptual coordinates for the understanding and measurement of interpersonal behavior. In D. Cicchetti & W. M. Grove (Eds.), *Thinking clearly about psychology: Essays in honor of Paul E. Meehl* (Vol. 2, pp. 89–113). Minneapolis: University of Minnesota Press.

Wright, J. C., & Bartsch, K. (2008). Portraits of early moral sensibility in two children's everyday conversation. *Merrill-Palmer Quarterly, 54*, 56–85. doi:10.1353/mpq.2008.0010

Zimbardo, P. G. (2007). The banality of evil, the banality of heroism. In J. Brockman (Ed.), *What is your dangerous idea? Today's leading thinkers on the unthinkable* (pp. 275–276). New York: Harper Perennial.

{ INDEX }

Note: The notation "n" indicates an entry in a footnote.